T0331691

Handbook of Research on Modeling, Analysis, and Application of Nature-Inspired Metaheuristic Algorithms

Sujata Dash
North Orissa University, India

B.K. Tripathy
VIT University, India

Atta ur Rahman
University of Dammam, Saudi Arabia

A volume in the Advances in Computational
Intelligence and Robotics (ACIR) Book Series

Published in the United States of America by
IGI Global
Engineering Science Reference (an imprint of IGI Global)
701 E. Chocolate Avenue
Hershey PA, USA 17033
Tel: 717-533-8845
Fax: 717-533-8661
E-mail: cust@igi-global.com
Web site: http://www.igi-global.com

Library of Congress Cataloging-in-Publication Data

Names: Dash, Sujata, 1969- editor. | Tripathy, B. K., 1957- editor. | Rahman,
  Atta Ur, 1982- editor.
Title: Handbook of research on the modeling, analysis, and application of
  nature-inspired metaheuristic algorithms / Sujata Dash, B.K. Tripathy, and
  Atta Ur Rahman, editors.
Description: Hershey, PA : Information Science Reference, [2018] | Includes
  bibliographical references.
Identifiers: LCCN 2017012030| ISBN 9781522528579 (hardcover) | ISBN
  9781522528586 (ebook)
Subjects: LCSH: Natural computation--Handbooks, manuals, etc. | Heuristic
  algorithms--Handbooks, manuals, etc. | Engineering mathematics--Handbooks,
  manuals, etc. | Science--Mathematics--Handbooks, manuals, etc.
Classification: LCC QA76.9.N37 H3646 2018 | DDC 006.3/8--dc23 LC record available at https://lccn.loc.gov/2017012030

This book is published in the IGI Global book series Advances in Computational Intelligence and Robotics (ACIR) (ISSN: 2327-0411; eISSN: 2327-042X)

British Cataloguing in Publication Data
A Cataloguing in Publication record for this book is available from the British Library.

All work contributed to this book is new, previously-unpublished material. The views expressed in this book are those of the authors, but not necessarily of the publisher.

For electronic access to this publication, please contact: eresources@igi-global.com.

Advances in Computational Intelligence and Robotics (ACIR) Book Series

Ivan Giannoccaro
University of Salento, Italy

ISSN:2327-0411
EISSN:2327-042X

MISSION

While intelligence is traditionally a term applied to humans and human cognition, technology has progressed in such a way to allow for the development of intelligent systems able to simulate many human traits. With this new era of simulated and artificial intelligence, much research is needed in order to continue to advance the field and also to evaluate the ethical and societal concerns of the existence of artificial life and machine learning.

The **Advances in Computational Intelligence and Robotics (ACIR) Book Series** encourages scholarly discourse on all topics pertaining to evolutionary computing, artificial life, computational intelligence, machine learning, and robotics. ACIR presents the latest research being conducted on diverse topics in intelligence technologies with the goal of advancing knowledge and applications in this rapidly evolving field.

COVERAGE

- Synthetic Emotions
- Robotics
- Artificial life
- Fuzzy systems
- Evolutionary computing
- Computational intelligence
- Computational Logic
- Brain Simulation
- Machine Learning
- Adaptive and Complex Systems

IGI Global is currently accepting manuscripts for publication within this series. To submit a proposal for a volume in this series, please contact our Acquisition Editors at Acquisitions@igi-global.com or visit: http://www.igi-global.com/publish/.

Titles in this Series

For a list of additional titles in this series, please visit: www.igi-global.com/book-series

Handbook of Research on Applied Cybernetics and Systems Science
Snehanshu Saha (PESIT South Campus, India) Abhyuday Mandal (University of Georgia, USA) Anand Narasim-hamurthy (BITS Hyderabad, India) Sarasvathi V (PESIT- Bangalore South Campus, India) and Shivappa Sangam (UGC, India)
Information Science Reference • copyright 2017 • 463pp • H/C (ISBN: 9781522524984) • US $245.00 (our price)

Handbook of Research on Machine Learning Innovations and Trends
Aboul Ella Hassanien (Cairo University, Egypt) and Tarek Gaber (Suez Canal University, Egypt)
Information Science Reference • copyright 2017 • 1093pp • H/C (ISBN: 9781522522294) • US $465.00 (our price)

Handbook of Research on Soft Computing and Nature-Inspired Algorithms
Shishir K. Shandilya (Bansal Institute of Research and Technology, India) Smita Shandilya (Sagar Institute of Research Technology and Science, India) Kusum Deep (Indian Institute of Technology Roorkee, India) and Atulya K. Nagar (Liverpool Hope University, UK)
Information Science Reference • copyright 2017 • 627pp • H/C (ISBN: 9781522521280) • US $280.00 (our price)

Membrane Computing for Distributed Control of Robotic Swarms Emerging Research and Opportunities
Andrei George Florea (Politehnica University of Bucharest, Romania) and Cătălin Buiu (Politehnica University of Bucharest, Romania)
Information Science Reference • copyright 2017 • 119pp • H/C (ISBN: 9781522522805) • US $160.00 (our price)

Recent Developments in Intelligent Nature-Inspired Computing
Srikanta Patnaik (SOA University, India)
Information Science Reference • copyright 2017 • 264pp • H/C (ISBN: 9781522523222) • US $185.00 (our price)

Ubiquitous Machine Learning and Its Applications
Pradeep Kumar (Maulana Azad National Urdu University, India) and Arvind Tiwari (DIT University, India)
Information Science Reference • copyright 2017 • 259pp • H/C (ISBN: 9781522525455) • US $185.00 (our price)

Advanced Image Processing Techniques and Applications
N. Suresh Kumar (VIT University, India) Arun Kumar Sangaiah (VIT University, India) M. Arun (VIT University, India) and S. Anand (VIT University, India)
Information Science Reference • copyright 2017 • 439pp • H/C (ISBN: 9781522520535) • US $290.00 (our price)

701 East Chocolate Avenue, Hershey, PA 17033, USA
Tel: 717-533-8845 x100 • Fax: 717-533-8661
E-Mail: cust@igi-global.com • www.igi-global.com

Editorial Advisory Board

List of Contributors

Table of Contents

Detailed Table of Contents

This chapter focuses on key applications of metaheuristic techniques in the field of gene selection and classification of microarray data. The metaheuristic techniques are efficient in handling combinatorial optimization problems. In this article, two different types of metaheuristics such as Genetic algorithm (GA) and Particle Swarm Optimization (PSO) are hybridized with fuzzy-rough (FR) method for optimizing the subset selection process of microarray data. The FR method applied here deals with impreciseness and uncertainty of microarray data. The predictive accuracy of the models is evaluated by an adaptive neural net ensemble and by a rule based classifier MODLEM respectively. Moreover, the learning efficiency of the ensemble is compared with base learners and with two classical ensembles. The rule based classifier generates a set of rules for disease diagnosis and prognosis and enables to study the function of genes from gene ontology website. The experimental results of both the models prove that, hybrid metaheuristic techniques are highly effective for finding potential genes.

Chapter 2

Nature-inspired algorithms have been productively applied to train neural network architectures. There exist other mechanisms like gradient descent, second order methods, Levenberg-Marquardt methods etc. to optimize the parameters of neural networks. Compared to gradient-based methods, nature-inspired algorithms are found to be less sensitive towards the initial weights set and also it is less likely to become trapped in local optima. Despite these benefits, some nature-inspired algorithms also suffer from stagnation when applied to neural networks. The other challenge when applying nature inspired techniques for neural networks would be in handling large dimensional and correlated weight space. Hence, there arises a need for scalable nature inspired algorithms for high dimensional neural network optimization. In this chapter, the characteristics of nature inspired techniques towards optimizing neural network architectures along with its applicability, advantages and limitations/challenges are studied.

C. M. Anish, Guru Ghasidas Vishwavidyalaya, India
Babita Majhi, Guru Ghasidas Vishwavidyalaya, India
Ritanjali Majhi, NIT Warangal, India

Net asset value (NAV) prediction is an important area of research as small investors are doing investment in there, Literature survey reveals that very little work has been done in this field. The reported literature mainly used various neural network models for NAV prediction. But the derivative based learning algorithms of these reported models have the problem of trapping into the local solution. Hence in chapter derivative free algorithm, particle swarm optimization is used to update the parameters of radial basis function neural network for prediction of NAV. The positions of particles represent the centers, spreads and weights of the RBF model and the minimum MSE is used as the cost function. The convergence characteristics are obtained to show the performance of the model during training phase. The MAPE and RMSE value are calculated during testing phase to show the performance of the proposed RBF-PSO model. These performance measure exhibits that the proposed model is better model in comparison to MLANN, FLANN and RBFNN models.

B. K. Tripathy, VIT University, India
Sooraj T. R., VIT University, India
R. K. Mohanty, VIT University, India

The term "memetic algorithm" was introduced by Moscato is an extension of the traditional genetic algorithm. It uses a local search technique to reduce the likelihood of the premature convergence. Memetic algorithms are intrinsically concerned with exploiting all available knowledge about the problem under study. MAs are population-based metaheuristics. In this chapter we explore the applications of memetic algorithms to problems within the domains of image processing, data clustering and Graph coloring, i.e., how we can use the memetic algorithms in graph coloring problems, how it can be used in clustering based problems and how it is useful in image processing. Here, we discuss how these algorithms can be used for optimization problems. We conclude by reinforcing the importance of research on the areas of metaheuristics for optimization.

Ayan Chatterjee, Sarboday Public Academy, India
Nikhilesh Barik, Kazi Nazrul University, India

Today, in the time of internet based communication, steganography is an important approach. In this approach, secret information is embedded in a cover medium with minimum distortion of it. Here, a video steganography scheme is developed in frequency domain category. Frequency domain is more effective than spatial domain due to variation data insertion domain. To change actual domain of entropy pixels of the video frames, uniform crossover of Genetic Algorithm (GA) is used. Then for data insertion in video frames, single layer perceptron of Artificial Neural Network is used. This particular concept of information security is attractive due to its high security during wireless communication. The effectiveness of the proposed technique is analyzed with the parameters PSNR (Peak Signal to Noise Ratio), IF and Payload (bpb).

Computational approaches like "Black box" predictive modeling approaches are extensively used technique applied in machine learning operations of today. Considering the latest trends, present study compares capabilities of two different "Black box" predictive model like ANFIS and ANN with a population-based evolutionary algorithm GEP for forecasting machining parameters of Inconel 690 material, machined in a CNC-assisted 3-axis milling machine. The aims of this article are to represent considerable data showing, every techniques performance under the criteria of root mean square error (RSME), Correlational coefficient R and Mean absolute percentage error (MAPE). In this chapter, we vigorously demonstrate that the performance of the GEP model is far superior to ANFIS and ANN model.

Simulated annealing is a probabilistic local search method for global combinatorial optimisation problems allowing gradual convergence to a near-optimal solution. It consists of a sequence of moves from a current solution to a better one according to certain transition rules while accepting occasionally some uphill solutions in order to guarantee diversity in the domain exploration and to avoid getting caught at local optima. The process is managed by a certain static or dynamic cooling schedule that controls the number of iterations. This meta-heuristic provides several advantages that include the ability of escaping local optima and the use of small amount of short-term memory. A wide range of applications and variants have hitherto emerged as a consequence of its adaptability to many combinatorial as well as continuous optimisation cases, and also its guaranteed asymptotic convergence to the global optimum.

Chapter 8

This chapter presents an overview of some widely accepted bio-inspired metaheuristic algorithms which would be helpful in solving the problems of software testing. Testing is an integral part of the software development process. A sizable number of Nature based algorithms coming under the per- view of metaheuristics have been used by researchers to solve practical problems of different disciplines of engineering and computer science, and software engineering. Here an exhaustive review of metaheuristic algorithms which have been employed to optimize the solution of test data generation for past 20 -30 years is presented. In addition to this, authors have reviewed their own work has been developed particularly to generate test data for path coverage based testing using Cuckoo Search and Gravitational Search algorithms. Also, an extensive comparison with the results obtained using Genetic Algorithms, Particle swarm optimization, Differential Evolution and Artificial Bee Colony algorithm are presented to establish the significance of the study.

Chapter 9

Vikas Bhatnagar, NIT Warangal, India
Ritanjali Majhi, NIT Warangal, India
S. L. Tulasi Devi, NIT Warangal, India

A lot of studies have been made on new product development process to make it an ideal procedure and many researchers have contributed significantly to achieve this by studying various factors associated with it. In this study, an attempt has been made to predict the optimal numbers of new products produced by electronics and metal & machinery industry by considering various factors those significantly affects the production pattern of these industries. For prediction purposes, functional linked artificial neural network (FLANN) with and without nature-inspired techniques have been used and comparison of performance for both the models have been done by using mean square error (MSE) and mean absolute percentage error (MAPE) as the measurement indices.

Chapter 10

Atta ur Rahman, University of Dammam, Saudi Arabia

Dynamic allocation of the resources for optimum utilization and throughput maximization is one of the most important fields of research nowadays. In this process the available resources are allocated in such a way that they are maximally utilized to enhance the overall system throughput. In this chapter a similar problem is approached which is found in Orthogonal Frequency Division Multiplexing (OFDM) environment, in which the transmission parameters namely the code rate, modulation scheme and power are adapted in such a way that overall system's data rate is maximized with a constrained bit error rate and transmit power. A Fuzzy Rule Base System (FRBS) is proposed for adapting the code rate and modulation scheme while Genetic Algorithm (GA) and Differential Evolution (DE) algorithm are used for adaptive power allocation. The proposed scheme is compared with other schemes in the literature including the famous Water-filling technique which is considered as a benchmark in the adaptive loading paradigm. Supremacy of the proposed technique is shown through computer simulations.

Chapter 11

Ch. Sanjeev Kumar Dash, Silicon Institute of Technology, India
Ajit Kumar Behera, Silicon Institute of Technology, India
Sarat Chandra Nayak, Kommuri Pratap Reddy Institute of Technology, India

This chapter presents a novel approach for classification of dataset by suitably tuning the parameters of radial basis function networks with an additional cost of feature selection. Inputting optimal and relevant set of features to a radial basis function may greatly enhance the network efficiency (in terms of accuracy) at the same time compact its size. In this chapter, the authors use information gain theory (a kind of filter approach) for reducing the features and differential evolution for tuning center and spread of radial basis functions. Different feature selection methods, handling missing values and removal of inconsistency to improve the classification accuracy of the proposed model are emphasized. The proposed approach is validated with a few benchmarking highly skewed and balanced dataset retrieved from University of California, Irvine (UCI) repository. The experimental study is encouraging to pursue further extensive research in highly skewed data.

This chapter will discuss and present a new model to perform a competency map in an educational institute which has moderate number of faculty members on whom the map has to be performed. Performing such a map is a tough but essential task. Hence utmost objectivity must be followed for the procedure. In this chapter the authors performed academic load assignment to the faculty members of a particular dept at the onset of a semester. Few parameters that have been considered as the input parameters are depth of knowledge, sincerity, class management, contribution towards research, text book publication. part from that one of the main concerns is the assignment is done by taking into consideration the preferences of a particular faculty in terms of teaching a subject. There are number of constraints which need to be considered while making the load assignment. The AICTE guidelines for teaching load allotment have been considered as a baseline. The MOPSO has been used to perform the competency map and the simulation results have been presented to show the effectiveness of the method.

One of the most studied methods to get approximate solutions in optimization problems are the heuristics methods. Heuristics are usually employed to find good, but not necessarily optima solutions. The primary purpose of the chapter at hand is to provide a survey of the Greedy Randomized Adaptive Search Procedures (GRASP). GRASP is an iterative multi-start metaheuristic for solving complex optimization problems. Each GRASP iteration consists of a construction phase followed by a local search procedure. In this paper, we first describe the basic components of GRASP and the various elements that compose it. We present different variations of the basic GRASP in order to improve its performance. The GRASP has encompassed a wide range of applications, covering different fields because of its robustness and easy to apply.

The class of Textiles produced from terephthalic acid and ethylene glycol by condensation polymerization has many end-uses for example these are used as filter fabric in railway track to prevent soil erosion, in cement industry these are used in boiler department as filter fabric to prevent the fly-ash from mixing in the atmosphere. Presently, the quality checking is done by the human in the naked eye. The automation of quality check of the non-Newtonian fabric can be termed as Image Analysis or texture analysis problem. A Simulation study was carried out by the process of Image Analysis which consists of two steps the former is feature extraction and the later part is recognition. Various techniques or tools that are presently studied in research for texture feature extraction are Grey level co-occurrence matrix(GLCM), Markov Random Field, Gabor filter. A GLCM matrix with 28 Haralick features were taken as input for this chapter.

Multi-Criteria Decision Making has evolved as an important tool for taking some of the most important decisions in the today's hi-tech engineering world. But due to some reasons like measurement difficulty, lack of data, faulty instruments, etc., or due to lack of absolute information about the topic, alternatives present and the criteria, decision making becomes very difficult as all parameter for modeling a decision making problem are not precise. In such scenario the importance of one with respect to the others are represented in terms of linguistic factor. Such cases could be tackled by considering the problem in fuzzy environment. In this chapter, the different hybrid fuzzy MCDM techniques are shown along with their application in different engineering problems. One problem is randomly selected and solved using different fuzzy MCDM techniques and compared the result with the existing literature.

Chapter 16

Due to advancement in technology, a huge volume of data is generated. Extracting knowledgeable data from this voluminous information is a difficult task. Therefore, machine learning techniques like classification, clustering, information retrieval, feature selection and data analysis has become core of recent research. These techniques can also be solved using Nature Inspired Algorithms. Nature Inspired Algorithms is inspired by processes, observed from nature. Feature Selection is helpful in finding subset of prominent components to enhance prescient precision and to expel the excess features. This chapter surveys seven nature inspired algorithms, namely Particle Swarm Optimization, Ant Colony Optimization Algorithms, Artificial Bees Colony Algorithms, Firefly Algorithms, Bat Algorithms, Cuckoo Search and Genetic Algorithms and its application in feature selections. The significance of this chapter is to present comprehensive review of nature inspired algorithms to be applied in feature selections.

Nature-Inspired algorithms have gained relevance particularly for solving complex optimization problems in engineering domain. An overview of implementation modeling of the established algorithms to newly developed algorithms is outlined. Mobile location management has vital importance in wireless cellular communication and can be viewed as an optimization problem. It has two aspects: location update and paging where the objective is to reduce the overall cost incurred corresponding to these two operations. The potential application of the Nature-Inspired algorithms to mobile location management is studied. Many such algorithms are recently being explored along with incremental modifications to the existing techniques. Finally, analysis and insights highlight the further scopes of the Nature-Inspired algorithms to mobile location management application.

Nature-inspired algorithms are still at a very early stage with a relatively short history, comparing with many traditional, well-established methods. Metaheuristics, in their original definition, are solution methods that orchestrate an interaction between local improvement procedures and higher level strategies to create a process capable of escaping from local optima and performing a robust search of a solution space. One major algorithm is Ant Colony Optimization which has been applied in varied domains to better the performance. Fuzzy Linear Programming models and methods has been one of the most and well-studied topics inside the broad area of Soft Computing. Its applications as well as practical realizations can be found in all the real-world areas. Here we wish to introduce how fuzziness can be included in a nature inspired algorithm like ant colony optimization and thereby enhance its functionality. Several applications of ACO with fuzzy concepts will be introduced in the chapter.

Chapter 19

In this chapter an effort has been made to develop a hybrid system using functional link artificial neural network (FLANN) and differential evolution (DE) for effective recognition of Odia handwritten numerals. The S-transform (ST) is chosen for feature extraction from handwritten numerals and these are further reduced by using principal component analysis (PCA). After reduction of feature the reduced features are applied to FLANN model for recognition of each numeral. Further differential evolution algorithm (DE) is used for the optimization of weights of FLANN classifier. For performance comparison, genetic algorithm (GA) and particle swarm optimization (PSO) based FLANN models (FLANN_GA and FLANN_PSO) are also designed and simulated under similar condition. The efficiency of proposed DE based FLANN (FLANN_DE) method is assessed through simulation with standard dataset consisting of 4000 handwritten Odia numerals. The results of three models are compared and it is observed that the FLANN_DE model provides the best result as compared to other models.

Chapter 20

In the new direction of understand the signal that is created from the brain organization is one of the main chores in the brain signal processing. Amid all the neurological disorders the human brain epilepsy is measured as one of the extreme prevalent and then programmed artificial intelligence detection technique is an essential due to the crooked and unpredictable nature of happening of epileptic seizures. We proposed an Improved Fuzzy firefly algorithm, which would enhance the classification of the brain signal efficiently with minimum iteration. An important bunching technique created on fuzzy logic is the Fuzzy C means. Together in the feature domain with the spatial domain the features gained after multichannel EEG signals remained combined by means of fuzzy algorithms. And for better precision segmentation process the firefly algorithm is applied to optimize the Fuzzy C-means membership function. This proposed algorithm result compared with other algorithms like fuzzy c means algorithm and PSO algorithm.

Chapter 21

Soumya Sahoo, C. V. Raman College of Engineering, India
Sushruta Mishra, C. V. Raman College of Engineering, India
Brojo Kishore Kishore Mishra, C. V. Raman College of Engineering, India
Monalisa Mishra, C. V. Raman College of Engineering, India

The growing complexity of real-world problems has motivated computer scientists to search for efficient problem-solving methods. Evolutionary computation and swarm intelligence meta-heuristics are outstanding examples that nature has been an unending source of inspiration. The behaviour of bees, bacteria, glow-worms, fireflies, slime moulds, cockroaches, mosquitoes and other organisms have inspired swarm intelligence researchers to devise new optimisation algorithms. Swarm Intelligence appears in biological swarms of certain insect species. It gives rise to complex and often intelligent behavior through complex interaction of thousands of autonomous swarm members. In this chapter, the ABC algorithm has been extended for solving constrained optimization problems and applied to a set of constrained problems.

Chapter 22

Sarat Chandra Nayak, Kommuri Pratap Reddy Institute of Technology, India
Bijan Bihari Misra, Silicon Institute of Technology, India
Himansu Sekhar Behera, Veer Surendra Sai University of Technology, India

Random fluctuations occur in the trend of financial time series due to many macroeconomic factors. Such fluctuations lead to sudden fall after a constant raise or a sudden rise after a constant fall, which are difficult to predict from previous data points. At the fluctuation point, previous data points that are not too close to the target price adversely influence the prediction trend. Far away points may be ignored and close enough virtual data points are explored and incorporated in order to diminish the adverse prediction trend at fluctuations. From the given data points in the training set, virtual data positions (VDP) can be explored and used to enhance the prediction accuracy. This chapter presents some deterministic and stochastic approaches to explore such VDPs. From the given data points in the training set, VDPs are explored and incorporated to the original financial time series to enhance the prediction accuracy of the model. To train and validate the models, ten real stock indices are used and the models developed with the VDPs yields much better prediction accuracy.

    Pijush Samui, National Institute of Technology Patna, India
    Viswanathan R., Galgotias University, India
    Jagan J., VIT University, India
    Pradeep U. Kurup, University of Massachusetts – Lowell, USA

This study adopts four modeling techniques Ordinary Kriging(OK), Generalized Regression Neural Network(GRNN), Genetic Programming(GP) and Minimax Probability Machine Regression(MPMR) for prediction of rock depth(d) at Chennai(India). Latitude (Lx) and Longitude(Ly) have been used as inputs of the models. A semivariogram has been constructed for developing the OK model. The developed GP gives equation for prediction of d at any point in Chennai. A comparison of four modeling techniques has been carried out. The performance of MPMR is slightly better than the other models. The developed models give the spatial variability of rock depth at Chennai.

Preface

In the past 25-30 years, a new approach of approximate algorithm has emerged which combines the basic heuristic methods in higher-level frameworks aiming to efficiently and effectively exploring a search space. These methods are referred to as *metaheuristics* and gaining tremendous attention from researchers of various domains. The term *metaheuristic*, first introduced in Gloves (1986), derives from the composition of two Greek words. *Heuristic* derives from the verb *heuriskein* which means 'to find', while the suffix *meta* means "beyond in an upper level". Before this term was widely adopted, metaheuristics were often termed as *modern heuristics* (Reeves, 1993). This class of algorithms includes Ant Colony Optimization (ACO), Evolutionary Computation (EC), Genetic Algorithms (GA), Iterated Local Search (ILS), Simulated Annealing (SA), and Tabu Search (TS). Till date, there is no commonly accepted definition for the term metaheuristic. It is just in the last few years that some researchers in the field tried to propose a definition. In the following, we quote some of them:

- *A metaheuristic is formally defined as an iterative generation process which guides a subordinate heuristic by combining intelligently different concepts for exploring and exploiting the search space, learning strategies are used to structure information in order to find efficiently near-optimal solutions* (Osman & Laporte, 1996).
- *A metaheuristic is an iterative master process that guides and modifies the operations of subordinate heuristics to efficiently produce high-quality solutions. It may manipulate a complete (or incomplete) single solution or a collection of solutions at each iteration. The subordinate heuristics could be a high (or low) level procedure, or a simple local search, or just a construction method* (Vob et al., 1999).
- *A metaheuristic is a set of concepts that can be used to define heuristic methods that can be applied to a wide set of different problems. In other words, a metaheuristic can be seen as a general algorithmic framework which can be applied to different optimization problems with relatively few modifications to make them adapted to a specific problem* (www.metaheuristic).

In short, we could say that metaheuristics are high-level strategies for exploring search spaces by using different methods. Of great importance hereby is that a dynamic balance is given between *diversification* and *intensification*. The term diversification generally refers to the exploration of the search space, whereas the term intensification refers to the exploitation of the accumulated search experience. These terms stem from the Tabu Search field (Glover & Laguna, 1997) and it is important to clarify that the terms *exploration* and *exploitation* are sometimes used instead, for example in the Evolutionary Computation field (Eiber & Schippers, 1998), with a more restricted meaning. In fact, the notions of exploitation and exploration often refer to rather short-term strategies tied to randomness, whereas intensification and diversification also refer to medium and long-term strategies based on the usage of memory. The search strategies of different metaheuristics are highly dependent on the philosophy of the metaheuristic itself. There are several different philosophies apparent in the existing metaheuristics. Some of them can be seen as intelligent extensions of local search algorithms. The goal of this kind of metaheuristic is to escape from local minima in order to proceed in the exploration of the search space and to move on to find hopefully better local minima which generally happens in Tabu Search, Iterated Local Search, Variable Neighbourhood Search, GRASP and Simulated Annealing.

CLASSIFICATION OF METAHEURISTIC ALGORITHMS

There are different ways to classify and describe metaheuristic algorithms. Depending on the characteristics selected to differentiate among them, several classifications are possible, each of them being the result of a specific viewpoint. We briefly summarize the most important ways of classifying metaheuristics.

- **Nature-Inspired vs. Non-Nature Inspired:** Perhaps, the most intuitive way of classifying metaheuristics is based on the origins of the algorithm. There are nature-inspired algorithms, like Genetic Algorithms and Ant Algorithms, and non-nature-inspired ones such as Tabu Search and Iterated Local Search. In our opinion, this classification is not very meaningful for the following two reasons. First, many recent hybrid algorithms do not fit either class (or, in a sense, they fit both at the same time). Second, it is sometimes difficult to clearly attribute an algorithm to one of the two classes. Therefore, for example, one might ask the question if the use of memory in Tabu Search is not nature-inspired as well.

- **Population-Based vs. Single Point Search:** Another characteristic that can be used for the classification of metaheuristics is the number of solutions used at the same time: Does the algorithm work on a population or on a single solution at any time? Algorithms working on single solutions are called *trajectory methods* and encompass local search-based metaheuristics, like Tabu Search, Iterated Local Search, and Variable Neighbourhood Search. They all share the property of describing a trajectory in the search space during the search process. Population-based metaheuristics, on the contrary, perform search processes which describe the evolution of a set of points in the search space.

- **Dynamic vs. Static Objective Function:** Metaheuristics can also be classified according to the way they make use of the objective function. While some algorithms keep the objective function given in the problem representation "as it is", some others, like Guided Local Search (GLS), modify it during the search. The idea behind this approach is to escape from local minima by modifying the search landscape. Accordingly, during the search the objective function is altered by trying to incorporate information collected during the search process.

- **One vs. Various Neighbourhood Structures:** Most metaheuristic algorithms work on one single neighbourhood structure. In other words, the fitness landscape topology does not change in the course of the algorithm. Other metaheuristics, such as Variable Neighbourhood Search (VNS), use a set of neighbourhood structures which gives the possibility to diversify the search by swapping between different fitness landscapes.

- **Memory Usage vs. Memory-Less Methods:** A very important feature to classify metaheuristics is the use they make of the search history, that is, whether they use memory or not. Memory-less algorithms perform a Markov process, as the information they exclusively use to determine the next action is the current state of the search process. There are several different ways of making use of memory. Usually we differentiate between the use of short term and long-term memory. The first usually keeps track of recently performed moves, visited solutions or, in general, decisions taken. The second is usually an accumulation of synthetic parameters about the search. The use of memory is nowadays recognized as one of the fundamental elements of a powerful metaheuristic.

CHARACTERISTICS OF METAHEURISTIC ALGORITHMS

The efficiency of metaheuristic algorithms can be attributed to the fact that they imitate the best features in nature, especially the selection of the fittest in biological systems which have evolved by natural selection over millions of years. Two important characteristics of metaheuristics are: intensification and diversification (Blum & Roli, 2003). Intensification intends to search locally and more intensively, while diversification makes sure the algorithm explores the search space globally (hopefully also efficiently).

Furthermore, intensification is also called exploitation, as it typically searches around the current best solutions and selects the best candidates or solutions. Similarly, diversification is also called exploration, as it strives to explore the search space more efficiently, often by large-scale randomisation.

The fine balance between these two components is very important to the overall efficiency and performance of an algorithm. Too little exploration and too much exploitation could cause the system to be trapped in local optima, which makes it very difficult or even impossible to find the global optimum. On the other hand, if too much exploration but too little exploitation, it may be difficult for the system to converge and thus slows down the overall search performance. The proper balance itself is an optimisation problem, and one of the main tasks of designing new algorithms is to find a certain balance concerning this optimality and/or trade-off. Obviously, simple exploitation and exploration are not enough. During the search, we have to use a proper mechanism or criterion to select the best solutions. The most common criterion is to use the *Survival of the Fittest* that is to keep updating the current best found so far. In addition, certain elitism is often used, and this is to ensure the best or fittest solutions are not lost, and should be passed onto the next generations.

There are many ways of carrying out intensification and diversification. In fact, each algorithm and its variants use different ways of achieving the balance of between exploration and exploitation. By analysing all the metaheuristic algorithms, we can categorically say that the way to achieve exploration or diversification is mainly by certain randomisation in combination with a deterministic procedure. This ensures that the newly generated solutions distribute as diversely as possible in the feasible search space. One of simplest and yet most commonly used randomisation techniques is to use:

$$xnew = L + (U - L) * \varepsilon u,$$

where L and U are the lower bound and upper bound, respectively. εu is a uniformly distributed random variable in $[0,1]$. This is often used in many algorithms such as harmony search, particle swarm optimisation, and firefly algorithm. It is worth pointing that the use of a uniform distribution is not the only way to achieve randomisation. In fact, random walks such as Lévy flights on a global scale are more efficient.

A more elaborate way to obtain diversification is to use mutation and crossover. Mutation makes sure new solutions are as far / different as possible, from their parents or existing solutions; while crossover limits the degree of over diversification, as new solutions are generated by swapping parts of the existing solutions. The main way to achieve the exploitation is to generate new solutions around a promising or better solution locally and more intensively. This can be easily achieved by a local random walk:

xnew = xold + s w,

where w is typically drawn from a Gaussian distribution with zero mean. Here is the step size of the random walk. In general, the step size should be small enough so that only local neighbourhood is visited. If s is too large, the region visited can be too far away from the region of interest, which will increase the diversification significantly but reduce the intensification greatly. Therefore, a proper step size should be much smaller than (and be linked with) the scale of the problem. For example, the pitch adjustment in harmony search and the move in simulated annealing are a random walk. If we want to increase the efficiency of this random walk (and thus increase the efficiency of exploration as well), we can use other forms of random walks such as Lévy flights where s is drawn from a Lévy distribution with large step sizes. In fact, any distribution with a long tail will help to increase the step size and distance of such random walks. Even with the standard random walk, we can use a more selective or controlled walk around the current best xbest, rather than any good solution. This is equivalent to replacing the above equation by:

xnew = xbest + s w.

Some intensification technique is not easy to decode, but may be equally effective. The crossover operator in evolutionary algorithms is a good example, as it uses the solutions/strings from parents to form offspring or new solutions. In many algorithms, there is no clear distinction or explicit differentiation between intensification and diversification. These two steps are often intertwined and interactive, which may, in some cases, become an advantage. Good examples of such interaction are the genetic algorithms (Holland, 1975), harmony search (Geem et al., 2001), and bat algorithm (Yang 2010b). Readers can analyse any chosen algorithm to see how these components are implemented.

In addition, the selection of the best solutions is a crucial component for the success of an algorithm. Simple, blind exploration and exploitation may not be effective without the proper selection of the solutions of good quality. Simply choosing the best may be effective for optimisation problems with a unique global optimum. Elitism and keeping the best solutions are efficient for multimodal and multi-objective problems. Elitism in genetic algorithms and selection of harmonics are good examples of the selection of the fittest. In contrast with the selection of the best solutions, an efficient metaheuristic algorithm should have a way to discard the worse solutions so as to increase the overall quality of the populations during evolution. Some form of randomisation and probabilistic selection criteria often achieves this. For example, mutation in genetic algorithms acts a way to do this. Similarly, in the cuckoo search, the castaway of a nest/solution is another good example (Yang & Deb, 2009).

Another important issue is the randomness reduction. Randomisation is mainly used to explore the search space diversely on the global scale, and also, to some extent, the exploitation on a local scale. As better solutions are found, and as the system converges, the degree of randomness should be reduced; otherwise, it will slow down the convergence. For example, in particle swarm optimisation, randomness is automatically reduced as the particles swarm together (Kennedy & Eberhart, 1995); this is because the distance between each particle and the current global best is becoming smaller and smaller. In other algorithms, randomness is not reduced and but controlled and selected. For example, the mutation rate is usually small so as to limit the randomness, while in simulated annealing, the randomness during iterations may remain the same, but the solutions or moves are selected and acceptance probability becomes smaller.

Finally, from the implementation point of view, the actual implementation does vary, even though the pseudo code should give a good guide and should not in principle lead to ambiguity. However, in practice, the actual way of implementing the algorithm does affect the performance to some degree. Therefore, validation and testing of any algorithm implementation are important (Talbi, 2009).

This book has covered all the aspects of nature-inspired metaheuristic algorithms including modelling, analysis, and applications and hence will provide a good insight of all aspects to the keen readers. After a very careful shortlisting process, contents of the book are selected from the diverse areas of study, including engineering, bio-informatics, telecommunication, big data, data mining and much more. Hence, for sure, the readers from any area of research will be equally benefitted from the book.

ORGANIZATION OF THE BOOK

The book is organized into 23 chapters. A brief description of each of the chapters follows:

Chapter 1 focuses on key applications of metaheuristic techniques in the field of gene selection and classification of microarray data. In this article, two different types of metaheuristics such as Genetic algorithm (GA) and Particle Swarm Optimization (PSO) are hybridized with fuzzy-rough (FR) method for optimizing the subset selection process of microarray data..

Chapter 2 emphasizes the characteristics of nature inspired techniques towards optimizing neural network architectures along with its applicability, advantages and limitations/challenges are studied.

Chapter 3 focused on Net asset value (NAV) prediction, as small investors are doing investment in there, Literature survey reveals that very few work has been done in this field. The reported literature mainly used various neural network models for NAV prediction. But the derivative based learning algorithms of these reported models have the problem of trapping into the local solution. Hence in chapter derivative free algorithm, particle swarm optimization is used to update the parameters of radial basis function neural network for prediction of NAV.

Chapter 4 has explored the applications of memetic algorithms to problems within the domains of image processing, data clustering and Graph coloring. i.e, how can use memetic algorithms in graph coloring problems, in clustering based problems and in image processing. Here, authors have highlighted how these algorithms can be used for optimization problems and concluded by reinforcing the importance of research on the areas of metaheuristics for optimization.

Chapter 5 developed a video steganography scheme in frequency domain category. Frequency domain is more effective than spatial domain due to variation data insertion domain. To change actual domain of entropy pixels of the video frames, uniform crossover of Genetic Algorithm (GA) is used. Then for data insertion in video frames, single layer perceptron of Artificial Neural Network is used. This particular concept of information security is attractive due to its high security during wireless communication. The effectiveness of the proposed technique is analyzed with the parameters PSNR (Peak Signal to Noise Ratio), IF and Payload (bpb).

Chapter 6 has compared capabilities of two different "Black box" predictive model like ANFIS and ANN with a population-based evolutionary algorithm GEP for forecasting machining parameters of Inconel 690 material, machined in a CNC-assisted 3 axis milling machine and concluded that the performance of the GEP model is far superior to ANFIS and ANN model.

Chapter 7 explains about simulated annealing which is a probabilistic local search method for global combinatorial optimization problems allowing gradual convergence to a near-optimal solution. It consists of a sequence of moves from a current solution to a better one according to certain transition rules while accepting occasionally some uphill solutions in order to guarantee diversity in the domain exploration and to avoid getting caught at local optima.

Chapter 8 presents some widely accepted Bio-inspired metaheuristic algorithms which would be helpful in solving the problems of software testing. Testing is an integral part of the software development process. A sizable number of Nature based algorithms coming under the perview of metaheuristics have been used by researchers to solve practical problems of different disciplines of engineering and computer science, and software engineering. Here an exhaustive review of metaheuristic algorithms which have been employed to optimize the solution of test data generation for past 20 -30 years is presented.

Chapter 9 has attempted to predict the optimal numbers of new products produced by electronics and metal & machinery industry by considering various factors those significantly affects the production pattern of these industries. For prediction purpose functional linked artificial neural network (FLANN) with and without nature inspired techniques have been used and comparison of performance for both the models have been done by using mean square error (MSE) and mean absolute percentage error (MAPE) as the measurement indices.

Chapter 10 proposed a Fuzzy Rule Base System (FRBS) for adapting the code rate and modulation scheme while Genetic Algorithm (GA) and Differential Evolution (DE) algorithm are used for adaptive power allocation. The proposed scheme is compared with other schemes in the literature including the famous Water-filling technique which is considered as a benchmark in the adaptive loading paradigm. Supremacy of the proposed technique is shown through computer simulations.

Chapter 11 presents a novel approach for classification of dataset by suitably tuning the parameters of radial basis function networks with an additional cost of feature selection. Authors have used information gain theory (a kind of filter approach) for reducing the features and differential evolution for tuning center and spread of radial basis functions. Different feature selection methods, handling missing values and removal of inconsistency to improve the classification accuracy of the proposed model are emphasized.

Chapter 12 discussed and presents a new model to perform a competency map in an educational institute which has moderate number of faculty members on whom the map has to be performed. Authors performed academic load assignment to the faculty members of a particular department at the onset of a semester. The MOPSO has been used to perform the competency map and the simulation results have been presented to show the effectiveness of the method.

Chapter 13 provides a survey of the Greedy Randomized Adaptive Search Procedures (GRASP). Authors have highlighted the basic components of GRASP and the various elements that compose it and different variations of the basic GRASP in order to enhance or improve its performance.

Chapter 14 has made a simulation study using the process of Image Analysis which consists of two steps the former is feature extraction and the second part is recognition. Various techniques or tools that are presently in research for texture feature extraction are Grey level co-occurrence matrix(GLCM), Markov Random Field, Gabor filter.

Chapter 15 has studied on Multi-Criteria Decision Making which is evolved as an important tool for taking some of the most important decisions in the today's hi-tech engineering world. Different hybrid fuzzy MCDM techniques are shown along with their application in different engineering problems. One problem is randomly selected and solved using different fuzzy MCDM techniques and compared the result with the existing literature.

Chapter 16 surveys seven nature inspired algorithms, namely Particle Swarm Optimization, Ant Colony Optimization Algorithms, Artificial Bees Colony Algorithms, Firefly Algorithms, Bat Algorithms, Cuckoo Search and Genetic Algorithms and its application in feature selections. The significance of this chapter is to present comprehensive review of nature inspired algorithms to be applied in feature selections.

Chapter 17 studied about the potential application of the Nature-Inspired algorithms to mobile location management. Many such algorithms are recently being explored along with incremental modifications to the existing techniques. Finally, analysis and insights highlight the further scopes of the Nature-Inspired algorithms to mobile location management application.

Chapter 18 has introduced how fuzziness can be included in a nature inspired algorithm like ant colony optimization and thereby enhance its functionality. Several applications of ACO with fuzzy concepts will be introduced in the chapter.

Chapter 19 In this chapter an effort has been made to develop a hybrid system using functional link artificial neural network (FLANN) and differential evolution (DE) for effective recognition of Odia handwritten numerals. The S-transform (ST) is chosen for feature extraction from handwritten numerals and these are further reduced by using principal component analysis (PCA). The efficiency of proposed DE based FLANN (FLANN_DE) method is assessed through simulation with standard dataset consisting of 4000 handwritten Odia numerals.

Chapter 20 proposed an Improved Fuzzy firefly algorithm, which would enhance the classification of the brain signal efficiently with minimum iteration. An important bunching technique created on fuzzy logic is the Fuzzy C means. Together in the feature domain with the spatial domain the features gained after multichannel EEG signals remained combined by means of fuzzy algorithms. And for better precision segmentation process the firefly algorithm is applied to optimize the Fuzzy C-means membership function.

Chapter 21 emphasizes the growing complexity of real-world problems has motivated computer scientists to search for efficient problem-solving methods. The behavior of bees, bacteria, glow-worms, fireflies, slime moulds, cockroaches, mosquitoes and other organisms have inspired swarm intelligence researchers to devise new optimization algorithms. This chapter focusses on ABC algorithm for solving constrained optimization problems and applied to a set of constrained problems.

Chapter 22 presents some deterministic and stochastic approaches to explore such VDPs. From the given data points in the training set, VDPs are explored and incorporated to the original financial time series to enhance the prediction accuracy of the model. To train and validate the models, ten real stock indices are used and the models developed with the VDPs yields much better prediction accuracy.

Chapter 23 This study adopts four modeling techniques Ordinary Kriging(OK), Generalized Regression Neural Network(GRNN), Genetic Programming(GP) and Minimax Probability Machine Regression(MPMR) for prediction of rock depth(d) at Chennai(India The performance of MPMR is slightly better than the other models. The developed models give the spatial variability of rock depth at Chennai.

REFERENCES

Blum, C., & Roli, A. (2003). Metaheuristics in combinatorial optimisation: Overview and conceptual comparision. *ACM Computing Surveys*, *35*, 268–308. doi:10.1145/937503.937505

Eiben, A. E., & Schippers, C. A. (1998). On evolutionary exploration and exploitation. *Fundamenta Informaticae*, *35*, 1-16.

Geem, Z. W., Kim, J. K., & Loganathan, G. V. (2001). A new heuristic optimisation: Harmony search. *Simulation*, *76*(2), 60–68. doi:10.1177/003754970107600201

Glover, F. (1986). Future paths for integer programming and links to artificial intelligence. *Comp. Oper. Res.*, *13*, 533-549.

Glover, F., & Laguna, M. (1997). *Tabu Search*. Kluwer Academic Publishers. doi:10.1007/978-1-4615-6089-0

Holland, J. (1975). *Adaptation in Natural and Artificial systems*. University of Michigan Press.

Kennedy, J., & Eberhart, R. (1995). Particle swarm optimization. *Proc. of the IEEE Int. Conf. on Neural Networks*, 1942-1948. doi:10.1109/ICNN.1995.488968

Osman, I. H., & Laporte, G. (1996). Metaheuristics: A bibliography. *Annals of Operations Research*, *63*, 513-623.

Reeves, C. R. (Ed.). (1993). *Modern Heuristic Techniques for Combinatorial Problems*. Oxford, UK: Blackwell Scientific Publishing.

Talbi, E. G. (2009). *Metahueristics: From Design to Implementation*. Wiley. doi:10.1002/9780470496916

Voß, S., Martello, S., Osman, I. H., & Roucairol, C. (Eds.). (1999). *Meta-Heuristics - Advances and Trends in Local Search Paradigms for Optimization*. Dordrecht, The Netherlands: Kluwer Academic Publishers.

Yang, X. S. (2010b). A new metaheuristic bat-inspired algorithm. In J. R. Gonzalez et al. (Eds.), *Nature Inspired Cooperative Strategies for Optimization (NICSO 2010)* (Vol. 284, pp. 65–74). Springer, SCI. doi:10.1007/978-3-642-12538-6_6

Yang, X. S., & Deb, S. (2009). Cuckoo search via L'evy flights. *Proc. of World Congress on Nature & Biologically Inspired Computing*, 210-214. doi:10.1109/NABIC.2009.5393690

Acknowledgment

The editors would like to acknowledge the help of all the people involved in this project and, more specifically, to the authors and reviewers that took part in the review process. Without their support, this book would not have become a reality.

First, the editors would like to thank each one of the authors for their contributions. Our sincere gratitude goes to the chapter's authors who contributed their time and expertise to this book.

Second, the editors wish to acknowledge the valuable contributions of the reviewers regarding the improvement of quality, coherence, and content presentation of chapters. Most of the authors also served as referees; we highly appreciate their double task.

Sujata Dash
North Orissa University, India

B. K. Tripathy
VIT University, India

Atta ur Rehman
University of Dammam, Saudi Arabia

Chapter 1
Metaheuristic–Based Hybrid Feature Selection Models

Sujata Dash
North Orissa University, India

ABSTRACT

This chapter focuses on key applications of metaheuristic techniques in the field of gene selection and classification of microarray data. The metaheuristic techniques are efficient in handling combinatorial optimization problems. In this article, two different types of metaheuristics such as Genetic algorithm (GA) and Particle Swarm Optimization (PSO) are hybridized with fuzzy-rough (FR) method for optimizing the subset selection process of microarray data. The FR method applied here deals with impreciseness and uncertainty of microarray data. The predictive accuracy of the models is evaluated by an adaptive neural net ensemble and by a rule based classifier MODLEM respectively. Moreover, the learning efficiency of the ensemble is compared with base learners and with two classical ensembles. The rule based classifier generates a set of rules for disease diagnosis and prognosis and enables to study the function of genes from gene ontology website. The experimental results of both the models prove that, hybrid metaheuristic techniques are highly effective for finding potential genes.

1. INTRODUCTION

Microarray technology produces high dimensional datasets by measuring the expression levels of tens of thousands of genes in a single experiment under varying conditions. It has become an indispensable tool for biological, medical and pharmaceutical researchers to get a better understanding of the diseases at genomic level. On the other hand, the inherent problem i.e., large number of features and small sample size of microarray dataset makes the analysis process difficult for the problem. Typically, are latively small numbers of features are found to be strongly correlated with the phenotypes in question? Therefore, to identify these discriminative features from gene expression dataset, a data mining tool (Witten, Frank & Hall, 2011) known as feature selection technique plays an important role. The methods specifically used for feature selection can be categorized into two major groups namely, filter and wrapper methods (Saeys, Inza&Larranaga, 2007; Guyon, Nikravesh, Zadeh, 2006; Dash& Patra, 2016a).

DOI: 10.4018/978-1-5225-2857-9.ch001

Filter methods select features considering individual characteristic of each feature without taking into account the mutual dependencies among features. Then the features are sorted by their assigned ranks. The top ranked features are kept for further analysis by removing low ranked features. Actually, these selected features are used to develop the diagnostic model to efficiently predict the diseases. On the contrary, in wrapper methods, a search algorithm is wrapped around a learning algorithm: so that an estimated learning accuracy for all subsets can be calculated to derive an optimal one. This method is computationally intensive in comparison to filter methods because to obtain an optimal subset of features all possible subsets need to be examined which is practically a difficult task. Thus, to alleviate this difficulty in wrapper methods a metaheuristic search strategy (Ghosh & Jain (Eds),2005; Akadi, Amine, Ouardighi & Aboutajdine, 2009; Dash, 2016) may be adopted from a set of heuristic or stochastic algorithms which can be able to generate an optimal subset effectively.

In the gene selection process, an optimal gene subset is always relative to a certain criterion. Several information measures such as entropy, mutual information (Ding& Peng, 2005)and *f*-information (Maji, 2009) have successfully been used in selecting a set of relevant and non redundant genes from a microarray data set. An efficient and effective reduction method is necessary to cope with large amount of data by most techniques. Growing interest in developing methodologies that are capable of dealing with imprecision and uncertainty is apparent from the large scale research that are currently being done in the areas related to fuzzy (Zadeh, 1965) and rough sets. Rough set theory (RST) was introduced by Pawlak (1982) and has been used widely by researchers as a classifier and selection technique. The success of rough set theory is due to three aspects of the theory. First, only hidden facts in the data are analyzed. Second, additional information about the data is not required for data analysis. Third, it finds a minimal knowledge representation for data. Due to this Rough set theory is used in complement with other concepts such as, fuzzy set theory. The two fields may be considered similar in the sense that both can tolerate inconsistency and uncertainty. The only difference among these two fields is the type of uncertainty and their approach to it. While fuzzy sets are concerned with vagueness, rough sets are concerned with indiscernibility. The fuzzy- rough set-based approach considers the extent to which fuzzified values are similar.

The ensemble learning approach constructs several classifier models for the original dataset and then combines the predictive outputs to identify an unknown sample. The motivation of combinings several classifiers is to improve the classification efficiency which in turn depends on the accuracy and diversity (Yang P., Yang H., Bing, Zomaya, 2010) of the base classifiers. The ensemble techniques very popular in the field of classification and pattern recognition as it increases the generalization and percentage of classification by aggregating (Chen, Hong, Deng, Yang, Wei & Cui, 2015) the outcome of finite number of neural network classifiers (Lee, Hong & Kim, 2009a). However, neural network ensemble learning has been used in many problems, such as, face recognition (Lee, Hong &Kim, 2009 b), digital image processing (Liu, Cui, Jiang & Ma, 2004) and medical diagnosis (Huang,Zhou, Zhang & Chen, 2000) and has given outstanding performance in terms of classification accuracy.

In the last 30 years, a new kind of approximate algorithm has emerged which basically tries to combine basic heuristic methods in higher level frameworks aimed at efficiently and effectively exploring asearch space. These methods are nowadays commonly called *metaheuristics*. The term *metaheuristic*, first introduced in (Glover, 1986), derives from the composition of two Greek words. *Heuristic* derives from the verb *heuriskein,* which means "to find", while the suffix *meta* means "beyond, in an upper level". Before this term was widely adopted, metaheuristics were often called *modern heuristics* (Reeves, 1993).This class of algorithms includes but is not restricted to, Ant Colony Optimization (ACO), Evolutionary Computation (EC) including Genetic Algorithms (GA), Iterated Local Search (ILS), Simulated Annealing (SA), and Tabu Search (TS). A metaheuristic is formally defined (Osman & Laporte, 1996) as an iterative generation process which guides a subordinateheuristic by combining intelligently different concepts for exploring and exploiting the search space; learning strategies are used to structure information in order to find efficiently near-optimal solutions. We could say that metaheuristics are high level strategies for exploring search spaces by using different methods. Of great importance hereby is that a dynamic balance is given between *diversification* and *intensification*. The term diversification generally refers to the exploration of the search space, whereas the term intensification refers to the exploitation of the accumulated search experience. These terms stem from the Tabu Search field (Glover & Laguna, 1997) and it is important to clarify that the terms *exploration* and *exploitation* are sometimes used instead, for example in the Evolutionary Computation field (Eiben & Schippers, 1998), with a more restricted meaning. In fact, the notions of exploitation and exploration often refer to rather short term strategies tied to randomness, whereas intensification and diversification also refer to medium and long term strategies based on the usage of memory. The balance between diversification and intensification as mentioned above is important, on one side to quickly identify regions in the search space with high quality solutions and on the other side not to waste too much time in regions of the search space which are either already explored or which do not provide high quality solutions.

In this study, a hybrid metaheuristic gene selection model (Dash & Patra, 2012a) is introduced by hybridizing fuzzy-rough filter model (FR) with an evolutionary genetic search based wrapper model (GSNN) (Dash& Patra, 2016b). The efficiency of the hybrid model (FRGSNN) (Dash & Patra, 2016a) is evaluated by the proposed adaptive neural net ensemble learning algorithm. Again to prove the learning capability of ensemble algorithm, performance of the component classifiers pairing with FR, GSNN and FRGSNN are compared with proposed hybrid metaheuristic FRGSNN based ensemble model. In addition to this, efficiency of neural net ensemble is compared with two classical ensemble learning algorithms. Another hybrid metaheuristic gene selection model is designed by combining Particle Swarm Optimization (PSO) and Fuzzy-Rough algorithm to address the problem of gene selection. Particle Swarm Optimization (PSO), developed by (Kennedy & Eberhart, 1995), is a population-based meta-heuristic on the basis of stochastic optimization, inspired by the social behavior of flocks of birds or schools of fish (Chen et al., 2011). A swarm of particles move toward the optimal position along the search path that is iteratively updated on the basis of the best particle position and velocity in PSO (Dash, 2015; Mohamad et al., 2009). Here we consider a rule induction algorithm called MODLEM, introduced by (Stefanowskiin, 2003). MODLEM is a rule based specific search induction algorithm, whose rules are one of the most popular type of knowledge used in practice. This is mainly because they are both very expressive and human-readable at the same time. This algorithm is most suitable for analyzing data containing a mixture of numerical and qualitative attributes.

The proposed approach is an integration of PSO searching algorithm with Fuzzy-Rough subset evaluator called FRPSO. Combining PSO with Fuzzy-Rough as an evaluator has rarely been investigated by many researchers. The performance of our proposed method will be evaluated by 4 microarray datasets collected from Bioinformatics Laboratory, University of Ljubljana, http://www.biolab.si/supp/biancer/projections/info/lungGSE1987.htm, 1987.

The paper is structured in the following way: section 2 furnishing the background of rough set theory, fuzzy-rough set, genetic algorithm (GA), PSO and MODLEM. Section 3 and 4 illustrate the proposed learning models and all microarray datasets respectively. Experimental setups, results, analysis of comparison of the model, discussion of results and future scope are presented in section 5. Section 6 presents concluding remarks followed by exhaustive references.

2. BACKGROUND

Here, in this chapter, how the feature selection can be reduced to a search problem is discussed, where one selects a good feature subset based on a selected evaluation measure. Each state in the search space represents a subset of possible features. As per (Kohavi & George, 1996), to design a feature selection algorithm one has to define three following components: *search algorithm* (technique that looks through the space of feature subsets), *evaluation function* (used to evaluate examined subsets of features), and *classifier* (a learning algorithm that uses the final subset of features). These elements can be integrated in two ways: (a) *filter approach* and (b) *wrapper* approach.

2.1. Fuzzy-Rough Data Reduction

Fuzzy-Rough feature selection (FRFS) method is devised on the basis of the fuzzy lower approximation to enable reduction of datasets containing real-valued features. This method becomes similar to the crisp approach when dealing with nominal well-defined features. The crisp positive region in Rough Set Theory (RST) is defined as the union of the lower approximations. By the extension principle, the membership of an object x $\in$ U, belonging to the fuzzy positive region can be defined by

$$\mu_{POSp(Q)^{(x)}} = \frac{1}{X \in \frac{U}{Q}}^{SUP} \mu px^{(x)} \tag{1}$$

Object x will belong to the positive region only if the equivalence class it belongs to is a constituent of the positive region. This is similar to the crisp version where objects belong to the positive region only if their corresponding equivalence classes do so. The new dependency function can be defined using the definition of the fuzzy positive region as,

$$\gamma p^{(Q)} = \frac{\left| \mu_{POSp(Q)^{(x)}} \right|}{|U|} = \frac{\sum x \epsilon u \mu_{POSp(Q)^{(x)}}}{|u|} \tag{2}$$

Here the dependency of *Q* on *P* is the proportion of objects that are discernible out of the entire dataset, similar to the crisp rough sets. This corresponds to determining the fuzzy cardinality of $\mu_{POS\,P(Q)}$ *(x)* divided by the total number of objects in the universe. This may give rise to a problem if compared to the crisp approach. In conventional rough set-based feature selection, a reduct is a subset R of the features which have the same information as the full feature set A. In terms of the dependency function this means that the values $\gamma(R)$ and(A) are identical and equal to 1, provided the dataset does not contain any contradictory information. However, in the fuzzy-rough approach this is not necessarily true just because the uncertainty encountered when objects belong to many fuzzy equivalence classes results in a reduced total dependency. This can be overcome by determining the degree of dependency of a set of decision features D upon the full feature set and use this as the denominator rather than $|U|$, allowing γ' to reach 1.

2.2. Genetic Algorithms

Genetic algorithms are metaheuristic optimization methods motivated by biological phenomenon of natural selection and evolution and have wide applications in many different problems (Dash &Patra, 2012; Dash & Patra, 2013). It generates new population of chromosomes that is considered as the candidate solutions in the iteration. Each chromosome is encoded as a string of binary/ real,etc., version of a candidate solution. The fitness of each string of chromosome is then evaluated by fitness function $f(x)$. Two fittest chromosomes having more fitness value are likely to be selected from the population and the genetic operator crossover and mutation are applied to generate new offspring from new population. The variation is introduced to the selected individuals for obtaining global optimum solution using crossover and mutation (Dash & Patra, 2016; Luque-Baena, Urda,Subirats, Franco & Jerez, 2014).

2.3. Particle Swarm Optimization (PSO)

PSO has been used by many applications of several problems. The algorithm of PSO emulates from behavior of animals societies that don't have any leader in their group or swarm, such as bird flocking and fish schooling. Typically, a flock of animals that have no leaders will find food by random, follow

Figure 1. Lower and upper approximations of a rough set X

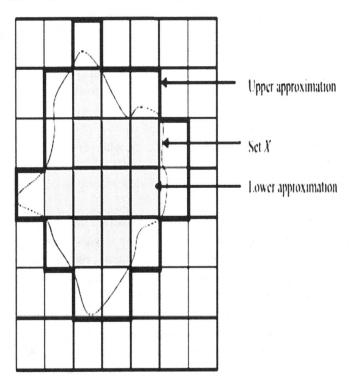

one of the members of the group that has the closest position with a food source (potential solution). The flocks achieve their best condition simultaneously through communication among members who already have a better situation. Animal which has a better condition will inform it to its flocks and the others will move simultaneously to that place. This would happen repeatedly until the best conditions or a food source discovered. The process of PSO algorithm in finding optimal values follows the work of this animal society. Particle swarm optimization consists of a swarm of particles, where particle represent a potential solution.

Exploration is the ability of a search algorithm to explore different region of the search space in order to locate a good optimum. Exploitation, on the other hand, is the ability to concentrate the search around a promising area in order to refine a candidate solution (Ahmed & Dey, 2005).With their exploration and exploitation, the particle of the swarm fly through hyperspace and have two essential reasoning capabilities: their memory of their own best position - *local best (lb)* and knowledge of the global or their neighborhood's best - *global best (gb)*.

2.4. Modlem Algorithm

It is a sequential covering algorithm, which treats nominal and numeric data in a similar way. It generates heuristically a minimal set of rules for every decision concept by finding best rule condition during rule induction from the attribute search space. It handles directly numerical attributes during rule induction when elementary conditions of rules are created, without using any preliminary discretization process. The rules induced from objects are represented as logical expressions of the following form:

IF (conditions) THEN (decision class);

where conditions are specified as conjunctions of elementary conditions on values of attributes, and decision part of the rule assigns a given class to an object which satisfies the condition. Due to the restriction in size of the paper, formal presentation of the algorithm is skipped and only the main objective of the algorithm is discussed. For more information (Chen et al., 2011) can be referred. The set of rules tries to cover all *positive examples* of the given concept and not to cover any *negative examples.* The procedure of rule induction starts by creating a first rule, i.e. choosing sequentially the best elementary conditions according to the criteria chosen (we have used *class entropy* in our experiments). Then the rule is matched with all positive learning examples. Moreover, when a rule is formed, all positive learning examples are required to be matched with the rule and the matching examples are needed to be removed from further consideration. The process is repeated iteratively as long as some positive examples of the decision concept remain still uncovered.

Then, the procedure is repeated sequentially for each decision class. The elementary conditions on numerical attributes are represented as either $(a < v_a)$ or $(a \leq v_a)$, where a denotes an attribute and v_a its value. Selection of the threshold v_a *is made* from checking several possible candidates and then all temporary conditions are evaluated over uncovered examples by means of the chosen evaluation measure. But, if the same attribute is selected twice while framing a single rule, one can obtain the condition $(a = [v1; v2))$ which results from an intersection of two conditions $(a < v2)$ and $(a \geq v1)$ such that $v1 < v2$. In case of nominal attributes, the equivalent conditions are represented as $(a = v_a)$. For more details about the function finding best elementary conditions see, (Mohamad et al., 2009).When the input data contains *inconsistent examples*, the rough sets theory can be used to handle them. In this theory inconsistencies are neither removed from consideration nor aggregated by probabilistic operations. Instead, lower and upper approximations of each class are computed. Basing on that two sets of rules corresponding to lower and upper approximations are induced. When the set of induced rules are applied to classify new examples, a classification strategy introduced by Grzymala in LERS system is used. This strategy considers completely matched rules but in some cases allows partially matching rules when it does not find the rules matching the description of tested examples.

3. THE PROPOSED LEARNING SCHEME

3.1. Hybrid Fuzzy-Rough-Genetic Search Method for Feature Selection

The first key element of the hybrid-FRGSNN model is its fuzzy-rough feature selection method which computes the reduct sets. Then an evolutionary search based wrapper model GSNN is employed on the outcome of filter FR method to select an optimal subset of features which is the outcome of the hybrid search FRGSNN model. Genetic algorithm is adopted here as a search tool to perform this operation. The reduct sets produced from fuzzy rough reduction process is used as the population of the genetic search which generates a reduced set of individuals in each new generation. In this scheme, *KNN* is used as a fitness function to evaluate the fitness of each individual elected from the population and then the operators like crossover and mutation are applied to reproduce new offspring. The primary motive of the proposed method is to optimize the search process to identify subset of features which improves the classification accuracy. It also focuses on reducing the size of the selected subset without compromising the accuracy rate of the problem. The detail configuration of genetic search is given below:

- **Encoding of Chromosome:** Each individual in the solution space is encoded in to a string of binary bits called chromosomes. Each bit of the string represents the state of each feature/genein the reduct set derived from fuzzy-rough filter model (1 if feature is selected else 0).
- **Crossover:** A two-point crossover mechanism is employed to swap the substrings between the two points selected to generate new offspring.
- **Mutation:** Crossover cannot provide a satisfactory result if the encoded information of the population is not sufficient to solve the given problem. In such cases, a flip bit mutation operator is applied to the new offspring to generate a new chromosome spontaneously.
- **Selection:** Selection operator selects eligible parents for mating for the next generation. The parents are selected with a selection probability which is proportional to their fitness values. This operation is analogous to survival of the fittest in theory of evolution. In the proposed hybrid-FRGSNN model a binary tournament procedure will be used for selection of parents in each generation.

3.2. Proposed Neural Network Ensemble for Classification

Adaptive neural network (Dash & Patra, 2016a; Luque-Baena, Urda, Subirats, Franco & Jerez,2014) consists of a large number of massively interconnected neurons which function simultaneously to find solution of problems. Adaptive neural network (Lee, Hong & Kim, 2009) has the ability to learn how to perform tasks based on the data given for training or initial experience. Neural networks are efficient in recognizing patterns and classifying data in a large dataset with little information. They are best suited for predicting high dimensional datasets like microarray datasets. The architecture of the multilayer neural network consists of three types of layers of neurons such as input, hidden and output layer. The behavior of the neural net increasingly depends on the connections between the components. These inputs and weighted connections between input and hidden layers determine the performance of the hidden layers. Similarly the performance of output layer is determined by the weight vector connecting hidden and output layer neurons. The objective of the network is to establish a mapping function which can minimize the error between desired and estimated output. A single neural network cannot build a stable and generalized learning model for finding optimal solution for some specific problems. In this paper, we have ensemble (Yang P., Yang H., Zhou & Zomaya, 2010) three variants of neural networks such as LVQ, SOM and BP, in an attempt to find an efficient solution to this problem. Usually, the learners show some biasness to different attribute selection models. The performance of the ensemble depends on the meta-algorithm which aggregates the output of individual classifiers. A simple combination rule like majority voting has been applied in combining the resultant of the classifiers. The majority voting consensus for k classifiers in a given n classifiers where:

$$k = \begin{cases} \dfrac{n}{2} + 1 \; if \, n \, is \, even \\ \dfrac{n+1}{2} \; if \, n \, is \, odd \end{cases}$$

The component classifiers used in the ensemble classifier namely LVQ, SOM and BP are combined and aggregated as a consensus committee. The subset of features produced by evolutionary fuzzy-rough feature selection phase will be fed into the ensemble classifier. The three base classifiers contained in this ensemble will use the input features to learn and classify the dataset separately. Finally, majority voting is used for calculating the consensus from the classification accuracy obtained from each classifier by using certain feature combination. Many significant advantages of ensemble learning algorithm over individual have been shown by many authors (Tan & Gilbert, 2003). The multi-net systems i.e., combination of a finite number of neural networks (Zhou, Jiang, Yang & Chen, 2002) has been used in different areas of research shown in Figure 2. The combined output of more than one classifier often provides improved accuracy over the output of individual network. However, the recent study of computational biology has witnessed an increasing use of ensemble learning because of the unique advantages in handling complex data structure, small sample size and high-dimensionality. The aim of this kind of ensemble learning is to achieve better generalization by combining the outputs of individual networks. The advantages of the ensemble learning i.e., how the problem of stability of the classifier can be improved compared to an individual classifier has been demonstrated in (Tan & Gilbert, 2003).

3.3. Proposed Fuzzy-Rough- PSO (FRPSO) Algorithm for Gene Selection

PSO algorithm is integrated with Fuzzy-Rough algorithm to address the gene selection problem. The important genes were identified by PSO algorithm employing Fuzzy-Rough as fitness function to verify the efficiency of the selected genes. We used a random function to initialize the particles of PSO. Good initial seed value leads to a better result.

Figure 2. Ensemble learning scheme

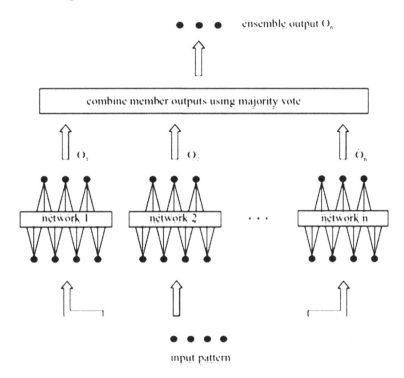

A particle represents a potential candidate solution (i.e., gene subset) in an n-dimensional space. Each particle is coded as a binary alphabetical string. We updated the dimension d of particle i by

$$x_{id}^{new} = \begin{cases} 1, if\ sigmoid\left(v_{id}^{new}\right) > u\left(0,1\right) \\ 0, \end{cases} \tag{3}$$

Where, the sigmoid function

$$v_{id}^{new} is \quad 1 \Big/ \left(1 + e^{-v_{id}^{new}}\right) \tag{4}$$

The fitness function of the particle is measured by Fuzzy-Rough evaluation algorithm. The pseudo-code explains the FRPSO procedure for gene selection.

3.4. Pseudocode of Fuzzy-Rough- PSO (FRPSO) Algorithm

```
input
c1, c2,r1,r2,w,vmin,vmax
```

```
output
GB
The fitness value of GB
begin
Initialize Population
while(max iteration or convergence criteria is not met) do
for i=1 to numbers of particles
Evaluate fitness value of the particle by PSO
if the fitness value of Xi is greater than that of PBi
then PBi= Xi
end if
if the fitness value of Xi is greater than that of GB
then GB = Xi
end if
for d=1 to no of genes
```

$v^{new}id= w * v^{old}id+ c1r1 \ (pb^{old}id- x^{old}id) \ +(c2r2 \ (pb^{old}id- x^{old}id)$

if $v^{old}id$>*vmax***then** $v^{new}id$= *vmax*

if $v^{old}id$<*vmax***then** $v^{new}id$= *vmin*

if *sigmoid* $(v^{new}id) > U \ (0,1)$

```
then
```
$x^{new}id$=1
```
else
```
$x^{new}id$=0
```
end if
next d
next i
end while
end
```

4. DATASETS ILLUSTRATION

A large amount of benchmark gene expression data is available in several public repositories. In this chapter, eight publicly available gene expression datasets are used to evaluate the performance of the proposed hybrid fuzzy-rough genetic feature selection method and neural network ensemble classification scheme. First five datasets, namely, DLBCL-NIH, DLBCL-Stanford, DLBCL-Harvard, CNS embryonic tumor outcome and Lung Harvard are collected from http://datam.i2r.a-star.edu.sg/datasets/krbd/ and last three, namely, ALL-AML, Brain Tumor and SRBCT are collected from http://www.gems-system. org/ which are illustrated in Table 1.

Again four microarray cancer datasets with different sizes, features, and classes have taken for experimental analysis to evaluate the effectiveness of hybrid fuzzy-rough-PSO algorithm for feature selection. The datasets were collected from "Bioinformatics Laboratory, University of Ljubljana", 1987, which include MLL, Lung Tumor, Childhood Tumor and DLBCL Tumor. Table 2 summarizes the character-

Table 1. Microarray datasets

Dataset	Number of genes	Training Samples	Test Samples	References
DLBCL - NIH	7399	160(72:88)	80 (30:50)	Andreas Rosenwald, et al (2002)
DLBCL - Stanford	4026	47 (24:23)	0	Ash A. Alizadeh, et al (2000)
DLBCL - Tumor	7129	77 (58:19)	0	Margaret A. Shipp, et al. (2002)
CNS	7129	60 (21:39)	0	Scott L. Pomeroy, et al. (2002)
ALL_AML_GEMS	7129	38 (27:11)	34(20:14)	Golub, et al. (1999)
Lung Harvard	12600	122 (58:21:20:6:17)	81(81:0:0:0:0)	Arindam Bhattacharjee, et al. (2001)
Brain_Tumor1_GEMS	5920	90 (60:10:10:4:6)	0	Pomeroy SL et al. (2002)
SRBCT_GEMS	2308	83 (29:11:18:25)	0	Khan J et al. (2001)

Table 2. Microarray data sets

Data Set	No. of Features	No. of Samples	No. of Classes	Particle Size PSO	No of Genes/Features Selected
MLL	12534	72	03	130	14
Childhood Tumours	9946	23	03	99	06
Lung Tumor	12601	203	05	135	20
DLBCL Tumor	7130	77	02	73	08

istics of those microarray datasets. The parameter values selected for FRPSO are as follows: number of particles in the population was set to the one-tenth number of genes (field of 'particle size" in Table 2). The parameter, c1 and c2, were both set at 2, whereas the parameter, lower (vmin) and upper bounds (vmax), were set at −4 and 4, respectively. The algorithm was repeated until either the fitness was 1.0 or the number of the repetitions was reached by the default value of T = 100.

5. EXPERIMENTAL RESULTS

5.1. FRGSNN Model

Eight microarray datasets are used to ascertain the validity of the projected hybrid FRGSNN scheme. Out of these eight datasets, five datasets i.e., DLBCL–NIH, DLBCL-Stanford, DLBCL-Harvard, Central Nervous system (CNS) and ALL-AML are binary samples and the remaining three i.e., Lung-Harvard, Brain-Tumor-GEMS and SRBCT-GEMS are multi-class samples. DLBCL data samples are taken from three different sources and studied their behavior by applying the proposed scheme. All the learning algorithms used in this work are taken from WEKA machine learning package.

The experimental method is composed of feature selection and classification method. In feature selection process, the proposed hybrid FRGSNN model is applied to all datasets to identify subset of potential genes/ biomarkers by reducing the computational complexity of the problem. Traditional feature selection methods such as FR-filter and GSNN-wrapper model are applied to all datasets for comparison purpose. The parameters of genetic search algorithm used in wrapper and hybrid model are set as follows in Box 1.

The potential genes identified by hybrid FRGSNN, FR-filter andGSNN-wrapper are recorded in Table 3 for all the datasets. Then the representative subset of genes obtained from the above processes is classified by the proposed ensemble model and other learning algorithms. In addition to this, the reduced set of features is classified by classical ensemble methods namely, bagging and boosting. The performance of the learning algorithms is validated by using test dataset for DLBCL-NIH, ALL-AML and Lung cancer and ten-fold cross validation was applied to measure the statistically reliable predictive accuracy for the remaining datasets.

The proposed neural network ensemble is trained with three component neural networks and then combines the outputs of all the networks into an integrated output using majority voting (Kuncheva, 2004). The subset of features is fed to each component classifiers, Bagging, Boosting and to the proposed ensemble for each dataset. Then the classification accuracy of each component classifiers and classical ensembles are compared with the accuracy obtained from proposed ensemble classifier. The parameters of all the base classifiers of the ensemble are set as follows:

1. **BP Learning:** Configured with 10 hidden nodes in a single hidden layer, output nodes equivalent to number of class of the datasets, learning rate varies from 0.01~0.10, momentum equals to 0.9 and maximum number of iterations fixed to 500.
2. **LVQ Learning:** Configured with codebook vectors fixed to 25, learning rate varies in the range 0.01~0.10, learning function is set to static, momentum sets to 0.1 and maximum iterations is 1000.
3. **SOM Learning:** 5 x 5 rectangle shape initial map is set with neighborhood size 16, learning function sets to static, learning rate varies within the range0.1~0.9 and maximum iterations is set to 2000.

When they are used as independent classifiers, a small variation is made to the above parameters for learning purpose. In this study, predictive accuracy (A_{cc}) and kappa statistic (k) are used to measure the performance of learning algorithms. Predictive accuracy is computed using four base line statistical components (Dash &Behera, 2016) namely, TP and FN denote the number of positive samples which are accurately and falsely predicted, respectively and TN and FP represent number of negative samples that are predicted accurately and wrongly, respectively. Kappa statistic (k), as a statistical metric, measures the percentage of agreement (Kuncheva, 2004) between accuracy and diversity of base learners, which is shown along with the ensemble performance. The reliability of classification is measured using the formula:

k = observed agreement – chance agreement / (1 – chance agreement)   (5)

Box 1.

cross-over probability = 0.6	mutation probability = 0.033
maximum generation=50	Population size = 100

The value of *k* ranges from 0 to 1, when k= 1 shows a better agreement than value 0.

Table 4 summarizes the classification accuracy of each component classifiers and proposed neural network ensemble on the subset of genes obtained from FR-filter, GSNN-wrapper and hybrid FRGSNN model. When results of the pair <FR-filter, classifier> and <GSNN-wrapper, classifier>compared with <hybrid-FRGSNN, classifier> methodology, it is observed that the pairing of proposed ensemble

Table 3. Selection of genes using FR-filter, GSNN-wrapper and hybrid FRGSNN method

Datasets	No. Of Genes Before Filtering	Selection of Genes Using FR-Filter	Selection of Genes Using GSNN-Wrapper	Selection of Genes Using Hybrid FRGSNN	% of Genes Selected by Hybrid FRGSNN
DLBCL-NIH	7399	294	3139	133	1.80
DLBCL-Stanford	4026	298	1205	124	3.08
DLBCL-Tumor	7129	162	2377	73	1.02
CNS	7129	162	2814	45	0.63
Lung Harvard	12600	234	3313	121	0.96
ALL-AML	7129	162	3442	58	0.81
Brain-Tumor	5920	267	2111	108	1.82
SRBCT-GEMS	2308	82	1041	20	0.87

Table 4. Best estimated classification accuracy of three elementary neural networks and proposed Ensemble method with estimated kappa statistic (k) value

Datasets	FRGS				GSNN				FRGSNN			
	LVQ	SOM	Back Propagation	Proposed Ensemble/*k*	LVQ	SOM	Back Propagation	Proposed Ensemble/*k*	LVQ	SOM	Back Propagation	Proposed Ensemble/*k*
DLBCL - NIH	63.75	62.5	64.375	**93.125/0.86**	64.125	63.125	66.25	**90.63/0.81**	64.126	64.375	68.3333	**97.00/0.93**
DLBCL - Stanford	80.851	59.57	80.85	**100.00/1.0**	87.234	78.7234	89.3617	**100.00/1.0**	91.4894	78.7234	91.4894	**100.00/1.0**
DLBCL - Tumor	68.8312	57.1409	74.026	**84.42/0.49**	92.2078	66.2338	81.8182	**94.81/0.84**	94.5195	72.7273	81.8182	**98.51/0.94**
CNS	68.33	66.6667	81.6667	**81.82/0.41**	68.33	66.6667	84.33	**96.67/0.92**	68.33	69.67	85.33	**99.67/0.99**
Lung Harvard	86.6995	77.8325	68.4729	**89.16/0.76**	89.6552	79.3842	80.3103	**92.61/0.84**	90.1478	79.3842	81.4729	**100.00/1.0**
ALL_AML	73.6111	59.7222	69.4444	**80.56/0.58**	90.8333	68.0556	70.8333	**94.44/0.99**	93.4544	70.8333	76.3889	**99.44/0.99**
Brain_Tumor1	74.444	66.6667	68.8889	**84.44/0.72**	78.8889	68.3333	70	**87.78/0.74**	83.3333	71.1111	71.6667	**90.22/0.89**
SRBCT	74.6988	56.6265	87.9518	**90.36/0.87**	86.747	62.6506	90.3976	**92.72/0.84**	90.3614	62.6506	93.9759	**93.98/0.91**

with hybrid-FRGSNN model yields better performance and also statistically significant difference is observed in all the datasets. It can also be observed from last column of Table 3 that hybrid FRGSNN model selects only 0.96% of genes from the largest Lung cancer dataset, 0.63%from CNS which is least and highest percentage 3.08% of genes from DLBCL-Stanford dataset.

The predictive accuracy of proposed ensemble algorithm for reduct set of genes obtained from FR-filter is better than the performance of component neural network learning algorithms. Similarly, for GSNN-wrapper model, comparison of results show a significant performance obtained by proposed ensemble method for six datasets achieving more than 90% accuracy. But, a highly remarkable performance is observed by ensemble method for the genes obtained from hybrid FRGSNN model for all the datasets in comparison to component classifiers. The analysis clearly indicates that the proposed learning scheme outperforms the predictive results of all three component classifiers. The same conclusion is agreed with the findings of (Lee, Hong & Kim, 2009).

Table 4 also provides a comparison between the classification accuracy of proposed ensemble and the value of kappa statistic (k) for all the subsets. The classification accuracy and the value of kappa statistic (k) obtained from the proposed learning scheme has established a proper balance between accuracy and diversity. It is worth to note that, a small value of k denotes high diversity among the learners. Kappa statistic k measures the diversity between the pair of base learners, which is shown along with the ensemble performance. Hence, proposed method has achieved proper balance between diversity and accuracy and at the same time fulfilled the objective of finding a generalized prediction model.

Table 5 summarizes the predictive accuracy of the proposed ensemble and other ensembles such as *Bagging and Boosting* for the subset of genes obtained from hybrid FRGSNN model for all the datasets. The analysis of the table proved that the other two ensembles work effectively for a particular microarray dataset, i.e., bagging performs well for ALL-AML, boosting does for Lung-Harvard using hybrid FRGSNN model. The predictive results obtained by Bagging and Boosting ensemble are not consistent across the datasets whereas the results obtained by neural network ensemble are remarkably significant across all the datasets.

Table4 shows the estimated accuracy obtained by all datasets using elementary classifiers such as LVQ, SOM, BP and the proposed neural network ensemble where Vote combines probability distribution of

Table 5. Comparison of 10 fold cross validated predictive accuracy of proposed ensemble with other ensembles using features obtained from hybrid-FRGSNN

Ensembles / Datasets	Bagging Accuracy (%)	Boosting Accuracy (%)	Proposed Ensemble Accuracy (%)
DLBCL - NIH	56.875	50.625	**97.00**
DLBCL - Stanford	78.7234	78.7234	**100.00**
DLBCL - Tumor	77.9221	83.1169	**98.5065**
CNS	61.6667	58.3333	**99.67**
Lung Harvard	88.67	95.0739	**100.00**
ALL_AML	93.0556	87.5000	**99.4444**
Brain_Tumor1	78.8889	80.00	**90.2222**
SRBCT	83.1325	86.747	**93.9759**

all three neural networks. We can see the accuracy obtained by ensemble is better for DLBCL-Harvard, ALL-AML, Lung-Harvard and Brain Tumor than other datasets. Here the performance of ensemble is enhanced by the hybrid FRGSNN feature selection method which selects optimal subset using genetic search. The accuracy of ensemble ranges from 69.375% ~ 98.3333% with average of 83.854% whereas for element classifiers it ranges from 64.126% ~ 93.9759% with average of 79.44683%. This analysis clearly demonstrates, the proposed neural network ensemble outperforms the efficiency of element classifiers for all three types of feature selection methods.

5.2. FRPSO Model

Table 6 shows, 10 certain rules which are generated from lower approximation involving 14 genes in which some are identified as strongly associated with 3 cancers i.e., ALL, AML and MLL when the model FRPSO is evaluated by MODLEM. Rules 3, 5 and 9 strongly identify all the 3 types of cancer than the other 7 induced rules. Gene 33589_at is strongly associated with all three cancers i.e., rule one: (38989_at >= 582.5)&(33589_at < 13)&(32189_g_at < 1046.5) => (class = ALL) (17/17, 70.83%), classify more than 70% ALL cancer data, rule 5: (41664_at >= 586)&(33589_at in [13, 543])&(32581_at < 31) => (class = MLL) (15/15, 75%) classify 75% MLL cancer and rule 9: (38989_at < 133)&(36045_at < 3.5) => (class = AML) (25/25, 89.29%) classify more than 89% AML cancer dataset. Gene 38989_at is also strongly associated with ALL and MLL. Conditional entropy is used as a conditional measure to find best elementary conditions to form rules.

Similarly, 6 important genes out of 9946 are identified by 5 rules in Childhood Tumor shown in Table 7. Rule 1 classifies more than 81% EWS, more than 66% eRMS by rule 3 and 100% aRMS by rule 5.

Table 8, demonstrates 12 induced rules generated from lower approximation for Lung Tumor which classify all 5 cancers from the dataset identifying 20 genes out of 12601. Gene 38138_at is strongly associated with all five cancers.

Table 6. Certain rules generated from lower approximation for MLL by MODLEM

Rule 1. (38989_at >= 582.5)&(33589_at < 13)&(32189_g_at < 1046.5) => (class = ALL) (17/17, 70.83%)
Rule 2. (41651_at >= 5066.5)&(32850_at < 1516) => (class = ALL) (7/7, 29.17%)
Rule 3. (32138_at < 199)&(34449_at < 135.5) => (class = ALL) (4/4, 16.67%)
Rule 4. (38627_at < -58) => (class = ALL) (3/3, 12.5%)
Rule 5. (41664_at >= 586)&(33589_at in [13, 543])&(32581_at < 31) => (class = MLL) (15/15, 75%)
Rule 6. (32799_at >= 2713)&(34449_at >= 888) => (class = MLL) (3/3, 15%)
Rule 7. (32799_at >= 2713)&(33589_at < -1134) => (class = MLL) (2/2, 10%)
Rule 8. (38866_at < 13)&(33589_at >= -286) => (class = MLL) (3/3, 15%)
Rule 9. (38989_at < 133)&(36045_at < 3.5) => (class = AML) (25/25, 89.29%)
Rule 10. (41651_at < 1672)&(33589_at < -286) => (class = AML) (15/15, 53.57%)

Table 7. Certain rules generated from lower approximation for childhood tumor by MODLEM

Rule 1. (2017_s_at >= 0.09) => (class = EWS) (9/9, 81.82%)
Rule 2. (32334_f_at >= 0.66) => (class = EWS) (6/6, 54.55%)
Rule 3. (38522_s_at >= 0.67) => (class = eRMS) (2/2, 66.67%)
Rule 4. (33500_i_at >= 0.58) => (class = eRMS) (1/1, 33.33%)
Rule 5. (32334_f_at < 0.54)&(37287_at < 0) => (class = aRMS) (9/9, 100%)

Table 8. Certain rules generated from lower approximation for lung tumor by MODLEM

Rule 1. (38138_at >= 377.86)&(37141_at >= 7.64)&(41549_s_at < 92.88)&(33693_at < 30.04) => (class = AD) (100/100, 71.94%)
Rule 2. (41151_at < 258.56)&(38138_at < 1788.99)&(37797_at >= -16.47)&(37187_at >= 23.28)&(37148_at < 177.38) => (class = AD) (87/87, 62.59%)
Rule 3. (35090_g_at >= 124.49)&(38442_at >= 298.22)&(38138_at >= 328.33) => (class = AD) (14/14, 10.07%)
Rule 4. (39805_at >= 62.22) => (class = AD) (8/8, 5.76%)
Rule 5. (749_at < 54.89)&(37148_at >= 102.74)&(33667_at >= 1792.99) => (class = NL) (16/16, 94.12%)
Rule 6. (32052_at >= 4253.91) => (class = NL) (5/5, 29.41%)
Rule 7. (36572_r_at >= 592.41)&(39023_at < 136.77) => (class = SMCL) (6/6, 100%)
Rule 8. (33693_at >= 106.75)&(38138_at >= 512.27) => (class = SQ) (14/14, 66.67%)
Rule 9. (38968_at < 44.24)&(36702_at < 76.58) => (class = SQ) (6/6, 28.57%)
Rule 10. (33667_at < 1870.71)&(547_s_at < 4.33)&(33843_g_at >= -58.08) => (class = SQ) (4/4, 19.05%)
Rule 11. (38138_at < 119.98) => (class = COID) (19/19, 95%)
Rule 12. (34265_at >= 390.66) => (class = COID) (18/18, 90%)

The classifier model of DLBCL contains 7 rules which classify DLBCL and FL by identifying 8 significant genes from the dataset shown in Table 9. Gene L38810_at is strongly associated with DLBCL and FL.

The results of these experiments are given in Table 10. For each data set, the first column shows the average classification accuracy obtained by the classifier over ten-fold-cross-validations. Mean absolute error and model building time in seconds is also given. The next column represents the number of rules generated by the classifier for each datasets.

6. DISCUSSION

From the experiment of FRGSNN model, it is observed that feature selection plays an important role in enhancing the classification accuracy of the problem. Potential features influence the predictive ability

Table 9. Certain rules generated from lower approximation for DLBCL by MODLEM

Rule 1. (X61123_at < 1444)&(S82024_at < 265.5) => (class = DLBCL) (20/20, 34.48%)
Rule 2. (L38810_at >= 512)&(U47101_at < 2662.5)&(D42073_at >= -93.5) => (class = DLBCL) (39/39, 67.24%)
Rule 3. (L38810_at >= 1164.5) => (class = DLBCL) (24/24, 41.38%)
Rule 4. (D28423_at < 444) => (class = DLBCL) (12/12, 20.69%)
Rule 5. (L38810_at < 585)&(X61123_at >= 1444)&(U57721_at < 479.5) => (class = FL) (10/10, 52.63%)
Rule 6. (U47101_at >= 2662.5)&(L38810_at < 1164.5) => (class = FL) (6/6, 31.58%)
Rule 7. (U65402_at >= 2030) => (class = FL) (3/3, 15.79%)

Table 10. Classification accuracy (%) validated with 10-fold CV

DATA SET	Percentage of Accuracy	Mean absolute error	No. of rules	Model building time (in seconds)
MLL	68.0556	0.213	10	27.54
Childhood Tumours	60.8696	0.2609	5	8.24
Lung Tumour	86.2069	0.0552	12	120.95
DLBCL Tumour	74.026	0.2597	7	4.85

of the classification model. In this study, the proposed method outperforms the results published by other authors. We found the discrimination ability of the ensemble classifier is highly significant when search strategy like filter, wrapper, and hybrid methods are concerned. Further, we used the same features for predicting component classifiers such as BP, SOM, and LVQ and for two other ensembles such as bagging and Boosting and found that the results are not better than the propose done. Hence, these significant improvements of the proposed scheme can be attributed to the fact that the evolutionary hybrid feature selection mechanism optimizes different combinations of genes that enhances the classification accuracy thereby improves the stability and generalization capability of the ensemble network.

The most important issue in ensemble learning is to establish a proper balance between the accuracy and diversity of the constituent base learners. In fact, the base learners used in an ensemble classifier need to have high classification accuracy and should avoid making misclassification errors. The diversity would be more among base learners if the misclassification error increases in the process of classification. It is also evident from Table 4 that the proposed methodology could provide a generalized prediction model which is the main objective of this research (Dash & Patra, 2016; Yang, Huei, Chuang & Yang C. Hong, 2009). In order to measure the level of agreement between a pair of base learners, a k-metric or kappa statistic (kuncheva, 2004) is used while correcting the chance. We believe that, ensemble classifiers are more appropriate for bioinformatics problems because it helps to design classifiers from noisy and incomplete data. Another inherent problem of microarray data is the relatively small number of samples compared to the dimension of the dataset. This problem is really a difficult task for a single learning classifier to induce an optimal hypothesis for this type of dataset. Ensemble learner which combines component can appropriately address this issue. As a result, the network becomes stable and attains global minima instead of being trapped in local minima. Nevertheless, how many component classifiers need to be combined to capture the true hypothesis is still an open problem.

The validation of the result of FRPSO model is shown in two ways. One is mathematical validation and another one real life functional classification of genes. The mathematical validation is based on the induced rules generated from the reducts obtained from Fuzzy-Rough-PSO and classification of whole dataset on the basis of that generated rules which have only few responsible genes. The accuracy of prediction of the diseases is verified by applying rule sets generated by MODLEM classifier on the datasets. The cross validated result, as shown in Table 10 indicates that these rules can accurately predict the data with total coverage 1. In all the datasets only few marker genes classify the entire datasets which validate our results.

To find biological relevance of the method, next part of validation need to be applied to find actual functional classification of those genes in human body. This is obtained from a Gene Ontology website called DAVID [http://david.abcc.ncifcrf.gov/] where it is available. If the lists of marker genes are provided as input with appropriate gene identifier, the website gives the function of these genes or proteins in human body. In addition to this, it is also possible to find genetic disease which happens due to variation in gene expressions. Table11 shows a sample of functional classification of marker genes for Leukemia dataset.

7. CONCLUSION

Experimental results show that the evolutionary feature selection techniques effectively selected subset of marker genes for each component learner and increased the discriminatory power of the neural net-

Table 11. Functional classification of marker genes for leukemia

Gene identifiers	Gene Name	Gene Symbol	Gene Functions Obtained From DAVID
34449_at	caspase 2, apoptosis-related cysteine protease (neural precursor cell expressed, developmentally down-regulated 2)	CASP2	This gene encodes a protein which is a member of the cysteine-aspartic acid protease (caspase) family. Sequential activation of caspases plays a central role in the execution-phase of cell apoptosis.
38866_at	GRB2-related adaptor protein 2	GRAP2	This gene encodes a member of the GRB2/Sem5/Drk family. This member is an adaptor-like protein involved in leukocyte-specific protein-tyrosine kinase signaling. polyA sites exist.
32189_g_at	myelin transcription factor 1	MYT1	The protein encoded by this gene is a member of a family of neural specific, zinc finger-containing DNA-binding proteins. The protein binds to the promoter regions of proteolipid proteins of the central nervous system and plays a role in the developing nervous system.
32850_at	nucleoporin 153kDa	NUP153	Nuclear pore complexes are extremely elaborate structures that mediate the regulated movement of macromolecules between the nucleus and cytoplasm. These complexes are composed of at least 100 different polypeptide subunits, many of which belong to the nucleoporin family.

work ensemble. In addition, it is evident from the study that ensemble classifier performs better than classical ensembles and component classifiers for all datasets. The proposed method has achieved the highest averaged generalization ability compared to its counterparts and established an acceptable level of diversity among the base learners for majority of the analysed benchmark datasets. The analysis of the second metaheuristic model has shown the involvement of specific genes in the form of rules.

The genetic information available in 4 microarray datasets such as MLL, Childhood Tumor, Lung Tumor and DLBCL Tumor has been used to diagnose human disease. It is also considered that the set of genes will behave in a general way in this investigation. With this constraint, a model has been proposed to provide optimize solution for two different purposes. First one is predicting disease using genetic information from microarray data and second one, identification of marker genes responsible for causing the disease. The algorithm of the model is developed using a hybrid metaheuristic FRPSO. The results obtained here is quite dependable. The validation of the predicted results has been carried out in two ways. The result shows more than 60% accuracy in prediction in the form of diagnosis of disease. The result also predicted marker genes for causing cancers. Then using these responsible genes, induction rules can be generated to classify the datasets. This may help in drug design for cancer with regulating the function of the marker genes or proteins by injecting drugs which will stop proliferation of cancer in human body. The real life validation can be carried out in the DAVID website.

REFERENCES

Ahmad, A., & Dey, L. (2005). A feature selection technique for classificatory analysis. *Pattern Recognition Letters*, *26*(1), 43–56. doi:10.1016/j.patrec.2004.08.015

Akadi, A. E., Amine, A., Ouardighi, A. E., & Aboutajdine, D. (2009). Feature selection for Genomic data bycombining filter and wrapper approaches. *INFOCMP Journal of Computer Science, 8*(4), 28-36.

Alizadeh, A. A., Eisen, M. B., Davis, R. E., Ma, C., Lossos, I. S., Rosenwald, A., & Staudt, L. M. et al. (2000). Distinct types of diffuse large B-cell lymphoma identified by gene expression profiling. *Nature*, *403*(6769), 503–511. doi:10.1038/35000501 PMID:10676951

Bhattacharjee, A., Richards, W. G., Staunton, J., Li, C., Monti, S., Vasa, P., & Meyerson, M. et al. (2001). Classification of human lung carcinomas by mRNA expression profiling reveals distinct adenocarcinomasubclasses, PNAS. *The National Academy of Sciences, USA*, *98*(24), 13790–13795. doi:10.1073/pnas.191502998 PMID:11707567

Chen, L. F., Su, C.-T., Chen, K.-H., & Wang, P.-C. (2011). Particle swarm optimization for feature selection with application in obstructive sleep apnea diagnosis. *Neural Computing & Applications*, *21*(8), 2087–2096. doi:10.1007/s00521-011-0632-4

Chen, L. F., Su, C.-T., Chen, K.-H., & Wang, P.-C. (2011). Particle swarm optimization for feature selection with application in obstructive sleep apnea diagnosis. *Neural Computing & Applications*, *21*(8), 2087–2096. doi:10.1007/s00521-011-0632-4

Chen, T., Hong, Z., Deng, F., Yang, X., Wei, J. & Cui, M. (2015). A novel selective ensemble classificationof microarray data based on teaching-learning-based optimization. *International Journal of Multimedia and Ubiquitous Engineering*, *10*(6), 203-218.

Dash, S. (2015). *A Rule Induction Model Empowered by Fuzzy-Rough Particle Swarm Optimization Algorithm for Classification of Microarray Dataset, Computational Intelligence in Data Mining* (Vol. 3). SIST. doi:10.1007/978-81-322-2202-6_26

Dash, S. (2016). *Hybrid Ensemble Learning Methods for Classification of Microarray Data. In Handbook of research on Computational Intelligence Applications in Bioinformatics* (pp. 17–36). Hershey, PA: IGI Global. doi:10.4018/978-1-5225-0427-6

Dash, S., & Behera, R. (2016). Sampling based Hybrid Algorithms for Imbalanced Data Classification. *International Journal of Hybrid-Intelligent-Systems*, *13*(2), 77–86. doi:10.3233/HIS-160226

Dash, S., & Patra, B. N. (2012). Rough Set Aided Gene Selection for Cancer Classification. *Proceedings of 7th International Conference on Computing and Convergence Technology (ICCCT)*, 290-294.

Dash, S., & Patra, B. N. (2013). Redundant Gene Selection based on Genetic and Quick-Reduct Algorithms. *International Journal on Data Mining and Intelligent Information Technology Application*, *3*(2), 1–9.

Dash, S., & Patra, B. N. (2016). Genetic diagnosis of cancer by evolutionary fuzzy-based neural network ensemble. *International Journal of Knowledge Discovery in Bioinformatics, 6*(1).

Dash, S., & Patra, B. N. (2016). *Knowledge Discovery using Machine Learning Algorithms*. Lambert Academic Publishing.

Dash, S., Patra, B. N., & Tripathy, B. K. (2012). A Hybrid Data Mining Technique for Improving the Classification Accuracy ofMicroarray Data Set. I.J. *Information Engineering and Electronic Business*, *4*(2), 43–50. doi:10.5815/ijieeb.2012.02.07

Ding, C., & Peng, H. (2005). Minimum redundancy feature selection from microarray gene expression data. *Journal of Bioinformatics and Computational Biology*, *3*(2), 185–205. doi:10.1142/S0219720005001004 PMID:15852500

Eiben, A. E., & Schippers, C. A. (1998). On evolutionary exploration and exploitation. *Fundamenta Informaticae, 35*(1), 16.

Ghosh, A., & Jain, L. C. (Eds.). (2005). *Evolutionary computation in data mining*. Berlin: Springer-Verlag. doi:10.1007/3-540-32358-9

Glover, F. (1986). Future paths for integer programming and links to artificial intelligence. *Comp. Oper. Res., 13*, 533-549.

Glover, F., & Laguna, M. (1997). *Tabu Search*. Kluwer Academic Publishers. doi:10.1007/978-1-4615-6089-0

Golub, T. R. (1999). Molecular classification of cancer: Class discovery and class prediction by gene expression monitoring, 1. *Science*, *286*(5439), 531–537. doi:10.1126/science.286.5439.531 PMID:10521349

Guyon, I., Gunn, S., Nikravesh, M., & Zadeh, L. A. (Eds.). (2006). *Feature Extraction: foundations and applications*. Berlin: Springer. doi:10.1007/978-3-540-35488-8

Huang, F., Zhou, Z., Zhang, H., & Chen, T. (2000). Pose invariant face recognition. *Proceedings of 4th IEEE International Conference. Automatic Face and Gesture Recognition*, 245–250.

Kennedy, J., & Eberhart, R. (1995). Particle swarm optimization. *IEEE Int. Conf Neural Networks - Conf Proc, 4*, 1942–1948. doi:10.1109/ICNN.1995.488968

Khan, J., Wei, J. S., Ringner, M., Saal, L. H., Ladanyi, M., Westermann, F., & Meltzer, P. S. (2001). Classification and diagnostic of cancers using gene expression profiling and artificial neural networks. *NCBI*, *7*(6), 673–679. PMID:11385503

Kuncheva, L. (2004). *Combining Pattern Classifiers*. John Wiley & Sons. doi:10.1002/0471660264

Lee, H., Hong, S., & Kim, E. (2009). A new genetic feature selection with neural network ensemble. *International Journal of Computer Mathematics*, *86*(7), 1105–1117. doi:10.1080/00207160701724760

Lee, H., Hong, S., & Kim, E. (2009). Neural Network Ensemble with probabilistic fusion and its application to gait recognition. *Neurocomputing*, *72*(7-9), 1557–1564. doi:10.1016/j.neucom.2008.09.009

Liu, B., Cui, Q., Jiang, T., & Ma, S. (2004). A combinational feature selection and ensemble neural network method for classification of gene expression data. *BMC Bioinform.*, *5*(1), 136–147. doi:10.1186/1471-2105-5-136 PMID:15450124

Luque-Baena, R. M., Urda, D., Subirats, J. I., Franco, L., & Jerez, J. M. (2014). Application of genetic algorithms and constructive neural networks for the analysis of microarray cancer data. *Theoretical Biology & Medical Modelling*, *11*(Suppl. 1), S7. doi:10.1186/1742-4682-11-S1-S7 PMID:25077572

Maji, P. (2009). f-information measures for efficient selection of discriminative genes from microarray data. *IEEE Transactions on Bio-Medical Engineering*, *56*(4), 1063–1069. doi:10.1109/TBME.2008.2004502 PMID:19272938

Mohamad, M. S. (2009). Particle swarm optimization for gene selection in classifying cancer classes. *Proceedings of the 14th International Symposium on Artificial Life and Robotics*, 762–765. doi:10.1007/s10015-009-0712-z

Mohamad, M. S. (2009). Particle swarm optimization for gene selection in classifying cancer classes. *Proceedings of the 14th International Symposium on Artificial Life and Robotics*, 762–765. doi:10.1007/s10015-009-0712-z

Osman, I. H., & Laporte, G. (1996). Metaheuristics: A bibliography. *Annals of Operations Research, 63*, 513-623.

Pawlak, Z. (1982). Rough sets. *Int. J. Inform. Comput. Sci., 11*(5), 341–356. doi:10.1007/BF01001956

Pomeroy, S. L., Tamayo, P., Gaasenbeek, M., Sturla, L. M., Angelo, M., McLaughlin, M. E., & Golub, T. R. et al. (2002). Prediction of central nervous system embryonal tumour outcome based on gene expression. *Nature, 415*(6870), 436–442. doi:10.1038/415436a PMID:11807556

Reeves, C. R. (Ed.). (1993). *Modern Heuristic Techniques for Combinatorial Problems*. Blackwell Scientific Publishing.

Rosenwald, A., Wright, G., Chan, W. C., Connors, J. M., Campo, E., Fisher, R. I., & Staudt, L. M. et al. (2002). The use of molecular profiling to predict survival after chemotherapy for diffuse large-B-cell lymphoma. *The New England Journal of Medicine, 346*(25), 1937–1947. doi:10.1056/NEJMoa012914 PMID:12075054

Saeys, Y., Inza, I., & Larranaga, P. (2007). A review of feature selection techniques in Bioinformatics. *Bioinformatics (Oxford, England), 23*(19), 2507–2517. doi:10.1093/bioinformatics/btm344 PMID:17720704

Shipp, M. A. et al.. (2002). The AP1-dependent secretion of gelectin-1 by Reed-Sternberg cells fosters immune privilege in classical Hodgkin lymphoma, PNAS. *The National Academy of Sciences, USA, 104*(32), 13134–13139.

Stefanowski. (2003). *Changing representation of learning examples while inducing classifiers based on decision rules, Artificial Intelligence Methods*. Bioinformatics Laboratory, University of Ljubljana. Retrieved from http://www.biolab.si/supp/bi-ancer/projections/info/lungGSE1987.htm

Tan, A. C., & Gilbert, D. (2003). Ensemble machine learning on gene expression data for cancer classification. *Applied Bioinformatics, 2*, S75–S83. PMID:15130820

Witten, I. H., Frank, E., & Hall, M. A. (2011). *Data mining: practical machine learning tools and techniques* (3rd ed.). Morgan Kaufmann.

Yang, P., Yang, Y. H., Zhou, B. B., & Zomaya, A. Y. (2010). A review of ensemble methods in bioinformatics. *Bioinformatics (Oxford, England), 5*(4), 296–308.

Zadeh, L. A. (1965). Fuzzy sets. *Information and Control, 8*(3), 338–353. doi:10.1016/S0019-9958(65)90241-X

Zhou, Z.-H., Jiang, Y., Yang, Y.-B., & Chen, S.-F. (2002). Lung cancer cell identification based on artificial neural network ensembles. *Artificial Intelligence in Medicine, 24*(1), 25–36. doi:10.1016/S0933-3657(01)00094-X PMID:11779683

KEY TERMS AND DEFINITIONS

Ensemble Method: In this method learning methods are embedded or cascaded with each other and organized in two ways and called homogeneous and heterogeneous ensemble. They classify new data points by taking weighted vote of their predictions.

Fuzzy-Rough Feature Selection (FRFS): Provides a means by which discrete or real-valued noisy data or a mixture of both can be effectively reduced without the need for user-supplied information.

Genetic Algorithm: Genetic algorithms are evolutionary optimization methods motivated by biological phenomenon of natural selection and evolution.

Hybrid Ensemble Learning: The potential of ensemble learning is augmented by combining the characteristics of another learning algorithm.

Neural-net Ensemble: Neural network ensemble can significantly improve generalization accuracy of networks by training several networks and combining their results.

Rule Based Algorithm: These algorithms extract knowledges in the form of rules from the classification model, which are easy to comprehend and very expressive. This algorithm is most suitable for analyzing data containing a mixture of numerical and qualitative attributes.

Chapter 2
Swarm–Based Nature–Inspired Metaheuristics for Neural Network Optimization

Swathi Jamjala Narayanan
VIT University, India

Boominathan Perumal
VIT University, India

Jayant G. Rohra
VIT University, India

ABSTRACT

Nature-inspired algorithms have been productively applied to train neural network architectures. There exist other mechanisms like gradient descent, second order methods, Levenberg-Marquardt methods etc. to optimize the parameters of neural networks. Compared to gradient-based methods, nature-inspired algorithms are found to be less sensitive towards the initial weights set and also it is less likely to become trapped in local optima. Despite these benefits, some nature-inspired algorithms also suffer from stagnation when applied to neural networks. The other challenge when applying nature inspired techniques for neural networks would be in handling large dimensional and correlated weight space. Hence, there arises a need for scalable nature inspired algorithms for high dimensional neural network optimization. In this chapter, the characteristics of nature inspired techniques towards optimizing neural network architectures along with its applicability, advantages and limitations/challenges are studied.

INTRODUCTION

Swarm based Optimization is a strategy that considers several agents collectively working to intelligently achieve a goal in the most optimal manner. Nature inspired techniques might include the consideration of these agents to be a flock of birds, a school of fish, a swarm of bees etc. Metaheuristic approaches are framed to form an analogy between the nature and computational systems and hence implement a

DOI: 10.4018/978-1-5225-2857-9.ch002

relevant behavior as a paradigm to perform the required task. Since 1990, several nature inspired meta-heuristic techniques have been proposed. There exist several applications areas where the metaheuristics like swarm based or evolutionary optimization algorithms play vital role. Several NP-hard optimization problems like Traveling Salesman Problem, Quadratic Assignment Problem, Graph problems are also solved using nature inspired techniques.

Classification is the task of assigning an object to a pre-defined class or group (Duda, 1973). Classifier can be considered as a mapping function of the form $Y_i = f(X_i, \Phi_1, \Phi_2, \ldots, \Phi_N)$, where f(.) is the classifier that maps the object X_i to class Y_i based on parameters $\Phi_1, \Phi_2, \ldots, \Phi_N$ that are related attributes of object X_i. Classification is widely used in business, science, industry, and medicine and addresses many real world problems such as bankrupt prediction, credit scoring, medical diagnosis, handwritten character recognition, and speech recognition.

In traditional statistical classifiers, classification decision depends on posterior probability which is derived based on the assumptions on underlying probability model. Prior knowledge required on data properties and model capabilities limits the scope of statistical classifiers in many real world problems. Emergence of Neural Network, a non-linear model that models real world complex problems provides solution for the conventional statistical classifiers. The advantage of neural networks lies in the following theoretical aspects. First, neural networks are data driven self-adaptive methods in that they can adjust themselves to the data without any explicit specification of functional or distributional form for the underlying model. Second, they are universal functional approximators in that neural networks can approximate any function with arbitrary accuracy (Cybenko 1989; Hornik, 1991; Hornik et al, 1989).

Since any classification procedure seeks a functional relationship between the group membership and the attributes of the object, accurate identification of this underlying function is doubtlessly important. Third, neural networks are nonlinear models, which makes them flexible in modelling real world complex relationships. Finally, neural networks are able to estimate the posterior probabilities, which provide the basis for establishing classification rule and performing statistical analysis. Neural networks are considered as data driven self-adaptive methods and universal functional approximators that estimates posterior probability with arbitrary accuracy.

To improve the performance of the neural networks by optimizing its parameters, the authors (Werbos, 1990, 1994; Williams et al.,1986; Gupta & Sexton, 1999; Wilamowski, 2002) have suggested that back propagation using gradient descent methods is the most widely used neural network training method to optimize the neural network parameters in supervised learning strategy. In recent years, many improved learning algorithms have been developed that aim to remove the shortcomings of the gradient descent based systems.

Zell (2002) developed The Stuttgart Neural Network Simulator (SNNS), which uses many different algorithms including Error Back Propagation developed by Fahlman (1988), Resilient Error Back Propagation developed by Riedmiller, & Braun (1993), Back percolation, Delta-bar-Delta, Cascade Correlation developed by Fahlman & Lebiere (1989) etc. All these algorithms are derivatives of steepest gradient search; hence the ANN training is relatively slow. To have a fast and efficient training method, second order learning algorithms are developed. The most effective method is Levenberg Marquardt (LM) algorithm proposed by Hagan & Menhaj (1994), which is a derivative of the Newton method. This is quite multifaceted algorithm since both the gradient and the Jacobian matrix is calculated. The LM algorithm was developed only for layer-by-layer ANN topology, which is far from optimal. LM algorithm is ranked as one of the most efficient training algorithms for patterns that are both small and medium sized. Wilamowski et al., (2007) suggest that it is a good combination of Newton's method and steepest descent. It borrows speed from Newton method and convergence capability of steepest descent method. It is best suited for training neural network which calculates the performance index using Mean Squared Error (MSE) but still fails at removing local minimum as suggested by Xue et al., (2010).

As classical training method get trapped to local minima and cost of the objective function evaluation is high, there is a need for applying nature inspired meta-heuristic techniques to train neural network parameters. San et al. (2013) proposed evolved block-based neural network (BBNN) for modeling and design of a noninvasive hypoglycemia monitoring system. One of the implications behind the proposed algorithm is that the overall network structure is organized by individual basic building blocks which are characterized by a feedforward neural network structure. To overcome the problems of getting trapped to local minima, a powerful random global learning optimization algorithm called hybrid particle swarm optimization (PSO) with wavelet mutation (HPSOWM) is used to optimize the neural network parameters. Further in 2014, the paper is extended to include the concept of rough sets and the author developed rough block-based neural network (R-BBNN) to study on hypoglycemia detection system. Hassanien (2014) introduced a hybrid approach that combines the advantages of fuzzy sets, ant-based clustering and multilayer perceptron neural networks (MLPNN) classifier, in conjunction with statistical-based feature extraction technique to study on breast cancer MRI images classification.

These works show that, metaheuristic techniques help in improving the accuracy of the neural network model. Meta heuristic techniques have better time performance and good quality solutions compared to standard training algorithms. Most of the metaheuristic techniques draw their inspiration from nature inspired optimization techniques like evolutionary algorithms, genetic algorithms, ant colony optimization, particle swarm optimization, differential evolution and artificial bee colony algorithm. Harmony search (HS) algorithm, which is obtained from improvisation processes done by musicians not from biological or physical processes, is also adopted for the training of NNs.

The various nature inspired meta-heuristics techniques can be placed under four categories namely Swarm based, Bio inspired, Physics and chemistry based and other algorithms. In this chapter, we present the details of how swarm based meta heuristic techniques can be used for optimizing the well-known neural network algorithms for improving its performance in terms of minimizing the error and improving the accuracy.

ARTIFICIAL NEURAL NETWORK

Neural Networks is a mechanism of modelling the human brain to perform information processing using a computational approach. It consists of a network of interconnected neurons that work collectively or in parallel to complete a certain task or solve a given problem. These neurons are organized into layers that have activation functions to process the data. The neural network has an input, an output and a hidden layer depending upon the complexity of the problem to be solved. The order of processing as shown in Figure 1 involves the input layer first, where the pattern is presented as a suitable input to the network followed by the hidden layer in which most of the processing is done and the finally the output layer where the solved output is presented in various forms depending on the requirement.

Weights are the measure of the strength of interconnection between two neurons in artificial neural networks which also biologically mean the ability to fire a neuron. Neural Networks can be trained by updating weights to perform calculations, approximations, pattern matching, determining associations

Figure 1. Basic structure of an artificial neural network

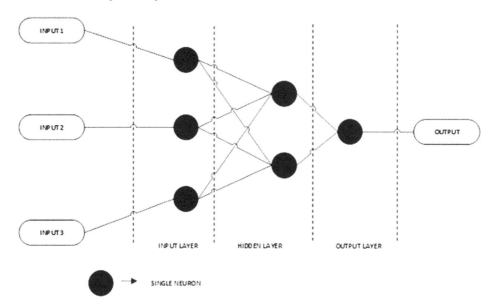

etc. ANNs learn by example, similar to how our biological senses do. The architecture and the training algorithms used contribute largely to the performance and characteristics exhibited by the network.

NEURAL NETWORK ARCHITECTURES

The design or the architecture of the artificial neural networks influences its performance characteristics. Various applications and problems show different compatibility with different designs. There are numerous architectures that exist for neural networks. Some of the widely used ones are feed forward neural networks, recurrent neural networks, hop field neural networks, Elman and Jordan neural network, long short term memory, bi-directional neural network, self-organizing map, etc., The choice of the neural architecture depends on various factors like the desired accuracy to be achieved, training time, learning strategy etc.,

FEED FORWARD NEURAL NETWORKS

In feed forward neural network models each node sends a signal to the nodes of the next layer, and each signal is then is multiplied by a separate weight value. The weighted inputs are summed, and passed through a limiting function. This further scales the output to a fixed range of values. The output of the limiter function is then broadcast to all the other nodes in the next layer. The output of every i_{th} node is obtained using Equation 1.

$$y_i = f_i\left(\sum_{j=1}^{n} w_{ij} x_j + b_i\right) \tag{1}$$

where y_i is the output of the node, x_j is the jth input to the node, w_{ij} is the connection weight between the node and input x_j, b_i is the threshold(or bias) of the node, and f_i is the node transfer function. Usually, the node transfer function is a nonlinear function such as a linear function, a sigmoid function, a Gaussian function, etc. Here, we assume the logarithmic sigmoid (Equation 2) transfer function at hidden and output layer neurons.

$$y = f(net) = \frac{1}{1 + e^{-net}} \tag{2}$$

RECURRENT NEURAL NETWORK

A recurrent neural network (RNN) includes a feedback mechanism with the basic architecture of a feed forward neural network. It is used for the sequential processing of data that has variable length. In this type of mechanism, every node in the hidden layer can have the same transition function. The RNN has many applications such as word prediction, image and video captioning etc. (see Figure 3)

Figure 2. Structure of feed forward neural networks with hidden layers

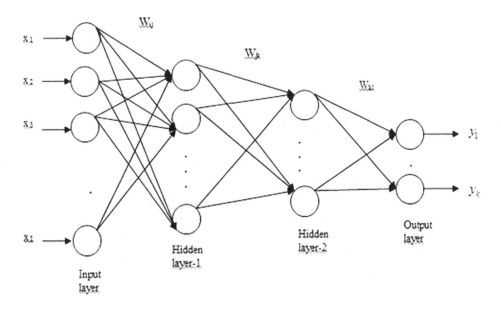

Figure 3. Simple architecture of RNN

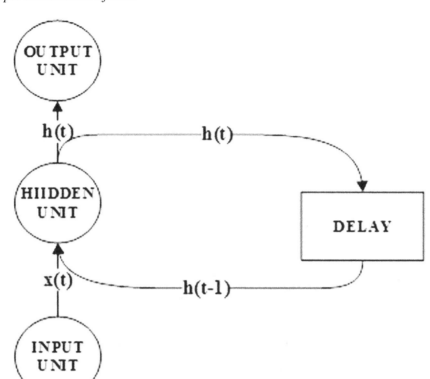

HOPFIELD NETWORK

John Hopfield in the year 1982 proposed a single layer RNN that is also somewhat similar to the human brain. This network does not have any hidden layers or self-loops. It consists of a storage and retrieval mechanism which includes a completely interconnected and complex design like that of human brain. Since the network has only one layer, all the neurons here are binary threshold units which means they act as both the input unit and the output unit. The updation of the nodes in this network happens randomly. The architecture of Hopfield network is shown in Figure 4.

ELMAN AND JORDAN ARTIFICIAL NEURAL NETWORK

Jeff Elman in the year 1990 designed the ENN with recurrent links and dynamic memory. Mostly suitable for temporal tasks, the ENN also has other applications that simple recurrent networks carry out. Apart from the input, output and hidden neurons, these networks also consist of newly designed context units arranged in three layers. There is also a connection from hidden unit to context unit with a feedback to the hidden layer which helps in maintaining the information of the state. This in turn helps the network to perform sequence predictions. The ENNs as shown in Figure 5 are used for speech recognition, segmentations, handwriting recognition etc.

Figure 4. Architecture of Hopfield network

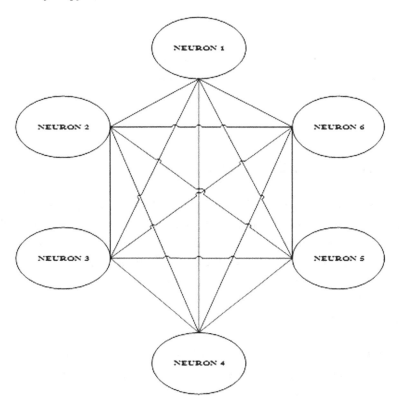

Figure 5. Architecture of ENN

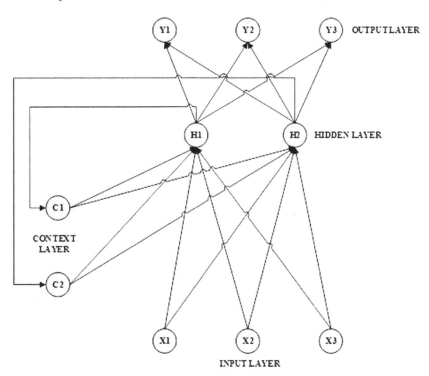

LONG SHORT TERM MEMORY (LSTM)

Hochreiter and Schmidhuber in 1997 proposed a gated RNN that is a LSTM. Features of this network include bridging time intervals of more than a thousand steps and overcome backflow error problems with very minimal time lag. The LSTM exhibits these features even in the presence of highly noisy inputs. The design of this network using the gradient descent strategy ensures constant error rate flow throughout all the internal nodes too.

BI-DIRECTIONAL NEURAL NETWORK

Schuster and Paliwal in 1997 designs the Bi-directional RNN that consists of a pair of separate RNNs among which one moves towards the tail end of the input and the other move towards the beginning of the input. Figure 6 depicts the architecture of the bidirectional neural network. Its applications involve strong linguistic approaches like translation and protein structure prediction.

SELF ORGANIZING MAP

The Self-Organizing Map (SOM) (Kohenon, 1990) is a competitive learning strategy that creates a representation of the features of input signals and their abstractions in a n dimensional space. A series

Figure 6. Architecture of bi-directional RNN

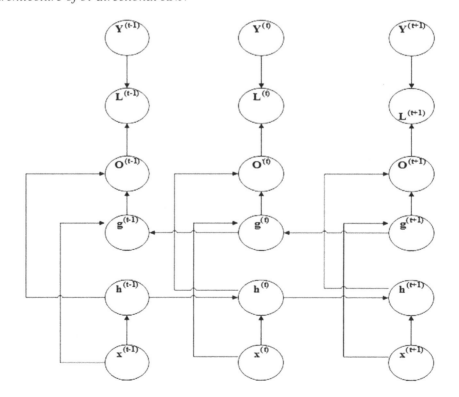

of fine tuning methods need to be applied to its weight vectors to perform well even with noisy signals. The number of neurons determines the scale or the granularity of the resulting model. Scale selection affects the accuracy and the generalization capability of the model. It must be taken into account that the generalization and accuracy are contradictory goals. By improving the first, we lose on the second, and vice versa. It has a wide range of application such as practical speech recognition, robotics, process control, and telecommunication.

APPLICATIONS OF NEURAL NETWORK

Neural networks have a wide range of applications. It is used in real world business for sales forecasting, industrial process control, customer search, data validation, risk management and target marketing. In the field of medical science, neural networks are used for drug prediction, pathology segmentation, medical image analysis and disease identification. Neural networks are also used in Gaming applications. Character recognition, Object detection and classification are some of the neural network applications related to image processing. Neural networks outperform in natural language processing and speech recognition.

NEURAL NETWORKS FOR PATTERN CLASSIFICATION

Given a set of n input-output training patterns $D = \left\{ \left(x^i, y^i \right) \mid i = 1, ..., n \right\}$, where each training pattern x^i has been described by a set of p conditional (or input) attributes $\left(x_1, ..., x_p \right)$ and one corresponding discrete class label y^i where $y^{(i)} \in (1, ..., q)$ and q is the number of classes. Classification problems assign patterns to classes. Class is considered to be a group of similar patterns. For example, Table 1 provides the sample patterns from Thyroid Gland dataset (UCI Repository).

The row vector represents the pattern. The column vector is the attribute. The values of the attribute T3-resin uptake test are 107, 89 and 120. There are five conditional attributes plus one decision attribute the "Class label". The conditional attributes can be numerical or categorical. The decision attribute is always considered as discrete in classification problem. Each of the patterns has to be classified into any of the three classes: 1 for normal, 2 for hyper, 3 for hypo. The neural networks can be used to classify the test patterns to the classes mentioned. As per the results mentioned in our earlier work, 69.76% of accuracy is obtained when Feed forward neural networks are used for classification (Swathi & Jayant,

Table 1. Sample patterns from thyroid gland dataset

T3-Resin Uptake Test	Total Serum Thyroxin	Total Serum Triiodothyronine	Basal Thyroid-Stimulating Hormone (TSH)	Maximal Absolute Difference of TSH	Class Label
107	10.1	2.2	0.9	2.7	1
89	14.3	4.1	0.5	0.2	2
120	6.8	2.1	10.4	38.6	3

2016). To further improve the accuracy of classification, the parameters namely the weights and biases of the neural networks are optimized as discussed in next few sections.

WHAT IS NEURAL NETWORK OPTIMIZATION?

In general, the optimization goal is to either minimize or maximize the objective function by tuning certain parameters. The optimization of neural network is the process of updating the weights and biases of the network in order to minimize the cost function. The most commonly used cost function is to minimize mean square error E.

$$E(\vec{w}(t)) = \frac{1}{N} \sum_{j=1}^{N} \sum_{k=1}^{K} (d_k - o_k)^2 \qquad (3)$$

where $E(\vec{w}(t))$ is the error at the tth iteration, $\vec{w}(t)$, the weights in the connections at the tth iteration, d_k and o_k represent the desired and actual values of kth output node, K is the number of output nodes and N is the number of patterns. The details of the neural network optimization are present based on feed forward neural networks. During the training process as the error E decreases, the accuracy of the neural networks towards the prediction of the label for the unknown pattern gets increased.

CLASSICAL METHODS FOR TRAINING NEURAL NETWORKS

In literature, there are several classical training methods available for tuning the parameters of neural networks. The most commonly and popularly used techniques are based on the concept of back propagation which was originally introduced in 1970s but got major focus when (Rumelhart et al. 1985;1988), came up with many neural networks and showed back propagation is working better. The main theme of backpropagation is, after the neural network is processed in the forward pass, the obtained error is back propagated and the weights and the biases of the output, hidden and input layers are updated by computing the partial derivatives $\frac{\partial C}{\partial w}, \frac{\partial C}{\partial b}$ of the cost function C with respect to weights (w) and biases (b) in order to reduce the error function. The finest combination of weights and biases which helps to reduce the error function forms as the solution for the learning problem considered. The back propagation is mainly based on the concept of computing the gradient of the error function for several iterations. Few other second order algorithms are based on the computation of Hessian Matrix.

Definition 1: Gradient is the first derivative of a scalar function $E(w)$ with respect to a vector

$$W = [w_1, w_2]^T$$

$$H = \nabla\nabla E(W) = \frac{d^2}{dw^2}E(W) = \begin{bmatrix} \dfrac{\partial^2 E}{\partial w_1^2} & \dfrac{\partial^2 E}{\partial w_1 w_2} \\ \dfrac{\partial^2 E}{\partial w_2 w_1} & \dfrac{\partial^2 E}{\partial w_2^2} \end{bmatrix} \tag{4}$$

Definition 2: Second derivative of $E(w)$ is termed as the Hessian matrix (H).

$$H = \nabla\nabla E(W) = \frac{d^2}{dw^2}E(W) = \begin{bmatrix} \dfrac{\partial^2 E}{\partial w_1^2} & \dfrac{\partial^2 E}{\partial w_1 w_2} \\ \dfrac{\partial^2 E}{\partial w_2 w_1} & \dfrac{\partial^2 E}{\partial w_2^2} \end{bmatrix} \tag{5}$$

In next sections, we discuss few of the classical training methods for neural network optimization.

GRADIENT DESCENT

The standard back propagation technique is the gradient descent algorithm in which the parameters of the neural networks (weights and the biases) are moved in the direction of negative gradient of the objective function (Rumelhart et al. 1985). The concept of moving the weights is based on the line search procedure which decides the direction of the move and then how far to move in that direction.

$$w_{ij}^{t+1} = w_{ij}^{t} - \eta\nabla(w_{ij}^{t}) \tag{6}$$

NEWTON'S METHOD

The Newton's method also called as Newton's Raphson method is a second order training algorithm based on Hessian Matrix. This method finds better training directions using second order derivatives. The basic idea of this method is to minimize the quadratic approximation of the objective function around the current point.

$$w_{ij}^{t+1} = w_{ij}^{t} - \left[\nabla^2 f(w_{ij}^{t})\right]^{-1} \nabla f(w_{ij}^{l}) \tag{7}$$

The first derivative is expressed as:

$$\nabla f(w_{ij}^t) = J^T(w_{ij}^t)e(w_{ij}^t) \tag{8}$$

The second derivative is expressed as:

$$\nabla^2 f(w_{ij}^t) = J^T(w_{ij}^t)J(w_{ij}^t) + \sum_{i=1}^{N} e_i(w_k)\nabla^2 e_i(w_k) \tag{9}$$

$J(w_{ij}^t)$ is the Jacobian matrix and the error is determined as:

$$e(w_{ij}^t) = T - y(w_{ij}^t) \tag{10}$$

T is the target vector and $y(w_{ij}^t)$ is the actual output of the network.

CONJUGATE GRADIENT DESCENT

Conjugate gradient descent methods are in between gradient descent and Newton's method. The main objective of this method is to improve the convergence speed allied to gradient descent. In general conjugate descent algorithms are based on the notion of quadratic error function with a positive definite Hessian matrix. As it is known that computation of Hessian is computationally costly, conjugate gradient method overcomes this issue by including a tricky relationship between direction and gradient vector and avoids the computation of inverse of Hessian matrix as essential in Newton's method. The computations are possible only using gradient as in first order methods. As the search in this method is towards the conjugate directions, we achieve faster convergence than gradient descent methods.

The new weight change in the next iteration doesn't change the component of the gradient along the previous direction. The new weight update is done using the equation (Bishop, 1995)::

$$w_{ij}^{t+1} = w_{ij}^t - \alpha\nabla f(w_{ij}^t) + \beta\nabla w_{ij}^t \tag{11}$$

The Polak-Ribière formula is used to calculate β. It is the conjugate gradient parameter determined using the equation given below:

$$\beta = \frac{[\nabla f(w_{ij}^t) - \nabla f(w_{ij}^t)]^T \nabla f(w_{ij}^t)}{\nabla f(w_{ij}^{t-1})^T \nabla f(w_{ij}^{t-1})} \tag{12}$$

QUASI-NEWTON METHOD

The Newton's method is more expensive as it involves more computations and operations like determining Hessian matrix and its inverse. To overcome this issue, Quasi-Newton's method approximates the inverse Hessian by another matrix G which is purely based on first partial derivatives. The two commonly used methods for inverse approximation G are from Davidon- Fletcher-Powell formula (DFP) and the Broyden-Fletcher-Goldfarb-Shanno formula (BFGS).

$$w_{ij}^{t+1} = w_{ij}^{t-1} + t\Delta w_{ij}^t \tag{13}$$

$$\Delta w_{ij}^t = -H_{t-1}^{-1} \nabla f(w_{ij}^{t-1}) \tag{14}$$

GAUSS- NEWTON METHOD

The Gauss-Newton method is an approximate Newton's method that works only with objective functions that can be expressed as a sum of squares. The Gauss-Newton method uses the approximate Hessian and exact gradient in Newton's method.

The Gauss Newton's modification provides the following update equation

$$w_{ij}^{k+1} = w_{ij}^k - [J^T(w_{ij}^k)J(w_{ij}^k)]^{-1}J^T(w_{ij}^k)e(w_{ij}^k) \tag{15}$$

LEVENBERG – MARQUARDT ALGORITHM

If the Hessian matrix in Gauss Newton's method is not positive definite, then the Levenberg Marquardt algorithm is used with the following update equation (Hagan and Menhaj, 1994).

$$w_{ij}^{k+1} = w_{ij}^{k} - [J^{T}(w_{ij}^{k})J(w_{ij}^{k}) + \mu I]^{-1} J^{T}(w_{ij}^{k})e(w_{ij}^{k}) \tag{16}$$

The modification made in Levenberg-Marquardt method against Gauss Newton method helps to make the hessian matrix positive definite by increasing μ until $\lambda + \mu > 0$. The Levenberg Marquardt algorithm is a second order training algorithm which works with gradient vector and the Jacobian matrix involving first derivatives instead of computing the exact Hessian Matrix. The speed of this algorithm increases as it converges to the minimum. This algorithm is not compatible for the cost function like root mean square error or the cost entropy error. The best suit for the cost function is the sum-of-squared error. As this algorithm stores a huge Jacobian matrix, this requires lot of memory and becomes infeasible for training huge datasets/ neural networks.

SWARM BASED NEURAL NETWORK OPTIMIZATION

The typical classical training methods like backpropagation algorithm (Williams et al., 1986), are used to adjust the weight and/or biases of the neural networks in order to minimize the error and increase classification accuracy. But the main drawback of the gradient descent methods is they often get trapped into local minima due to their strategy of trajectory searching. To overcome this issue, global optimization algorithms like evolutionary, swarm based optimization techniques emerged and these are now widely used for training neural networks. In this section we briefly describe nine swarm based optimization techniques for training the parameters of neural networks. The characteristics of these algorithms are given in Table 2.

ANT COLONY OPTIMIZATION

Dorigo (1992) proposed ant colony optimization (ACO) algorithm. The algorithm is based on the behavior of the ants in finding the shortest path between their nest and food source. Each ant provides a solution satisfying the objective function. The deposit of pheromone trails acts as a communication medium among the ants. The communication is established between the ants using the pheromone trails deposited in the path of travel. The concentration of pheromone substance deposited in the path determines the quality of the solution and the path with high quality is chosen to be the shortest path. In ACO technique, the local best solution is chosen as the global solution.

The procedure for applying ACO technique for neural network training is given below:

The following notations are used:

τ : Attractiveness of ant towards an edge

η : Visibility (desirability) of choosing an edge

Table 2. Characteristics of Swarm based Optimization Techniques

Algorithms	Basic Principle	Solution Representation	Evolutionary Operators	Fitness	Selection Process	Type of Decision Variables
Ant colony optimization	Cooperative group of ants	Graph	None	Scaled objective value	Probabilistic, preservative	Mainly for discrete values
Artificial Bee colony	Collective knowledge of bees	Real –valued	None	Objective function value	Probabilistic, preservative	Both discrete and continuous
Bacterial Foraging	Foraging behavior of *Escherchia coli* bacteria	Result is: bacteria will die/ migrate based on split/adapt nutrient values which are real valued	None	Objective function value	Deterministic	Mainly for continuous values
BAT	Echolocation behavior of micro bats	Real- valued	None	Objective function value	Metaheuristic (stochastic)	Discrete and Continuous
CAT swarm	Based on cat behavior	Real- valued	None	Objective function value	Metaheuristic (stochastic)	Mainly for Discrete values
Cuckoo	Cunning breeding behavior of cuckoos (obligate brood parasitism)	Nests are ranked as best/worse	None	Objective function value	Metaheuristic (stochastic)	Discrete and Continuous
Firefly	Flashing patterns of fireflies	Real valued (Fireflies are ranked as best to worst depending on attractiveness)	None	Objective function value	Metaheuristic (stochastic)	Both discrete and continuous, but variants include an approach only for discrete values (DFA)
Fish Swarm Algorithm	Imitate fish behavior such as preying, swarming, etc.	Real valued.	None	Objective function value	Deterministic	Position is vector value, step is a discrete length, Crowd factor has values with a range of (0,1)
Particle Swarm optimization	Cooperative group of swarm intelligence	Real- Valued	None	Objective function value	Deterministic, extinctive	continuous values and discrete

Pseudocode:

Step 1: Initialize the base attractiveness (τ) as $\tau_{ij} = \dfrac{1}{n_0 + n_h + n_i}$ and visibility (η) for each element of initial Multi layered Perceptron's (MLPs) having the number of hidden nodes as n_h, number of output nodes as n_o and the number of input nodes as n_i.

Step 2: for each iteration do:

```
Step 3:    for each ant do:
Make a probabilistic choice using attractiveness and visibility to make a next
move to      determine new weights and biases
Place the move to the Tabu list for each ant
Repeat until each ant completed a solution
end
 Step 4: for each ant that completed a solution do:
Update attractiveness τ for each edge that the ant traversed using the equa-
tion,
```

$$\tau_{ij} = \tau_{ij} + \Delta_{ij}^{best} \tag{17}$$

```
 end
Step 5: If local best MLP weights and biases are better than global solution
then save MLP as global solution; end
Step 6:  end // when maximum iteration is reached;
```

ARTIFICIAL BEE COLONY

Artificial Bee Colony (ABC) is one of the most recently defined algorithms by Karaboga (2007) motivated by the intelligent behavior of honey bees. It is as simple as Particle Swarm Optimization (PSO) and Differential Evolution (DE) algorithms, and uses only common control parameters such as colony size and maximum cycle number. ABC as an optimization tool provides a population-based search procedure in which individuals called foods positions are modified by the artificial bees with time and the bee's aim is to discover the places of food sources with high nectar amount and finally the one with the highest nectar. In ABC system, artificial bees fly around in a multidimensional search space and some (employed and onlooker bees) choose food sources depending on the experience of themselves and their nest mates, and adjust their positions. Some (scouts) fly and choose the food sources randomly without using experience. If the nectar amount of a new source is higher than that of the previous one in their memory, they memorize the new position and forget the previous one. Thus, ABC system combines local search methods, carried out by employed and onlooker bees, with global search methods, managed by onlookers and scouts, attempting to balance exploration and exploitation process.

The following notations are used in the pseudocode given below:

SN : Number of food sources

MCN : Maximum cycle number

p_i : Is the probability value associated with the food source.

x_{ij} : Food source at two positions i and j

ϕ_{ij} : Random number between [-1,1]

Pseudocode:

Step 1: Initialize the population of Multi layered Perceptron solutions x_{ij} where: $i = 1..SN$, $j = 1..D$

Step 2: Evaluate the Fitness of the population

Step 3: For each iteration do

Step 4: Produce new solutions v_{ij} for the employed bees using equation (18) and evaluate the fitness

$$v_{ij} = x_{ij} + \phi_{ij}\left(x_{ij} - x_{kj}\right) \tag{18}$$

Step 5: Apply the greedy selection process

Step 6: Calculate the probability values P_{ij} for the solutions x_{ij} using equation (19)

$$p_i = \frac{fit_i}{\sum_{n=1}^{SN} fit_n} \tag{19}$$

Step 7: Depending on the P_{ij} value, produce the new solutions v_{ij} for the onlookers from the selected solutions x_{ij} and evaluate for its fitness.

Step 8: Apply the greedy selection process

Step 9: Determine the abandoned solution for the scout, if exists, and replace it with a new randomly produced solution x_{ij} by Equation (20)

$$x_i^j = x_{\min}^j + rand(0,1)(x_{\max}^j - x_{\min}^j) \tag{20}$$

Step 10:   Memorize the best MLP weights and biases achieved so far

Step 11: End for

BACTERIAL FORAGING OPTIMIZATION

Passino (2002) developed the bacterial foraging algorithm which is based on the chemotaxis behavior and patterns of the bacteria, M.xanthus and E.coli while they are in the search of food (refers to the process of foraging here). The bacterium uses a strategy where they sense chemical gradients or nutrients and determine the direction of the food based on the attracting and repelling chemicals they secrete in the environment. The search is carried out stochastically by the swarm to achieve the optima. It is achieved through four main processes on a simulated cell, namely – The Chemotaxis stage which depicts the movements of the bacteria on a cost surface and each random sized step taken by the bacteria is shown as a vector. The next stage is the group behavior of the specie, where these bacteria try to move up their nutrient gradient by forming a ring using a cell to cell signaling as an objective function. The third stage involves reproduction where only those bacteria split asexually which have performed well during their course of foraging. Thus, the lowest objective function value is selected for this process. The final stage is elimination-dispersal where the population is replaced because of the bacteria being killed due to environmental factors and hence new random samples with low probability values are selected.

The following notations are used in the pseudocode given below:

θ_i^t : Represents the position of the ith bacterium in the tth - chemotaxis step.

$C(i)$: Is the step length during the ith chemotaxis.

$\phi(i)$: Is a unit vector which stands for the swimming direction after a tumble.

N_s : Is the maximum run step

N_c : Is the number of chemotactic steps

N_{re} : Is the number of reproduction steps

S: Is the size of the population

P_e : Is the predetermined number

N_{ed} : Is the number of eliminate- dispersal events happen.

```
Pseudocode:
Step 1: Initialization the Multi layered Perceptron solutions
Step 2: For i= 1: N_ed
Step 3:    For j = 1: N_re
Step 4:       For k = 1: N_c
Step 5:          For n = 1: S
Step 6:             J_last = J(n)
Step 7:                Generate a tumble angle for bacterium n
Step 8:                Update the position of bacterium n by
```

$$\theta_i^{t+1} = \theta_i^t + C(i)\Phi(i) \tag{21}$$

```
where
```

$$\phi(i) = \frac{\Delta_i}{\sqrt{\Delta_i^T \Delta_i}} \tag{22}$$

```
and Δ_i is a randomly produced vector of the same dimension of the problem and
the step length C is calculated by using the equation
```

$$C = C_s - \frac{(C_s - C_e) * nowEva}{TotEva} \tag{23}$$

where Cs is the step length at the beginning and Ce is the steplength at the end and *nowEva* is the current fitness evaluation count and *TotEva* is the total fitness evaluations. The bacteria's step length might vary due to the nutrition. This is calculated by the equation below:

$$C(i) = \left\{ \frac{C}{Nutrient(i)}, [if(Nutrient(i)) > 0]; C, otherwise \right. \tag{24}$$

Step 9:   Recalculate the $J(n)$

Step 10: $m = 0$

Step 11:   While ($m < N_s$)

Step 12:   If $J(n) < J_{last}$
                          $J_{last} = J(n)$

Step 13:   Run one more step using equation 6;

Step 14:   Recalculate the $J(n)$;

Step 15: $m = m + 1$

Step 16:   Else

Step 17: $m = N_s$

Step 18:   End if

Step 19:   End while

Step 20:   End for

Step 21:   Update the best value achieved so far;

Step 22:   End for

Step 23:   Sort the population according to J;

Step 24:   For m = 1: S/2

Step 25:   Bacterium (k + S/2)= Bacterium (k);

Step 26:   End For

Step 27: End for

Step 28:   For l =1: S

Step 29:   If rand < P_e

Step 30:   Move Bacterium l to a random position

Step 31:   End if

Step 32:   End for

Step 33: End for

BAT

The Bat Swarm Optimization (BSO) is a metaheuristic optimization strategy that considers virtual bats that fly randomly with a velocity(v_i) and position(x_i) and vary their pulse rates, emission frequencies and loudness. These parameters change when the bat finds its prey. It uses the concept of echolocation, where it detects objects/prey by the use of sound waves or echo (Yang, 2010). A random walk is used to determine the path of the bat which might consist of successive random steps. This would further intensify the search and hence help in achieving the global optimum. A frequency tuning technique is used to handle the dynamic and chaotic behaviour of the bats. This would balance the exploration and exploitation strategies in the algorithm by fine tuning of the factors that influence the algorithm. The updation of parameters continues until the set stopping criteria is met. The main disadvantage in BSO is that it most often gets trapped in the local minima and thus suffers from premature convergence. This can be solved by using chaotic strategies or various hybrid approaches. In all, it constitutes a good global optimization strategy.

The following notations are used in the pseudocode given below:

v_i : Velocity at x_i position with pulse frequency

f_i : Pulse frequency

x_* : Is the current global best location (solution) which is located after comparing all the solutions among all n bats.

β: Belongs to an uniform distribution in the range [0,1]

Pseudocode:
Step1: Initialize n Multi layered Perceptron solutions (bat population) representing x_i (i = 1, 2... n) and v_i

Step 2: Define pulse frequency f_i at x_i

Step 3: Initialize pulse rates r_i and the loudness A_i

Step 4: while (t< Max number of iterations)
Generate new weights and biases by adjusting frequency, and updating velocities and locations/solutions using the following equations

$$f_i = f_{\min} + (f_{\max} - f_{\min})\beta,$$
$$v_i^t = v_i^{t-1} + (x_i^t - x_*)f_i, \tag{25}$$
$$x_i^t = x_i^{t-1} + v_i^t$$

Step 5:   if (rand> r_i)
Select a solution among the best solutions
Generate a local solution around the selected best solution
end if
Step 6: Generate a new solution by flying based on updating the position by

using the equation $x_{new} = x_{old} + \varepsilon < A_t >$ where $<A_t>$ is the average loudness of all the bats and ε is the constant in the range [-1,1]. Update the loudness using the equation $A_i^{t+1} = \alpha A_i^t$ where α is a constant. The emission rate is updated using the equation $r_i^{t+1} = r_i^0[1 - \exp(-\gamma t)]$, where r_i^0 is the emission rate at t=0 and γ is a constant.

Step 7: Rank the MLPs(bats) and find the current best MLP with low MSE
Step 8: end while

CAT SWARM OPTIMIZATION

Modelling the behavior of cats (Chu et al., 2006) for optimization is done by observing the curiosity pattern that is whether the cat is in seeking mode – it is resting and looking around to seek the next position to move to (or) tracing mode – the cat is currently tracing some targets. Each solution set of a cat has a m-dimensional position, velocities for each dimension, fitness value and seeking or tracing mode flag. Positions and velocities of the cats are updated suitably, considering the inertia weight of the cat and the mode it is currently in. Suitable parameters are assigned to both the modes and the quest for a global optimal is desired. The algorithm is said to be a better global optimizer when compared with other algorithms like the ant colony or particle swarm optimization. The complexity is the reason why sometimes the pure CSO takes a longer time to converge and cannot achieve the accurate solution. For solving this problem and improving the convergence accuracy level, other dynamic and adaptive strategies could be adopted.

Notations used:

SMP: Seeking Memory Pool
SPC: Self Position Consideration
CDC: Count of dimensions to Change
SRD: Seeking of a Dimension
FS: Fitness values

```
Pseudocode
Step 1: Initialize a set of Multi layered Perceptron solutions (cats)
Step 2: Randomly sprinkle the cats into the M dimensional solution space and
randomly give values, which are in-range of the maximum velocity, to the ve-
locities of every cat. Then haphazardly pick number of cats and set them into
tracing mode, and the others set into seeking mode.
Step 3: Evaluate the MSE of each cat and store the best cat solution
Step 4: Move the cats according to their flags, if cat_k is in seeking mode,
apply the cat to the seeking mode process using,
Create j copies of the current position of cat_k, where j = SMP.
If (SPC is true),
  let j = SMP & retain the current position
```

```
In each copy, according to CDC -
    Add / subtract randomly the SRD percentage to current values
    Replace old values with current
Compute fitness values (FS) for all candidate data points
If (FS_i <> FS_j), compute the probability of selecting the candidate data point.
Else, set the probability of selecting the candidate point to 1
Pick a random point to move and replace the position of cat_k using,
```

$$P_i = \frac{|FS_i - FS_j|}{FS_{max} - FS_{min}} \qquad (26)$$

```
otherwise apply it to the tracing mode process.
Step 5: Re-pick number of cats and set them into tracing mode, then set the
other cats into seeking mode.
Update the velocity using the equation
```

$$V_{kM} = V_{kM} + rnd * c_1 * (x_{bestM} - x_{kM}), M = 1,2,3,...N \qquad (27)$$

```
where rnd is a random number in the range [0,1], C1 is a constant value and
```
x_{bestM} is the cat having the best fitness value for the dth dimension.
```
Check if computed new velocity is in the range(V_max) computed till now. If not,
set the newly computed velocity as V_max
Update the position using the equation
```

$$x_{kM} = x_{kM} + V_{kM} \qquad (28)$$

```
Step 6: Check the termination condition, if satisfied, terminate the program,
and otherwise repeat Step 3 to Step 5.
```

CUCKOO SEARCH

The cuckoo birds follow the brood parasitism strategy of laying their eggs in other bird's nests so that the host bird would consider the egg as its own and nurture it to birth (Yang & Deb, 2009). There is a probability that the host bird finds out the egg doesn't belong to its own family and may discard it. These eggs are depicted as 'alien eggs'. Another strategy involved is that the host bird may disown the nest, if there is an egg from any alien bird found in its nest. The algorithm proposed is a metaheuristic strategy that uses the concept of Levy flights and random walks. A probability 'p' is assumed for the discovery of an alien egg in the host's nest. The numbers of host nests are fixed and each cuckoo lays an egg each time in a randomly chosen nest. The next generation is composed by the selection of the best quality nests that is the one in which they survived.

```
Pseudocode:
Step 1: Generate n initial set of Multi layered Perceptron solutions (host
nests)
Step 2: while terminating condition not met
Step 3: Get a cuckoo randomly by Levy flights
Step 4: evaluate MSE (Fᵢ)
Step 5: Choose a nest j among n
Step 6: if if(Fᵢ > Fⱼ)
  randomly replace j by the new weights and biases;
end
Step 7: A fraction of worse MLP weights and biases are abandoned and new ones
are built;
Step 8: Store the best MLPs with low MSE
Step 9: Rank the solutions and find the current best MLP with low MSE
Step 10: end while
```

In the pseudocode, Step 4 evaluates the mean squared error F_i, Step 6 contains the conditional $if(F_i > F_j)$.

FIREFLY ALGORITHM

Yang (2010) developed the firefly algorithm as a metaheuristic optimization approach. The firefly uses the luminescence strategy. There are a set of fireflies that are attracted to each other in a swarm based on the intensity of the firefly. As fireflies are unisexual, any of them among the swarm can be attracted to one another based on the brightness. The greater the distance of the firefly from each other, the lesser would be the intensity and hence they would not move towards each other. The intensity of brightness is a large determining parameter in the objective function. Other parameters include the distance travelled, Ψ -the vector of Gaussian distribution, α - the step size. The attractiveness is computed as a direct proportionality to the distance and a randomly generated parameter is also used.

```
Pseudocode:
Step 1:  Generate n initial population of Multi layered Perceptron solutions
(fireflies);
Step 2:  Formulate light intensity I ; I(r) = I₀e^{-γr²}
Step 3: Define absorption coefficient, Ψ;
Step 4: While max generation not reached
Step 5: For i= 1 to n (all n fireflies)
Step 6:              For j=1 to n (all n fireflies)
```

Step 2 formulates the light intensity I as $I(r) = I_0 e^{-\gamma r^2}$.

```
Step 7:                           If ( I_j > I_i ) then
move firefly i towards j;
                 Update
```

$$x_i^{t+1} = x_i^t + \beta * e^{-\Psi r_{ij}^2} * [x_j^t - x_i^t] + \alpha_t \varepsilon_t \tag{29}$$

where the attractiveness $\beta = \beta_0 e^{-\gamma r^m}$ (m>1) and the distance r is computed using the equation $r_{ij} = \sqrt{\sum_{k=1}^{d} (x_{i,k} - x_{j,k})^2}$

```
End if
End if
Step 8:         Evaluate new solutions and update light intensity;
Step 9:    End For j;
Step 10: End For i;
Step 11: Select and populate global best solution until now
Step 12: Rank the MLPs (fireflies) and find the current best (with low MSE);
Step 13: End while.
```

FISH SWARM OPTIMZIATION ALGORITHM

The behavior and movement of school of fishes inspires the FSO (Li et al., 2002) to exploit intelligent strategies for solving optimization problems. The social interaction of fishes among colonies, their immigration footprints, reaction to dangers and preying are studied for a particular environment and suitable parameters are determined. The search space in this problem is depicted along directions in which the fish explores for food. This measure parameterizes the learning capacity of the fish. Various behaviours like the swarming behavior, random behavior, searching behavior, chasing and leaping behavior summarizes the series of instinctive strategies the fishes follow when searching food. The algorithm is found to have high accuracy, fault tolerance and better convergence speed. However, it lacks the balance between local and global search and low running time complexity. The algorithm could be better enhanced to work well when the school of fishes benefit from the experiences of each other, which would help them to make next moves while in search for food.

The procedure for applying FSO technique for neural network training is given below:

```
Pseudocode:
Step 1: Random initialize Multi layered Perceptron solutions (Fish Swarm)
Step 2: While Termination condition not reached
Step 3:    For each Fish
              Measure fitness for fish
Step 4:             Do Step Follow
Step 5:             If(Follow fails) then
              Do step Swarm
```

```
Step 6:              If(Swarm fails) then
                  Do step Prey
Step 7:              End If
Step 8:      End If
Step 9:   End For
Step10: End while
```

PARTICLE SWARM OPTIMIZATION (PSO)

The PSO technique proposed by Kennedy and Ederhart (1995; 2011) mimics the flocking behavior of the birds to determine the optimum solution. Each solution determined by the bird is called the particle. The birds fly in a solution space and the shortest path determined by the bird is considered as local best (lbest) solution and the best path found by any particle at a particular instance is stored as global best (gbest) solution. The basic concept behind PSO is that at each time step, the velocity of each particle is accelerated towards the lbest and gbest. Based on the local and global best solutions, birds learn and communicate with each other to find the most optimum best solutions.

The procedure for applying PSO technique for neural network training is given below:

Notations

p_{best} : Is the previous best value and related to only a particular particle.

g_{best} : Is the best value of all the particles.

V_{jd} : Represents the velocity of j particle with d dimensions respectively.

X_{jd} : Represents the position of j particle with d dimensions respectively.

rand₁ and *rand₂* are two uniform random functions.

W : Inertia weight whose dynamic range is between 0.2 and 1.2

c_1 : Cognition coefficient and c_2 - social coefficient.

Step 1: Initialize a population of Multi-layered perceptron's (particles) with random positions and velocities of d dimensions in the problem space.

Step 2: For each particle, evaluate the desired optimization fitness function MSE (Mean Square Error)

Step 3: Compare particle's fitness evaluation with particles p_{best}.

If current value is better than p_{best}, then set p_{best} value equal to the current value and the p_{best} location equal to the current location in d-dimensional space.

Step 4: Compare MSE with the population's overall previous best. It the current value is better than g_{best} then reset g_{best} to the current particle's array index and value.

Step 5: Change the velocity and position of the particle according to equation (30) and (31) respectively.

$$V_{t+1} = W \times V_t + c_1 \times rand_1 \times \left(P_{best}^t - X_t \right) + c_2 \times rand_2 \times \left(G_{best}^t - X_t \right) \tag{30}$$

$$X_{t+1} = X_t + V_{t+1} \tag{31}$$

Step 6: Repeat step 2 until a Minimum MSE value is achieved or a maximum number of Iterations/ epochs is reached.

SWARM BASED TECHNIQUES FOR TRAINING DEEP LEARNING NEURAL NETWORKS

In the recent era, swarm based metaheuristic techniques are widely used for optimizing neural networks. Albeahdili et al. (2015) proposed and demonstrated a new hybrid training process called Particle Swam Optimization- Stochastic Gradient Decent (PSO-SGD) algorithm, for training Convolution Neural Network (CNN). The hybrid training method avoids occurring in local optimum and premature saturation inspired by using single algorithm. Syulistyo et al. (2016) introduced utilization of Particle Swarm Optimization (PSO) in Convolutional Neural Networks (CNNs) to optimize the results of the solution vectors on CNN in order to improve the recognition accuracy using a hybrid approach called CNNPSO. Jiang et al. (2016) proposed a deep learning approach, which hybridizes a deep belief networks (DBNs) and a nonlinear kernel-based parallel evolutionary SVM (ESVM), to predict evolution states of complex systems in a classification manner using PSO. Cai et al. (2007) proposed a hybrid PSO-EA algorithm to train recurrent neural networks to predict time series data. In their work, an initial population is created and evaluated. Winners are selected based on the fitness value and these winners are enhanced by PSO. Using these enhanced winners, offspring are generated using evolutionary operators, and these offspring replace less fit members of the population. Desell et al. (2015) presented a novel strategy for using ant colony optimization (ACO) to evolve the structure of deep recurrent neural networks with up to 5 hidden and 5 recurrent layers for the challenging task of predicting general aviation flight data. Soll (2015) proposed a method is presented using Cuckoo Search to find images which mislead deep neural networks (Example: AlexNet) into incorrectly labelling these images. Moreover, CSO is used to improve the classification performance of artificial neural network.

ADVANTAGES OF SWARM BASED TECHNIQUES

1. Swarm intelligent based algorithms are highly scalable. They can be well utilized starting from using few individuals up to millions of individuals for generating optimal solutions. This clearly shows that the working or control mechanism of the SI techniques is not based on the swarm size, as long as it is not very small.
2. SI algorithms adapt well for even rapidly changing environments and they are more flexible with inherent auto configuration and self –organizing capabilities.

3. The SI based systems are more robust as they work collectively without any central control mechanism. Hence, the applicability of the algorithms for neural network optimization is more reliable.
4. Though the SI algorithms are based on simple individuals and their behaviours, the techniques cooperatively work well to show case as the refined group behaviour.

LIMITATIONS / CHALLENGES OF SWARM BASED TECHNIQUES

Though the capability of swarm intelligence for getting optimal solutions is indeed far reaching for most of the optimization problems, still there are few challenges:

1. The swarm based techniques are well explored for most of the optimization problems but still there is lot of research work is needed to explore their capabilities to work on time critical applications.
2. Most of the swarm algorithms are parameter dependent. Most of the time, the parameters are predetermined using trial and error approach. Optimizing these parameters is another challenge for the researchers when applying the same for optimization problems.
3. Since the swarm intelligent techniques don't have a central control and they work in collaborative manner, there is a chance that they suffer from the problem of stagnation. But still, this issue can be addressed well if the algorithm parameters are carefully set.

CONCLUSION

Among several machine algorithms, Feed Forward Neural Networks are one of the widely used machine learning techniques for pattern classification. Generally, to improve the obtained classification accuracy results, we optimize the parameters (weights and bias) of the neural networks. The optimization aims to minimize the mean square error (MSE) calculated using the actual output produced by the feedforward network and the desired output. The back-propagation (BP) training algorithm is the most prominent approach for optimization in supervised learning strategy. Due to the problem of getting stuck in local minima, by taking advantage of social collective behaviour of swarms, recently, several nature-inspired metaheuristic techniques are widely used for training neural networks. Nature inspired swarm techniques generally aim towards global optimization and they are computationally inexpensive, robust, and simple.

FUTURE WORK

The future research direction would be to develop scalable nature inspired metaheuristic techniques to handle the inherent high dimensionality of weight space. To explore real world applications with strong theoretical foundation to use Neural Networks with swarm based optimizations. Further, there is a need to investigate existing nature-inspired techniques and to develop efficient techniques to overcome the challenges. The other possibility would be to find methods to shorten the optimization cycle. There is large scope for wide-range of successful applications in different areas as the studies on metaheuristic techniques are exponentially growing and going on.

REFERENCES

Albeahdili, H. M., Han, T., & Islam, N. E. (2015). Hybrid Algorithm for the Optimization of Training Convolutional Neural Network. *International Journal of Advanced Computer Science & Applications*, *1*(6), 79–85.

Bishop, C. M. (1995). *Neural Networks for Pattern Recognition*. Clarendon Press.

Cai, X., Zhang, N., Venayagamoorthy, G. K., & Wunsch, D. C. II. (2007). Time series prediction with recurrent neural networks trained by a hybrid PSO–EA algorithm. *Neurocomputing*, *70*(13), 2342–2353. doi:10.1016/j.neucom.2005.12.138

Chu, S. C., Tsai, P. W., & Pan, J. S. (2006, August). Cat swarm optimization. In *Pacific Rim International Conference on Artificial Intelligence* (pp. 854-858). Springer Berlin Heidelberg.

Cybenko, G. (1989). Approximation by superpositions of a sigmoidal function. *Mathematics of Control, Signals, and Systems*, *2*(4), 303–314. doi:10.1007/BF02551274

Desell, T., Clachar, S., Higgins, J., & Wild, B. (2015, April). Evolving Deep Recurrent Neural Networks Using Ant Colony Optimization. In *European Conference on Evolutionary Computation in Combinatorial Optimization* (pp. 86-98). Springer International Publishing. doi:10.1007/978-3-319-16468-7_8

Dorigo, M. (1992). *Optimization, learning and natural algorithms* (Ph. D. Thesis). Politecnico di Milano, Italy.

Duda, P. O., & Hart, P. E. (1973). *Pattern Classification and Scene Analysis*. New York: Wiley.

Eberhart, R. C., & Kennedy, J. (1995, October). A new optimizer using particle swarm theory. In *Proceedings of the sixth international symposium on micro machine and human science* (Vol. 1, pp. 39-43). doi:10.1109/MHS.1995.494215

Elman, J. L. (1990). Finding structure in time. *Cognitive Science*, *14*(2), 179–211. doi:10.1207/s15516709cog1402_1

Fahlman, S. E. (1988). *Faster-learning variations on back-propagation: An empirical study*. Academic Press.

Fahlman, S. E., & Lebiere, C. (1989). *The cascade-correlation learning architecture*. Academic Press.

Gupta, J. N., & Sexton, R. S. (1999). Comparing backpropagation with a genetic algorithm for neural network training. *Omega*, *27*(6), 679–684. doi:10.1016/S0305-0483(99)00027-4

Haberman, B. K., & Sheppard, J. W. (2012). Overlapping particle swarms for energy-efficient routing in sensor networks. *Wireless Networks*, *18*(4), 351–363. doi:10.1007/s11276-011-0404-1

Hagan, M. T., & Menhaj, M. B. (1994). Training feedforward networks with the Marquardt algorithm. *IEEE Transactions on Neural Networks*, *5*(6), 989–993. doi:10.1109/72.329697 PMID:18267874

Hassanien, A. E., Moftah, H. M., Azar, A. T., & Shoman, M. (2014). MRI breast cancer diagnosis hybrid approach using adaptive ant-based segmentation and multilayer perceptron neural networks classifier. *Applied Soft Computing*, *14*, 62–71. doi:10.1016/j.asoc.2013.08.011

Hochreiter, S., & Schmidhuber, J. (1997). Long short-term memory. *Neural Computation, 9*(8), 1735–1780. doi:10.1162/neco.1997.9.8.1735 PMID:9377276

Hopfield, J. J. (1982). Neural networks and physical systems with emergent collective computational abilities. *Proceedings of the National Academy of Sciences of the United States of America, 79*(8), 2554–2558. doi:10.1073/pnas.79.8.2554 PMID:6953413

Hornik, K. (1991). Approximation capabilities of multilayer feedforward networks. *Neural Networks, 4*(2), 251–257. doi:10.1016/0893-6080(91)90009-T

Hornik, K., Stinchcombe, M., & White, H. (1989). Multilayer feedforward networks are universal approximators. *Neural Networks, 2*(5), 359–366. doi:10.1016/0893-6080(89)90020-8

Jiang, P., Chen, C., & Liu, X. (2016, April). Time series prediction for evolutions of complex systems: A deep learning approach. In *2016 IEEE International Conference on Control and Robotics Engineering (ICCRE)* (pp. 1-6). IEEE. doi:10.1109/ICCRE.2016.7476150

Karaboga, D., & Basturk, B. (2007). A powerful and efficient algorithm for numerical function optimization: Artificial bee colony (ABC) algorithm. *Journal of Global Optimization, 39*(3), 459–471. doi:10.1007/s10898-007-9149-x

Kennedy, J. (2011). Particle swarm optimization. In Encyclopedia of machine learning (pp. 760-766). Springer US.

Kohonen, T. (1990, September). The self-organizing map. *Proceedings of the IEEE, 78*(9), 1464–1480. doi:10.1109/5.58325

Li, X. L., Shao, Z. J., & Qian, J. X. (2002). An optimizing method based on autonomous animats: Fish-swarm algorithm. *System Engineering Theory and Practice, 22*(11), 32–38.

Passino, K. M. (2002). Biomimicry of bacterial foraging for distributed optimization and control. *IEEE Control Systems, 22*(3), 52-67.

Riedmiller, M., & Braun, H. (1993). A direct adaptive method for faster backpropagation learning: The RPROP algorithm. In *Neural Networks, 1993., IEEE International Conference on* (pp. 586-591). IEEE.

Rumelhart, D. E., Hinton, G. E., & Williams, R. J. (1985). *Learning internal representations by error propagation (No. ICS-8506)*. California Univ San Diego La Jolla Inst for Cognitive Science.

Rumelhart, D. E., Hinton, G. E., & Williams, R. J. (1988). Learning representations by back-propagating errors. *Cognitive Modeling, 5*(3), 1.

San, P. P., Ling, S. H., & Nguyen, H. (2014). Evolvable rough-block-based neural network and its biomedical application to hypoglycemia detection system. *IEEE Transactions on Cybernetics, 44*(8), 1338-1349.

San, P. P., Ling, S. H., & Nguyen, H. T. (2013). Industrial application of evolvable block-based neural network to hypoglycemia monitoring system. *IEEE Transactions on Industrial Electronics, 60*(12), 5892–5901. doi:10.1109/TIE.2012.2228143

Schuster, M., & Paliwal, K. K. (1997). Bidirectional recurrent neural networks. *IEEE Transactions on Signal Processing, 45*(11), 2673–2681. doi:10.1109/78.650093

Soll, M. (2015). *Fooling deep neural networks using Cuckoo Search*. Academic Press.

Swathi, J. N., & Jayant, G. R. (2016). A Review On Metaheuristic Techniques To Train Feedforward Neural Networks And Its Application To Predict Patient Medical Behaviour. *Int J Pharm Bio Sci*, 300-309.

Syulistyo, A. R., Purnomo, D. M. J., Rachmadi, M. F., & Wibowo, A. (2016). Particle swarm optimization (PSO) for training optimization on convolutional neural network (CNN). *Jurnal Ilmu Komputer dan Informasi, 9*(1), 52-58.

Werbos, P. J. (1990). Backpropagation through time: What it does and how to do it. *Proceedings of the IEEE, 78*(10), 1550–1560. doi:10.1109/5.58337

Werbos, P. J. (1994). *The roots of backpropagation*. John Wiley & Sons.

Wilamowski, B. (2002). *Neural networks and fuzzy systems*. The Microelectronic Handbook.

Wilamowski, B. M., Cotton, N., Hewlett, J., & Kaynak, O. (2007, June). Neural network trainer with second order learning algorithms. In *2007 11th International Conference on Intelligent Engineering Systems* (pp. 127-132). IEEE. doi:10.1109/INES.2007.4283685

Williams, D. R. G. H. R., & Hinton, G. E. (1986). Learning representations by back-propagating errors. *Nature, 323*(6088), 533–536. doi:10.1038/323533a0

Xue, Q., Yun, F., Zheng, C., Liu, Y., Wei, Y., Yao, Y., & Zhou, S. (2010, October). Improved LMBP algorithm in the analysis and application of simulation data. In *2010 International Conference on Computer Application and System Modeling (ICCASM 2010)* (Vol. 6, pp. V6-545). IEEE.

Yang, X. S. (2010). A new metaheuristic bat-inspired algorithm. In Nature inspired cooperative strategies for optimization (NICSO 2010) (pp. 65-74). Springer Berlin Heidelberg. doi:10.1007/978-3-642-12538-6_6

Yang, X. S. (2010). Firefly algorithm, stochastic test functions and design optimisation. *International Journal of Bio-inspired Computation, 2*(2), 78–84. doi:10.1504/IJBIC.2010.032124

Yang, X. S., & Deb, S. (2009, December). Cuckoo search via Lévy flights. In *Nature & Biologically Inspired Computing, 2009. NaBIC 2009. World Congress on* (pp. 210-214). IEEE.

Zell, A. (2002). *SNNS Stuttgart Neural Network Simulator*. Retrieved from http://www-ra. informatik. uni-tuebingen. de

KEY TERMS AND DEFINITIONS

Back Propagation (BP): Is a commonly used method for back propagating errors while training artificial neural networks.

Deep Learning (DL): Is a branch of machine learning with a set of algorithms modelling high level abstractions in data using deep graphs having multiple processing layers.

Feed Forward Neural Network: In this network, there are no cycles formed. The information moved forward from input layer to hidden layer and from hidden to output layer.

Gradient: Is an increase or decrease that happens when moving from one point to another.

Hessian: Is a square matrix of second order derivatives.

Mean Square Error (MSE): Commonly used objective function to evaluate the performance of classification algorithms. It is defined as the variance of the estimator.

Nature Inspired Optimization: The optimization techniques which emerged based on the behavior of the nature including the behavior of ants, birds, bees, bats, cat, cuckoo, fireflies, etc.

Neural Network (NN): A system modelled based on the working mechanism of human brain and nervous system.

Chapter 3
A Novel Hybrid Model Using RBF and PSO for Net Asset Value Prediction

C. M. Anish
Guru Ghasidas Vishwavidyalaya, India

Babita Majhi
Guru Ghasidas Vishwavidyalaya, India

Ritanjali Majhi
NIT Warangal, India

ABSTRACT

Net asset value (NAV) prediction is an important area of research as small investors are doing investment in there, Literature survey reveals that very little work has been done in this field. The reported literature mainly used various neural network models for NAV prediction. But the derivative based learning algorithms of these reported models have the problem of trapping into the local solution. Hence in chapter derivative free algorithm, particle swarm optimization is used to update the parameters of radial basis function neural network for prediction of NAV. The positions of particles represent the centers, spreads and weights of the RBF model and the minimum MSE is used as the cost function. The convergence characteristics are obtained to show the performance of the model during training phase. The MAPE and RMSE value are calculated during testing phase to show the performance of the proposed RBF-PSO model. These performance measure exhibits that the proposed model is better model in comparison to MLANN, FLANN and RBFNN models.

1. INTRODUCTION

Financial forecasting plays an important role by the corporation to do financial planning. The planning includes an assessment of their future financial needs. The accurate prediction of financial time series are usually subject to high risk as the series are more complex than other conventional data due to the

DOI: 10.4018/978-1-5225-2857-9.ch003

irregular movement, seasonal and cyclical variation, chaotic in nature and influenced by economical, political, psychological factors. Financial data forecasting is important for optimal utilization of resources, planning of production and human resources in the firms and for efficient investment of firm funds. Most common financial indices which are forecasted by the researchers are stock indices, exchange rate, interest rate, net asset value etc. Apart from the corporate planner, small investors are also handling many kind of investment scheme. Mutual fund (MF) is one of them; MF is an established investment scheme that aggregates the funds collected from the stockholders and the manager invest this money to stocks, bonds, money market instruments and commodities such as precious metals etc. The success of the investment strategies is depending upon the fund managers knowledge and management for earning high returns with minimum risk. The common investors, firms, and brokers etc. faces the difficulties to anticipate the ups and downs in the mutual funds by using conventional methods like least mean square (LMS).

In financial data mining, in order to predict financial data series accurately and efficiently, many researcher shows great interest to develop a robust model using machine learning techniques. This technique can be either conventional statistical models or soft computing techniques or combination of both the models. The conventional statistical methods include exponential smoothing, the moving average, autoregressive moving average, autoregressive integrated moving average and generalized autoregressive conditional heteroskedasticity (GARCH) models (Franses & Ghijsels, 1999). These models are simple and work on the principle that the data of various time series are linearly correlated. But the real time financial data are non-linear and dynamic in nature. To overcome these deficiencies Atsalakis and Valavanis (2009 a,b) suggested soft and evolutionary computing methods to forecast the time series. Moreover, many researchers have applied computational intelligence methods for efficient prediction of various financial data like artificial neural network, fuzzy information systems, support vector machine, evolutionary computations, machine learning techniques etc. Different neural network based techniques like multi layer perception network (MLPN), back propagation neural network (BPNN), radial basis function neural network (RBF-NN), functional link artificial neural network (FLANN), wavelet neural network (WNN), recurrent neural network (RNN), etc. are also extensively used in financial data prediction.

2. LITERATURE REVIEW

On the basis of historical data, the neural network families having inherent features to model complex real world systems as ANN has non-linear nature, which casually point out the complicated relationship of non-linearity in the financial time series. ANN estimates any non-linear function to a desired accuracy with a high degree of input data. Different artificial neural network used by the researchers (Song et al., 2007; Ma et al., 2010; Oliveira et al., 2011) show its viable alternative to statistical conventional techniques to predict the dynamics of non-linear behavior and complicated features of the financial time series data. In some works, probabilistic neural networks (PNN) (Kim & Chun, 1998), generalized regression neural networks (GRNN) (Mostafa, 2010) and cerebellar neural networks (CNN) (Lu & Wu, 2011) are also proposed for forecasting purposes. In the paper, Kumar and Ravi (2007) reported the prediction of bankruptcy of banks and firms. According to this review, a neural network method shows superior performance than other methods and also shows better result when they combine with other methods. In another review done by (Gooijer & Hyndman, 2006) the authors reported many statistical and simulation methods like exponential smoothing (ES), auto regressive integrated moving average

(ARIMA), autoregressive conditional heteroskedasticity (ARCH), GARCH, non-linear models etc., their advantages and disadvantages, points out their future scope in the different research fields. They also pointed the issues in the ANN while utilization and implementing to outperforms with other methods. In another research, Kozarzewski (2010) proposed a prediction model for predicting the future values based on wavelet preprocessing and neural networks clustering. In Yu and Rong (2010), proposed a model to achieve higher accuracy by approximate the non-linear function in stock market forecasting using MLP. To overcome the limitation of ANN which suffer from slow convergence, over fitting, local minima, large computational cost, required huge iteration etc., functional link artificial neural network (FLANN) has been proposed (Pao,1989). FLANN possess a high degree of convergence and keeps the computational cost lesser than other neural networks such as multilayer artificial neural network (MLANN) architecture. Recently various researcher develop wide variety of FLANNs using different expansion functions: orthogonal trigonometric functions (Dehuri et al., 2012; Mili & Hamdi, 2012), legendre orthogonal polynomial (George & Panda, 2012; Rodriguez, 2009; Das & Satapathy, 2011; Patra & Bornand, 2010), languere polynomial (Patra et al., 2009) and chebyshev polynomial (Mishra et al., 2009; Li et al., 2012). Back propagation algorithm (BPA) is common learning method used to update the weights of FLANN. But researchers adopt different evolutionary techniques to update the weights. In Yogi et al. (2010), a novel method is developed for equalization of digital communication channels using particle swarm optimization (PSO) based training of trigonometric expansion based FLANN.

Neural network modeling for solving the dynamic nature of time series is a complicated process as it is needed to adjust the real time data series with the behavior of the model. Recently lots of work has been carried out by various researchers to solve static and dynamic prediction problems. It is always been a challenging task to design a robust neural network model for handling the dynamic prediction problems which is simple in architecture, use less memory for storage, required few neurons, low computational time and high accuracy. RBF-NN is gaining interest among researchers to design a model and control the non-linear nature of the system due to the iterative free learning ability and architecture simplicity. In RBF-NN, radial basis function is commonly used as an activation function of the neurons. Due to the simple architecture and iterative less learning ability, RBF-NN is universal accepted for various applications like prediction, classification, clustering etc.

Several novel techniques are applied to the RBF-NN parameters like the number of centers, spreads and the weights which determine the speed and accuracy of the network and hence improve the conventional RBF-NN learning mechanism. To increase the performance of the RBF neural network different techniques have been developed by various researchers. Few of them are listed as: A hybrid model is proposed by Rubio-Solis and Panoutsos (2015) which combines the interval type-2 fuzzy logic along with RBF neural network and use back propagation algorithm (BPA) as a training algorithm. In Lian (2014), the fuzzy rules are obtained by using radial basis-function neural network for a self-organizing fuzzy controller which regulates membership function. Ko (2012), proposed a model where the learning rates of the RBF neural network is optimized using a time varying learning algorithm based on PSO .The centers, RBF parameters and weight values of the RBF-NN are determined by using support vector regression (SVR) method. In another work, Alexandridis (2013) has developed a model in which the parameters of RBF model are tuned using fuzzy techniques. Further PSO optimization approach is used to select the optimal partition of fuzzy in the input search space. Babu and Suresh (2013) proposed a technique to classify a data set using a RBF network with sequential projection based meta-cognitive learning rules. This network adopts the learning mechanism by using cognitive and meta-cognitive components.

Substantial work has been reported on use of RBF-NN and their application to various real life problems such as fault detection (Chai & Qiao, 2014), temperature prediction (Yao et. al., 2002), forecasting (Yu et al., 2008), car fuel consumption (Wu & Liu, 2012), gene classification (Francisco et. al., 2012) and other areas (Park et al., 2011). RBF-NN attracts the researcher as compared to other neural network models due to the simple architecture and faster convergence ability. Pen et al. (2006) has reported few disadvantages of RBF architecture for designing a model like selecting input vectors, fixing of nodes in hidden layer and deciding RBF parameters. The survey of research papers, exhibited that the researchers try to solve the problem of network size optimization and also update the parameters of RBF-NN. Pen et al. (2006) has suggested optimizing both the network size and RBF-NN parameters at the same time to obtain good results. Aladag (2011) has reported that there is no analytical method available to optimize the network size and network parameters. Most preferable techniques adopted by many researchers are focused only to determine the RBF parameters instead of choosing the various hidden neurons and the input vector to make it simple.

In the past, Chen et al. (2011) has reported a complex value in RBF neural network. It uses a complex value for the weights in RBF structure and a real value in activation function and uses different learning algorithms for parameter updating. In another work, Jianping et al. (2002) and Deng et al. (2000) has used the Gaussian function as a activation function in the hidden layer to map the inputs to hyper dimensional feature inputs. That means the mapping in the hidden layer is one to one. In the recent year, Suresh et al. (2013) has derived a new activation function using a hyperbolic secant function is named as fully complex valued RBF neural network (FCRBFNN). Hence the gradient descent algorithm is read to local optima solution, so research efforts have been made to design a model with neural networks using evolutionary computation methods by different researchers (Chen et. al., 2011; Araújo, 2010; Chang, 2013; Wu et. al., 2013; Yu, 2012).

However for time series forecasting, a single forecast model cannot predict all the streams of the forecasting problem efficiently. Thus many researchers have proposed the combination of more than one forecast models. This hybrid model shows superior performance compared to that of a single forecast model. In Atsalakis and Valavanis, (2009b), for the short term forecasting of trends of stock market, an adaptive neuro-fuzzy inference system (ANFIS) is used. Lai et al. (2009) has integrated the data clustering technique along with the fuzzy decision tree and genetic algorithm (GA) for stock market forecasting. Huang and Tsai (2009) have to propose a self-organizing feature map (SOFM) along with SVR for stock market forecasting. Forecasting model that combines the neural networks and genetic fuzzy system to optimize the results are reported in Hadavandi et al. (2010). Khashei and Bijari (2010, 2011) has reported a hybrid model using ARIMA and ANN to further enhance the results already obtained by ANN. Rout et al. (2014) developed a new adaptive model of auto regressive moving average (ARMA) model for forecasting of currency exchange rate which are further optimize by an evolutionary algorithm, differential evolution (DE), based training scheme for higher rate of accuracy. Prediction of Hong Kong stock market index price trend using different techniques of data mining has been reported in Ou and Wang (2009). This ten different techniques are noted as linear discriminant analysis, quadratic discriminant analysis, K-nearest neighbor classification, tree based classification, Bayesian classification, support vector machine, least squares support vector machine, neural network, naïve bayes and logit model.

The training of RBF network is made by using evolutionary algorithms by many researchers (Shcta & Jong, 2001; Leung et al., 2003; Lee & Ko, 2009; Harpham et al., 2004; Lacerda et al., 2005). Some researchers optimize both the RBF-NN architecture and basis function parameters simultaneously. Yu et al. (2009) has suggested integrating PSO and BPA for training of the RBF-NN. A novel encoding scheme for RBF architecture and parameter is developed to train RBF with genetic algorithm (GA) in Du and Zhang (2008). RBF architecture and neural network parameters are optimized by employing an improved GA technique is proposed in Leung et al. (2003).In another work, Zhan et al. (2009) proposed a modified adaptive particle swarm optimization algorithm to train the RBF parameters.

Recently, many authors have proposed different soft computing techniques and applied this techniques for prediction of various economical time series data such as multiobjective particle swarm optimization (MOPSO) and non-dominating sorting genetic algorithm version II (NSGA-II) (Anish & Majhi, 2015a), support vector with chaos firefly (Kazem et. al., 2013), empirical mode decomposition (Wei, 2016), genetic algorithm (Tsai, Yang & Peng, 2011), artificial neural network (Majhi, Panda & Sahoo, 2009), and many more. In recent past a number of researchers has presented various types of neural network techniques to predict net asset value of mutual fund such as neural network (Li,Zhou & Cai, 2010;Chiang & Urban, 1996), neural network with back propagation (BPNN) (Yan et. al., 2010), functional link artificial neural network (FLANN) (Anish & Majhi,2016) and RBF-FLANN ensemble model(Anish & Majhi,2015b) .

From the literature it is also been noted that various population based evolutionary and swarm intelligence have been applied to non-linear time series forecasting which are derivative free such as genetic algorithm (GA), particle swarm optimization (PSO), differential evolution (DE), bacteria foraging (BF), cat swarm optimization (CSO), fish swarm optimization (FSO) etc. These new population or swarm based learning rules have been developed to used as a backbone of various prediction models to accomplish the global solution.

It is also clear from the literature review that, many authors have used artificial neural network for net asset value (NAV) prediction. A single method cannot efficiently handle the entire spectrum of the prediction problems. So, there is a need to develop a hybrid model that is more efficient than compared to a single model for NAV prediction (Anish & Majhi, 2015b; Haykin, 1999).

In this chapter, an adaptive predictive model (PSO-RBFNN) has been suggested compose of the derivative free nature inspired learning technique, particle swarm optimization (PSO) and radial basis function neural network for net asset value prediction of various Indian mutual funds. This model alleviates the problem of fall the model into local minima while using derivative based learning techniques. PSO is used as a training algorithm to update the center, variance and weights of a radial basis functional neural network model.

Rest of the chapter is organized into following sections. Methodology used for the hybrid model is described in Section 3. Section 4 describes the development and overview of the proposed RBF-PSO model. Section 5 deals with different performance measures used in the proposed NAV prediction. In Section 6, computer simulation based study and the results obtained after the experiment is discussed. Section 7 describes the conclusion.

3. METHODOLOGY

3.1. Radial basis Function Neural Network (RBF-NN)

In this chapter, the radial basis function neural network (RBF-NN) is used in a proposed hybrid predictive model. RBF-NN is feed forward network compose of RBF supervised learning function which is proposed by Broomhead & Lowe (1988) comprises of three layers: the input layer, hidden layer and the output layer. Each neuron in the RBF $\left(\varphi\left(n\right)\right)$ acts as an activation function in the hidden layer. The schematic diagram of a three layered RBF-NN with PSO algorithm for prediction of net asset value with N inputs, H hidden nodes and one output is shown in the Figure 1. According to the Broomhead and Lowe the structure of a RBF-NN model is consists of three layers. This are discussed as follows:

- **Input Layer:** The first layer is the input layer. This layer is used to connect all the input feature patterns to the hidden layer nodes.
- **Hidden Layer:** The second layer is the hidden layer. This layer contains a number of RBF nodes. Each RBF nodes is associated with center $\left(c_k\right)$ and varience σ_k. This layer applies a non-linear transformation using RBF nodes to the input vectors. The Euclidean distance $\left(d_k\right)$ in the RBF node is computed by:

$$d_k = \left\| x - c_k \right\| = \sqrt{\sum_{i=1}^{N}\left(x_i - c_{ik}\right)^2} \tag{1}$$

where $k = 1$ to $H.N$ and H are the number of nodes in the input and hidden layer respectively. Out of the many basis function in the hidden layer (Guassian, multiquadratic, inverse multiquadratic, inverse quadratic, poly harmonic spline and thin plate splines), the popular Gaussian function is used as an activation function in the proposed RBF-PSO predictor. The Gaussian function $\left(\varphi\right)$ is calculated as:

$$\varphi\left(d_k\right) = \exp\left(-\frac{H}{d_{\max}^2}.d_k^2\right) \tag{2}$$

where $d_{\max}$ represents the highest distance obtain among all the selected centers.

- **Output Layer**: The last layer is the output layer. This layer contains all the predicted output obtains from the proposed network model, which is computed by:

$$y\left(n\right) = w_0 + \sum_{j=1}^{M} w_k.\varphi\left(d_k\right) \tag{3}$$

where $w_k, 0 \leq k \leq M$ contains all the weights in the output layer.

The width (spread) of all the Gaussian radial functions is calculated by

$$\sigma = \frac{d_{\max}}{\sqrt{2m}} \tag{4}$$

For the given set of inputs $x(n)$, a unique center is connected with each neuron in the hidden layer. A non-linear transformation maps the input patterns to the hidden neurons with the presence of activation function. The output of the hidden layer is obtained by computing the resemblance between the input vector and the center of each hidden nodes. The output of the RBF is computed by the weighted sum of the hidden output with the connecting weights (w_k). The error $(e(n))$ is computed by subtracting the output $(y(n))$ with the desired value $(d(n)); n = 1, 2, 3, ...N$. (Schwenker et. al. 2001) has suggested that the performance of the RBF network which is trained with two-phase learning can be improved further by three phase-learning by using back propagation (BP) algorithm. Thus in the proposed RBF-PSO hybrid prediction model the three-phase learning technique is used during training, where the whole set of parameters such as RBF centers, spreads and all weights are updated using PSO. The algorithm of RBF training of the proposed model is describes as follows:

```
Algorithm 1: Algorithm for computation of RBF based training of the proposed
model
1. Let us assume the number of hidden nodes, H
2. Randomly initialize the parameters of the RBF-NN structure (centers,
spreads and weights).
3. Read the next training input vector (x(n)) with elements x_i(n) in the
```
input layer as n increases from 1 to H and find the closest RBF center (c_k) by:
$$\min \left(\left\| c_1 - x_n \right\|, \left\| c_2 - x_n \right\|, ..., \left\| c_H - x_n \right\| \right).$$
```
4. Modify this RBF center (c_k) closest to the training input vector x(n) in
the Euclidean distance by using the equation
```

$$c_k(new) = c_k(old) + \alpha \left[x(n) - c_k(old) \right] \tag{5}$$

```
where α denotes the learning rate of the RBF neural network.
5. Step 3 and 4 is repeated for all the input vectors.
6. Update the RBF parameters (centers, spreads and weights) by using learning
algorithms.
7. Calculate the mean square error (MSE) from the trained network.
8. Repeat the step 3 to 6 until the MSE attains the minimum possible value and
network parameters are almost remains constant for a maximum number of itera-
tions. Freeze the parameters for next iteration.
```

3.2. Particle Swarm Optimization (PSO)

Particle swarm optimization (PSO) is a meta-heuristic search technique developed by James Kennedy and Russell Eberhart (Kennedy & Eberhart, 1995a; Eberhart & Kennedy, 1995b; Eberhart & Shi, 2001). In PSO algorithm, the system is initialized with a population of particles in the domain space. Then randomly generate the initial position and velocity of a particle and each particle monitors themselves their own position and velocity in the search domain. Let in the n-dimensional search space, the ith particle of the position vector $\left(\overrightarrow{P_i}\right)$ be represented as $\overrightarrow{P_i} = (p_{i1}, p_{i2}, \ldots\ldots, p_{in})$ and the velocity vector $\overrightarrow{(V_i)}$ be represented as:

$$\overrightarrow{V_i} = (v_{i1}, v_{i2}, \ldots\ldots, v_{in}),$$

where n represent the number of particles.

The first best value is the best solution or *pbest* of the particle achieved so far and *gbest* represents the best position so far in the neighborhood. Let the *pbest* of the ith particle be denoted as $\overrightarrow{p_i^b} = (p_{i1}^b, p_{i2}^b, p_{i3}^b, \ldots, p_{in}^b)$ and the *gbest* be denoted as $\overrightarrow{P_i^g} = (p_{i1}^g, p_{i2}^g, \ldots\ldots, p_{in}^g)$. Then the position vector and velocity vector of the particles is updated using equation (6) and (7) after every experiment until the desired value is reached.

$$\overrightarrow{V_{ij}} = w * V_{ij} + c_1 * rand_1 * (P_{ij}^b - P_{ij}) + c_2 * rand_2 * (p_{ij}^g - p_{ij}) \tag{6}$$

$$P_{ij} = P_{ij} + V_{ij} \tag{7}$$

where $j = 1, 2, \ldots\ldots, n$. Inertia weight is w and acceleration coefficients is c_1, c_2 both are always greater than 0, $rand_1$ and $rand_2$ are random numbers between 0 to 1. The algorithm for the PSO is described in the Algorithm 2.

```
Algorithm 2: Algorithm for particle swarm optimization (PSO)
1. In the search domain, randomly initialize the particles such that each
particle represents as the candidate solution.
2. Initialize constants c₁,c₂, maximum iterations.
3. For each particle Pᵢ in the search space, go to step (4).
4. Compute the fitness value fᵥ of the particle Pᵢ.
5. If fᵥ is greater than the pbest, then
6. Set pbest = Pᵢ.
7. Select the particle having global best fitness value as the gbest.
8. Do step (9) and (10) for each particle Pᵢ in the space
9. Evaluate the velocity of particle Vᵢ using eq. (6)
10.Update the particle position Pᵢ of the search space using eq. (7)
11.Repeat the step (4) to (9) for the maximum number of iteration or the value
of gbest is no further change.
```

4. DEVELOPMENT OF NAV PREDICTION MODEL
USING PSO BASED RBF MODEL

The proposed RBF-PSO based prediction model for NAV is shown in Figure 1. Firstly select the features from the time series. This feature vector is representing as input pattern. Then each set of input feature patterns are applied to the RBF neural network to give predicted output which are discussed in the Algorithm 1. Then the particle swarm optimization (PSO) algorithm is used as a learning algorithm to update the Guassian center, spreads and weights of the RBF neural network. The flowchart for the proposed RBF-PSO illustrated in Figure 2.

The algorithm of developing an RBF-PSO based NAV prediction model is proceeds as follows:

```
Algorithm 3: Algorithm for computation of RBF-PSO based NAV prediction model
1. Randomly initialize the parameters (centers, spreads and weights) of the
RBF-NN structure.
2. Compute the predicted output for each input patterns by applying the RBF
techniques as discussed in Algorithm 1.
3. [Initialization]: Apply the PSO learning algorithm by randomly generate a
population of N particles with random positions and velocities. The position
vector of a particle represents the weights, heights of the centre and spread
of the Guassian function. The initial position represents the current pbest    .
4. [Evaluate fitness function]: Fitness function is used to evaluate the fit-
ness value of all the particles in the generated population.
5. [Find pbest ]: Particle's pbest is obtained by comparing particles current
fitness value with particle previous pbest .
```

if $current(f_v) < pbest$

$$pbest = current(f_v)$$

Figure 1.

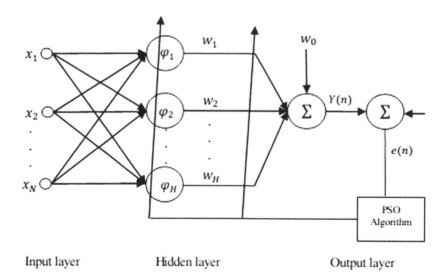

Input layer   Hidden layer   Output layer

Figure 2.

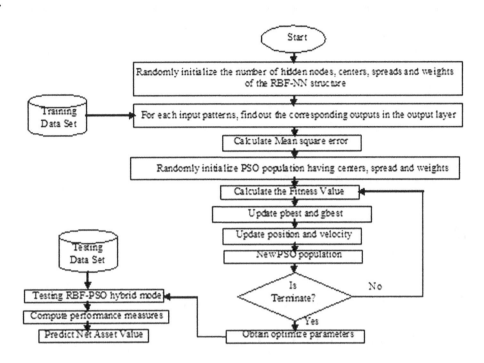

$$loc(pbest) = loc(current(f_v))$$

End

6. [Find *gbest*]: *gbest* is obtained by comparing the current fitness value with the overall previous best in the population.

$$if \quad current(f_v) < gbest$$
$$gbest = current(f_v)$$

End

7. The network parameters (weights, Guassian center and spreads) of the RBF-PSO hybrid prediction model are updated iteratively by changing the velocity and position of all the particles in the search domain as defined in equations (6) and (7).

8. After one movement of particle the minimum MSE (MMSE) is computed and the training characteristic is obtained to observe the convergence characteristics.

5. PERFORMANCE MEASURE USED

Generally the forecasting of time series data in the optimization problem is treated as a single objective problem, in order to evaluate the prediction performance of the proposed RBF-PSO hybrid model, mean square error (MSE) is used as the cost function. During the testing phase, the prediction performance of the RBF-PSO hybrid model is evaluated and analyzed by comparing the forecast results obtained by calculation of the mean absolute percentage error (MAPE) and the root mean square error (RMSE). Let the actual value are $A_i = \{A_1, A_2, A_3, ..., A_N\}$ and the predicted values are $P_i = \{P_1, P_2, P_3, ..., P_N\}$ for the N number of testing patterns. Then mean absolute percentage error (MAPE) is computed as:

$$MAPE = \frac{\sum_{i=1}^{N} \left| \frac{A_i - P_i}{A_i} \right|}{N} \times 100 \tag{8}$$

and root mean square error (RMSE) is computed as:

$$RMSE = \sqrt{\sum_{i=1}^{n} \left(A_i - P_i \right)^2 / N} \tag{9}$$

6. COMPUTER SIMULATION AND PREDICTED RESULTS

6.1. Data Collection and Feature Extraction

The net asset value (NAV) data for the simulation of the RBF-PSO hybrid model are collected from the website (http://smartinvestor.business-standard.com) for the top rated Indian Mutual Funds. The details of collected data from various mutual funds in each day is listed in Table 1. Table 1 also shows the number of training patterns and testing patterns of various mutual funds used for the simulation. For simulation, firstly each data patterns that are collected is normalized to a range of [0, 1] by dividing each value by the maximum value of that data set. Feature is selected in the second step with a running window size of 12, containing the present and previous 11 data .The 12th number data, mean and variance of 12 data are calculated to form one input feature pattern.

Then the window is shifted towards right by one position and mean and variance of new feature pattern is computed. This process is repeated to extract all the features of the data set. In the similar manner, we generate 1065 data patterns for Birla Sunlife equity fund (growth) and similar method is used to compute the data patterns for other mutual funds which is listed in Table 1. From various test and trial the best performance achieved from the model is the size of the window to 12. The ratio of the input data from

Table 1. Details of training and testing data patterns available from various mutual funds

Mutual Fund	Data Year	Total Data Patterns	Available Training Patterns	Available Testing Patterns
Birla Sunlife Equity Fund-Growth	27/08/1998 to 31/12/2002	1065	852	213
HDFC Top200- Growth	01/01/1997 to 31/12/2001	1225	980	245
ICICI pro. Top100-Growth	19/06/1998 to 31/12/2002	1097	878	219
UTI Equity Fund-Growth	01/01/1998 to 31/12/2002	1123	898	225

the whole patterns which is used for the training and testing purpose of the proposed model is 80% and 20% respectively for each mutual fund.

6.2. Training and Testing of PSO Based RBF Model

The training of the RBF-PSO model is acquired by determining the random swarm of particles which represent radial basis function parameters (weights, Guassian center and spreads) in the form of vectors having random position and velocity. In the proposed hybrid model each input feature of each pattern composes the input layer. The hidden layer transfers the data from the input layer to the hidden layer non-linearly and finally the output is calculated by a weighted sum of the radial basis function. An error is computed by subtracting the predicted source output with the desired NAV value for each input pattern. With the help of this error the RBF network parameters of the hybrid model are updated according to the PSO algorithm given in section (3). In the similar fashion all the training patterns are sequentially employed to the proposed model and evaluate its error values. Then MSE is computed for each experiment according to the equation (10)

$$MSE(i) = \frac{1}{N} \sum_{i=1}^{N} e^2(n) \qquad (10)$$

The training of the RBF-PSO hybrid model is completed after achieving the MSE to minimum value and at that stage the RBF parameters are frozen. Figure 3 (a) to (d) show the comparison of convergence characteristic of the forecasting model for MSE and corresponding experiment number during training period for various mutual fund. The different parameters of PSO based RBF model used for the simulation are: number of center=3, number of iteration=500, particle size=30, $c_1 = c_2 = 1.042$ and $w=15$.

Rest of the 20 percent of the feature patterns are applied to get output from the proposed model for evaluating and analyzing its performance. In order to assess the forecasting performance of the RBF-PSO hybrid model, two performance evaluation measures mean absolute percentage error (MAPE) and the root mean squares error (RMSE) is calculated.

6.3. Simulation Results

In this section, the prediction performance of the proposed RBF-PSO hybrid model for NAVs prediction is validate through the prediction results obtained through simulation study at the time of testing. It is clear from the results that the RBF-PSO hybrid prediction model is better candidate for prediction of NAV compared to the single neural network forecasting models. The simulated results of the RBF-PSO hybrid model are compared with the experimental results obtained by the multi linear artificial neural network (MLANN), FLANN and RBF-NN based prediction models. The MLANN architecture model which is used for the experiment consists of a structure 3:4:1. In the FLANN model, each input pattern undergoes trigonometric expansion as discussed in the paper (Anish & Majhi, 2015 a,b). The parameters used in the RBF model for the simulation are number of center=3, spread=0.1, μ =0.01. The number of epoch used by each single forecast model is 500.

Table 2. The comparative results of various Indian mutual funds in terms of performance measure value

	MLANN Predictive Model		FLANN Predictive Model		RBF-NN Predictive Model		RBF-PSO Predictive Model	
	RMSE	MAPE	RMSE	MAPE	RMSE	MAPE	RMSE	MAPE
Birla Sunlife Equity Fund(G)	0.0650	2.4420	0.3123	0.9352	0.3126	0.9349	0.3096	**0.9230**
HDFC Top 200(G)	0.0820	4.8510	0.2111	1.1141	0.2056	1.0938	0.2039	**1.0751**
ICICI Pro.Top 100 (G)	0.0380	2.5440	0.2453	0.9927	0.2417	0.9574	0.3009	**0.9435**
UTI Equity Fund(G)	0.0340	2.8960	0.1285	0.9538	0.1450	1.1339	0.1432	**1.0405**

Figure 3.

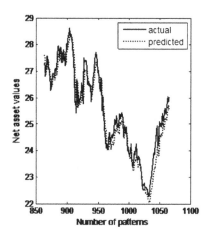

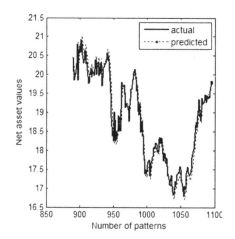

Figure 3(a): Comparison of actual and predicted value of RBF-PSO during Testing for BirlaSunlife Equity Fund-Growth

Figure 3(c): Comparison of actual and predicted value of RBF-PSO during Testing for ICICI Pro.Top100 –Growth

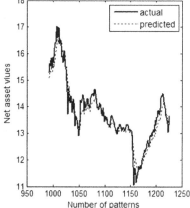

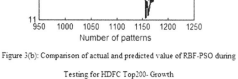

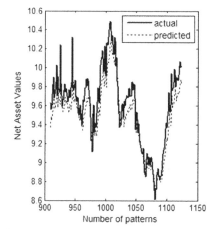

Figure 3(b): Comparison of actual and predicted value of RBF-PSO during Testing for HDFC Top200- Growth

Figure 3(d): Comparison of actual and predicted value of RBF-PSO during Testing for UTI Equity Fund- Growth

Figures 3(a)-(d) shows the comparison of actual and predicted values obtained at the time of testing phase of the predictor using RBF-PSO hybrid model for different mutual funds. The potentiality of the proposed model is observed from these figures which indicates its superior prediction performance in respect to accuracy It is also clear from these figures that for NAV prediction, proposed hybrid model can successfully predicts with an accuracy of more than 98.9% obtained from various mutual funds for one day ahead prediction.

The values listed in Table 2 shows the predicted performance measure of various NAV values. The MAPE value of the RBF-PSO hybrid model is below 1.1% for all NAVs is observed from the table. It is also observed that the RMSE value is very low in the RBF-PSO hybrid model, which exhibits that the proposed RBF-PSO model is superior prediction model than the individual MLANN, FLANN and RBF based prediction models.

7. CONCLUSION

In this chapter, the derivative free PSO based RBF network model has been developed as a predictor for net asset value (NAV) of various mutual funds. It alleviates the problem of trapping the model into the local minima which is commonly seen in the conventional prediction model. PSO is used as a learning algorithm to update the center, variance and weights of the radial basis functional (RBF) neural network model. During the simulation the same set of the data is fed to the MLANN, RBF-NN and FLANN models for comparison. The results of various simulation using proposed model shows a better prediction performance in points of convergence plot, MAPE and RMSE values. The proposed hybrid model can be further extended to predict other similar time series such as exchange rate, interest rate etc. For the future work the NAV's prediction task will be solved by various other hybrid models or multi-objective evolutionary algorithms. Also some new learning techniques can be applied in NAV prediction.

REFERENCES

Aladag, C. H. (2011). A new architecture selection method based on tabu search for artificial neural networks. *Expert Systems with Applications*, *38*(4), 3287–3293. doi:10.1016/j.eswa.2010.08.114

Alexandridis, A. (2013). RBF network training using a non symmetric partition of the input space and particle swarm optimization. *IEEE Transactions on Neural Networks and Learning Systems*, *24*(2), 219–230. doi:10.1109/TNNLS.2012.2227794 PMID:24808277

Anish, C. M., & Majhi, B. (2015a). Multiobjective optimization based adaptive models with fuzzy decision making for stock market forecasting. *Neurocomputing*, *167*, 502–511. doi:10.1016/j.neucom.2015.04.044

Anish, C. M., & Majhi, B. (2015b). An ensemble model for net asset value prediction. *Proceeding of IEEE International Conference on Power, Communication and information technology (PCITC)*, 392-396. doi:10.1109/PCITC.2015.7438197

Anish, C. M., & Majhi, B. (2016).Prediction of mutual fund net asset value using low complexity feedback neural network. *Proceeding of IEEE International Conference on Current Trends in advanced Computing (ICCTAC)*, 1-5. doi:10.1109/ICCTAC.2016.7567345

Araújo, R. A. (2010). Swarm-based translation-invariant morphological prediction method for financial time series forecasting. *Information Science, 180*, 4784–4805. doi:10.1016/j.ins.2010.08.037

Atsalakis, G. S., & Valavanis, K. P. (2009a). Surveying stock market forecasting techniques – Part II: Soft computing methods. *Expert Systems with Applications, 36*(3), 5932–5941. doi:10.1016/j.eswa.2008.07.006

Atsalakis, G. S., & Valavanis, K. P. (2009b). Forecasting stock market short term trends using a neuro-fuzzy based methodology. *Expert Systems with Applications, 36*(7), 10696–10707. doi:10.1016/j.eswa.2009.02.043

Babu, G. S., & Suresh, S. (2013). Sequential projection-based meta cognitive learning in a radial basis function network for classification problems. *IEEE Transactions on Neural Networks, 24*(2), 194–206. doi:10.1109/TNNLS.2012.2226748 PMID:24808275

Broomhead, & Lowe, D. D. (1998). Multivariable functional interpolation and adaptive networks. *Complex System, 2*, 321-355.

Chai, W., & Qiao, J. (2014). Passive robust fault detection using RBF neural modeling based on set membership identification. *Engineering Applications of Artificial Intelligence, 28*, 1–12. doi:10.1016/j.engappai.2013.10.005

Chang, Y. W. (2013). New parameter-free simplified swarm optimization for artificial neural network training and its application in the prediction of time series. *IEEE Transaction on Neural Networks Learning System, 24*(4), 661–665. doi:10.1109/TNNLS.2012.2232678 PMID:24808385

Chen, Y., Yang, B., Meng, Q., Zhao, Y., & Abraham, A. (2011). Time-series forecasting using a system of ordinary differential equations. *Information Science, 181*(1), 106–114. doi:10.1016/j.ins.2010.09.006

Chiang, W. C., & Urban, T. L. (1996). A Neural Network Approach to Mutual Fund Net Asset Value Forecasting. OMEGA. *International Journal of Management Sciences, 24*(2), 205–215.

Das, K. K., & Satapathy, J. K. (2011). Legendre neural network for non-linear active noise cancellation with non-linear secondary path. *International Conference on Multimedia, Signal Processing and Communication Technologies*, 40–43.

Dehuri, S., Roy, R., Cho, S. B., & Ghosh, A. (2012). An improved swarm optimized functional link artificial neural network (ISO-FLANN) for classification. *Journal of Systems and Software, 85*(6), 1333–1345. doi:10.1016/j.jss.2012.01.025

Deng, J., Sundararajan, N., & Saratchandran, P. (2000). Complex-valued minimal resource allocation network for non-linear signal processing. *International Journal of Neural Science, 10*(02), 95–106. doi:10.1142/S0129065700000090

Eberhart, R. C., & Kennedy, J. (1995b). A new optimizer using particle swarm theory. *Proceeding of sixth International Symposium on Micro Machine and Human Science*, 39-43. doi:10.1109/MHS.1995.494215

Eberhart, R. C., & Shi, Y. (2001). Particle swarm optimization: Developments, Applications and Resources. *Proceeding of IEEE International Conference on Evolutionary Computation, 1*, 81-86. doi:10.1109/CEC.2001.934374

Francisco, F. N., César, H. M., Roberto, R., & Jose, C. R. (2012). Evolutionary Generalized Radial Basis Function neural networks for improving prediction accuracy in gene classification using feature selection. *Applied Soft Computing, 12*(6), 1787–1800. doi:10.1016/j.asoc.2012.01.008

Franses, P. H., & Ghijsels, H. (1999). Additive outliers. GARCH and forecasting volatility. *International Journal of Forecasting, 15*(1), 1–9. doi:10.1016/S0169-2070(98)00053-3

George, N. V., & Panda, G. (2012). A reduced complexity adaptive Legendre neural network for non-linear active noise control. *19th International Conference on Systems, Signals and Image Processing (IWSSIP)*, 560–563.

Gooijer, J. G. D., & Hyndman, R. J. (2006). 25 years of time series forecasting. *International Journal of Forecasting, 22*(3), 443–473. doi:10.1016/j.ijforecast.2006.01.001

Hadavandi, E., Shavandi, H., & Ghanbari, A. (2010). Integration of genetic fuzzy systems and artificial neural networks for stock price forecasting. *Knowledge-Based Systems, 23*(8), 800–808. doi:10.1016/j.knosys.2010.05.004

Harpham, C., Dawson, C. W., & Brown, M. R. (2004). A review of genetic algorithms applied to training radial basis function networks. *Neural Computing & Applications, 13*(3), 193–201. doi:10.1007/s00521-004-0404-5

Haykin, S. (1999). *Neural Networks: A Comprehensive Foundation* (2nd ed.). Prentice-Hall.

Huang, C. L., & Tsai, C. Y. (2009). A hybrid SOFM-SVR with a filter-based feature selection for stock market forecasting. *Expert Systems with Applications, 36*(2), 1529–1539. doi:10.1016/j.eswa.2007.11.062

Jianping, D., Sundararajan, N., & Saratchandran, P. (2002). Communication channel equalization using complex-valued minimal radial basis function neural networks. *IEEE Transactions on Neural Networks, 13*(3), 687–696. doi:10.1109/TNN.2002.1000133 PMID:18244465

Kazem, A., Sharifi, E., Hussain, F. K., Saberi, M., & Hussain, O. K. (2013). Support vector regression with chaos-based firefly algorithm for stock market price forecasting. *Applied Soft Computing, 13*(2), 947–958. doi:10.1016/j.asoc.2012.09.024

Kennedy, J., & Eberhart, R. C. (1995a). Particle swarm optimization. *Proceeding of IEEE international conference on Neural Networks (ICNN)*, 4, 1942-1948. doi:10.1109/ICNN.1995.488968

Khashei, M., & Bijari, M. (2010). An artificial neural network (p, d, q) model for time series forecasting. *Expert Systems with Applications, 37*(1), 479–489. doi:10.1016/j.eswa.2009.05.044

Khashei, M., & Bijari, M. (2011). A novel hybridization of artificial neural networks and ARIMA models for time series forecasting. *Applied Soft Computing, 11*(2), 2664–2675. doi:10.1016/j.asoc.2010.10.015

Kim, S. H., & Chun, S. H. (1998). Graded forecasting using an array of bipolar predictions: Application of probabilistic neural networks to a stock market index. *International Journal of Forecasting, 14*(3), 323–337. doi:10.1016/S0169-2070(98)00003-X

Ko, C. N. (2012). Identification of non-linear systems using radial basis function neural networks with time-varying learning algorithm. *IET Signal Processing, 6*(2), 91–98. doi:10.1049/iet-spr.2011.0025

Kozarzewski, B. (2010). A neural network based time series forecasting system. *3rd International Conference on Human System Interaction*, 59–62. doi:10.1109/HSI.2010.5514591

Kumar, P. R., & Ravi, V. (2007). prediction in banks and firms via statistical and intelligent techniques – A review. *European Journal of Operational Research*, *180*(1), 1–28. doi:10.1016/j.ejor.2006.08.043

Lacerda, E., Carvalho, A. C., Braga, A. P., & Ludermir, T. B. (2005). Evolutionary radial basis functions for credit assessment. *Applied Intelligence*, *22*(3), 167–181. doi:10.1007/s10791-005-6617-0

Lai, R. K., Fan, C. Y., Huang, W. H., & Chang, P. C. (2009). Evolving and clustering fuzzy decision tree for financial time series data forecasting. *Expert Systems with Applications*, *36*(2), 3761–3773. doi:10.1016/j.eswa.2008.02.025

Lee, C. M., & Ko, C. N. (2009). Time series prediction using RBF neural networks with a non-linear time-varying evolution PSO algorithm. *Neurocomputing*, *73*(1), 449–460. doi:10.1016/j.neucom.2009.07.005

Leung, F. H., Lam, H. K., Ling, S. H., & Tam, P. K. (2003). Tuning of the structure and parameters of a neural network using an improved genetic algorithm. *IEEE Transactions on Neural Networks*, *14*(1), 79–88. doi:10.1109/TNN.2002.804317 PMID:18237992

Li, H., Zhou, H., & Cai, Q. (2010).An Asset Evalution Method Based on Neural Network. *The 2nd IEEE International Conference on information management and engineering (ICIME)*, 582-585.

Li, M., Liu, J., Jiang, Y., & Feng, W. (2012). Complex Chebyshev functional link neural network behavioral model for broadband wireless power amplifiers. *IEEE Transactions on Microwave Theory and Techniques*, *60*(6), 1979–1989. doi:10.1109/TMTT.2012.2189239

Lian, R. J. (2014). Adaptive self-organizing fuzzy sliding-mode radial basis-function neural-network controller for robotic systems. *IEEE Transactions on Industrial Electronics*, *61*(3), 1493–1503. doi:10.1109/TIE.2013.2258299

Lu, C. J., & Wu, J. Y. (2011). An efficient CMAC neural network for stock index forecasting. *Expert Systems with Applications*, *38*(12), 15194–15201. doi:10.1016/j.eswa.2011.05.082

Ma, W., Wang, Y., & Dong, N. (2010). Study on stock price prediction based on BP neural network. *IEEE International conference on Emergency Management and Management Sciences (ICEMMS)*, 57–60.

Majhi, R., Panda, G., & Sahoo, G. (2009). Development and performance evaluation of FLANN based model for forecasting of stock markets. *Expert Systems with Applications*, *36*(3), 6800–6808. doi:10.1016/j.eswa.2008.08.008

Mili, F., & Hamdi, M. (2012). A hybrid evolutionary functional link artificial neural network for data mining and classification. *International Journal of Advanced Computer Science and Applications*, *3*(8), 89–95. doi:10.14569/IJACSA.2012.030815

Mishra, S. K., Panda, G., & Meher, S. (2009). Chebyshev functional link artificial neural networks for denoising of image corrupted by salt and pepper noise. *International Journal of Recent Trends in Enginering*, *1*(1), 413–417.

Mostafa, M. M. (2010). Forecasting stock exchange movements using neural networks: Empirical evidence from Kuwait. *Expert Systems with Applications*, *37*(9), 6302–6309. doi:10.1016/j.eswa.2010.02.091

Oliveira, F. A., Zarate, L. E., & Reis, M. A. (2011). The use of artificial neural networks in the analysis and prediction of stock prices. *IEEE International Conference on Systems, Man and Cybernetics (SMC)*, 2151–2155.

Ou, P., & Wang, H. (2009). Prediction of stock market index movement by ten data 549 mining techniques. *Modern Applied Science*, *3*(12), 28. doi:10.5539/mas.v3n12p28

Pao, Y. H. (1989). *Adaptive Pattern Recognition and Neural Networks*. Reading, MA: Addison-Wesley Publishing Co., Inc.

Park, H. S., Chung, Y. D., Oh, S. K., Pedrycz, W., & Kim, H. K. (2011). Design of information granule-oriented RBF neural networks and its application to power supply for high-field magnet. *Engineering Applications of Artificial Intelligence*, *24*(3), 543–554. doi:10.1016/j.engappai.2010.11.001

Patra, J. C., & Bornand, C. (2010). Non-linear dynamic system identification using Legendre neural network. *International Joint Conference on Neural Networks (IJCNN)*, 1–7.

Patra, J. C., Bornand, C., & Meher, P. K. (2009). Laguerre neural network based smart sensors for wireless sensor networks. *IEEE Conference on Instrumentation and Measurement Technology*, 832–837. doi:10.1109/IMTC.2009.5168565

Pen, J. X., Li, K., & Huang, D. S. (2006). A hybrid forward algorithm for RBF neural network construction. *IEEE Transactions on Neural Networks*, *17*(6), 1439–1451. doi:10.1109/TNN.2006.880860 PMID:17131659

Rodriguez, N. (2009). Multiscale Legendre neural network for monthly anchovy catches forecasting. *Third International Symposium on Intelligent Information Technology Application*, 598–601. doi:10.1109/IITA.2009.466

Rout, M., Majhi, B., Majhi, R., & Panda, G. (2014). Forecasting of currency exchange rates using an adaptive ARMA model with differential evolution based training. *Journal of King Saud University-Computer and Information Sciences*, *26*(1), 7–18. doi:10.1016/j.jksuci.2013.01.002

Rubio-Solis, A., & Panoutsos, G. (2015). Interval type-2 radial basis function neural network: A modeling framework. *IEEE Transactions on Fuzzy Systems*, *23*(2), 457–473. doi:10.1109/TFUZZ.2014.2315656

Sheta, A. F., & Jong, K. (2001). Time-series forecasting using GA-tuned radial basis functions. *Information Sciences*, *133*(3), 221–228. doi:10.1016/S0020-0255(01)00086-X

Song, Y., Chen, Z., & Yuan, Z. (2007). New chaotic PSO based neural network predictive control for nonlinear process. *IEEE Transactions on Neural Networks*, *18*(2), 595–600. doi:10.1109/TNN.2006.890809 PMID:17385644

Suresh, S., Sundararajan, N., & Savitha, R., (2013). A fully complex-valued radial basis function network and its learning algorithm. *Studies in Computational Intelligence, 421*, 49-71.

Tsai, T. J., Yang, C. B., & Peng, Y. H. (2011). Genetic algorithms for the investment of the mutual fund with global trend indicator. *Expert Systems with Applications*, *38*(3), 1697–1701. doi:10.1016/j.eswa.2010.07.094

Wei, L. Y. (2016). A hybrid ANFIS model based on empirical mode decomposition for stock time series forecasting. *Applied Soft Computing*, *42*, 368–376. doi:10.1016/j.asoc.2016.01.027

Wu, J., & Liu, J. C. (2012). A forecasting system for car fuel consumption using a radial basis function neural network. *Expert Systems with Applications*, *39*(2), 1883–1888. doi:10.1016/j.eswa.2011.07.139

Wu, Q., Law, R., Wu, E., & Lin, J. (2013). A hybrid-forecasting model reducing Gaussian noise based on the Gaussian support vector regression machine and chaotic particle swarm optimization. *Information Science*, *238*, 96–110. doi:10.1016/j.ins.2013.02.017

Yan, H., Liu, W., Xiuying, Kong, H., & Lv, C. (2010). Predicting Net Asset Value of Investment Fund Based On BP Neural Network. *IEEE International Conference on Computer Application and system modeling (ICCASM)*, *10*, 635-637.

Yao, X., Wang, Y., Zhang, X., Zhang, R., Liu, M., Hu, Z., & Fan, B. (2002). Radial basis function neural network-based QSPR for the prediction of critical temperature. *Chemometrics and Intelligent Laboratory Systems*, *62*(2), 217–225. doi:10.1016/S0169-7439(02)00017-5

Yogi, S., Subhashini, K. R., & Satapathy, J. K. (2010). A PSO based functional link artificial neural network training algorithm for equalization of digital communication channels. *5th International Conference on Industrial and Information Systems, ICIIS*, 107–112. doi:10.1109/ICIINFS.2010.5578726

Yu, H., Xie, T., Paszczyñski, S., & Wilamowski, B. M. (2011). Advantages of radial basis function networks for dynamic system design. *IEEE Transactions on Industrial Electronics*, *58*(12), 5438–5450. doi:10.1109/TIE.2011.2164773

Yu, L. (2012). An evolutionary programming based asymmetric weighted least squares support vector machine ensemble learning methodology for software repository mining. *Information Science*, *191*, 31–46. doi:10.1016/j.ins.2011.09.034

Yu, L., Lai, K. K., & Wang, S. (2008). Multistage RBF neural network ensemble learning for exchange rates forecasting. *Neurocomputing*, *71*(16), 3295–3302. doi:10.1016/j.neucom.2008.04.029

Yu, L. Q., & Rong, F. S. (2010). Stock market forecasting research based on neural network and pattern matching. *International Conference on E-Business and E-Government*, 1940–1943. doi:10.1109/ICEE.2010.490

Zhan, Z. H., Zhang, J., Li, Y., & Chung, H. S. H. (2009). Adaptive particle swarm optimization. *IEEE Transactions on Systems, Man, and Cybernetics*, *39*(6), 1362–1381. doi:10.1109/TSMCB.2009.2015956 PMID:19362911

Chapter 4
Memetic Algorithms and Their Applications in Computer Science

B. K. Tripathy
VIT University, India

Sooraj T. R.
VIT University, India

R. K. Mohanty
VIT University, India

ABSTRACT

The term "memetic algorithm" was introduced by Moscato is an extension of the traditional genetic algorithm. It uses a local search technique to reduce the likelihood of the premature convergence. Memetic algorithms are intrinsically concerned with exploiting all available knowledge about the problem under study. MAs are population-based metaheuristics. In this chapter we explore the applications of memetic algorithms to problems within the domains of image processing, data clustering and Graph coloring, i.e., how we can use the memetic algorithms in graph coloring problems, how it can be used in clustering based problems and how it is useful in image processing. Here, we discuss how these algorithms can be used for optimization problems. We conclude by reinforcing the importance of research on the areas of metaheuristics for optimization.

INTRODUCTION

Optimization algorithms can be roughly divided into two categories: Exact algorithms and heuristics. Exact algorithms are designed in such a way that they will find optimum solution in a finite amount of time. However, for very difficult optimization problems (e.g. NP-hard) the finite amount of time may increase exponentially with respect to the dimensions of the problem. Heuristics do not have this guarantee, and therefore generally return solutions that are worse than optimal. However, heuristic algorithms usu-

DOI: 10.4018/978-1-5225-2857-9.ch004

ally find "good" solutions in a "reasonable" amount of time. The best solution cannot be found through heuristics, but heuristics can find a realizable solution with limited time and information. For design optimization using heuristics, however, an acceptable solution can be found, but there is no practical way of determining how close to a global optimum the final design is (Coley and Schukat, 2002).

Many heuristic algorithms are very specific and problem-dependent. On the other hand, a meta-heuristic is a high-level problem-independent algorithmic frame-work that provides a set of guidelines or strategies to develop heuristic optimization algorithms. But a concrete definition has been elusive and in practice many researchers and practitioners interchange these terms. Thus, the term metaheuristic is also used to refer to a problem specific implementation of a heuristic optimization algorithm according to the guidelines expressed in such a framework. In contrast to heuristics, meta-heuristics designate a computational method that optimizes a problem by trying iteratively to improve a candidate solution with regard to a given measure of quality. It can search very large option spaces of candidate solutions.

A metaheuristics is an algorithm designed to solve approximately a wide range of hard optimization problems without having to deeply adapt to each problem. Indeed, the Greek prefix ''Meta'', present in the name, is used to indicate that these algorithms are ''higher level'' heuristics, in contrast with problem-specific heuristics. Metaheuristics are generally applied to problems for which there is no satisfactory problem-specific algorithm to solve those (Boussaïd et al., 2013).

Memetic Algorithms

A memetic algorithm is an extension of the traditional genetic algorithm. It uses a local search technique to reduce the likelihood of the premature convergence. The term "memetic algorithm" was introduced by Moscato in his technical report in 1989. Memetic algorithms are intrinsically concerned with exploiting all available knowledge about the problem under study. MAs are population-based metaheuristics. This means that the algorithm maintain a population of solutions for the problem at hand, i.e., a pool comprising several solutions simultaneously. Each of these solutions is termed "individual" in the EA jargon, following the nature-inspired metaphor upon which these techniques are based

APPLICATIONS OF MEMETIC ALGORITHMS

In this section we discuss some of the applications of memetic algorithms.

Clustering

Clustering can be considered the most important unsupervised learning problem. Clustering is the process of organizing objects into groups whose members are similar in some way. In this section, various applications of clustering are mentioned. i.e., how memetic algorithms are used in clustering. The essence of the clustering problem is to partition a set of objects into an a priori unknown number of clusters while minimizing the within-cluster variability and maximizing the between cluster variability. Data clustering is a common technique for statistical data analysis and has been used in a variety of engineering and scientific disciplines such as biology (e.g., to study genome data (Baldi & Hatfield, 2002; Tavazoie et al., 1999; Wu, Liew, Yan & Yang, 2004) and computer vision; e.g. to segment images (Frigui & Krishnapuram, 1999; Jain & Flynn, 1996; Shi& Malik, 2000).

Many clustering algorithms have been proposed in the literature. Generally, they can be divided into two main categories, namely, hierarchical and partitional (Jain & Dubes, 1988). Hierarchical clustering constructs a hierarchy of partitioning, represented as a dendrogram in which each partitioning is nested within the partitioning at the next level in the hierarchy. In hierarchical clustering, problems due to initialization and local optima do not arise. However, thisapproach considers only local neighbors in each step and ignores the global shape and size of clusters. Moreover, hierarchical clustering is static; that is, data objects committed to a given cluster in the early stages cannot move to a different cluster.In partitional clustering, each data object is represented by a vector of features. Most partitional algorithms assume all features to be equally important for clustering in the sense that they do not distinguish among different features, but this approach to clustering can create significant limitations in an unsupervised learning context. The problem is that not all features are equally important; indeed, some of the features may be redundant, some may be irrelevant, and some can even mislead the clustering process. This is one of the reasons that many clustering algorithms do not perform well in the face of high-dimensional data, and the task of selecting the best feature subset, the process known as feature selection, is therefore important. In addition, feature selection may lead to more economical clustering algorithms (in terms of both storage and computational effort) and contribute to the interpretability of the models generated. Generally, for a data set of nontrivial size, finding the optimal clustering solution is a challenging problem (Garey & Johnson, 1979) and becomes even more challenging if an appropriate feature set also needs to be selected.

One way of approaching this challenge is to use stochastic optimization schemes, prominent among which is an approach based on genetic algorithms (GAs). The GA, first developed by Holland (Holland, 1975), is biologically inspired and embodies many mechanisms mimicking natural evolution. It has a great deal of potential in scientific and engineering optimization or search problems. Recently, hybrid methods (Areibi & Yang, 2004; Merz & Freisleben, 1998; Whitley, 1995), which incorporate local searches with traditional GAs, have been proposed and applied successfully to solve a wide variety of optimization problems. These studies show that pure GAs are not well suited to fine-tuning structures in complex search spaces and that hybridization with other techniques can greatly improve their efficiency. GAs that have been hybridized with local searches are also known as memetic algorithms (MAs).

Niching Memetic Algorithm

In this section, we discuss the algorithm proposed by Sheng et al. (2004). It is a niching MA for simultaneous clustering and feature selection (NMA_CFS) by optimizing the unified criterion J_2. The unified criterion selected is for simultaneous clustering and feature selection. The algorithm works with variable composite chromosomes, which are used to represent solutions.The operation of the algorithm consists of using a niching selection method for selecting pairing parents for reproduction, performing different genetic operators on different parts (i.e., feature selection vector and cluster centers) of the paired parents, applying local search operations (i.e., feature add and remove procedures and one step of K Means) to each offspring, and carrying out a niching competition replacement. The evolution is terminated when the fitness value of the best solution in the population has not changed for g generations. The output of the algorithm is the best solution encountered during the evolution. The flow of the algorithm (Algorithm 1) is given as follows:

```
Algorithm 1: NMA_CFS
Step1. Randomly initialize p sets of solutions, which encode both feature se-
lection and cluster centers with different numbers of clusters, by using a
variable composite representation.
Step2. Calculate J₂ for each solution in the initial population and set its
fitness value as f = J₂.
Step3. Repeat the following steps until the stopping criterion is met:
1. Select pairing parents based on a niching selection method. This procedure
is repeated until p/2 parent pairs are selected.
2. Generate intermediate offspring by applying different genetic operators on
the different parts (i.e., feature selection vector and cluster centers) of
the paired parents.
3. Apply feature add and remove procedures to the offspring.
4. Run one step of K Means on the offspring.
5. Pair the offspring with the most similar solution found during a restricted
competition replacement
6. Calculate J₂ for each of the offspring. If the fitness of the offspring is
better than its paired solution, then the latter is replaced.
Step4. Provide the feature subset and cluster centers of the solution from the
terminal population with the best fitness.
```

In the following section, we discuss the major steps involved in the above algorithm.

Representation and Initialization

In the NMA_CFS procedure, a variable composite chromosome is devised, which can encode both feature selection and cluster centers with a variable number of clusters. The feature selection vector in the chromosome is a string with D binary digits (D is the total number of available features in the data to be clustered), and each binary digit represents an individual feature, with values 1 and 0 denoting selected and ignored, respectively. The cluster centers in the chromosome consist of $D \times k_i$ real numbers, where k_i is the number of clusters. The first D positions represent the D dimensions of the first cluster center, the next D positions represent those of the second cluster center, and so on. For example, in five-dimensional data, the chromosome

$$< 11001\ 0.5_1 0.1_1 0.7_0 0.5_0 0.6_1 0.2_1 0.9_1 0.8_0 0.7_0 0.3_1\ 0.8_1 0.9_1 0.5_0 0:6_0 0:2_1 >$$

encodes centers of three clusters (i.e., (0.5, 0.1, 0.6), (0.2, 0.9, 0.3), and (0.8, 0.9, 0.2)), with the first, second, and fifth features being selected. It should be noted that only values of the elected features (values with subscript "1") are used to form the cluster centers and the others (values with subscript "0") are ignored. Each solution in the population is constructed using the variable composite chromosome. The values are initialized by random assignment of binary digits and real numbers to the feature selection vector and the k_i cluster centers, respectively. The initial values of the cluster centers are constrained to be in the range (determined from the data set) of the feature to which they are assigned but are otherwise random. The initial number of clusters k_i is calculated according to *RandInt*(2,k_{max}). Here, *Rand-*

Int() is a function returning a natural number in the range from 2 to k_{max} (inclusive), and k_{max} is the upper bound of the number of clusters and is taken to be $\sqrt{n}$ (n is the number of objects in the data set to be clustered), which is a rule of thumb used by many investigators in the clusteringliterature. The number of clusters for the solutions in the population will therefore range from 2 to k_{max}.

Crossover and Mutation

In the composite representation, feature selection and cluster centers are encoded in a single solution. Accordingly, we have to apply different genetic operators, which are sensitive to the corresponding context, on feature selection vector and cluster center parts of the paired parents. For the feature selection vector part, the m-point crossover and flip mutation are applied. The m-point crossover, which is performed on each set of paired parents, chooses m cutting points at random and alternately copies each segment from the two parents. For example, given a parent pair

Parent$_1$:< 1|1|0|0|1 0.50.10.70.50.6 0.20.90.80.70.30.80.90.50.60.2 >,

Parent$_2$:< 1|0|1|1|0 0:40:20:80:40:5 0:90:70:30:50:10.10.80.60.90.2 0.40.50.30.40.1 >;

suppose that three cutting points are chosen at positions 1, 3, and 4 (denoted by "|") in the feature selection vector. After the m-point crossover, the two intermediate offspring generated would be

Offspring$_1$:< 10100 0.50.10.70.50.6 0.20.90.80.70.30.80.90.50.60.2>,

Offspring$_2$:< 11011 0.40.20.80.40.5 0.10.80.60.90.20.90.70.30.50.1 0.40.50.30.40.1>.

After crossover, each bit of the offspring is considered for mutation. Mutation consists of flipping the value of the chosen bit from 1 to 0, or vice versa. Both crossover and mutation operations are likely to generate an offspring, with no features being selected. When such an offspring emerges, repeat the operations until a proper offspring is produced or until a limit on the number of trials is reached.

For the cluster center part, use a crossover operation analogous to the traditional two-point crossover (Goldberg,1989). During crossover, the cluster centers are considered to be indivisible(i.e., the crossover points can only lie in between two clusters' centers). For this purpose, the crossover operation is defined as follows: Let paired parents P_1 and P_2 encode k_1 and k_2 cluster centers $\left(k_1 \leq k_2\right)$, respectively. Then, x_1 and x_2, the crossover points in P_1, are generated according to *RandInt(0, k_1-1)*. If x_1 is greater than x_2, then swap the value of x_1 and x_2 to make sure that $x_2 > x_1$. The cross points x_3 and x_4 in P_2 are then generated as x_3=*RandInt(0, k_2-|x_2-x_1|-1)* and x_4=x_3+|x_2-x_1|, where |x_2-x_1| is the length of segment between cross points of x_2 and x_1. After that, the segment information between x_1 and x_2 in P_1 exchanges with the segment information between x_3 and x_4 in P_2. Continuing with the above example, given the two intermediate offspring after the *m*-point crossover

Offspring$_1$:< 10100 0.50.10.70.50.6 | 0.20.90.80.70.3|0.80.90.50.60.2 >,

Offspring$_2$:< 11011 0.40.20.80.40.5 |0.90.70.30.50.1 |0:10:80:60:90:2 | 0:40:50:30:40:1 >;

suppose that the crossover points x_1, x_2, x_3, and x_4 are generated at positions 1, 2, 2, and 3, respectively (denoted by "|"). After the crossover, the two offspring would become

Offspring$_1$: < 10100 0.50.10.70.50.6 0.10.80.60.90.20.80.90.50.60.2 >,

Offspring$_2$: < 11011 0.40.20.80.40.5 0.90.70.30.50.10.20.90.80.70.3 0.40.50.30.40.1 >.

It can be seen that according to the above rules, the number of clusters of the offspring will be equal to either k_1 or k_2. The crossover is performed on each set of paired parents. After crossover, a low probability of Gaussian mutation is applied on the offspring. Gaussian mutation adds a unit Gaussian distributed random value to the chosen feature. The new feature value is clipped if it falls outside the lower or upper bounds of that feature.

Local Searches

Pure GAs is not well suited to fine-tune solutions that are close to optima (Goldberg & Richardson, 1987), and this results in their having a long runtime. To improve the time efficiency, incorporation of local searches into the regeneration step of GAs, creating the so-called MAs, is essential if competitive GAs are to be used (Areibi & Yang, 2004). Several local search operations to effectively design an MA for simultaneous clustering and feature selection will be discussed next. Feature add and remove are those operations. Sequential forward selection (SFS) and sequential backward selection (SBS) (Foroutan & Sklasky, 1987) are two classical heuristic feature selection algorithms developed for supervised learning. SFS starts with an empty set of features, and at each iteration, the algorithm tentatively adds each available feature and selects the feature that results in the highest estimated performance. The search terminates when the accuracy of the current subset cannot be improved by adding any other feature. SBS works in an analogous way but starts from the full set of available features and tentatively deletes each feature not deleted previously. SFS and SBS are simple and fast. However, they are prone to being trapped in locally optimal solutions.

The following two basic operations—add (based on the SFS) and remove (based on the SBS)—as noted in the following are used and are incorporated into the GA to fine-tune the feature selection encoded in the solution for clustering:

- **Add:** Choose a feature from the unselected feature subset that, when combined with the currently selected features, yields the largest value of the criterion J_1 and changes its status to "selected."
- **Remove:** Choose a feature from the selected feature subset that makes the least contribution to the criterion J_1 and changes its status to "ignored."

The above operations generate local improvements by adding the most significant feature or removing the least significant feature and aim at speeding up the search for the best feature subset. Each of the operations is applied once (the add operation followed by the remove operation) to all new offspring after the crossover and mutation operations.

K-Means operation: K-Means (MacQueen, 1967) is an iterative scheme attempting to minimize the within-cluster sum of squares errors (SSE):

$$SSE = \sum_{i=1}^{n} \sum_{j=1}^{k} z_{ji} \left\| x_i - m_j \right\|^2$$

where $z_{ij} = 1$ if x_i is an element of cluster j, otherwise 0. m_j is the mean of cluster j.

Starting from an initial distribution of cluster centers in the data space, each data object is assigned to a cluster with the closest center, after which each center itself is updated asthe center of data objects belonging to that particular cluster. This procedure is repeated until there is no reassignment of any data object from one cluster to another or the SSE value ceases to decrease significantly. This iterative scheme is known to converge fast. However, it depends highly on the initialization of cluster centers.

In order to improve the computational efficiency, one step of K-means is applied to the cluster centers encoded in all the new offsprings during each generation after the feature add and remove operations. This is done by assigning each data object to one of the clusters with the nearest center encoded in the solution. After that, the cluster centers encoded in the solution are replaced by the means of the respective clusters.

Niching Method

One of the key elements in overcoming less promising locally optimal solutions of a difficult optimization problem with a GA approach is to preserve the population diversity during the search (Sareni & Krahenbu, 1998). Sheng et al. (2004) modified the niching method and integrated it into GA to preserve the population diversity during the simultaneous search for clustering and feature selection. The niching method presented in Sheng et al. (2004) was designed for clustering where no feature selection is required and the number of clusters is known beforehand. In this method, a niching selection with a restricted competition replacement was developed to encourage mating among similar solutions while allowing for some competitions among dissimilar solutions. During the niching selection, one parent p_1 isselected randomly from the population, and its mate is selected from a group of solutions called the selection group, picked randomly from the population. The one most similar (determined by the Euclidean distance based on a phenotypic metric) to p_1 is chosen as its mate p_2. During the restricted competition replacement, each offspring is compared with agroup of solutions called the replacement group, picked randomly from the population, and is then paired with the most similar one. If the fitness of the offspring is better than its paired solution, then the latter is replaced. With appropriate sizes of the selection and replacementgroups, this method can maintain the population diversity with respect to the cluster centers with a fixed number of clusters encoded in the solutions. However, for the problem considered here, it is more important to preserve the population diversity with respect to the number of clusters, since the solutions with different numbers of clusters have rather different feature selection and cluster centers. For this purpose, Sheng et al. (2004), modified the niching selection to encouragemating among solutions with similar numbers of clusters and extend the restricted competition replacement to encourage replacement among solutions with the same number of clusters while allowing for some competitions among the solutions with different numbers of clusters. The modified niching method is implemented as follows:

During the niching selection, one parent p_1 is still randomly selected from the population. Its mate p_2 is now chosen from the selection group with the most similar number of clusters as for p_1. If this results in a group with more than one candidate solution, the similarity of feature selection and cluster centers is further used to select the most similar one. During the restricted competition replacement, we can compare the offspring with each solution that has the same number of clusters as the offspring in the competition group, and we pair it up with the one having the most similar feature selection and cluster centers if this exists; otherwise, we pair it with a solution with the lowest fitness. If the fitness of the offspring is better than its paired solution, then the latter is replaced. Crossover among solutions with a large difference in cluster numbers often produces low-performance offspring. The modified niching selection tries to promote mating among solutions with similar numbers of clusters. When the size of the selection group is equal to one, it is basically a random selection. As the size increases, there is a greater possibility of selecting parent pairs with the same number of clusters. However, the size should be small enough to allow mating among solutions with different numbers ofclusters. The extended restricted competition replacement is mostly used to balance competitions during replacement among solutions with different numbers of clusters. A largereplacement group size will restrict the replacement among solutions with the same number of clusters. Decreasing the size will promote more competitions among the solutions with different numbers of clusters. An appropriate value should be set to allow both thorough exploration of the search space with the same number of clusters and competitions among solutions with different numbers of clusters. By measuring the similarity of solutions based ontheir feature selection and cluster centers during replacement, we are also attempting to preserve the diversity among the solutions of the same number of clusters with respect to feature selection and cluster centers.

Complexity

The major computational load during each generation of the above algorithm is in the feature addand remove procedures, one step of the K Means operator, and the fitness evaluation. The feature add procedure takes $O(nk_{max}D^2)$ time. Similarly, the feature remove procedure has $O(nk_{max}D^2)$ time complexity in the worst case. The one-step K Means operator and the fitness evaluation of a given solution take $O(nk_{max}D)$ and $O(nD)$ time respectively. Therefore, the overall complexity of the proposed algorithm is $O(nk_{max}D^2)pg$, where p is the population size, and g is the number of generations.

Graph Coloring Problem

Graph coloring problem (GCP) assigns different colors to the adjacent vertices of a graph using minimum number of colors. The GCP is illustrated with a simple graph in Figure 1, where six colors are needed to color eleven vertices. In Figure 1, the vertex number is shown within the circle and the color number is shown outside the circle. The GCP is a well known NP-hard problem (Kubale, 2004). The notable applications of GCP are seen in pattern recognition (Chen & Yun, 1998), map coloring (Gwee, Lim & Ho, 1993), radio frequency assignment (Hale, 1980), bandwidth allocation (Gamst, 1986) and timetable scheduling (Cauvery, 2011).

Assume that a graph G = (V, E) is to be colored with numbers of colors. The objective is to color all the vertices reducing *n* dynamically so that minimum chromatic number, denoted by X(G), is found, that is, n = X(G) is reached. It has been an established fact that metaheuristic approaches such as evolutionary algorithms (EA) are best suited for this class of optimization problem.

Figure 1. GCP

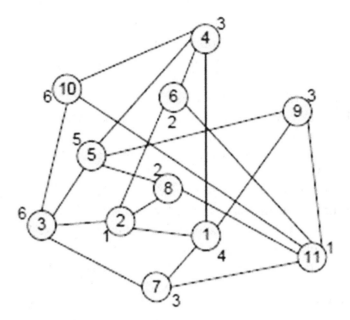

One of the most recent works on GCP (Hindi & Yampolskiy, 2012) combines wisdom of artificial crowds (WoAC) approach with the genetic algorithm (GA) and k-coloring approach is used. Wisdom of artificial crowds is a novel swarm based nature-inspired metaheuristic algorithm for global optimization. WoAC is a post-processing algorithm in which independently-deciding artificial agents aggregate their individual solutions to arrive at an answer which is superior to all solutions in the population.In this approach, multiple parent selection and multiple mutations based on the closeness of the solution to the global optima are used. The algorithm is run several times for several decreasing values of k and the minimum possible k value is taken as the minimum chromatic number. Another work used hierarchical parallel genetic algorithm for GCP (Foroutan & Sklasky, 1987), where the authors extended genetic algorithm with genetic modification operator introduced by them. A guided genetic algorithm for GCP called MSPGCA is reported in (Ray, Pal, Bhattacharyya & Kim, 2010), where the authors fine-tuned the initial chromosomes using a simple genetic algorithm and then the deterministic MSPGCA algorithm is run to dynamically reduce the chromatic number. Tabu Search as a GCP solving approach was used in (Lim,Zhu,Lou& Rodrigues, 2005). A hybrid immune algorithm is also applied in GCP (Cutello, Nicosia & Pavone, 2003). All the above mentioned approaches used integer encoding for the chromosomes.

Chowdhury et al. [33] introduced a classical crossover operation as the main variation operator and a deterministic local improvement technique. They used binary encoded chromosomes for graph coloring problems, which makes both the crossover and the local improvement easier. In the traditional evolutionary algorithm (EA) for GCP, k-coloring is used and the EA is run repeatedly until the lowest possible k is reached. But Choudhury et al. (2013) started with the theoretical upper bound of chromatic number and in the process of evolution some of the colors are made unused to dynamically reduce the number of colors. Thus, the solution is found in a single run of the MA reducing the total execution time in comparison to running k-coloring for several times.

Chowdhury's Encoding Scheme

Integer encoding is used in the previous works on GCP. However, binary encoding has dominating success in the evolutionary computing for describing solution structure in depth. On the other hand, in a dynamic learning system, it is more feasible to understand learning progress and to improve quality of population at any point. Considering these facts, Chaudhury et al. used a binary encoding scheme for chromosomes in this MA, which allows to implement the crossover operator easily and to deterministically improve the solution quality dynamically. The encoding scheme is illustrated in Figure 2 for the undirected graph of Figure 1.

In this encoding as atwo-dimensional array, each row corresponds to a color and each column corresponds to a vertex. Let the jth vertex be colored using the ith color, then the (i, j)th element of the array will be 1 and the other elements will be 0. Thus, in a valid chromosome, every column must have a single 1 and a row will have one or more than one 1s placed on non-adjacent columns for different vertices. A row may also have all 0s, in which case the color is not used in the solution. If a column has all 0s (the vertex is not colored) or more than one 1s (more than one color is assigned to that vertex), then the encoding is invalid. This situation may arise after crossover operation as discussed later, where two 1s may be present in one column. On the other hand, if a row has 1s in adjacent vertices columns (same color is assigned to adjacent vertices), then theencoding is invalid. This situation may arise during initialization. The process of correcting a chromosome when it becomes invalid is discussed in the following. If a row has all 0s, then that color is not used in the vertex coloring. Thus, the number of rows having at least one 1 is the number of used colors and is used as the fitness function in our MA. Binary encoding technique will allow us to deterministically improve the quality of the solution.

Memetic Algorithm for Graph Coloring

Memetic algorithm (MA) for graph coloring problem (GCP) is shown below and each step of the MA is discussed separately.

Figure 2. Chromosome encoding of graph of Figure 1

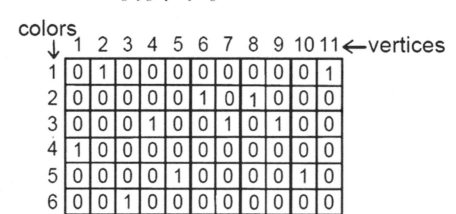

```
Memetic Algorithm for GCP ():
Step 1:  population = initialization ()
Step 2: population = correction (population)
Step 3: fitness = evaluation (population)
Step 4: while (termination condition not reached) do
1. parents = parentSelection (population)
2. offsprings = crossover (parents)
3. offsprings = correction (offsprings)
4. offsprings = improvement (offsprings)
5. offsprings_fitness = evaluation (offsprings)
6. population = replacement (population, offsprings)
Step 5: end
```

The initialization procedure of step1 generates the chromosomes of the initial population. Chromosomes are initialized with m + 1 colors, where m is the maximum out-degree of the graph. The theoretical upper bound of the chromatic number is m + 1. The initial chromosome is generated by putting a single 1 under each column at a randomly selected row and filling up the remaining elementsby 0s. During the initialization, a chromosome for the graph of Figure 1 may be as shown in Figure 3(a). In this chromosome,adjacent vertices 7 and 11 are colored by color 1 and adjacentvertices 4 and 6 are colored by color 2, which is an invalidchromosome. Therefore, correction is needed to make it avalid chromosome. For the correction procedure of step 2, oneof the conflicting 1s is chosen randomly and then the chosen 1.

The evaluation procedure of step3 determines the fitness of each chromosome. The fitness of a chromosome is equal to the number of used colors in the chromosome. In the termination condition of step4, if both average and best fitness remain constant for a pre-determined number of generations then the algorithm is terminated.

In the parent selection procedure of step 4(i), two parents are randomly selected from the population. In the crossover procedure of step 4(ii), a crossover point is randomly selected and the rows above the crossover point are interchanged between the two parents. Two parent chromosomes for the graph of Figure 1 and the generated offsprings are shown in Figure 4. In our MA, the crossover operation is applied with high probability. The crossover operation may produce invalid offsprings. Two possible problems may occur – 1) a column may have two 1s or 2) a column may have all 0s. In Figure 4, both the generated offsprings are invalid and both have the two possible problems. In the correction procedure of step 4(iii), the invalid offsprings are corrected. For case 1), one of the two 1s is randomly deleted. For the case 2), a 1 is inserted at a randomly selected row among used color clusters so that no conflict is created at that row. If such a used color row is not available, then a 1 is inserted at a randomly selected row among unused color clusters.

Improvement procedure of step 4(iv) deterministically improves the quality of the offsprings. For each offsprings, a lowest used color cluster is selected randomly. Then 1s of that selected color cluster are moved to other rows of the used color clusters so that no conflict is created at that row. If any 1 of the selected color cluster cannot be moved to any of the rows of the used color clusters, then it is left in the original color cluster. This local improvement procedure makes a color unused improving the fitness of the offspring. The improvement procedure is applied with a low probability. One possible chromosome for the graph of Figure 1 and its improved version is shown in Figure 6. In Figure 6 (a), colors 2 is the lowest used. The 1 of the 2nd row can be moved to row 2, 3, 4, or 6 without conflict. It is moved to row

Figure 3. Invalid chromosome during initialization and its correction

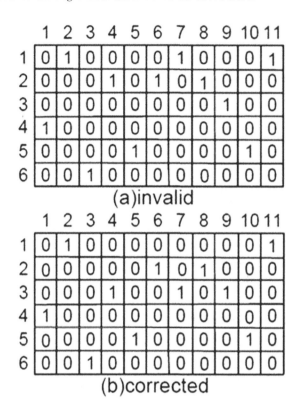

(a)invalid

(b)corrected

4 to produce the improved chromosome of Figure 6 (b). The fitness of the chromosome of Figure 6 (a) is six and that of the Figure 6 (b) is five.

Tabu Search Techniques for Graph Coloring

Tabu search techniques are used for moving step by step towards the minimum value of a function. A tabu list of forbidden movements is updated during the iterations to avoid cycling and being trapped in local minima. Such techniques are adapted to graph coloring problems.

Tabu Search Technique

In rough terms the Tabu search method can be sketched as follows:

We want to move step by step from an initial feasible solution of a combinatorial optimization problem towards a solution giving the minimum value of some objective function. For this, we may represent each solution by a point in some space and we have to define a neighborhood N (s) of each point s.

The basic step of the procedure consists in starting from a feasible point s and generating a sample (with fixed size rep) of solutions in N (s); then we choose the best neighbor s* generated so far and we move to s* whether f(s*) is better than f(s) or not.The interesting feature of tabu search is precisely the construction of a list T of Tabu moves: these are moves which are not allowed at the present iteration.

Figure 4. The crossover operation

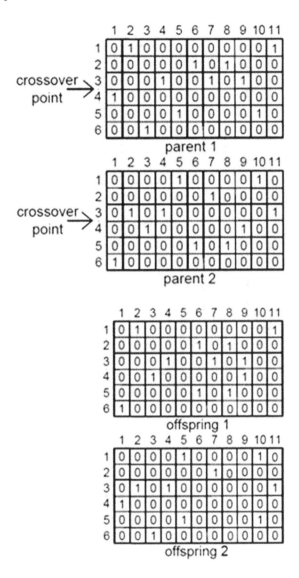

The reason for this list is to exclude moves which would bring us back where we were at some previous iteration. Now a move remains a Tabu move only during a certain number of iterations, so that we have in fact a cyclical list T where at each move s→s* the opposite move s* →s is added at the end of T while the oldest move in T is removed from T.

In conclusion the basic step consists in generating randomly a fixed number rep (number of neighbors) of possible moves from s (whenever a move in T is generated, it is destroyed and a new move is generated). Then the best one of the generated moves is realized and the Tabu list T is updated accordingly.

The stopping rule can be defined as the maximum (nbmax) number of iterations. However, here an estimation f* of the minimum value of the objective function f(s) is used. As soon as the value is close enough to (or when f* is reached) the whole procedure is stopped.

Figure 5. Correction of invalid offspring

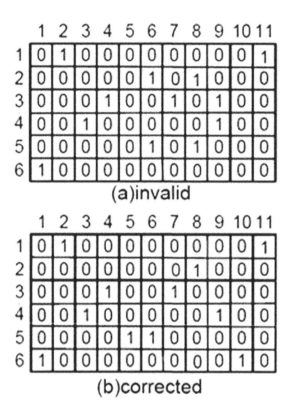

(a)invalid

(b)corrected

Figure 6. Local improvement of a chromosome

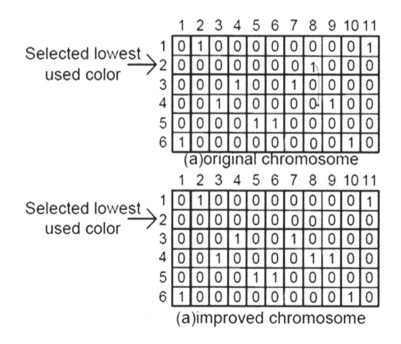

(a)original chromosome

(a)improved chromosome

Application to Node Colorings

Let G is the graph given and k is the fixed number of colors. Given a graph G = (V, E) a feasible solution will be a partition s = (V_1, V_2, V_k) of the node set V into a fixed number k of subsets. If E (V_i) is the collection of edges of G with both endpoints in V_i, we may define the objective function f as the number of edges for which both endpoints are in the same V_i (i.e. have the same color):

$$f(s) = \sum_{i=1}^{k} \left| E\left(V_i\right)\right| \tag{1}$$

Clearly s will be a coloring of the nodes of G with k colors if and only if f (s) = 0. In fact, we can estimate the best possible value of f(s) with f* = 0; this will give us a stopping condition in the algorithm. From s we generate a neighbor s' (i. e. another partition into k subsets of nodes) as follows:

We choose a random node x among all those which are adjacent to an edge in $E\left(V_1\right) \cup ... \cup E\left(V_1\right)$.

Then assuming $x \in V_i$, we choose a random color $j \neq i$ and we obtain s' from $s = \left\{V_1, ..., V_k\right\}$ by setting:

$$V_j' = V_j \cup \left\{x\right\}; \quad V_j' = {V_j}/{\{x\}}; \quad V_r' = V_r \quad \text{for r=1,...,k;r} \neq \text{i,j.} \tag{2}$$

Having generated rep neighbors of s (which do not lead to Tabu moves), we pick upthe best one and we move to it. The tabu list is obtained as follows: whenever a node x is moved from V_i to V_j to get the new solution, the pair (x, i) becomes Tabu: node x cannot be returned to V_i for some iterations. As described before the list T of Tabu moves is cyclic. Now, we shall continue the iterations until either we get a solution s such that f(s) =f* or until we reach the maximum number nbmax of iterations. In this case, we will not have obtained a coloring if for the last solution s we have f(s)>0.

The TBUCOL Algorithm

```
Input: G = (V, E)
      k =number of colors
      |T| =size of tabu list.
      rep = number of neighbors in sample
      nbmax =maximum number of iterations.
Initialization
Generate a random solution  s = {V₁,...,Vₖ}
      nbiter: =0; choose an arbitrary tabu list T.
While (f(s) >0)and(nbiter<nbmax)
generate rep neighbourss  of s with move  s→sᵢ ∈T or  f(sᵢ) ≤ A(f(s))
      (as soon as we get an sᵢ with f(sᵢ)<f(s) we stop the generation).
      Let s ' be the best neighbor generated
      update Tabu list T
      (introduce move s→s' and remove oldest tabu move)
```

```
     s:=s'
     nbiter: = nbiter + 1
endwhile
```

Output: If f (s) =0, we get a coloring of G with k colors: V_1, V_k are the color sets. Otherwise nocoloring has been found with k colors.

Image Processing Applications

Synthetic aperture radar (SAR) is a form of radar that is used to create images of objects, such as landscapes – these images can be either two or three dimensional representations of the object.Few memetic algorithms are used for data processing of synthetic aperture radar (SAR) imagery. The genetic approach used for processing of SAR imagery to find a region of pre-defined criterion. Aydemir et al.(2003) used memetic algorithm in SAR imagery. They used memetic algorithm for search method.

SAR (Synthetic Aperture Radar) has found wide range of applications in satellite imaging. Evaluation of SAR images is one of the most important steps of the process. The application of a global optimization procedure to the detection of pre-defined terrain regions is studied by Aydemir. An efficient recursive analytical procedure is used for the image processing. Starting by a random pixel population, the iterative minimization of the functional is performed by a new optimization method called memetic algorithm. SAR images contain highly uncorrelated data. Two approaches are usually followed to face this problem. The first one concerns the use of linearized procedures, which allows quick finding of local minimums. The second approach is the stochastic search algorithms, in which iterative approaches are utilized for the inspection of highly contrasted inhomogeneities.

SAR Image Processing

SAR image processing is shown in figure. 7. Efficient target detection schemes in SAR geometry are based on a hierarchical approach where each step in the hierarchy operates on a smaller amount of data with algorithms of increasing computational complexity.

Early steps perform low-complexity rejection (prescreening) of non-target areas while subsequent steps refine the detection (or classification) using for instance, feature-based false alarm discrimination In Figure 8, an output of SAR MTI algorithm is shown. For determining the target, prescreening of some different colored areas is needed. Considering large image sizes, search methods may become favorable to direct pixel comparison methods. The next step is determining the population structure of the Memetic Algorithm.

Memetic Algorithm Parameter Search

Memetic algorithms are optimization methods that belong to the family of evolutionary methods. The basic idea of the memetic algorithm is to emulate the idea transmission process. A meme is a unit of information that can be transmitted when people exchange ideas. Memetic algorithms are population-based algorithms, in which every "idea" is an individual. Since people process any idea to obtain a personal optimum before propagating it, each individual is a point of local minima of the cost function.

Figure 7. SAR Image Processing

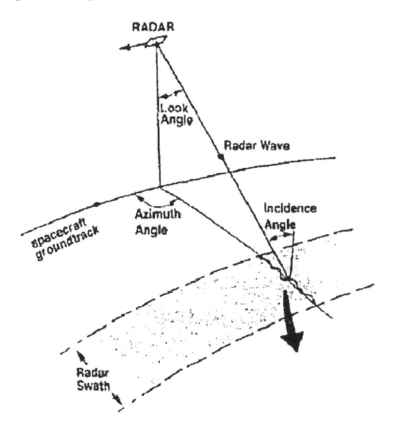

Figure 8. Output of SAR MTI algorithm

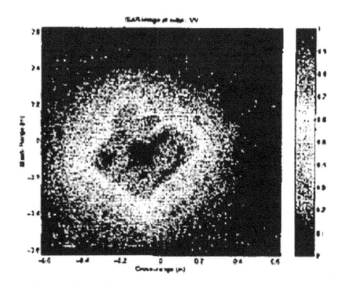

The evolution of the population is modeled by using the same operators of the genetic algorithm, i.e., selection, crossover and mutation. Since these operators are not generally able to produce local optima, an optimization procedure is needed. The general schema of a memetic algorithm is shown in Figure 9.

Consider a generic individual denoted by x_k.

$$x_k = \left(x_k^1, ..., x_k^m \right) \tag{3}$$

where x_k^1 belongs to R, where R is the real number set. The population of the algorithm is composed by N individuals.

Figure 9. The memetic algorithm flow chart

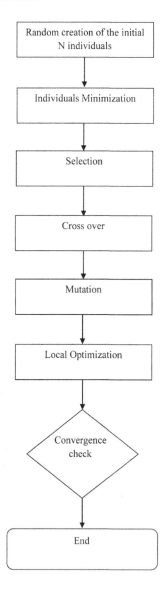

$$P_i = \{x_k : k = 1, ..., N\} \tag{4}$$

where the subscript "i" indicates the generation's number. An initial population P_0 is generated by randomly choosing N arrays in the search domain. Generally, these arrays are not points corresponding to local minima of the cost function; consequently, a local optimization procedure is applied to every vector x_k in order to obtain a point of minimum x_k. The algorithm core is composed by three operations, i.e., selection, reproduction and mutation, which are applied sequentially. These operations are the same with the genetic algorithm.

The main difference from the Genetic algorithm is the local optimization.

FUTURE SCOPE

Recently soft computing techniques are growing rapidly.So, we can use memetic algorithms in uncertainty based models such as fuzzy set, rough sets, soft sets(Molodtsov, 1999). Even though there exists clustering techniques (Tripathy& Ghosh, 2011), we can apply the memetic algorithms with the hybrid models of rough sets and soft sets (Tripathy & Arun, 2015; Sooraj, Mohanty, Tripathy, 2016; Tripathy, Sooraj, Mohanty, 2016).

CONCLUSION

Recently, evolutionary algorithms have been widely proposed for solving optimization problems. In this chapter we discussed some of the applications of memetic algorithms in computer science including clustering, graph coloring and image processing and how it can be helpful to solve optimization problems.

REFERENCES

Areibi, S., & Yang, Z. (2004). Effective Memetic Algorithms for VLSI Design Automation = Genetic Algorithms + Local Search + Multi- Level Clustering. *Evolutionary Computation, 12*(3), 327–353. doi:10.1162/1063656041774947 PMID:15355604

Baldi, P., & Hatfield, G. W. (2002). *DNA Microarrays and Gene Expression.* Cambridge Univ. Press.

Cauvery, N. K. (2011). Timetable scheduling using graph coloring. International Journal of P2P Network Trends and Technology, 1(2), 57-62.

Chen, C. W. K., & Yun, D. Y. Y. (1998). Unifying graph-matching problem with a practical solution. *Proceedings of International Conference on Systems, Signals, Control, Computers.*

Cutello, V., Nicosia, G., & Pavone, M. (2003). A hybrid immune algorithm with information gain for the graph coloring problem. *Proceedings of GECCO 2003*, 171-182.

EmreAydemir, M., Gunel, T., & Kumaz, S. (2003). A h'ovcl Approach for Synthetic Aperture Radar Image Processing Based On Genetic Algorithm. *Proceedings of RAST 2003 Conference.*

Foroutan, I., & Sklasky, J. (1987). Feature Selection for Automatic Classification of Non-Gaussian Data. *IEEE Transactions on Systems, Man, and Cybernetics, 17*(2), 187–198. doi:10.1109/TSMC.1987.4309029

Frigui, H., & Krishnapuram, R. (1999, May). A Robust Competitive Clustering Algorithm with Applications in Computer Vision. *IEEE Transactions on Pattern Analysis and Machine Intelligence, 21*(5), 450–465. doi:10.1109/34.765656

Gamst, A. (1986). Some lower bounds for class of frequency assignment problems. *IEEE Transactions on Vehicular Technology, 35*(1), 8–14. doi:10.1109/T-VT.1986.24063

Goldberg, D. E. (1989). Genetic Algorithms in Search, Optimization, and Machine Learning. Addison-Wesley.

Goldberg, D. E., & Richardson, J. (1987). Genetic Algorithms with Sharing for Multimodal Function Optimization. *Proceedings of Second Int'l Conf. Genetic Algorithms (ICGA '87)*, 41-49.

Gwee, B. H., Lim, M. H. & Ho, J. S. (1993). Solving four-colouring map problem using genetic algorithm. *Proceedings of Artificial Neural Networks and Expert Systems*.

Hale, W. K. (1980). Frequency assignment: Theory and applications. *Proceedings of the IEEE, 12*(12), 1497–1514. doi:10.1109/PROC.1980.11899

Hindi, M. M., & Yampolskiy, R. V. (2012). Genetic algorithm applied to the graph coloring problem. *Proceedings of 23rd Midwest Artificial Intelligence and Cognitive Science Conf.*, 61-66.

Holland, J. H. (1975). *Adaptation in Natural and Artificial Systems*. Ann Arbor, MI: Univ. of Michigan.

Jain, A. K., & Dubes, R. C. (1988). Algorithms for Clustering Data. Prentice Hall.

Jain, A. K., & Flynn, P. (1996). *Image Segmentation Using Clustering*. Advances in Image Understanding.

Kubale, M. (2004). Graph colorings. American Mathematical Society.

Lim, A., Zhu, Y., Lou, Q., & Rodrigues, B. (2005). Heuristic methods for graph coloring problems. *Proceedings of Symposium on Applied Computing*.

MacQueen, J. (1967). Some Methods for Classification and Analysis of Multivariate Observations. *Proceedings of Fifth Berkeley Symp. Math. Statistics and Probability*, 281-297.

Merz, P., & Freisleben, B. (1998). *Memetic Algorithms and the Fitness Landscape of the Graph Bi-partitioning Problem*. LNCS. doi:10.1007/BFb0056918

Ray, B., Pal, A. J., Bhattacharyya, D., & Kim, T. (2010). An efficient GA with multipoint guided mutation for graph coloring problems. *International Journal of Signal Processing, Image Processing and Pattern Recognition, 3*(2), 51–58.

Sareni, B., & Krahenbuhl, L. (1998). Fitness Sharing and Niching Methods Revisited. *IEEE Transactions on Evolutionary Computation, 2*(3), 97–106. doi:10.1109/4235.735432

Sheng, W., Tucker, A., & Liu, X. (2004). Clustering with Niching Genetic K-Means Algorithm. *Proceedings of Genetic and Evolutionary Computation Conf. (GECCO '04)*, 162-173. doi:10.1007/978-3-540-24855-2_15

Shi, J., & Malik, J. (2000). Normalized Cuts and Image Segmentation. *IEEE Transactions on Pattern Analysis and Machine Intelligence, 22*(8), 888–905. doi:10.1109/34.868688

Tavazoie, S., Hughes, D., Campbell, M. J., Cho, R. J., & Church, G. M. (1999). Systematic Determination of Genetic Network Architecture. *Nature Genetics, 22*(3), 281–285. doi:10.1038/10343 PMID:10391217

Whitley, D. (1995). Modeling Hybrid Genetic Algorithms. In G. Winter, J. Periaux, M. Galan, & P. Cuesta (Eds.), *Genetic Algorithms in Eng. and Computer Science* (pp. 191–201). John Wiley.

Wu, S., Liew, A. W. C., Yan, H., & Yang, M. (2004). Cluster Analysis of Gene Expression Database on Self-Splitting and Merging Competitive Learning. *IEEE Transactions on Information Technology in Biomedicine, 8*(1).

Chowdhury, H. A. R., Farhat, T., & Khan, H. A. (2013). Memetic Algorithm to solve Graph Coloring Problem. *International Journal of Computer Theory and Engineering, 5*(6).

Molodtsov, D. (1999). Soft set theory - First results. *Computers & Mathematics with Applications (Oxford, England), 37*(4-5), 19–31. doi:10.1016/S0898-1221(99)00056-5

Sooraj, T. R., Mohanty, R. K., & Tripathy, B. K. (2016). Fuzzy soft set theory and its application in group decision making. *Advances in Intelligent Systems and Computing, 452*, 171–178. doi:10.1007/978-981-10-1023-1_17

Tripathy, B. K., & Arun, K. R. (2015). A new approach to soft sets, soft multisets and their properties. *International Journal of Reasoning-based Intelligent Systems, 7*(3-4), 244–253. doi:10.1504/IJRIS.2015.072951

Tripathy, B. K., & Ghosh, A. (2011). SDR: An algorithm for clustering categorical data using rough set theory. *IEEE Recent Advances in Intelligent Computational Systems, RAICS 2011*, 867-872.

Tripathy, B. K., Sooraj, T. R., & Mohanty, R. K. (2016). A new approach to fuzzy soft set theory and its application in decision making. *Advances in Intelligent Systems and Computing, 411*, 305–313. doi:10.1007/978-81-322-2731-1_28

KEY TERMS AND DEFINITIONS

GCP: Graph coloring problem is to assign colors to certain elements of a graph subject to certain constraints.

Memetic Algorithm: A memetic algorithm is an extension of the traditional genetic algorithm. It uses a local search technique to reduce the likelihood of the premature convergence.

Meta Heuristic Algorithm: In computer science and mathematical optimization, a metaheuristic is a higher-level procedure or heuristic designed to find, generate, or select a heuristic (partial search algorithm) that may provide a sufficiently good solution to an optimization problem, especially with incomplete or imperfect information or limited computation capacity.

SAR Image: Synthetic aperture radar (SAR) is a form of radar that is used to create images of objects, such as landscapes – these images can be either two or three dimensional representations of the object.

Chapter 5
A New Data Hiding Scheme Combining Genetic Algorithm and Artificial Neural Network

Ayan Chatterjee
Sarboday Public Academy, India

Nikhilesh Barik
Kazi Nazrul University, India

ABSTRACT

Today, in the time of internet based communication, steganography is an important approach. In this approach, secret information is embedded in a cover medium with minimum distortion of it. Here, a video steganography scheme is developed in frequency domain category. Frequency domain is more effective than spatial domain due to variation data insertion domain. To change actual domain of entropy pixels of the video frames, uniform crossover of Genetic Algorithm (GA) is used. Then for data insertion in video frames, single layer perceptron of Artificial Neural Network is used. This particular concept of information security is attractive due to its high security during wireless communication. The effectiveness of the proposed technique is analyzed with the parameters PSNR (Peak Signal to Noise Ratio), IF and Payload (bpb).

INTRODUCTION

Steganography is the art of hiding secret data or secret information at the time of wireless communication (2013). In this special approach, the existence of communication among sender and intended receiver(s) can be hidden from unintentional receiver(s) or hacker(s). In the particular system of methodology, the secret information is embedded in a cover medium, such as- image, audio, video etc. and the embedded file is transferred through communication channel. In Image steganography, image pixels are used for inserting secret data (2014). In video steganography, video frames are used to embed the data. Each video frame is treated as an image. The fact is that video files are safer than image files, because- video files take a large no. of image pixels over image files. So, obviously, insertion of data in video files

DOI: 10.4018/978-1-5225-2857-9.ch005

consists of less distortion over image files. There are two major categories of steganography- spatial domain and frequency domain. In spatial domain steganography, the secret data is inserted directly in the image domain.

In frequency domain steganography, the actual domain of cover medium is converted to another medium using some mathematical transformation. This transformed domain is used for inserting secret data. Comparing these two different categories, it is observed that the distortion between actual cover medium and stego medium is generally less in spatial domain steganography over frequency domain steganography. In other words, peak signal to noise ratio (PSNR) and MSE (Mean Squared Error) generally give better result in spatial domain. But it can be easily hacked by unintended receiver(s) using pseudo random number generator (PRNG). Frequency domain steganography is better than spatial domain with respect to PRNG and other statistical attacks. Different mathematical transformations, such as- Discrete Cosine Transformation (DCT), Discrete Wavelet Transformation (DWT), Discrete Fourier Transformation (DFT), Fast Fourier Transformation (FFT) etc are used to transform the actual domain of cover medium. Also, in data compression, different stochastic optimization schemes are used. Among them, Genetic Algorithm (GA), Fuzzy logic etc are very important. Genetic Algorithm (GA) is basically a soft computing based optimization approach. But, the hereditary properties of animal, the concepts of which are used in this particular approach, are very much effective in various fields rather than optimization. Among them, image processing, information security, artificial intelligence etc. are very much important. Basically, GA is developed with three different properties- selection of chromosomes, crossover and mutation. According to the variation of these three operations, various types of GA are developed. GA is generally very much effective for NP hard problems. Another important tool in soft computing is Artificial Neural Network (ANN). In engineering field, this is a sequence of patterns like neurons of human being. In generally, at the time of implementation of all soft computing based approaches, given information and corresponding ingredients are taken as input. Target or goal is obtained Output in all the approaches. The speciality of the approach ANN is that the source pattern and target are taken as input and corresponding ingredients are obtained as output. This speciality makes ANN more effective than other schemes. Depending on variation of source pattern and target, different ANN schemes are developed. Among them, single layer perceptron, multi layer perceptron etc. are very much important. In this paper, a particular approach of frequency domain steganography is developed by using crossover operator of GA and single layer perceptron of ANN. In the next section, some related works are discussed. Then the proposed data hiding scheme is illustrated followed by the algorithm. After that the efficiency of the scheme is analyzed with different type experiments. At last, conclusion of the scheme is given followed by future direction of the work.

BACKGROUND

In this section, some data hiding schemes with cover medium video and tools GA and/or ANN are discussed. In the scheme Optimized Video Steganography using GA (2013), weighted sum approach of multi objective GA is used to make optimizer at the time of encoding. According to the architecture of that scheme is that at first cover video is divided into frames and audio using splitter. After that, in the carrier frame(s), secret data is embedded and stego frame is made. Then an optimizer is developed for steganalysis purpose. In other words, if it is observed that the stego video passes through anti-steganalysis test, then these frames are taken as final stego frames. At the time of using optimizer, two objective functions are considered. These are Mean squared error (MSE) and Human vision system deviation (HVS). Using weighted sum approach, formed single objective function is,

$$f = w_1 \times MSE + w_2 \times HVS \tag{1}$$

Here, the values of w_1 and w_2 are taken 0.8 and 0.2 respectively. RGB pixel values after inserting data in the frames are taken as chromosomes. Then simple mutation with mutation probability 0.05 and single point crossover are performed sequentially. In another scheme, GA based steganography using DCT, at first the actual domain is converted to another domain using Discrete Cosine Transformation (DCT). After that, secret message is embedded in 2nd and 3rd lower frequency component position. At the time of Te- transformation, combined DCT and GA are used. In the scheme LSB based steganography using GA and visual cryptography, genetic algorithm is used for changing pixel position of stego image. In the output of GA, the algorithm of visual cryptography is used. In this particular proposed scheme, only uniform crossover operator of genetic algorithm is used to transform the actual domain and after that using single layer perceptron of Artificial Neural Network (ANN) to make cipher corresponding to the original information and then the cipher is inserted through LSB substitution of the changed domain. The proposed scheme with sender and receiver sides algorithms are illustrated in the next section.

DATA HIDING SCHEME

In this section, proposed data hiding scheme is discussed followed by the algorithms of sender and receiver side separately. This is a frequency domain steganography approach. So, domain transformation of cover medium is required at first. According to the proposed scheme, the basic architectures of sender and receiver side procedures are shown in Figure 1 and Figure 2 respectively.

According to the diagram of the procedure of embedding data, it is observed that at first domain of cover video is transformed to another domain using Genetic Algorithm with secret keys. After that, in that domain, the secret information is embedded by using a particular concept of Artificial Neural

Figure 1. Diagram of data embedding procedure of the proposed scheme (sender side)

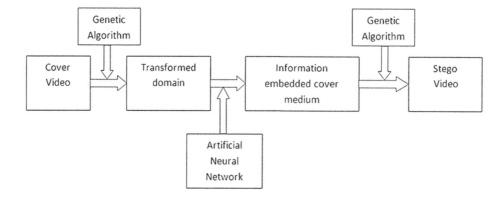

Figure 2. Diagram of data extraction procedure of the proposed scheme (receiver side)

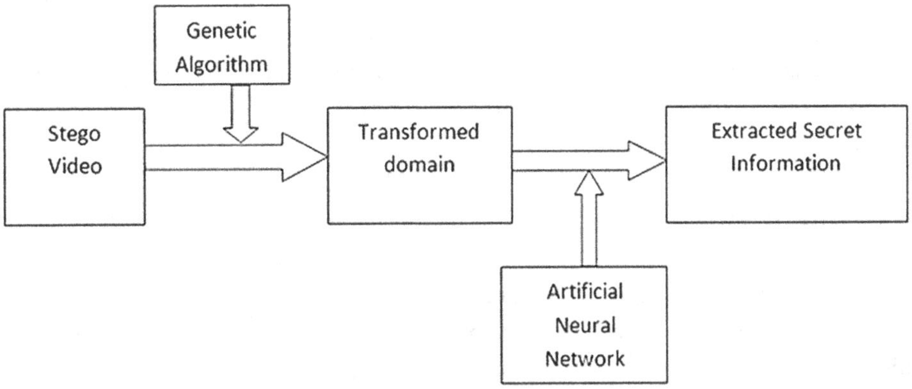

Network (ANN). Then, using the same idea of GA, inverse transformation is applied to form the stego video. In similar way, at the receiver end, the stego video is transformed to the other domain by using GA with the secret keys, which were used in sender side previously. Next, Neural Network is applied to extract the data from stego video. So, description of total scheme is divided into five parts. Among them, first three parts are the responsibilities of the sender and remaining two parts are of the receiver. So, the parts of sender side procedure are transformation of domain of actual cover video, insertion of secret information in the transformed domain and inverse transformation after insertion of secret information in the cover video. The parts of receiver side process are transformation of domain of stego video and extraction of secret information.

Transformation of Domain of Actual Cover Video

At first, a cover video is divided into video frames and audio separately. Then each video frame is divided into 8×8 entropy pixel blocks. After that, uniform crossover operator of Genetic Algorithm is applied to each block. Actually, the pixels are chosen pair wise sequentially and uniform crossover is applied between them with predefined secret key positions. The key positions are same in all the pixel blocks. The idea of uniform crossover is applied to all the blocks as well as to all the video frames. As a result, a new transformed domain is formed over the actual cover video frames and the domain is used to insert the secret message.

Insertion of Secret Information

After performing the transformation phase, the secret message is divided into 8 bits segment form. In other words, each transformed video frame is used to insert 8 bits secret data. A particular 8×8 block of a frame is taken as a secret key block and that is predefined among sender and receiver before communication. Suppose the 8 bits size message segment is $a_1 a_2 .... a_8$. Here, a single layer perceptron problem of Artificial Neural Network (ANN) is formulated as:

$$\{X_i^T = [i - th \text{ row of the key matrix block}], \text{ the value of } a_i\}; \; i = 1, 2, .., 8 \tag{2}$$

After forming the particular problem, corresponding weight matrix and bias are evaluated. Here are 8 input patterns and therefore the order of weight matrix is 8×1. So, 8 values of weight matrix and bias are inserted into 9 blocks of that particular frame sequentially (except the secret key block) by LSB substitution in the transformed domain. In similar way, the next 8 bits of the message are inserted to the second transformed video frame and so on. In this way, full message is embedded in the transformed domain of the video frames of a particular cover video.

Formation of Stego Video

After insertion of secret message in the transformed domain of video frames, uniform crossover is applied to the blocks and the chromosomes for crossover are selected pair wise and sequentially with secret key positions, which were used at the time of transformation of actual cover video. After the crossover operation, video frames are concatenated. At last, stego video is built up by merging video frames and audio.

The stego video is sent to the receiver through communication channel. After receiving the stego video at the receiver side, the video is divided into video frames and audio. To extract information from the stego video frames, next two steps are performed by the receiver.

Transformation of Domain of Stego Video Frames

At the receiver end, the stego video is partitionized into 8×8 blocks. Uniform crossover operator is applied to the blocks individually by taking the values pair wise and sequentially. To apply uniform crossover, secret key positions are required and these are predefined among sender and receiver before communication. This transformation is applied to all the video frames and the transformed domain is used to extract secret information.

Extraction of Secret Information

Secret matrix block is chosen from first video frame initially. Then, 8 values of weight matrix and bias are extracted from 9 sequential blocks of the frame. Therefore, the weight matrix $[w_{ij}]_{8\times1}$ and bias (b) are obtained. From the secret block, 8 input patterns are obtained as,

$$X_i^T = [i-th \text{ row of the key matrix block}], \quad i = 1, 2, .., 8 \tag{3}$$

Each bit of the message is evaluated as,

$$m_i = \phi(X_i^T w + b); \quad i = 1, 2, .., 8 \tag{4}$$

and

$$\phi(x) = 1, \text{ if } x \geq 0 \text{ and } \phi(x) = 0, \text{ if } x \prec 0 \tag{5}$$

here m_i is the $i-th$ bit of 8 bit segment of the message.

In this way, first 8 bits of the message is obtained from the first video frame. Similarly, second 8 bits of the message are obtained from the second frame and the process is continued until full message is extracted at the receiver side.

Procedure

Sender Side

- **Input:** A cover video, secret message
- **Output:** Stego Video
- **Secret Keys:** Secret key positions for crossover, secret key block of the video frames

Algorithm

Step 1: Divide the video into audio and video frames
Step 2: Each video frame is divided into 8×8 entropy pixel blocks
Step 3: Apply uniform crossover pair wise sequentially in each block with key position values to all video frames
Step 4: Divide the full secret message into 8 bits segments sequentially
Step 5: Select the first video frame
Step 6: Take the secret key block of the frame and formulate a problem with 8 bit segmented message in the format of single layer perceptron as equation (1)
Step 7: Find accurate weight matrix (w) and bias (b) using the algorithm of single layer perceptron by maintaining the step function (4)
Step 8: Insert 8 values of weight matrix and bias in the blocks sequentially starting from first block (except the secret key block) by LSB substitution
Step 9: Take the next video frame and next 8 bits segment of the message and go to step 6 until insertion of full message, Otherwise go to step 10
Step 10: Perform the operation same as step 3
Step 11: Combine the frames and audio, as a result stego video is formed

Receiver Side

- **Input:** Stego video
- **Output:** Secret message
- **Secret Keys:** Secret key positions for crossover, secret key block of the video frames

Algorithm

Step 1: Divide the video into audio and video frames
Step 2: Each video frame is divided into 8×8 entropy pixel blocks

Step 3: Apply uniform crossover pair wise sequentially in each block with key position values to all video frames

Step 4: Select the first video frame

Step 5: Take the secret key block of the frame and formulate 8 input patterns using the format (2)

Step 6: Take the 8 values of the weight matrix and bias from the blocks of the frame sequentially

Step 7: Form the weight matrix using these 8 values in 8×1 format

Step 8: Evaluate 8 bit message segment using the formats (3) and (4) respectively

Step 9: Select the next video frame and go to step 5 until obtaining the full message, otherwise go to step 10

Step 10: Combine all the message bits sequentially and obtain the full secret message

EXPERIMENTS AND RESULTS

In this section, efficiency and effectiveness of the proposed data hiding scheme is analyzed through different parameters. Among them, Peak Signal to Noise Ratio (PSNR), Mean Squared error (MSE), Image Fidelity (IF) and Payload (bpB) are important parameter related to this purpose. The working formulae of PSNR and MSE are

$$MSE = \frac{1}{mn} \sum_{i=0}^{m-1} \sum_{j=0}^{n-1} \left\| I(i,j) - K(i,j) \right\|^2 \tag{6}$$

$$PSNR = 20 \log_{10}(\frac{MAX_i}{\sqrt{MSE}}) \tag{7}$$

Here, MAX_i is maximum pixel value of original cover frame and $MAX_i = 2^b - 1$, b is the bit depth of cover frame. In other words, it is observed that MSE is the distortion among cover video frame (I) and stego frame (K). PSNR is anti proportionally related with MSE. Therefore, high PSNR and low MSE represent the efficiency of a data hiding scheme. So, in comparison with the scheme optimized video steganography using GA, the parameters PSNR, IF and payload (bpB) are considered. Here, a small secret message of 800 bits is taken and using the data hiding scheme, this is embedded into 3 different video files and obtained PSNR, IF and payload (bpB) are given in table. The detail structures of the videos and comparative results with other two popular video steganography schemes are also represented in Table 1.

According to the experimental table, it is observed that the proposed data hiding scheme is something better than the previous schemes. Also, it is safe from different statistical attacks, such as- Chi square attack, histogram attack etc for its dynamisms.

Table 1. Comparison of PSNR, IF and Payload tested in various video files using different data hiding schemes

Video files	No. of frames	Results using GA as optimizer over base method			Results using base video steganography 3-3-2 LSB			Results using proposed method		
		PSNR	IF	Payload (bpB)	PSNR	IF	Payload (bpB)	PSNR	IF	Payload (bpB)
Tree.avi	450	39.374	0.99	2.66	38.03	0.87	2.66	37.64	0.83	2.66
Globe.avi	107	34.372	0.99	2.66	32.67	0.89	2.66	32.61	0.87	2.66
Computer.avi	510	41.613	0.99	2.66	39.21	0.86	2.66	38.32	0.85	2.66

FUTURE TRENDS

In this paper, the data hiding scheme is developed only for videos as cover medium. But, in steganography, various cover mediums, such as- audio, image files can be used for hiding data. So, In future, this method can be implemented in different mediums also. Also, to implement this method in the video files, it is observed that a large video, i.e. a video with large number of frames is required for inserting a particular secret message. This problem also can be tried to remove in future.

CONCLUSION

In this paper, an approach of video steganography is built up during communication through wireless network by assortment of Genetic Algorithm (GA) and Artificial Neural Network (ANN). The idea of uniform crossover operator of GA is used to transform the actual entropy pixel values to different domain. In other words, it is used to transform the actual domain. After that, single layer perceptron of Artificial Neural Network is used to develop a ciphertext corresponding to the secret message by using a particular block of a frame of a video file. The particular approach is striking for selecting the secret key pixel block and becomes very much secured from various steganography attacks. Also, the scheme gives better PSNR, IF and Payload over some popular previous data hiding approaches maintaining basic conditions of information security, i.e. confidentiality, integrity and availability of secret important data among authorized users.

REFERENCES

Chakrapani, G., & Lokeswara Reddy, V. (2014). Optimized Videotapr Steganography Using Genetic Algorithm (GA). *IJCS*, *15*, 1–6.

Dasgupta, K., Mondal, J. K., & Dutta, P. (2013). *Optimized Video Steganography using Genetic Algorithm (GA)*. Paper presented in International Conference on Computational Intelligence: Modeling, Techniques and Applications (CIMTA) 2013, Department of Computer Science & Engineering, University of Kalyani, West Bengal, India.

Deb, K., Pratap, A., Agarwal, S., & Meyarivan, T. (2002). A Fast and Elitist Multiobjective Genetic Algorithm. *IEEE Transaction Evolutionary Computation, 6*(2), 182–197. doi:10.1109/4235.996017

Dutt, D., & Hedge, V. (2015). AAKRITI[ed]: An Image and Data Encryption-Decryption Tool. *International Journal of Computer Science and Information Technology Research, 2*(2), 264-268.

Gokul, M., & Umeshbabu, R. (2012). Hybrid Steganography using Visual Cryptography and LSB Encryption Method. *International Journal of Computer Applications, 59*(14), 5-8.

Jain, R., & Kumar, N. (2012). Efficient data hiding scheme using lossless data compression and image steganography. *International Journal of Engineering Science and Technology, 4*(8), 3908-3915.

Khamrui, A., & Mandal, J. K. (2013). A Genetic Algorithm based Steganography using Discrete Cosine Transformation (GASDCT). *International Conference on Computational Intelligence: Modeling Techniques and Applications (CIMTA).* doi:10.1016/j.protcy.2013.12.342

Lin, Y.-K. (2014). A data hiding scheme based upon DCT coefficient modification. *Computer Standards & Interfaces, 36*(5), 855–862. doi:10.1016/j.csi.2013.12.013

Mishra, A., & Johri, P. (2015). A Review on Video Steganography using GA. *International Journal of Innovative & Advancement in Computer Science, 4*(SI), 120-124.

Nehru, G., & Dhar, P. (2012). A Detailed look of Audio Steganography Techniques using LSB and Genetic Algorithm Approach. *International Journal of Computer Science Issues, 9*(1), 402-406.

Roy, S., & Venkateswaran, P. (2014). Online Payment System using Steganography and Visual Cryptography. *IEEE Students' Conference on Electrical, Electronics and Computer Science.*

Singla, D., & Syal, R. (2012). Data Security Using LSB & DCT Steganography In Images. *International Journal of Computational Engineering Research, 2*(2), 359-364.

Soleimanpour, M., Tabeli, S., & Azadi-Motlag, H. (2013). A Novel Technique for Steganography Method Based on Improved Genetic Algorithm Optimization in Spatial Domain. *Iranian Journal of Electrical & Electronics Engineering, 9*(2), 67–74.

Zamani, M., Manaf, A. A., Ahmed, R. B., Zeki, A. M., & Abdullah, S. (2009). A Genetic Algorithm Based Approach for Audio Steganography, International Journal of Computer, Electrical, Automation. *Control and Information Engineering, 3*(6), 1562–1565.

KEY TERMS AND DEFINITIONS

Artificial Neural Network (ANN): An important tool to set up linkage between provided input and required output and it is developed on the basis of the set up of communicating nervous system of human being.

Genetic Algorithm: A special algorithmic optimization procedure, developed on the basis of simple hereditary property of animals and used for both of constrained and unconstrained problem. In Artificial Intelligence (AI), it is used as heuristic search also.

Peak Signal to Noise Ratio (PSNR): An expression is used to realize the distortion of quality of a cover medium at the presence of noise during wireless communication.

Steganalysis: Security analysis system at the time of sending data through wireless communication by the schemes of steganography.

Video Steganography: Process of authenticated communication by hiding secret information from unauthorized user(s) through a video file as cover medium.

Wireless Communication: Communication process with independent of wire among a finite set of users, who are in a long distance.

Chapter 6

A Statistical Scrutiny of Three Prominent Machine-Learning Techniques to Forecast Machining Performance Parameters of Inconel 690

Binayak Sen
NIT Agartala, India

Uttam Kumar Mandal
NIT Agartala, India

Sankar Prasad Mondal
Midnapore College (Autonomous), India

ABSTRACT

Computational approaches like "Black box" predictive modeling approaches are extensively used technique applied in machine learning operations of today. Considering the latest trends, present study compares capabilities of two different "Black box" predictive model like ANFIS and ANN with a population-based evolutionary algorithm GEP for forecasting machining parameters of Inconel 690 material, machined in a CNC-assisted 3-axis milling machine. The aims of this article are to represent considerable data showing, every techniques performance under the criteria of root mean square error (RSME), Correlational coefficient R and Mean absolute percentage error (MAPE). In this chapter, we vigorously demonstrate that the performance of the GEP model is far superior to ANFIS and ANN model.

DOI: 10.4018/978-1-5225-2857-9.ch006

1. INTRODUCTION

Amongst the various technological advancement adopted in defining premeditated pathways to meet up the cutting force-surface roughness-cutting temperature trade off in a milling machine, CNC systems with its unique capability to concurrently provide a significantly abridged cutting force-surface roughness-cutting temperature footprint as compared to a conventional milling machine. A greater dedication of CNC machine manufacturer to appreciably reduced cutting force, surface roughness and cutting temperature dilemma has greatly augmented.

Inconel alloys are the most extensively used super alloys especially used in aerospace industries. Due to its incredible strength and hardness, it posses very dumpy machinability. Therefore, machinability of Inconel materials has turn out to be a very decisive subject for exploration. Considering machinability of Inconel some noteworthy studies were found in the precedent literature. But the gigantic majority of the accessible literature focuses on Inconel 718 (Obikawa et al 2008; Ezugwu et al 2005; Dudzinski et al 2004; Coelho et al 204; Narutaki 1993).

On the other hand, Predictive models are advantageous, as they curtail the need for experiments, which are typically costly and time-consuming. Machine learning techniques offer a feasible solution where the pertinent machine behavior is emulated by appropriate plant model embodying the underlying physics of the problem.

Even though a significant number of Artificial Intelligence based predictive methods have been projected previously by different authors for modeling machining performance parameters, but ANN strategies have been extensively subjugated in the field of simulations of machining performance parameters. But still, now modeling of machining parameters is one of the prime fascinating topics in engineering research. Therefore, it is desirable to build up some new predictive models of machining parameters.

Hence, the current chapter endeavors to launch three predictive models of machining parameters of Inconel 690 alloy based on four draw frame variables, namely, speed, feed, depth of cut and width of cut. To explore the reliability of the developed models, they have been comprehensively compared with themselves to address the identical objectives as in the present study.

2. THE MOTIVATION OF THE PRESENT STUDY

Due to the wide usage of heat resistive alloys, the machining of Inconel materials has turn out to be a very crucial subject for investigation in the arena of manufacturing. In this chapter, a tentative inquiry was carried out to recognize the machinability behavior of Inconel 690. Generally, Inconel alloys are portrayed by excellent oxidation, high strength, creep resistance at elevated temperature. These properties are accountable for low machinability, high tool wear, high cutting temperature, and high cutting force. Thus, it is very demanding to machined Inconel alloys in the industrial ambiances. However, computational systems with its unique capability to concurrently get across an appreciably reduced surface roughness, resultant cutting force and cutting temperature footmark as paralleled to conventional milling have been correctly considered to be an imperative technical revolution to grace the milling machines of today.

Numerous alternatives crop up as a solution to these machinability problems; the use of novel tool materials with special cutting geometry, new lubrication strategies and use of refrigerant fluids. In fact, to advance the process efficiency, latest tool materials such as coated carbide tools, coated CBN, PCBN and whisker reinforced ceramics cutting tool are regularly used as cutting tools for machining of Inconel

718 (Li 2006, Muammer et al 2007; Costes, 2007).Where the usage of superior pressure Jet-assisted cooling technology during the machining of heat resistive super-alloys, delivers temperature diminution at the cutting zone (Colak 2012)..Nitrogen has also being worn as a coolant in the milling of diverse heat resistive alloys.

"Black box" predictive approach like ANN does have a confirmed reputation of sensation for certain specific problem fields. But the neural network is still viewed by many of investigators as being magical hammers which can explain any machine learning problems and consequently, tend to apply it indiscriminately to problems for which they are not appropriate.

In this article the machining parameters of Inconel 690 super alloy have been sculpted by three prominent machine learning techniques (GEP, ANFIS and ANN) where speed, feed, depth of cut and width of cut were chosen as input parameters and this article also enthusiastically demonstrate that the enactment of the GEP model is far superior to ANFIS and ANN model.

3. EXPERIMENTAL ENDEAVOR

The dry milling experiments were executed on a three axis milling machine with uncoated cemented carbide cutting tool. Every specimen of Inconel 690 exploited for experiment having a dimension of 60 mm*40 mm. The workpieces were mounted on a dynamometer to compute the applied cutting forces and 3D profilometer with 20*magnification is employed for surface roughness measurement. For cutting temperature measurement, a specially developed LESAR gun was used. Machining was accomplished with constant cutting speed, feed, depth of cut, width of cut and design of experiment was scheduled with the help of RSM as detailed in Table 1

4. THE ARCHITECTURE OF THE GEP

GEP was invented by Ferreira in 1999.GEP is the natural development of the genetic algorithm and genetic programming. It is a genotype-phenotype algorithm, where expression trees are an expression of the genome (Ferreira, 2006).

GEP embraces of five important factors: - i) function set ii) terminal set iii) fitness function iv) control parameters and v) stop condition which necessitates to be pre-set when using GEP to resolve a problem (Fallahpour, 2013).The characters are programmed as linear strings of stationary size (genome) in GEP, which are communicated later as non-linear individuals with altered size and shapes; and are well-known as Expression Trees (Ferreria, 2002) as shown in Figure 1.

Table 1. Experimental level of the independent variables and coding

Factor/Level	-1	0	1
Cutting speed(m/min)	100	120	140
Feed(mm/tooth)	0.1	0.15	0.2
Depth of Cut(mm)	0.5	0.75	1.0
Width of cut(mm)	0.2	1.0	1.8

Figure 1. An example of GEP expression tree (ET)

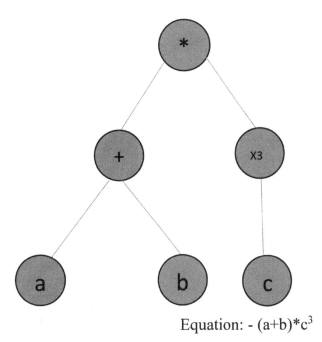

Equation: - $(a+b)*c^3$

This type of diagram representation is infect the phenotype of GEP chromosomes, being the genotype easily inferred from phenotype as follows (see Table 2).

Figure 2 illustrates the GEP algorithm. The genes of GEP have composed of a head and a tail. The head holds symbols that signify both functions and terminals, while the tail contains only terminals. For every problem, the length of the head h is chosen, where the length of the tail t is a function of h and the number of arguments n of the function with additional arguments (also called *maximum arity*) (Ferreira 2006) and is evaluated by the equation:

$$T= (a-1)*h + 1 \tag{1}$$

In the current study, basic arithmetic operators (+,-,*,/) and diverse mathematical functions (Pow, Sqrt, Exp, Ln, Log, 1/x, x2, x3, Cube root, Sin, Cos) were employed to develop the anticipated GEP model.

The recent study was assumed to accomplish an unambiguous relationship between response variables (cutting force, surface roughness and cutting temperature) with the verdict variables (speed, feed, depth of cut and width of cut).

Table 2.

0	1	2	3	4	5
*	+	X3	a	b	c

Figure 2. A generic flowchart of the GEP algorithm

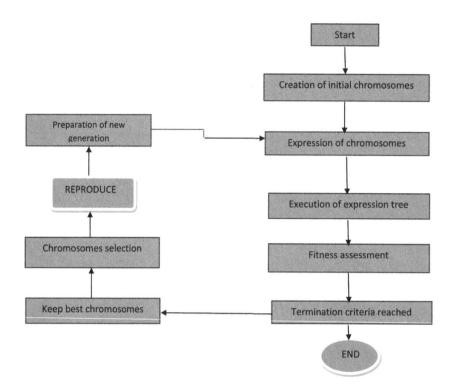

Table 3. Simulation Parameters of the GEP model

Mathematical functions	+, _, *,/, Pow, Sqrt, Exp, Ln(x), Log, Inv(1/x), x^2, x^3, Cube root(3Rt), Sin, Cos
Number of Chromosomes	30,60,90,120,150
Number of genes	2,3,4,5,6
Head size	5,10,15,20
Linking function	addition
Mutation rate	0.044
Inverse rate	0.1
One-point recombination rate	0.3
Two-point recombination rate	0.3
Gene recombination rate	0.1
Gene transportation rate	0.1

So, cutting force, surface roughness, cutting temperature = f (speed, feed, depth of cut and width of cut) (Figures 3-5), permitting a faster and more complete indulgent of the Boolean structure. The best categorical formula exhumed by the developed GEP models for cutting force, surface roughness and Cutting Temperature are denoted by the following Equations:

Figure 3. Expression Tree for the resultant cutting force

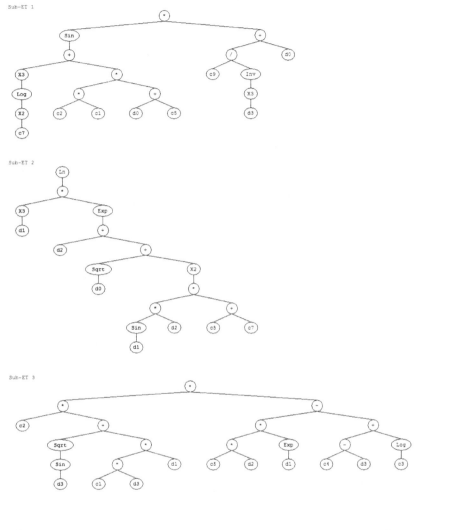

$$\text{Cutting force} = \left[\left(\sin\left(\left(\log\left(c_7^2 \right) \right)^3 \right) \right) + \left(\left(c_2 * c_1 \right) * \left(d_0 + c_5 \right) \right) * \left(\left(c_9 \middle/ \left(1 \middle/ \left(d_3 \right)^3 \right) \right) + d_0 \right) \right]$$

$$+ \left[d_1^3 * e^{\left[d2 + \left(\sqrt{d0} + \left(\left(\left(\text{sind1*d2} \right) * \left(\text{c5+c7} \right) \right)^2 \right) \right) \right]} \right]$$

$$+ \left[\left(\left(c_2 * \left(\left(\sqrt{\sin d_3} \right) + \left(\left(c_1 * d_3 \right) * d_1 \right) \right) \right) \right. \right.$$
$$\left. \left. * \left(\left(\left(c_5 * d_2 \right) * e^{d_1} \right) - \left(\left(c_4 - d_3 \right) + \log c_3 \right) \right) \right) \right]$$

$$(2)$$

Figure 4. Expression Tree for surface roughness

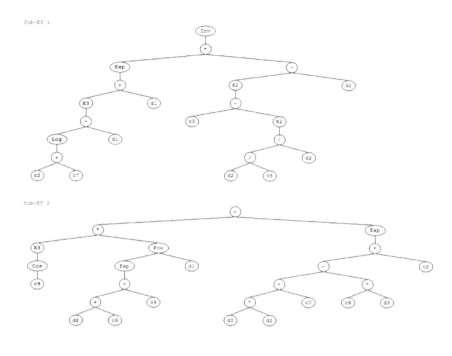

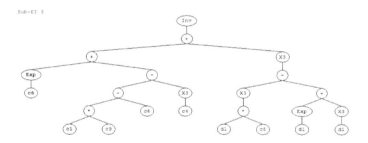

$$\text{Surface roughness} = \left[1 \middle/ \left[\left(\left(\log\left(c_2 + c_7\right)\right) + d_1\right) * \left[c_5 - \left(\left(\left(d_2/c_8\right)\middle/d_2\right)^2\right)\right]^2 - d_2\right)\right]\right]$$

$$+ \left[\left[\left(\left(\cos c_9\right)^3\right) * \left(e^{\left((\text{d2}+\text{c6})+\text{c4}\right)^{d_1}}\right)\right] + \left(\left(\left(d_0 * d_2\right) + c_0\right) - \left(c_6 * d_3\right) * c_2\right)\right] \quad (3)$$

$$+ \left[1 \middle/ \left(\left(e^{c_6}\right) + \left(\left(c_1 * c_9\right) - c_6\right) - c_4^3\right) + \left(\left(\left(d_1 * c_8\right)^3\right) - \left(e^{d_1} + d_1^3\right)\right)^3\right]$$

Figure 5. Expression Tree for cutting Temperature

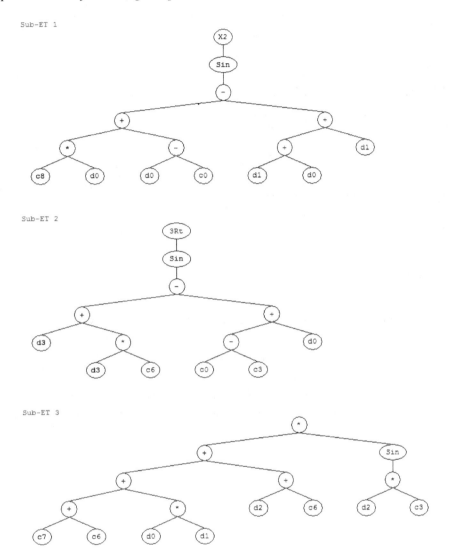

$$\text{Cutting Temperature} = \sin^2\left[\left(\left(c_8 * d_0\right) + \left(d_0 - c_0\right)\right) - \left(\left(d_1 + d_0\right) + d_1\right)\right]$$
$$+ \sin^{1/3}\left[\left(d_3 + \left(d_3 * c_6\right)\right) - \left(\left(c_0 - c_3\right) + d_0\right)\right] \qquad (3)$$
$$+ \left\{\left[\left(\left(c_7 + c_6\right) + \left(d_0 * d_1\right)\right) + \left(d_2 + c_6\right)\right] * \sin\left(d_2 * c_3\right)\right\}$$

where do, d_1, d_2 & d_3 represents speed, feed, Depth of cut and width of cut respectively.
Value of Numerical Constants used in Equations (see Table 4).

Table 4.

G1C9 = -7.50810083841908	G1C2 = -9.59287349070711	G1C1 = 1.6365114291818
G1C5 = -6.76848662678915	G1C7 = 10.0026682332835	G2C5 = 8.5270713214078
G2C7 = 43.155681428633	G3C2 = -9.14513813717945	G3C5 = -8.863424726410
G3C4 = 3.43767883791314	G3C3 = 7.01690394093858	G3C1 = 6.35482685773144
G1C8 = -8.41607768873252	G2C2 = -7.57874539774754e-02	G2C9 = 4.05846227111560
G2C4 = -9.27593421872162	G2C0 = -9.20636552018799	G2C6 = -11.078992171880
G3C6 = -10.1862525229127	G3C4 = -7.42146101138478	G3C1 = -1.5486392384700
G3C9 = 14.7804133573610	G3C8 = -9.25079288294473	
G1C8 = 6.04174633106174	G1C0 = -1.0696737571337	G2C6 = -4.78133487960448
G2C0 = 2.77016510513627	G2C3 = 6.36916684469131	G3C6 = -2.76254860072634
G3C3 = 0.533405295361187	G3C7 = 3.14605578783532	

5. THE ARCHITECTURE OF ANFIS

ANFIS is a fuzzy inference system implemented in the framework of adaptive networks. Using a hybrid learning procedure, the proposed ANFIS can build an input-output mapping derived from both human knowledge and predetermined input-output data pairs. The ANFIS architecture consists of five different layers. They are input layer, fuzzification layer, inferences process layer, defuzzification layer and a final output layer. Each layer performs a particular task to forward the signals. Such an ANFIS model is shown in Figure 7. It is a network structure consists of a number of nodes attached through direct links (Takagi 1985; Sugeno, 1988). Here Figure 6 illustrates the ANFIS algorithm.

Figure 6. A Flow chart for predicting machining performance parameters using ANFIS

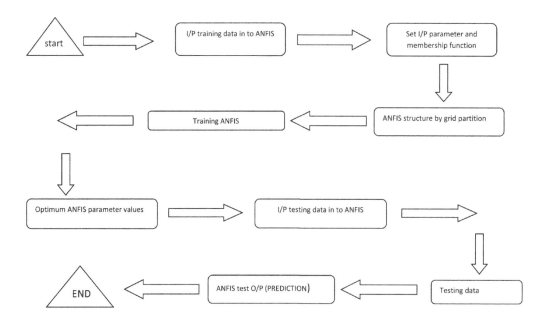

Figure 7. The architecture of ANFIS

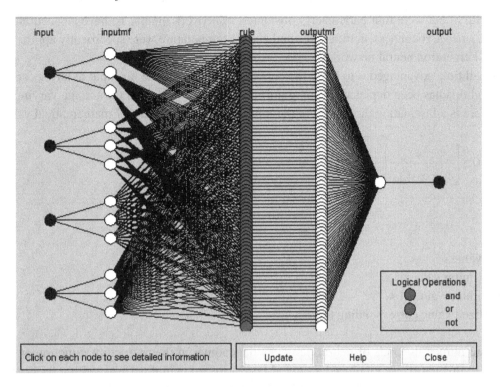

29 pairs of data are employed that 15 of them are employed for training and others for validation. All data are normalized and set in the range of [0,1]. For each input variable three membership functions have been taken, consequently, there are 3^4 numbers of rules for each ANFIS model. The output of AN-FIS is intended by employing subsequent parameters. The output error is cast-off to adjust the principle parameters by means of a standard back prop algorithm. In this process, three kinds of membership functions are tested as triangular, trapezoidal and bell, then number of input Membership Functions and direction of Sugeno fuzzy inference system are changed. But the comparison of three membership function designates that trapezoidal membership function accomplishes slightly superior predicting accuracy than others.

6. THE ARCHITECTURE OF THE ANN

ANN has been developed as simplifications of precise models of biological nervous systems. The fundamental processing constituents of neural networks are called artificial neurons. In a simplified model of the neuron, the effects of the synapses are symbolized by connecting weights which transform the effect of the associated input signals, and the nonlinear characteristic demonstrated by neurons is signified by a transfer function. The neuron impulse is then calculated as the weighted sum of the input signals, converted by the transfer function. The learning ability of an artificial neuron is accomplished by regulating the weights in accord to the preferred learning algorithm (Fausett, 1994; Mandie et al, 2001, McCulloch, 1943, Mandie and Chambers, 2001).

In this study, twenty-nine experimental datas are used for modeling. The speed, feed rate, depth of cut and width of cut were four parameters considered as network inputs. To have an accurate and reliable model, surface roughness, cutting force and cutting temperature were specifically approximated by means of a Perceptron neural network.

It is for all time advantageous to bring the data to a negotiable scale for input to any soft computing methods and this has been depicted by doing normalization using Eq. (5) for a range varying from 0.1 to 0.9 as there is a fascinating distinction in the input data range in terms of mathematical value,

$$y = 0.1 + 0.8 \left(\frac{x - x_{min}}{x_{max} - x_{min}} \right) \tag{5}$$

where,

x = actual value,
X_{max} = maximum value of x,
X_{min} = minimum value of x,
y = normalized value corresponding to x.

There are numerous kinds of neural networks depending on their structure, function and training algorithm. In this paper, we employed a typical Feed forward neural network with a back prop learning algorithm to train it. The performance of the training network was proved by determining the error between practical value and predicted value. All the topological and training setting parameters are revealed in Table 5 and 6.

7. PERFORMANCE ASSESSMENT OF THE PROJECTED MODELS

For evaluating the performance of the three predictive models the norms used in this article were, RSME, correlation coefficient and MAPEwhere,

$$RMSE = \sqrt{\frac{1}{n} \sum_{i=1}^{n} \left(E_i - P_i \right)^2} \tag{6}$$

Table 5. Topology settings

Parameter	Value
Number of input variables	04
Number of output variables	03
Number of hidden layers	02
Node of 1st hidden layer	10
Node of 2nd hidden layer	05

Table 6. Training settings

Parameter	Value
Learning rate	0.01
Momentum coefficient	0.1
Transfer function	Hyperbolic tangent
Max. of training cycle	100000
Target error	1E − 07
Analysis update interval(cycles)	1000

$$MAPE = \frac{1}{n} \sum_{i=1}^{n} \left(\frac{E_i - P_i}{E_i} \right) * 100 \qquad (7)$$

where; 'n' is the number of pattern in the data set, 'E' is the experimental output and 'P' is the predicted output value.

8. RESULT AND DISCUSSION

The three machine learning processes were cast off to predict cutting force, surface roughness and cutting temperature for Inconel 690. Mean absolute percentage error, correlation coefficient and root mean square errors are employed to estimate and compare the three predictive models. The comparisons of three predictive models for Inconel 690 are demonstrated in Table 5.

On close scrutiny of the Figures 8-10, it imitates the reliable and admirable concurrency of the all forecasted values with that of the real investigational observations for the integral series of operation.

Based on the obtained results, minimum and maximum RMSE and MAPE in the GEP model were 0.017290%, 0.694523% and 1.814442%, 4.235789% respectively. Therefore, it was obvious that the GEP function was able to closely follow the trend of actual data.

Figure 8. Comparison of GEP predicted data with experimental data

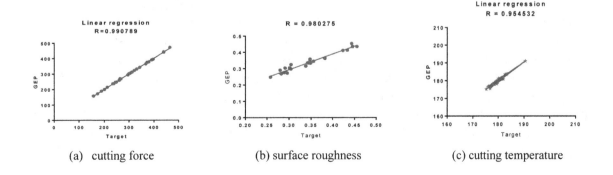

(a) cutting force   (b) surface roughness   (c) cutting temperature

Figure 9. Comparison of ANFIS predicted data with experimental data

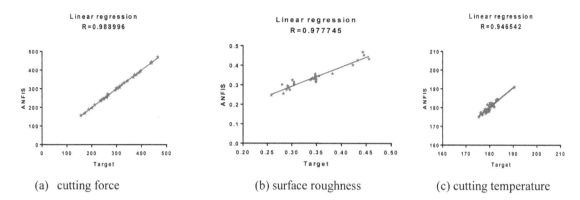

(a) cutting force   (b) surface roughness   (c) cutting temperature

Figure 10. Comparison of ANN predicted data with experimental data

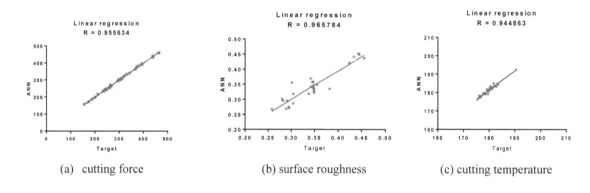

(a) cutting force   (b) surface roughness   (c) cutting temperature

As it is clear in Figure 11 (a), 11 (b), 11 (c) that there was a closer match between actual and predicted data. But GEP generations are superior to the other two strategies which confirmed the excellent capability of GEP model in predicting machining performance parameters of Inconel 690.

9. CONCLUSION

Three mathematical models between the cutting parameters of speed, feed, depth of cut and width of cut were produced by GEP, ANFIS and ANN for the purpose of predicting cutting force, surface roughness and cutting temperature for Inconel 690 material. The results of the developed models have been assessed on a statistical platform of RMSE, Corr. coff R and MAPE, in comparison to the investigational results. Actually, the concepts of RMSE, Corr. coff R and MAPE scores have been developed for qualitative judgment of the reliability and robustness of three forecasting mathematical models. The MAPE, Corr. coff R and RMSE scores were perceived by GEP, ANFIS and ANN model are in acceptable margins. But it was manifest from the performance evaluation, that the GEP predicted data synchronized the experimental data with high overall accuracy. This recommends the inherent sensitivity and robustness of the GEP model.

Table 7. Comparison between GEP, ANFIS and ANN for Inconel 690

Parameter	Model	RMSE (%)	Corr. Coefficient R	MAPE (%)
Cutting force(N)	GEP	0.017290	0.990789	1.814442
	ANFIS	0.044804	0.988996	4.684087
	ANN	0.049956	0.955634	4.875462
Surface roughness(μm)	GEP	0.445775	0.980275	1.979754
	ANFIS	0.455361	0.977745	3.879652
	ANN	0.564235	0.965784	4.587456
Cutting temperature(°C)	GEP	0.694523	0.954532	4.235789
	ANFIS	0.745632	0.946542	7.456275
	ANN	0.758641	0.944863	6.998547

Figure 11. Comparison of three machine learning process predicted cutting force with experimental data

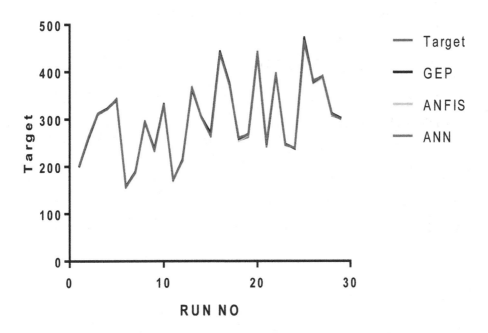

Figure 12. Comparison of three machine learning process predicted surface roughness with experimental data

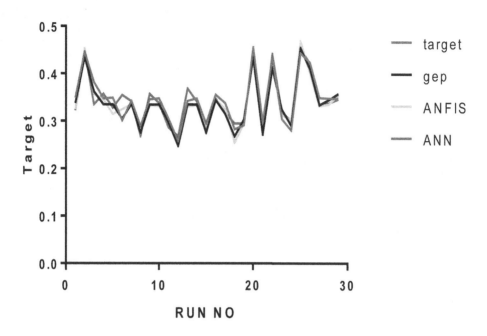

Figure 13. Comparison of three machine learning process predicted cutting temperature with experimental data

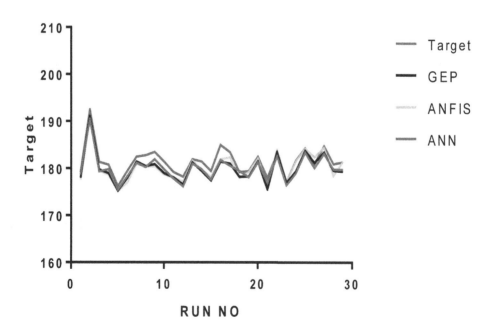

9.1. Future Scope

Future works can be done as follows: finding sensitivity and robustness of GA-ANFIS, GMDH, ARIMA and ARIMA-ANN model to predict machining performance parameters of Inconel 690 in 3-axis CNC milling machine. To Quantify Uncertainties in present study Monte Carlo Simulation can also be applied.

ACKNOWLEDGMENT

The authors would like to acknowledge HOD of Production Engineering Department, NIT Agartala and all the technical and non-technical staffs of Production Engineering Department, NIT Agartala, for their valuable assistance and guidance while performing the experimental work.

REFERENCES

Coelho, R. T., Silva, L. R., Braghini, A. Jr, & Bezerra, A. A. (2004). Some effects of cutting edge preparation and geometric modifications when turning Inconel 718 (TM) at high cutting speeds. *Journal of Materials Processing Technology*, *148*(1), 147–153. doi:10.1016/j.jmatprotec.2004.02.001

Çolak, O. (2012). Investigation on Machining Performance of Inconel 718 under High Pressure Cooling Conditions. *Journal of Mechanical Engineering*, *5811*(11), 683–690. doi:10.5545/sv-jme.2012.730

Costes, J., Guillet, Y., Poulachon, G., & Dessoly, M. (2007). Tool-life and wear mechanisms of CBN tools in machining of Inconel 718. *International Journal of Machine Tools & Manufacture*, *47*(7–8), 1081–1087. doi:10.1016/j.ijmachtools.2006.09.031

Dudzinski, D., Devillez, A., Moufki, A., Larrouquère, D., Zerrouki, V., & Vigneau, J. (2004). A review of developments towards dry and high speed machining of Inconel 718 alloy. *International Journal of Machine Tools & Manufacture*, *44*(4), 439–456. doi:10.1016/S0890-6955(03)00159-7

Ezugwu, E. O., Fadare, D. A., Bonney, J., Silva, R. B., & Sales, W. F. (2005). Modelling the correlation between cutting and process parameters in high-speed machining of Inconel 718 alloy using an artificial neural network. *International Journal of Machine Tools & Manufacture*, *45*(12-13), 1375–1385. doi:10.1016/j.ijmachtools.2005.02.004

Fallahpour, A. R., &Moghassem, A. R. (2013). Yarn Strength Modelling Using Adaptive Neuro-Fuzzy Inference System (ANFIS) and Gene Expression Programming (GEP). *Journal of Engineered Fibers and Fabrics, 8*(4).

Fausett, L. (1994). *Fundamentals of Neural Networks*. Prentice Hall.

Ferreira, C. (2001). Gene Expression Programming: A New Adaptive Algorithm for Solving Problems. *Complex Systems*, *13*(2), 87–129.

Ferreira, C. (2002). Gene Expression Programming: Mathematical Modeling by an Artificial Intelligence. Angra do Heroismo, Portugal

Ferreira, C. (2006). *Gene Expression Programming: Mathematical Modeling by an Artificial Intelligence* (2nd ed.). Springer-Verlag.

Li, H. Z., Zeng, H., & Chen, X. Q. (2006). An experimental study of tool wear and cutting force variation in the end milling of Inconel 718 with coated carbide inserts. *Journal of Materials Processing Technology, 180*(1-3), 296–304. doi:10.1016/j.jmatprotec.2006.07.009

Mandic, D., & Chambers, J. (2001). *Recurrent Neural Networks for Prediction: Learning Algorithms, Architectures and Stability*. New York: John Wiley & Sons. doi:10.1002/047084535X

Mandic, D., & Chambers, J. (2001). *Recurrent Neural Networks for Prediction: Learning Algorithms, Architectures and Stability*. New York: John Wiley & Sons. doi:10.1002/047084535X

McCulloch, W. S., & Pitts, W. H. (1943). A Logical Calculus of the Ideas Immanent in Nervous Activity. *The Bulletin of Mathematical Biophysics, 5*(4), 115–133. doi:10.1007/BF02478259

Muammer, N., Abdullah, A., & Hasan, G. (2007). The effect of cutting speed and cutting tool geometry on machinability properties of nickel-base Inconel 718 super alloys. *Materials & Design, 28*(4), 1334–1338. doi:10.1016/j.matdes.2005.12.008

Narutaki, N., Yamane, Y., Hayashi, K., Kitagawa, T., & Uehara, K. (1993). High speed machining of Inconel 718 with ceramic tools. *Annals of CIRP, 42*(1), 103–106. doi:10.1016/S0007-8506(07)62402-0

Obikawa, T., Kamata, Y., Asano, Y., Nakayama, K., & Otieno, A. W. (2008). Micro-liter lubrication machining of Inconel 718. *International Journal of Machine Tools & Manufacture, 48*(15), 1605–1612. doi:10.1016/j.ijmachtools.2008.07.011

Rogen Jang, J. S., & Sun, C. T. (1995). Nuero fuzzy modeling control. *Proc IEEE, 83*, 378-404.

Sugeno, M., & Kang, G. T. (1988). Structure identification of fuzzy model. *Fuzzy Sets Syst, 28*, 15-33.

Takagi, T., & Sugeno, M. (1985). Fuzzy identification of systems and its applications to modeling and control. *IEEE Trans Syst Man Cybernet, 15*(1), 116-132.

Chapter 7
Insights Into Simulated Annealing

Khalil Amine
Mohammed V University, Morocco

ABSTRACT

Simulated annealing is a probabilistic local search method for global combinatorial optimisation problems allowing gradual convergence to a near-optimal solution. It consists of a sequence of moves from a current solution to a better one according to certain transition rules while accepting occasionally some uphill solutions in order to guarantee diversity in the domain exploration and to avoid getting caught at local optima. The process is managed by a certain static or dynamic cooling schedule that controls the number of iterations. This meta-heuristic provides several advantages that include the ability of escaping local optima and the use of small amount of short-term memory. A wide range of applications and variants have hitherto emerged as a consequence of its adaptability to many combinatorial as well as continuous optimisation cases, and also its guaranteed asymptotic convergence to the global optimum.

INTRODUCTION

Combinatorial optimisation purpose is basically to find optimal, or at least best reached, solutions out of a finite set. When the set of solutions get larger, the combinatorial optimisation is faced to an exhaustive search which is rather memory and computing time consuming. Due to the failure of exact methods to provide optimal solutions within economical computing time and memory allocation, problem-independent (or generic) methods called meta-heuristics were introduced in the 1940s, around which a wide range of studies have been emerged on account of the ease of application and implementation for many optimisation problems, despite the solid mathematical foundations behind. Meta-heuristics includes three main categories, namely evolutionary optimisation that includes genetic algorithms; swam intelligence that includes stochastic diffusion search (Bishop, 1989), ant colony optimisation (Dorigo, 1992), and Particle swarm optimisation (Kennedy & Eberhart, 1995); and local search optimisation that includes hill climbing, tabu search (Glover, 1986), and simulated annealing (Kirkpatrick, Gelatt, & Vecchi, 1983).

DOI: 10.4018/978-1-5225-2857-9.ch007

Simulated annealing is a local search method for global combinatorial optimisation problems introduced by Kirkpatrick et al. (1983). This meta-heuristic consists at each iteration of generating a candidate solution that will be whether accepted as a result of a comparison with a current one. It aims at improving the current solution (in the context of minimisation, as presented herein) by means of a certain transition rule while accepting occasionally some uphill solutions in order to guarantee diversity in the domain exploration and to avoid getting caught at local optima. The process is managed by a certain cooling schedule which can be static or dynamic whereby the number of iterations is controlled. Many variants have been introduced in the literature in order to fasten the simulated annealing execution and to simplify the tuning of the different parameters. Furthermore, an extension to the multi-objective case has been developed that allows a construction of near-Pareto optimal solutions. It consists basically of using an archive that catches the non-dominated solutions while exploring the feasible domain.

This chapter provides insights into simulated annealing. It presents the fundamentals of the meta-heuristic as well as an understanding of the choice and the design of its different parameters and discusses many related concerns.

PRINCIPLES OF SIMULATED ANNEALING

Local search represents a main category of meta-heuristics that includes hill climbing, tabu search (Glover, 1986), simulated annealing (Kirkpatrick et al., 1983), and variable neighbourhood search (Mladenovic & Hansen, 1997). Local search algorithm is based on the idea consisting of starting at a given feasible solution and making, at each iteration, a sequence of moves from the current solution to a neighbouring one that improve the objective function. A neighbouring solution is determined according to a certain defined neighbourhood structure. For instance, for a solution consisting of a vector of a certain length, all vectors differing from by one component would be considered as neighbouring solutions. The iterative process is continuously repeated until reaching a (global) optimal solution or a near-optimal one if a time or iteration bound was erected. This heuristic has been initially known as hill climbing or iterative improvements. The subsequent meta-heuristics within this category have been developed with the aim to deal with some identified issues relevant to the search loop size and being caught at local optima.

Simulated annealing has been introduced based on the Metropolis algorithm (Metropolis, Rosenbluth, Rosenbluth, Teller, & Teller, 1953) introduced in equilibrium statistical mechanics. It mimics the metallurgical process of careful annealing which consists of heating a metal or alloy to a high temperature until the molecules become melted. A slow cooling is applied thereafter until the molecules coalesce into a crystalline form called the ground state. As long as the cooling is perfectly slow, the ground state is reached, which corresponds to the most solid state of the considered metal or alloys. The simulated annealing terms, summarized in Table 1, derive from both the physical mechanics and the optimisation nomenclatures. From a combinatorial optimisation perspective, simulated annealing has extended the hill climbing algorithm by introducing an occasional acceptance mechanism of uphill solutions guaranteeing thereby diversity in the domain exploration and avoiding getting caught at local optima. The process is managed by a certain, either static or dynamic, cooling schedule. The algorithm is practically expected to stop when no significant improvement still be possible or when a cooling limit is reached. Figure 1 represents the flowchart of the algorithm pointing out its two main components, namely the neighbouring solutions generation and the energy improvement evaluation.

Table 1. Analogy between metallurgic annealing, simulated annealing, and combinatorial optimisation nomenclature

Combinatorial Optimisation	Simulated Annealing	Metallurgic Annealing
Feasible solution	Solution / Configuration	State (microstate)
Objective function	Cost / Energy	Energy
Optimal solution	Optimal solution	Ground state / Stable state
Iterative control / Parameter control	Temperature	Temperature
Local optimum	Local optimum	Stable state
Local search	Configuration variation	Rapid quenching / Rapid cooling
	Simulated annealing	Careful annealing
Decision variables		Molecular positions
	Equilibrium condition	Thermodynamic equilibrium
Iteration	Iteration	Move / Transition
Heuristic/Efficient solution	Efficient solution	Frozen state
Search space	Landscape	Energy surface

Figure 1. Flowchart of the (generic) simulated annealing algorithm

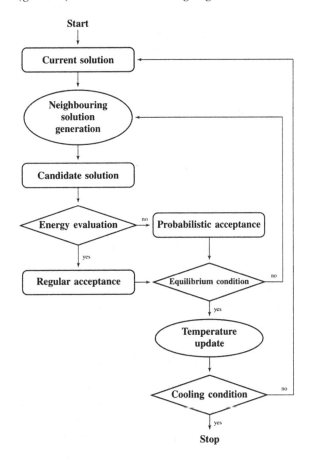

CHOICE OF SIMULATED ANNEALING PARAMETERS

Temperature and Cooling Schedule Considerations

Simulated annealing is controlled by means of a certain plan, so-called cooling schedule, according to which the temperature parameter is decreased during the algorithm execution. It comprises four elements, namely an initial and a final temperature values, a cooling scheme that controls the temperature variation, and an equilibrium condition that controls the number of iterations at each temperature. The choice of these parameters should be rather case-specific and preliminary experiments are therefore required. Nevertheless, such a choice should ensure that the process starts at a sufficiently high temperature value and terminates at sufficiently low temperature value according to a sufficiently slow cooling scheme. As much as these conditions are respected, the found solution is satisfactory.

The starting temperature value requires to be carefully chosen giving a good balance between being too high and too low. If the initial temperature is too high, the acceptance probability gets larger allowing moves to any neighbouring solution. This is inherited from statistical mechanics where molecules are likely to move in any direction when the temperature is hot enough, that is the metal or alloy is in the liquid state. The algorithm tends then to perform a large number of non-improving moves, thereby resulting in a random search heuristic behaviour – at least in the early stages. If the initial temperature is too low, the acceptance probability gets smaller and moves to neighbouring solutions are restricted. The algorithm tends then to perform few non-improving moves, thereby resulting in a hill climbing heuristic behaviour. Determining an appropriate value of the initial temperature is then of interest. Unfortunately, there is no specific rule to determine such a value for a whole range of problems. Nevertheless, some calculating methods do exist for some specific cases. Kirkpatrick (1984) proposed to find the *'melting temperature'* corresponding to the temperature value for which the probabilistic acceptance ratio is equal to a certain value χ_0, for example 80%. Accordingly, van Laarhoven (1988) has proposed an initial value:

$$T_0 = \frac{\overline{\Delta E}}{\ln\left(\chi_0\right)}$$

For problems where $\overline{\Delta E}$ – the maximum distance (in terms of the objective function) between two neighbouring solutions, is known in advance. Sait and Youssef (1999) extended the approach by considering χ_0 as the ratio between all acceptance occurrences, including both regular acceptance of improving solutions and probabilistic acceptance of non-improving solutions, and the number of all trails. Yet, this approach requires a preliminary empirical study to determine an accurate initial temperature.

The final temperature design presents a less difficulty – It should be mainly set to zero. Indeed, it has been proven (Aarts, Korst, & van Laarhoven, 1997; Geman & Geman, 1984; Hajek, 1988; Hajek & Sasaki, 1989; Ingber, 1989) that, under particular conditions, the simulated annealing algorithm converges to the global optimum if the temperature sequence tends to zero when the number of iterations tends to infinity. That is, precisely, the probability of founding a global optimum tends to 1 when the temperature tends to 0. However, practically there is no need to let the algorithm reach the temperature zero because the acceptance probability become almost the same near zero and the chance of accepting non-improving moves becomes rare – From a physical perspective, the system, in this case, is said to reach the so-called frozen state.

A cooling scheme consists of a decreasing sequence of temperature at every which a certain number of transitions will be performed until reaching the equilibrium condition. The choice of an appropriate cooling scheme is crucial to ensure successful convergence. Unfortunately, the convergence keeps slow to reach a global optimum, even if a final temperature value is set. Therefore, faster cooling schedules are adopted in practical implementations (Blum & Roli, 2003) which guarantee only convergence to an efficient solution rather than an optimal one. Thus, many cooling schemes have been introduced in the literature which can be classified into two categories: static – consisting of a monotonic decreasing function controlling the temperature variation, and dynamic – consisting of an adaptive annealing in accordance to the quality of the current move.

Static cooling schemes usually have a functional form of the next temperature involving one or more parameter from the initial temperature, the final temperature, and the current iteration index. The following schemes have been widely considered in the literature:

- Geometric scheme has been widely used proposing at each iteration a proportional temperature to the previous one. Precisely, following the formula:

$$T_k = \alpha T_{k-1}$$

where α is a constant that belongs to $\left[0,1\right]$. Practically, it should be between 0.5 and 0.99 (Talbi, 2009). This scheme is sometimes referred to as exponential scheme. Indeed, given the initial temperature T_0, the formula becomes:

$$T_k = \alpha^k T_0$$

- A trivial scheme is the linear one consisting of updating the temperature by subtracting a constant amount at each iteration. That is:

$$T_k = T_{k-1} - \beta$$

where β is a positive constant with an arbitrary value. Again, given the initial temperature T_0, the formula is equivalent to:

$$T_k = T_0 - k\beta$$

- Logarithmic scheme consists of using the following formula:

$$T_k = \frac{T_0}{\ln\left(k+1\right)}$$

and which guarantees the convergence towards the global optimum (Geman & Geman, 1984).

- Lundy and Mees (1986) proposed a very slow decreasing scheme consisting of the following:

$$T_k = \frac{T_{k-1}}{1 + \beta T_{k-1}}$$

which is nothing but:

$$T_k = \frac{T_0}{1 + k\beta T_0}$$

The scheme implies a large number of temperature instances, to deal with this situation, only one iteration is allowed at each temperature.

An empirical study has been carried out by Triki, Collette, and Siarry (2005) leading to demonstrate that almost all classical cooling schemes are equivalent in sense that they can be tuned to give similar decrease of the temperature parameter in the course of the algorithm execution.

Adaptive cooling scheme, initially named very fast annealing, has been introduced by Ingber (1989) compromising a mechanism of heating and re-annealing according to the acceptance sequence conduct. Along the algorithm progress, the temperature decreases when moves are satisfactory, and increases when more diversification is needed. Figure 2 shows a monotonic exponential cooling scheme vs an adaptive one. Generally, the cooling scheme takes the following form:

$$T_k = \alpha\left(S_c\right) T_{k-1}$$

where α is a function depending on the candidate solution S_c that takes a value less than 1 if S_c improves the objective function in comparison to the best solution found so far, and greater than 1 otherwise.

The equilibrium condition controls the inner loop of the algorithm by limiting the number of iterations at every temperature level. It represents a thermal equilibrium when the algorithm can no more find an

Figure 2. Monotonic cooling scheme vs adaptive cooling scheme

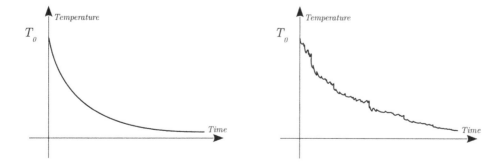

improving solution within the current explored neighbourhood. In spite of its effect on the computational cost, the bigger is the equilibrium condition, the deeper is the exploration and therefore the better is the result. Practically, an equilibrium condition can be simply preset to a certain upper bound of iterations, allowed at each temperature level, plausibly proportional to the current solution neighbourhood cardinality. When this upper bound is preset to be equal to 1, the equilibrium condition adopted by Lundy and Mees (1986) is recovered where only one iteration is allowed at each temperature. For adaptive cooling schedules, the equilibrium condition can be related to the quality of solution found, thereby affecting the cooling scheme. Yet, with the lack of a general agreement, this upper bound should be determined according to the nature of the considered problem.

Cooling Condition, Acceptance Rule, and Stopping Criterion

Simulated annealing performs an exploration of the feasible domain by moving from a current solution to another one. At every move attempt, the candidate solution undergoes an evaluation phase to detect whether the energy of the metal or alloy is minimized, that is whether the objective function of the considered combinatorial problem is improved. If the candidate solution adhere to a certain acceptance rule, it is accepted as the current solution. This process is repeated until reaching a certain stopping criterion so-called a cooling condition.

The cooling condition controls the outer loop of the algorithm and often corresponds to the final temperature due. Yet, it can plausibly set to a certain parameter related to the sequence of improvements conduct. If no further improving solution has been found during a long period of annealing, that is at numerous temperature levels, the algorithm terminates with the current solution. This is of interest in case where the starting solution was taken, by chance, close or equal to the optimal solution, or when the algorithm reaches an efficient solution after few iterations.

As to the acceptance rule, simulated annealing algorithm involves the inherent regular acceptance of improving solutions, in addition to which it considers accepting some uphill solutions in order to skip local optima. The acceptance of a candidate solution S_c, which corresponds to the probability of transition from the current solution to S_c, usually follows the Metropolis rule given by the following probabilistic formula

$$\text{P}(\text{Accept } S_c) = \min\left(1 \; ; \exp\left(-\frac{\Delta E}{kT}\right)\right)$$

where ΔE is the energy variation that corresponds to the objective function of the problem, and T is the current temperature. k is called Boltzmann constant and often assumed to be equal to 1. Actually, according to Dowsland and Thompson (2012), the simulated annealing parameter, referred to as temperature, corresponds to the product of the Boltzmann constant and the physical temperature, and therefore considered as a single constant. The exponential function in the formula allows frequent non-improving solutions acceptance at the beginning of the process, and rare acceptance as far as the process progresses. Furthermore, this function more likely allows small deteriorations than large ones (Suman & Kumar, 2006).

Neighbourhood Structure Considerations

A solution corresponds essentially to a certain configuration of a finite number of components that may consist of even quantitative values (e.g. the value of a vector of decision variables) or any conceptual entities (e.g. a sequence of nodes that represent a graph). In fact, solutions of decision problems are usually considered in a certain indirect representation that allows ease handling. Accordingly, a neighbouring solution of a current one is any solution that is somehow similar; that is the two configurations differ in certain components or may have close energy values. A neighbourhood of a solution refers then to the set of candidate solutions having similar configuration. It is characterized by means of a neighbourhood structure that defines how moves from a configuration to another one should be performed as well as the number of the possible moves at each iteration. Typically, a neighbourhood structure is defined by means of a mapping function N from the feasible domain D to its power set 2^D that assigns for each solution S a certain subset $N(S) \subset D$. It is typically represented by the intersection of the feasible domain and a ball centred at S and of radius equal to a certain positive ε. Figure 3 represents a neighbourhood structure for both the continuous and discrete cases: the hatched area represents the set of neighbouring solutions of S in the continuous case, whereas they are represented by blacked nodes in the discrete case.

The definition of a neighbourhood structure depends strongly on the problem under consideration as well as on the adopted representation of configurations. It is worth noting that the neighbourhood structure affects the concept of local optimality (Aarts, Korst, & Michiels, 2014; Talbi, 2009); indeed and despite the classical conception of optimisation problems where few local optima would be identified in the feasible domain, a local optimum exists at every neighbourhood that will be hopefully reached by the algorithm before reaching the equilibrium condition. Nevertheless, it is often difficult to declare explicitly the neighbourhood function. Particularly for combinatorial problems, a generation procedure is usually introduced that consists of a series of certain perturbations (swaps or mutations) applied to the current configuration components. For instance, the neighbourhood of a vector $(0,0,1)$ would contain $(0,0,0)$, $(0,1,1)$, $(1,0,1)$, and so on.

A neighbourhood structure is supposed to provide a restricted number of possible transitions as well as fast generation and evaluation of neighbouring solutions. As a subset of the feasible domain, the neighbourhood size should be large enough to ensure diversity exploitation and quick moves around the

Figure 3. Neighbourhood structure for two-dimension continuous and discrete cases according to the Euclidean distance

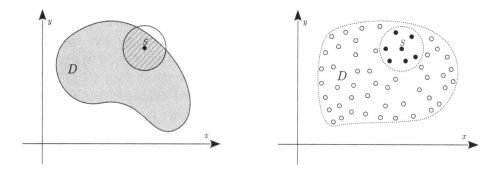

local optimum, without being too large so that the process results in a random search heuristic behaviour. Yet, it was observed that early studies has often underestimated the impact of the neighbourhood choice on the simulated annealing performance (Alizamir, Rebennack, & Pardalos, 2008; Goldstein, 1988). In fact, apart from the variable neighbourhood search meta-heuristic where the neighbourhood structure is systematically changing, meta-heuristics, including simulated annealing, consider the same structure over the course of the algorithm execution. Besides, the structure definition is usually chosen according to some empirical information and trivial considerations. Few studies (Rodriguez-Cristerna & Torres-Jimenez, 2012; Lin, Bian, & Liu, 2016) have recently proposed a hybridisation of simulated annealing and variable neighbourhood search.

SIMULATED ANNEALING VARIANTS

In order to either speed up the simulated annealing execution or to soften the challenging tuning of the different parameters, several variants of simulated annealing have been proposed in the literature that include the following. Besides, a multi-objective extension has been introduced giving rise to a wide range of studies.

Microcanonical Annealing

Microcanonical annealing has been introduced by Creutz (1983). Unlike simulated annealing, microcanonical annealing deals with the total energy of the system which is defined as the sum of the potential energy and the kinetic energy of the current state. While this energy keep preserved, the potential energy is considered as the objective function. Despite the disadvantage of non-guaranteed convergence to a global optimum, that is the algorithm would be trapped in a local optimum, microcanonical annealing does not require the evaluation of many parameters during the process, thereby reducing the execution time.

Threshold Accepting Method

The threshold accepting method has been introduced by Dueck and Scheuer (1990) and in a very similar way by Moscato and Fontanari (1990). It consists of a simulated annealing method-like that involves a positive threshold parameter, as only one parameter to be dependent on and according to which whether the acceptance of a candidate solution is allowed. Unlike the simulated annealing method which involves two different acceptance patterns (regular and probabilistic), the threshold accepting method does not require any probabilistic computation and would accept, in a deterministic way, every new solution which is not much worse than the current one. That is, any generated solution for which the objective function variation ΔE is less than the considered threshold T is accepted, that is:

$$\Delta E < T$$

The threshold parameter is lowered gradually in the course of the algorithm in order to mimics the simulated annealing strategy of accepting uphill solutions more often in early stage of iterations and restrictively in late stage. The threshold parameter is a combination of both the temperature and the acceptance rule concepts. Figure 4 represents the flowchart of the threshold accepting method.

Many empirical studies (e.g. Abboud, Sakawa, & Inuiguchi, 1998; Liu, 2011) have shown the satisfactory performance of the method for different applications. Given an appropriate threshold sequence, Althöfer and Koschnick (1991) presented some results on the convergence of the threshold accepting method. Nevertheless, Jacobson and Yücesan (2004) have proven that the general implementation of the threshold accepting does not asymptotically converge to the global optimum.

Nevertheless, a construction of an optimal threshold sequence still challenging and presents rather similar difficulty as the choice of cooling scheme in simulated annealing presents. Winker and Fang (1997) and Gilli, Këllezi, and Hysi (2006) suggested a procedure for generating the threshold sequence using a data driven method. Tarantilis and Kiranoudis (2002) introduced a list-based threshold accepting method where the threshold sequence is taken from a list that would be rejuvenated and adapted according to the nature (topology) of the feasible domain. Unlike the original threshold accepting method which is based on a priori setting of an initial threshold and a reduction strategy, the list-based threshold accepting method involves a mechanism of automatic determination of these two parameters. A direct implication of this reflection is the accuracy of each threshold taken value according to the neighbourhood structure, thereby allowing more likely to accept improving solutions and to escape local optima.

Figure 4. Flowchart of the threshold accepting method

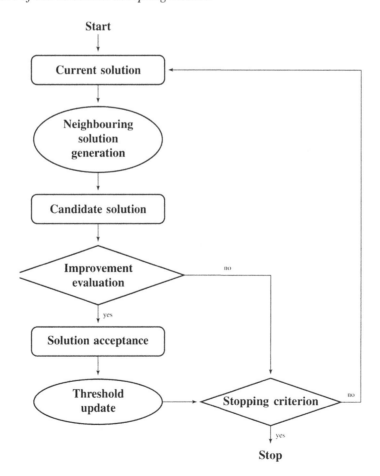

List-based threshold accepting method has been applied to different problems including job shop scheduling (Lee, Vassiliadis, & Park, 2002, 2004; Tarantilis & Kiranoudis, 2002) and vehicle routing (Tarantilis, Kiranoudis, & Vassiliadis, 2002, 2003). Furthermore, an extension to the numerical optimisation has been introduced and applied to a protein structure prediction problem (Lin & Zhong, 2015). The idea of using a list for the threshold parameter has been used for the cooling schedule parameter to develop a list-based simulated annealing algorithm for the traveling salesman problem (Zhan, Lin, Zhang, & Zhong, 2016).

Great Deluge Method

Great deluge method has been introduced by Dueck (1993) on the basis of both simulated annealing and threshold method. It mimics the metaphor of a hill climber jumping from a position to a higher one to escape a great deluge, sometimes the hill climber jumps to a position of lower altitude if one's feet will keep dry, that is above the current water level. Obviously, the method is very similar to the threshold accepting method. Indeed, the water level represents a threshold parameter which is controlled dynamically by means of a rain speed parameter that will be subtracted from (or added to in the maximisation context) the water level after each acceptance occurrence. As a consequence, the acceptance threshold is linearly decreasing in the course of the method execution. A more flexible acceptance condition has been introduced by Burke and Bykov (2016) involving a flexibility coefficient $0 \leq k_f \leq 1$ where any move from a current solution S with energy $E(S)$ to any candidate solution S_c with energy $E(S_c)$ would be accepted if it respects one of the following conditions:

$$E(S_c) \leq E(S) + k_f(W - E(S)) \quad \text{if} \quad E(S) < W$$

$$E(S_c) \leq E(S) \qquad\qquad \text{if} \quad E(S) \geq W$$

where W is the current water level. The case where $k_f = 0$ corresponds to the greedy hill climbing, while the case where $k_f = 1$ corresponds to the original great deluge method.

Record-To-Record Travel Method

Dueck (1993) has introduced another variant called record-to-record travel that consists of accepting any candidate solution not much worse that the best recorded energy value so far – called the record. Actually this method follows the same idea as the great deluge method does. The water level has been replaced by a formula involving the record and a tolerated deterioration – called the deviation. Given the objective function E, a record R, and a deviation D, any candidate solution S_c is accepted if the following formula follows

$$E(S_c) < R + D$$

The record is updated when the energy function is improved by the current candidate solution, that is $E(S_c) < R$.

Multi-Objective Simulated Annealing

Multi-objective simulated annealing is an extension of the classical simulated annealing that dates back to the work of Serafini (1994) where many probabilistic acceptance rules have been discussed. The regular acceptance, that is the situation where candidate solutions are accepted with probability 1, has been enlarged within two alternative approaches with the aim to increase the acceptance of the potential non-dominated solutions, that is solutions non-dominated by any generated solution so far. The first alternative consists of accepting with probability 1 only improving moves, that is to accept any candidate solution that dominates the current one. This strong acceptance criterion allows a deep exploration of the feasible domain, but leads to only one near-optimal solution. The second alternative focuses on dominated solutions. It consists of accepting with probability strictly less than 1 only a dominated solution. Which implies to accept with probability 1 weakly improving solutions, that is any candidate solution is either dominating or non-comparable with the current one. This weak acceptance criterion is expected to allow diversity in the exploration of the feasible domain.

Considering m objective functions E_i, m scalar weights ω_i for $i = 1, \ldots, m$, and a candidate solution S_c, the strong acceptance rule is expressed in the following form:

$$P\left(\text{Accept } S_c\right) = \prod_{i=1}^{m} \min\left(1 \, ; \exp\left(\frac{\omega_i \Delta E_i}{T}\right)\right)$$

and the weak acceptance rule is expressed in the following one:

$$P\left(\text{Accept } S_c\right) = \min\left(1 \, ; \max_{i=1,\ldots,m}\left(\exp\left(\frac{\omega_i \Delta E_i}{T}\right)\right)\right)$$

The two alternatives lead to a quite different Markov chain for which non-dominated solutions were proven to have higher stationary probability. A combined rule has been proposed to retain the advantages of both the two approaches, that consists of:

$$P\left(\text{Accept } S_c\right) = \alpha \prod_{i=1}^{m} \min\left(1 \, ; \exp\left(\frac{\omega_i \Delta E_i}{T}\right)\right)$$
$$+ (1 - \alpha) \min\left(1 \, ; \max_{i=1,\ldots,m}\left(\exp\left(\frac{\omega_i \Delta E_i}{T}\right)\right)\right)$$

where $\alpha \in [0,1]$ and $\dfrac{T}{\omega_i}$ is considered as a temperature T_i related to the function E_i. This work has dealt with the multi-objective case by considering weighted combination of the objective functions under consideration which is expected to express a certain preference structure. A slow random modification of the weights has been proposed in order to guarantee entire exploration of the Pareto set.

Many multi-objective simulated annealing paradigms have been proposed in the literature (e.g. Alrefaei & Diabat, 2009; Czyżak & Jaszkiewicz, 1998; Suman, 2003; Suppapitnarm, Seffen, Parks, & Clarkson, 2000; Teghem, Tuyttens, & Ulungu, 2000; Tekinalp & Karsli, 2007; Ulungu, Teghem, Fortemps, & Tuyttens, 1999) that almost all of them have in common the idea of gathering near-Pareto optimal solutions by means of an archive that catches the non-dominated solutions while exploring the feasible domain. Furthermore, the asymptotic convergence to the Pareto solutions set has been proved under certain choice of the acceptance probabilities (Villalobos-Arias, Coello, & Hernández-Lerma, 2006).

CONCLUSION

Simulated annealing is a probabilistic local search method that guarantees gradual convergence to a near-optimal solution. It was inspired from the metallurgical process of careful annealing and provides two main advantages, namely the ability of escaping local optima and being memoryless. A wide range of applications have hitherto emerged due to its adaptability to many combinatorial as well as continuous optimisation cases. Nevertheless, the following remarks are observed:

- Simulated annealing was initially introduced for global combinatorial optimisation problems giving rise to a wide range of results concerning the convergence and the complexity of the algorithm. Many results have been successfully extended to the continuous optimisation case.
- Comparing to other meta-heuristics, simulated annealing is a powerful tool for many applications due to its asymptotic convergence. However, the algorithm process is rather slow especially for some cooling schemes and using other heuristic seems to give better result for problems with few optima.
- Considering an appropriate representation of solutions as well as an appropriate neighbourhood structure has a great impact on the performance of the algorithm. Moreover, simulated annealing is problem dependent and the choice of appropriate parameters is rather a challenging task.

REFERENCES

Aarts, E., Korst, J., & Michiels, W. (2014). Simulated annealing. In E. K. Burke & G. Kendall (Eds.), *Search methodologies: Introductory tutorials in optimization and decision support techniques* (2nd ed.). Boston, MA: Springer US; doi:10.1007/978-1-4614-6940-7_10

Aarts, E. H. L., Korst, J. H. M., & van Laarhoven, P. J. M. (1997). Simulated annealing. In E. H. L. Aarts & J. K. Lenstra (Eds.), *Local Search in Combinatorial Optimization* (pp. 91–120). Chichester, UK: Wiley-Interscience.

Abboud, N., Sakawa, M., & Inuiguchi, M. (1998). School scheduling using threshold accepting. *Cybernetics and Systems*, *29*(6), 593–611. doi:10.1080/019697298125533

Alizamir, S., Rebennack, S., & Pardalos, P. M. (2008). Improving the Neighborhood Selection Strategy in Simulated Annealing using the Optimal Stopping Problem. In C. M. Tan (Ed.), Simulated Annealing (pp. 363–382). Rijeka, Croatia: InTech. doi:10.5772/5571

Alrefaei, M. H., & Diabat, A. H. (2009). A simulated annealing technique for multi-objective simulation optimization. *Applied Mathematics and Computation*, *215*(8), 3029–3035. doi:10.1016/j.amc.2009.09.051

Althöfer, I., & Koschnick, K. (1991). On the convergence of Threshold Accepting. *Applied Mathematics & Optimization*, *24*(1), 183–195. doi:10.1007/BF01447741

Bishop, J. M. (1989). Stochastic Searching Networks. *Proceedings of the 1st IEE International Conference on Artificial Neural Networks*, 329–331.

Blum, Ch., & Roli, A. (2003). Metaheuristics in combinatorial optimization: Overview and conceptual comparison. *ACM Computing Surveys*, *35*(3), 268–308. doi:10.1145/937503.937505

Burke, E. K., & Bykov, Y. (2016). An Adaptive Flex-Deluge Approach to University Exam Timetabling. *INFORMS Journal on Computing*, *28*(4), 781–794. doi:10.1287/ijoc.2015.0680

Creutz, M. (1983). Microcanonical Monte Carlo simulation. *Physical Review Letters*, *50*(19), 1411–1414. doi:10.1103/PhysRevLett.50.1411 PMID:10047098

Czyżak, P., & Jaszkiewicz, A. (1998). Pareto simulated annealing - a metaheuristic technique for multiple objective combinatorial optimization. *Journal of Multi-Criteria Decision Analysis*, *7*(1), 34–47. doi:10.1002/(SICI)1099-1360(199801)7:1<34::AID-MCDA161>3.0.CO;2-6

Dorigo, M. (1992). *Optimization, Learning and Natural Algorithms* (Unpublished doctoral dissertation). Politecnico di Milano, Italy.

Dowsland, K. A., & Thompson, J. M. (2012). Simulated Annealing. In G. Rozenberg, Th. Bäck, & J. N. Kok (Eds.), *Handbook of Natural Computing* (pp. 1623–1655). Berlin: Springer-Verlag; doi:10.1007/978-3-540-92910-9_49

Dueck, G. (1993). New optimization heuristics, the great deluge and the record to record travel. *Journal of Computational Physics*, *104*(1), 86–92. doi:10.1006/jcph.1993.1010

Dueck, G., & Scheuer, T. (1990). Threshold accepting: A general purpose optimization algorithm appearing superior to simulated annealing. *Journal of Computational Physics*, *90*(1), 161–175. doi:10.1016/0021-9991(90)90201-B

Geman, S., & Geman, D. (1984). Stochastic Relaxation, Gibbs Distributions, and the Bayesian Restoration of Images. *IEEE Transactions on Pattern Analysis and Machine Intelligence*, *6*(6), 721–741. doi:10.1109/TPAMI.1984.4767596 PMID:22499653

Gilli, M., Këllezi, E., & Hysi, H. (2006). A Data-Driven Optimization Heuristic for Downside Risk Minimization. *Journal of Risk*, *8*(3), 1–18. doi:10.21314/JOR.2006.129

Glover, F. (1986). Future paths for integer programming and links to artificial intelligence. *Computers & Operations Research, 13*(5), 533–549. doi:10.1016/0305-0548(86)90048-1

Goldstein, L., & Waterman, M. (1988). Neighborhood size in the simulated annealing algorithm. *American Journal of Mathematical and Management Sciences, 8*(3-4), 409–423. doi:10.1080/01966324.1988.10737247

Hajek, B. (1988). Cooling schedules for optimal annealing. *Mathematics of Operations Research, 13*(2), 311–329. doi:10.1287/moor.13.2.311

Hajek, B., & Sasaki, G. (1989). Simulated annealing – to cool or not. *Systems & Control Letters, 12*(5), 443–447. doi:10.1016/0167-6911(89)90081-9

Ingber, L. (1989). Very fast simulated re-annealing. *Mathematical and Computer Modelling, 12*(8), 967–973. doi:10.1016/0895-7177(89)90202-1

Jacobson, Sh. H., & Yücesan, E. (2004). Global Optimization Performance Measures for Generalized Hill Climbing Algorithms. *Journal of Global Optimization, 29*(2), 173–190. doi:10.1023/B:JOGO.0000042111.72036.11

Kennedy, J., & Eberhart, R. (1995). Particle Swarm Optimization. *Proceedings of the 4th IEEE International Conference on Neural Networks*, 1942–1948. doi:10.1109/ICNN.1995.488968

Kirkpatrick, S. (1984). Optimization by simulated annealing – quantitative studies. *Journal of Statistical Physics, 34*(5-6), 975–986. doi:10.1007/BF01009452

Kirkpatrick, S., Gelatt, C. D., & Vecchi, M. P. (1983). Optimization by simulated annealing. *Science, 220*(4598), 671–680. doi:10.1126/science.220.4598.671 PMID:17813860

Lee, D. S., Vassiliadis, V. S., & Park, J. M. (2002). List-Based Threshold-Accepting Algorithm for Zero-Wait Scheduling of Multiproduct Batch Plants. *Industrial & Engineering Chemistry, 41*(25), 6579–6588. doi:10.1021/ie010570n

Lee, D. S., Vassiliadis, V. S., & Park, J. M. (2004). A novel threshold accepting meta-heuristic for the job-shop scheduling problem. *Computers & Operations Research, 31*(13), 2199–2213. doi:10.1016/S0305-0548(03)00172-2

Lin, J., & Zhong, Y. (2015). Multi-agent list-based threshold-accepting algorithm for numerical optimisation. *International Journal of Computing Science and Mathematics, 6*(5), 501–509. doi:10.1504/IJCSM.2015.072970

Lin, Y., Bian, Z., & Liu, X. (2016). Developing a dynamic neighborhood structure for an adaptive hybrid simulated annealing – tabu search algorithm to solve the symmetrical traveling salesman problem. *Applied Soft Computing, 49*, 937–952. doi:10.1016/j.asoc.2016.08.036

Liu, Y.-H. (2011). Incorporating scatter search and threshold accepting in finding maximum likelihood estimates for the multinomial probit model. *European Journal of Operational Research, 211*(1), 130–138. doi:10.1016/j.ejor.2010.10.038

Lundy, M., & Mees, A. (1986). Convergence of an annealing algorithm. *Mathematical Programming, 34*(1), 111–124. doi:10.1007/BF01582166

Metropolis, N., Rosenbluth, A. W., Rosenbluth, M. N., Teller, A. H., & Teller, E. (1953). Equation of State Calculations by Fast Computing Machines. *The Journal of Chemical Physics, 21*(6), 1087–1092. doi:10.1063/1.1699114

Mladenovic, N., & Hansen, P. (1997). Variable neighborhood search. *Computers & Operations Research, 24*(11), 1097–1100. doi:10.1016/S0305-0548(97)00031-2

Moscato, P., & Fontanari, J. F. (1990). Stochastic versus deterministic update in simulated annealing. *Physics Letters. [Part A], 146*(4), 204–208. doi:10.1016/0375-9601(90)90166-L

Rodriguez-Cristerna, A., & Torres-Jimenez, J. (2012). A Simulated Annealing with Variable Neighborhood Search Approach to Construct Mixed Covering Arrays. *Electronic Notes in Discrete Mathematics, 39*, 249–256. doi:10.1016/j.endm.2012.10.033

Sait, S. M., & Youssef, H. (1999). *Iterative Computer Algorithms with Applications in Engineering: Solving Combinatorial Optimization Problems.* Los Alamitos, CA: IEEE Computer Society Press.

Serafini, P. (1994). Simulated annealing for multiple objective optimization problems. In G. H. Tzeng, H. F. Wang, U. P. Wen, & P. L. Yu (Eds.), *Multiple Criteria Decision Making: Proceedings of the Tenth International Conference: Expand and Enrich the Domains of Thinking and Application* (pp. 283–292). New York, NY: Springer-Verlag. doi:10.1007/978-1-4612-2666-6_29

Suman, B. (2003). Simulated annealing based multiobjective algorithm and their application for system reliability. *Engineering Optimization, 35*(4), 391–416. doi:10.1080/03052150310001597765

Suman, B., & Kumar, P. (2006). A survey of simulated annealing as a tool for single and multiobjective optimization. *The Journal of the Operational Research Society, 57*(10), 1143–1160. doi:10.1057/palgrave.jors.2602068

Suppapitnarm, A., Seffen, K. A., Parks, G. T., & Clarkson, P. J. (2000). A simulated annealing algorithm for multiobjective optimization. *Engineering Optimization, 33*(1), 59–85. doi:10.1080/03052150008940911

Talbi, E.-Gh. (2009). *Metaheuristics: From design to implementation.* Hoboken, NJ: John Wiley & Sons. doi:10.1002/9780470496916

Tarantilis, C. D., & Kiranoudis, C. T. (2002). A list-based threshold accepting method for job shop scheduling problems. *International Journal of Production Economics, 77*(2), 159–171. doi:10.1016/S0925-5273(01)00231-6

Tarantilis, C. D., Kiranoudis, C. T., & Vassiliadis, V. S. (2002). A list based threshold accepting algorithm for the capacitated vehicle routing problem. *International Journal of Computer Mathematics, 79*(5), 537–553. doi:10.1080/00207160210948

Tarantilis, C. D., Kiranoudis, C. T., & Vassiliadis, V. S. (2003). A list based threshold accepting metaheuristic for the heterogeneous fixed fleet vehicle routing problem. *The Journal of the Operational Research Society, 54*(1), 65–71. doi:10.1057/palgrave.jors.2601443

Teghem, J., Tuyttens, D., & Ulungu, E. L. (2000). An intractive heuristic method for multiobjective combinatorial optimization. *Computers & Operations Research, 27*(7-8), 621–634. doi:10.1016/S0305-0548(99)00109-4

Tekinalp, O., & Karsli, G. (2007). A new multiobjective simulated annealing algorithm. *Journal of Global Optimization, 39*(1), 49–77. doi:10.1007/s10898-006-9120-2

Triki, E., Collette, Y., & Siarry, P. (2005). A theoretical study on the behavior of simulated annealing leading to a new cooling schedule. *European Journal of Operational Research, 166*(1), 77–92. doi:10.1016/j.ejor.2004.03.035

Ulungu, E. L., Teghem, J., Fortemps, P., & Tuyttens, D. (1999). MOSA method: A tool for solving multiobjective combinatorial optimization problems. *Journal of Multi-Criteria Decision Analysis, 8*(4), 221–236. doi:10.1002/(SICI)1099-1360(199907)8:4<221::AID-MCDA247>3.0.CO;2-O

van Laarhoven, P. J. M. (1988). *Theoretical and computational aspects of simulated annealing* (Unpublished PhD dissertation). Erasmus University, Rotterdam, The Netherlands.

Villalobos-Arias, M., Coello, C. A. C., & Hernández-Lerma, O. (2006). Asymptotic convergence of a simulated annealing algorithm for multiobjective optimization problems. *Mathematical Methods of Operations Research, 64*(2), 353–362. doi:10.1007/s00186-006-0082-4

Winker, P., & Fang, K. (1997). Application of threshold-accepting to the evaluation of the discrepancy of a set of points. *SIAM Journal on Numerical Analysis, 34*(5), 2028–2042. doi:10.1137/S0036142995286076

Zhan, Sh., Lin, J., Zhang, Z., & Zhong, Y. (2016). List-Based Simulated Annealing Algorithm for Traveling Salesman Problem. *Computational Intelligence and Neuroscience, 2016,* 1–12. doi:10.1155/2016/1712630 PMID:27034650

ADDITIONAL READING

Ben-Ameur, W. (2004). Computing the Initial Temperature of Simulated Annealing. *Computational Optimization and Applications, 29*(3), 369–385. doi:10.1023/B:COAP.0000044187.23143.bd

Burke, E. K., & Bykov, Y. (2016). The Late Acceptance Hill-Climbing Heuristic. *European Journal of Operational Research, 258*(1), 70–78. doi:10.1016/j.ejor.2016.07.012

Dréo, J., Pétrowski, A., Siarry, P., & Taillard, E. (2006). *Metaheuristics for Hard Optimization: Methods and Case Studies* (A. Chatterjee, Trans.). Berlin, Germany: Springer-Verlag Berlin Heidelberg. (Original work published 2003), doi:10.1007/3-540-30966-7

Fouskakis, D., & Draper, D. (2002). Stochastic Optimization: A Review. *International Statistical Review, 70*(3), 315–349. doi:10.1111/j.1751-5823.2002.tb00174.x

Ledesma, S., Aviña, G., & Sanchez, R. (2008). Practical Considerations for Simulated Annealing Implementation. In Ch. M. Tan (Ed.), Simulated Annealing (pp. 401–420). Rijeka, Croatia: InTech. doi:10.5772/5560

Monticelli, A. J., Romero, R., & Asada, E. N. (2008). Fundamentals of Simulated Annealing. In K. Y. Lee & M. A. El-Sharkawi (Eds.), *Modern Heuristic Optimization Techniques: Theory And Applications To Power System* (pp. 123–146). Hoboken, New Jersey: John Wiley & Sons; doi:10.1002/9780470225868.ch7

Nikolaev, A. G., & Jacobson, Sh. H. (2010). Simulated Annealing. In M. Gendreau & J.-Y. Potvin (Eds.), *Handbook of Metaheuristics* (pp. 1–39). Boston, MA: Springer; doi:10.1007/978-1-4419-1665-5_1

Salamon, P., Sibani, P., & Frost, R. (2002). *Facts, conjectures, and improvements for simulated annealing*. Philadelphia, PA: SIAM. doi:10.1137/1.9780898718300

Shojaee, K., Shakouri, H., & Taghadosi, M. B. (2010). Importance of the Initial Conditions and the Time Schedule in the Simulated Annealing. In R. Chibante (Ed.), Simulated Annealing: Theory with Applications (217–234). Rijeka, Croatia: InTech. doi:10.5772/46942

Siddique, N., & Adeli, H. (2016). Simulated annealing, its variants and engineering applications. *International Journal on Artificial Intelligence Tools, 25*(6), ArticleID 1630001, 24 p. doi: 10.1142/S0218213016300015

Suman, B. (2004). Study of simulated annealing based multiobjective algorithm for multiobjective optimization of a constrained problem. *Computers & Chemical Engineering, 28*(9), 1849–1871. doi:10.1016/j.compchemeng.2004.02.037

Xinchao, Z. (2011). Simulated annealing algorithm with adaptive neighborhood. *Applied Soft Computing, 11*(2), 1827–1836. doi:10.1016/j.asoc.2010.05.029

KEY TERMS AND DEFINITIONS

Careful Annealing: A process in metallurgy consisting of heating a metal or alloy to a high temperature until the molecules become within a melted state and applying thereafter a slow cooling until they achieve a ground state.

Greedy Algorithm: A constructive algorithm that takes the best alternative in every component choice without taking into account the quality of the whole solution.

Heuristic: A low level method allowing to construct a feasible solution for a given problem. Due to its constructive aspect, meta-heuristics often involve one or more heuristic to construct initial or intermediate solutions.

Metropolis Algorithm: An algorithm of statistical physics for sampling from a probability distribution by means of a sequence of Markov chains construction. It is often used under an extended version called Mestropolis-Hastings algorithm.

Multi-Objective Optimisation: Also Multicriteria or Multi-attribute optimisation. The mathematical field dealing with optimisation problems that involve more than one objective function to be simultaneously optimised.

Pareto Optimality: The quality of being optimal for a solution of any given multi-objective optimisation problem. Compared to mono-objective optimisation, the Pareto optimality is attained by means of a set of solutions, called Pareto set, rather than a single solution. A Pareto optimal solution corresponds to the best trade-off between all considered objective functions and implies no other solution exists that can improve at least one of the objective functions without any deterioration for any one of the others.

Preference Structure: A term of decision science that refers to a generalisation of the concept of aggregating the objective functions under consideration into one objective function. It is a set of qualitative relations between the objectives or alternatives for which the resolution leads to a certain trade-off.

Statistical Mechanics: The mathematical physics field using probability theory to deal with thermodynamic behaviour of systems with large number of states.

Chapter 8
Automatic Test Data Generation Using Bio-Inspired Algorithms:
A Travelogue

Madhumita Panda
North Orissa University, India

Sujata Dash
North Orissa University, India

ABSTRACT

This chapter presents an overview of some widely accepted bio-inspired metaheuristic algorithms which would be helpful in solving the problems of software testing. Testing is an integral part of the software development process. A sizable number of Nature based algorithms coming under the per- view of metaheuristics have been used by researchers to solve practical problems of different disciplines of engineering and computer science, and software engineering. Here an exhaustive review of metaheuristic algorithms which have been employed to optimize the solution of test data generation for past 20 -30 years is presented. In addition to this, authors have reviewed their own work has been developed particularly to generate test data for path coverage based testing using Cuckoo Search and Gravitational Search algorithms. Also, an extensive comparison with the results obtained using Genetic Algorithms, Particle swarm optimization, Differential Evolution and Artificial Bee Colony algorithm are presented to establish the significance of the study.

INTRODUCTION

It would not be wrong to say that software has become the life line of our human civilization and like electricity we cannot survive without it. As the quality of software is playing the crucial role in determining the user's satisfaction therefore it is becoming more and more crucial for the software development team to build the product right. Out of the several phases of software development life cycle the most important phase is the testing phase which ensures the correctness as well as the quality of the software before release.

DOI: 10.4018/978-1-5225-2857-9.ch008

Now a days gradually the complexity of the systems are increasing and the software handling those complex systems needs to be error free, safe, secure and reliable from the users perspective. The competing market is influencing testers to implement new approaches, methodologies and strategies to enhance quality and reduce the testing time and development cost of systems. Test case selection and optimization is an NP complete problem. Therefore cannot be solved using existing heuristic algorithms.

Till data a number of metaheuristic algorithms have been proposed, that are nature based search algorithms designed by observing the natural process of evolution followed by nature as well as the intelligent selection and search strategies adopted by natural species for better adaption to their habitat as well as selection of best offspring to carry forward their races to the next generation. Metaheuristic bio inspired algorithms have been used by different researchers in their respective fields of engineering and mathematics for obtaining optimized and best results within a particular period of time or satisfying certain predefined constraints. Some of the most popular and widely used metaheuristic algorithms specifically in the field of software engineering include Genetic Algorithms (GA), Particle swarm optimization (PSO), Artificial Bee Colony algorithm (ABC), Firefly algorithm and Cuckoo Search Algorithm (CS).

A recent area of software testing has emerged in last few decades known as search based software testing (SBST) where the researchers are applying metaheuristic optimization algorithms to solve the critical problems of software testing(De Oliveira, 2015). More than fifty percent of research work of this area involves test data generation using Genetic Algorithms (GA), Particle swarm optimization (PSO), Artificial Bee Colony algorithm (ABC), and multiobjective Genetic Algorithms for performing structural, functional and mutation testing.

The proposed work emphasizes on giving an overview of the automated process of test data generation using metaheuristic algorithms for unit testing of structured programs, targeting complete path coverage of the program under test.This chapter is organized into following sections, Section 2 presents the basic techniques applied to software testing and test data generation, Section 3 gives an exhaustive review of the existing literature, especially in the field of test data generation Section 4 describes a detailed overview of the Bio-inspired metaheuristic algorithms including Genetics Algorithms, Particle Swarm optimization Algorithm, Differential Evolution Algorithm, Artificial bee colony algorithm, Gravitational search algorithm and Cuckoo Search Algorithm, Section 5 includes our proposed methodology and experimental results finally Section 6 concludes the chapter with future directives and discussions.

BASIC CONCEPTS OF TEST DATA GENERATION

Software testing mainly includes the detailed verification and validation of the entire process of software development ensuring its correctness and quality. In earlier days people were not technical literate and neither well acquainted with the use of software and its underlying technologies. With the passage of time and advent of modern technology gradually program complexity, as well as common user's technical knowledge start growing at an explosive rate. Thus it became mandatory to ensure the quality and correct functioning of each and every specification, before successful lunching of any new software, as well as maintenance of existing software.

Testing

Software testing includes black box testing, also known as functional testing, structural testing commonly known as white box testing, gray box testing used for object oriented testing and non-functional testing (Hitesh, 2011). Black box testing is performed to check the correct functioning of different modules by comparing the system generated outputs with the expected outputs, on the basis of specified inputs. In black box testing, no attempt is made to find out the logical or program level errors. Many automatic tools are available nowadays to perform black box testing.

White box testing also known as glass box testing is performed to find out the logical errors present in the program structure. It needs the entire program structure and normally performed at unit level.

Grey box testing is a combination of both black box as well as white box testing. This testing strategy is applied for testing object oriented software. Here instead of program structure, test cases are prepared from design models developed using UML and similar modeling languages.

Non-functional testing includes the testing strategies adapted to test different non-functional components of the software.

Test Data

Test data is the input data, carefully selected from the software specification document SRS document) to ensure the correct functionality of different components of the system under test. These inputs are carefully selected satisfying specific test adequacy criteria and percent of coverage. Test data generation research area is a very mature area originated since 1970 (Yenigun,2016) and till data research is going on to completely automate this process of test data generation (Hitesh and Bichitra et al., 2011).

In black box testing, also known as specification based testing or functional testing, test data is provided as input to find out what out put the system or specific module is producing and this value is matched with the expected output previously calculated. Black box testing is conducted to find out missing logical faults. It is performed at unit level, integration level, as well as system level. It is also performed during regression testing.

In white box testing there are many test adequacy criteria as here the overall program structure is tested (Madhumita, 2013), therefore test data are carefully calculated or selected satisfying those requirements. It is performed during unit testing and integration testing (Mauro and Michal et al., 2007).

Similarly in model based testing, models are developed to automate the process of test data generation of software testing.

Test Adequacy Criteria

The test adequacy criteria are design rules or a set of test obligations that help to identify the inadequacies of test cases or test suites (Mauro and Michal et al., 2007; Rutherford et al., 2008). A test suite consisting of a set of test cases satisfies an adequacy criterion, if all the test cases pass or execute successfully giving the expected outputs or results.

Coverage

Coverage is a very useful index to ensure the thoroughness or adequacy of a particular test suit (Mauro and Michal, 2007). It is normally measured in terms of percentage and is relatively calculated on the basis of the amount of test adequacy criteria fulfilled by a particular test suite.

Several techniques support test data generation including symbolic execution, random test data generation and search based test data generation etc. (Alessandro, Rothermel, 2014).

Here in this chapter the main emphasis is given on search based test data generation techniques using Bio-inspired metaheuristic algorithms.

In Structural software testing a number of tests adequacy criteria are followed to find out whether a software system has been tested adequately or not. The structural testing is done at the level of unit testing (Alzabidi, 2007). Some common test adequacy criteria include control flow-based criteria, data flow based criteria, fault based criteria and error-based criteria .The control flow based criteria include branch coverage, condition coverage and path coverage. Out of the three control flow based criteria, path coverage is the most effective testing criteria as it includes the other two, branch coverage and condition coverage criteria.

Path Testing

The path based software testing includes four steps, first step includes the construction of a data flow based or control flow based graphical representation of the program under test. The graphical representation helps the testers to identify the basic feasible paths and critical paths present in the program. The common graphical representation used by researchers is the Control flow graph (CFG). The second step of path based testing is the target path selection; normally the target path includes critical paths, i.e. the paths which are critical and crucial to be covered to ensure good quality of the software under test. After control flow graph construction and target path selection, metaheuristic search algorithms can be used to automatically generate new test cases or test data in the third step. In the final step the generated test data are executed to cover the targeted paths. Finally the coverage is determined by evaluating the path coverage capability of the generated test data.

Control Flow Graph

Control flow graph is a flow graph showing the control flow of a program, it's a directed graph depicted by a set of vertices and edges. In this graph the continuous sequential blocks of program statements without any branches or loops are represented as nodes, the edges between the nodes indicate the control flow between those nodes. A control flow graph consists of a start node, an end node, decision nodes, junction nodes, edges and bound regions (Rajib,2014).

Cyclomatic Complexity

Cyclomatic complexity is a metric used to measure the logical complexity of a program on the basis of its control flow graph. It was introduced by McCabe (Rajib, 2014).

Cyclomatic complexity is also used to correctly predict the upper bound of the number of feasible paths present in the program and the program complexity. Here only the independent, feasible paths are taken into consideration. Following equation is used to compute the Cyclomatic complexity.

$$V(G) = E - N + 2 \qquad (1)$$

where, $V(G)$ number of independent paths in a control flow graph

E = Number of edges present in the control flow graph
N = Number of nodes of the control flow graph

Graph Matrix

A graph matrix is a square matrix, its rows and columns are equal to the number of nodes present in the control flow graph. Each row and column of the matrix identifies one specific node present in the control flow graph. The entries in this matrix represent a connection between the nodes (Naresh, 2010), which is helpful in tracing feasible paths present in the program structure.

Connection Matrix

A matrix defined with link weights is known as connection matrix (Rajib, 2014; Naresh, 2010). This matrix is very similar to graph matrix, in this matrix the link weights are added to each cell entry. When any connection exist the link weight is one otherwise it is zero. The connection between different nodes or path between different nodes of a control flow graph can be easily calculated by using this connection matrix.

Metaheuristic algorithms can be applied to path testing but prior to that, we need an intermediate representation to identify target paths and an appropriate fitness function to choose test data directing control flow to the specified paths (Harman, 2015; Bertolino, 2007).

BACKGROUND

Test data is essential for Software testing; if the input test data is erroneous then it is not possible to test the correct functionality of the different modules as well as the software as a whole. The manual prediction, design or selection of test data is an error prone process which may lead to incorrect test data leading to the failure of testing process as a whole. Thus rigorous research in the domain of automated test data generation is carried forward since1976, more than three decades before and still continuing considering new programming and testing paradigms.

The term Search based software engineering (SBSE) and Search based software testing (SBST)were coined by Harman in (Harman and Jones, 2001). The search based software testing(SBST) domain of software testing tries to solve the complexities of software testing considering the entire testing process as a search problem and includes metaheuristic algorithms to get best, optimized results within less time covering a very large solution space which is almost impossible to solve using heuristic or traditional classic algorithms. Though the area has become mature but still a lot more research is needed for its concrete establishment as an independent discipline.

Metaheuristics are iterative generation processes which guide the subordinate heuristics intelligently, combining the approaches of exploration and exploitation. The metaheuristic are widely recognized and efficient approaches for many problems of hard optimization, problems which are unsolvable within a particular time limit or through any deterministic approach. Almost all metaheuristic share some common characteristics like,

- They are designed mimicking the nature's behavior, some principles of physics, biology, ethology etc.
- They use stochastic variables
- They do not use gradient or Hessian matrix of function.

Many metaheuristic algorithms have been proposed(Kar,2016) since 1982, including Simulated Annealing (Kirkpatrick, 1982), Tabu Search (Glover, 1986), Artificial Immune system (Farmer, 1988), Genetic programming(Korz,1992), Genetic Algorithms(Goldberg, 1989), Ant Colony Optimization (Dorigo, 1992), Artificial Bee colony (Walker, 1993), Particle swarm optimization(Kennedy, 1995), Differential Evolution Algorithm (Storn, 1997), Bacteria foraging Algorithm (Passino, 2002), Firefly Algorithm(Yang, 2008), Cuckoo Search algorithm(Yang and Dev, 2010), Bat Algorithm(Yang,2010))etc.

The metaheuristic algorithms are either population based or single solution based. The solution based metaheuristic algorithms use more exploitation and the population based metaheuristic algorithms use more exploration. The population based metaheuristics are popular at providing a set of suitable solutions and therefore widely used in testing domain as here the need is a set of best solutions from a large number of solutions.

The population based metaheuristics are related to the algorithms developed following the theory of evolution or swarm intelligence. In Evolutionary algorithms the solution space is explored using recombination and mutation operators. Where as the swarm based algorithms are developed mimicking the approach and intelligentsia shown by natural species like Cuckoo, Ant, Bacteria, Birds, Fish, Bee etc., for getting food and better survival.

Optimization techniques include a large number of algorithms and out of them the most widely used optimization algorithms in the area of software testing are local search techniques, Randomized algorithms, Genetic Algorithms, Genetic programming, Particle Swarm optimization etc. (Mark Harman, 2007). Software testing includes a variety of testing goals like structural, functional, stress, mutation, integration, safety, robust etc.. Whatsoever testing goal may be chosen the crucial role is played by the fitness function. The fitness function is framed in such a manner that it picks the best solution and is the primary guide of the search process (Mark Harman, 2007). In search based test data generation approach, the entire set of possible inputs (test data) form the search space and the test adequacy criterion is designed as the fitness function, for example to achieve branch coverage the fitness function determines which set of inputs are suitable for executing the nearest uncovered branches.

Andreas Windisch (2007) used Particle Swarm Optimization (PSO) technique to perform code based evolutionary structural testing of about 13 complex industrial objects and claimed that PSO out performs GA in terms of its efficiency and effectiveness.

Moataz A. Ahmed (2008) used Genetic Algorithms for performing white box testing of software. They used path coverage as the test adequacy criteria for test data generation, compared their work with the existing work of two authors (Lin, 2000; Pei, 1997) considering the same problems and found that their approach is working better. Some of the limitations of their work includes, most of the steps of the proposed methodology are done manually which needs intelligence and careful planning of the tester. They suggested that the approach can be automated and further extended using object oriented testing approach.

Wasif Afzal (2009) stated that the application of metaheuristic techniques to software testing is a very promising approach as exhaustive testing of software is not possible with the existing approaches due to its large size and complexity. At the same time application of search techniques to the non-functional testing is still ad-hoc and complex as the techniques are problem specific therefore the area needs a lot of reconsideration. In this paper the authors have given a comparative analysis of the different fitness functions used, the different non-functional properties of software as well as the search techniques like Tabu search, Simulated Annealing, Genetic Algorithms, Particle Swarm optimization etc. in 35 selected articles within the period of 1996 to 2007.

Shaukat Ali (2010) says that metaheuristics are capable of providing an efficient and cost effective solution to the test case generation process. Here the authors have stated that as search based testing (SBST) techniques are mostly heuristic in nature therefore a detailed empirical investigation of their cost effectiveness and efficiency in satisfying the test objective and their realistic application to development artifacts. They have provided a framework to be used as a guideline for guiding the data collection and empirical study purpose. They state that no doubt metaheuristic search is a very effective technique in solving the software testing process and most of the papers published are dealing with structured programs. The algorithms effectiveness and efficiency can be proved only through statistical data analysis which is lacking in many papers therefore the proposed framework would be very effective in empirically analysing the capability and performance of different metaheuristic algorithms.

Hitesh Tahbildar (2011) provided a brief and well defined classification of different testing and test data generation techniques as well as four types of generalized architecture for software test data generation, along with their merits and demerits. They have given a clear idea of the future directions, challenges of research and industrialization of the process of automated test data generation. Here the authors have not taken into consideration the topics of test data generation using UML and object oriented methodologies, but this work could be referred as a standard for understanding the concept of software testing techniques and specifically the different techniques of automatic test data generation.

Harman (2012) have described this field as an excellent and attractive approach, providing semi-automated or fully automated solutions for those problems involving high complexity, with a large solution space holding a variety of competing and conflicting solutions. Rendered a detailed classification of literature available in the arena of search based software engineering (SBSE) using popular search based optimization (SBO) algorithms also identified the recent research areas of SBSE. Here they expressed that the main strength of search based approach is the automated techniques work without any bias and always the best solution is selected satisfying the objective function, and with each iteration the search process is more filtered improving the solution and here the main role of human being is designing better fitness functions enclosing their knowledge and intuition.

Gentian (2012) provided a comparison among three search algorithms, Particle Swarm Optimization, Simulated Annealing and Genetic Algorithms for path based test data generation. They have shown that the algorithms are useful for reducing execution time and generating target path oriented test data.

Praveen (2012) used metaheuristic Cuckoo Search algorithm to generate optimized test data for software testing. Here the author ensures that the proposed methodology gives full transition coverage.

They have shown that Cuckoo Search is showing total transition coverage with very less amount of redundancy in comparison to Genetic Algorithms and Ant Colony Optimization (ACO).

Saswat (2013) represented a well-organized survey of the well appreciated techniques of test cases generation. The beauty of this paper is each category of the survey is written by well-known and established researchers of that field discussing the basic ideas, associated methodologies, current trends as well as future perspectives of those areas. In the search based testing section the author describes search based testing is the process of automatic generation of test cases mainly test inputs using search algorithms being guided by a fitness function based on test objective along with a stochastic process to transit through the solution space till stopping criteria is reached. Here the researchers have suggested using a hybridized approach using dynamic symbolic execution and search based software testing as those two approaches complement each other.

Madhumita (2013) presented a performance analysis of three metaheuristic algorithms, Artificial Bee Colony (ABC), Differential Evolution (DE) and Genetic Algorithms. Taking into consideration the bench mark triangle classification problem they have shown that DE algorithm out performs the other two algorithms, GA and PSO in generating test data within less time and less number of iterations.

Alessandro (2014) have provided a brief survey of the most successful researches performed in software testing domain within 2000 to 2014.This paper can act as a bible for researchers working in the area of software testing as this not only accounts the most successful researches performed in the testing domain it also throws light on all important open challenges and opportunities for future research related to testing.

Kar (2016) have analyses twelve bio-inspired algorithms including their inherent principles and different scope of applications.

Vardhini (2016) described the popular swarm based algorithms and applied these algorithms to different problems of power load balancing, cost estimation, optimal routing, color segmentation etc. and also performed a detailed study of the convergent as well as constraint of each of those algorithms.

BIO-INSPIRED METAHEURISTIC ALGORITHMS

Bio-inspired metaheuristic algorithms are the heuristic algorithms modeled mimicking the intelligentsia applied by nature and its organisms to obtain better adaptability, offspring or food etc. These algorithms have already shown their efficiency in providing good solutions to optimization problems within a particular range of data or at a particular point of time.

In search based testing the researchers are using search based techniques for finding the suitable test data or test cases satisfying a particular test adequacy criteria, (Alessandro et al.; 2014). The researchers are trying to generate optimized test data automatically using search algorithms like Simulated Annealing, Tabu Search, Genetic Algorithms, Particle Swarm Optimization etc.

In this paper the bio-inspired metaheuristic algorithms including Genetics Algorithms, Particle Swarm optimization Algorithm, Differential Evolution Algorithms, Artificial bee colony algorithms, Gravitational search algorithm and Cuckoo Search Algorithm, have been used to generate path coverage based test data for white box testing of structured programs. Though these algorithms are widely used for solving problems of other engineering branches but their use in search based testing area is negligible except Genetic Algorithms and Particle Swarm Optimization. A brief description of these algorithms has been given in out earlier papers (Madhumita, 2013, Madhumita, 2015).

Genetic Algorithms (GA)

Genetic Algorithms are Bio-inspired metaheuristic search algorithms inspired from the theory of evolution followed by nature to select and preserve the offspring bearing best traits for adaptability and survival. The Genetic algorithms accept a possible set of (inputs solutions) known as chromosomes and apply three nature inspired operators, selection, crossover and mutation for selecting best solutions from a possible set of solution space. Chromosome representation of the solutions and correct fitness function design and evaluation play the key role in the success of GA applications. The beauty of Genetic algorithms comes from its simplicity and quality as robust search algorithms as well as from its power to explore good solutions promptly for difficult high-dimensional problems covering large solution spaces.

Differential Evolution Algorithm (DE)

Differential Evolution algorithm is a little bit different from other evolutionary algorithms, as it begins with a population of constant size of Np individual candidate solutions, where Np is the size of population. Here each member of the population is a d-dimensional real-parameters vector representing a solution in the solution space S. The population size of new candidate solutions obtained generation by generation remains same in the solution space. The subsequent generations are denoted by $g = 0, 1, g_{max}$.

In each generation the vectors are changed by a differential operator as the standard crossover and mutation operators of genetic Algorithms are not used here. Differential Evolution uses the mutation operator, and unlike Genetic Algorithms here the mutation value is calculated by adding an amount to the difference of two randomly selected individuals from current population. In differential evolution another operator is also used, the selection operator which selects the locally best candidate, without sorting or ranking the population. Differential evolution algorithm generates new parameter vectors by adding the weighted difference among two population vectors to a third vector. Those obtained parameter vectors are then crossed with the parameters of trial vector to yield new trial vectors. Trial vector with better fitness value replaces target vector in the next generations and the overall process is known as selection. Each population vector serves at least once as target vector.

Artificial Bee Colony (ABC) Algorithm

The Artificial Bee Colony Algorithm is a swarm based optimization algorithm, recently proposed mimicking the food foraging behavior of Honey Bees (Karaboga, 2005).

In Artificial Bee Colony (ABC) algorithm there are three types of honey bees to search food source. They are named as employed bees, onlooker bees and scouts bees. The main role of the employed bees is to establish the hive in such a place where ample food source is available near and then they collect nectar from the food source present around the hive and provide food and look after the eggs laid by queen bee. The bees search for food source available nearby and pass this information to other bees through a dance known as waggle dance. A bee present in the dance area and watching the dance for making decision to choose a food source is known as an onlooker bee similarly a bee regularly collecting food from the food source previously visited by itself is named as an employed bee. A bee carrying out stochastic search to find out new food source is called a scout bee. In ABC algorithm the entire work of food searching, nectar foraging around the hive and taking care of eggs and baby bees are carried out together by employed, onlooker and scouts bees. In the ABC algorithm, almost half of the colony consists of employed artificial bees and the other half comprises of the onlookers. For each food source, there is only one employed bee. The number of employed bees is always equal the number of food sources present around the bee hive. The employed bee whose food source is exhausted again becomes a scout searching for new food source.

Particle Swarm Optimization Algorithm

The particle swarm optimization PSO) is a population based metaheuristic algorithm widely accepted by the researchers (Eberhart, 1995). The concept of this heuristic search algorithm is inspired by the social behavior of birds flocking. Later the inertia weight w is introduced into the initial algorithm. In PSO, a number of particles candidate solutions, constitute a population which flies around in the search space to find the global optimal solution. Meanwhile, every particle positions are controlled by their own best position, personal best, p_{best} and overall best, global best, g_{best} so far in their paths.

Each particle in the population represents the current position in the search space with the current velocity, it changes its velocity and position by considering the distance to p_{best} and the distance to g_{best}.

Gravitational Search Algorithm

The gravitational search algorithm (GSA) is a new optimization algorithm developed by Rashedi et al. in (Rashedi, 2009). This algorithm is based on Newton's laws of gravity and mass interaction, which says: "Every particle in the universe attracts every other particle with a force that is directly proportional to the product of their masses and inversely proportional to the square of the distance between them(Rashedi, 2009). In this algorithm, candidate solutions known as agents are taken into consideration as objects and their performances are measured by their masses proportional to the fitness values. In the evolution process, all masses attract each other by the gravitational forces between them. The heavier the mass, the bigger is the force of attraction. As the heavier masses have higher fitness values, they represent good optimal solutions to the problem and move slowly than lighter masses representing worse solutions. In Gravitational search algorithm, each mass has four characteristics: its position X_i, inertial mass M, active gravitational mass, and passive gravitational mass. The position of the mass in the search space represents a solution of the problem and its gravitational and inertial masses are determined using a fitness function of the problem(Rashedi, 2009).

Cuckoo Search Algorithm

Cuckoo search (CS) is a metaheuristic search algorithm inspired from the parasitic reproductive strategy adopted by Cuckoo birds, (Yang and Dev, 2010; Walton 2011; Srivastava, 2012). Cuckoo is a very interesting bird with its mesmerizing sweet voice and parasitic breeding pattern.

The cuckoo lays its egg in the nest of other host birds of different species. The cuckoo eggs as well as the newly hatched cuckoo chick try to mimic the pattern and behavior of host eggs and chicks, so that they could not be identified by the host birds.

The characteristic features of this algorithm includes three basic idealistic rules, first of all one cuckoo lays one egg and dumps it on a randomly selected host nest. The number of nests is fixed and only a few number of nests are abandoned if the host manages to identify the cuckoo egg with a probability Pa(0,1). A fraction of nests containing the best egg or solutions will carry over to the next generation.

The cuckoo search algorithm has the feature of preserving the best nests to the next generation same as elitism of genetic algorithms. It incorporates both the features of exploitation through local random walks as well as exploration through levy flights.

PROPOSED METHODOLOGY

We have proposed the following methodology, for generating test data, targeting path coverage based testing,

Proposed Methodology for Path Coverage Based Testing

Our proposed methodology is presented in a systematic manner in the following steps,

Step 1: Accept a program written in C programming language
Step 2: Instrument the program lines of code
Step 3: Generate a control flow graph for the target program
Step 4: Prepare a connection matrix from the control flow graph
Step 5: Find out all feasible path sequences from the control flow graph
Step 6: Find out the Cyclomatic complexity of the graph to get the maximum feasible path number
Step 7: Apply metaheuristic search algorithms to automatically generate test data
Step 8: Compare traced paths with Cyclomatic number
Step 9: Stop execution

Parameter Settings for Test Data Generation

Test data are the set of inputs to be provided at the time of execution of a program to find out the correct functioning of a specific module or the entire software under test(Bertolino,2007).

These inputs are carefully selected according to test adequacy criteria. A test adequacy criteria specifies the conditions that must be fulfilled on the basis of some test requirements. Here we have used path coverage as the test adequacy criteria, and this requires all the available paths in the program must be covered once.

Fitness Function

Search based optimization is applied to the field of software engineering in two steps. First a suitable representation for the program under test is selected and then a fitness function is defined, fulfilling the test adequacy criteria (Harman, 2015). This fitness function is used to evaluate the suitability of the candidate solution satisfying the targeted objective. Our test adequacy criterion is path coverage, so we have taken the weighted path based coverage as our fitness function (Srivastava, 2009). Here satisfying the test adequacy criteria it is needed to identify the paths of the program under test. First the upper bound of path numbers are identified from the control flow graph using Cyclomatic complexity (Rajib,2014).

To trace the traversed paths by the set of inputs, weights are assigned to each edge traversed. The initial weight for sequential statements is taken 100, then weight 20 is assigned to every false edge (satisfying false condition) encountered and weight 80 to every true edge(satisfying true condition) encountered during traversal, for example in an if -else statement the condition satisfying the if condition is the true edge and the condition satisfying the else condition is the false edge. Finally the total edge weight of every path from start node to end node is calculated. The sum of this edge weight is taken as the fitness value of each path.

$$f(x) = \sum_{i=1}^{n} P_i \tag{2}$$

where, P_i = fittest path.

$$P_i = \sum_{i=1}^{n} W_i \tag{3}$$

where, W_i = total path weight

The above mentioned fitness function is evaluated, to generate the total path weight of the feasible paths and then this path weight is used to generate coverage based input test data covering every feasible paths of the program.

EXPERIMENTS AND RESULTS

When we performed an elaborated study of existing literature in the field of test data generation, we found that the triangle classification problem is the most suitable and bench mark problem for path based testing. The triangle classification program is a bench mark problem for many researchers in the field of software testing. This problem classifies a triangle into one of the four categories, invalid, scalene, equilateral and isosceles by accepting the length of the three sides of a triangle as input. In our implementation first we instrumented the triangle classification program and prepared a control flow graph of this example program. Then we identified the path numbers in our example triangle classification problem as four, using McCabe's Cyclomatic complexity matrix. The identified paths from the control flow graph of our example triangle classification problem are as shown below,

Path 1: 1-2-3-8 (Sclene)
Path 2: 1-2-4-5-8 (Isosceles)
Path 3: 1-2-4-6-8 (Equilateral)
Path 4: 1-7-8 (Not a Triangle)

Parameter Settings for DE

Given below are the parameter setting for DE algorithm.

- The different variants of the scaling factor, F(0.25,0.75,1.0 and1.6)
- CR(0.5,0.6,0.7,0.8)
- The population size is fixed from 100 to 500.
- Generation size from 50 to 200.

Parameter Settings for GA

Following are the parameter setting for GA.

- **Population Size:** Initially 100 then 500.
- **No. of Generations:** 50 to 500.
- Chromosome Length $\mathbf{p_n}$ bits. Where P in number of parameters and n is number of bits, where **n=0,15**.
- Cross over probability 0.7.
- Random probability 0.5.
- Mutation probability 0.01.

Parameter Settings for ABC

Following are the parameter setting for ABC.

- The colony size is the sum of the number of employed bees and onlooker bees.
- Number of food sources are equal to the half of colony size.
- Limit of visit to the food source by employed bee is 10.
- population size 200, 400, 500.
- **No. of Generations:** 50 to 500

RESULTS

when we focused on the best results obtained using the different bio-inspired algorithms, we found that the cuckoo search algorithm with its excellent exploration and exploitation capability is the best choice to get optimal result in the search space, to generate appropriate test data covering every path of the example triangle classification problem. ABC explores the search space in a better way for all the four paths in comparison to DE and GA. In addition to that DE also gives better exploration for path1, path2 and path4 and GA's exploration is better only for path1 and path4. In terms of time complexity the execution time for Cuckoo Search algorithm is less than DE algorithm, GA and ABC algorithms. The five algorithms were executed ten times with same number of generation (10) and population size(50) and it was found that the average execution time for Cuckoo was the least.

Figure 1. Results obtained using Cuckoo Search [CO]

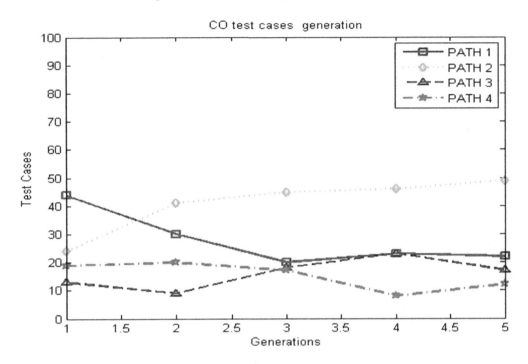

Figure 2. Results obtained using ABC

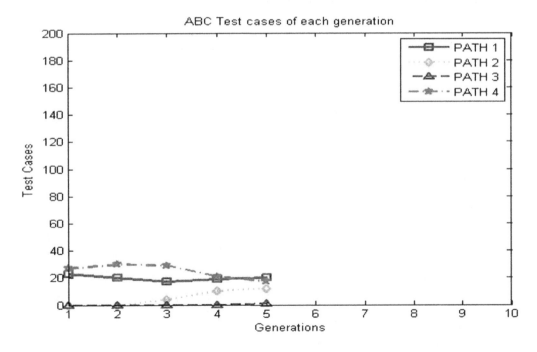

Figure 3. Results obtained using DE

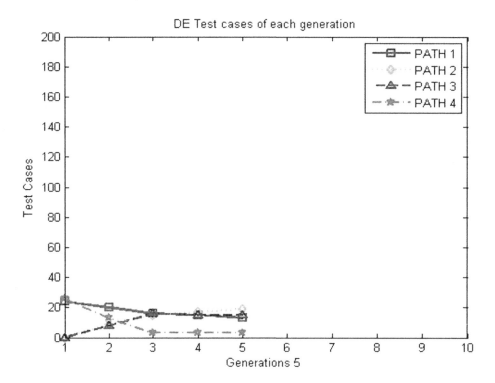

Figure 4. Results obtained using GSA

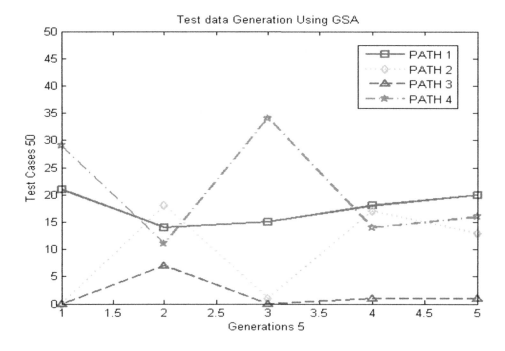

Figure 5. Results obtained using GA

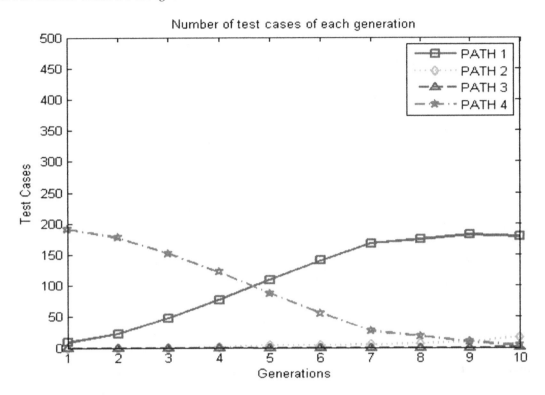

Figure 6. Results obtained using PSO

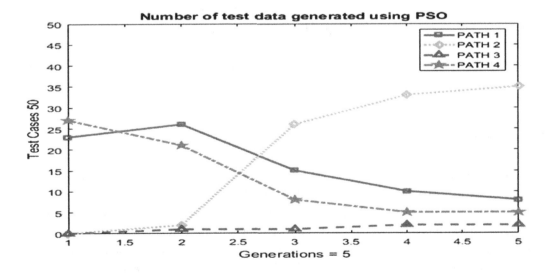

Figure 7. A comparative analysis of Results obtained using all the six Algorithms

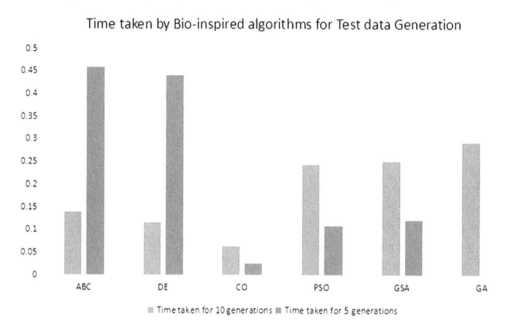

FUTURE SCOPE

Search based software testing is a recently developed domain of software testing, and this area is showing promising results towards the automation of test data generation process of software testing. Till date a number of bio-inspired algorithms have been proposed and used for solving different problems of engineering (Kar, 2016; Vardhini, 2016). This main problem of using the metaheuristic algorithms in software testing is development of intermediate structure and generation of connection matrix, and then formulation of fitness function,finally parameter tuning. A lot of research needs to be done to solve all those above described problems.

CONCLUSION

In this chapter we have given a detailed overview of six most popular nature inspired metaheuristic algorithms, Genetic algorithms(GA), Differential evolution algorithms(DE), Artificial bee colony algorithm(ABC), Gravitational search algorithm(GSA), Particle Swarm optimization algorithm(PSO), Cuckoo search algorithm(CS) successfully employed for solving different engineering optimization problems. We have also studied and developed a new methodology to generate test data for path coverage based testing using those popular metaheuristic algorithms, and performed an extensive comparison with the results obtained using those algorithms to establish the significance of the study. While comparing the results we found that the Cuckoo search algorithm outperforms all other algorithms in generating test data due to its excellent exploration and exploitation capability within less time showing better coverage and in comparatively fewer number of generations. We have also found that the parameter setting plays a major role in all the above algorithms especially Cuckoo Search and Differential evolution.

REFERENCES

Chauhan, N. (2010). *Software Testing: Principles and Practices*. Oxford University Press.

De Oliveira, B. M., & Labiche, Y. (2015). *Search-Based Software Engineering: 7th International Symposium*. Springer.

Elghondakly, R., Moussa, S., & Badr, N. (2016, March). A Comprehensive Study for Software Testing and Test Cases Generation Paradigms. *Proceedings of the International Conference on Internet of things and Cloud Computing*, 50. doi:10.1145/2896387.2896435

Harman, M. (2007). The current state and future of search based software engineering. Future of Software Engineering, 342-357. doi:10.1109/FOSE.2007.29

Harman, M., Jia, Y., & Zhang, Y. (2015). Achievements, open problems and challenges for search based software testing. *Software Testing, Verification and Validation ICST, 8th International Conference*, 1-12.

Harman, M., & Jones, B. F. (2001). The SEMINAL workshop: Reformulating software engineering as a metaheuristic search problem. *Software Engineering Notes*, *26*(266), 62–66. doi:10.1145/505532.505548

Harman, M., & Jones, B. F. (2001). Search-based software engineering. *Information and Software Technology*, *43*(4314), 833–839. doi:10.1016/S0950-5849(01)00189-6

Harman, M., Mansouri, S. A., & Zhang, Y. (2009). *Search based software engineering: A comprehensive analysis and review of trends techniques and applications*. Department of Computer Science, King's College London, Tech. Rep. TR-09-03.

Kar, A. K. (2016). A Bio inspired computing – A review of algorithms and scope of applications. *Expert Systems with Applications*, *59*, 20–32. doi:10.1016/j.eswa.2016.04.018

Madhumita, P., & Durga, P. M. (2014). Generating Test Data for Path Coverage Based Testing Using Genetic Algorithms. *Proceedings of ICICIC Global Conference*.

Madhumita, P. & Partha, S. (2013). Performance Analysis of Test Data Generation for Path Coverage Based Testing Using Three Meta-heuristic Algorithms. *International Journal of Computer Science and Informatics*, (32), 2231–5292.

Mall, R. (2014). *Fundamentals of software engineering*. PHI Learning Pvt., Ltd.

Maragathavalli, P. (2011). *Search-based software test data generation using evolutionary computation*. arXiv preprint arXiv:1103.0125

McMinn, P. (2004). Search-based software test data generation: A survey. *Software Testing Verification and Reliability*, (142), 105-156.

McMinn, P., Harman, M., Fraser, G., & Kapfhammer, G. M. (2016, May). Automated search for good coverage criteria: moving from code coverage to fault coverage through search-based software engineering. *Proceedings of the 9th International Workshop on Search-Based Software Testing*, 43-44. doi:10.1145/2897010.2897013

Mohanty, H., Mohanty, J. R., & Balakrishnan, A. (2016). *Trends in Software Testing.* Springer.

Nimpa, J. L., & Lichter, H. (2016). An Overview on Automated Test Data Generation. *Full-Scale Software Engineering/Current Trends in Release Engineering, 31.*

Orso, A., & Rothermel, G. (2014). Software testing: a research travelogue 2000–2014. In *Proceedings of the on Future of Software Engineering* (pp. 117-132). ACM.

Sadiq, M., & Sultana, S. (2015). A Method for the Selection of Software Testing Techniques Using Analytic Hierarchy Process. Computational Intelligence in Data Mining, (1), 213-220.

Shi, Y. (2001). Particle swarm optimization: developments, applications and resources. *Proceedings of the 2001 Congress on Evolutionary Computatio.*

Srivastava, P. R., Ramachandran, V., Kumar, M., Talukder, G., Tiwari, V., & Sharma, P. (2008). Generation of test data using meta heuristic approach. In *TENCON IEEE Region 10 Conference* (pp. 1–6). IEEE. doi:10.1109/TENCON.2008.4766707

Srivastava, P. R., Sravya, C., Ashima, N. A., Kamisetti, S., & Lakshmi, M. (2012). Test sequence optimisation: An intelligent approach via cuckoo search. *International Journal of Bio-inspired Computation, 4*(43), 139–148. doi:10.1504/IJBIC.2012.047237

Sthamer, H., Wegener, J., & Baresel, A. (2002).Using evolutionary testing to improve efficiency and quality in software testing. *Proceedings of the 2nd Asia-Pacific Conference on Software Testing Analysis& Review.*

Vardhini, K. K., & Sitamahalakshmi, T. (2016). A Review on Nature-based Swarm Intelligence Optimization Techniques and its Current Research Directions. *Indian Journal of Science and Technology, 9*(10).

Walton, S., Hassan, O., Morgan, K., & Brown, M. R. (2011). Modified cuckoo search: A new gradient free optimisation algorithm. *Chaos, Solitons, and Fractals, 44*(449), 710–718. doi:10.1016/j.chaos.2011.06.004

Yang, X. S. (2009). Firefly algorithms for multimodal optimization. In *International symposium on stochastic algorithms* (pp. 169-178). Springer.

Yang, X. S. (2010). A new metaheuristic bat-inspired algorithm. *Nature Inspired Cooperative Strategies for Optimization*, 65-74.

Yang, X. S., & Deb, S. (2010). Engineering optimisation by cuckoo search. *International Journal of Mathematical Modelling and Numerical Optimisation*, (14), 330-343.

Yenigun, H., Yilmaz, C., & Andreas, U. (2016). Advances in test generation for testing software and systems. *International Journal of Software Tools and Technology Transfer, 18*(3), 1–5. doi:10.1007/s10009-015-0404-z

KEY TERMS AND DEFINITIONS

Bio-Inspired Algorithm: It includes all the metaheuristic algorithms developed mimicking the food and foraging behavior of different organisms as well as the intelligentsia developed by nature for better species selection as well as adaptation to the environment.

Coverage: The percent of code tested by a particular set of input data or by adopting a specific testing strategy is known as coverage.

Feasible Path: All traceable paths of the program structure where we can traverse from start node to end node of a program structure, are known as the the feasible paths of that program structure.

Search Based Testing: It is a domain of software testing where bio inspired search algorithms are applied to solve the critical problems of software testing.

Test Adequacy Criteria: It is the minimum and sufficient criteria required to perform a particular type of testing.

Test Data: The set of inputs carefully calculated or selected to test a software or any specific module of a software.

160

Chapter 9
Development of an Efficient Prediction Model Based on a Nature-Inspired Technique for New Products:
A Case of Industries From the Manufacturing Sector

Vikas Bhatnagar
NIT Warangal, India

Ritanjali Majhi
NIT Warangal, India

S. L. Tulasi Devi
NIT Warangal, India

ABSTRACT

A lot of studies have been made on new product development process to make it an ideal procedure and many researchers have contributed significantly to achieve this by studying various factors associated with it. In this study, an attempt has been made to predict the optimal numbers of new products produced by electronics and metal & machinery industry by considering various factors those significantly affects the production pattern of these industries. For prediction purposes, functional linked artificial neural network (FLANN) with and without nature-inspired techniques have been used and comparison of performance for both the models have been done by using mean square error (MSE) and mean absolute percentage error (MAPE) as the measurement indices.

DOI: 10.4018/978-1-5225-2857-9.ch009

INTRODUCTION

Allocating scarce resources and utilizing them in best possible manner is the biggest challenge being faced by the scientist and research community all over the world in recent time (Manufacturing & Industrial: Waste Minimization). As demand for limited resources has been shooting up exponentially with time; industries are coming up with new and innovative products to survive and mark their success. In real time, it seems to be very obscure to estimate the exact numbers of new products needs to be produced to remain competitive in the market without wasting scant resources (Tomkovick & Miller, 2000) (Nayak). Considering this alarming situation of depleting resources and continuous boost in their demand; it is anticipated to predict proficiently the numbers of new products to be produced. Metal & Machinery and Electronics industries from manufacturing sector have been chosen to study their production pattern because of huge growth seen in these industries during last few decades. Real time data related to the production of the new products have been collected from the numbers of firms those are operating in these industries on different parameters like; age of firm, export experience, numbers of products produced by firm, expenditure on research and development, numbers of employees in firm, percentage input from domestic market, gross national income of the country where firm operates, total sales amount realized by firm, technology used for the production. Artificial neural networks (ANNs) are the techniques which imitate the working of human brain and as human learn from their past experiences ANN learn from the data provided to them. These techniques have found applications in numerous real time problems ranging from study of human behavior, medical studies, product and process improvement, image and signal processing and many more. In this study, a variant of ANN called functional linked artificial neural network (FLANN) technique have been used. FLANN is known for its simple structure with lesser computational requirements as compared to other available ANN techniques like multilayer perceptron (MLP). The best part of using ANNs is that they do not have many assumptions about the input data except the same format of input stream for getting significant results. Data collected on different variables has come from different sources and their values are distinctive in nature and to put them on the same scale normalization of data has been done. Randomization has been introduced in the input data sequences to avoid saturation during training and testing phase with the added benefit of testing the robustness of the model. Different functional expansions like trigonometric, legendre, chebyshev and power series are fused with the basic FLANN structure and two different models have been developed on the basis of feedback algorithm. In one model least mean square (LMS) for other bio-inspired particle swarm optimization (PSO) has been implemented as the weight updating / feedback algorithms. Mean square error (MSE) and mean absolute percentage error (MAPE) are taken as performance indices and comparison of the models have been made on the basis of results obtained from the simulation study. Working efficiency and prediction accuracy of the models have been shown using MSE plots and MAPE values respectively in the result section. Managerial implications along with limitation and future direction for the study have been discussed at last, which could help decision makers in maintaining the production level and may also help managers to use resources wisely while keeping the wastage at minimal.

LITERATURE REVIEW

A study was made on successful new product projects found that only 58% of such projects ended as successful one (Booz, Hamilton, & Allen, 1968) (Page, Assessing new product development practices and performance: Establishing crucial norms, 1993) (Page, Result from PDMA's best practices study: The best practices of high impact new product programs, 1994) which suggests approximately half of the efforts and resources were gone in vain. For every single project of new product development firm has to invest lot of resources and if product fails to perform in potential market then firm has to bear three fold losses first investment made on resources; second competitors got the upper hand; and third firm losses a golden opportunity to capture the market. Metal & Machinery and Electronics industries have been selected for this study because of their remarkable growth under new products categories during last few decades (IHS Newsroom) (EU SME Centre, 2011) (Ian) (Electronics manufacturing industry overview) and intensive usage of dearth raw resources for the production. No new product could be developed in isolation since many factors either internal or external to firm contribute towards it. Some critical factors have been identified by various researchers those are affecting the new product development process either on individual or combined basis e.g. the time of operation of firm from the day of start or in other words age of firm (Naldi & Davidsson, 2013) (Abernathy & Corcoran, 1983), export experience of firm (Glick, 1982) (Wren, Souder, & Berkowitz, 2000) (Dominguez & Cirigliano, 1997) (Soete, 1987) (Gupta & Sapienza, 1992), gross national income (gni) (Roessner, Bond, Okubo, & Planting, 2013) as the economic measure of the country where firm operates, numbers of permanent employees (Roure & Keeley, 1990) (Bourgron, 2007)working in the firm which also gives a measure of size of the firm, the percentage of input supplies from domestic market (Laursen & Andersen, 2016) (Mazzola, Bruccoleri, & Perrone, 2015) (Primo & Amundson, 2002) (Junfeng & Ping, 2016), technology used for the production (Park, Gunn, Lee, & Shim, 2015) (Xu, Huang, & Gao, 2012) (Grupp, 1994), expenditure on research and development (Pandit & Siddharthan, 1998) (Bender, Pyle III, Westlake, & Douglas, 1976) (Tsai, Hsieh, & Hultink, 2011) (Frankort, 2016), total sales (Chang & Chen, 2004) (McDougall, 1989) amount realized by the company in a year, total number of new products produced (Frankenhoff & Granger, 1971) by the firm in a year. All these critically important factors are affecting directly or in-directly the production process and hence considered as independent variables whereas numbers of new products produced is taken as dependent variables which needs to be estimated. The relationship between the independent and dependent variable for product development process is vague and ill-defined (University of Wisconsin-Madison) since by incrementing or decrementing input data values there is no proportional change on the output values which makes it difficult to estimate the output using conventional methods of approximation. The non linear network techniques such as artificial neural networks models could be useful in such situations because of inherent non linearity in their structure (Soteris, 2001) (Narendra & Parthasarathy, 1990). Development and widespread usage of neural networks techniques is evident in recent time and numbers of ANNs models have been developed (Yasdi, 2000) (Marini, 2009) like functional linked neural network (FLANN), radial basis neural network (RBF), multilayer perception neural network (MLP) etc. MLP is the basic and first designed neutral network having three layers, input layer, hidden or intermediate layer, and output layer with numbers of neurons embedded in them and connected to each other in a predefined manner (Basheer & Hajmeer,

2000). FLANN is a single layer single neuron network whereas RBF has closely matched structure with MLP but here instead of neurons it has nodes in different layers. All these techniques have been used to get solution for real time problems like stock market prediction problem (Xiaohua, Phua, & Weidong, 2003), climate condition estimation (Emery, Ferenc, Mary, & Emmanuel, 2003), fault detection and diagnosis (V., R., & Y., 1990), automotive guidance system (Gomez & Miikkulainen, 2003), EEG and ECG analysis (Nicos, Telemachos, Konstantinos, Costas, & Michael, 1998), routing system and many more numerous applications in diverse fields ranging from engineering, medical to management. Almost in every sphere of human world the usage of ANNs is evident and results from these techniques approximate the real life solution very closely which make these techniques very popular and a topic of interest for engineers and scientists.

RESEARCH METHODOLOGY

The research methodology used in this study has been discussed in this section. Data have been collected from numbers of firms operating in electronics and metal & machinery industries. The collected data is tabulated and validated by removing the missing and outlier values. It is a pre-requisite for ANN architecture that input data streams should be in normalized form i.e. bounded in the same interval for all the input variables or else abrupt result may occur. The ANN models used for this study have been developed with or without nature inspired techniques for different functional expansion. Least mean square (LMS) as simple and particle swarm optimization (PSO) as nature inspired techniques have been considered for the weight updating algorithm with FLANN architecture. Simulation study has been made on the validated data and results have been compared for both the developed models. Different plots showing the convergence and accuracy of prediction for both the models have been provided for clear understanding of working of the models. Conclusion has been made on the basis of results obtained from simulation study and at last limitations of the study as well as managerial implications have been discussed along with future directive to facilitate further research on the subject matter.

DATA COLLECTION AND VALIDATION

A real time data has been collected from electronics and metal & machinery industries on various parameters as mentioned in Table 1. These parameters have been identified from surveying intensive literature available for the new product development and its process pertaining to the industries belonging to manufacturing sector. Data statistics for both the selected industries are shown in Table 2, where collected data implies the total number of firms from which data have been acquired, and validated data indicate the set of data used for analysis after removing missing and outlier values. As a prior requirement of normalized data to work with ANNs, validated data is converted into normalized form with values lying between -1 to 1. One inherent advantage of normalizing data is it does not let affect adversely the weights updating schema of different weight updating / feedback algorithms implemented in the model. Randomization of normalized data have been done for avoiding the saturation in prediction accuracy and for assigning optimal weights to the bias and weight units by providing different combinations of input patterns. Randomization also helps in robust building of model and in achieving higher prediction accuracy even in case of entirely new input pattern applied to it.

Table 1. Independent and dependent variable

Independent Variable/Factor/Parameter	Dependent Variable/Factor/Parameter
Age of firm	
Export experience of firm	
Number of permanent employees	
Gross national income of the country where firm operates	
Percentage of domestic input supply	Number of new products produced in a year
Total products produced by a firm in a year	
Total sales amount realized by a firm in a year	
Technology used for production	
Expenditure on research and development in a year	

Table 2. Data statistics for electronics and metal & machinery industry

Data → Industry ↓	Collected Data	Validated Data
Electronics	398 firms data on 10 variables (9 independent input variables and 1 dependent output variable)	327 firms data on 10 variables (9 independent input variables and 1 dependent output variable)
Metal & Machinery	663 firms data on 10 variables (9 independent input variables and 1 dependent output variable)	464 firms data on 10 variables (9 independent input variables and 1 dependent output variable)

MODEL DEVELOPMENT

A FLANN model has been proposed to predict the numbers of new products produced by the different firms belonging to manufacturing sector. FLANN has less computational complexity because of its simple structure as compared to other ANN architectures. Different functional expansions like power, legendre, chebyshev, and trigonometric series are incorporated in FLANN for introducing necessary non linearity in the model (Majhi, Panda, & Sahoo, 2009). LMS was the first and most widely used method that has been implemented with the FLANN model for updating the weights and for training of model to its optimal level (the level from where no further decrease in error is possible). LMS is based on the stochastic gradient descent procedure where only present value of the difference between actual value and predicted value (by model) is taken into consideration for updating the weights associated with different input streams to the model. LMS is a bit old algorithm for updating weights and has its own limitations e.g. possibility of being trapped to the local minima or maxima and not able to converge to the optimal solution (Gal, Matan, Nir, & Dale, 2002). Many new algorithms have been proposed by the researchers and scientists like nature inspired techniques in comparison to LMS method as weight updating scheme for ANNs. PSO is a nature inspired technique which has shown significant increase in performance for numbers of applications than its counterpart LMS (Zbigniew, 1994). This study has implemented both the simple (LMS) and nature inspired (PSO) weight updating algorithms as two different models for the simulation study.

The basic block diagram for training phase of FLANN with LMS and FLANN with PSO models have been shown in Figure 1 and for testing phase in Figure 2. Input data streams are consists of normalized values of critically important variables for a firm identified by literature survey and a bias value of +1. These inputs values except bias are non-linearly expanded for different number of expansions like 3, 5... up to 11per input variable using different functional expansions like trigonometric, legendre, chebyshev and power series. Initially random weights have been assigned to all the inputs of model i.e. expanded inputs and a bias input. The weights and the corresponding inputs multiplied with each other and summed up to get the single output value. This value has been passed through tangent hyperbolic activation function which makes a non-linear decisive periphery because of its bounded nature. A difference has been computed between the predicted (output of activation function) and the actual value of the output variable. During training period the difference between predicted and actual value is termed as error in prediction which is propagated back to the model using LMS or PSO weight updating algorithms. The epoch procedure for training of model have been adopted where all the input patterns are given to model and average of all the error values have been propagated to update the weights in a single go and so on. This procedure will continue and the stopping criterion is either the numbers of iterations are exhausted or the mean square error between actual and predicted values reached at the desired level specified by the user.

Modeling of model in mathematical form is as follows:

Let 'A' denotes the input data matrix where row contains different industries and column contains data on different variables affecting the output. Single industry data on various factors i.e. individual row of the 'A' matrix is represented by 'a'.

Suppose if input data matrix has 'p' column and 'q' rows. Then, n^{th} row of the matrix including bias signal will be written as follows:

Figure 1. FLANN Block Diagram with LMS/PSO weight updating algorithm during training

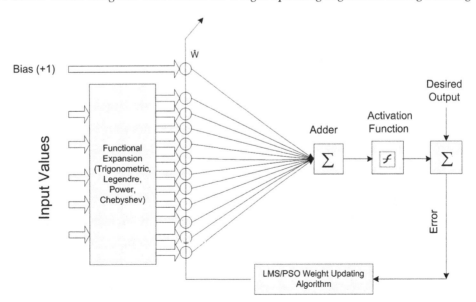

Figure 2. FLANN Block Diagram for testing after fixing weights

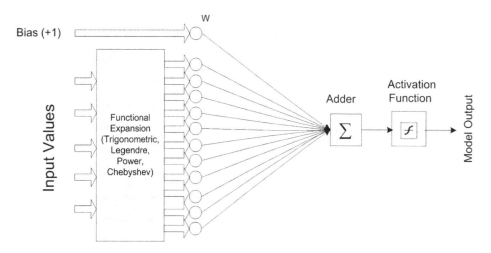

$$A\left(n\right) = \left[1, a\left(n, 1\right), a\left(n, 2\right), \ldots, a\left(n, p\right)\right] \tag{1}$$

where first term in the expansion is bias input.

Depending on the expansion type and number of expansions A(n) has been expanded.

The general equations of the four different expansions used are as follows:

Trigonometric series expansion =

$$\left[x, sin\pi\left(x\right), cos\pi\left(x\right), sin2\pi\left(x\right), cos2\pi\left(x\right), sin3\pi\left(x\right), cos3\pi\left(x\right)\ldots\right] \tag{2}$$

Chebyshev series expansion =

$$[1, x, \left\{2 * x^2 - 1\right\}, \left\{(4 * x^2 - 2) - x\right\}\ldots] \tag{3}$$

Legendre series expansion =

$$\left[1, x, \left\{\frac{3}{2} * x^2 - 1\right\}, \left\{\frac{5}{2} * x^3 - 3 * x\right\}, \ldots\right] \tag{4}$$

Power series expansion =

$$\left[x^1, x^2, x^3, x^4, x^5, \ldots\right] \tag{5}$$

where, x is the input which needs to be expanded.

For training and testing of the models only odd numbers of expansions have been considered because trigonometric series expansion does not hold valid for even number of expansions in case of inclusion of sine and cosine components along with the input term. For the purpose of comparison of model efficiency with different functional expansions only odd numbers of expansions have been used throughout the analysis.

For the demonstration purpose let suppose power series expansion has been used with three numbers of expansions. Here expanded input will look like as follows

$$A^e\left(n\right) = [\{1\}, \{\left(a\left(n,1\right)*x^1\right), \left(a\left(n,1\right)*x^2\right), \left(a\left(n,1\right)*x^3\right)\},$$
$$\{\left(a\left(n,2\right)*x^1\right), \left(a\left(n,2\right)*x^2\right), \left(a\left(n,3\right)*x^3\right)\}, \dots \qquad (6)$$
$$\{\left(a\left(n,p\right)*x^1\right), \left(a\left(n,p\right)*x^2\right), \left(a\left(n,p\right)*x^3\right)\}$$

where $A^e(n)$ stand for extended input after functional expansion.

With every input of the extended input one random weight has been assigned which result in $3p+1$ numbers of weights.

$$\widehat{W}\left(n\right) = \begin{bmatrix} w\left(1\right), w\left(2\right), \dots \\ w\left(p-1\right), w\left(p\right), w\left(p+1\right), \dots \\ w\left(3*p-1\right), w\left(3*p\right), w\left(3*p+1\right) \end{bmatrix} \qquad (7)$$

where, $\hat{W}$ stands for the variable weight matrix which will change its value after every epoch training of the model and become fix either when all the iterations are exhausted or the error value reach to the desired level specified by the user.

Every input is multiplied with its assigned weight and the result is summed up which is shown as follows

$$b\left(n\right) = \begin{bmatrix} \{\left(1\right)*\left(w\left(1\right)\} + \{\left(a\left(n,1\right)*x^1\right)*w\left(2\right)\} \\ +\{\left(a\left(n,1\right)*x^2\right)*w\left(3\right)\} + \dots \\ +\{\left(a\left(n,p\right)*x^3\right)*w\left(3*p+1\right)\} \end{bmatrix} \qquad (8)$$

This b(n) value is pass through activation function, here tangent hyperbolic function have been considered to meet the purpose.

$$B\left(n\right) = \begin{bmatrix} \dfrac{e^{2b\left(n\right)}-1}{e^{2b\left(n\right)}+1} \end{bmatrix} \qquad (9)$$

The B(n) value is the output predicted by the model of one firm and by comparing this value with the actual value of output for the firm an error value has been computed.

$$E(n) = C(n) - B(n) \tag{10}$$

where E(n) = Error value, B(n) = Predicted output, C(n) = Actual output

This E(n) value is stored and this process will continue till all the error values corresponding to given input data streams have been calculated. Average of all these error values have been propagated back to the model using LMS or PSO updating algorithm after one epoch to adjust the assigned weights. In this way epoch training has been carried out and continued till there is no more significant difference in error value observed or when the error value remains constant i.e. reached at the level specified by the user. At this point training is stopped and the last updated weights are fixed as the final weights for the model and model is ready for testing purpose. For simulation study eighty percent of randomized dataset have been used for training and rest of the twenty percent dataset for testing purpose.

MSE is used as the stopping criteria during training phase of the model development. MAPE and MSE are considered as performance indices for comparison the results obtained from both the models for different types of functional and number of expansions used in the analysis.

FLANN With LMS as Weight Updating Algorithm

The least mean square algorithm has been used for updating the weights associated with the expanded inputs and the bias input. This approach for updating weights was first used by Bernard Widrow and Ted Hoff in 1960 where only present difference in the actual value and predicted value (by model) were used. This algorithm is based on stochastic gradient descent method. Equation used for updating weight in LMS algorithm is:

$$W(n+1) = W(n) + 2 * \mu * x(n) * e(n) \tag{11}$$

Here updated value of weight W(n+1) depends on the present weight value W(n), input corresponding to the weight x(n), error propagated back to the model e(n) and μ which is the learning parameter for the model whose value lies in between 0 to 1. μ is responsible for making model learn at different speeds if μ value is small, model will learn slowly and have better convergence. On the contrary if μ has higher value it will make model learn fast with moderate convergence capability. Initial weights have been assigned as random values lying in between -0.5 to 0.5.

FLANN With PSO as Weight Updating Algorithm

The first practical implementation of Particle swarm optimization has been done in 1995 by Kennedy and Eberhart. It is based on collective movements of bird's which was first studied by Heppner where every bird wanted to be at best possible position with respect to other birds without any collision in group. For implementing PSO an initial assumption has made that bird is already at its local best position and to find the global best position it keep looking for the other bird position and iteratively tries to reach to the global best position in the group. The global best position of any bird in this algorithm depends on two parameters one is position itself and other is velocity. Birds fly in a group which makes them absolutely necessary to maintain their velocity and position at optimal place with respect to other birds moving in the same group. It should be noted that velocity of the bird is considered instead of speed since speed is a scalar quantity and has no knowledge about the direction but velocity is a vector quantity which shows direction of movement as well. When group of birds' fly, the movements seems to be very random with varied directions suggesting that movement of birds' may come under space – time dimension. Every bird has to maintain its speed along with the varying direction of movement. The position of bird again is an important aspect with respect to other bird's position as synchronization among them needs to be maintained all the time otherwise there will be no optimal movement and collision may happen. To maintain this synchronization all the birds needs to keep changing their position and velocity which is given by the Kennedy and Eberhart as follows:

$$V^{up} = V^{pr} + c1 * rand * \left(L^{best} - P^p \right) + c2 * rand * \left(G^{best} - P^p \right) \qquad (12)$$

$$P^{up} = P^p + V^{up} \qquad (13)$$

where V^{up} stands for updated velocity, V^{pr} means present velocity, c1 and c2 are learning factors those take the same value which means c1 and c2 are numerically equal and for the present problem of predicting number of new products produced by the firm pertaining to particular industry it is taken as 1.042 which turns out to be giving best results during simulation study, rand is the randomly generated number whose value lies in between 0 to 1, L^{best} is the best local position of the bird, P^p is the present position of the bird, G^{best} is the global best position of the bird, P^{up} is the updated position of the bird. Initial weights have been assigned as random values lying in between -0.5 to 0.5. For studying present problem with this algorithm, firm data have been considered in place of bird's parameters.

SIMULATION STUDY AND RESULTS

Experiments simulated using developed models by incorporating predefined parameters along with numbers of combinations of non-linear functions and numbers of expansions have generated different results those are shown in Table 3 for Metal & Machinery industry and in Table 4 for Electronics industry. These results were obtained by using 1000 numbers of epoch iterations, learning factor as 0.01, odd numbers of expansions ranging from 3 to 11, non-linear functional expansions like trigonometric, legendre, power and chebyshev series for FLANN with LMS model. On the other hand for FLANN with PSO only 200 epoch iterations, 50 reference particles initialized, c1 and c2 values were initialized to 1.042, odd numbers of expansions ranging from 3 to 11, non-linear functional expansions like trigonometric, legendre, power and chebyshev series have been used. Figure 3, Figure 4 and Figure 5 shows mean square error curve, training dataset plot and testing dataset plot respectively for actual and predicted values of Metal & Machinery industry using FLANN with LMS model whereas Figure 6, Figure 7 and Figure 8 shows mean square error curve, training dataset plot and testing dataset plot respectively for actual and predicted

Table 3. Result statistics for Metal & Machinery industry for both the developed models

Metal & Machinery Industry		FLANN With LMS				FLANN With PSO			
Expansion		Training		Testing		Training		Testing	
Type	Number	MSE Values	MAPE Values	MSE Values	MAPE Values	MSE Values	MAPE Values	MSE Values	MAPE Values
Power	3	0.002	3.430	0.005	3.851	0.001	2.568	0.001	2.809
	5	0.003	3.646	0.003	3.767	0.001	2.414	0.004	3.217
	7	0.002	3.179	0.002	3.075	0.001	2.403	0.002	3.022
	9	0.002	3.165	0.011	3.861	0.001	2.563	0.039	4.738
	11	0.003	3.178	0.041	5.365	0.001	2.476	0.021	4.692
Legendre	3	0.002	3.275	0.002	3.182	0.001	2.694	0.002	3.015
	5	0.002	3.196	0.006	4.334	0.001	2.477	0.001	2.378
	7	0.003	3.411	0.003	3.751	0.001	2.630	0.004	3.766
	9	0.002	3.292	0.002	3.321	0.002	2.806	0.043	6.361
	11	0.003	3.107	0.004	3.887	0.001	2.708	0.002	3.155
Chebyshev	3	0.002	3.277	0.002	3.733	0.001	2.5311	0.002	3.439
	5	0.002	3.179	0.002	3.165	0.001	2.631	0.003	3.777
	7	0.004	3.307	0.006	3.893	0.002	3.076	0.003	3.595
	9	0.003	3.664	0.002	3.768	0.002	2.970	0.005	3.469
	11	0.002	3.134	0.004	3.365	0.001	2.737	0.011	4.617
Trigonometric	3	0.005	3.703	0.010	4.329	0.001	2.674	0.010	2.934
	5	0.003	3.299	0.002	3.465	0.002	3.003	0.054	3.477
	7	0.005	3.694	0.008	4.727	0.001	2.803	0.024	3.149
	9	0.004	3.903	0.003	3.751	0.002	3.124	0.038	3.650
	11	0.005	3.984	0.018	4.465	0.002	2.923	0.011	3.482

values of Metal & Machinery industry using FLANN with PSO model. Similarly Figure 9, Figure 10 and Figure 11 shows mean square error curve, training dataset plot and testing dataset plot respectively for actual and predicted values of Electronics industry using FLANN with LMS model whereas Figure 12, Figure 13 and Figure 14 shows mean square error curve, training dataset plot and testing dataset plot respectively for actual and predicted values of Electronics industry using FLANN with PSO model. Plots were shown only for the type and number of expansion where best results were obtained during the simulation study. Results obtained from the study suggests that for Metal and Machinery industry the best performing type and numbers of expansions is coming out to be power series expansion and for 7 numbers of expansions terms for the FLANN with LMS model. Also for the same industry using FLANN with PSO model the best type and numbers of expansions is coming out to be legendre series expansion and for 5 numbers of expansions terms. Similarly for Electronics industry the best perform-ing type and numbers of expansions is coming out to be power series expansion and for 7 numbers of expansions terms for both the developed model i.e., FLANN with LMS and FLANN with PSO model.

Table 4. Result statistics for Electronics industry for both the developed models

Electronics Industry		FLANN With LMS				FLANN With PSO			
Expansion		Training		Testing		Training		Testing	
Type	Number	MSE Values	MAPE Values	MSE Values	MAPE Values	MSE Values	MAPE Values	MSE Values	MAPE Values
Power	3	0.006	5.940	0.005	5.355	0.005	5.339	0.005	5.043
	5	0.007	6.118	0.005	5.418	0.005	5.270	0.006	5.502
	7	0.007	6.066	0.005	5.126	0.004	4.887	0.005	5.019
	9	0.006	5.865	0.005	5.442	0.004	5.037	0.006	5.341
	11	0.006	5.923	0.006	5.829	0.005	5.143	0.006	5.354
Legendre	3	0.006	5.796	0.006	5.443	0.005	5.2715	0.006	5.284
	5	0.005	5.607	0.006	5.539	0.005	5.268	0.007	5.705
	7	0.007	6.312	0.009	6.331	0.006	5.301	0.006	5.179
	9	0.008	6.288	0.011	7.294	0.005	5.254	0.007	5.743
	11	0.008	6.264	0.008	5.970	0.005	5.037	0.028	8.724
Chebyshev	3	0.006	6.005	0.006	5.576	0.005	5.605	0.006	5.410
	5	0.008	6.434	0.006	5.423	0.006	5.154	0.006	5.221
	7	0.007	5.841	0.010	7.142	0.006	5.531	0.011	6.382
	9	0.008	6.507	0.008	6.440	0.006	5.654	0.094	12.521
	11	0.006	5.786	0.010	6.346	0.006	5.280	0.009	6.179
Trigonometric	3	0.006	6.184	0.005	5.593	0.005	5.207	0.006	5.586
	5	0.007	6.074	0.009	6.354	0.005	4.980	0.006	5.585
	7	0.007	6.184	0.024	8.471	0.006	5.293	0.061	9.165
	9	0.008	6.175	0.011	6.537	0.007	5.877	0.007	5.669
	11	0.009	6.717	0.034	9.706	0.006	5.449	0.007	5.857

Figure 3. Mean Square Error curve of Metal & Machinery industry for FLANN with LMS

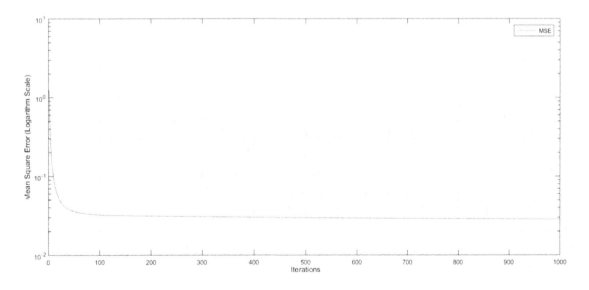

Figure 4. Training plot of Metal & Machinery industry for FLANN with LMS

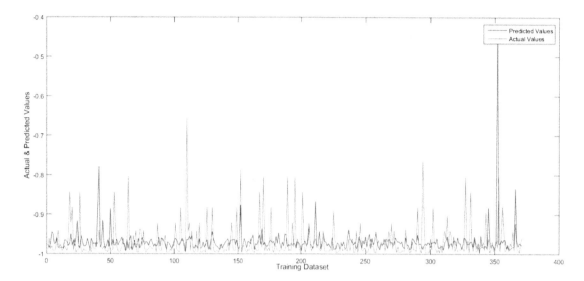

Figure 5. Testing plot of Metal & Machinery industry for FLANN with LMS

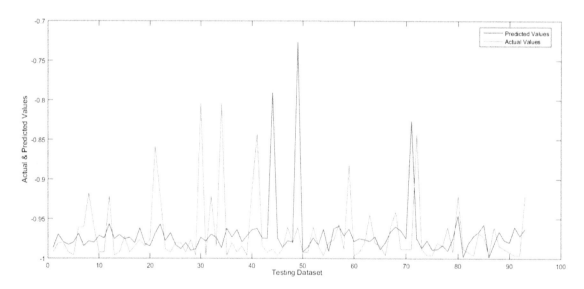

MSE and MAPE value during training phase signifies the closeness or approximation of model to the actual output for the input data provided to the model. Lower the MSE and MAPE values during training better the model prediction accuracy at the time of testing. But the real model efficiency and accuracy could be estimated only with the MSE and MAPE values obtained during testing phase of the model. It shows that how much accurately we can tell the output value only by knowing the input values which is the real test for the model. In this study different types and numbers of expansions have been used to study their effect on the prediction efficiency on both the models and results have been shown in Table 3 and Table 4 for both the industries. Same model constants have been used throughout the analysis for

Figure 6. Mean Square Error curve of Metal & Machinery industry for FLANN with PSO

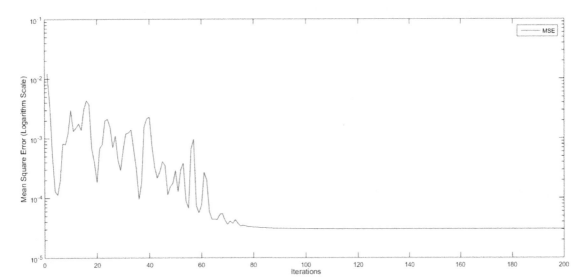

Figure 7. Training plot of Metal & Machinery industry for FLANN with PSO

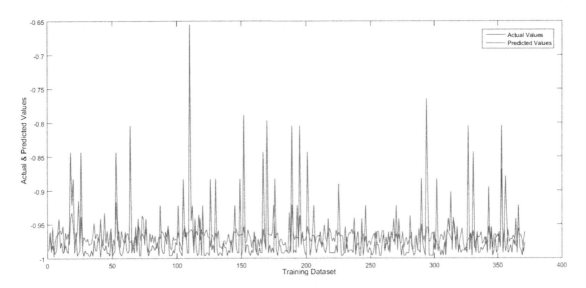

facilitating comparison of both the models. The constant values used in analysis were decided after hit and trial method with different number of values in the acceptable range and the best values on which model is working most efficiently in term of running time and less complexity have been selected for further training and testing with different dataset.

From the results obtained from simulation study it is found that power series expansion is the most efficient type of expansion in predicting the output in case of metal & machinery as well as electronics

Figure 8. Testing plot of Metal & Machinery industry for FLANN with PSO

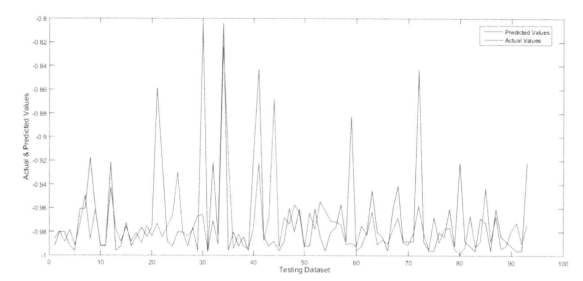

Figure 9. Mean Square Error curve of Electronics industry for FLANN with LMS

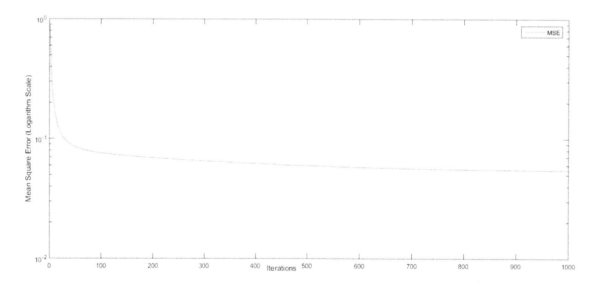

industry with FLANN with LMS model whereas for the metal & machinery industry legendre series expansion and for electronics industry power series expansion is giving the best result in comparison to all the other types of expansions used for simulation study with FLANN with PSO model. Table 3 and Table 4 shows that value of MAPE varies directly with the MSE value e.g. wherever MAPE value is least the corresponding value of MSE is the smallest.

Figure 10. Training plot of Electronics industry for FLANN with LMS

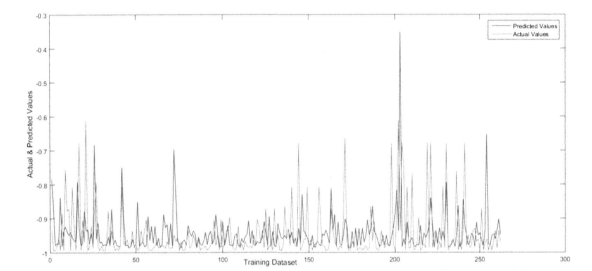

Figure 11. Testing plot of Electronics industry for FLANN with LMS

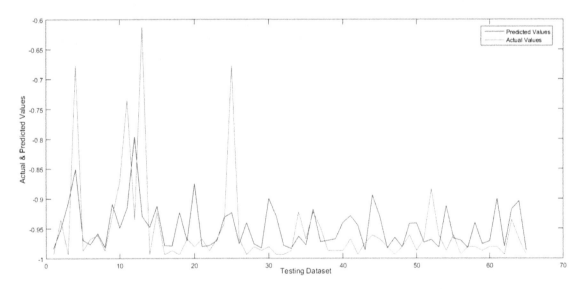

CONCLUSION

Simulation study on the two industries using artificial neural network with or without nature inspired techniques proves that ANN with PSO (nature inspired technique) outperform the ANN with LMS in numbers of ways. In the case of metal & machinery industry the prediction accuracy of the nature inspired technique is far better than its counterpart both in terms of MSE and MAPE except in one type of expansion. For electronics industry nature inspired technique has given better simulation results for all different types of expansions studied. Overall we can say that performance of FLANN with PSO is far

Figure 12. Mean Square Error curve for Electronics industry for FLANN with PSO

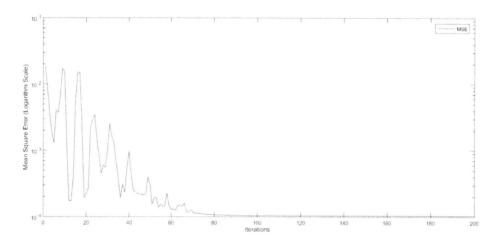

Figure 13. Training plot of Electronics industry for FLANN with PSO

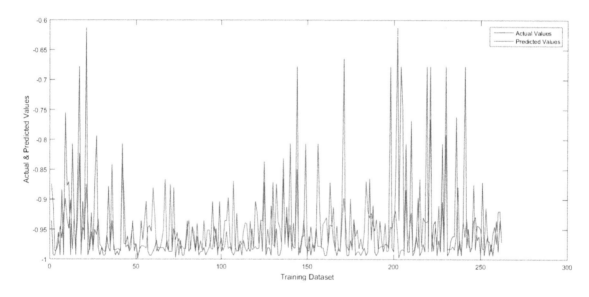

better than FLANN with LMS model which is evident from the results obtained from simulation study. The results obtained from the simulation study suggest that nature inspired techniques could be extended to solve numbers of real time complex problems with good efficiency with respect to other counterpart techniques where it is difficult to map the relationship between the variables.

MANAGERIAL IMPLEMENTATION

Industries are very well aware of the fact that people are more focused on eco friendly products and in other words people are willing to buy those products only where either no or negligible environmental

Figure 14. Testing plot of Electronics industry for FLANN with PSO

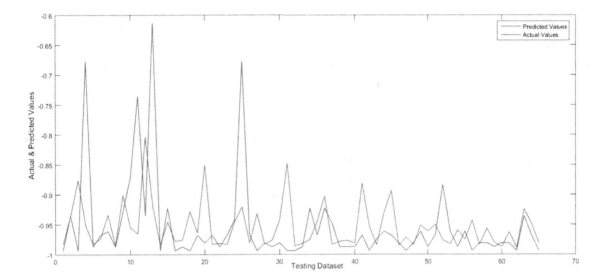

damage had happened (Robbins & Garcia). It is the corporate social responsibility of every industry (Smith, Read, & Rodriguez) to keep the environment safe and healthy which could be possible if there would be no wastage and firm produces the optimal number of new products. Managers could use the findings of this study to maintain the new product production level which may result in lesser wastage and more profitability to firm. Scant resources could be save which may improve the social image of the firm and will benefit the firm in long run. New firms those are going to open in the same industry if they may know in advance the safer number of new products to be produced for sustaining in the market could minimize wastage and disposal problem because of non consumption or failure of products. Moreover, different variables have been discussed in this study those are affecting directly or in-directly the number of new products to be produced by the firm which can be of great help to the managers for checking the production capacity as well as rate of production for their firm.

LIMITATION

This study has some generic limitations as well like dataset is limited if more dataset could be available better training and testing results may be obtained. Also to find out the total number of new products to be produced by the firm is dependent on many factors some factors could be measured directly like quantitative variables but others are difficult to measure like qualitative variables hence difficult to incorporate in the analysis. However if somehow such variables are measured then again to line up them with other quantitative variables is a big challenge. All the developed models works on some basic underlying assumptions if these assumptions have not met working of model could not be guaranteed.

FUTURE RESEARCH DIRECTIONS

In this chapter comparative study have been made between the artificial neural networks with and without nature inspired techniques for the two industries data by identifying some critically important variables those affects the number of new products produced by these industries. For future work some other combinations of inputs could be use or some new relevant inputs can be added to increase the prediction accuracy and to decrease the effect of uncertainty. Incorporating more relevant inputs can help in generalization of problem more accurately which may result in less uncertainty. Predicting number of new products to be produced is a complex phenomenon and depends on numbers of internal and external variables where quantization of variables again poses a difficult situation for the researcher. Hence for future work it is suggested that select only those relevant factors who can explain the maximum effect or phenomenon under study. Also other different types of expansions series and number of expansions could be tried to increase the prediction efficiency of the developed models.

REFERENCES

Abernathy, W. J., & Corcoran, J. E. (1983). Relearning from the old masters: Lessons of the American system of manufacturing. *Journal of Operation Management*, 155-167.

Basheer, I. A., & Hajmeer, M. (2000). Artificial neural networks: Fundamentals, computing, design, and application. *Journal of Microbiological Methods*, *43*(1), 3–31. doi:10.1016/S0167-7012(00)00201-3 PMID:11084225

Bender, A. D., Pyle III, E. B., Westlake, W. J., & Douglas, B. (1976). Simulation of R&D investment strategies. *OMEGA, International Journal of Management Science*, 67-77.

Booz, E. G., Hamilton, C. L., & Allen, J. L. (1968). *Management of new products*. Chicago: Booz, Allen & Hamilton.

Bourgron, L. (2007). Staffing approach and condition for collective learning in project teams: The case of new product development projects. *International Journal of Project Management*, *25*(4), 413–422. doi:10.1016/j.ijproman.2007.01.014

Chang, P. L., & Chen, K. L. (2004). The influence of input factors on new leading product development projects in Taiwan. *International Journal of Project Management*, *22*(5), 415–423. doi:10.1016/j.ijproman.2003.11.002

Dominguez, L. V., & Cirigliano, M. (1997). Chocolates EI Rey: Industrial Modernization and Export Strategy. *Journal of Business Research*, *38*(1), 35–45. doi:10.1016/S0148-2963(96)00116-6

Electronics Manufacturing Industry Overview. (n.d.). Retrieved June 12, 2016, from http://policy.electronicsb2b.com/industry/electronics-manufacture-industry-overview/

Emery, C. J., Ferenc, S., Mary, P., & Emmanuel, C. (2003). Artificial Neural Network Approach for Predicting Transient Water Levels in Multilayered Groundwater System Under Variable State, Pumping, and Climate Conditions. *Journal of Hydrologic Engineering*, 348–360.

EU SME Centre. (2011). *The machinery sector in China*. Retrieved June 12, 2016, from https://www.ccilc.pt: https://www.ccilc.pt/sites/default/files/machinery_sectorreport_v3_en.pdf

Frankenhoff, W. P., & Granger, C. H. (1971, April). Strategic Management: A new managerial concept for an era of rapid change. *Long Range Planning*, *3*(3), 7–12. doi:10.1016/0024-6301(71)90015-X

Frankort, H. T. (2016). When does knowledge acquisition in R&D alliances increase new product development? The moderating roles of technological relatedness and product-market competition. *Research Policy*, *45*(1), 291–302. doi:10.1016/j.respol.2015.10.007

Gal, E., Matan, N., Nir, F., & Dale, S. (2002). Data perturbation for escaping local maxima in learning. *Eighteenth National Conference on Artificial Intelligence*, 132-139.

Glick, R. (1982). *R& D effort and US exports and foreign affiliate production of manufactures*. North-Holland Publishing Company.

Gomez, F. J., & Miikkulainen, R. (2003). Active Guidance for a finless rocket using neuroevolution. *Genetic and Evolutionary Computation Conference* (pp. 2084-2095). Chicago, IL: Springer Berlin Heidelberg. doi:10.1007/3-540-45110-2_105

Grupp, H. (1994). *The measurement of technical performance of innovations by technometrics and its impact on established technology indicators*. North-Holland Research Policy.

Gupta, A. K., & Sapienza, H. J. (1992). Determinants of venture capital firmss preferences regarding diversity and geographic scope of their investments. *Journal of Business Venturing*, *7*(5), 347–362. doi:10.1016/0883-9026(92)90012-G

Ian, P. (n.d.). *Electronics component and Industry forecast for 2016*. Retrieved June 12, 2016, from http://www.radio-electronics.com/articles/distribution-supply/electronics-component-industry-forecast-for-168

Junfeng, Z., & Ping, W. W. (2016). Leveraging internal resources and external business networks for new product success: A dynamic capabilities perspective. *Industrial Marketing Management*.

Laursen, L. N., & Andersen, P. H. (2016). Supplier involvement in NPD: A quasi-experiment at Unilever. *Industrial Marketing Management*, *58*, 162–171. doi:10.1016/j.indmarman.2016.05.023

Majhi, R., Panda, G., & Sahoo, G. (2009). Development and performance evaluation of FLANN based model for forecasting of stock markets. *Expert Systems with Applications*, *36*(3), 6800–6808. doi:10.1016/j.eswa.2008.08.008

Manufacturing & Industrial: Waste Minimization. (n.d.). Retrieved June 12, 2016, from https://www.wm.com/sustainability-services/documents/insights/Waste%20Minimization%20Insight.pdf

Marini, F. (2009). 3.14 - Neural Networks. *Comprehensive Chemometrics*, 477-505.

Mazzola, E., Bruccoleri, M., & Perrone, G. (2015). Supply chain of innovation and new product development. *Journal of Purchasing and Supply Management, 21*(4), 273–284. doi:10.1016/j.pursup.2015.04.006

McDougall, P. P. (1989). International versus domestic entrepreneurship: New venture strategic behaviour and industry structure. *Journal of Business Venturing, 4*(6), 387–400. doi:10.1016/0883-9026(89)90009-8

Naldi, L., & Davidsson, P. (2013). Entrepreneurial growth: The role of international knowledge acquisition as moderated by firm age. *Journal of Business Venturing*, 687–703.

Narendra, K. S., & Parthasarathy, K. (1990). Identification and control of dynamic systems using neural networks. *IEEE Transactions on Neural Networks, 1*(1), 4–27. doi:10.1109/72.80202 PMID:18282820

Nayak, B. (n.d.). *Lean Manufacturing and Value Management Convergence of Divergent Tools*. Retrieved June 12, 2016, from http://www.value-eng.org/knowledge_bank/attachments/200629.pdf

Newsroom, I. H. S. (n.d.). *Rise of the Machines: Industrial Machinery Market Growth to Double in 2014*. Retrieved June 12, 2016, from http://press.ihs.com/press-release/design-supply-chain/rise-machines-industrial-machinery-market-growth-double-2014

Nicos, M., Telemachos, S., Konstantinos, D., Costas, P., & Michael, S. (1998). ECG pattern recognition and classification using nonlinear transformations and neural networks: A review. *International Journal of Medical Informatics*, 191–208. PMID:9848416

Page, A. L. (1993). Assessing new product development practices and performance: Establishing crucial norms. *Journal of Product Innovation Management, 10*(4), 273–290. doi:10.1016/0737-6782(93)90071-W

Page, A. L. (1994). Result from PDMA's best practices study: The best practices of high impact new product programs. *The EEI/PDMA Conference*.

Pandit, B. L., & Siddharthan, N. S. (1998). Technological acquisition and investment: Lessons from recent indian experience. *Journal of Business Venturing, 13*(1), 43–55. doi:10.1016/S0883-9026(97)00003-7

Park, J., Gunn, F., Lee, Y. H., & Shim, S. (2015). Consumer acceptance of a revolutionary technology-driven product: The role of adoption in the industrial design development. *Journal of Retailing and Consumer Services, 26*, 115–124. doi:10.1016/j.jretconser.2015.05.003

Primo, M. A., & Amundson, S. D. (2002). An exploratory study of the effects of supplier relationships on new product development outcomes. *Journal of Operation Management*, 33-52.

Robbins, A., & Garcia, J. P. (n.d.). *Consumer Willingness to Pay for Renewable Bilding Materials: An Experimental Choice Analysis and Survey*. Retrieved June 12, 2016, from https://digital.lib.washington.edu/researchworks/bitstream/handle/1773/35443/WP96WillingnessToPayRenewableBuildingMatrls.pdf?sequence=1

Roessner, D., Bond, J., Okubo, S., & Planting, M. (2013). The economic impact of licensed commercialized inventions originating in university research. *Research Policy, 42*(1), 23–34. doi:10.1016/j.respol.2012.04.015

Roure, J. B., & Keeley, R. H. (1990). Predictors of success in new technology based ventures. *Journal of Business Venturing, 5*(4), 201–220. doi:10.1016/0883-9026(90)90017-N

Smith, N. C., Read, D., & Rodriguez, S. L. (n.d.). *Consumer Perceptions of Corporate Social Responsibility: The CSR Halo Effect.* Retrieved June 12, 2016, from https://flora.insead.edu/fichiersti_wp/inseadwp2010/2010-16.pdf

Soete, L. (1987). *The impact of technological innovation on international trade patterns: The evidence reconsidered.* North Holland Research Policy.

Soteris, A. K. (2001). Artificial neural networks in renewable energy systems applications: A review. *Renewable & Sustainable Energy Reviews,* 373–401.

Tomkovick, C., & Miller, C. (2000). Perspective-Riding the wind: Managing new products development in an age of change. *Journal of Product Innovation Management, 17*(6), 413–423. doi:10.1016/S0737-6782(00)00056-4

Tsai, K. H., Hsieh, M. H., & Hultink, E. J. (2011). External technology acquistion and product innovativeness: The moderating roles of R&D investment and configurational context. *Journal of Engineering and Technology Management, 28*(3), 184–200. doi:10.1016/j.jengtecman.2011.03.005

University of Wisconsin-Madison. (n.d.). *A Basic Introduction To Neural Networks.* Retrieved August 22, 2016, from University of Wisconsin-Madison: http://pages.cs.wisc.edu/~bolo/shipyard/neural/local.html

V., V., R., V., & Y., Y. (1990). Process fault detection and diagnosis using neural networks-I. steady-state processes. *Computers & Chemical Engineering,* 699-712.

Wren, B. M., Souder, W. E., & Berkowitz, D. (2000). Market orientation and new product development in global industrial firms. *Industrial Marketing Management, 29*(6), 601–611. doi:10.1016/S0019-8501(00)00120-6

Xiaohua, W., Phua, P. K., & Weidong, L. (2003). Stock market prediction using neural networks: Does trading volume help in short-term prediction? *Proceedings of the International Joint Conference on Neural Networks,* 2438-2442. doi:10.1109/IJCNN.2003.1223946

Xu, K., Huang, K. F., & Gao, S. (2012). Technology sourcing, appropriability regimes, and new product development. *Journal of Engineering and Technology Management, 29*(2), 265–280. doi:10.1016/j.jengtecman.2012.03.003

Yasdi, R. (2000). A Literature Survey on Applications of Neural Networks for Human-Computer Interaction. *Neural Computing & Applications, 9*(4), 245–258. doi:10.1007/s005210070002

Zbigniew, M. (1994). GAs: What are they? Genetic Algorithm+ Data Structures = Evolution Programs. *Genetic and Evolutionary Computation Conference* (pp. 13-30). Chicago: Springer Berlin Heidelberg.

KEY TERMS AND DEFINITIONS

Dependent Variable/Factor/Parameter: These variables are bound to other variables or in other words variations in these variables are affected by the variations in other variables. These variables serve the purpose of studying any phenomenon by observing these variables.

Independent Variable/Factor/Parameter: These variables do not bound to any other variable or in other words variations in these variables do not depends on the variation of any other variables. These variables are used as the input data streams for any phenomenon to study.

Nature Inspired Technique: Techniques or methods those are devised or copycat from nature are called as nature inspired techniques since these are motivated from the phenomenon happening in the nature as a daily routine e.g. the movement of groups of birds in sky, movement of ants in a single line and many more.

New Products: Products those give different utility and feeling to the consumers rather than the traditional old products are considered to be new products.

Qualitative Variables: These variables cannot have exact numerical values but we can measure them on some particular scale like likert 5 point scale e.g., financial status of firm can be measured on a 5 point scale from very good, good, average, poor, very poor. Later we can assign any numerical value to these scales for representation.

Quantitative Variables: These are the variables those could have get numerical values. For example age of a person, number of pen one person is holding etc.

Simulation Study: Creating an artificial environment satisfying all the real time conditions or creating exact duplicate of the phenomenon. In this way we can simulate the copy of real time problem and can check the result by using different input variables and other conditions which could save lot of resources and according to results obtained different strategies may be devise for future action plan.

Chapter 10
Applications of Hybrid Intelligent Systems in Adaptive Communication

Atta ur Rahman
University of Dammam, Saudi Arabia

ABSTRACT

Dynamic allocation of the resources for optimum utilization and throughput maximization is one of the most important fields of research nowadays. In this process the available resources are allocated in such a way that they are maximally utilized to enhance the overall system throughput. In this chapter a similar problem is approached which is found in Orthogonal Frequency Division Multiplexing (OFDM) environment, in which the transmission parameters namely the code rate, modulation scheme and power are adapted in such a way that overall system's data rate is maximized with a constrained bit error rate and transmit power. A Fuzzy Rule Base System (FRBS) is proposed for adapting the code rate and modulation scheme while Genetic Algorithm (GA) and Differential Evolution (DE) algorithm are used for adaptive power allocation. The proposed scheme is compared with other schemes in the literature including the famous Water-filling technique which is considered as a benchmark in the adaptive loading paradigm. Supremacy of the proposed technique is shown through computer simulations.

INTRODUCTION

Demand of high data rates, mobility and enhanced quality of service (QoS) in wireless communication systems is increasing day by day due to the advent of various applications like cloud computing with thin client architecture, services like online conferencing, video streaming and many more. To meet these requirements, conventional fixed and static communication techniques are far from satisfaction.

This situation demands adaptive and dynamic communication systems to meet the day to day communication requirements and integrity of data. In adaptive communication, different transmission parameters like transmit power, modulation scheme, number of subcarriers and forward error correcting (FEC) code rate are adjusted according to the varying channel state information (CSI) and QoS demand

DOI: 10.4018/978-1-5225-2857-9.ch010

by the user during that transmission interval. Though, adaptive communication is not a new idea as it was started about two decades ago, however, its necessity in current communication systems is much more than ever because of the shift from wired communication links to wireless communication, need of mobility and numerous services demanding high data rates with quality. Moreover, initially the adaptive communication systems were based on conventional optimization techniques because number of transmission parameters being adapted were limited to one or two like adaptive modulation and/or adaptive code rate; even if both code rate and modulation schemes were to adapt, one of the two aspects was kept fixed while other was adapted; that is adaptive modulation with fixed code rate and vice versa.

Adaptive communication is a highly non-linear and dynamic phenomenon due to three major aspects. First, number of parameters being optimized increased; second, most of the modern communication systems shift from single carrier (SC) to multicarrier (MC) systems like orthogonal frequency division multiplexing (OFDM) systems where each subcarrier experiences a different channel behavior and third, flexible data rate demands on different subcarrier or group of subcarriers to satisfy user or application demand while satisfying several constraints. So, optimum selection of these parameters in presence of certain constraints like transmit power and target bit error rates (BER), is a hottest area of research. Also, it is proven to be a non-convex optimization problem that cannot be optimized by conventional optimization techniques unless it is made convex first (Bockelmann et al, 2000).

On the other hand, applications of evolutionary algorithms and soft-computing techniques like Genetic algorithms (GAs), Differential Evolution, Fuzzy Systems (FS and their combinations (hybrid intelligent systems) has been increasing tremendously over the past decade for the solution to highly non-linear and non-convex optimization problems, identical to the one mentioned above.

In this chapter, applications of soft and evolutionary computing techniques with their hybrid versions to solve the above cited optimization problem is presented. Majorly, this chapter summarizes the work done by Atta-ur-Rahman et al. (2012-2017). This chapter is organized as follows.

- Basic concept of adaptive communication is presented in first section
- Section two contains related work and problem definition
- Section three contains the system model and coded modulations and their performance
- Section four contains the design of Fuzzy Rule Based System
- Section five contains the simulation results
- Section six contains adaptive power background and techniques
- Section seven contain applications of GA and DE in combination to FRBS
- Section eight contain simulation results and conclusions

BACKGROUND

Adaptive Communication

Adaptive communication has gained attention of most of the current and future communication systems. Many 3rd generation (3G) and 4th generation (4G) systems have employed it as the main feature of communication while 5th generation (5G) is in research phase. These systems are mainly Orthogonal Frequency Division Multiplexing (OFDM) based systems. In OFDM systems, one large data stream is divided into several low data rate streams. Then these streams are modulated over different orthogonal subcarriers. These subcarriers exhibit different channel conditions during transmission.

Adaptive communication is a technique in which different transmission parameters like code rate, modulation symbol, power and subcarriers etc. are chosen according to varying channel state information (CSI) of the sub-channels. It is done in such a way that the overall throughput of OFDM system is maximized while satisfying certain number of constraints like bit error rate (BER) and total transmit power etc., at the same time. So, it is a constrained optimization problem and the concept of adaptive communication ultimately leads to the optimum utilization of resources in a communication system environment. Different terminologies like adaptive resource allocation, dynamic resource allocation and optimum resource allocation are also referred in the literature to the same phenomenon.

From an extensive literature review it is observed that Adaptive coding and modulation is one of the hottest areas of research in wireless communication especially in Wireless Broadband Access (WBA) like IEEE802.11 (WIFI), IEEE802.16/e (WiMAX) etc. Adaptive modulation and adaptive coding is used to maximize throughput and minimize the BER for OFDM environment.

According to Keller et al. (2000) there are three steps in adaptive communication. First step is channel estimation in which the receiver estimates the channel state information (CSI). Second step is adapting the parameters according to CSI estimated in previous step. Third step is synchronization in which the chosen parameters are acknowledged by the transmitter so that new parameters may be used in the next transmission interval.

In the literature survey, we have observed that the second step is most critical where parameters are intelligently adapted while remaining two steps are mostly assumed to be known in many contributions. Like Bockelmann et al. (2009) and Al-Askary (2006) proposed schemes for adaptive communication assuming that channel state information is known at transmitter and receiver both. Sastry *et al.* (2010) proposed a Fuzzy logic based scheme for channel estimation and adaptive modulation with an assumed synchronization. Moreover, fuzzy logic interface was used to estimate the channel and this was called non-data aided SNR estimation.

Following approaches have been made for adapting parameters according to the given channel state information,

1. Adaptive modulation without using any practical channel coding scheme. This kind of work is carried out by Kelet (1989), Chow et al. (1995), Cyzlwic (1996) and Sastry *et al.* (2010).
2. Adaptive modulation with a fixed code rate for all subcarriers during the transmission interval as by Faezah *et al.* (2009), Li *et al.* (2007), Stierstorfer et al (2007) etc. This approach is also named as Adaptive Coded Modulation.
3. Adaptive code rate with a fixed modulation order for all subcarriers during the transmission interval like Al-Askary (2006).
4. Adaptive code rate and modulation with flat power distribution for all subcarriers during the transmission interval like Bockelmann et al. (2009)

As such no combined approach is investigated that uses adaptive coding, adaptive modulation and adaptive power for each subcarrier in an efficient way based upon some criteria. This is perhaps because there is no closed form expression available in the literature that encompasses the whole phenomenon. Moreover, in the literature, the decision for next modulation/coding is mainly based upon the following.

1. Average received SNR from all the subcarriers or chunk of subcarriers
2. Previous modulation/coding scheme especially for slowly varying channels (IEEE indoor channels) like Peng et al. (2007)
3. Type of channel like fading type, frequency selective/non-selective, Doppler effect etc

The problems with these schemes are as under;

Firstly, the decision for adapting parameters was based upon average channel conditions on all the subcarriers instead of individual channel conditions. Hence same set of parameters will be used for all subcarriers during the transmission interval; however, the suggested parameters would not be suitable for many of the subcarriers. For example, the chosen modulation symbol and code rate might be suitable for subcarriers with good channel conditions but on the subcarriers with poor channel conditions, performance of the modulation and coding scheme will be deteriorated.

Secondly, the adaptive criteria are not very efficient as few wide range signal-to-noise ratio (SNR) thresholds were used for adapting the parameters. For example, if average received SNR lies in the range [20dB-30dB] then a specific code rate and modulation symbol will be used. In this way, the chosen parameters would never be equally good for subcarriers having marginal values of average received SNR e.g., 20dB and 30dB. So with this discussion, we formulate the problem as under;

Instead of using adaptive modulation and coding individually, a combined approach will be used which is called Adaptive Coding and Modulation (ACM). The decision of next transmission interval modulation code pair (MCP) will be taken by individual subcarrier conditions rather than average or group subcarrier conditions. In this way every subcarrier may have a different code rate and modulation symbol after each transmission interval.

Problem Statement

In a typical OFDM environment the available channel bandwidth is divided into a number of orthogonal subcarriers. As each subcarrier, may experience a different channel behavior, using a fixed modulation and coding scheme for all the subcarrier and for all the time may not be a good idea. In literature, a number of adaptive communication techniques have been investigated, they do adapt the parameters like code rate and/or modulation scheme after each transmission interval; but once the parameters are chosen same combination of parameters is applied on all subcarriers.

Moreover, the decision for the next transmission parameters used is mostly done by average received signal to noise ratio (SNR) thresholds. In this way the chosen parameters may be very good for some subcarriers but for the rest it may not be a good choice. Consequently the throughput of the system cannot be optimized. Another limiting factor in this regard is that SNR thresholds quite wide like same modulation code combination is inferred for 10dB SNR spectrum.

To overcome these limitations a Fuzzy Rule Base System is proposed for the solution of the constrained optimization problem that can be stated as,

Maximize the overall data rate of OFDM system by varying the code rate and modulation scheme such that the bit error rate and total transmit power should remain under certain thresholds.

Mathematically, this problem can be written as;

$$\max \quad R_{Total} = \frac{1}{N} \sum_{n=1}^{N} r_n$$

$$\text{s.t,}$$

$$BER_n \leq BER_{QoS_n} \tag{1}$$

$$\text{and}$$

$$\sum_{n=1}^{N} p_n < P_T$$

where $r_n = (\log_2(M))_n R_n$ is bit rate of the *n*th subcarrier, which is product of code rate R_n and bits per modulation symbol used $(\log_2(M))_n$ at *n*th subcarrier also known as *modulation code product*, P_T is the available transmit power and BER_{QoS_n} is the target BER that depends upon a specific quality of service (QoS) request or application requirement over *n*th subcarrier, while N denotes the total number of subcarriers in OFDM system.

System Model

The system model considered is an Orthogonal Frequency Division Multiplexing (OFDM) equivalent baseband model with N number of subcarriers. It is assumed that complete channel state information (CSI) is known at both transmitter and receiver sides. The frequency domain representation of system is given by;

$$r_n = h_n \cdot \sqrt{p_n} \cdot x_n + z_n; \quad n = 1, 2, \ldots, N \tag{2}$$

where $r_n, h_n, \sqrt{p_n}, x_n$ and z_n denote received signal, channel coefficient, transmit power, transmit symbol and the additive while Gaussian noise (AWGN) at the subcarrier $n = 1, 2, \ldots, N$, respectively. The overall transmit power of the system is $P_T = \sum_{n=1}^{N} p_n = Np$ since power is considered same (flat) for all the subcarriers, and the noise distribution is complex Gaussian with zero mean and unit variance.

It is assumed that signal transmitted on the *n*th subcarrier is propagated over an independent non-dispersive single-path Rayleigh Fading channel and where each subcarrier faces a different amount of fading independent of each other. Hence, the channel coefficient of the *n*th subcarrier can be expressed as:

$$h_n = \alpha_n e^{j\theta_n}; n = 1, 2, \ldots, N \tag{3}$$

where α_n is Rayleigh distributed random variable of *n*th subcarrier, and the phase θ_n is uniformly distributed over $[0, 2\pi]$. And j represents the complex number notation 'iota'. Figure 1 shows the schematic diagram of the proposed system. According to this diagram, upon receiving the signal, channel coefficients and quality of service demands for all subcarriers is fed into the proposed fuzzy rule base system block, which in turn would decide the new modulation and coding scheme. The information about the new parameters in sent to the receiver via a feedback channel. Upon receiving the parameters transmitter starts using them and so on.

Figure 1. Schematic of proposed adaptive system

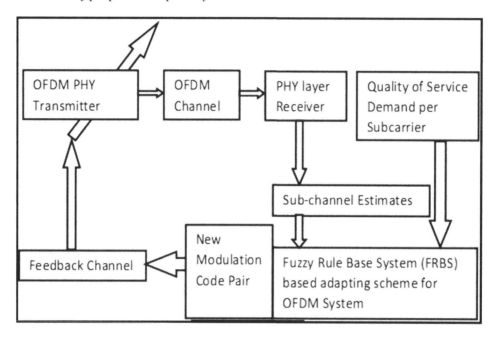

Coded Modulation

For the solution of above cited problem, different combinations of coding and modulation schemes are plotted over AWGN channel. Later these plots become the starting point of design of the proposed Fuzzy Rule Base System. Following classes of coding and modulation schemes are used for experimentation.

Coding Scheme

The codes used in this paradigm are non-recursive convolutional codes with code rates taken from the set $C = \{1/4, 1/3, 1/2, 2/3, 3/4\}$ with constraint length 3. For decoding, standard soft output Viterbi decoder is used originally proposed by Hagenauer et al. (1989). The reason for selection of these codes is that these codes are practically being used in many OFDM based 3rd Generation (3G) and 4th Generation (4G) communication systems nowadays.

Modulation Scheme

In this system Quadrature Amplitude Modulation (QAM), with rectangular constellation is used as modulation scheme. The modulation sizes are taken from the set $M = \{2,4,8,16,32,64,128\}$. This scheme is currently being used in many practical OFDM systems.

Performance Graphs

For experimentation the sequence of operations is carried out in same way as given in the Figure 2. The transmitted signal is first encoded using standard feed-forward convolutional encoder having code rate

Figure 2. Simulation block diagram

SNR-->>		Q1	Q2	Q3	Q4	Q5	Q6	Q7	Q8	Q9	Q10	Q11	Q12	Q13	Q14	Q15	Q16
	L0	P2	P2	P2	P2	P2	P2	P2	P1	P1	P1	P1	P1	P1	P1	P1	P1
	L1	P3	P3	P2	P2	P2	P2	P2	P2	P2	P2	P1	P1	P1	P1	P1	P1
	L2	P4	P3	P3	P2	P2	P2	P2	P2	P2	P2	P2	P2	P1	P1	P1	P1
	L3	P7	P7	P7	P7	P7	P7	P7	P2	P2	P2	P2	P2	P1	P1	P1	P1
	L4	P7	P7	P7	P7	P7	P7	P5	P5	P5	P5	P3	P3	P1	P1	P1	P1
	L5																
	L6																
	L7																
	L8																
	L9																
	L10																
	L11																
	L12																
	L13																
	L14																
	L15																
	L16																
	L17																
	L18																
	L19																
	L20																
	L21																
	L22																
	L23																
	L24																
	L25																
	L26																
	L27																
	L28																
	L29																
	L30																

QoS-->>

from the set *C* and then the encoded signal is modulated using the QAM from the set *M*. Similarly, upon receiving signal is first demodulated then decoded.

All codes belong to set C and modulation symbols from set M are plotted. By cross product of sets *C* and *M* following modulation code pairs (MCPs) are obtained;

$$P = CxM = \{(c_i, m_j); \forall c_i \in C, \forall m_j \in M\} \tag{4}$$

Then graph for each pair is obtained over an Additive White Gaussian Noise (AWGN) channel. The selection of this channel is suitable in a sense that it reflects the proper relationship between signal to noise ratio (SNR) and data rate achievable under a specific target bit error rate (BER). Also, other channel characteristics like fading types etc. can be compensated easily. Few of the graphs are depicted in the Figure 3, Figure 4 and Figure 5 with code rate 1/4, 1/3 and 1/2 respectively. These graphs will be used for data acquisition and rules formulation in the proposed Fuzzy Rule Base System subsequently.

Figure 3. BER comparison of different QAM schemes using rate 1/4 convolutional Code

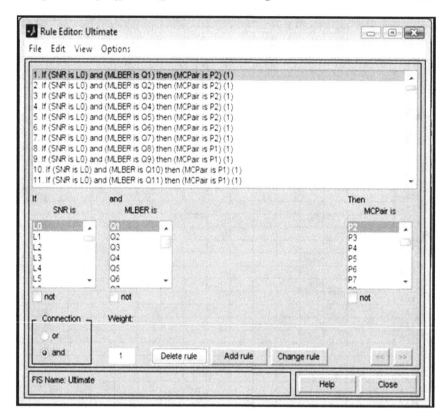

Figure 4. BER comparison of different QAM schemes using rate 1/3 convolutional Code

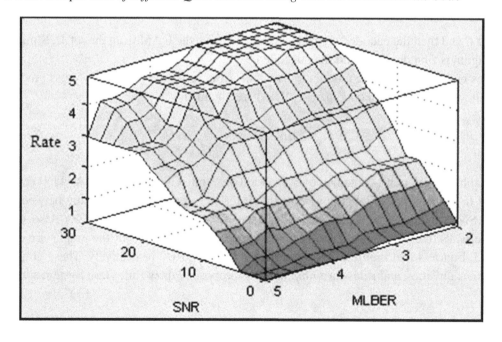

Figure 5. BER comparison of different QAM schemes using rate 1/2 convolutional code

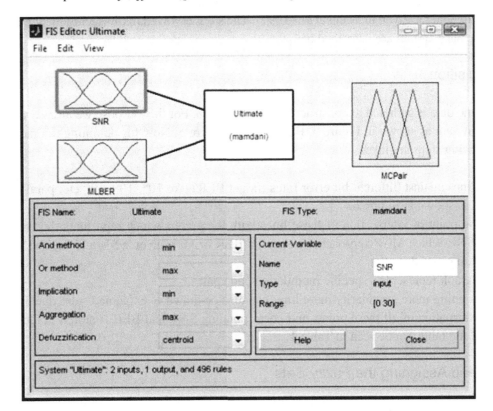

The Proposed Fuzzy Rule Base System

A fuzzy rule base system (FRBS) is proposed and designed, which is capable of deciding the best modulation code pair (MCP) for the next transmission interval on a specific subcarrier, based upon the current channel state information (CSI) and quality of service demand of that subcarrier. The FRBS being designed is used to optimize the cost function given in Equation 3. It will be decided that which modulation code pair is optimum (that will provide the highest throughput) for a specific subcarrier based upon the individual CSI and the Quality of Service (QoS) demand at the subcarriers while satisfying the target BER constraint on per subcarrier basis and overall transmit power constraint. Without loss of generality this can be expressed as a function;

$$
\begin{aligned}
R &= \frac{1}{N}\sum_{i=1}^{N} r_i \\
&= \frac{1}{N}\sum_{i=1}^{N} (\log_2(M))_i R_{C,i} \\
&= \frac{1}{N}\sum_{i=1}^{N} FRBS(\alpha_i, QoS_i)
\end{aligned}
\tag{5}
$$

There are a number of methods to construct fuzzy rule base systems, the one we have used, is called Table Lookup Scheme given in Wang *et al.* (1997). The steps involved in this technique for the creation of fuzzy rule base system are described below.

Data Acquisition

In this step the data is gathered to construct the fuzzy system. For this purpose we already have plotted the analytical data as shown in Figure 3, Figure 4 and Figure 5. Now for obtaining the facts from the graphs following steps are taken;

- Draw lines against different bit error rates (target BER) like 10^{-2}, 10^{-3}, 10^{-4} etc. parallel to x-axis (SNR) as shown in Figure 6.
- Find the point of intersection of these lines with the graphs which represents the fact that for a given SNR which MCP approaches a specific BER or for a given SNR and desired BER which MCP can be used.
- Every graph represents a specific modulation code pair
- For obtaining more granularity more lines can also be drawn as explained subsequently
- The information of all these points and corresponding SNR and BER is stored in table. Few entries of the table can be seen in Table 1.

Deciding and Assigning the Fuzzy Sets

Now the rule for every pair enlisted in Table 1 is obtained by the appropriate fuzzy set used. This is done in the following manner;

1. First of all decide sufficient number of fuzzy sets for each input and output variable in order to cover the input output spaces.
2. In our case we have two input variables namely SNR and QoS. There is one output variable name MCP.
3. The range of first input variable i.e. SNR is from 0 to 30. This range represents received SNR from any specific subcarrier. So accordingly, we have taken thirty-one fuzzy sets named as L0 to L30.
4. The range of second input variable is from 2 to 5. This number basically represents a specific quality of service demand from a certain subcarrier. Since QoS is a number that represents a specific target BER. So to make this relationship following conversion is done.

$$MLBER = -\log(BER)$$
$$\text{as} \quad BER = 10^{-q} \tag{6}$$
$$MLBER = -\log(10^{-q}) = q$$

There are sixteen fuzzy sets used for second input variable Minus Log BER (MLBER).

5. After this conversion we name this variable as minus log bit error rate (MLBER). As this is a real number so we have drawn more lines parallel to SNR axis to get more and more information like 4×10^{-3} etc. In this way more information can be taken from the graphs. The more information is extracted more number of rules can be formulated and a robust system can be designed.

6. There is one output variable that is modulation code pair (MCP) that represents a specific MCP number from a list. In this list a unique number is allotted to each MCP. In this way we have used twenty-five fuzzy sets for output variable labeled from P1 to P25.

7. These input output sets are shown in Figure 6, Figure 7 and Figure 8 respectively.

8. There are two input variables namely the receive SNR and MLBER while there is one output variable named MCP.

Rules Formulation

Each entry of the Table 1 is plugged into the fuzzy sets shown above. Once the value is entered its membership is calculated and it is noted that this very input lies in which variable. That will end up in a rule. For example; the entry SNR=5, QoS=3 and MCP=4 would result in a rule that is;

{IF SNR=L5 and MLBER=Q6 THEN MCP=P4}.

So in this fashion all the rules are generated. Mathematically, it can be expressed as;

Figure 6. Process of finding MCP against SNR and BER

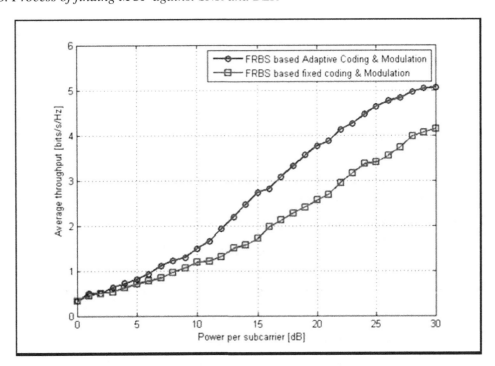

Figure 7. Fuzzy sets for first input variable SNR

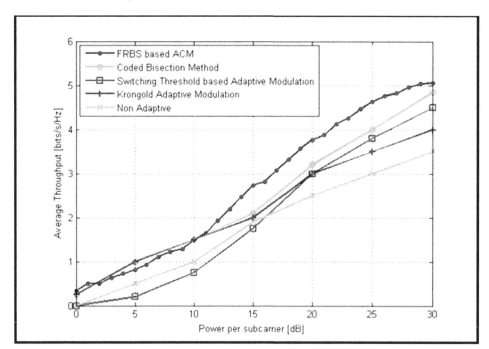

Figure 8. Fuzzy sets for second input variable MLBER

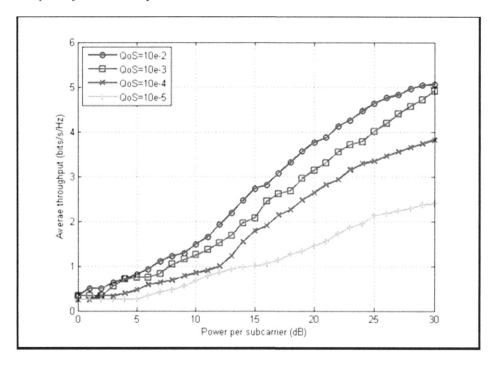

Table 1. NR, BER and MCP relationship table

SNR	BER	MCP	SNR	BER	MCP
1.72	10e-2	[4,1/4]	1.529	10e-4	[2,1/3]
8.732	10e-2	[8,1/4]	5.093	10e-4	[4,1/3]
10.18	10e-2	[16,1/4]	12.25	10e-4	[8,1/3]
13.63	10e-2	[32,1/4]	13.59	10e-4	[16,1/3]
18.08	10e-2	[64,1/4]	16.98	10e-4	[32,1/3]
21.45	10e-2	[128,1/4]	21.63	10e-4	[64,1/3]
0.143	10e-2	[2,1/3]	24.27	10e-4	[128,1/3]
4.109	10e-3	[4,1/3]	17.62	10e-5	[32,1/3]
11.16	10e-3	[8,1/3]	22.68	10e-5	[64,1/3]
12.56	10e-3	[16,1/3]	24.83	10e-5	[128,1/3]

$$(x_1^s, x_2^s; y^s); s = 1, 2, 3 \ldots\ldots S \tag{7}$$

without loss of generality we can say that a rule is generated from each entry in the (Table 1). These rules are enlisted in a table that is known as "the rule lookup table". This table is shown in Figure 10.

Elimination of Conflicting Rules

The rules having same IF part but different THEN parts are known as conflicting rules. This appears when more than one modulation code pair (MCP) are available for given SNR and MLBER. Say for instance, there is a rule whose THEN part contains three different MCP namely [8, 1/2], [16, 2/3] and [16, 3/4]. Now [16, 3/4] is best among the rest since its throughput is 4x3/4=3 while others have 3x1/2=1.5 and 4x2/3=2.67 respectively.

Similarly, sometime there could be two different pairs with same throughput like [2, 1/2] and [4, 1/4] both have same throughput that is 1x1/2=0.5, then [2, 1/2] will be chosen since it exhibits less modulation/demodulation and coding/decoding cost.

Completion of Lookup Table

Since in lookup table scheme we may not have complete number of input output pairs, then those parts are filled by heuristic or expert knowledge. We have suggested following heuristics. For example, a modulation code pair is suggested by rule for a certain SNR and QoS. Then that rule can also be used for slightly above SNR and poor QoS.

For instance, [128, 3/4] is suggested for 25dB SNR and BER 10^{-3} then this pair can be used for 26-30dB SNR and 10^{-2} BER cases as well. Since if a modulation code pair performs for lower SNR, then it can easily sustain in higher SNR situations. Similarly, if a MCP performs for a good QoS then it certainly can sustain for poor QoS demands. Figure 10 shows the lookup table.

Figure 9. Fuzzy sets for the output variable MCP

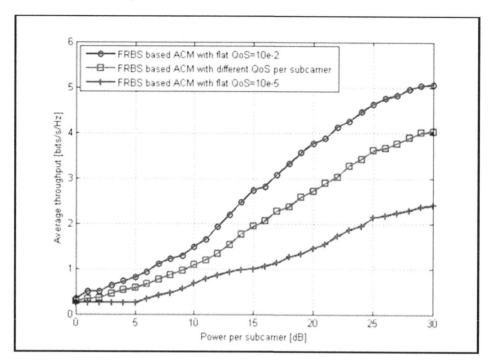

Figure 10. The lookup table

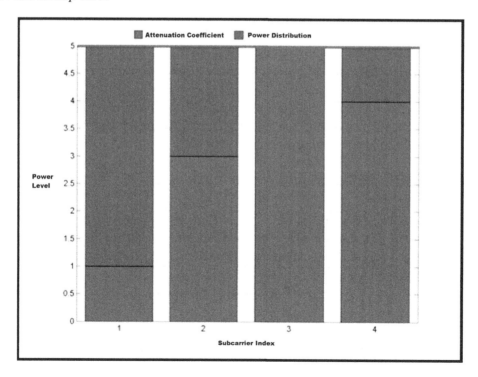

Fuzzy Rule Base Creation

Finally, the fuzzy rule base system is created that is purely based upon the lookup table explained above. FRBS is created in Matlab 7.8.0 (R2009a). The parameters used in creation of this fuzzy rule base system are given below.

1. **Fuzzifier:** Standard triangular fuzzifier is used with AND as MIN and OR as MAX. These functions can be seen in Figure 6, Figure 7 and Figure 8 respectively.
2. **Rule Base:** Rule base contains rules against all possible input output pairs. As there are thirty-one sets (L0 to L30) for first input variable named SNR and about sixteen sets (Q1 to Q16) for input variable MLBER.

Hence there are four-hundred-ninety-six rules in rule base. Rule base is complete in a sense that rules are defined for all possible combinations of input spaces.

The rule base editor is shown in Figure 11 while the rule surface is given in Figure 12. Figure 13 contains the rule base system at a glance. Rule surface depicts the soul of fuzzy rule base system. One can deduce that changing values of SNR and MLBER how throughput is varied.

Like for SNR=30 and MLBER=2, throughput approaches 5bits/s/Hz, this is because target bit error rate is relaxed and SNR is high so FRBS will choose MCPs with high data rates.

3. **Inference Engine:** Standard Mamdani Inference Engine (MIE) is used that will infer which input pair will be mapped on to which output point.
4. **De-Fuzzifier:** Standard Center Average Defuzzifier (CAD) is used for defuzzification due to its suitability to the problem in terms of efficiency and less computation cost.

Simulation Results

In this section the proposed FRBS based Adaptive Coding and Modulation Scheme is compared with various adaptive as well as non-adaptive techniques. Power per subcarrier in assumed to be flat in the simulations. Rayleigh flat fading channel is used for simulations. Figure 14 shows significance of the adaptive coding and modulation scheme over the fixed modulation and coding. Both cases are supervised by Fuzzy Rule Base System. In first case, every subcarrier may have a different MCP depending upon its own CSI.

While in second case, same MCP is used for all OFDM subcarriers after each adaptation interval. In this simulation, the value for fixed modulation code pair (MCP) is found by same fuzzy rule base system. But the decision of next MCP is taken on behalf of average received SNR from all subcarriers and the suggested MCP is used for all the subcarriers regardless of their individual channel conditions. In this way, some subcarriers may have the appropriate MCP but some may not, since the decision is made on average channel conditions rather than individual channel conditions. While the main advantage of the proposed scheme is that the decision for appropriate modulation code pair for a specific subcarrier is taken by channel state information and quality of service demand of that subcarrier. This may be written as;

Figure 11. Rule editor

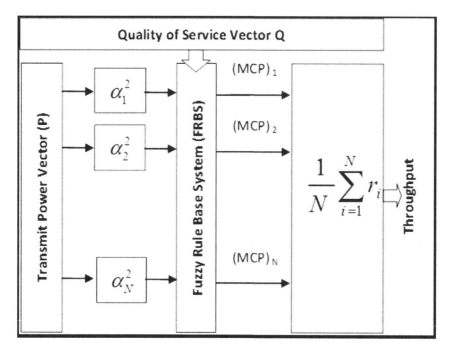

Figure 12. The rule surface

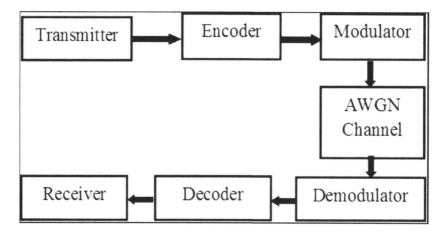

$$r_i = (\log_2(M))_i R_i$$
$$= MCP_i$$ \hfill (8)
$$= FRBS(SNR_i, QoS_i)$$

Figure 15 shows the comparison of FRBS assisted adaptive coding and modulation with various well known schemes. First comparison is done with the scheme by Bockelmann *et al.* (2009), where authors used a Coded Bisection Method to choose the appropriate modulation code pair for next transmission.

Figure 13. Fuzzy rule base system at a glance

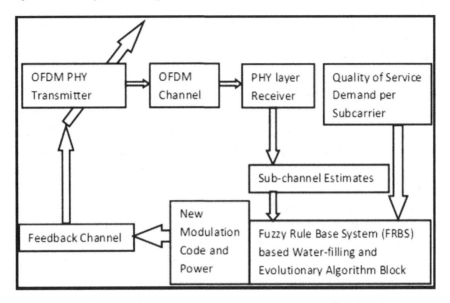

Figure 14. Comparison of FRBS based AMC with Fixed Modulation and Coding using QoS=10^{-2} and N=256

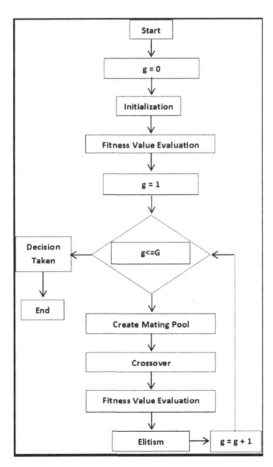

Second comparison is given with Faezah *et al.* (2010); in which there were used SNR based Switching Thresholds to adapt the appropriate modulation scheme for next interval. In this scheme subcarriers were grouped, then based upon the average group channel conditions modulation was chosen for that group. Though in this paper there given coded modulation as well that is adaptive modulation (AM) with fixed code rate but we compare with the best case in that paper.

Third comparison is given with another adaptive modulation scheme that was proposed by Krongold *et al.* (2000). In this technique decision for suitable modulation was taken by virtue of average received SNR then switching thresholds were used to decide the type of modulation to be used. This result shows that only Adaptive Modulation could not achieve that throughput alone which can be achieved by combined adaptive coding and modulation. A significant superiority of the proposed scheme can be observed in the simulation. Lastly, FRBS performance was compared with non-adaptive case, there is superiority of proposed scheme was more than 1.5bits/s/Hz.

Performance of Fuzzy Rule Base System for different fixed Quality of Services for all subcarriers is demonstrated in Figure 16. It shows that for high power per subcarrier and relatively poor QoS values throughput of the system approaches above 5bits/s/Hz while for high QoS achievable throughput is 2.5bits/s/Hz at 30dB of power per subcarrier.

Figure 17 reveals the performance of FRBS for different QoS per subcarrier, which is more practical scenario. In this case, each subcarrier has a different QoS demand. Results show that with even a diverse scenario, performance of Fuzzy Rule Base System is remarkable and more than 4bits/s/Hz throughput is achievable. This very performance is compared with two fixed QoS for all subcarriers that is 10^{-2} and 10^{-5}. These two cases put the lower and upper bound on its performance, respectively. It means the performance of random QoS cannot be more than 10^{-5} and less than 10^{-2}.

Figure 15. Comparison of FRBS based AMC with various scheme

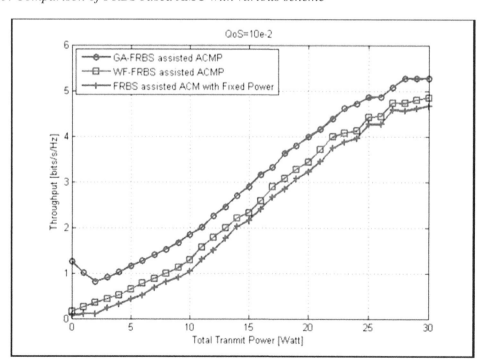

Figure 16. Performance of FRBS based AMC for fixed QoS for all the subcarrier and N =256

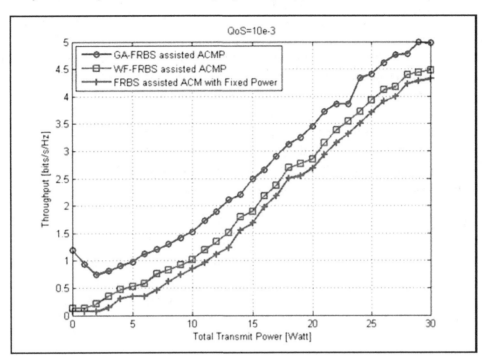

Figure 17. Performance comparison of FRBS based AMC for different QoS for each subcarrier with fixed QoS for all subcarriers while N =256

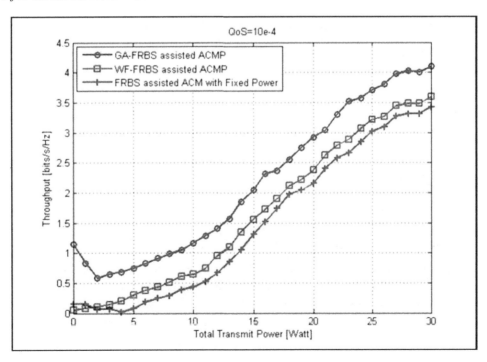

This scenario is practical in s sense that it perfectly matches with IEEE wireless standards like IEEE802.16 and IEEE802.16/e (2006), where variety of mobile users having different reception power levels and different Quality of Service Demands are present.

In most of the adaptive communication schemes for OFDM systems, those subcarriers are chosen to shut down where channel conditions are very poor. Once a subcarrier is chosen to shut down the resources like power are redistributed among rest of the subcarriers like in Faezah et al (2009), Al-Askary (2006). But as far as the proposed scheme is concerned transmission is even possible at a subcarrier with such a hostile scenario. This is because, in proposed scheme the communication at the subcarrier with poor channel state information is survived because a low code rate like 3/4, 5/6 can be used similarly a smaller modulation size like binary phase shift keying (BPSK) can be used. In such a scenario although the throughput touches it lower bound but still communication survives.

Adaptive Power Techniques

To make the power adaptive, several techniques have been investigated in conjunction with the proposed Fuzzy Rule Base System (FRBS). These techniques will be used for adaptive power one by one while FRBS will be used for adapting code rate and modulation. Also, once the power is adapted the throughput is calculated using FRBS. Following the detail about each technique is given.

Water-Filling Principle

Water-filling principle has been used for multicarrier loading problems. It is one of the basic and effective techniques for adaptive loading. It is restated here for sake of reference. According to Haykin (2001),

Maximize the total bit rate R_{Total} for the entire multi-carrier transmission systems through an optimal sharing of the total transmit power P_T between the N sub-carriers, subject to the constraint that P_T is maintained constant.

We have proposed FRBS based Water-filling principle for adaptive power in OFDM Systems. In contrast to our system this phenomenon can be expressed mathematically as,

$$p_i + \frac{\sigma_i^2}{\left|H(f_i)\right|^2} = K; 1 \leq i \leq N \tag{9}$$

where p_i is transmit power, σ_i^2 is noise variance (noise power) and $\left|H(f_i)\right|$ is the magnitude response at subcarrier i respectively. The choice of constant K depends upon application and it is under designer control. That is, the sum of the transmit power and noise variance (power) scaled by inverse of square of channel (subcarrier) magnitude response must be maintained constant for each subcarrier. This can also be written as;

$$p_i + \frac{1}{(CNR)_i} = K; 1 \leq i \leq N \tag{10}$$

where

$$(CNR)_i = \frac{|H(f_i)|^2}{\sigma_i^2} \tag{11}$$

Another subset contribution of the proposed scheme is that the value of the constant K is calculated analytically and given below while derivation can be found in Atta-ur-Rahman et al. (2013).

$$K = P_{avg} + \frac{1}{N}\sum_{i=1}^{N} \frac{1}{(CNR)_i} \tag{12}$$

It is derived as;

$$p_i + \frac{1}{(CINR)_i} = K$$

$$\sum_{i=1}^{N} p_i = \sum_{i=1}^{N} (K - \frac{1}{(CINR)_i})$$

$$P_T = \sum_{i=1}^{N} K - \sum_{i=1}^{N} \frac{1}{(CINR)_i}$$

$$P_T = NK - \sum_{i=1}^{N} \frac{1}{(CNR)_i}$$

$$K = \frac{P_T}{N} + \frac{1}{N}\sum_{i=1}^{N} \frac{1}{(CINR)_i}$$

$$K = P_{avg} + \frac{1}{N}\sum_{i=1}^{N} \frac{1}{(CINR)_i}$$

It can be stated as the analytical value of the constant K for ith subcarrier can be found by a adding average transmit power and average of inverse of channel to interference noise ratio (CNR). where P_{avg} is the average transmit power per subcarrier and $(CNR)_i$ is given in equation 11. This algorithm basically makes use of the fact that, pumping more power to those subcarriers who has low attenuation coefficient would result in decreased channel to interference noise ratio (CINR) and hence throughput can be maximized. Similarly, allocating less transmit-power to those subcarriers whose attenuation coefficient is high, since this would result in an increased channel to interference noise ratio and throughput will be decreased. This phenomenon is depicted in Figure 18.

Figure 18. The water filling algorithm

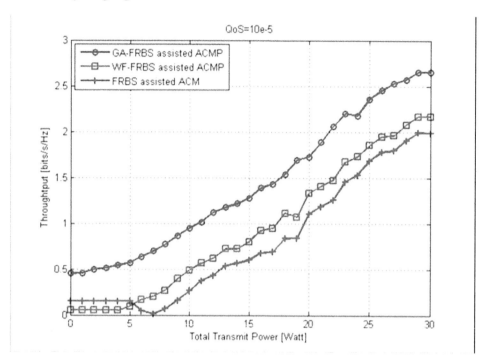

The throughput of this loading algorithm will be calculated by Equation 1, while the power vector P will be found by Water-filling algorithm using Equation 10. So after this, the Equation 5 will become;

$$
\begin{aligned}
R &= \frac{1}{N} \sum_{i=1}^{N} r_i \\
&= \frac{1}{N} \sum_{i=1}^{N} (\log_2(M))_i R_{C,i} \\
&= \frac{1}{N} \sum_{i=1}^{N} FRBS(p_i^{WF} \alpha_i, QoS_i)
\end{aligned}
\tag{13}
$$

where p_i^{WF} is the transmit-power suggested by Water-filling principle, α_i is channel coefficient and QoS_i is quality of service demand on ith subcarrier, respectively. For a given channel state information and QoS demand, Water filling algorithm finds the power vector then FRBS finds the throughput by Equation 13.

The diagram that visualizes Equation 13 is given in Figure 19. This diagram simply shows that upon providing a specific power vector and quality of service demand respective modulation code pairs (MCPs) can be found. An MCP represents a modulation code product that gives throughput. After adding and averaging the individual throughputs, overall orthogonal frequency division multiplexing (OFDM) system's throughput can be obtained.

The adaptation procedure can be seen by the Figure 20. In this way, upon receiving the channel coefficients and quality of service on per subcarrier basis, a power vector is found using Water-filling

Figure 19. FRBS based throughput calculation diagram

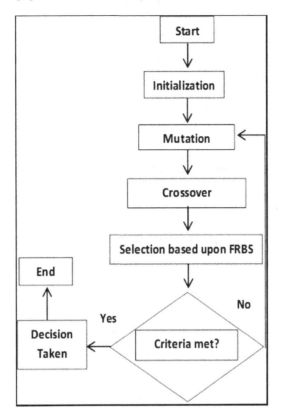

Figure 20. Adaptation diagram using FRBS and various algorithms

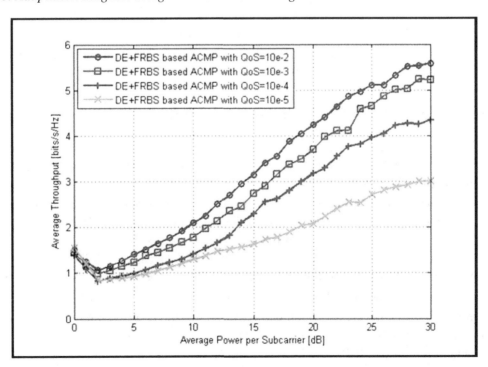

principle. Using this power vector the modulation code pairs are chosen by Fuzzy Rule Based System and throughput is calculated as discussed above.

All the intelligence is contained within the Fuzzy Rule Base System inference engine. No matter what values of channel coefficients and quality of service appear as input, fuzzy inference engine can suggest the suitable modulation code pairs are appeared as output. Moreover, the decision is not taken at average signals to noise ratio (SNR) but individual SNRs from different subcarriers.

Genetic Algorithm

Genetic Algorithms (GA) belong to the class of Evolutionary algorithms. It is a biologically inspired evolutionary algorithm based upon the motive "survival of the fittest". These algorithms are very famous for finding the optimum vector in a large vector space. Here we propose FRBS based Genetic Algorithm for finding the optimum power vector for all subcarriers that maximizes the throughput and satisfies the certain constraints. In this way once given the channel coefficient and quality of service vectors from all subcarriers, GA will be used to search the optimum power vector for this situation. Equation 13 can be written as;

$$
\begin{aligned}
R &= \frac{1}{N} \sum_{i=1}^{N} r_i \\
&= \frac{1}{N} \sum_{i=1}^{N} (\log_2(M))_i R_{C,i} \\
&= \frac{1}{N} \sum_{i=1}^{N} FRBS(p_i^{GA}\alpha_i, QoS_i)
\end{aligned}
\tag{14}
$$

where p_i^{GA} represents the transmit power vector obtained by Genetic Algorithm. The fitness function for the algorithm can be viewed in Figure 19. That is, for given vectors of channel coefficients and quality of service (QoS), which power vector maximizes the throughput. The algorithm used is given below while flowchart of the Genetic Algorithm is given in Figure 21.

Simulation Results Using Water-Filling and Genetic Algorithm

In this section proposed FRBS based Water-filling and Genetic Algorithm schemes are demonstrated and compared with other schemes. Simulation parameters are enlisted in table 2, while the simulation results are given in Figure 22 to Figure 25.

Figure 22 to Figure 25 show the comparison of proposed Fuzzy Rule Base System with Genetic Algorithm (FRBS-GA) assisted Adaptive Coding, Modulation and Power (ACMP) scheme; proposed Fuzzy Rule Base System with Water-Filling (FRBS-WF) assisted ACMP; and simple FRBS assisted Adaptive Coding and Modulation (ACM) with fixed power per subcarrier. In these figures Quality of Service (QoS) demands or target bit error rates (BER) per subcarrier were assumed to be $10^{-2}, 10^{-3}, 10^{-4}$ and 10^{-5} respectively.

In Figure 22, three schemes are being compared with a fixed target bit error rate or quality of service demand of 10e-2 for all subcarriers. As the target bit error rate is relaxed, so all the schemes possess a high throughput. Proposed FRBS based GA scheme outperforms compared to all the schemes. The

Figure 21. Flow chart of genetic algorithm

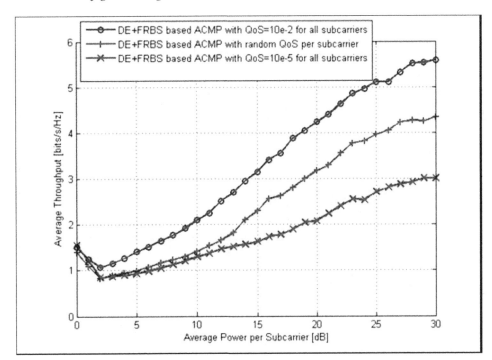

Table 2. Simulation parameters for FRBS based GA and WF algorithm

Sr.	Parameter	Value
1	OFDM Standard used	IEEE 802.11n Indoor channel
2	Adaptive parameters	Code rate, Modulation, Power
3	Channel Type	Rayleigh Fading
3	Channel Coefficient range	$0.1 \leq \alpha_i \leq 0.4; i = 1, 2, ..., N$
4	Number of subcarriers N	128
5	Adapting criteria	FRBS based GA and WF
6	Chromosome Length	128
7	Population Size	50
8	Stopping criteria	No of populations=50

maximum overall throughput approached 5.4bits/s/Hz at a 30dB transmitted power. This is because adaptive power using GA plays its role. Second scheme that is FRBS based Water-filling algorithm performs second best. Highest throughput approaches to 4.9bits/s/Hz, while FRBS based ACM with fixed power scheme approaches to 4.8bits/s/Hz.

Figure 22. Comparison of proposed schemes at QoS=10e-2 per subcarrier

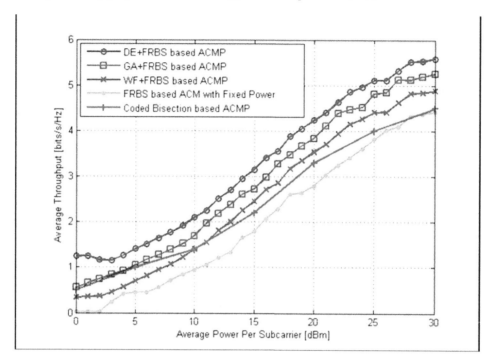

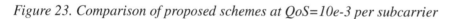

Figure 23. Comparison of proposed schemes at QoS=10e-3 per subcarrier

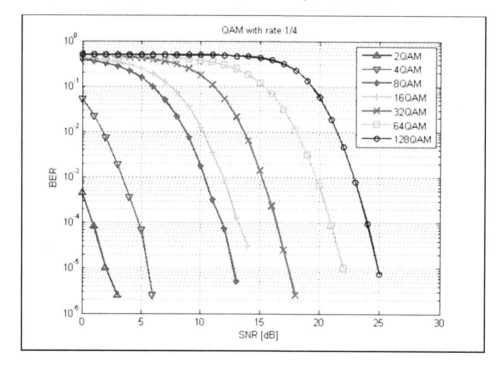

Figure 24. Comparison of proposed schemes at QoS=10e-4 per subcarrier

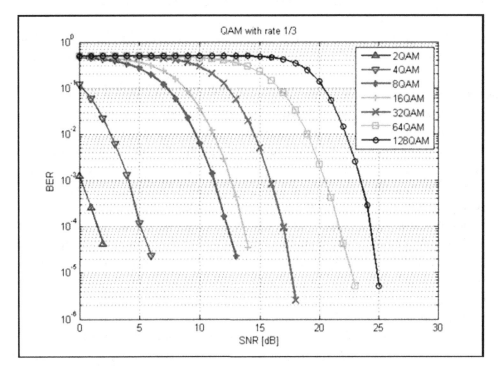

Figure 25. Comparison of proposed schemes at QoS=10e-5 per subcarrier

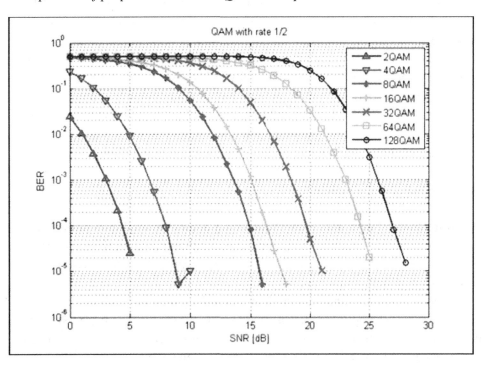

Similarly, in Figure 23, same three schemes are being compared with a fixed target bit error rate or quality of service demand of 10e-3 for all subcarriers. As the target bit error rate is still somewhat relaxed, hence all the schemes possess a better throughput. Proposed FRBS based GA scheme outperforms compared to all the schemes. The maximum overall throughput approached 5bits/s/Hz at a 30dB transmitted power.

Second scheme that is FRBS based Water-filling algorithm performs second best. Highest throughput approaches to 4.5bits/s/Hz, while FRBS based ACM with fixed power scheme approaches to 4.4bits/s/Hz. It can be noted that in order to fulfill the target BER demand, throughput is slightly compromised.

In Figure 24, almost same facts are repeated and same schemes are being compared with a fixed target bit error rate or quality of service demand of 10e-4 for all subcarriers. As the demanded quality of service high so a significant degradation in average throughput can be noted. But the proposed FRBS based GA scheme still outperforms compared to the other schemes.

The maximum overall throughput approached 4.1bits/s/Hz at a 30dB transmitted power. Second scheme that is FRBS based Water-filling algorithm, performs second best. Highest throughput approaches to 3.6bits/s/Hz, while FRBS based ACM with fixed power scheme approaches to 3.4bits/s/Hz.

In Figure 25, proposed scheme is compared with the other schemes at a fixed target bit error rate or quality of service demand of 10e-5 for all subcarriers. As the demanded quality of service very high so a significant degradation in average throughput can be noted. But the proposed scheme still sustains and outperforms compared to the other schemes. The maximum overall throughput approaches to 2.7 bits/s/Hz at a 30dB transmitted power. Second scheme that is FRBS based Water-filling algorithm the throughput approaches to 2.2bits/s/Hz, while FRBS based ACM with fixed power scheme approaches to 2bits/s/Hz.

From the comparisons given in these figures it can easily be deduced that proposed FRBS-GA assisted Adaptive coding, modulation and power scheme performs better than proposed FRBS-WF assisted ACMP while FRBS-WF assisted ACMP scheme performs better than that of FRBS assisted ACM with fixed transmit power.

It can also be noted down that Water-filling scheme with ACMP is not much better than that of ACM with fixed transmit power. This is because the motive of Water-filling algorithm is that give more power to those subcarriers that is good or the channel with small attenuation factor to increase the throughput and vice versa. But the channels with poor conditions are given less power that ends up with degradation in the throughput. While in case of ACM with fixed power; every subcarrier is equally treated in terms of power so throughput is slightly less than (0.2bits/s/Hz) that of Water-filling algorithm.

Differential Evolution Algorithm

Differential Evolution (DE) algorithm is an evolutionary algorithm originally proposed by Storn *et al.* (1997). In many aspects, it is comparable to Genetic Algorithm (GA), but the main feature that makes it superior than GA, is its fast convergence rate. Here we have proposed FRBS based Differential Algorithm (FRBS-DE) for ACMP.

In this way once given the channel coefficient and quality of service vectors from all subcarriers, DE will be used to search the optimum power vector for this situation. There are four operations in DE namely initialization, mutation, crossover and selection. A flowchart of the algorithm is given in Figure 26. Description of each step pertaining to our problem is given below.

Figure 26. Differential evolution algorithm flowchart

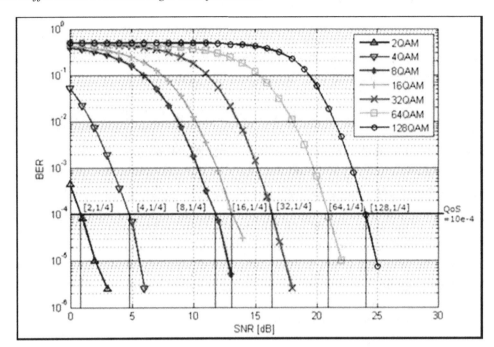

1. **Initialization:** The first power vector taken in the scheme would be the flat power for all subcarrier.

    Power vector length is equal to number of subcarriers N. Then initial population is generated randomly around the initial vector, so that the power constraint remained satisfied.

2. **Mutation:** Standard mutation operation is used as described originally in the basic algorithm. That is a weighted difference of two power vectors is added to third vector.
3. **Crossover:** Standard crossover method is used to generate the trial vector.
4. **Selection:** Whether to keep a vector or not is based upon a fitness value used in greedy criterion. We have employed Fuzzy Rule Base System for this purpose, as shown in Figure V-1.

    That is, fitness is equal to sum rates after applying the chosen vector to the system that is;

$$
\begin{aligned}
R &= \frac{1}{N} \sum_{i=1}^{N} r_i \\
&= \frac{1}{N} \sum_{i=1}^{N} (\log_2(M))_i R_{C,i} \\
&= \frac{1}{N} \sum_{i=1}^{N} FRBS(p_i^{DE} \alpha_i, QoS_i)
\end{aligned}
\tag{15}
$$

where p_i^{DE} represents the optimum power-vector searched by Differential Evolution.

Simulation Results Using Differential Evolution

In this section, all the proposed techniques will be demonstrated and compared with each other as well as other techniques given in literature. The parameters used in the simulations are listed in table V-2. So, the proposed scheme is compared with the following schemes.

- FRBS with Genetic Algorithm (FRBS-GA) based Adaptive Coding, modulation and Power (ACMP)
- FRBS with Water filling algorithm (FRBS-WF) based ACMP
- FRBS based Adaptive Coding and Modulation (ACM) with flat power for all subcarriers
- ACMP scheme using Bisection Approach by Bockelmann *et al.* (2009)

Figure 27 shows performance of proposed scheme with various Quality of Service (QoS) requests for the subcarriers. In this figure the target bit error rates were assumed like 10e-2 to 10e-5 for all sub-carriers. Say for the instance, that target bit error rate is 10e-2; it means all subcarriers demands that bit error rate must not go beyond this limit. The throughput approaches to almost 5.6bit/s/Hz for the quality of service 10e-2 because it is comparatively relax condition while for value of QoS 10e-5 it is 3bits/s/Hz because it's a high quality of service demand from all subcarriers.

This figure explains that as QoS demand increases mean the required bit error rate (BER) is decreased the average throughput is decreased since the focus is to meet the BER threshold. In this case; FRBS chooses those MCPs that possess a good BER but then comparatively low throughput is achieved. On the other hand for a relaxed BER, average throughput goes high. This is because the FRBS is suggesting modulation code pairs that provide high data rates, which results in a high throughput. So roughly we can say that QoS is inversely proportional to the average throughput. Another view of the figure is that for a fixed quality of service (target BER), average throughput of the system is almost directly proportional to the average transmit power per subcarrier.

Figure 28 shows the upper and lower bounds on the performance of the proposed DE-FRBS based adaptive coding modulation and power scheme. So, there are three cases given. First case when all subcar-

Table 3. Simulation parameters for FRBS based DE algorithm

Sr.	Parameter	Value
1	OFDM Standard used	IEEE 802.11n Indoor (WIFI)
2	Number of Subcarriers N	1024
3	Fitness Function for DE	Fuzzy Rule Base System
4	Parameters being updated	Code rate, modulation scheme, power
5	Type of Channel	Rayleigh Fading
6	Channel Coefficients range	[0.1-0.4]
7	Size of chromosome	1024
8	Population Size	50
9	Stopping Criteria	No of populations=50
10	Complexity	O (Population size x No. of population)

Figure 27. Comparison of proposed scheme for different QoS

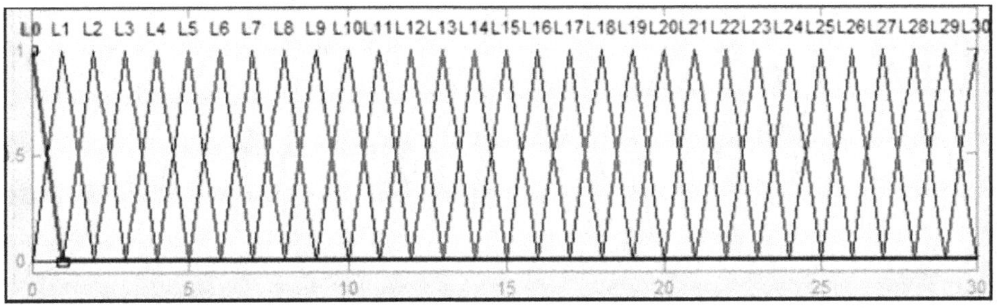

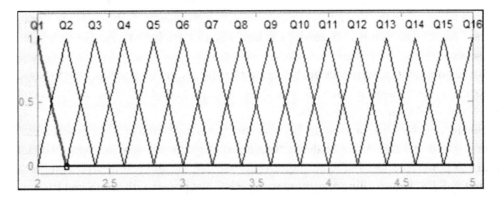

Figure 28. Upper and lower bound on performance

riers have same quality of service demand that is BER=10e-2, then the average throughput approaches to its highest value that is 5.6bits/s/Hz. That can be said as the upper bound on performance. Second case is more practical where every subcarrier may have a different quality of service demand. In this case the quality of service demand vector was generated randomly. The average throughput approaches approximately 4.4bits/s/Hz. Third case is when all subcarriers demand for the highest quality of service that is target BER equal to 10e-5. This may be designated as the lower bound on the performance.

Figure 29 shows the comparison of proposed scheme with three schemes presented in previous sections that are GA+FRBS based ACMP (Section 5.2.2), WF+FRBS based ACMP (Section 5.2.1), FRBS based ACM with flat power (Section 4.5) and another scheme namely the Bisection method proposed by the Bockelmann *et al.* (2009). First scheme in this regard the so called Bisection method is also used for choosing appropriate modulation code pair and the power. Its performance approaches to 4.4bits/s/Hz at the highest value of average transmit power.

Second scheme being compared is FRBS based adaptive coding and modulation scheme where flat and fixed power per subcarrier is assumed. This has almost same performance as the Bisection method.

Third scheme being compared is well known Water-filling algorithm a famous loading algorithm for multicarrier systems. In this scheme the power vector is chosen by Water-filling principle, and then the throughput is calculated using proposed Fuzzy Rule Base System. This scheme is better that previous two schemes and in this scheme the throughput approaches to 4.9bits/s/Hz.

Fourth scheme being compared is Genetic Algorithm and FRBS based adaptive coding, modulation and power scheme. In this scheme the power vector is chosen using Genetic Algorithm under a specific

Figure 29. Comparison proposed scheme with other schemes

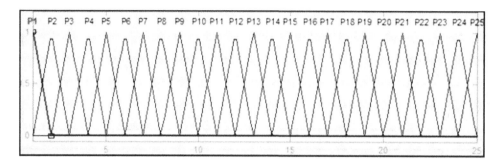

set of channel conditions and quality of service demands. Once chosen this vector, fuzzy rule base system is used to calculate the throughput. This scheme approaches to 5.3bits/s/Hz in throughput that is next to the fifth scheme that is Differential Evolution and FRBS based adaptive coding, modulation and power scheme.

It can also be noted that performance of Differential Evolution and FRBS (DE-FRBS) based Adaptive Coding, Modulation and Power scheme approaches to the highest that is 5.6bits/s/Hz. Hence DE-FRBS outperforms compared to all other schemes.

Simulation results show that proposed scheme outperforms compared to all other schemes. A detailed comparison is given in Table 4. Table shows the vitality of proposed scheme over other schemes. At 30dBm transmit power, proposed scheme outperforms 0.4, 0.7, 1.2 and 1.1bits/s/Hz compare to Genetic Algorithm with FRBS, Water-filling algorithm with FRBS, flat power with FRBS and Bisection method based adaptive coding and modulation by Bockelmann et al. (2009) respectively.

Table 4. Comparison of proposed schemes

Sr.	Scheme	Average Power Level	Average Throughput
1	DE+FRBS	30dB	5.6 bits/s/Hz
2	GA+FRBS	30dB	5.2bits/s/Hz
3	WF+FRBS	30dB	4.9bits/s/Hz
4	Flat+FRBS	30dB	4.4bits/s/Hz
5	Bisection method by Bockelmann et al. (2009)	30dB	4.5bits/s/Hz
6	DE+FRBS	20dB	4.3bits/s/Hz
7	GA+FRBS	20dB	3.9bits/s/Hz
8	WF+FRBS	20dB	3.6 bits/s/Hz
9	Flat+FRBS	20dB	3.4bits/s/Hz
10	Bisection method by Bockelmann *et al.* (2009)	20dB	2.85bits/s/Hz

CONCLUSION

In this chapter, a Fuzzy Rule Base System (FRBS) is proposed for adaptive coding and modulation in Orthogonal Frequency Division Multiplexing (OFDM) systems. This is done by formulating a constrained optimization problem in which the throughput of the OFDM system is maximized by choosing appropriate modulation code pair based upon FRBS such that two constraints must be satisfied first the target bit error rate and second the total transmit power.

Significance of the proposed scheme is demonstrated in terms of simulations. Proposed scheme is compared with well-known schemes in the literature for this purpose. Simulation results show that the proposed scheme performs significantly better than rest of the adaptive schemes.

In the later part of this chapter; adaptive coding, modulation and power schemes are proposed by using Fuzzy Rule Base System (FRBS) and various evolutionary algorithms as loading algorithms of Orthogonal Frequency Division Multiplexing (OFDM) systems. Proposed FRBS has been used for taking care of adaptive coding and modulation while Water-filling algorithm and evolutionary algorithms like Genetic Algorithm, Differential Evolution algorithm are used to adapt the power. Genetic Algorithm and Differential Evolution algorithm both performs better than Water-filling principle. But as far as complexity is concerned Water-filling has very low complexity compared to GA and DE. This makes GA and DE impractical for real time systems.

REFERENCES

Al-Askary, O. (2006). *Coding and iterative decoding of concatenated multi-level codes for the Rayleigh fading channel* (PhD thesis). KTH Information and Communication Technology, Stockholm, Sweden.

Atta-ur-Rahman. (2011, December). Adaptive Coding and Modulation for OFDM Systems using Product Codes and Fuzzy Rule Base System. *International Journal of Computers and Applications*, *35*(4), 41–48.

Atta-ur-Rahman. (2012). Adaptive Resource Allocation in OFDM Systems using GA and Fuzzy Rule Base System. *World Applied Sciences Journal*, *18*(6), 836–844. doi:10.5829/idosi.wasj.2012.18.06.906

Atta-ur-Rahman. (2012). A Fuzzy Rule Base Assisted Adaptive Coding and Modulation Scheme for OFDM Systems. *J. Basic Appl. Sci. Res.*, *2*(5), 4843–4853.

Atta-ur-Rahman. (2013). Comparison of Coding Schemes over FRBS aided AOFDM Systems. *Journal of Networking and Innovative Computing*, *1*, 183–193.

Atta-ur-Rahman. (2014). Dynamic Resource allocation for OFDM Systems using Differential Evolution and Fuzzy Rule Base System. *Journal of Intelligent & Fuzzy Systems*, *26*(4), 2035–2046.

Atta-ur-Rahman. (2016). QoS and Rate Enhancement in DVB-S2 using Fuzzy Rule Base System. *Journal of Intelligent & Fuzzy Systems*, *30*(1), 801–810.

Atta-ur-Rahman. (2017). Applications of Softcomputing in Adaptive Communication. *International Journal Control Theory and Applications*, *10*(18), 81–93.

Atta-ur-Rahman, Qureshi, I.M., Malik, A.N., & Naseem, M.T. (2014). A Real Time Adaptive Resource Allocation Scheme for OFDM Systems using GRBF-Neural Networks and Fuzzy Rule Base System. *International Arab Journal of Information Technology, 11*(6), 593-601. http://ccis2k.org/iajit/PDF/vol.11,no.6/6305.pdf

Atta-ur-Rahman, Qureshi, I.M., Muzaffar, M.Z., & Naseem, M.T. (2012). A Fuzzy Rule Base Aided Rate Enhancement Scheme for OFDM Systems. *IEEE Conference on Emerging Technologies (ICET'12)*, 151-156.

Atta-ur-Rahman, Qureshi, I.M., Muzaffar, M.Z., & Naseem, M.T. (2012). FRBS based Rate Enhancement Scheme for OFDM Systems using Product Codes. *IEEE 15th International Multi-topic Conference (INMIC'12)*, 339-344.

Atta-ur-Rahman, Qureshi, I.M., Naseem, M.T., & Muzaffar, M.Z. (2012). A GA-FRBS based Rate Enhancement Scheme for OFDM based Hyperlans. *10th IEEE International Conference on Frontiers of Information Technology (FIT'12)*, 153-158.

Atta-ur-Rahman, Qureshi, I.M., Muzaffar, M.Z., & Naseem, M.T. (2012). Adaptive Resource Allocation for OFDM Systems using Fuzzy Rule Base System Water-filling Principle and Product Codes. *12th International Conference on Intelligent Systems Design and Applications (ISDA'12)*, 811-816.

Atta-ur-Rahman, & Qureshi, I.M. (2013). Optimum Resource Allocation in OFDM Systems using FRBS and Particle Swarm Optimization. Nature and Biologically Inspired Computing (NaBIC'13), 174-180.

Atta-ur-Rahman, Qureshi, I.M., Salam, M.H., & Naseem, M.T. (2013). Efficient Link Adaptation in OFDM Systems using a Hybrid Intelligent Technique. *13th International Conference on Hybrid Intelligent Systems (HIS'13)*, 12-17.

Atta-ur-Rahman, Qureshi, I.M., Naseem, M.T., & Muzaffar, M.Z. (2013). An Intelligent Link Adaptation Scheme for OFDM based Hyperlans. *5th International Conference of SoftComputing for Pattern Recognition (SoCPaR'13)*, 361-366.

Atta-ur-Rahman, Qureshi, I.M., Salam, M.H., & Muzaffar, M. Z. (2013). Adaptive Communication using Soft-computing Techniques. *5th International Conference of Soft-Computing for Pattern Recognition (SoCPaR'13)*, 19-24.

Bockelmann, C., Wübben, D., & Kammeyer, K. D. (2009). Rate Enhancement of BICM-OFDM with Adaptive Coded Modulation via a Bisection approach. *IEEE 10th Workshop on Signal Processing Advances in Wireless Communications, SPAWC '09*, 658-662.

Chow, P. S., Cioffi, J. M., & Bingham, J. A. C. (1995). A practical discrete multi-tone transceiver loading algorithm for data transmission over spectrally shaped channels. *IEEE Transactions on Communications, 48*, 772–775.

Cyzlwik, A. (1996). Adaptive OFDM for wideband radio channels. *Global Telecommunications Conference*, 1, 713-718.

Faezah, J., & Sabira, K. (2009). Adaptive Modulation for OFDM Systems. *International Journal of Communication Networks and Information Security*, 1(2), 1–8.

Hagenauer, J., & Hoeher, P. (1989). A Viterbi algorithm with soft-decision outputs and its applications. *Proc. IEEE GLOBECOM*, 11-17. doi:10.1109/GLOCOM.1989.64230

Haykin, S. S. (2001). *Communication Systems*. Wiley Johns and Sons.

Kalet, I. (1989). The multitone channel. *IEEE Transactions on Communications*, 37(2), 119–124. doi:10.1109/26.20079

Keller, T., & Hanzo, L. (2000). Adaptive modulation techniques for duplex OFDM transmission. *IEEE Transactions on Vehicular Technology*, 49(5), 1893–1906. doi:10.1109/25.892592

Krongold, B. S., Ramchandran, K., & Jones, D. L. (2000). Computationally Efficient Optimal Power Allocation Algorithm for Multicarrier Communication Systems. *IEEE Transactions on Communications*, 48(1), 23–27. doi:10.1109/26.818869

Li, Y., & Ryan, W. E. (2007). Mutual-Information-Based Adaptive Bit-Loading Algorithms for LDPC-Coded OFDM. *IEEE Transactions on Wireless Communications*, 6(5), 1670–1680. doi:10.1109/TWC.2007.360369

Peng, F., Zhang, J., & Ryan, W. E. (2007). Adaptive Modulation and Coding for IEEE 802.11n. *IEEE Wireless Communications and Networking Conference*, 656-661. doi:10.1109/WCNC.2007.126

Sastry, K.S., & Babu, M.S.P. (2010). Fuzzy Logic based Adaptive Modulation using Non Data Aided SNR Estimation for OFDM Systems. *International Journal of Engineering Science and Technology*, 2(6), 2384-2392.

Stierstorfer, C., & Fischer, R. F. H. (2007). Gray Mapping for Bit-Interleaved Coded Modulation. *IEEE Vehicular Technology Conference*, 1703-1707. doi:10.1109/VETECS.2007.354

Storn, R., & Price, K. (1997). Differential Evolution - A Simple and Efficient Heuristic for Global Optimization over Continuous Spaces. *Journal of Global Optimization*, 11(4), 341–359. doi:10.1023/A:1008202821328

Wang, L. X. (1997). *A Course in Fuzzy Systems and Controls*. Prentice Hall Publications.

Chapter 11
DE–Based RBFNs for Classification With Special Attention to Noise Removal and Irrelevant Features

Ch. Sanjeev Kumar Dash
Silicon Institute of Technology, India

Ajit Kumar Behera
Silicon Institute of Technology, India

Sarat Chandra Nayak
Kommuri Pratap Reddy Institute of Technology, India

ABSTRACT

This chapter presents a novel approach for classification of dataset by suitably tuning the parameters of radial basis function networks with an additional cost of feature selection. Inputting optimal and relevant set of features to a radial basis function may greatly enhance the network efficiency (in terms of accuracy) at the same time compact its size. In this chapter, the authors use information gain theory (a kind of filter approach) for reducing the features and differential evolution for tuning center and spread of radial basis functions. Different feature selection methods, handling missing values and removal of inconsistency to improve the classification accuracy of the proposed model are emphasized. The proposed approach is validated with a few benchmarking highly skewed and balanced dataset retrieved from University of California, Irvine (UCI) repository. The experimental study is encouraging to pursue further extensive research in highly skewed data.

DOI: 10.4018/978-1-5225-2857-9.ch011

1. INTRODUCTION

Classification is one of the fundamental tasks in data mining and pattern recognition. Over the years many models have been proposed. However, it is a consensus that the accuracy of the discovered model (i.e., a neural networks (NNs), rules, decision tree strongly depends on the quality of the data being mined. Hence inconsistency removal and feature selection brings lots of attention of many researchers. If the inconsistent data is simply deleted or classified as a new category then inevitably some useful information will be lost. The method used in this article for making the dataset consistent is based on Bayesian statistical method. Here the inconsistent data is classified as the most probable one and the redundant data records are deleted as well. So the loss of information due to simple deletion or random classification of inconsistent data is reduced and the size of the dataset is also reduced.

Feature selection is the process of selecting a subset of available features to use in empirical modeling. Like feature selection, instance selection is to choose a subset samples to achieve the original purpose of a classification tasks, as if the whole dataset is used. Many variants of evolutionary and non-evolutionary based approaches are discussed in literatures. The ideal outcome of instance selection is a model independent, minimum sample of data that can accomplish tasks with little or no performance deterioration. Unlike feature selection and instance selection, feature extraction at feature level fusion recently attracts data mining/machine learning researchers to give special focus while designing a classifier.

Feature selection can be broadly classified into two categories: i) filter approach (it depends on generic statistical measurement); and ii) wrapper approach (based on the accuracy of a specific classifier). In this work, the feature selection is performed based on information gain theory (entropy) measure with a goal to select a subset of features that preserves as much as possible the relevant information found in the entire set of features. After selection of the relevant set of features the fine tuned radial basis function network is modeled using differential evolution for classification of both balanced and unbalanced datasets. In imbalance classification problems occurs that the number of instances of each class can be very different.

Over the decade radial basis function (RBF) networks have attracted a lot of interest in various domain of interest. One reason is that they form a unifying link between function approximation, regularization, noisy interpolation, classification, and density estimation. It is also the case that training RBF networks is usually faster than training multi-layer perceptron networks. RBF network training usually proceeds in two steps: First, the basis function parameters (corresponding to hidden units) are determined by clustering. Second, the final-layer weights are determined by least square which reduces to solve a simple linear system. Thus, the first stage is an unsupervised method which is relatively fast, and the second stage requires the solution of a linear problem, which is also fast.

One of the advantages of RBF neural networks, compared to multi-layer perceptron networks, is the possibility of choosing suitable parameters for the units of hidden layer without having to perform a nonlinear optimization of the network parameters. However, the problem of selecting the appropriate number of basis functions remains a critical issue for RBF networks. The number of basis functions controls the complexity, and hence the generalization ability of RBF networks. An RBF network with too few basis functions gives poor predictions on new data, i.e., poor generalization, since the model has limited flexibility. On the other hand, an RBF network with too many basis functions also yields poor generalization since it is too flexible and fits the noise in the training data. A small number of basis functions yields a high bias, low variance estimator, whereas a large number of basis functions yields a low bias but high variance estimator. The best generalization performance is obtained via a compromise between the conflicting requirements of reducing bias while simultaneously reducing variance. This trade-off highlights the importance of optimizing the complexity of the model in order to achieve the best generalization. However, choosing an optimal number of kernels is beyond the focus of this article.

In training procedure of RBFNs revealing center of gravity and width is of particular importance for the improvement of the performance of the networks. There are many approaches along the line with their own merits and demerits. This article discusses the use of differential evolution to reveals hidden centers and spreads. The motivation using differential evolution (DE) over other EAs such as GAs is that in DE string encoding are typically represented as real valued vectors, and the perturbation of solution vectors is based on the scaled difference of two randomly selected individuals of the current population. Unlike GA, the resulting step size and orientation during the perturbation process automatically adopt to the fitness function landscape. The justification behind combining the idea of feature selection, data inconsistency removal with classification is to reduce the space, time, and thereby enhancing accuracy.

Differential evolution (DE) invented by Storn et al. in 1995 is a population based meta-heuristic search algorithm which typically operates on real valued chromosome encodings. Like GAs, DE maintains a pool of potential solutions which are then perturbed in an effort to uncover yet better solutions to a problem in hand. In GAs, the individuals are perturbed based on crossover and mutation. However in DE, individuals are perturbed based on the scaled difference of two randomly chosen individuals of the current population. One of the advantages of this approach is that the resulting 'step' size and orientation during the perturbation process automatically adapts to the fitness function landscape.

Over the years, there are many variants of DE algorithms developed however, we primarily describe a version of the algorithm based on the DE/rand/1/bin scheme. The different variants of the DE algorithm are described using the shorthand DE/x/y/z, where x specifies how the base vector (of real values) is chosen (rand if it is randomly selected, or best if the best individual in the population is selected), y is the number of difference vectors used, and z denotes the crossover scheme (bin for crossover based on independent binomial experiments, and exp for exponential crossover).

Multi-layer perceptron (MLP) network models are the popular network architectures used in most of the application areas (Bishop, 1995). In an MLP, the weighted sum of the inputs and bias term are passed to activation level through a transfer function to produce the output (i.e., $p(\vec{x}) = f_s\left(w_0 + \sum_{i=1}^{D} w_i x_i\right)$,

where $\vec{x}$ is an input vector of dimension D, $w_i, i = 1, 2, .., D$ are weights, w_0 is the bias weight, and

$f_s(o) = \dfrac{1}{1 + e^{-ao}}, a$ is the slope) and the units are arranged in a layered feed-forward topology called Feed Forward Neural Network (Callan, 1998). The network is then trained by back-propagation learning scheme. An MLP with back-propagation learning is also known as Back-Propagation Neural Networks (BPNNs). In BPNNs a common barrier is the training speed (i.e., the training speed increases as the number of layers, and number of neurons in a layer grow) (Haykin, 1994). To circumvent this problem a new paradigm of simpler neural network architectures with only one hidden layer has been penetrated to many application areas with a name of Radial Basis Function Neural Networks (RBFNs) (Acosta, 1995; Bors, 2001; Buhmann, 1990, 1993a, 1993b, 1995, 1998, 2000, 2003; Buhmann & Chui, 1993; Buhmann & Ron, 1994; Buhmann & Mehaute, 1995; Caiti et al., 1994; Wu, 1995). RBFNs were first introduced by Powell (Powell, 1987a, 1987b, 1992, 1999) to solve the interpolation problem in a multi-dimensional space requiring as many centers as data points. Later Broomhead and Lowe (Broomhead & Lowe, 1988) removed the 'strict' restriction and used less centers than data samples, so allowing many practical RBFNs applications in which the number of samples is very high. An important feature of RBFNs is the existence of a fast, linear learning algorithm in a network capable of representing complex non-linear mapping. At the same time it is also important to improve the generalization properties of RBFNs (Gyorfi et al., 2002). Today RBFNs has been a focus of study not only in numerical analysis but also in machine learning researchers.

Being inherited from the concept of biological receptive field (Broomhead & Lowe, 1988) and followed, Park and Sandberg prove, "RBFNs were capable to build any non-linear mappings between stimulus and response (Park & Sandberg, 1991). The growth of RBFNs research has been steadily increased and widespread in different application areas (c.f., Sections 5, 6, and 7 for more detailed discussion along with a number of indicative cited works). The research in RBFNs is grouped into three categories: i) development of learning mechanism (include heuristics and non-heuristics), ii) design of new kernels, and iii) areas of application.

Recently, Patrikar (Patrikar, 2013) has studied that RBFNs can be approximated by multi-layer perceptron with quadratic inputs (MLPQ). Let the MLPQ with one hidden layer consisting of M units and the output unit with linear activation function. Let $w_0(o)$ be the bias weight for the output unit and let $w_i(o)$ be the weights associated with the connection between hidden unit i and output unit o. the output of the MLPQ can be computed as:

$$Q(\vec{x}) = w_0(o) + \sum_{i=1}^{M} \frac{w_i(o)}{1 + \exp(-w_{i0} - \sum_{j=1}^{D} w_{Lij} x_j - \sum_{j=1}^{D} w_{Qij} x_j^2)}, \tag{1}$$

where for each hidden unit i, w_{io} is the bias weight, w_{Lij} are the weights associated with linear terms x_j, and w_{Qij} are the weights associated with quadratic terms x_j^2. For an RBFN with same hidden units, the output is given by:

$$R(\vec{x}) = \sum_{i=1}^{M} w_i \exp(-\beta(\vec{x} - \vec{\mu}_i)^T (\vec{x} - \vec{\mu}_i)), \tag{2}$$

where w_i are the weights of unit i, $\vec{\mu}_i$ is the center vector of unit i, and β is the parameter. Using approximation equation (2) can be approximated as

$$R(\vec{x}) \approx \sum_{i=1}^{M} w_i (H / (1 + \exp(-c\beta(\vec{x} - \vec{\mu}_i)^T (\vec{x} - \vec{\mu}_i)) - d), \tag{3}$$

where H, c, and d are constants.

This work is set out as follows. Section 2 gives overview RBFN architecture. Section 3 of this work is devoted to the multi-criteria issues of RBFNs and discussed some potential contributions. Different RBFN tools are discussed in section 4. Section 5-7 discusses the various application of RBFNs. Future research direction is discussed in section 8.

2. RBFNS ARCHITECTURE

The idea of RBFNs is derived from the theory of function approximation. The Euclidean distance is computed from the point being evaluated to the center of each neuron, and a radial basis function (RBF) (also called a kernel function) is applied to the distance to compute the weight (influence) for each neuron. The radial basis function is so named because the radius distance is the argument to the function. In other words, RBFs represent local receptors; its output depends on the distance of the input from a given stored vector. That means, if the distance from the input vector $\vec{x}$ to the center $\vec{\mu}_j$ of each RBF φ_j i.e., $\left\| \vec{x} - \vec{\mu}_j \right\|$ is equal to 0 then the contribution of this point is 1, whereas the contribution tends to 0 if the distance $\left\| \vec{x} - \vec{\mu}_j \right\|$ increases.

RBF networks broadly consist of three layers.

1. **Input Layer:** The input layer can have more than one predictor variable where each variable is associated with one independent neuron. The output of the input layer neurons, then feed the values to each of the neurons in the hidden layer.
2. **Hidden Layer:** The hidden layer can have multiple numbers of neurons. The selection of neurons in this layer is a challenging task. Mao and Huang (2005) have suggested a data structure preserving criterion technique for selection of neurons in the hidden layer.

Each neuron in the hidden layer consists of an RBF centered at a point, depending on the dimensionality of the input/output predictor variables. The hidden unit activations are given by the basis functions $\varphi_j(\vec{x}, \vec{\mu}_j, \sigma_j)$ (e.g., Gaussian basis functions), which depend on the parameters { $\vec{\mu}_j, \sigma_j$ } and input activations { $\vec{x}$ } in a non standard manner.

$$\varphi_j(\vec{x}) = \exp\left(-\frac{\left\| \vec{x} - \vec{\mu}_j \right\|^2}{2\sigma_j^{\,2}} \right) \tag{4}$$

The spread (radius) of the RBF function may be different for each dimension. The centers and spreads are determined by the training process of the network.

3. **Summation Layer:** Each neuron is associated with weights $\left(w_1, w_2, ..., w_N \right)$. The value coming out of a neuron in the hidden layer is multiplied by the weight associated with the neuron and passed to the summation which adds up the weighted values and presents this sum as the output of the network. A bias value is multiplied by a w_0 and fed into the summation layer.

Figure 1 shows a standard architecture of a RBFN network. In Figure 1, there are M neurons in the input layer and is decided based on the number of predictor variables. There are N neurons in the hidden layers (decided based on the problem complexity, some of the works in this direction have been mentioned in item number 2) and one output neuron in the output layer is assumed.

Figure 1. Architecture of RBFN network

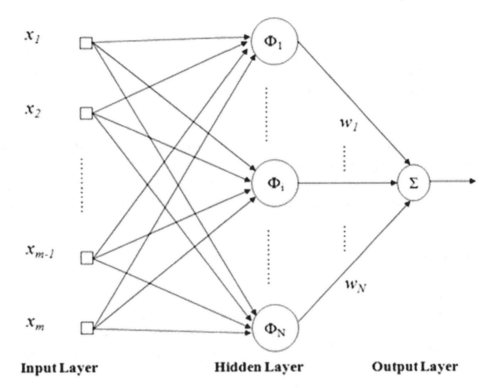

It is interesting to note that RBFNs are closely related to Gaussian Mixture Model (GMM) if Gaussian basis functions are used (Uykanet et al., 2000). RBFNs with N hidden units with one output neuron in the output layer can be represented as (equation 2) with a simple replacement of M by N. A Gaussian mixture density is a weighted sum of component densities given by:

$$g(\vec{x} \mid \lambda) = \sum_{i=1}^{N} \alpha_i b_i(\vec{x}),$$

where

$$\sum_{i=1}^{N} \alpha_i = 1.$$

$$b_i(\vec{x}) = \frac{1}{(2\pi)^{D/2} \left| \sum_i \right|^{1/2}} \exp(-\tfrac{1}{2}(\vec{x} - \vec{\mu})^T \sum_i{}^{-1}(\vec{x} - \vec{\mu})) \tag{5}$$

with mean vector $\vec{\mu}_i$ and covariance matrix $\sum_i$.

2.1. Learning in RBFNs

Learning or training a neural network is a process by means of which the network adapts itself to a stimulus by making proper parameter adjustment, resulting in the production of desired response. Hence, in order to achieve the similar approximation/classification accuracy and in addition to the required number of RBF units, the following parameters are determined by the training process of RBFNs (Schwenker et al., 1994).

1. The number of neurons in the hidden layer. [Ideally the number of neurons (M) in the hidden layer should be much less than data points (N)];
2. The coordinates of the center of each hidden-layer RBF, determined by the training algorithm;
3. The radius (spread) of each RBF in each dimension, determined by the training algorithm; and
4. The weights applied to the RBF outputs as they are passed to the summation layer.

2.2. Kernels in RBFN

The Gaussian kernel is a usual choice for kernel functions. Equation (5) is the most generic form of Gaussian kernel. The inverse of the covariance matrix is used to capture the correlations between different features, providing to each kernel an n-dimensional ellipsoid shape. It is generally more versatile than using the simple distance to kernel centroid that assumes strict variable independence. However, if the covariance matrix is singular or very ill conditioned, the use of the inverse can produce meaningless results or strong numerical instability. Therefore, a spectral decomposition suggested in (Falcao et al., 2006) can be applied to covariance matrix, producing the eigen system $\sum = P\Lambda P^t$ in which P is the matrix composed of the eigenvectors and Λ the respective eigenvalues in a diagonal matrix format.

The standard practical form of Gaussian kernel (i.e., equation 4) present a very selective response with high activation for close samples and very small activation for distant samples. It can also take different forms, including Cauchy RBF, defined by:

$$\varphi_j(\vec{x}) = \frac{1}{\left(1 + \dfrac{\left\|\vec{x} - \vec{\mu}_j\right\|}{\sigma_j^{\,2}}\right)} \tag{6}$$

and inverse multiquadric RBF, given by,

$$\varphi_j(\vec{x}) = \frac{1}{\left(1 + \dfrac{\left\|\vec{x} - \vec{\mu}_j\right\|}{\sigma_j^{\,2}}\right)^{1/2}} \tag{7}$$

Equations (6) and (7) have larger tails than equation (4) i.e., their activations for patterns far from the centroid of the RBF which is greater than the activation of the standard form (equation (4)) for these patterns. For sufficiently large distance norms, the decay of the equation (6) and (7) is very slow. In addition, equations (4), (6), and (7) do not fall asymptotically to zero. Fernández-Navarro et al. (2011) have presented q-Gaussian RBFs as an alternative to Gaussian RBF. The q-Gaussian RBF for the ith unit is defined as:

$$
\varphi_j(\vec{x}) = \begin{cases} \left(1 - (1 - q)\left(\dfrac{\|\vec{x} - \vec{\mu}_j\|^2}{\sigma_j^2}\right)\right)^{\frac{1}{1-q}}, & if\ 1 - (1 - q)\left(\dfrac{\|\vec{x} - \vec{\mu}_j\|^2}{\sigma_j^2}\right) \geq 0 \\ \qquad\qquad 0 & otherwise \end{cases}
\tag{8}
$$

where q is a real valued parameter. The q-Gaussian RBF allows different RBFs to be represented by updating the new parameter q. Yamada et al. (1993) has discussed different properties of Gaussian function in his work. In addition to standard Gaussian kernels, a range of other basis functions can be used in RBFNs. Table 1 summarizes the commonly used RBFs.

In multiquadric function (Buhmann, 1990) the matrix representation of basis function has an important spectral property: it is almost negative definite. Franke (Franke & Schaback, 1998) found that this radial basis function provides the most accurate interpolation surface in two dimensions. Franke (1982) found that the inverse multiquadric basis function can provide excellent approximations, even when the number of centers is small. However, presents that sometimes a large value of σ can be useful. In contrast, there is no good choice of σ known at present in the case of multi-quadric basis function.

The thin plate spline basis function has more global nature than the Gaussian function i.e. A small perturbation of one of the control points always affect the coefficients corresponding to all other points as well. Similarly, the polynomial basis functions like cubic and linear has some degree of influence in certain applications. An overview of RBFs and its corresponding models are described in (Acosta, 1995). The use of above list of kernels along with Gaussian kernels can be obtained in (Hon et al., 2003; Chen et al., 2007; Cherrie et al., 2002; Bors et al., 1996; Bors, 1999; Bors, 2001). However, we observe

Table 1. Different kernels used in RBFN

Name of the Kernel	Mathematical Representation
Generalized Multi-Quadric Functions	$\Phi(r) = (r^2 + c^2)^\beta, c > 0, 1 > \beta > 0$
Generalized Inverse Multi-Quadric Functions	$\Phi(r) = (r^2 + c^2)^{-\alpha}, c > 0, \alpha > 0$
Thin Plate Spline Function	$\Phi(r) = r^2 \ln(r)$
Cubic Function	$\Phi(r) = r^3$
Linear Function	$\Phi(r) = r$

in most of the neural network literature the Gaussian RBFs is widely used in diversified domain like medical/biological science, computational finance, defense systems, engineering, etc.

2.3. Learning of Kernel Parameters and Weights

One major advantage of RBF networks of choosing suitable hidden unit/basis function parameters without having to perform a full non-linear optimization of the whole network. The coordinates of center of each hidden-layer in RBF function can be calculated by using any of the following unsupervised methods:

2.3.1. Fixed Centers Selected at Random

This is a simple and fast approach for setting the RBF parameters, where the centers are kept fixed at M points selected at random from the N data points. Specifically, we can use normalized RBFs centered at $\{\mu_j\}$ defined by:

$$\phi_j(x) = \exp\left(-\frac{\|X - \mu_j\|^2}{2\sigma_j^2}\right)$$

where

$$\{\mu_j\} \subset \{X^p\}$$

and

$$\sigma_j \tag{9}$$

is spread.

2.3.2. Clustering

Clustering techniques can be used to find a set of centers which more accurately reflect the distribution of the data points. The K-means clustering algorithm (Lim et al., 2008) selects the number K of centers in advance, and then follows a simple re-estimation procedure to divide the data points $\{X^p\}$ into K disjoint sub-sets S_j and N_j data points in order to minimize the sum of squared clustering function.

$$J = \sum_{j=1}^{K} \sum_{p \in S_j} \|X^p - \mu_j\|^2 \tag{10}$$

where, μ_j is the mean/centroid of the data points in set S_j given by the equation (11):

$$\mu_j = \frac{1}{N_j} \sum_{p \in S_j} X^p \tag{11}$$

There are, however, two intrinsic disadvantages associated with the use of K-means. The first is due to its iterative nature, which can lead to long convergence times, and the second originates from its inability to automatically determine the number of RBF centers, thus resulting in a time-consuming trial-and-error procedure for establishing the size of the hidden layer.

2.3.3. Orthogonal Least Squares (OLS)

One of the fine tuned approaches to selecting a sub-set of data points as the basis function centers is based on the technique of orthogonal least squares. OLS is a forward stepwise regression procedure, where OLS sequentially selects the center that results in the largest reduction of sum-of-square-error at the output. OLS constructs a set of orthogonal vectors Q for the space spanned by the candidate centers. In this orthogonal subspace, computation of pseudo-inverse is avoided since $Q'Q$ becomes diagonal. OLS construct a set of orthogonal vectors Q for the space spanned by basis vectors ϕ_k such that $\Phi = Q A$ where, A is an upper triangular matrix. Using this orthogonal representation, the RBF solution is expressed as:

$$T = \Phi W = QG \tag{12}$$

and the LS solution for the weight vector G in the orthogonal space is given as:

$$G = \left(Q'Q\right)^{-1} Q'T \tag{13}$$

3. DIFFERENTIAL EVOLUTION

Differential evolution (DE) (Storn et al., 1995, 1997, 1999) is a population based stochastic search algorithm which typically operates on real valued chromosome encodings. Like GAs, DE maintains a population of potential solution encodings which are then perturbed in an effort to uncover yet better solutions to a problem in hand. In GAs, the basic steps are selection, crossover and mutation. However in DE, individuals are represented as real-valued vectors, and the perturbation of solution vectors is based on the scaled difference of two randomly chosen individuals of the current population. One of the advantages of this approach is that the resulting 'step' size and orientation during the perturbation process automatically adapts to the fitness function landscape.

Although several DE algorithms available in literature (Price et al., 2005; Das et al., 2011) we primarily describe a version of the algorithm based on the DE/rand/1/bin scheme (Storn et al., 1995). The different variants of the DE algorithm are described using the shorthand DE/x/y/z, where x specifies how the base vector (of real values) is chosen (rand if it is randomly selected, or best if the best individual in the population is selected), y is the number of difference vectors used, and z denotes the crossover scheme (bin for crossover based on independent binomial experiments, and exp for exponential crossover).

A population of n, d-dimensional vectors $x_i = \left(x_{i1}, x_{i2}, .., x_{id}\right)$, $i = 1...n$ each of which encode a solution is randomly initialized and evaluated using a fitness function f(.). During the search process, each individual (i) is iteratively refined. The following three steps are required while execution.

1. **Mutation:** Create a donor vector which encodes a solution, using randomly selected members of the population.
2. **Crossover:** Create a trial vector by combining the donor vector with i .
3. **Selection:** By the process of selection, determine whether the newly-created trial vector replaces i in the population or not.

Under the mutation operator, for each vector $x_i(t)$ a donor vector $v_i(t+1)$ is obtained by equation (14).

$$v_i\left(t+1\right) = x_k\left(t\right) + f_m * \left(x_l\left(t\right) - x_m\left(t\right)\right) \tag{14}$$

where k, l, m $\in$ 1...n are mutually distinct, randomly selected indices, and all the indices $\neq$ i $\left(x_k(t)\right)$ is referred to as the base vector and $(x_l(t) - x_m(t))$ is referred as difference vector). Selecting three indices randomly implies that all members of the current population have the same chance of being selected, and therefore influencing the creation of the difference vector. The difference between vectors x_l and x_m is multiplied by a scaling parameter f_m [called mutation factor and a range for the parameter must be associated to it, that is $f_m \in \left[0, 2\right]$. The mutation factor controls the amplification of the difference between x_l and x_m which is used to avoid stagnation of the search process. There are several alternative versions of the above process for creating a donor vector.[see (Price et al.,2005;Das et al. 2011) for details of these].

A notable feature of the mutation step in DE is that it is self-scaling. The size/rate of mutation along each dimension stems solely from the location of the individuals in the current population. The mutation step self-adapts as the population converges leading to a finer-grained search. In contrast, the mutation process in GA is typically based on (or draws from) a fixed probability density function.

Following the creation of the donor vector, a trial vector $u_i(t+1) = (u_{i1}, u_{i2}, u_{i3}, ..., u_{id})$ $u_i\left(t+1\right) = \left(u_{i1}, u_{i2}, u_{ie}, ..., u_{id}\right)$ is obtained by equation (3).

$$u_i\left(t+1\right) = \begin{cases} v_{ip}\left(t+1\right), & if \ \left(rand \leq c_r\right) \ or \ \left(i = rand(ind)\right) \\ x_{ip}(t), & if \ \left(rand > c_r\right) \ and \ \left(i \neq rand(ind)\right) \end{cases} \tag{15}$$

$$u_i\left(t+1\right) = \begin{cases} v_{ip}\left(t+1\right), & if \ \left(rand \leq c_r\right) \ or \ \left(i = rand(ind)\right) \\ x_i p(t), & if \ \left(rand > c_r\right) \ and \ \left(i = rand(ind)\right) \end{cases}$$

where p = 1,2,....,d, rand is a random number generated in the range (0, 1), c_r is the user-specified crossover constant from the range (0, 1), and rand(ind) is a randomly chosen index, chosen from the range (1, 2, ..., d). The random index is used to ensure that the trial vector differs by at least one element from $x_i(t)$. The resulting trial (child) vector replaces its parent if it has higher fitness (a form of selection); otherwise the parent survives unchanged into the next iteration of the algorithm.

Finally, if the fitness of the trial vector exceeds that of the fitness of the parent then it replaces the parent as described in equation (4).

$$x_i(t+1) = \begin{cases} u_i(t+1), & if \quad (f(u_i(t+1)) > f(x_i(t)) \\ x_i(t), & otherwise \end{cases} \qquad (16)$$

Price and Storn (2005) provide a comprehensive comparison of the performance of DE with a range of other optimizers, including GA, and report that the results obtained by DE are consistently as good as the best obtained by other optimizers across a wide range of problem instances. Many variants of DE can be obtained from a recent study by Das et al. (2011).

Rationale for a RBF-DE Integration: There are a number of reasons to suppose that an evolutionary methodology, (particularly GA) coupled with a RBF can prove fruitful in classification tasks. The selection of quality parameters for classifiers represents a high-dimensional problem, giving rise to potential use of evolutionary methodologies. Combining these with the universal approximation qualities of a RBF produces a powerful modeling methodology.

4. NOISY DATA IN CLASSIFICATION PROBLEM

Data gathered from real-world problems are never perfect and often suffer from corruptions that may hinder the performance of the system in terms of the classification accuracy, size and interpretability of the classifier. A large number of components determine the quality of a dataset. Among them, the class labels and the attribute values directly influence the quality of a classification dataset. The quality of the class labels refers to whether the class of each example is correctly assigned; otherwise, the quality of the attributes refers to their capability of properly characterizing the examples for classification purposes – obviously, if noise affects attribute values, this capability of characterization and therefore, the quality of the attribute is reduced. Based on these two information sources, two types of noise can be distinguished in a given dataset:

- **Noise in Attributes:** It is given by the errors occurred during the entrance of the values of the attributes. Among the sources of this type of noise are: variable with missing values, and redundant data.
- **Noise in Classes:** It is given by the errors introduced during the assignment of the instances to the classes. The presence of this kind of noise may be due to subjectivity, errors in the data entry process, and incorrect information for assigning a instance to a class.

There are two possible sources of class noise: i) Inconsistent instances. These are instances with the same attribute values but belonging to two or more different classes of the dataset, and ii) Error in the classification. Here we are focusing on inconsistence instances.

Dataset Consistency

A dataset is said to be consistent if it does not contain any inconsistent instances or patterns. A pattern is inconsistent if there are at least two instances which have the same value for all corresponding features but different class labels.

For example the instances t1=(1, 0, 2) and t2=(1, 0, 3) are inconsistent as they have the same value for corresponding features but different class labels which is the last value in the instances.

So t1 and t2 are inconsistent instances. We can also say the pattern (1, 0) is inconsistent.

The method used in this paper to make the dataset consistent is described below with the help of an example.

Let us take a dataset having n instances. Here the dataset D has n=9 instances and two feature variables. Table 2 gives the description of the data set.

D= {i1, i2, i3, i4, i5, i6, i7, i8, i9}

Let there be k classes. Here k=2. Then the class set C= {c1=1, c2=2}.
The steps are as follows:

Step 1: The dataset is divided into groups according to patterns. If there are t patterns than the dataset is divided into t-disjoint sets.

D contains 3 patterns: p1= (a, b); p2= (b, c); p3=(c, d).So the (t=3) disjoint sets according to patterns are:d1= {i1, i2, i3}, d2= {i4, i5}, d3= {i6, i7, i8, i9}

Step 2: The same dataset is also divided into groups according to classes into k disjoint sets.

Table 2. Description of dataset D

i1	a	b	1
i2	a	b	2
i3	a	b	1
i4	b	c	2
i5	c	d	2
i6	c	d	1
i7	c	d	2
i8	c	d	1
i9	c	d	1

Since D has 2 classes, so the (k=2) disjoint sets according to classes are:

c1= {i1, i3, i6, i8, i9} c2= {i2, i4, i5, i7}

Step 3: A category proportion matrix (R) is constructed according to the formula

$$Rmn= |dm \cap cn|/ |dm|$$ (17)

where $(1 \leq m \leq t, 1 \leq n \leq k; t=3 ; k=2)$

| S | represents the cardinality of the set S.

Table 3 shows the category proportion matrix for the dataset D.

Step 4: In this step it is checked if the dataset is consistent or not.

If for all Rmn: 0 or 1 then the dataset is consistent.
If for any Rmn: $0 \leq Rmn \leq 1$ then the dataset is inconsistent.
Here R11, R12, R31, R32 have values between 0 and 1.
Hence D is inconsistent. The corresponding disjoint sets d1 and d3 are inconsistent data subsets or the pattern p1 and p3 are inconsistent. To make the dataset uniform all inconsistent data subsets are made uniform.

Step 5: The most probable class for the inconsistent pattern is found out in this step. The probability of a pattern ps belonging to category cn is given by the formula

$$P(cn | ps)= \{P(ps | cn)* P(cn)\}/P(ps),$$ (18)

where $P (cn) = |cn|/|D|$, $P(ps | cn) = |dm \cap cn|/|cn|$, $P(ps) = |dm|/|D|$
The most probable class for the pattern ps is the one for which P (cn | ps) is maximum. But if the class distribution of a pattern is quite even then the above probability may give a wrong most probable class. For example if a pattern Ps has three class values c1, c2, c3 then the corresponding probability is 0.34, 0.33, 0.33 respectively. In this case it is inappropriate to classify the pattern as c1. For this situation a threshold α is introduced.

Table 3. Category of proportion matrix

2/3=0.6666	1/3=0.3333
0/3=0	2/2=1
3/4=0.75	1/4=0.25

So, only when P(cq | ps) > P(cn | ps) and P(cq | ps) > α then the pattern ps is classified as cq.

If the probability for all classes for a pattern is below the threshold then the inconsistent data subset containing this pattern is deleted from the dataset.

Taking α=0.5, the inconsistent data subsets d1 and d3 can be unified as c1=1. The dataset is also compressed into 3 instances.

Table 4 presents the final consistent dataset D.

5. ENTROPY BASED FEATURE SELECTION

In our approach we rank the features or attributes according to information gain ratio and then delete an appropriate number of features which have least gain ratio. [see (Aruna et al.2012)]. The exact number of features deleted varies from dataset to dataset. The expected information needed to classify a tuple in D is given by

$$Info(D) = -\sum_{i=1}^{m} p_i \log_2(p_i),$$

(19)

where pi is the non-zero probability that an arbitrary tuple in D belongs to class Ci and is estimated by $|C_{i,D}| / |D|$. A log function to the base 2 is used, because the information is encoded in bits. Info(D) is the average amount of information needed to identify the class level of a tuple in D. Info(D) is also known as entropy of D and is based upon only the properties of classes[9].

For an attribute 'A' entropy "$Info_A(D)$" is the information still required to classify the tuples in D after partitioning tuples in D into groups only on its basis.

$$Info_A(D) = \sum_{j=1}^{v} \frac{|D_j|}{|D|} \times Info(D_j)$$

(20)

where v is the number of distinct values in the attribute A, $|D|$ is the total number of tuples in D and $|D_j|$ is the number of repetitions of the jth distinct value.

Information gain is defined as the difference between the original information requirement and new requirement (after partitioning on A)

Table 4. Description of consistent dataset D

i1	a	b	1
i2	b	c	2
i3	c	d	3

$$Gain(A) = Info(D) - Info_A \left(D\right) \tag{21}$$

Information gain applies a kind of normalization to information gain using split information value defined analogously with $Info(D)$ as:

$$SplitInfo_A \left(D\right) = \sum_{j=1}^{v} \frac{\left|D_j\right|}{\left|D\right|} \times \log_2 \left(\frac{\left|D_j\right|}{\left|D\right|}\right) \tag{22}$$

This value represents the potential information generated by splitting the training data set, D, into v partitions, corresponding to the v outcomes of test on attribute A. For each outcome, it considers the number of tuples having the outcome with respect to the total number of tuples in D. The gain ratio is defined as

$$GainRatio(A) = Gain(A) \,/\, SplitInfo(A). \tag{23}$$

The more the gain ratio of an attribute the more important it is. In our approach first feature selection is done using information gain ratio and then the reduced dataset is used for automatic training and determination of the parameters of RBF network using DE.

In the third phase, we are focusing on the learning of the classifier. As mentioned there are two steps within the learned procedure. In step one differential evolution is employed to reveal the centers and width of the RBFNS. Although centers, widths, and weights that connect kernel nodes and output node simultaneously be evolved using DE, but here we restrict ourselves with evolving only centers and spreads. This ensures efficient representation of an individual of DE. If all these parameters are encoded, then the length of the individual would be too long and hence the search space size becomes too large, which results in a very slow convergence rate. Since the performance of the RBFNs mainly depends on center and width of the kernel, we just encode the centers and widths into an individual for stochastic search.

Figure 2 presents the structure of individual. Suppose the maximum number of kernel nodes is set to $K_{\max}$, then the structure of the individual is represented as follows:

In other words each individual has three constituent parts such as center, width and bias. The length of the individual is $2K_{\max} + 1$.

The fitness function which is used to guide the search process is defined in equation (24).

Figure 2. Structure of the individual

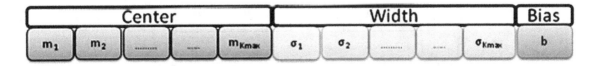

$$f(x) = \frac{1}{N} \sum_{1}^{N} \left(t_n - \widehat{\Phi} \left(\overrightarrow{x_i} \right) \right)^2 \tag{24}$$

where N is the total number of training sample t_n is the actual output and is the estimated output of RB-FNs. Once the centers and widths are fixed, the task of determining weights in second phase of learning reduces to solving a simple linear system. In this work the pseudo inverse method is adopted to find out a setoff optimal weights. Figure 3 illustrates the two step learning procedure adopted in this work.

The algorithmic framework of RBFN-DE is described as follows:

Initially, a set of n_p individuals (i.e. n_p is the size of the population) pertaining to networks centers, width, and bias are created.

$$x_i^{(t)} = \left\langle x_{i1}^{(t)}, x_{i2}^{(t)}, ..., x_{id}^{(t)} \right\rangle, \; i = 1, 2, ..., n_p$$

and $d = 2K_{max} + 1$, where $d = 2.h_{max} + 1$ t is the iteration number.

At the start of the algorithm this n_p set of individuals are initialized randomly and then evaluated using the fitness function f(.).

In each iteration, e.g., iteration t, for individual $x_i^{(t)}$ undergoes mutation, crossover and selection as follows:

- **Mutation:** For vector $x_i^{(t)}$ a perturbed vector $V_i^{(t+1)}$ called donor vector is generated according to equation (25):

$$V_i^{(t+1)} = x_{r1}^{(t)} + m_f * \left(x_{r2}^{(t)} - x_{r3}^{(t)} \right), \tag{25}$$

where m_f is the mutation factor drawn from (0,2], the indices $r_1, r_2 \; and \; r_3$ are selected randomly from $\{1, 2, 3, ..., n_p\}$, $r_1 \neq r_2 \neq r_3 \neq i$.

- **Crossover:** The trial vector is generated as follows (equation (26)):

Figure 3. Two step learning procedure

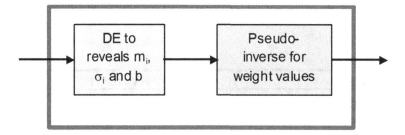

$$u_i^{(t+1)} = u_{i1}^{(t+1)}, u_{i2}^{(t+1)}, \ldots, u_{id}^{(t+1)}$$

$$u_{ij}^{(t+1)} = \begin{cases} v_{ij}^{(t+1)} & if\ (rand \leq c_r)\ \ or\ \ (i = rand(1,2,..,d)) \\ x_{ij}^{(t)} & if\ (rand > c_r)\ \ and\ \ (i \neq rand(1,2,..,d)) \end{cases} \qquad (26)$$

where j=1, 2, …,d, rand is a random number generated in the range (0,1) c_r is the user specified cross-over constant from the range (0,1) and rand(1,2,…,d) is a randomly chosen index from the range(1,2,…,d). The random index is used to ensure that the trial solution vector differs by at least on element from x_i^t. The resulting trial (child) solution replaces its parent if it has higher accuracy (a form of selection), otherwise the parent survives unchanged into the next iteration of the algorithm. Figure 4 illustrates this operation in the context of revealing center, width and bias.

- **Selection:** Finally, we obtain target vector $x_i^{(t+1)}$ as follows in equation (27):

$$x_i^{(t+1)} = \begin{cases} u_i^{(t+1)} & if\ \ f(x_i^{(t+1)}) \leq f(x_i^{(t)}) \\ x_i^{(t)} & otherwise. \end{cases} \qquad (27)$$

Figure 4. Selection of individuals

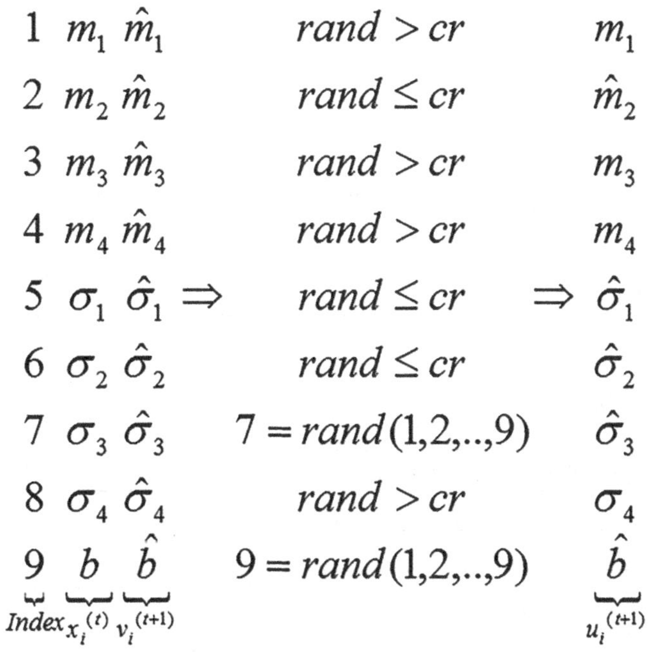

$$\begin{array}{llll}
1 & m_1\ \hat{m}_1 & rand > cr & m_1 \\
2 & m_2\ \hat{m}_2 & rand \leq cr & \hat{m}_2 \\
3 & m_3\ \hat{m}_3 & rand > cr & m_3 \\
4 & m_4\ \hat{m}_4 & rand > cr & m_4 \\
5 & \sigma_1\ \hat{\sigma}_1 \Rightarrow & rand \leq cr & \Rightarrow \hat{\sigma}_1 \\
6 & \sigma_2\ \hat{\sigma}_2 & rand \leq cr & \hat{\sigma}_2 \\
7 & \sigma_3\ \hat{\sigma}_3 & 7 = rand(1,2,..,9) & \hat{\sigma}_3 \\
8 & \sigma_4\ \hat{\sigma}_4 & rand > cr & \sigma_4 \\
9 & b\ \hat{b} & 9 = rand(1,2,..,9) & \hat{b}
\end{array}$$

$$\underbrace{}\ \underbrace{}\ \underbrace{} \qquad\qquad \underbrace{}$$

$$Index\ \ x_i^{(t)}\ \ v_i^{(t+1)} \qquad\qquad\qquad u_i^{(t+1)}$$

where j=1,2,…,d.

Given that the centers, widths, and bias are computed from training vector, they may be written in the matrix from as:

$$Y = W\Phi$$

$$\Rightarrow W = \left(\Phi^T \Phi\right)^{-1} \Phi^T Y.$$

6. DESCRIPTION OF DATASET AND PARAMETERS

The datasets used in this work were obtained from the UCI machine learning repository (Frank & Asuncion, 2010). Three datasets have been chosen to validate the proposed method. The details about the three datasets are given below. Table 5 summarizes the data sets used in this work and their characteristics.

In our experiment, every dataset is divided into two mutually exclusive parts: training sets and test sets. Table 6 summarizes the simulation parameters used for validating our proposed method.

7. RESULTS AND ANALYSIS

Table 7-16 summarizes the experimental results. Through the empirical validation we have reported the results of the classifier under three categories.

Table 5. Description of datasets

Data Set	Instances	Attributes	Classes	Class 1	Class2
MAMMOGRAPHIC MASSES	961	6	2	516	445
HABERMEN	306	4	2		
BLOOD TRANSFUSION	748	5	2	500	248

Table 6. Parameters used for simulation

Parameter	Mammographic Masses	Habermen	Blood Transfusion
Maximum Iteration	100	100	150
Population	50	50	50
Mutation	0.8	0.8	0.8
Crossover	0.8	0.8	0.8

Table 7. Results of DE-RBF (95% confidence level)

Data Set	Average Accuracy Result After 10 Iterations.	Average Accuracy Result After 20 Iterations.	Average Accuracy After 30 Iterations.
MAMMOGRAPHIC MASSES	81.6744±.034	81.5233±.034	81.7442±.034
HABERMEN	88.7097±.050	88.7097±.050	88.7097±.050
TRANSFUSION	85.7664±.035	85.7664±.035	85.7664±.035

Table 8. Results Obtained from DE-RBF (98% confidence level)

Data Set	Average Accuracy Result After 10 Iterations	Average Accuracy Result After 20 Iterations	Average Result After 30 Iterations
MAMMOGRAPHIC MASSES	81.6744±.041	81.5233±.041	81.7442±.041
HABERMEN	88.7097±.059	88.7097±.059	88.7097±.059
TRANSFUSION	85.7664±.041	85.7664±.041	85.7664±.041

Table 9. Results of DE-RBF with feature selection (95% confidence level)

Data Set	Feature Removed	Average Result After 10 Iterations.	Average Result After 20 Iterations	Average Result After 30 Iterations.
MAMMOGRAPHIC MASSES	5	82.3023±.034	82.2907±.034	82.1318±.034
HABERMEN	2	88.7097±.050	88.7097±.050	88.7097±.050
TRANSFUSION	2	85.7664±.035	85.7664±.035	85.7664±.035

Table 10. Results Obtained from DE-RBF with feature selection (98% confidence level)

Data Set	Feature Number Removed From Dataset	Average Result After 10 Iterations.	Average Result After 20 Iterations	Average Result After 30 Iterations
MAMMOGRAPHIC MASSES	5	82.3023±.040	82.2907±.040	82.1318±.40
HABERMEN	2	88.7097±.059	88.7097±.059	88.7097±.059
TRANSFUSION	2	85.7664±.042	85.7664±.042	85.7664±.042

1. Average classification accuracy of 10, 20 and 30 iteration in terms of 95% and 98% percentage confidence level without selecting any features;
2. Average classification accuracy of 10, 20 and 30 iteration in terms of 95% and 98% percentage confidence level after removing 1/3rd of the features based on filter approach.

Table 11. Results Obtained from DE-RBF after feature consistency (95% confidence level)

Data Set	Average Result After 10 Iterations.	Average Result After 20 Iterations.	Average Result After 30 Iterations.
MAMMOGRAPHIC MASSES	85.12±.031	85.06±.031	85.0933±.031
HABERMEN	94.5578±.035	94.5578±.035	94.5578±.035
TRANSFUSION	92.9825±.025	92.9825±.025	94.5578±.025

Table 12. Results Obtained from DE-RBF after feature consistency (98% confidence level)

Data Set	Average Result After 10 Iterations.	Average Result After 20 Iterations.	Average Result After 30 Iterations.
MAMMOGRAPHIC MASSES	85.12±.037	85.06±.037	85.0933±.031
HABERMEN	94.5578±.042	94.5578±.042	94.5578±.042
TRANSFUSION	92.9825±.030	92.9825±.030	94.5578±.030

Table 13. Results of DE-RBF with feature consistency and feature selection (95% confidence level)

Data Set	Feature Umber Removed From Dataset	Average Accuracy Result of 10 Iterations	Average Accuracy Result of 20 Iterations.	Average Accuracy Result of 30 Iterations.
MAMMOGRAPHIC MASSES	5	86.2174±.030	86.1087±.030	86.4638±.030
HABERMEN	2	96.8421±.027	96.8421±.027	96.8421±.027
TRANSFUSION	1	94.3662±.023	94.3662±.23	94.3662±.023

Table 14. Results of DE-RBF with feature consistency and feature selection (98% confidence level)

Data Set	Feature Number Removed From Dataset	Average Accuracy of 10 Iterations	Average Accuracy Result of 20 Iterations	Average Accuracy Result of 30 Iterations.
MAMMOGRAPHIC MASSES	5	86.2174±.036	86.1087±.036	86.4638±.036
HABERMEN	2	96.8421±.032	96.8421±.032	96.8421±.032
TRANSFUSION	1	94.3662±.027	94.3662±.027	94.3662±.027

3. Average classification accuracy of 10, 20 and 30 iteration in terms of 95% and 98% percentage confidence level after feature consistency approach.

4. Average classification accuracy of 10, 20 and 30 iteration in terms of 95% and 98% percentage confidence level after feature consistency approach and feature selection.

5. Finally Average accuracy result of above method of 10, 20 and 30 iterations.

Table 15. Average results of 10, 20 and 30 iteration Obtained from DE-RBF, DE-RBF with feature selection, DE-RBF with feature consistency and DE-RBF with feature consistency and feature selection (95% confidence level)

Data Set	Average Accuracy of DE-RBF(10,20 and 30 iteration)	Average Accuracy Result of (DE-BF With Feature Selection	Average Accuracy Result of (DE-RBF With Feature Consistency	Average Accuracy of DE-RBF With Feature Consistency and Feature Selection
MAMMOGRAPHIC MASSES	81.6473±.034	82.2416±.034	85.0911±.031	86.2633±.030
HABERMEN	88.7097±.050	88.7097±.050	94.5578±.035	96.8421±.027
TRANSFUSION	85.7664±.035	85.7664±.035	92.9825±.025	94.3662±.023

Table 16. Average results of 10, 20 and 30 iteration Obtained from DE-RBF, DE-RBF with feature selection, DE-RBF with feature consistency and DE-RBF with feature consistency and feature selection (98% confidence level)

Data Set	Average Accuracy of DE-RBF (10, 20 and 30 iteration)	Average Accuracy Result of (DE-RBF With Feature Selection	Average Accuracy Result of (DE-RBF With Feature Consistency	Average Accuracy Result of DE-RBF With Feature Consistency and Feature Selection
MAMMOGRAPHIC MASSES	81.6473±.041	82.2416±.040	85.0911±.037	86.2633±.036
HABERMEN	88.7097±.059	88.7097±.059	94.5578±.042	96.8421±.032
TRANSFUSION	85.7664±.041	85.7664±.041	92.9825±.030	94.3662±.027

8. CONCLUSION

In this work, a synergy of Bayesian statistics based inconsistency removal, filter based feature selection and differential evolution trained RBFNs is functioning towards removal of inconsistency, reduction of irrelevant features, and maximization of predictive accuracy of the classifier. The method of encoding an RBF network into an individual is given, where only the centers and the spread of the hidden units are encoded. The connection weights between hidden layer and output layer are obtained by pseudo-inverse method. The performance under synergistic approach is encouraging to use in more diversified engineering applications. In the future scope of research, lots of avenues are here, e.g., i) the synergy of fuzzy entropy based feature selection and DE trained RBFNs with consistency removal, ii) testing this proposed method in large number of highly skewed data, and iii) a very rigorous comparative analysis with other classifiers who are simultaneously reducing the features and maximizing the classification accuracy.

REFERENCES

Acosta, F. M. A. (1995). Radial Basis Functions and Related Models: An Overview. *Signal Processing*, *45*(1), 37–58. doi:10.1016/0165-1684(95)00041-B

Aruna, S., Nandakishore, & Rajagopalan, L. V. S. P. (2012). A Hybrid Feature Selection Method based on IGSBFS and Naïve Bayes for the Diagnosis of Erythemato - Squamous Diseases. *International Journal of Computer Applications, 41*(7).

Bishop, C. (1995). *Neural Networks for Pattern Recognition*. Oxford University Press.

Bors, A. G. (2001). Introduction of the Radial Basis Function Networks. *Online Symposium for Electronics Engineers, 1*(1), 1-7.

Bors, A. G., & Pitas, I. (1996). Median Radial Basis Functions Neural Network. *IEEE Transactions on Neural Networks, 7*(6), 1351–1364. doi:10.1109/72.548164 PMID:18263530

Bors, A. G., & Pitas, I. (1999). Object Classification in 3-D images using Alpha-trimmed Mean Radial Basis Function Network. *IEEE Transactions on Image Processing, 8*(12), 1744–1756. doi:10.1109/83.806620 PMID:18267451

Broomhead, D. S., & Lowe, D. (1988). Multi-variable Functional Interpolation and Adaptive Networks. *Complex Systems, 2*, 321–355.

Buhmann, M. D. (1990). Multivariate Cardinal Interpolation with Radial Basis functions. *Constructive Approximation, 6*(3), 225–255. doi:10.1007/BF01890410

Buhmann, M. D. (1993a). On Quasi-Interpolation with Radial Basis Functions. *Journal of Approximation Theory, 72*(1), 103–130. doi:10.1006/jath.1993.1009

Buhmann, M. D. (1993b). New Developments in the Theory of Radial Basis Function Interpolation. In K. Jette & F. Utreras (Eds.), *Multivariate Approximation: From CAGD to Wavelets* (pp. 35–75). Singapore: World Scientific Publishing. doi:10.1142/9789814503754_0003

Buhmann, M. D. (1995). Pre-Wavelet on Scattered Knots and from Radial Function Spaces: A Review. In R. R. Martin (Eds.), *6th IMA Conference on the Mathematics of Surfaces*. Clarendon Press.

Buhmann, M. D. (1998). Radial Functions on Compact Support. *Proceedings of the Edinburgh Mathematical Society, 41*(1), 33–46. doi:10.1017/S0013091500019416

Buhmann, M. D. (2000). Radial Basis Functions. *Acta Numerica, Cambridge University Press, 9*(0), 1–38. doi:10.1017/S0962492900000015

Buhmann, M. D. (2003). *Radial Basis Functions: Theory and Implementations. 12*. Cambridge University Press. doi:10.1017/CBO9780511543241

Buhmann, M. D., & Chui, C. K. (1993). A Note on the Local Stability of Translates of Radial Basis Functions. *Journal of Approximation Theory, 74*(1), 36–40. doi:10.1006/jath.1993.1051

Buhmann, M. D., & Mehaute, A. L. (1995). Knot Removal with Radial Basis Function Interpolation. *Comptes Rendus de l'Académie des Sciences. Série 1, Mathématique, 320*, 501–506.

Buhmann, M. D., & Ron, A. (1994). Radial Basis Functions: Lp-Approximation Orders with Scattered Centers in Wavelets, Images, and Surface Fitting. A. K. Peters.

Callan, R. (1998). *The Essence of Neural Networks*. Prentice Hall PTR Upper Saddle River.

Chen, S., Gibson, G. J., Cowan, C. F. N., & Grant, P. M. (1991). Reconstruction of Binary Signals using an Adaptive Radial-Basis-Function Equalizer. *EURASIP Signal Processing*, *22*(1), 77–93. doi:10.1016/0165-1684(91)90030-M

Chen, S., Hong, X., Luk, B. L., & Harris, C. J. (2009). Construction of Tunable Radial Basis Function Networks Using Orthogonal Forward Selection. *IEEE Transactions on Systems, Man, and Cybernetics. Part B, Cybernetics*, *39*(2), 457–466. doi:10.1109/TSMCB.2008.2006688 PMID:19095548

Chen, S., McLaughlin, S., & Mulgrew, B. (1994). Complex-valued Radial Basis Function Network, Part I: Network Architecture and Learning Algorithms. *Signal Processing*, *35*(1), 19–31. doi:10.1016/0165-1684(94)90187-2

Chen, S., Wang, X. X., Hong, X., & Harris, C. J. (2006). Kernel Classifier Construction Using Orthogonal Forward Selection And Boosting With Fisher Ratio Class Separability Measure. *IEEE Transactions on Neural Networks*, *17*(6), 1652–1656. doi:10.1109/TNN.2006.881487 PMID:17131680

Chen, T., & Chen, H. (1995). Approximation Capability to Functions of Several Variables, Nonlinear Functional and Operators by Radial Basis Function Neural Networks. *IEEE Transactions on Neural Networks*, *6*(4), 904–910. doi:10.1109/72.392252 PMID:18263378

Cherrie, J. B., Beatson, R. K., & Newsam, G. N. (2002). Fast Evaluation of Radial Basis Functions: Methods for Generalized Multi-quadrics in Rn. *SIAM Journal on Scientific Computing*, *23*(5), 1549–1571. doi:10.1137/S1064827500367609

Das, S., & Suganthan, P. N. (2011). Differential Evolution: A Survey of the State-of- the- Art. *IEEE Transactions on Evolutionary Computation*, *15*(1), 4–31. doi:10.1109/TEVC.2010.2059031

Dash, C. S. K., Dash, A. P., Dehuri, S., Cho, S. B., & Wang, G. N. (2013). DE+ RBFNs Based Classification: A Special Attention to Removal of Inconsistency and Irrelevant Features. *Engineering Applications of Artificial Intelligence*, *26*(10), 2315–2326. doi:10.1016/j.engappai.2013.08.006

Falcao, A., Langlois, T., & Wichert, A. (2006). Flexible Kernels for RBF Networks. *Neurocomputing*, *69*(16-18), 2356–2359. doi:10.1016/j.neucom.2006.03.006

Fernandez-Navarro, F., Hervas-Martinez, C., Cruz-Ramirez, M., Gutierrez, P. A., & Valero, A. (2011). Evolutionary q-Gaussian Radial Basis Function Neural Network to Determine the Microbial Growth/no Growth Interface of Staphylococcus Aureus. *Applied Soft Computing*, *11*(3), 3012–3020. doi:10.1016/j.asoc.2010.11.027

Frank, A., & Asuncion, A. (2010). UCI Machine Learning Repository. Irvine, CA: University of California, School of Information and Computer Science. Retrieved from http://archive.ics.uci.edu/ml

Franke, C., & Schaback, R. (1998). Convergence Orders of Meshless Collocation Methods using Radial Basis Functions. *Advances in Computational Mathematics*, *8*(4), 381–399. doi:10.1023/A:1018916902176

Gyorfi, L., Kohler, M., Krzyzak, A., & Walk, H. (2002). *A Distribution Free Theory of Non- Parametric Regression*. Springer Verlag, New York Inc.

Haykin, S. (1994). *Neural Networks: a Comprehensive Foundation*. Upper Saddle River, NJ: Prentice Hall.

Hon, Y. C., & Mao, X. Z. (1999). A Radial Basis Function Method for Solving Options Pricing Model. *Journal of Financial Engineering*, *8*, 31–49.

Hon, Y. C., & Schaback, R. (2001). On UnSymmetric Collocation by Radial Basis Functions. *Applied Mathematics and Computation*, *119*(2-3), 177–186. doi:10.1016/S0096-3003(99)00255-6

Hon, Y. C., Schaback, R., & Zhou, X. (2003). An Adaptive Greedy Algorithm for Solving Large RBF Collocation Problems. *Numerical Algorithms*, *32*(1), 13–25. doi:10.1023/A:1022253303343

Lim, E. A., & Zainuddin, Z. (2008). An Improved Fast Training Algorithm for RBF Networks using Symmetry-Based Fuzzy C-Means Clustering. *Matematika*, *24*(2), 141–148.

Patrikar, A. M. (2013). Approximating Gaussian Mixture Model on Radial Basis Function Networks with Multilayer Perceptron. *IEEE Transactions on Neural Networks*, *24*(7), 1161–1166. doi:10.1109/TNNLS.2013.2249086 PMID:24808530

Powell, M. J. D. (1987a). Radial Basis Functions for Multivariable Interpolation: A Review. In J. C. Mason & M. G. Cox (Eds.), *Algorithms for the Approximation* (pp. 143–167). Clarendon Press.

Powell, M. J. D. (1987b). Radial Basis Function Approximations to Polynomials. In D. F. Griths & G. A. Watson (Eds.), *Numerical Analysis 87* (pp. 223–241). Longman Publishing Group.

Powell, M. J. D. (1992). The Theory of Radial Basis Function Approximation in 1990. *Advances in Numerical Analysis*, *2*, 105–210.

Powell, M. J. D. (1999). *Recent Research at Cambridge on Radial Basis Functions*. New Developments in Approximation Theory, International Series of Numerical Mathematics. doi:10.1007/978-3-0348-8696-3_14

Price, K., Storn, R., & Lampinen, J. (2005). *Differential Evolution: A Practical Approach to Global Optimization*. Springer.

Ron, A. (1992). The L2-approximation Orders of Principal Shift-Invariant Spaces Generated by a Radial Basis function. In D. Braess & L. L. Schumaker (Eds.), *Numerical Methods in Approximation Theory* (pp. 245–268). doi:10.1007/978-3-0348-8619-2_14

Schwenker, F., & Dietrich, C. (2000). Initialization of Radial Basis Function networks by Means of Classification Trees. *Neural Network World*, *10*, 473–482.

Schwenker, F., Kestler, H. A., Palm, G., & Höher, M. (1994). Similarities of LVQ and RBF Learning - A Survey of Learning Rules and the Application to the Classification of Signals from High-Resolution Electrocardiography. *Proceedings IEEE SMC*, 646-651. doi:10.1109/ICSMC.1994.399913

Stron, R., & Price, K. (1995). *Differential Evolution-A Simple and Efficient Adaptive Scheme for Global Optimization over Continuous Spaces*. Technical Report TR-05-012: International Computer Science Institute, Berkeley.

Stron, R., & Price, K. (1997). Differential Evolution- Simple and Efficient Heuristic for Global Optimization over Continuous Spaces. *Journal of Global Optimization*, *11*(4), 341–359. doi:10.1023/A:1008202821328

Wu, X. L. (2007). Consistent Feature Selection Reduction About Classification Dataset. *Computer Engineering and Applications*, *42*(18), 174–176.

Yamada, T., & Wrobel, L. C. (1993). Properties of Gaussian Radial Basis Functions in the Dual Reciprocity Boundary Element Method. *Zeitschrift für Angewandte Mathematik und Physik*, *44*(6), 1054–1067. doi:10.1007/BF00942764

Chapter 12
Competency Mapping in Academic Environment:
A Swarm Intelligence Approach

Sushri Samita Rout
Silicon Institute of Technology, India

Bijan Bihari Misra
Silicon Institute of Technology, India

ABSTRACT

This chapter will discuss and present a new model to perform a competency map in an educational institute which has moderate number of faculty members on whom the map has to be performed. Performing such a map is a tough but essential task. Hence utmost objectivity must be followed for the procedure. In this chapter the authors performed academic load assignment to the faculty members of a particular dept at the onset of a semester. Few parameters that have been considered as the input parameters are depth of knowledge, sincerity, class management, contribution towards research, text book publication. part from that one of the main concerns is the assignment is done by taking into consideration the preferences of a particular faculty in terms of teaching a subject. There are number of constraints which need to be considered while making the load assignment. The AICTE guidelines for teaching load allotment have been considered as a baseline. The MOPSO has been used to perform the competency map and the simulation results have been presented to show the effectiveness of the method.

INTRODUCTION

In the recent past there has been a lot of hue & cry about the increasing un-employability of technical graduates in this country. Lot many research activities and studies have been conducted to gain insight into the actual problem behind this menace. There is no concrete evidence to attribute the problem to a particular reason. But generically speaking it has been found that the right kind of skills are not imbibed in the technical graduates and there is a huge gap in what the graduates can do and what the industry requires. One of the prime factors which shape the technical graduates as employable individuals is the

DOI: 10.4018/978-1-5225-2857-9.ch012

Faculty members who are largely associated with the students in their formative years of professional education. Hence it is quite essential that the faculty members be motivated enough to perform their duties & responsibilities with utmost zeal & dedication. But what happens when somebody is entrusted in doing something he/she is not interested in? May be less effort will be put in and ultimately the end result will be hampered in a negative way. The same happens, when a faculty teaches a subject he is not interested in or lacks the pre-requisites to teach the subject. In technical schools there are large numbers of faculty members may be with the same background qualifications but not with same skill set, expertise or experience. And moreover each of them has different priorities in terms of teaching.

This process of academic load allocation i.e. assigning/allocating subjects to faculty members is normally done by the HODs (Head of departments) manually. Since there are several objectives and constraints to be satisfied it is quite difficult for them to design the best allotment in spite of having the required resources. Simple reason being the inability of the human mind to process a huge amount of information. So the objective of this chapter is to elaborate on the nature of the problem, its implications and propose a computational strategy to generate solutions for the problem and last but not the least performing simulations on actual data to show the efficacy of the method proposed.

Till date there is negligible literary evidence regarding any method based on computational intelligence for academic load allocation. But similar kinds of tasks have been undertaken in other domains. Those have been discussed in the section on related work

BACKGROUND

Any academic institute imparting any kind of course has to undergo the task of load assignment/allotment to the concerned teachers or faculty members at the beginning of the academic year or semester. In technical institutions normally this is done by some senior faculty members and the Heads of department. But exactly there is no specified norm. For large departments the concerned heads spend a number of days to make such an allotment. And the basis of allotment is subjective assessment of HOD's generally guided by heuristics & instincts. Past performance of the faculty members in terms of student feedback, student results, years of experience etc normally contribute to those assessments.

But what are the implications of such an allotment? Compliance with the regulations, satisfaction of the departmental needs, satisfaction of the faculty members and most importantly the right map between the subject, faculty & student. Now with the manual process of allotment, most of the time the objectives are not satisfied. Moreover as the strength of the department increases it's difficult to find solutions which comply with most of the objectives. Hence a manual allotment often results in a sub-optimal solution which leads to resentment and demotivation among faculty members.

This necessitates a well-defined methodology which can generate optimal solutions taking care of all the objectives simultaneously. In this context the most important constructs are competency, competency mapping in academic scenario, optimal solutions & objective satisfaction. This narrows down to three broad aspects namely- *Competency, Academics & Mutli-Objective optimal solutions*. The mentioned aspects have been discussed in the next section with reference to relevant literature wherever necessary.

COMPETENCY

In this chapter, the term competency which was coined by David McClelland in the early 70's, refers to the aggregate set of skills, knowledge, and exhibited behavior patterns which are needed by an individual to perform a task at hand with the required level of proficiency. Skills are the component competencies that collectively establish the overall competency. Since the advent of the concept several researchers have taken keen interest and proposed a myriad of uses, application in different domains and have also extended the concept to engulf the entire gamut of Human Resource (HR) activities of an organization (McClelland, 1973). Some of the key inferences that have emerged out of the various studies are presented below (Shermon, 2004; Yuvaraj, 2011; Uddin, Tanchi & Alam, 2012):

- Though several researchers have proposed several attributes as the key components of competency, the one's which top the list are knowledge, skills, attitude, problem-solving capabilities, technical skills and communication.
- The key components of competency indicate a very strong link with the psychological aspects of the employees and the organization as well.
- Detailed guidelines for the implementation of a competency mapping exercise have been proposed by several researchers but there is very less work on the actual implementation using case studies & real data.
- Advanced studies on whether competencies can be acquired using ANN(Artificial Neural Networks)

COMPETENCY MAPPING IN ACADEMICS

If literary evidence is to be relied upon very less has been done in the domain of applying competency mapping in academics or academic institutions to be specific. In academics, this implies, maintaining a comprehensive list of competencies against which each faculty would be assessed and at the time of any academic assignment map those assessed competencies with requirements of the department . During the mapping several objectives and constraints have to be taken care of. To gain clarity into the process and the problems the current process of load allocation/assignment has been discussed below. Though this process may differ from organization to organization the core steps would remain the same. The same has been discussed below:

1. **Finalizing the Papers:** Prior to the commencement of a session/semester the HODs finalize the list of subjects to be offered along with specific requirements like laboratory & tutorials etc. The credits associated with each subject, the total number of students to be taught, the strength of each class is taken into account. The purpose of the whole activity is to find out the total number of faculty members required and the required skill set to teach the subjects offered in that semester
2. **Obtaining Option From the Teacher:** After finalizing the list of subjects to be offered during a particular semester/session, the HODs communicate the list to all faculty members of his branch and makes a request to apprise him with their priority/preference for the set of subjects they want to take during the said semester.

3. **Analysis of the Teachers Option and Rectifications:** Once the faculty members give their options, the HODs analyze them so as to find out if there are any subjects for which nobody or less people have given preference. Based on the analysis experienced faculty members are requested to opt for the same. And then a final list of subjects and faculty preferences is prepared.

4. **Analysis of Past Performance:** Data from different sources like personal data, feedback, appraisal etc is used judge the suitability of a faculty for a particular subject.

5. **Analysis of Present Scenario:** The scenario for each semester/session is then analyzed to find out exceptional conditions like proposal of long-term & short-term leaves, maternity leaves, sabbaticals, higher-studies etc. This information is necessary to get the actual strength that can be mapped moreover it will help in preparing a contingency plan.

6. *Final Allotment of Subjects*: The final allotment is done taking into consideration the maximum load that can be given to a particular faculty member. The maximum hours that can be given is based on the designation and the administrative responsibilities of a particular faculty. Sometimes the maximum load is relaxed due to unavoidable circumstances. Then the teaching load has to be balanced between different faculties.

At the outset the above-mentioned process might appear very trivial. But if we consider a standard technical institute with thousands of students and hundreds of faculty members, performing the said task becomes quite cumbersome & most of the time it will not yield the desired solution. The end result dissatisfaction of faculty members & students as well which might lead to vicious cycle of un-productivity. Further the procedure has to deal & satisfy several constraints as discussed earlier. Hence the said problem can be classified as non-trivial (Rout, Misra & Samanta, 2014).

Multi-Objective Optimization

As already mentioned in the background this problem has multiple objectives as well as constraints and qualifies to be a multi-objective optimization (MOO) problem. Hence it becomes imperative to discuss multi-objective optimization, its variants and applications in order to understand the relevance of MOO in the said problem. **Multi-objective optimization /** *multi-objective programming /pareto optimization/* **multi-criteria / multi-attribute** optimization, is the process of simultaneously optimizing two or more conflicting objectives subject to certain constraints (Sawaragi, Nakayama & Tanino, 1985; Steuer,1986).

When we formulate problems with more than one objective or a vector of objectives, they can be represented as:

$$F(x) = [F_1(x), F_2(x),...,F_m(x)]$$

Here each objective is subjected to number of constraints. But as the number of objectives increase determining the trade-off between the different constraints becomes increasingly complex and formulating a quantitative representation of the objectives becomes practically impossible (Arbnor & Bjerke, 2008).

While trying to find solutions for such problems, when one objective is improved, it sometimes so happens that another objective is further compromised or degraded. A candidate or tentative solution is called Non-dominated or Pareto-optimal solution if replacing the current solution with another solution will not yield any improvement in a particular objective without degrading another. The goal of a multi-objective optimization problem is to find such pareto efficient solutions, and represent the trade-offs required to satisfy different objectives quantifiably. But after finding such non-dominated solutions, it is upon to the decision maker to pick the best solution amongst all the non-dominated solutions. A multiobjective optimization problem may include a set of parameters (decision variables), a set of objective functions, and a set of constraints. Objective functions and constraints are functions of the decision variables.

Multi-Objective optimization algorithms have forayed into a wide range of application domains, the most common classification being: Engineering, Scientific and Industrial. Some of them are Electrical, Hydraulic, Structural, Aeronautics, Robotics and Control Engineering. A sample of Industrial application is Design, Manufacturing, Scheduling and Management, and a array of Scientific applications like Chemistry, Physics, medicine and Computer Science. There are certain other application areas like Cellular Automata, Bio-informatics, Data Mining, Pattern Recognition and a host of financial applications.

Our problem here - mapping competency of faculties and in turn allocating academic load to them taking care of all the constraints, is an apt candidate for being solved using Multi-objective optimization algorithms. Though existing literatures do not indicate any exact work that has been done in this field, there are few related domains in which these algorithms have been successfully applied. I-Tung Yang and Jui-Sheng Chou, in their work "Multi-objective optimization for manpower assignment in consulting engineering firms" proposed a multi-objective optimization model – **MUST**, to facilitate the staff-to-job assignment in consulting engineering firms. In addition to the objective of maximizing profits, other human resource related objectives like balancing workloads, avoiding excessive overtime, and eliminating demoralizing idleness while giving preference to projects with specified priorities. The optimization problem was of significant complexity (nonlinear, non-smooth, and combinatorial) and has been proved NP- and #P-complete. To handle all the difficulties, MUST incorporated a particle swarm optimization algorithm to approximate the tradeoff surface consisting of non-dominated solutions. The application of MUST was demonstrated through a numerical case of assigning six engineering teams to fifteen incoming projects. It has been shown that non-dominated solutions generated by MUST helped decision makers choose the compromised assignment plan which is otherwise hard and time-consuming to obtain. The comparisons with SPEA2 and LINGO verify the effectiveness and efficiency of MUST. It has been shown that non-dominated solutions generated by MUST helped decision makers choose the compromised assignment plan which is otherwise hard and time-consuming to obtain.

The problem consisted of assigning 'n' engineering teams to 'm' projects over a planning time horizon with several objectives subjected to a number of constraints. Results from this system in personnel staffing show the high capability of the model in making a high quality personnel selection while satisfying the goals of maximizing the overall profit, minimizing the variation of workload, minimizing the maximal overtime and maximizing the average utilization percentage (Yang & Chou, 2011). There are several other instances of the algorithm being used in human resource allocation problems and mapping of competency, mostly adopting multi-objective particle swarm optimization(MOPSO) for finding candidate solutions (Rout, Misra & Samanta, 2014).

Developments in Multi-Objective Optimization

Evolutionary approaches are the most common techniques to solve multi-objective optimization problems. David Schaffer in the mid-80's proposed the vector evaluated genetic algorithm (VEGA), which was considered to be the first Multi-Objective evolutionary algorithm. Since then many other algorithms have been proposed, some of which are mentioned below in alphabetical order (Coello, 2006; Ghosh & Dehuri, 2004; Zitzler, 1999)

- **AbYSS:** AbYSS stands for (Archive-Based Hybrid Scatter Search) is a hybrid metaheuristic algorithm which follows the scatter search structure using mutation and crossover operators. AbYSS combines ideas PAES, NSGA-II & SPEA2 for solving MOPs.
- **FastPGA:** Fast Pareto genetic algorithm (FastPGA). FastPGA uses a fitness assignment and ranking strategy which simultaneously optimizes multiple objectives, and where each solution is computationally- and/or financially-expensive. This is normally used when there is a time or resource constraint involved in computing the solution.
- **MOCeLL:** MoceLL is a cellular genetic algorithm which uses an external archive to store the non-dominated solutions found during the search. Using an feedback mechanism in each generation, a number of individuals in the current population is replaced by randomly chosen solutions from the external archive, in order to enhance the preservation of diversity. MOCell excels in terms of achieving convergence.
- **Multi-Objective Evolutionary Algorithm Based on Decomposition (MOEA/D):** This algorithm decomposes a multi-objective optimization problem into N single objective optimization problems using aggregation, where is subproblem is related to the other through a neighbourhood. N is set by the user, as a parameter to control the spacing between a set of uniformly distributed points approximating the Pareto front.
- **Multi-Objective Genetic Algorithm (MOGA):** MOGA implements a variant of the Pareto ranking where non-dominated individuals hold a rank equal to 1, while the dominated ones are penalized according to the population density in the corresponding region of the surface of the trade-off solutions. Fitness value is then assigned to each individual, by interpolating from the best (rank 1) to the worst.
- **Non-Dominated Sorting Genetic Algorithm (NSGA,):** NSGA is a non-elitist algorithm which classifies individuals as per the following. The population is ranked on the basis of non-domination: all non-dominated individuals are classified into one category, with a dummy fitness value proportional to the population size. Then this group of classified individuals is ignored and another layer of non-dominated individuals is considered. The process continues until all individuals in the population are classified into a particular category. Thereafter selection takes place.
- **Non-Dominated Sorting Genetic Algorithm:** II (NSGA-II)- In this approach selection is done based on a crowded-comparison operator which takes into account the non-dominated rank of an individual and its crowding distance. NSGA-II estimates the density of solutions surrounding a particular solution in the population by computing the average distance of two points on either side of this reference solution along each of the objectives. This value is called crowding distance.
- **Pareto Archived Evolution Strategy (PAES):** PAES is an elitist strategy which uses an adaptive grid in the external archive to store the non-dominated solutions generated during the search. Once the external archive reaches a particular set limit, new solutions are allowed only if they occupy the less densely populated grids, thus allowing proper distribution of the non-dominated solutions along the pareto front.
- **Pareto Envelope-based Selection Algorithm (PESA):** PESA like PAES, uses a small internal population and a larger external population. Additionally, the adaptive grid is used to filter out the solutions entering the external archive.

- **Strength Pareto Evolutionary Algorithm 2 (SPEA2):** SPEA2 stores the non-dominated solutions found during the search in an external archive and updates it at each generation. This update is done by estimating the neighborhood density for each solution. A "strength value" is computed for each individual in the external archive, based on the number of solutions that it dominates and to the number of solutions that dominate it.

- **Vector Evaluated Genetic Algorithm (VEGA):** VEGA decomposes the population into a number of sub-populations which is equal to the number of objective functions. In each sub-population, the solutions are evaluated based on only one objective and the survivors are selected by a roulette-wheel mechanism. This model has a certain limitation that it is unable to identify appropriate trade-offs regions since it is designed to consider solutions that are the best only with respect to one objective.

From the review of the MOO literature, the inferences are presented below in terms of application areas, limitations and research trends (Coello, 2006; Ghosh & Dehuri, 2004).

- Multi objective optimization algorithms specifically MOEAs are being incorporated for optimization in a wide variety of application domains.

- Engineering applications, which are the most popular in terms of literature study include electrical engineering, hydraulic engineering, structural engineering, aeronautical engineering & robotics and control (Censor, 1977).

- Industrial applications include design and manufacturing, scheduling, and wide variety of management applications as well.

- It is also being exploited in basic scientific applications representing chemistry, physics, and medicine and computer science as well.

- The application of multi-objective optimization is sometimes limited due to some methodological issues like maximizing the number of the solutions in the Pareto-optimal set, minimizing the distance of the Pareto front with respect to the global Pareto front. The issues are quite difficult to deal with in real world applications.

- Maintaining the required diversity sometimes poses as a serious concern in the implementation of MOEAs. MOO algorithms specifically MOEAs have found application in many industrial, scientific and engineering applications. But one major area where the potential of MOEAs is still untapped is management. Though MOEAs have been applied to operations management, financial applications quite successfully, a lot many intricate problems related to marketing, human resource management, supply chain, sustainability still remain outside the purview of MOEA applications.

- Incorporation of Swarm Intelligence in MOO.

Swarm Intelligence

Problem-solving devices inspired by the collective behavior of social insect colonies and other animal societies". It is basically a meta-heuristic algorithm to find optimal solutions in a given problem situation. The crux of such an algorithm is exploration and exploitation (Netjinda, Achalakul & Booncharoen Sirinaovakul, 2015). Exploration mechanism in the algorithm search the whole search space to find alternative solutions and exploitation mechanism try to find the best possible solution in a specific area of the search space. Some of the most popular swarm intelligence algorithms are: (Netjinda, Achalakul & Booncharoen Sirinaovakul, 2015; Zhang, Lee, Chan & Choy, 2015).

- Ant colony optimization based on ants foraging.
- Artificial bee colony algorithm based on bees gathering honey.
- Particle swarm optimization, based on birds flocking together.

Russell Eberhart and James Kennedy introduced PSO in the year 1995 inspired by the movement aesthetics of a bird flock trying to get closer to the food source. There is a reason behind birds flocking together from one place to another in search of food. While searching for food, there is always a bird which is closest to the food source. The bird closest to the food source transmits its location information to other birds by chirping loudly. The other birds in the flock, then try to veer towards that direction by adjusting their velocities with respect to the desired position. This process is repeated, whenever a bird finds itself closest to the food source and continues until the food source is found. Here the flock of birds can be considered particles referring to the swarm of solutions. The particles have to fly through the solution space by adjusting their velocities with respect to the position of the optimal solution. Each particle at any point of time keeps track of its own co-ordinates and stores that value as its pbest which is the best position it has come across during the search. Whenever movement occurs it has to update its information, in terms of three parameters: the current velocity, the personal best (pbest) and global best (gbest). gbest is the best value obtained by any particle in the entire population or search space. The pbest and gbest values are updated by a particle every time the particle moves towards a better position. This procedure continues in an iterative manner until the terminating condition or stopping condition is met. The gbest during that time may be considered to be the preferred solution (Zhang, Lee, Chan & Choy, 2015; Eberhart & Kennedy, 1995; Aote, Raghuwanshi & Malik, 2013; Song & Gu, 2004; Urade & Patel, 2012; Rout, Misra & Samanta, 2014). In a nutshell each individual particle ies through the search space and dynamically adjusts itself according to its own flying experience and the flying experience of neighborhood particles. Over a number of iterations, a group of particles / individuals have their velocities adjusted closer to the particle whose value is closest to the gbest.

Basic Algorithm/Flow Diagram

```
For each particle
        Initialize particle
                Do until maximum iterations/minimum error condition
                    For each particle
                            Compute data fitness value
                                    If fitness value better than
pBest
                                            Set pBest=Current fit-
ness value
                                    If pBest is better than gBest
                                        Set gBest=pBest
                For each particle
```

```
                                    Compute particle velocity
                      Use gBest and velocity to update par-
ticle data
```

Multi-Objective Particle Swarm Optimization

MOPSO is a multi-objective technique that combines or incorporates the concept of Pareto-dominance into a PSO algorithm to make it capable of handling multiple objective functions. While incorporating PSO in multi-objective optimization the algorithm has to keep track of the local best for every solution (particle) with time. The multi-objective PSO differs from the original PSO in terms of calculation of the local and global best values. To find the gbest for each particle an external archive is used to store all non-dominated particles. The archive is continuously updated and the size of the archive is controlled using a hyper grid. A particular particle will be selected from the archive for the gbest depending upon the density of the area surrounding the particle (Carlos, 2006; Deb, 2001; Elloumi & Almi, 2010; Knowles & Come, 2000 ; Jia & Gong, 2008 ; Ponsich, Jaimes & Coello, 2013 ; Zitzler, 1999 ; Yang & Chou, 2011).

Though PSO has been widely accepted as an efficient optimization technique in engineering domains, its application and consequent effectiveness is still undermined in the field of management. But of late several implementations have proved the efficiency of this technique in solving management problems specifically multi-objective optimization problems. Few but exemplary research has been done on the application of PSO specifically MOPSO in the field of competency mapping in Human Resource management (Jia & Gong, 2008; Yang & Chou, 2011).

Rationale Behind MOPSO

It is evident from the review of literature that PSO has been widely used across all do-mains. Though the usage of evolutionary computing techniques is limited in the area of management particularly human resource management, but PSO has been used in several human resource management applications like task allocation, resource allocation and scheduling etc. It has yield better results in comparison with traditional techniques. Though PSO lacks a strong theoretical foundation, it can be successfully used for the kind of problem dealt with in this chapter, as the results of the simulation can be validated by com-paring with the results of the traditional techniques. Moreover the speed of search is fast, the algorithm poses less computational burden and the storage and system requirements are comparatively negligible.

MOPSO (Multi-objective particle swarm optimization) incorporates the concept of pareto-dominance into the PSO algorithm in order to handle multiple objectives simultaneously.

Pseudo-Code for a MOPSO

```
Begin
        Initialize swarm, velocities and best positions
        Initialize external archive (initially empty)
        While (stopping criterion not satisfied) do
                For each particle
```

```
            Select a member of external archive
            Update velocity and position
            Evaluate new position
            Update best position and external archive
            End for
        End While
End
```

The concerned problem of academic load allocation using the concept of competency mapping has several objectives and constraints which need to handled simultaneously. Hence this problem can be safely classified as a multi-objective optimization problem. As per literary evidence swarm optimization techniques have been pre-dominantly used in the recent past for solving optimization problems. Amongst them Particle swarm optimization is the frontrunner. Mostly the PSO variant of multi-objective optimization has been used for similar tasks like resource allocation, scheduling, selection & task allocation problems, but mostly in allied domains (Wang & Zheng, 2011; Rout, Misra & Samanta, 2014; Shahhosseini & Sebt, 2011 ;Wang, Gong & Yan, 2009).

PROBLEM FORMULATION

In this chapter the data from the Department of Computer Science & Engineering has been used to make the academic load allocation using MOPSO. Keeping in mind the considerations of the problem the following objectives & constraints have been identified.

1. Objectives
   a. Priority of subject by the faculty is given from [0, 10] where larger priority value for a particular subject has to be given higher preference during allocation. This objective needs to be **maximized.**
   b. Depth of knowledge and contribution is from [0, 10] which is assigned by HOD and group of senior members. Larger the value higher the preference. This objective is also to be **maximized.**
   c. Sincerity and Class Management from [0, 10] assigned by HOD and group of senior members. This feature does not directly affect the allotment of subjects. For example, let assignment of a subject between two faculties with equal load, and both faculties has got equal level of priority and knowledge depth. Then this attribute will play a role for selection of faculty for the assignment of the subject. This objective is also to be **maximized.**
   d. Balancing the teaching load between faculties at same level. Random assignment always increases weakly teaching load than that is required. This objective is to be **minimized**.
2. Constraints
   a. No faculty should be assigned less than one theory subject.
   b. Depending on the designation and position of the faculty, maximum teaching load per faculty is predefined. No faculty member should be assigned teaching load beyond his maximum limits.
   c. Preferably, no faculty should be assigned more than two theory subjects.

d.   Both assignments of theory papers should not have lab component, one may have lab component and other only theory.

e.   The lab component of a theory paper is performed in two different sections of three hours each. If a theory subjects has a lab component, preferably the faculty assigned with theory should be assigned the lab component.

f.   No faculty should be assigned more than two lab assignments.

All other soft constraints like leaves, resignations, and higher studies are considered by adding suitable penalty

Let the total number of sections= *TS*, and total faculties=*TF*.

Then the search space for allotment will be:

$$S \approx \underbrace{{}^{TS}C_2 \times {}^{TS-2}C_2 \times \ldots \times {}^{4}C_2 \times {}^{2}C_2}_{TF \text{ terms}} = \underbrace{\frac{TS \times (TS-1)}{2} \times \frac{(TS-2) \times (TS-3)}{2} \times \ldots \times \frac{4 \times 3}{2} \times \frac{2 \times 1}{2}}_{TF \text{ terms}} = \frac{TS!}{2^{TF}}$$

In the data collected there were 22 subjects offered for 74 sections, excluding the lab allotments, among 36 faculties. Generally, every faculty gives about 10 options with order of preference and on an average each faculty is assigned with two theory papers. The allotment progresses initially 2 out of 74, then 2 out of 73, and so on. Then the search space can be viewed as:

$$S = \frac{74!}{2^{36}} = \frac{3.3079e+107}{6.8719e+010} = 4.8136e+096$$

During the actual subject allotment the constraints also need to be taken care of. If there are 'n' constraints to be handled then the search space increases to S^n, where S is the search space defined above. The search space defined here leads to a NP hard problem even for medium size of sections & faculty members.

Since the HODs make the allocation manually using different kind of heuristics, a proper competency map cannot be expected. Hence MOPSO has been used to obtain an optimal solution in terms of competency mapping.

The particle representation in a swarm is given below in Figure 1.

Figure 1. Particle representation

F_1				....	F_{TF}		
S_{11}	S_{12}	...	S_{11C}	...	S_{TF1}	S_{TF2}	...	S_{TFLC}

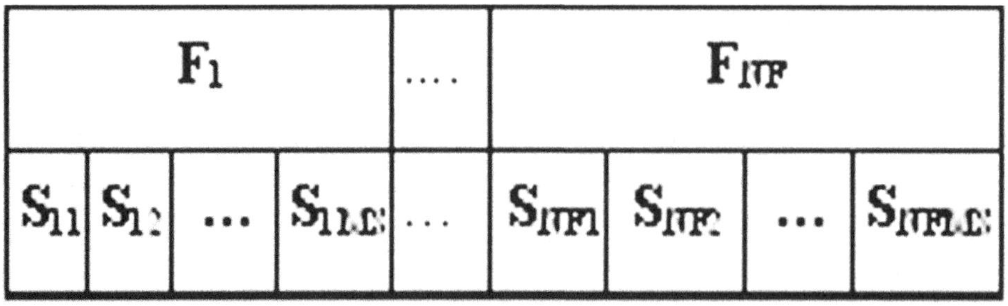

In Figure1, F_1 to F_{NF} represents individual faculties, where, NF is the total number of faculties. S_{i1} to S_{iMS} represents the subjects allotted to F_i, MS represents the maximum permissible allocation to any faculty.

SOLUTIONS/RESULTS

To satisfy the associated constraints maximization functions have been added with negative penalty and minimization functions with positive penalty. One of the feasible solutions in regards to the four objectives specified in the Problem formulation section has been discussed below with the help of bar charts (Rout, Misra & Samanta, 2014).

To explain a typical scenario, the requirement of a particular semester has been considered for a particular department in a premier engineering college. There are about 36 faculties excluding 3 those are on study leave and the requirement of section for which faculties to be assigned is 74. Table 1 shows the parameters considered for simulation of MOPSO.

To satisfy the constraints, the maximization functions are added with negative penalty and the minimization functions are added with positive penalty. The types of penalties used are presented in Table 2 (Rout, Misra & Samanta, 2014).

Table 3 shows the constraints considered and the type and units of penalty applied on it. Penalty applied on the evaluated value of the objective functions are unit times the respective penalty value. The category of constraints relating to leaves and relaxation are not considered here directly. Only the database of faculties under study leave is restricted from access during simulation.

The level of satisfaction to different objectives, have been discussed here.

In the figure above one of the objectives i.e. maximizing the priority or preference of faculty has been presented. Most of the faculty members have been allotted papers for which they given higher preference

Table 1. Parameters considered for the simulation of MOPSO

Parameters	Values
Population Size	200
Maximum Iterations	10000
Inertia Weight	0.729844
Cognitive Parameter	1.49445
Social Parameter	1.49445

Table 2.Types of penalty used for the simulation of MOPSO

Penalty Type	Values
Small	5
Medium	10
Large	15
Very large	20
Extremely large	50

Table 3. Types and quantum of penalty applied for simulation of MOPSO

Constraint Type	Units	Penalty Type
Allotment without preference	1	Very large
No subject allotment	1	Extremely large
Papers allotted differ allotment limit	Abs(Papers allotted – allotment limit)	Small
Hours allotted differ hour limit	Abs(Hours alotted- hour limit)	Small
More sections allotted than required sections per subject	Number of sections allotted-required sections	Small
Less sections allotted than required sections per subject	Required sections- number of sections allotted	Large

Figure 2. Number of subjects allotted for each priority level

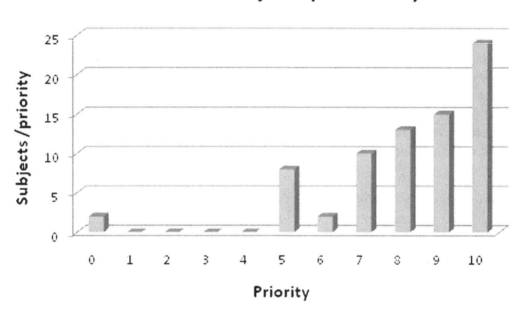

like 9 & 10. No allotment has been made at preference level 1-4. It can also be inferred that majority of the subjects have been allotted to faculty members where the preference level was 9 or more than 9.

As per the above charts the solutions also yielsds fair allotment for maximizing the depth of knowledge & contribution. Most of the allotments have been done to faculty members having a score of 5-7. Not many allotments are done in the score of 8-10 as there are very less or no faculty who have got a score in that range.

It is quite apparent from the above charts that most of the subject allocation have been done to faculties who have a class management & sincerity level of 9 and 10.

There are certain guidelines in regards to how many hours of teaching load can be given to a particular faculty, there might be some variations in order to handle certain factors like credit points& lab etc. In

Figure 3. Number of faculties satisfied with different level of preferences

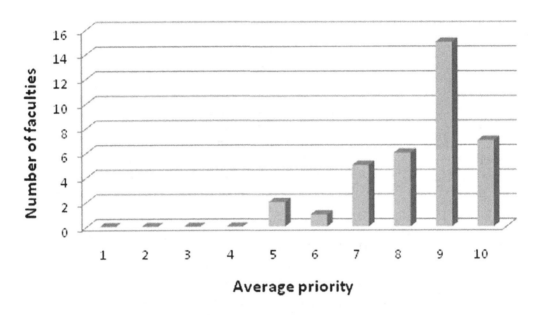

Figure 4. Number of subjects allotted for different levels of the depth of knowledge and contribution

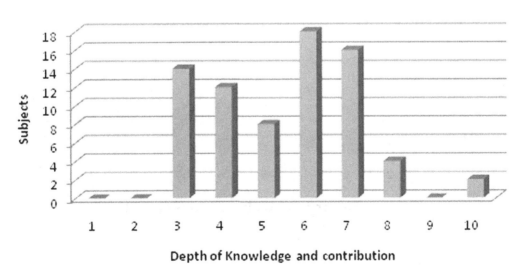

Figure 5. Allotment of papers satisfying different depth of knowledge and contribution levels

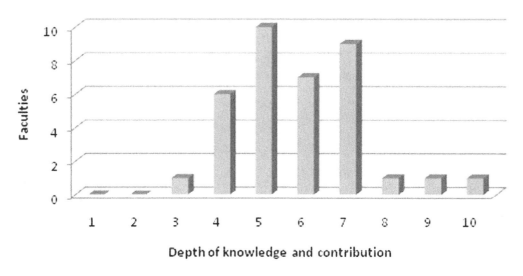

Figure 6. Number of subjects allotted for different sincerity and class management levels

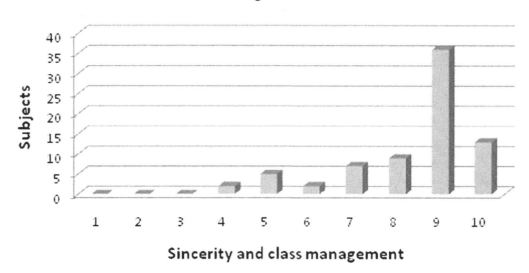

Figure 7. Sincerity and class management levels of faculty

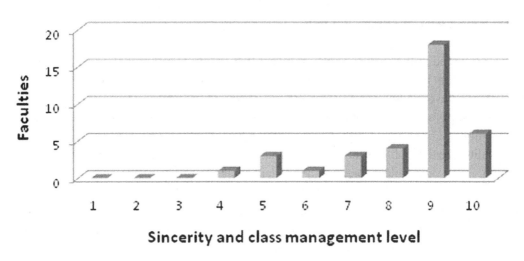

Figure 8. Weekly teaching load of faculty members

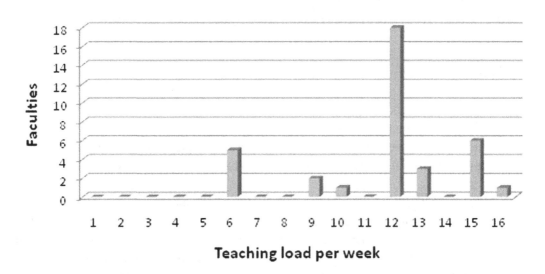

this simulation authors designated a standard of 12 hours maximum to be assigned to each faculty. But in case a faculty has got two subjects each with 4 credit points (4 hours of theory class) then he will have 2 hours extra load as against somebody who has two subjects with three credit points (3hours of theory class). The objective was to minimize the variance of load between faculty members. The above chart shows that this objective has also been satisfied to quite a large extent as 50% of the faculty members have got exactly 12 hours of load. Some of them have got more than that to satisfy certain constraints. And some have got less considering their designation and additional responsibilities

FUTURE RESEARCH DIRECTIONS

The results discussed in the previous section reveal that the proposed model or method works pretty efficiently to perform the competency mapping task in an academic environment. The same model can be easily extended to the administrative and other departments as well.

This model helps in selecting those solutions wherein if a faculty has been assigned a particular theory the same faculty will be assigned with the associated lab component. This ensures that there is no clash while scheduling the time table as the theory and lab sessions will be scheduled in different slots for the same section, in the time table. Moreover the model enables us to select a balanced workload which in turn reduces the time-table scheduling process.

At the same time other variants of PSO and evolutionary computing techniques like Genetic Algorithm, Ant Colony optimization etc can be used to compute optimal solutions in the same scenario and compare them in terms of satisfaction of the laid objectives.

Since the model yields a number of pareto-optimal solutions it can also be used to cater to the changing needs of an organization. Job suitability analysis can be performed using this method. In this particular simulation all the input data have been taken in a range 1 to 10 avoiding decimal numbers. The work can be fine-tuned to handle fuzzy inputs which will make it easier and user-friendly in terms of implementation. The algorithm can be tuned to handle more parameters which can be considered for obtaining an accurate & precise map (Xu & Wang, 2009; Wu, 2004; Wood & Pitt, 1998).

CONCLUSION

Very less or insignificant work has been done in the field of management or human resource management using computational intelligence. There is ample scope to exploit the potential of nature inspired computational techniques specifically swarm intelligence techniques. Studies can be taken up to use those techniques in the field of recruitment, selection, performance appraisal & succession planning to name a few.

Though the use of MOPSO has gain widespread acknowledgement in diverse fields it needs to be used more in practical situations for proper validation. The results & validations can only provide further insights into the lacunae and improvement required. The proposed model in this chapter gives a fair solution to the problem at hand. The validation comes easily with the comparison of the simulation results with the results of the traditional method. Apparently the major advantages of the proposed model over the traditional technique are: No scope of any biased decision, little or no scope of human error and last but not the least it's a very flexible and agile model suitable for any kind of organization who wants to perform such a mapping task.

REFERENCES

Aote, S. S., Raghuwanshi, M. M., & Malik, L. (2013). A brief review on particle swarm optimization: Limitations & future directions. *International Journal on Computer Science and Engineering, 14*(1), 196–200.

Arbnor, I., & Bjerke, B. (2008). *Methodology for creating business knowledge.* Sage Publications Ltd.

Bai, Q. (2010). Analysis of particle swarm optimization algorithm. *Computer and Information Science, 3*(1), 180.

Banks, A., Vincent, J., & Anyakoha, C. (2008). A review of particle swarm optimization. Part II: Hybridisation, combinatorial, multicriteria and constrained optimization, and indicative applications. *Natural Computing, 7*(1), 109–124. doi:10.1007/s11047-007-9050-z

Censor, Y. (1977). Pareto optimality in multiobjective problems. *Applied Mathematics & Optimization, 4*(1), 41–59. doi:10.1007/BF01442131

Coello, C. C. (2006). Evolutionary multi-objective optimization: A historical view of the field. *IEEE Computational Intelligence Magazine, 1*(1), 28–36. doi:10.1109/MCI.2006.1597059

Deb, K. (2001). *Multi-objective optimization using evolutionary algorithms* (Vol. 16). John Wiley & Sons.

Eberhart, R., & Kennedy, J. (1995, October). A new optimizer using particle swarm theory. In *Micro Machine and Human Science, 1995. MHS'95., Proceedings of the Sixth International Symposium on* (pp. 39-43). IEEE. doi:10.1109/MHS.1995.494215

Elloumi, W., & Alimi, A. M. (2010, May). A more efficient MOPSO for optimization. In *ACS/IEEE International Conference on Computer Systems and Applications-AICCSA 2010* (pp. 1-7). IEEE. doi:10.1109/AICCSA.2010.5587045

Ghosh, A., & Dehuri, S. (2004). Evolutionary algorithms for multi-criterion optimization: A survey. *International Journal of Computing & Information Sciences, 2*(1), 38–57.

Jia, Z., & Gong, L. (2008, December). Multi-criteria human resource allocation for optimization problems using multi-objective particle swarm optimization algorithm. In *Computer Science and Software Engineering, 2008 International Conference on* (Vol. 1, pp. 1187-1190). IEEE. doi:10.1109/CSSE.2008.1506

Knowles, J. D., & Corne, D. W. (2000). Approximating the nondominated front using the Pareto archived evolution strategy. *Evolutionary Computation, 8*(2), 149–172. doi:10.1162/106365600568167 PMID:10843519

McClelland, D. C. (1973). Testing for competence rather than for" intelligence. *The American Psychologist, 28*(1), 1–14. doi:10.1037/h0034092 PMID:4684069

Netjinda, N., Achalakul, T., & Sirinaovakul, B. (2015). Particle Swarm Optimization inspired by starling flock behavior. *Applied Soft Computing, 35*, 411–422. doi:10.1016/j.asoc.2015.06.052

Ponsich, A., Jaimes, A. L., & Coello, C. A. C. (2013). A survey on multiobjective evolutionary algorithms for the solution of the portfolio optimization problem and other finance and economics applications. *IEEE Transactions on Evolutionary Computation, 17*(3), 321–344. doi:10.1109/TEVC.2012.2196800

Rout, S. S., Misra, B. B., & Samanta, S. (2014). Load Allocation in Academic Environment: A Multi Objective PSO Approach. *GSTF Journal on Computing, 3*(4), 9. doi:10.7603/s40601-013-0036-7

Sawaragi, Y., Nakayama, H., & Tanino, T. (Eds.). (1985). Theory of multiobjective optimization (Vol. 176). Elsevier.

Shahhosseini, V., & Sebt, M. H. (2011). Competency-based selection and assignment of human resources to construction projects. *Scientia Iranica, 18*(2), 163–180. doi:10.1016/j.scient.2011.03.026

Shermon, G. (2004). *Competency based HRM.* McGraw-Hill.

Song, M. P., & Gu, G. C. (2004, August). Research on particle swarm optimization: a review. In *Machine Learning and Cybernetics, 2004. Proceedings of 2004 International Conference on* (*Vol. 4*, pp. 2236-2241). IEEE.

Steuer, R. E. (1986). *Multiple criteria optimization: theory, computation, and applications.* Wiley.

Uddin, M. I., Tanchi, K. R., & Alam, M. N. (2012). Competency mapping: A tool for hr excellence. *European Journal of Business and Management, 4*(5).

Urade, H. S., & Patel, R. (2012). *Performance Evaluation of Dynamic Particle Swarm Optimization.* IJCSN.

Wang, Q., & Zheng, H. C. (2011, April). Optimization of task allocation and knowledge workers scheduling based-on particle swarm optimization. In *Electric Information and Control Engineering (ICEICE), 2011 International Conference on* (pp. 574-578). IEEE. doi:10.1109/ICEICE.2011.5778029

Wang, S. Q., Gong, L. H., & Yan, S. L. (2009, July). The allocation optimization of project human resource based on particle swarm optimization algorithm. In *Services Science, Management and Engineering, 2009. SSME'09. IITA International Conference on* (pp. 169-172). IEEE. doi:10.1109/SSME.2009.113

Wood, R., & Pitt-Payne, T. (1998). *Competency-based recruitment and selection.* John Wiley & Sons.

Wu, R. T. (2004). *The Impact of Globalization on Career and Technical Education in Taiwan, Republic of China.* Online Submission.

Xu, H. H., & Wang, Y. H. (2009). Training system design for middle-level manager in coal enterprises based on post competency model. *Procedia Earth and Planetary Science, 1*(1), 1764–1771. doi:10.1016/j.proeps.2009.09.270

Yang, I. T., & Chou, J. S. (2011). Multiobjective optimization for manpower assignment in consulting engineering firms. *Applied Soft Computing, 11*(1), 1183–1190. doi:10.1016/j.asoc.2010.02.016

Yuvaraj, R. (2011). Competency Mapping. *International Journal of Scientific & Engineering Research, 2*(8).

Zhang, S., Lee, C. K., Chan, H. K., Choy, K. L., & Wu, Z. (2015). Swarm intelligence applied in green logistics: A literature review. *Engineering Applications of Artificial Intelligence*, *37*, 154–169. doi:10.1016/j.engappai.2014.09.007

Zitzler, E. (1999). *Evolutionary algorithms for multiobjective optimization: Methods and applications.* Academic Press.

KEY TERMS AND DEFINITIONS

Academic Load Allocation: is the process of assigning teaching load to the faculty members of an educational institution.

Competence: The ability of a person to perform efficiently and effectively in a situation or job using a combination of skills, attitude and knowledge.

Competency Mapping: is the process of identifying the key competencies required for a job at hand and mapping it to the strengths and weakness of employees who are supposed to perform that job.

Multi-objective Optimization: is the process of simultaneously optimizing two or more conflicting objectives subject to certain number of constraints.

Particle Swarm Optimization: is an optimization algorithm inspired by the movement aesthetics of a bird flock or a fish school trying to get closer to the food source and finally reach the target. Each individual in the flock represents a particle with a particular velocity, where each of them represents a feasible solution in the solution space.

Chapter 13

An Overview of the Last Advances and Applications of Greedy Randomized Adaptive Search Procedure

Airam Expósito Márquez
Universidad de La Laguna, Spain

Christopher Expósito-Izquierdo
Universidad de La Laguna, Spain

ABSTRACT

One of the most studied methods to get approximate solutions in optimization problems are the heuristics methods. Heuristics are usually employed to find good, but not necessarily optima solutions. The primary purpose of the chapter at hand is to provide a survey of the Greedy Randomized Adaptive Search Procedures (GRASP). GRASP is an iterative multi-start metaheuristic for solving complex optimization problems. Each GRASP iteration consists of a construction phase followed by a local search procedure. In this paper, we first describe the basic components of GRASP and the various elements that compose it. We present different variations of the basic GRASP in order to improve its performance. The GRASP has encompassed a wide range of applications, covering different fields because of its robustness and easy to apply.

1. INTRODUCTION

Over the last few decades, a wide range of effective solution techniques have been developed to solve many challenging optimization problems arisen in multitude of application areas. Optimization problems are common in various domains as diverse as biology, economics, transportation, medicine, industry, and logistics, among others. Solving optimization problems in these domains gives rise to significant environmental, economic, and social impacts. Some representative examples of optimization problems are routing problems, scheduling operations in manufacturing areas, facility location problems in public

DOI: 10.4018/978-1-5225-2857-9.ch013

and private sectors, network optimization in telecommunications, assignment problems, segmentation of images to detect potential tumours, problems associated with supply chain management, etc.

Broadly speaking, in the field of optimization problems, we are concerned with finding solutions which are optimal or near-optimal with respect to some given set of optimization criteria. Depending on the application field, the criteria are usually defined by practitioners, stakeholders, or decision makers, among others. From a practical perspective, in most of cases it is not possible to enumerate all the feasible solutions of the optimization problem under analysis and evaluate them on the basis of the imposed criteria. This is due to the fact that the volume of potential solutions often grows exponentially as the dimensions of the incumbent optimization problem. Thus, we cannot expect to be able to solve problem instances of realistic dimensions to optimality in most of cases. For this reason, depending on the size of the problem instance or the available computational resources -expressed in terms of time and memory-, we must conform with computing approximate solutions. In this regard, a great effort has gone into designing, implementing, and validating new approximate optimization techniques over the last years with the aim of reporting high-quality solutions of real-world optimization problems within reasonable computational time.

The computational complexity of most of real-world optimization problems gives rise to exact methods -those which report optima solutions in finite time- are not suitable for being applied in practice due to their high computational requirements. In fact, some optimization problems could never have an optimization technique to solve them (Sudkamp & Cotterman, 1988). For these reasons, these problems -termed intractable- demand new intelligent approaches to be solved effciently. In order to cope with these optimization problems, alternative approximate techniques have been progressively developed over the last decades. These techniques do not guarantee the optimality of the solutions reported but they are able to provide at least a feasible solution in reasonable computational time to fulfill the requirements imposed by the decision maker.

The approximate optimization techniques have found inspiration from diverse sources. Some of them are termed nature-inspired algorithms due to the fact that they borrow the foundations behind natural phenomena. Representative examples are Genetic Algorithms (Holland, 1975), Ant Colony Optimization Algorithms (Dorigo et al., 1996), Particle Swarm Optimization Algorithms (Kennedy & Eberhart, 1995), and Artificial Bee Colony Algorithms (Karaboga, 2005), among others. In these cases, the aforementioned algorithms are aimed at mimicing some evolutionary ideas associated with natural selection and genetics, behaviour of ants to find paths between the home colony and food sources, behaviour of particles in nature, and behaviour of a honey bee swarm, respectively. In the previous cases, the algorithms are based on evolving a population of solutions of the problem under study. However, alternative algorithms are single-solution-based approaches due to the fact that they work with only one solution. In all the cases, a general classification of the algorithms can be proposed according with the way the solution to manage is provided. One or several solutions provided by some procedure are transformed during the search process by using exploration operators in iterative algorithms, whereas values of the decision variables are assigned to an initial empty solution until a feasible solution is generated in greedy algorithms.

The chapter at hand seeks to provide the reader a systematic description of one of the most successful meta-heuristic techniques proposed in the scientific literature concerning the domain of optimization so far: the Greedy Randomized Adaptive Search Procedure, in short GRASP. Specifically, its basic theoretical foundations, main components, highlighted variants, advantages and disadvantages are here discussed. At the same time, due to its high effectiveness and effciency when solving a wide range of challenging optimization problems, this chapter also reviews the most relevant works about GRASP and its main variants.

The remainder of the chapter at hand is organized as follows. Firstly, Section 2 introduces the main concepts associated with the GRASP. Later, Section 3 overviews some of its most successful variants. Afterwards, Section 4 presents a literature review, analysing the highlighted contributions found in previous works. Finally, Section 5 summarizes the main conclusions extracted from the chapter.

2 GREEDY RANDOMIZED ADAPTIVE SEARCH PROCE-DURE

The Greedy Randomized Adaptive Search Procedure, in short GRASP, is an efficient meta-heuristic optimization method that has been successfully applied when solving a wide range of heterogeneous optimization problems. Its fundamentals were presented in the seminal paper (Feo & Resende, 1989) but many sophisticated variants have been gradually developed so far with the aim of tackling challenging optimization problems. This fact is discussed in Section 3.

Before presenting the GRASP, it is necessary to introduce some notations to contextualize formally the domain of application. It is assumed that we are intended to solve a given combinatorial optimization problem, termed P, defined over a finite ground set $E = \{1, 2,..., n\}$ and for which S denotes the set of feasible solutions. Without loss of generality, we are interested on finding the global optimal solution of P. This solution is denoted as s^*. That is, that feasible solution such that $f(s^*) \leq f(s)$; $\forall s \in S$, where $f(\cdot)$ is an analytical objective function to minimize with the form $f: 2^E \rightarrow R$. It should be noted that, in the case of maximization problems, we would be equivalently interested on that solution which maximizes $f(\cdot)$.

In general terms, the GRASP can be seen as an iterative multi-start procedure aimed at solving combinatorial optimization problems. For this purpose, at each iteration, two well-defined phases are sequentially carried out. The former builds incrementally a new feasible solution of the optimization problem to solve from scratch by adding a single element in each step and according with a defined utility criterion. Furthermore, the second phase seeks to improve the quality of the solution obtained in the first phase by exploring its neighbourhood until reaching a local optimum solution.

2.1. Overview

The general pseudo-code of the GRASP is depicted in Algorithm 1. The main part of the execution of the algorithm is embedded into a multi-start procedure. At each iteration, a new solution is constructed. This solution is herein termed s. In most of cases, the local optimality of this solution is not guaranteed. For this reason, a local search procedure is applied to s with the aim of reaching a local optimum solution. This local optimum solution is termed s'. Once s' has been defined, its objective function value is compared with that of the best solution reached during the search process so far. If the newest solution is that with the highest quality found around the search space of the optimization problem to solve -its objective function value is lower than that of the best solution so far-, the best solution is updated appropriately. These steps are repeated until a given stop criterion is fulfilled. A maximum number of iterations or computational time is usually set for this purpose. Finally, the best solution found during the search process is reported.

Algorithm 1

Algorithm 1: General pseudo-code of the Greedy Randomized Adaptive Search Procedure

---

Data: $\mathcal{P}$, optimization problem to solve

Result: Best solution found for optimization problem $\mathcal{P}$

1 $s_{best} \leftarrow \emptyset$

2 **while** *(stop criterion is not satisfied)* **do**

3 | $s \leftarrow$ Construct solution

4 | $s' \leftarrow$ Apply local search to s

5 | **if** $(f(s') < f(s_{best}))$ **then**

6 | | $s_{best} \leftarrow s'$

7 Return s_{best}

2.2. Constructive Phase

A simple and efficient approach to generate feasible solutions for any optimization problem is based upon building them progressively from scratch. In this framework, a candidate element out of the ground set E is added to a partial solution at each step. The elements are iteratively incorporated until the partial solution is feasible.

One of the main questions arisen from the previous framework is how to determine the next element to incorporate into the partial solution under construction. In a first approach, all the potential candidates to be selected could be ranked on the basis of an evaluation function, $g(\cdot)$. In the following, we denote as E^* the set of all feasible candidates to incorporate into the solution to build and $g(i)$ the evaluation of the candidate $i \in E^*$ by the aforementioned evaluation function. In most of cases, the evaluation function indicates the increase in the objective function value of the partial solution when the selected element has been incorporated. In a greedy approach, that candidate with the lowest increase is thus intuitively selected. That is:

$$e^* = arg\ min\{g(i): i \in E^*\} \tag{1}$$

It is worth pointing out that, given a partial solution, some elements could not be part of E^* due to the fact that they lead to potential infeasibilities. By way of illustration, consider the well-known knapsack problem (Kellerer et al., 2004). In this case, E^* is composed of only those objects whose incorporation into the knapsack does not result in an overweight.

Unfortunately, the deterministic behaviour of the previous greedy framework gives rise to, in most of cases, the quality of the solutions obtained is not suitable for its application environment. In fact, no feasible solutions can be obtained for some optimization problems under this approach. In these latter cases, repair procedures are applied with the aim of attempting to achieve feasibility. Some representative examples of these procedures can be found in the works (Duarte et al., 2006) and (Mateus et al., 2011). As discussed in (Resende & Ribeiro, 2014), the previous shortcomings give rise to the greedy solutions are usually destined to constitute initial solutions to improve by complementary optimization techniques.

2.2.1. Restricted Candidate List

In order to avoid the shortcomings associated with the deterministic behaviour of the previous greedy framework, semi-greedy algorithms are usually applied in the constructive phase of the GRASP. This type of algorithms was preliminary introduced in (Hart & Shogan, 1987).

The semi-greedy constructive algorithm in the GRASP is based upon the use of a restricted candidate list, in short RCL. This RCL is built at each iteration of the solution construction with the aim of identifying the most promising candidates to be incorporated into the partial solution under construction. With this goal in mind, the RCL is composed of the best candidates from E^* according with the evaluation function $g(\cdot)$. That is, the RCL is composed of those candidates whose impact on the objective function value is as low as possible after their incorporation into the partial solution.

In general terms, two main approaches are used to build the RCL in the general framework of the GRASP. In the former, the $p > 0$ best candidates from E^* in terms of $g(\cdot)$ are included into the RCL, whereas the RCL in the latter case is composed of those candidates $i \in E^*$ which satisfy the following expression:

$$g_{min} \leq g(i) \leq g_{min} + \alpha \cdot (g_{max} - g_{min}); \qquad (2)$$

where $g_{min} = \{g(i): i \in E^*\}$, $g_{max} = \{g(i): i \in E^*\}$, and α is a parameter defined in the range *[0..1]*, which controls the randomization level of the approach. It is easy to check that, when $\alpha = 0$, the RCL is composed of only the best candidate from E^*, and therefore the approach is equivalent to the completely greedy scenario discussed above. Furthermore, $RCL = E^*$ when $\alpha = 1$. Lastly, intermediate levels of randomization are obtained when $0 < \alpha < 1$.

Once the RCL is built, a candidate, e^*, is selected from the RCL at each step to be incorporated into the partial solution. However, in contrast to the greedy framework, e* is selected according with some randomized selection procedure. Multitude of selection procedures have been proposed in the scientific literature so far, but two general approaches are predominant. The former assigns a similar probability to be selected to each candidate in the RCL, whereas probabilities proportional to the evaluation of the candidates are assigned in the last. After the selected candidate e* has been already incorporated into the partial solution, those included into the RCL are re-evaluated according with $g(\cdot)$. Algorithm 2 depicts the pseudocode of the semi-greedy algorithm.

The procedure by which the solutions are built in the GRASP bring to light three attractive features of this meta-heuristic algorithm: greediness, randomization, and adaptiveness. These are derived from the composition of the RCL. The former is related to the way that only the best candidates are considered to be incorporated into the partial solution. The randomization of the GRASP is associated with the randomized selection procedure to identify the next candidate to incorporate, and the latter stems from the re-evaluation of the feasible candidates to be incorporated at each iteration of the search process.

2.3. Improvement Phase

As previously pointed out, the optimality of the solutions reported by the constructive phase described in Section 2.2 is not guaranteed. In fact, repair procedures are necessary to achieve feasibility in some cases.

In order to improve the quality of the solutions reported by the constructive phase, some improvement procedure can be applied. Without loss of generality, this procedure is a local search algorithm in most

Algorithm 2

Algorithm 2: Pseudo-code of the semi-greedy algorithm

Data: $\mathcal{P}$, optimization problem to solve

Result: Semi-greedy solution for optimization problem $\mathcal{P}$

1   $s \leftarrow \emptyset$

2   $E^* \leftarrow \{i \in E : s \cup \{i\}$ is not feasible$\}$

3   **while** $(E^* \neq \emptyset)$ **do**

4      $RCL \leftarrow$ Subset of best elements from E^* according with $g(\cdot)$

5      $e^* \leftarrow$ Select element from RCL according with selection procedure

6      $s \leftarrow s \cup \{e^*\}$

7      $E^* \leftarrow \{i \in E \setminus \{e^*\} : s \cup \{i\}$ is not feasible$\}$

8   Return s

---

of algorithmic approaches found in the scientific literature, but Tabu Search, Simulated Annealing, or Variable Neighbourhood Search have been also applied at this point. Starting from an initial solution, the improvement phase seeks to identify high-quality solutions in near regions of the search space. Specifically, the current solution is iteratively replaced by another feasible solution, which is considered to be near and has a higher quality. In this environment, the proximity between solutions within the search space is determined on the basis of a neighbourhood function, $N(\cdot)$. This process is finished when no better neighbour solution can be found in the neighbourhood of the current solution. The achieved solution, s_{local}, is termed local optimum due to the fact that has a higher quality than all of its neighbour solutions. That is, $f(s_{local}) \leq f(s)$, $\forall s \in N(s_{local})$. A general pseudo-code of a basic local search algorithm is depicted in Algorithm 3. In this case, it is assumed that the initial solution, s, is that provided by the constructive phase. Lastly, it is worth pointing out that the solution reported by the local search algorithm is always at least as good as the solution reported by the constructive phase.

Algorithm 3

Algorithm 3: Pseudo-code of the local search algorithm

Data: $\mathcal{P}$, optimization problem to solve

Data: s, initial solution

Result: Local optima solution for optimization problem $\mathcal{P}$

1   $s_{local} \leftarrow s$

2   $improvement \leftarrow true$

3   **while** $(improvement)$ **do**

4   Find neighbour solution $s' \in N(s_{local})$ with $f(s') < f(s_{local})$

5   **if** $(s'$ exists$)$ **then**

6         $s_{local} \leftarrow s'$

7   **else**

8         $improvement \leftarrow false$

9   Return s_{local}

2.4. Illustrative Example

In the following, we illustrate the behaviour of a basic GRASP when solving the well-known Quadratic Assignment Problem, in short QAP. This is known to be an NP-hard optimization problem introduced in (Koopmans & Beckman, 1957). It has received a lot of attention over the last decades due to its wide range of practical applications. Input data of the QAP are composed of a set of facilities, denoted as $F = \{1, 2,..., n\}$, and a set of locations, denoted as $L = \{1, 2,..., n\}$. In this case, each pair of facilities, $(i, j) \in F$, demands a certain flow, denoted as $f_{ij} \geq 0$. Also, the distance between the locations $k, l \in L$ is denoted as $d_{kl} \geq 0$. It is worth mentioning that the flows and distances are here symmetric (*i.e.*, $f_{ij} = f_{ji}$, $\forall \ i, j \in F$ and $d_{kl} = d_{lk}$, $\forall \ k, l \in L$) and the flow/distance between a given facility/location and itself is zero (*i.e.*, $f_{ii} = 0$, $\forall \ i \in F$ and $d_{kk} = 0$, $\forall \ k \in L$).

The optimization objective of the QAP consists of minimizing the cost associated with the distance and flows among the existing facilities. This objective is formally expressed as follows:

$$\min \Sigma^{n}_{i=1} \Sigma^{n}_{j=1} \ f_{ij} d_{s(i)s(j)}, \tag{3}$$

$$s \in S$$

where s is a solution belonging to the set composed of all the feasible permutations (*i.e.*, $s: F \rightarrow L$). S denotes the set of feasible solutions. The cost derived from assigning the facility i to location $s(i)$ and the facility j to facility $s(j)$ is $f_{ij} d_{s(i)s(j)}$, see equation (3). Furthermore, let us denote as $f(s)$ the objective function value of the solution $s \in S$.

Let us suppose we have a problem instance of the QAP to solve which is characterised by the flows and distances presented in Table 1. In this case, both flows between facilities and distances between locations are included into the range *[0..10]*. Also, the evaluation function, $g(\cdot)$, used in the example represents the increase of the objective function value after including a given candidate. That is, a facility assigned to a given location. Lastly, the restricted candidate list is built by selecting the $p = 4$ best candidates in terms of $g(\cdot)$.

We focus our attention only on the constructive phase of the GRASP due to the fact that excellent works dedicated to improvement strategies are available. With this goal in mind, the interested reader is refered to (Michiels et al., 2007). Figure 1 depicts the incorporation of elements into a solution created from scratch. In this case, the instance of the QAP is represented by means of a complete graph, where vertices represent the existing facilities whereas edges represent the distances between them. The number into the vertices indicate the existing locations. The execution of the GRASP starts by building a feasible solution from scratch, $s = \emptyset$ With this goal in mind, one feasible candidate is selected to be included at each step. This candidate is red in Figure 1 and its index is displayed in parentheses next to the corresponding location index. It is worth mentioning that no infeasibilities are obtained when including a new element into the partial solution of the QAP so any candidate is ruled out beforehand. In this case, all the candidates are equally attractive to be included into the initial empty solution. For this reason, one of the facilities is selected at random. This facility is the fourth, as can be seen in the upper left of the Figure 1. This way, the solution under construction is as follows at this step:

Table 1. Input data of the illustrative example of Quadratic Assignment Problem. The left table shows the ows between facilities and the right table shows distances between locations

	1	2	3	4	5	6	7	8	9		1	2	3	4	5	6	7	8	9
1	0	5	9	4	9	9	5	4	9	1	0	10	10	10	2	2	9	3	9
2	5	0	9	3	9	5	6	7	7	2	10	0	1	8	4	3	9	9	3
3	9	9	0	6	5	5	5	5	3	3	10	1	0	4	6	3	2	1	6
4	4	3	6	0	3	7	7	1	2	4	10	8	4	0	6	6	7	7	4
5	9	9	5	3	0	2	8	5	3	5	2	4	6	6	0	10	7	8	8
6	9	5	5	7	2	0	2	8	5	6	2	3	3	6	10	0	2	5	5
7	5	6	5	7	8	2	0	9	5	7	9	9	2	7	7	2	0	10	8
8	4	7	5	1	5	8	9	0	4	8	3	9	1	7	8	5	10	0	5
9	9	7	3	2	3	5	5	4	0	9	9	3	6	4	8	5	8	5	0

Figure 1. Steps carried out to build a feasible solution of the Quadratic Assignment Problem by the constructive phase of the Greedy Randomized Adaptive Search Procedure

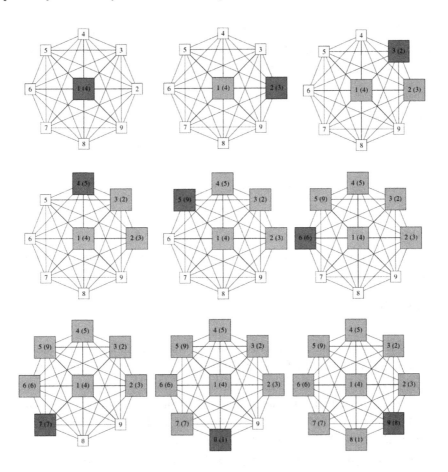

$s = [4, -, -, -, -, - , -, -, -]$

which indicates that the fourth facility is assigned to the first facility, $s(1) = 4$. It is worth mentioning that an efficient strategy to perform the first two assignments simultaneously is proposed in (Li et al., 1993).

Once we have decided the first facility to assign, we compute the attractiveness of the remaining candidates. In this case, $g(1) = 100$, $g(2) = 80$, $g(3) = 40$, $g(5) = 60$, $g(6) = 60$, $g(7) = 70$, $g(8) = 70$, and $g(9) = 40$. The third facility is selected as one of the four best candidates to be included into the partial solution. This way, the solution under construction is as follows at this step:

$s = [4, 3, -, -, -, - , -, -, -]$

The objective function value of s at this point is $f(s) = 40$.

The partial solution has to be completed by including the remaining facilities. In this case, the evaluation of the candidates is as follows: $g(1) = 360$, $g(2) = 162$, $g(5) = 216$, $g(6) = 162$, $g(7) = 162$, $g(8) = 144$, and $g(9) = 180$. The second facility is selected at this point, which means that the solution is as follows:

$s = [4, 3, 2, -, -, - , -, -, -]$

whose objective function value is now $f(s) = 202$. Later, this process is repeated until the feasibility is achieved. This is carried out iteratively by including the facilities *5, 9, 6, 7, 1,* and *8*. The solution reported by the constructive phase is as follows:

$s = [4, 3, 2, 5, 9, 6, 7, 1,$ $8]$

whose objective function value is $f(s) = 2376$.

3. VARIANTS

We present some highlighted variants of the Greedy Randomized Adaptive Search Procedure, GRASP, that have been proposed in the scientific literature and which have demonstrated to be highly competitive when solving a great spectrum of optimization problems.

3.1. Bias Functions

When a candidate is selected in the construction phase of the basic GRASP, it is incorporated into the partial solution. In its conception, the GRASP assigns equal probabilites of being chosen to candidates in the RCL. Nevertheless, it is possible to use any probability distribution to bias the candidate selection mechanism towards some particular candidates. A selection procedure using several biased probability distributions based on the ranking of candidates is presented in (Bresina, 1996). Several bias functions restricted to the elements of the RCL are introduced in the cited paper. Specifically, random bias $bias(r_i)$ $= 1$ (used by standard GRASP), logarithmic bias $bias(r_i) = log^{-1}(r + 1)$, polynomial bias $bias(r_i) = r^{-n}$ of order n, linear bias $bias(r_i) = 1/r$, exponential bias $bias(r_i) = e^{-r}$, being r_i the rank of candidate i and $bias(r_i)$ one of the bias function defined previously. In order to assign a probability to each element of the RCL, the bias values are evaluated for each element. Thereafter, the probability function $P(i)$ defines the propability of selecting the candidate i and is calculated as follows:

$$P\ (i) = \frac{bias(r_i)}{\sum_{i' \epsilon} RCLbias\left(r_{i'}\right)}$$

3.2. Reactive GRASP

The main idea of Reactive GRASP is that the basic parameter which restricts the candidate list is self-adjusted during the construction phase. This is done according to the quality of the solutions found previously. This way, it can be argued that the Reactive GRASP is a strategy to incorporate a learning mechanism in the construction phase of the basic GRASP. Accordingly to the section 2.2, we can suppose that the value of the parameter wich control the randomization of the RCL is not fixed, but it changes at each interation. The changes of the parameter α are influenced by the objective function values of the solutions found during previous iterations. A method to carry out this approach is proposed in (Prais et al., 1998). Specifically, being $\alpha\text{-}values = \alpha_1, ..., \alpha_m$, the set of possible values for α, the probabilities to choose a value of are all initailly to $p_i = 1/m$, $i = 1, ..., m$. Additionally, being s the incumbent solution and A_i the average of solutions found using $\alpha = \alpha_i$, $i = 1, ..., m$. The probabilites of selection new values of α are calculated as $p_i = q_i / \Sigma^m_{j=1} q_j$, where $q_i = s / A_i$ for $i = 1, ..., m$.

Those values of $\alpha = \alpha_i$ that guide the search to the best solutions correspond with larger values of q_i. In addition, probabilities associated with the most appropriate values will increase with each reevaluation of the probabilities. In general terms, the Reactive GRASP improves the performance of the basic GRASP in terms of objective function value, due to its higher diversification level and lower dependence on parameter tuning.

3.3. Proximate Optimality Principle

A GRASP based on a interpretation of Proximate Optimality Principle (POP) is presented in (Fleurent & Glover, 1999). Briefly, POP is based on the conception that "good solutions at one level are likely to be found close to good solutions at an adjacent level" (Glover & Laguna, 1997). Specifically, it justifies that bad decisions derived from the construction phase in the GRASP can be overcome using the local search phase during its construction phase. Given the implications in the efficiency of the GRASP, it is important to consider when to apply local search. In many approaches, this local search is only applied to limited set of solutions reported by the constructive phase, instead of being applied to all of them.

3.4. Smart Construction

The basic GRASP does not have mechanisms to take advantage of and make use of the information obtained in previous iterations. This means that it does not make use of long-term memory. In (Fleurent & Glover, 1999), a long-term memory is proposed with the aim of improving the search. The authors of the cited paper consider a set of elite solutions that will have a function during the construction phase of GRASP. A solution can become part of the set of elite solutions in two ways; if it is better solution than the best solution of the set of elite solutions or if it is better solution than the worst solution of the elite set and make a difference with respect to other solutions of the set of elite solutions. Using the concepts of consistent and strongly determined variables during the construction phase, they introduce intensification into the algorithm. Those characteristics of a solution that share in common high-quality solutions are termed consistent variables. Strongly determined variables are those characteristics of the solution that, if removed from the solution, the objective function value would degraded significally.

3.5. Path Relinking

Another essential improvement technique to apply to the basic GRASP procedure in order to report high-quality solution is termed Path-Relinking, in short PR, originally proposed in (Glover, 1997). PR is conceived as intensification technique to explore trajectories connecting elite solutions obtained by the Tabu Search. The purpose of PR is to be a strategy that incorporates attributes of high-quality solutions, by favoring these attributes in the selected movements. With one or more elite solutions, paths are generated and explored in the space of solutions that lead to other elite solutions in the search for better solutions. This is achieved by selecting movements that introduce attributes contained in the guidance solutions. The first use of PR with GRASP, as an intensification phase applied to each local optimum solution, was proposed in (Martins et al., 2000). More generally, there are two basic strategies for applied PR; as a post-optimization step to all pairs of elite solutions and as an intensication strategy to each local optimum obtained after the local search phase.

3.6. Hybridization GRASP

Other fast-growing variant is the Hybrid GRASP, where the major aim is enhancing the weaknesses of the algorithm by hybridizing it with other techniques. Efficient hybridizations of GRASP with other meta-heuristic techniques, such as Tabu Search, Variable Neighborhood Search, Iterated Local Search, and Genetic Algorithms, among others, have been reported in the literature so far.

The construction phase contains the random component of the GRASP, due the the fact that the local search always finishes at the first local optimum found during exploration. However, the VNS is able to escape from local optimal through the randomization of the process. Consequently, both meta-heuristic can be combined naturally. Representative examples can be found in the works (Hller et al., 2008), (Yin & Wang, 2012), (de Armas et al., 2015). Some hybridizations of GRASP and Genetic Algorithms have been proposed so far. In most of cases, the construction phase of a GRASP is applied to generate the initial population for the Genetic algorithm. Some examples of this can be found in (Ahuja et al., 2000) and (Armony et al., 2000). Tabu Search is another of the easily hybridizable meta-heuristics with GRASP. An example is presented in (Wang et al., 2013). In this case, an implementation of the Probabilistic GRASP-Tabu Search, in which the local search phase is strengthened by Tabu Search. The Tabu Search is also applied to the solutions obtained in memory-based GRASP in the work (Yang et al., 2013). Furthermore, a hybrid GRASP-ILS is presented in (Haddadene et al., 2016). The construction phase of the GRASP produces a feasible solution which is improved by the ILS, which replaces the local search phase. Finally, the algorithm proposed in (Coelho et al., 2016a), dubbed GILS-VND, combines an ILS, a GRASP, and a VND. In this case, the GRASP is used to generate the initial solution.

4. LITERATURE REVIEW

Over the last years, the Greedy Randomized Adaptive Search Procedure, GRASP, and its multitude of variants have been successfully applied when solving a wide range of practical applications. Some examples of extensive literature reviews with these applications, developments, and updates can be found in (Resende, M. G., & Ribeiro, C. C., 2014), (Resende, M. G., Mateus, G. R., & Silva, R., 2012), and (Resende, M. G., & Ribeiro, C. C., 2013). Throughout this section, we analyse some of the most highlighted contributions associated with the GRASP and its variants.

A wide variety of scheduling problems have been solved by using a GRASP. The following papers illustrate this fact. The problem addressed in (Chassaing et al., 2014) is the Job Shop Scheduling Problem, in short JSSP. A GRASP-ELS solution approach is proposed for solving this problem. The solution approach is evaluated using the well-known 40 Laurence benchmark with medium- and large-scale instances. The proposed method competes with the best published methods in solution quality and computational time. In (Bilyk et al., 2014), it is considered a Variable Neighborhood Search, VNS, scheme and a GRASP for solving a scheduling problem for parallel batch machines where the jobs have ready times. The performance of the solution approach is assessed using a large set of randomly generated problem instances and based on instances from the literature. The paper (de C. M. Nogueira et al., 2014) considers a parallel machine scheduling problem with the objective of minimizing the total earliness and tardiness penalties. Three different heuristics are proposed: a simple GRASP heuristic, an intensification procedure based on Path-Relinking, an Iterated Local Search as improvement phase of the GRASP. The central process of steel shaping in the steel industry is termed continuous casting. Commonly, there are parallel continuous casters, which demand to be balanced and scheduled. The requests of slabs to be casted are not assigned to a specific caster. A production planning has to decide about the assignment of slabs to casters as well as the sequence of slabs on individual casters. In (Wichmann & Spengler, 2015), a framework with a MIP-model formulation and a GRASP is proposed to solve this problem. The results indicate that the framework is able to obtain feasible solutions with high quality in comparison with an industry benchmark. The Ship Routing and Scheduling Problem with Discretized Time Windows is dealt in (de Armas et al., 2015). In order to solve this problem, a hybrid GRASP-VNS is proposed. The results are better than those of previous heuristics found in the literature in all the cases. In (Ribas & Companys, 2015), the minimization of the total flow time of a Blocking Flow Shop Problem is addressed. This paper proposes constructive heuristics and a GRASP to solve the problem under analysis. The performance of the proposed solutions was evaluated against other heuristics from the literature using the known instances by Taillard instances. The results show that the heuristics presented are competitive. An integrated Production and Transportation Scheduling Problem with capacity constraints and a short shelf life product with several vehicles is dealt in (Lacomme et al., 2016). To solve this problem, an efficient GRASP and an Evolutionary Local Search is introduced. The solution proposed is able to report solutions better than previous published ones in shorter computational times. An evolution of the GRASPxELS for the Flexible Job-shop problem is proposed in (Kemmoé et al., 2016). The results are compared with recent proposals, demonstrating that this meta-heuristic approach is e ective.

GRASP has been applied to multiple routing problems. A Generalized Vehicle Routing Problem involves finding a minimum-length set of vehicle routes passing through a set of clusters. This problem is solved in (H et al., 2014) by using a branch-and-cut algorithm and a combined approach based upon GRASP and ELS. The computational experiments demonstrate the high performance of the proposed algorithms. A variant of the classical VRP arising in two-level transportation systems, such as those encountered in the context of city logistics, the Two-Echelon Vehicle Routing Problem, is proposed in (Zeng et al., 2014). This problem is solved by a hybrid heuristic composed of a GRASP with a route first cluster-second procedure embedded and a Variable Neighborhood Descent. The results show that the algorithm is both effective and efficient and outperforms the best existing heuristics. Three sets of benchmarks from the literature were considered. A Multi-Depot Covering Tour Vehicle Routing Problem is studied in (Allahyari et al., 2015) where the assumption of visiting each customer does not hold. A hybrid meta-heuristic which combines GRASP, ILS, Simulated Annealing is proposed to solve the problem. The results clearly reveal the e effectiveness of the developed heuristic. A Close-Open Vehicle Routing Problem with Time Windows, in which all the vehicles are not required to return to the depot after completing their service, is proposed in (Brito et al., 2015). Also, vague and imprecise information on parameters is considered. To solve the problem, a meta-heuristic that combines an Ant Colony Optimization, GRASP, and VNS is used. In this paper, (Coelho et al., 2016b), a VRP variant inspired on a real case of a large distribution company is studied. In order to solve the problem a trajectory search heuristic called GILS-VND that combines ILS, GRASP and VND is designed. This heuristic is able to obtain competitive solutions. A real world bicycle reposition problem with selective pickup and delivery is studied in (Ho & Szeto, 2016). In this problem, the demand at each delivery node has to be satisfied by the supply collected from a subset of pickup nodes. Minimizing the total travel cost is the objective considered. To solve the problem, a GRASP with Path-Relinking is proposed. In this regard, the experimental results show that the approach improves the existing results in the literature using short computing times.

Location problems have been broadly addressed by GRASP. A Fixed Charge Location Problem which considers location specific costs and inventory replenishment costs is solved in (Silva & Gao, 2013) by means of a GRASP. In (Peir et al., 2014), a GRASP is proposed to solve the Uncapacitated r-Allocation p-Hub Median Problem by using a GRASP with three local searches aimed at locating, assigning, and routing. A hub location problem in which the hubs to be located must form a set of interconnecting lines is tackled in (Martins de Sá et al., 2015). A Benders-branch-and-cut algorithm, mathematical programming formulation, and several heuristic algorithms based on VNS, GRASP, and Adaptive Large Neighborhood Search are presented and compared to solve the problem in two sets of benchmark instances. Selecting a subset of p facilities from a given set of possible locations maximizing the sum of the distances between each customer and its nearest facility is termed as the Obnoxious p-Median Problem (Colmenar et al., 2016). An advanced GRASP which avoids applying local search method to low-quality solutions is proposed to solve the problem. The Single Row Facility Layout Problem, presented in (Rubio-Sánchez et al., 2016), consists of finding and optimal arrangement of a set of rectangular facilities, locating them next to each other along a line. This work combines a GRASP and Path-Relinking in order to obtain high-quality solutions for the SRFLP. Experiments show that proposed approach outperforms state of the art methods.

Moreover, manufacturing is a field in which a lot of work based on the framework of the GRASP has been done so far. For instance, the independent multi-plant, multi-period, and multi-item capacitated lot sizing problem is addressed in (Nascimento et al., 2010). A GRASP is developed to find cost effective solutions for this problem. The computational tests show that the GRASP reports better results than previous heuristics described in the literature. In (Zhu et al., 2013), the m-machine no wait flow shop scheduling problem with sequence dependent setup times is studied for the manufacturing process in iron and steel manufacturing systems. A new meta-heuristic is proposed, which is based on the GRASP and ELS, for the considered problem. Experimental results show that proposed heuristic improves the existing results in the literature and is able to optimize the manufacturing process in steelworks. An extension of the classical job shop scheduling problem, where each operation has to be executed by one machine and this can work at different speed is studied in (Kemmoe Tchomte & Tchernev, 2014). This application is related with reducing CO2 emission and associated carbon footprint consumption for manufacturing scheduling is addressed. In order to solve this problem, a GRASP-ELS was developed and tested using new instances based on the well-known instances by Laurence. The performance is evaluated in comparison with the optimal solutions. A non-linear integer programming for a mixed-model assembly line considering the detection uncertainty in a RFID network is dealt in (Tang et al., 2015). The proposed model is applied to an industrial case of an automobile mixed-model assembly. To solve this problem a Genetic Algorithm integrating a divide-and-conquer GRASP is designed. The results of the computational experiment demonstrate the effectiveness of the proposed algorithm. A lot-sizing problem is studied in (Zouadi et al., 2015) to deal with the production planning and control problem of a single product involving combined manufacturing and remanufacturing operations. A Memetic Algorithm and a hybrid algorithm with GRASP and Path-Relinking is proposed to solve this problem. Numerical experiments were conducted on a set of 300 instances with up to 48 periods. Computational experiments show that both heuristics provide high-quality solutions in moderate computational time.

Other transportation problems have been addressed with GRASP. A Pickup and Delivery Problem is studied for a daily route planning problem at a regional air carrier who was trying to determine the benefits of transhipment in (Qu & Bard, 2012). A GRASP was developed in order to find suitable solutions, but considering an ALNS in the improvement phase. Due to the absence of instances for the problem in the literature, a set of randomly instances was generated. Also, computational experiments were done on several existing PDP instances. The performance of the proposed GRASP was comparable to the best-known heuristics. In (Fei et al., 2013), a network design problem related with finding the set of optimal sensor locations under uncertainty is analysed. A non-linear two-stage stochastic bi-objective model is presented. To solve the problem, an iterative heuristic solution algorithm, hybrid GRASP, is developed. The proposed solution approach is tested on the Coordinated Highways Action Response Team network (Washington DC-Baltimore, Maryland corridor), in a mesoscopic traffic simulator. Test results show that, under stochastic conditions, the sensor location plan obtained has better performance than plans developed for deterministic conditions. A problem related with the optimal layout of an intermodal terminal network is dealt in (Sörensen & Vanovermeire, 2013). A bi-objective model that minimizes both the transportation cost for the users of the terminal network and the location cost for the terminal operators was developed. In order to solve the problem, a specific GRASP was developed introducing a parameter that set the allowed calculation time and is used to improve the Pareto set approximation. Furthermore, a GRASP is developed in (Sharif & Salari, 2015) for solving a transportation problem arising in disaster relief situations. The authors propose two mathematical models enriched by introducing valid inequalities. Different sets of instances were used to test the performance of the GRASP. The results show that the proposed GRASP is able to obtain high-quality solutions. An integrated recovery of both aircraft routing and passengers with a mathematical model based on both the flight connection network and the passenger reassignment relationship is studied in (Hu et al., 2016). A GRASP is developed to solve the problem. Its effectiveness was tested with synthetic and real-world datasets.

The GRASP has been applied to several class of problems from the graph theory. Several versions of the GRASP is proposed to solve the generalized minimum spanning tree problem in (Ferreira et al., 2012). In this case, it includes additional mechanisms such as ILS and Path-Relinking. Computational experiments indicate that the most efficient versions of the GRASP are those that use improvement mechanisms. The obtained solutions are better than most the known solutions in the literature with short computational times. In (Figueiredo & Frota, 2014), the problem of finding a subgraph of a signed graph that is balanced and maximizes the cardinality of its vertex set is analysed. A GRASP is developed and computational experiments are carried out on a set of random instances. Comparative computational experiments indicate that GRASP is the best heuristic solution approach when time limit was not a constraint in the search process. The k-Labelled Spanning Forest Problem is dealt in (Consoli & Prez, 2015). Several algorithms were developed for the problem including backtracking procedure, pilot method, Genetic Algorithms, GRASP, and VNS. To test the performance of the algorithms 20 different datasets were run. A greedy adaptive algorithm and a GRASP is proposed in (Musmanno & Ribeiro, 2016) to solve the Generalized Median Graph Problem. Exact methods for solving this problem are capable to handle only small graphs. Computational results indicate that both heuristics can be used to obtain high-quality approximate solutions.

Lastly, the GRASP has been applied to solve a large set of optimization problems found in other domains. However, due to the space limitations of this chapter, it is not our intention to provide an in depth study of the applications of the GRASP in all its domains. In (Palmieri et al., 2016), re-optimizing communication paths between virtual machines and big data sources so that more virtual machines can be allowed to access the needed big data sources with adequate bandwidth, is dealt as an optimization problem. This problem is tackled with a GRASP and Path-Relinking. Another kind of application is tackled in (Cordone & Lulli, 2013). Specifically, the Weighted Gene Regulatory Network. It consists in pruning a regulatory network obtained from DNA microarray gene expression data, in order to identify a reduced set of candidate elements which can explain the expression of all other genes. A GRASP and three alternative Path-Relinking-based strategies were developed to solve this problem. Furthermore, the power economic dispatch regarding power system operations is a problem dealt in (Neto et al., 2017). Its objective is to minimize the total generation cost of the generating units while satisfying various constraints of the units and system. In this work, a combination of a Continuous GRASP and Differential Evolution, C-GRASP-DE, is proposed to solve the problem. In (Baykasolu et al., 2015), a combination of GRASP and a quadratic programming model is proposed in order to solve Cardinality Constrained Port-folio Optimization. The stock selection is tackled for GRASP and once the stocks are selected the problem reduces to a quadratic programming problem. In (Díez-Pastor et al., 2014), two new methods for tree ensemble construction are presented, G-Forest and GAR-Forest. The tree construction process uses the same strategy used in the GRASP for generating random and adaptive solutions. In particular, the GRASP is used at each node of the trees. The results conclusively demonstrate that G-Forest and GAR-Forest outperform state of the art methods. The set k covering problem is an extension of the Set Covering Problem, but each object is required to be covered at least k times. The computational biology and design of communication networks are common applications of this problem. This problem is addressed in (Pessoa et al., 2013). A GRASP with Path-Relinking is described in this work, as well as the template of a family of Lagrangean heuristics. In (Barbalho et al., 2013), a hybrid version of the GRASP that incorporates a data mining process is applied for different combinatorial problems, such as the Set Packing Problem, the Maximum Diversity Problem, the Server Replication for Reliable Multicast Problem and the p-Median Problem. In the hybrid proposal, after executing a significant number of iterations, the data mining process extracts patterns from an elite set of suboptimal solutions. These patterns present characteristics of near-optimal solutions and can be used to guide the following GRASP iterations in the search through the combinatorial solution space. Two algorithms combining GRASP and Tabu Search for solving Unconstrained Binary Quadratic Programming is proposed in (Wang et al., 2013). Firstly, it proposes a simple GRASP-Tabu Search algorithm working with a single solution and then reinforce it by introducing a population management strategy.

5. CONCLUSION

The primary purpose of the chapter at hand is to provide a survey of the Greedy Randomized Adaptive Search Procedure, GRASP, proposed in (Feo & Resende, 1989). The GRASP is an iterative multistart meta-heuristic for solving complex optimization problems. Each GRASP iteration consists of a constructive phase followed by an improvement phase. In the constructive phase, a feasible solution is iteratively constructed, inserting a single candidate element to be part of the solution in each iteration. With the feasible solution built during the constructive phase, a single-solution-based algorithm works in an iterative fashion by successively replacing the current solution by a better solution in its neighborhood. Its execution finishes when no better solution is found in the neighborhood. In this chapter, we firstly describe the basic components of GRASP and the various elements that compose it. We present different variations of the basic GRASP in order to improve its performance. Multiple effective variants of the GRASP have been proposed in the scientific literature so far to adapt the general method to a wide range of optimization problems. Enhanced solution construction mechanisms and techniques to improve the search are also described.

The GRASP has encompassed a wide range of applications, covering different fields because of its robustness and easy to apply. The GRASP has been successfully applied when solving optimization problems associated with fields such as biology, covering and partition, decision sciences, routing and transportation, logic and partitioning, graph theory, location and assignment, manufacturing, telecommunications, power systems, timetabling and scheduling, VLSI design, etc. This chapter also aims to collect the latest applications of the GRASP.

In short, this chapter is expected to serve as a starting point to all researchers interested in the standard GRASP, variants, improvement mechanisms, hybridization strategies, and practical applications.

REFERENCES

Ahuja, R. K., Orlin, J. B., & Tiwari, A. (2000). A greedy genetic algorithm for the quadratic assignment problem. *Computers & Operations Research, 27*(10), 917–934. doi:10.1016/S0305-0548(99)00067-2

Allahyari, S., Salari, M., & Vigo, D. (2015). A hybrid metaheuristic algorithm for the multi-depot covering tour vehicle routing problem. *European Journal of Operational Research, 242*(3), 756–768. doi:10.1016/j.ejor.2014.10.048

Armony, M., Klincewicz, J. G., Luss, H., & Rosenwein, M. B. (2000). Design of stacked self-healing rings using a genetic algorithm. *Journal of Heuristics, 6*(1), 85–105. doi:10.1023/A:1009665726946

Barbalho, H., Rosseti, I., Martins, S. L., & Plastino, A. (2013). A hybrid data mining GRASP with path-relinking. *Computers & Operations Research, 40*(12), 3159–3173. doi:10.1016/j.cor.2012.02.022

Baykasoglu, A., Yunusoglu, M. G., & Özsoydan, F. B. (2015). A GRASP based solution approach to solve cardinality constrained portfolio optimization problems. *Computers & Industrial Engineering, 90,* 339–351. doi:10.1016/j.cie.2015.10.009

Bilyk, A., Mönch, L., & Almeder, C. (2014). Scheduling jobs with ready times and precedence constraints on parallel batch machines using metaheuristics. *Computers & Industrial Engineering, 78,* 175–185. doi:10.1016/j.cie.2014.10.008

Bresina, J. L. (1996). Heuristic-biased stochastic sampling. AAAI-96, 271-278.

Brito, J., Martínez, F., Moreno, J., & Verdegay, J. (2015). An aco hybrid metaheuristic for closeopen vehicle routing problems with time windows and fuzzy constraints. *Applied Soft Computing, 32,* 154–163. doi:10.1016/j.asoc.2015.03.026

Chassaing, M., Fontanel, J., Lacomme, P., Ren, L., Tchernev, N., & Villechenon, P. (2014). A GRASP - ELS approach for the job-shop with a web service paradigm packaging. *Expert Systems with Applications, 41*(2), 544–562. doi:10.1016/j.eswa.2013.07.080

Coelho, V., Grasas, A., Ramalhinho, H., Coelho, I., Souza, M., & Cruz, R. (2016a). An ils-based algorithm to solve a large-scale real heterogeneous eet fVRPg with multi-trips and docking constraints. *European Journal of Operational Research, 250*(2), 367–376. doi:10.1016/j.ejor.2015.09.047

Coelho, V., Grasas, A., Ramalhinho, H., Coelho, I., Souza, M., & Cruz, R. (2016b). An ils-based algorithm to solve a large-scale real heterogeneous eet vrp with multi-trips and docking constraints. *European Journal of Operational Research, 250*(2), 367–376. doi:10.1016/j.ejor.2015.09.047

Colmenar, J. M., Greistorfer, P., Martí, R., & Duarte, A. (2016). Advanced greedy randomized adaptive search procedure for the obnoxious p-median problem. *European Journal of Operational Research, 252*(2), 432–442. doi:10.1016/j.ejor.2016.01.047

Consoli, S., & Pérez, J. A. M. (2015). Variable neighbour-hood search for the k-labelled spanning forest problem. *Electronic Notes in Discrete Mathematics, 47,* 29–36. doi:10.1016/j.endm.2014.11.005

Cordone, R., & Lulli, G. (2013). A GRASP metaheuristic for microarray data analysis. *Computers & Operations Research, 40*(12), 3108–3120. doi:10.1016/j.cor.2012.10.008

de Armas, J., Lalla-Ruiz, E., Expósito-Izquierdo, C., Landa-Silva, D., & Melián-Batista, B. (2015). A hybrid GRASP-VNS for ship routing and scheduling problem with discretized time windows. *Engineering Applications of Artificial Intelligence, 45,* 350–360. doi:10.1016/j.engappai.2015.07.013

de C. M. Nogueira, J. P., Arroyo, J. E. C., Villadiego, H. M. M., & Gonçalves, L. B. (2014, February). Hybrid GRASP Heuristics to Solve an Unrelated Parallel Machine Scheduling Problem with Earliness and Tardiness Penalties. *Electronic Notes in Theoretical Computer Science*, *302*, 53–72. doi:10.1016/j.entcs.2014.01.020

Díez-Pastor, J. F., García-Osorio, C., & Rodríguez, J. J. (2014). Tree ensemble construction using a GRASP-based heuristic and annealed randomness. *Information Fusion*, *20*, 189–202. doi:10.1016/j.inffus.2014.01.009

Dorigo, M., Maniezzo, V., & Colorni, A. (1996). Ant system: optimization by a colony of cooperating agents. Systems, Man, and Cybernetics, Part B: Cybernetics. *IEEE Transactions on*, *26*(1), 29–41.

Duarte, A. R., Ribeiro, C. C., Urrutia, S., & Haeusler, E. H. (2006). Referee assignment in sports leagues. In *International Conference on the Practice and Theory of Automated Timetabling* (pp. 158-173). Springer.

Fei, X., Mahmassani, H. S., & Murray-Tuite, P. (2013). Vehicular network sensor placement optimization under uncertainty. *Transportation Research Part C, Emerging Technologies*, *29*, 14–31. doi:10.1016/j.trc.2013.01.004

Feo, T. A., & Resende, M. G. (1989). A probabilistic heuristic for a computationally di cult set covering problem. *Operations Research Letters*, *8*(2), 67–71. doi:10.1016/0167-6377(89)90002-3

Ferreira, C. S., Ochi, L. S., Parada, V., & Uchoa, E. (2012). A GRASP-based approach to the generalized minimum spanning tree problem. *Expert Systems with Applications*, *39*(3), 3526–3536. doi:10.1016/j.eswa.2011.09.043

Figueiredo, R., & Frota, Y. (2014). The maximum balanced subgraph of a signed graph: Applications and solution approaches. *European Journal of Operational Research*, *236*(2), 473–487. doi:10.1016/j.ejor.2013.12.036

Fleurent, C., & Glover, F. (1999). Improved construc-tive multistart strategies for the quadratic assignment problem using adaptive memory. *INFORMS Journal on Computing*, *11*(2), 198–204. doi:10.1287/ijoc.11.2.198

Glover, F. (1997). *Tabu Search and Adaptive Memory Programming - Advances*. Applications and Challenges. doi:10.1007/978-1-4615-6089-0_1

Glover, F., & Laguna, M. (1997). *Tabu Search*. Kluwer Academic Publishers. doi:10.1007/978-1-4615-6089-0

Ha, M. H., Bostel, N., Langevin, A., & Rousseau, L.-M. (2014). An exact algorithm and a metaheuristic for the generalized vehicle routing problem with exible eet size. *Computers & Operations Research*, *43*, 9–19. doi:10.1016/j.cor.2013.08.017

Haddadene, S. R. A., Labadie, N., & Prodhon, C. (2016). A GRASP ILS for the vehicle routing problem with time windows, syn-chronization and precedence constraints. *Expert Systems with Applications*, *66*, 274–294. doi:10.1016/j.eswa.2016.09.002

Hart, J. P., & Shogan, A. W. (1987). Semi-greedy heuristics: An empirical study. *Operations Research Letters*, *6*(3), 107–114. doi:10.1016/0167-6377(87)90021-6

Ho, S. C., & Szeto, W. (2016). GRASP with path relinking for the selective pickup and delivery problem. *Expert Systems with Applications*, *51*, 14–25. doi:10.1016/j.eswa.2015.12.015

Holland, J. H. (1975). *Adaptation in natural and artificial systems: an introductory analysis with applications to biology, control, and artificial intelligence*. University of Michigan Press.

Höller, H., Melián, B., & Voss, S. (2008). Applying the pilot method to improve VNS and GRASP metaheuristics for the design of SDH/WDM networks. *European Journal of Operational Research*, *191*(3), 691–704. doi:10.1016/j.ejor.2006.12.060

Hu, Y., Song, Y., Zhao, K., & Xu, B. (2016). Integrated recovery of aircraft and passengers after airline operation disruption based on a GRASP algorithm. *Transportation Research Part E, Logistics and Transportation Review*, *87*, 97–112. doi:10.1016/j.tre.2016.01.002

Karaboga, D. (2005). *An idea based on honey bee swarm for numerical optimization*. Technical report, Technical report-tr06, Erciyes University, Engineering Faculty, Computer Engineering Department.

Kellerer, H., Pferschy, U., & Pisinger, D. (2004). *Knap-sack problems*. Springer Berlin Heidelberg. doi:10.1007/978-3-540-24777-7

Kemmoé, S., Lamy, D., & Tchernev, N. (2016). A GRASP embedding a bi-levelels for solving exible job-shop problems. *IFAC-PapersOnLine*, *49*(12), 1749–1754. doi:10.1016/j.ifacol.2016.07.835

Kemmoe-Tchomte, S., & Tchernev, N. (2014). A GRASPxELS for Scheduling of Job-Shop Like Manufacturing Systems and CO2 Emission Reduction. Springer Berlin Heidelberg.

Kennedy, J., & Eberhart, R. (1995). Particle swarm optimization. *Neural Networks, 1995. Proceedings. IEEE International Conference on, 4*, 1942-1948. doi:10.1109/ICNN.1995.488968

Koopmans, T., & Beckman, M. (1957). Assignment problems and the location of economic activities. *Econometrica*, *25*(1), 53–76. doi:10.2307/1907742

Lacomme, P., Moukrim, A., Quilliot, A., & Vinot, M. (2016). The integrated production and transportation scheduling problem based on a GRASPxELS resolution scheme. *IFAC-PapersOnLine, 49*(12), 1466 - 1471.

Li, Y., Pardalos, P. M., & Resende, M. G. C. (1993). A greedy randomized adaptive search procedure for the quadratic assignment problem. In P. M. Pardalos & H. Wolkowicz (Eds.), *Quadratic Assignment and Related Problems, Proceedings of a DIMACS Workshop* (pp. 237-262). DIMACS/AMS.

Martins, S., Resende, M., Ribeiro, C., & Pardalos, P. (2000). A parallel GRASP for the Steiner tree problem in graphs using a hybrid local search strategy. *Journal of Global Optimization*, *17*(1), 267–283. doi:10.1023/A:1026546708757

Martins de Sá, E., Contreras, I., & Cordeau, J. F. (2015). Exact and heuristic algorithms for the design of hub networks with multiple lines. *European Journal of Operational Research*, *246*(1), 186–198. doi:10.1016/j.ejor.2015.04.017

Mateus, G. R., Resende, M. G., & Silva, R. M. (2011). GRASP with path-relinking for the generalized quadratic assignment problem. *Journal of Heuristics*, *17*(5), 527–565. doi:10.1007/s10732-010-9144-0

Michiels, W., Aarts, E., & Korst, J. (2007). *Theoretical aspects of local search.* Springer Science & Business Media.

Musmanno, L. M., & Ribeiro, C. C. (2016). Heuristics for the generalized median graph problem. *European Journal of Operational Research, 254*(2), 371–384. doi:10.1016/j.ejor.2016.03.048

Nascimento, M. C., Resende, M. G., & Toledo, F. M. (2010). Grasp heuristic with path-relinking for the multi-plant capacitated lot sizing problem. *European Journal of Operational Research, 200*(3), 747–754. doi:10.1016/j.ejor.2009.01.047

Neto, J. X. V., Reynoso-Meza, G., Ruppel, T. H., Mariani, V. C., & dos Santos Coelho, L. (2017). Solving non-smooth economic dispatch by a new combination of continuous GRASP algorithm and diferential evolution. *International Journal of Electrical Power & Energy Systems, 84*, 13–24. doi:10.1016/j.ijepes.2016.04.012

Palmieri, F., Fiore, U., Ricciardi, S., & Castiglione, A. (2016). Grasp-based resource re-optimization for e ective big data access in federated clouds. *Future Generation Computer Systems, 54*, 168–179. doi:10.1016/j.future.2015.01.017

Peiró, J., Corberán, Á., & Martí, R. (2014). Grasp for the uncapacitated r-allocation p-hub median problem. *Computers & Operations Research, 43*, 50–60. doi:10.1016/j.cor.2013.08.026

Pessoa, L. S., Resende, M. G., & Ribeiro, C. C. (2013). A hybrid Lagrangean heuristic with GRASP and path-relinking for set k-covering. *Computers & Operations Research, 40*(12), 3132–3146. doi:10.1016/j.cor.2011.11.018

Prais, M., & Ribeiro, C. C. (2000). Reactive GRASP: An application to a matrix decomposition problem in TDMA traffic assignment. *INFORMS Journal on Computing, 12*(3), 164–176. doi:10.1287/ijoc.12.3.164.12639

Qu, Y., & Bard, J. F. (2012). A GRASP with adaptive large neighborhood search for pickup and delivery problems with transshipment. *Computers & Operations Research, 39*(10), 2439–2456. doi:10.1016/j.cor.2011.11.016

Resende, M. G., Mateus, G. R., & Silva, R. (2012). *Manual da computacao evolutiva e metaheuristica, chapter GRASP: Busca gulosa, aleatorizada e adaptativa.* Coimbra: Coimbra University Press.

Resende, M. G., & Ribeiro, C. C. (2013). *Metaheuristicas em pesquisa operacional, chapter GRASP: Procedimentos de busca gulosos, aleatorios e adaptativos.* Curitiba: Omnipax Editora. doi:10.7436/2013.mhpo.01

Resende, M. G., & Ribeiro, C. C. (2014). GRASP: Greedy randomized adaptive search procedures. In Search methodologies (pp. 287-312). Springer US. ISO 690.

Resende, M. G., & Ribeiro, C. C. (2014). GRASP: Greedy randomized adaptive search procedures. In Search methodologies (pp. 287-312). Springer.

Ribas, I., & Companys, R. (2015). Efficient heuristic algorithms for the blocking flow shop scheduling problem with total flow time minimization. *Computers & Industrial Engineering, 87*, 30–39. doi:10.1016/j.cie.2015.04.013

Rubio-Sánchez, M., Gallego, M., Gortázar, F., & Duarte, A. (2016). GRASP with path relinking for the single row facility layout problem. *Knowledge-Based Systems*, *106*, 1–13. doi:10.1016/j.knosys.2016.05.030

Sharif, M. T., & Salari, M. (2015). A GRASP algorithm for a humanitarian relief transportation problem. *Engineering Applications of Artificial Intelligence*, *41*, 259–269. doi:10.1016/j.engappai.2015.02.013

Silva, F., & Gao, L. (2013). A joint replenishment inventory-location model. *Networks and Spatial Economics*, *13*(1), 107–122. doi:10.1007/s11067-012-9174-2

Sörensen, K., & Vanovermeire, C. (2013). Bi-objective optimization of the intermodal terminal location problem as a policy-support tool. *Computers in Industry*, *64*(2), 128–135. doi:10.1016/j.compind.2012.10.012

Sudkamp, T. A., & Cotterman, A. (1988). *Languages and machines: an introduction to the theory of computer science* (Vol. 2). Addison-Wesley.

Tang, L., Cao, H., Zheng, L., & Huang, N. (2015). RFID network planning for wireless manufacturing considering the detection uncertainty. *IFAC-PapersOnLine*, *48*(3), 406–411. doi:10.1016/j.ifacol.2015.06.115

Wang, Y. L. Z., Glover, F., & Hao, J. K. (2013). Probabilistic GRASP-tabu search algorithms for the UBQP problem. *Computers & Operations Research*, *40*(12), 3100–3107. doi:10.1016/j.cor.2011.12.006

Wichmann, M. G. & Spengler, T. S. (2015). Slab scheduling at parallel continuous casters. International Journal of Production Economics. *Current Research Issues in Production Economics*.

Yang, Z., Wang, G., & Chu, F. (2013). An effective GRASP and tabu search for the 0–1 quadratic knapsack problem. *Computers & Operations Research*, *40*(5), 1176–1185. doi:10.1016/j.cor.2012.11.023

Yin, P. Y., & Wang, T. Y. (2012). A GRASP-VNS algorithm for optimal wind-turbine placement in wind farms. *Renewable Energy*, *48*, 489–498. doi:10.1016/j.renene.2012.05.020

Zeng, Z. Y., Xu, W. S., Xu, Z. Y., & Shao, W. H. (2014). A hybrid GRASP+vnd heuristic for the two-echelon vehicle routing problem arising in city logistics. *Mathematical Problems in Engineering*, (1): 1–11.

Zhu, X., Li, X., & Wang, Q. (2013). An adaptive intelligent method for manufacturing process optimization in steelworks. In *Computer Supported Cooperative Work in Design (CSCWD), 2013 IEEE 17th International Conference on* (pp. 363-368). doi:10.1109/CSCWD.2013.6580989

Zouadi, T., Yalaoui, A., Reghioui, M., & El Kadiri, K. E. (2015). Lot-sizing for production planning in a recovery system with returns. *RAIRO-Operations Research*, *49*(1), 123–142. doi:10.1051/ro/2014044

Chapter 14
Defect Detection of Fabrics by Grey–Level Co–Occurrence Matrix and Artificial Neural Network

Dilip k. Choudhury
GIET Gunupur, India

Sujata Dash
North Orissa University, India

ABSTRACT

The class of Textiles produced from terephthalic acid and ethylene glycol by condensation polymerization has many end-uses for example these are used as filter fabric in railway track to prevent soil erosion, in cement industry these are used in boiler department as filter fabric to prevent the fly-ash from mixing in the atmosphere. Presently, the quality checking is done by the human in the naked eye. The automation of quality check of the non-Newtonian fabric can be termed as Image Analysis or texture analysis problem. A Simulation study was carried out by the process of Image Analysis which consists of two steps the former is feature extraction and the later part is recognition. Various techniques or tools that are presently studied in research for texture feature extraction are Grey level co-occurrence matrix(GLCM), Markov Random Field, Gabor filter. A GLCM matrix with 28 Haralick features were taken as input for this chapter.

INTRODUCTION

The class of Textiles produced from terephthalic acid and ethylene glycol by condensation polymerization has many end-uses for example these are used as filter fabric in railway track to prevent soil erosion, in cement industry these are used in boiler department as filter fabric to prevent the fly-ash from mixing in the atmosphere. Presently, the quality checking is done by the human in naked eye. The automation of quality check of the non-Newtonian fabric can be termed as Image Analysis or texture analysis problem

DOI: 10.4018/978-1-5225-2857-9.ch014

.We have done a Simulation study by the process of Image Analysis which consists of two steps the former is feature extraction and the second part is recognition. Various techniques or tools that are presently in research for texture feature extraction are GLCM (Brad, 2007), Markov Random Field (Dorrity, Vachtsevanos & Jasper, 1995), and Gabor filter (Dorrity, Vachtsevanos & Jasper, 1996). We have used here GLCM with 20 Haralick features.

The authors had done a simulation Study for defect detection and estimation by taking 25 nice sample and 25 defective still image samples and then extracted 28 Haralick features. Also, 20 polynomial entropy features were taken .When combined it has given 48 features. The pattern recognition problem for fault detection problem of Non-Newtonian fluid is done by Back propagation neural network, recurrent neural network, and Radial basis function neural network and Learning Vector Quantization neural network.

LITERATURE SURVEY

A comprehensive review on the automated fabric defect detection can be found in (Conci & Proenca, 2000; Schiffaueroval & Thomson, 2006). A segmentation of fabric image based on multi-scale Markov random field (MRF) of a fabric image is presented (Nickolay, Schicktanz & Schamlfuss, 1993). Multi-scale MRF is applied to segment the fabric images combined with the edge information obtained using the modulus maximum of Wavelet Transform. Experimental results show that the segmentation algorithm associated with edge information can reduce both the computing time and misclassification. Cohen et al. (1986) have used a MRF model for the detection of defects in fabrics. Sylla (2002) has implemented an MRF based method on TMS320C40 parallel processing system for the real time inspection of defects in a fabric. Ozdemir and Ercil (1996) have used Gauss MRF to detect the common defects in the textile fabrics. Arivazhagan et al. (2006) have applied the Gabor-wavelet transform for the detection of defects in fabrics. The defects in the regular texture can be found easily by the transform. Proper thresholding ensures the elimination of the defects from the texture background. The results obtained using this method vindicates its effectiveness. Krueger and Sommer (2000) have used an imaginary part of a Gabor function as the transfer function of the hidden layer in a wavelet network, and introduced the concept of Gabor- wavelet network for solving 2D problems in the pattern recognition (Dorrity, Vachtsevanos & Jasper, 1996). (Bodnarova et al., 2002) uses an optimal Gabor filters for the detection of flaws in textiles. When applied on the non- defective texture, the filter response maximizes a Fisher cost function. A pixel of potentially flawed texture is classified as an defective or non- defective based on the Gabor filter response. Yuan Shu et. al. (2004) have presented a flaw detection system in fabrics based on Gabor filter. It is based on the energy response from the convolution of Gabor filter bank in different frequencies and orientations. Using the image fusion to combine all response feature images and finally thresholding this fused images produces a simple binary image consisting of defects. The simulation results on fabric samples show the effectiveness of this method. Bu, Wang & Huang (2009) have developed a fabric defect detection system based on multiple fractal features to overcome the inability of the single fractal feature in dealing with flaw detection in fabrics. Multiple fractal features are needed to mitigate the problems of the box-counting method as well as the inherent characteristics.

Conci et al. (1998) have used the estimate of fractal dimension for the inspection of fabrics to detect defects. The approach used for decision in (Conci et al. 1998) though computationally is simple but the experimental results of 90% are validated on a small database involving eight types of defects. The localization accuracy of these detected defects is very poor raising high false alarm. Escofet et al. (1998)

also describe a general textile web inspection system for the local defects in the textile fabrics using symmetric and asymmetric Gabor filters. Kumar et al. (2002) have suggested a texture segmentation method using the real Gabor function (RGF). A bank of multi-orientation and multi-resolution RGFs followed by intra and inter- scale image fusion is used to find the textile defects. Bu, Wang & Huang (2009) have presented a novel multiple fractal features extraction framework along with its application to the detection of fabric defects, Xiuping Liu et al. (2013) have devised a novel method to detect the defects in fabrics based on slub extraction using Gabor filter. Kim et. al. (1998) have developed a fabric defect detection scheme using wavelet analysis on 1-D projection of signals. Two 1-D signals are generated from every inspection image by the gray-level summation of the pixels along the rows and columns. The Mexican hat wavelets over the three scales are used to decompose each of the 1-D signals. The wavelet coefficients of each of the decomposed signals are used to compute the respective signal to noise ratio (SNR) which is helpful to determine the defects. Sari-Sarraf et. al. (1999) have developed a fabric defect detection system based on the wavelet Transform which is capable of detecting defects as small as 0.2 inch with an overall detection rate of 89%. Their defect detection scheme uses the low- pass and the high-pass "Daubachies" D2 filters. As shown in (Sari-Sarraf et al. 1999), two fractal – based measurements, local Roughness R(m,n) and global homogeneity can be used to quantify surface characteristics of the real fabric images. However, owing to the dyadic nature of wavelet scales, problems can arise in the accurate localization of defects. To avert these problems, Li et al., (2015) have proposed multiscale representation of fabrics using B- spline transform for the detection of defects in fabrics.

A system dealing with the detection of defects and identification of details is developed using fuzzy wavelet analysis in which wavelet coefficients over several scales is combined nonlinearly by the fuzzy inferencing. The decision on defective fabric samples is made by comparing the fuzzy features extracted with the stored template features. By this process three types of defects, viz., point, line and area are identified from the defective fabrics.

Stojanovic et al. (2000) have implemented quality of woven fabrics using a vision based system. It utilizes both hardware and software to solve the problem of fabric defect detection in real-time and employs the improved binary, textural and neural network algorithms. It has good localization accuracy, low rate of false alarms, and compatibility with the standard inspection tools. Srinivasan et al. (1992) have developed a Fabric Defects Analysis System (FDAS) for the analysis of defects in the woven fabrics.

Yang et al. (2001) have presented a discriminative fabric defect detection using adaptive wavelets. The design of such adaptive orthonormal wavelet bases is also adopted by them to achieve the best performance in the characterization of fabric defects. Serdaroglu et. al., (2006) have investigated the detection of fabric defects using the wavelet packet decomposition and independent component analysis (ICA). Fuziwara et al. (2001) have considered the fabric texture as noise and removed using the wavelet shrinkage. However, they have observed that the noise based approach cannot detect defects when there are subtle changes in fabric texture. Siew et al., (1988) have made an assessment of the carpet wear using the spatial Gray Level Dependence Matrix (SGLDM), Gray Level Run Length Matrix (GLRLM). Tsai et. al., (1999) conclude from experiments that the gray level co-occurrence matrix is one of the most popular statistical texture analysis tools for the detection of defects in fabrics. Huart et al. (1994) have employed the classical approaches such as statistical moments (e.g. mean and variance) or parameters for the quick characterization of fabric images. However, the methods based on higher ordered statistics (e.g. co-occurrence matrix (Tsai et. al., 1999), GLRLM, SGLDM) though provide more information but they are entangled in high complexity both in time and memory. The fabric detection system based on co-occurrence matrix by Rosler (1992) can detect defects of size $1mm^2$. For the best performance the angle and distance used in the co-occurrence matrix must conform to the orientation of the fabric pattern and pattern period respectively.

Fractals are ways of characterizing geometries found in nature using mathematical terms and were first introduced by Benoit Mandelbrot. Fractals exhibit self-similarity, i.e. the whole structure is approximately similar in shape to its constituent parts.

In this work, fractal based approaches are investigated for the analysis and detection of defects in fabrics. Traditional approaches like Box-Counting have already been implemented for computation of fractal dimension. This chapter is organized as follows. Section 2 gives an overview of defects in fabrics and Section 3 describes the methodologies applied for extracting features. Section 4 discusses results obtained from the experiment and Section 5 gives the conclusions of the present work.

Overview of Defects in Fabric

Conci and Proença (1998) used Fractal Dimension (FD) to detect fabric defects. They implemented differential box counting method to process large amount of image data. Experimental results suggest 96% accuracy of detection. Stojanovic et al. (2001) developed a fabric inspection system that uses bi-level thresholding for noise removal followed by local averaging to identify eight categories of defects with 86.2% accuracy and 4.3% of false alarm. Huart and Postaire (1994) use threefold strategy to detect the fabric defects. The defects in the weft and warp directions are calculated separately using 1-D pixel data from the line-scan cameras. The defect detection from two separate 1-D signals is achieved by thresholding, whose limit is determined from the defect-free fabric. When a defect in the warp direction (usually long) begins, a short-time alarm is generated so that the defect can be corrected. Mallick-Goswami and Datta (2000) used laser-based morphological operations for the detection of fabric defects. Their approach filters out the periodic structure of fabric in the optical domain. Thus, the morphological operations are performed on periodic images containing defects. However, Detection of fabric defects using fuzzy decision tree the experimental results do not suggest any advantage over other approaches. De Natale (1986) used rank-order functions for the detection of artificially introduced defects in Brodatz textures. Experimental results indicate that the rank distance functions are better than histogram-based approaches for the detection of the fabric defects. Hung and Chen (2001) used back propagation neural network along with the fuzzy logic for the classification of eight types of fabric defects including the defect-free fabric. Zhang et al. (2010) presented a Radial Basis Function (RBF) network improved by Gaussian Mixture Model (GMM) that clusters the feature set and estimates the parameters the of Gaussian RBF for the classification of fabric defects using the features extracted from the grey level arrangement in the neighborhood of each pixel. The raw features are subjected to PCA that takes the between class scatter matrix as its generation matrix to eliminate the features with the same variance. A hybrid approach, that combines the statistical decision theory, multi-scale and multi-directional analysis and Probabilistic Neural Network (PNN), was proposed by Tolba (2011) for the detection of defects in textile fabrics. The statistical features that localise to detect defects are extracted from the log Gabor filter bank responses from the images and these are classified by PNN that helps in the fast defect classification based on their maximum posterior probability. 2.2 Spectral approaches Tsai and Heish (1999) detect defects in the directional textures that exist in the fabrics by using a combination of Discrete Fourier Transform (DFT) and Hough transform. The DFT of the texture shows high-frequency components, which are detected by 1-D Hough transform. To recover the images in the spatial domain Inverse Discrete Fourier

Transform (IDFT) is used. The IDFT preserves only local defects and removes all homogeneous and directional textures. The DFT based approach is not effective in those fabrics in which frequency components of the defective and non-defective textures are highly mixed. Campbell and Murtagh (1998) used a Windowed Fourier Transform (WFT) to detect the defects in denim fabrics. A window of size 16 × 16 pixels is employed to extract amplitude spectrum features using WFT, from the defective and defect-free images, and defects are identified using Neyman–Pearson criterion. Experimental results show that WFT is a better approach than DFT as it is more suitable for local defects. Shu and Tan (2004) conduct detection of defects based on multichannel and multi-scale Gabor filtering by employing the energy response from the convolution of Gabor filter banks in different frequency and orientation domains. The improved Gabor filters are employed by Jing et al. (2011) for the detection of certain flaws in textile fabrics. The filters have two scales and six orientations. The results confirm the satisfied performance and low-computational cost. Hou and Parker (2005) used Support Vector Machines (SVM) along with Gabor wavelet features for detecting defects on textured surfaces. Instead of using all the filters in the Gabor wavelets, an adaptive filter selection scheme is applied to reduce the computational cost on feature extraction while keeping a reasonable detection rate. Sari-Sarraf and Goddard (1999) used low-pass and high-pass 'Daubechies' D2 filters for the detection of defects. Local roughness and global homogeneity are the two measurements that are used to define texture characteristics. Experimental results show that defects with a size of .2 inches can be detected with an overall accuracy of 89%. 2.3 Model-based approaches Cohen et al. (1991) used Gauss Markov Random Field (GMRF) for the detection of defects in fabrics. The GMRF parameters are estimated from the defect-free training samples at a given orientation and scale. For the classification of defective and non-defective textures, test is conducted on Maximum Likelihood Estimate (MLE) of GMRF. Brzakovic et al. (1995) used Poisson's model for the detection of defects. Results show that difference between the estimated and actual measurements from the defect free image is within 10%. Testing between these two measurements is done to detect the fabric defects. Campbell et al. (1997) used a model based clustering to detect the defects in denim fabric. Bayesian Information Criterion (BIC) is used for the detection of defects. A sequence of pre-processing steps such as thresholding, opening, labelling, finding object centroid is done before estimating BIC from the textures. Experimental results show that BIC is a reliable indicator of the presence of defects. Song et al. (1995) used a color clustering scheme for the detection of defects in colored texture images. They used K-means clustering and perceptual merging. Experimental results show that this method works better for the color images. They presented a novel texture descriptor Local Directional Pattern (LDP), which is computed on the edge response values in all eight directions at each pixel position and generate a code from the relative strength magnitude. Texture images can be characterized better with the key features called textons. Some authors utilized Scale Invariant Feature Transform (SIFT) algorithm to generate local features for texture classification. A texton dictionary is built based on the local features. To establish the texton dictionary, an adaptive mean shift clustering algorithm is run with all local features to generate key features (called textons) for texton dictionary. They presented a novel scale and rotation invariant interest point detector and descriptor speeded up Robust Features. The method uses integral images for image convolutions by building on the strengths of the existing detectors and descriptors (specially using a Hessian matrix based measure for the detector, and a distribution-based descriptor), and by simplifying these methods. 2.4 Patterned textile fabrics. The defects in the patterned fabrics are found from the patterned texture decomposed into lattices and motifs.

Methodology

The co-occurrence matrix method of texture description is based on the repeated occurrence of some gray-level configuration in the texture. We are taking a window of size 256 x 256 go on sliding until the completion of the total image which is depicted in Table1.

The texture is measured according to the following formulas.

$$P_0^0, d\left(a, b\right) = |\left\{\left[(k, l), (m, n)\right]\right\} \varepsilon\ D:$$
$$k - m = 0, |l - n| \ (k, l) = a, f\left(m, n\right) = b\} |$$

Here angle between two pixels $\alpha = 0^0$, distance $d = 1$ means all the gray patters at a pixel distances 1 are counted for calculating the frequency count of a particular pattern.

Similarly angles at different orientations are being considered. The Angle positive 135^0 means all the pattern which are lying in the principal Diagonals are being considered

$$P_{45}^0, d\left(a,\ b\right) = |\left\{\left[(k,\ l), (m,\ n)\right]\right\} \varepsilon\ D:$$
$$\left(k - m = d,\ l - n = -d\right)\ OR$$

$$\left(k - m = -d,\ l - n = d\right)\ f\left(k,\ l\right) = a\ f\left(m,\ n\right) = b\} |$$

$$P_{90}^0, d\left(a,\ b\right) = |\left\{\left[(k,\ l), (m,\ n)\right]\right\} \varepsilon\ D:$$
$$|k - m| = d,\ l - n = 0,$$
$$f\left(k,\ l\right) = a,\ f\left(m,\ n\right) = b\} |$$

$$P_{135}^0, d\ \left(a,\ b\right) = |\left\{\left[(k,\ l), (m,\ n)\right]\right\}\ \varepsilon\ D:$$
$$\left(k - m = d, l - n = d\right)\ OR$$
$$\left(k - m = -d, l - n = -d\right),$$
$$f\left(k, l\right) = a, f\left(m, n\right) = b\} |$$

The input image size for the theoretical purpose, the author has chosen the window size as 5 x 5.

```
0  0  0  1  2
1  1  0  1  1
2  2  0  1  1
1  1  0  2  0
0  0  1  0  1
```

P $_{135, 1}$

8	2	1
2	6	2
0	2	0

It is to be noted that P(0,0)=8,P(0,1)=2,P(0,2)=1

P(1,0)=2,P(1,1)6,P(1,2)=2

P(2,1)=2

All other P values of the 256 x 256 size array are zero for 135 degree and distance Equal to 1. Similar case is applied for all other Orientation and distances.

Different parameters to measure texture

- Energy
- Contrast.
- Hanmandlu Entropy Function
- Maximum Probability.
- Inverse Difference Moment

Energy

It is defined as the angular second moment, the more the energy, the image is more homogeneous in the direction Θ.

$$\sum_{a,b} P^2_{\theta,d}(a,b)$$

a, b = gray values.
Θ = direction of scanning.
d = distance between two pixels.

Contrast

$$\sum_{a,b} |a-b|^K P^\lambda_{\theta,d}(a,b)$$

A measure of local image variation.

K = order of moment.

λ = a homogeneous constant

Polynomial Entropy Function

$$I_k = \sum_{10 \leq a,b} \sum_{c,d \leq 200} e^{-\left[a*P(i,j)^\wedge 3 + b*P(i,j)^\wedge 2 + c*P(I,j) + d\right]}$$

Maximum Probability

$$\frac{\max\limits_{a,b} P_{\theta,d}(a,b)}{\sum\limits_{a,b} P_{\theta,d}(a,b)}$$

Table 1. Results of Entropy Function for different values of k

K	A	B	C	d
ent(1)	10	10	10	10
ent(2)	10	10	10	10
ent(3)	10	10	10	10
ent(4)	10	10	10	10
ent(5)	20	20	20	20
ent(6)	50	50	50	50
ent(7)	100	100	100	100
ent(8)	200	200	200	200
ent(9)	20	20	20	20
ent(10)	50	50	50	50
ent(11)	100	100	100	100
ent(12)	200	200	200	200
ent(13)	20	20	20	20
ent(14)	50	50	50	50
ent(15)	100	100	100	100
ent(16)	200	200	200	200
ent(17)	20	20	20	20
ent(18)	50	50	50	50
ent(19)	100	100	100	100
ent(20)	200	200	200	200

0<= a, b<=255

Pattern (a, b) occurs frequently.

Homogenity

$$f_5 = \sum_{i=0}^{255} \sum_{j=0}^{255} \frac{1}{1 + (i-j)^2} P(i,j)$$

Inertia

$$f_6 = \sum_{i=0}^{255} \sum_{j=0}^{255} (i-j)^2 P(i,j)$$

Correlation

$$f_7 = \frac{\sum_{i=0}^{255} \sum_{j=0}^{255} (i-1)(j-1)P(i,j) - \mu_x \mu_y}{\sigma_x \sigma_y}$$

where μ_x, μ_y, σ_x and σ_y are the means and standard deviation of p_x and p_y. p_y is the transpose of p_x.

Defect Detection by Artificial Neural Network

We have got 7 x 4 Haralik features in 4 orientation totals into 28 features. We have got 20 Hanmandulu features, total into (20+28) 48 features. The database for the 48 features is shown in Table2. There are 50 patterns.

The above features selection was done by Hanmandlu, Choudhury & Dash, (2014 & 2016) by using GLCM and Classified by Minimum distance Classifier. We are doing classification by four ANN Techniques i.e. Back propagation, Recurrent Neural Network, earning Vector Quantization and Radial Basis function. In this experiment we have got total 50 tuples having (48 +1) fields.

Defective samples are lying between recno(1) to recno(25). Nice samples are lying between recno (26) to recno (50). Each of the above record contains 48 features. The 49th column contains the class level. The class level -1 (recno(1-25) is for defective samples and +1(26-50) is for nice samples. In the present machine learning expt. Supervised Learning is followed. Recno (1-18 && 26-43) are kept for training the machine. Recno(19-25) && (44-50) are kept for testing the samples.

Figure 1. Feature data base

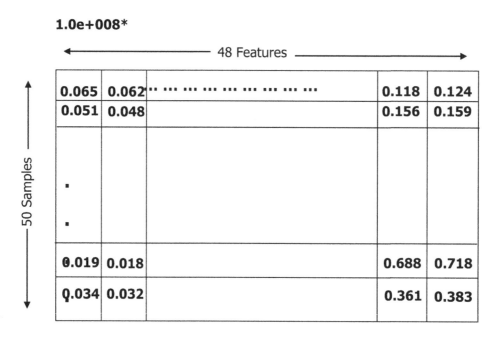

Four types of Artificial Neural Networks are utilized for testing the samples. They are:

1. Backpropagation Algorithm (BPN)
2. Recurrent Neural Algorithm (RNN)
3. Radial basis function Algorithm (RBF)
4. Learning Vector Quantization Algorithm (LVQ)

RESULTS AND DISCUSSION

Results of the classifiers are shown in Table 2. It is evident form Table 2, that RNN gives the best Result in comparison to other classifiers.

Table 2. Classification results

TYPE OF ANN	BNN	RNN	LVQ	RBF
CO-OCCURRENCE MATRIX	90%	96%	85%	60%

CONCLUSION

The above experiments can be extended to multi-class defect detection of fabrics having different types of defects. It will be convenient for detecting a particular defect which occurs frequently.

REFERENCES

Bodnarova, A., Bennamoun, M., & Latham, S. (2002). Optimal gabor filters for textile flaw detection. *Pattern Recognition*, *35*(12), 2973–2991. doi:10.1016/S0031-3203(02)00017-1

Brzakovic, D., & Vujovic, N. (1996). Desiging defect classification systems: A case study. *Pattern Recognition*, *29*(8), 1401–1419. doi:10.1016/0031-3203(95)00166-2

Bu, H., Wang, J., & Huang, X. (2009). Fabric defect detection based on multiple fractal features and support vector data description. *Engineering Applications of Artificial Intelligence*, *22*(2), 224–235. doi:10.1016/j.engappai.2008.05.006

Campbell, J.G., Hashim, A. A., & Murtagh, F.D. (1997). *Flaw Detection in Woven Textiles using Space-dependent Fourier Transform*. University of Ulster, Faculty of Informatics, Magee College, 8, Preprint INFM-97-004.

Cohen, F. S., Fan, Z., & Attali, S. (1991). Automated inspection of textile fabric using textural models. *IEEE Transactions on Pattern Analysis and Machine Intelligence*, *13*(8), 803–808. doi:10.1109/34.85670

Conci, A., & Proenca, C. B. (1998). A fractal image analysis system for fabric inspection based on a box-counting method. *Computer Networks and ISDN Systems*, *30*(20-21), 1887–1895. doi:10.1016/S0169-7552(98)00211-6

De Natale, F. G. B. (1986). Article. *International Journal of Pattern Recognition and Artificial Intelligence*, *10*(8).

Escofet, J., Navarro, R., Millan, M. S., & Pladelloreans, J. (1998). Detection of local defects in textiles webs using Gabor filters. *Optical Engineering (Redondo Beach, Calif.)*, *37*(8), 2297–2307. doi:10.1117/1.601751

Fujiwara, Y., Mori, K., Fujii, Y., Sawada, Y., & Okumura, S. (2001). Measurement of surface roughness of coated wood by laser scanning. *Proc. on the 15th Wood Machining Seminar*.

Hanmandlu, M., Choudhury, D., & Dash, S. (2015). Detection of defects in fabrics using topothesy fractal dimension features. *Signal Image and Video Processing*, *9*(7), 1521–1530. doi:10.1007/s11760-013-0604-5

Hanmandlu, M., Choudhury, D., & Dash, S. (2016). Detection of Fabric Defects using Fuzzy Decision Trees. *International Journal of Signal and Imaging Systems Engineering*, *9*(3), 184–198. doi:10.1504/IJSISE.2016.076230

Huart, J., & Postaire, J. G. (1994). Integration of computer vision onto weavers for quality control in the textile industry. *Proc. SPIE Mach. Vis. Appl. Ind. Insp., 2183*, 155–163. doi:10.1117/12.171205

Hung, C. C., & Chen, I. C. (2001). Article. *Textile Research Journal, 71*(3), 220–224. doi:10.1177/004051750107100306

Jing, J., Zhang, H., Wang, J., Li, P., & Jia, J. (2013). Fabric defect detection using Gabor filters and defect classification based on LBP and Tamura method. *Journal of the Textile Institute, 104*(1), 18–27. doi:10.1080/00405000.2012.692940

Jonathan, G. C., & Fionn, M. (1998). Automatic visual inspection of woven textiles using a two-stage defect detector. *Optical Engineering (Redondo Beach, Calif.), 37*(9), 2536–2542. doi:10.1117/1.601692

Kim, S., Lee, M. H., & Woo, K. B. (1998). Wavelet Analysis to defects detection in weaving processes. *Proc. IEEE Int. Symp. Industrial Electronics*, 3, 1406-1409.

Krueger, V., & Sommer, G. (2000), Gabor wavelet network for object representation. *DAGM Symposium*, 13–15.

Kumar, A. (2008). (2008), Computer vision –based fabric defect detection: A syrvetm IEEE. *Transactions on Industrial Electronics, 55*(1), 348–363. doi:10.1109/TIE.1930.896476

Kumar, A., & Pang, G. (2002). Defect detection in textured materials using optimized filters. *IEEE Transactions on Systems, Man, and Cybernetics, 32*(5), 553–570. doi:10.1109/TSMCB.2002.1033176 PMID:18244861

Kumar, A., & Pang, G. K. H. (2002). Defect Detection in Textured Materials Using Gabor Filters. *IEEE Transactions on Industry Applications, 38*(2), 425–440. doi:10.1109/28.993164

Li, P., Zhang, H., Jing, J., Li, R., & Zhao, J. (2015). Fabric defect detection based on multi-scale wavelet transform and Gaussian mixture model method. *Journal of the Textile Institute, 106*(6), 587–592. doi:10.1080/00405000.2014.929790

Mallick-Goswami, B., & Datta, A. K. (2000). Detecting defects in fabric with laser-based morphological image processing. *Textile Research Journal, 70*(9), 758–762. doi:10.1177/004051750007000902

Özdemir, S., & Erçil, A. (1996). Markov random fields and Karhunen-Loève transforms for defect inspection of textile products. *Proceedings of IEEE Emerging Technologies and Factory Automation Conference (EFTA)*, 2, 697-703.

Rosler, R. N. U. (1992). Defect detection in fabrics by image processing. *Melliand Texilber., 73*, 635–636.

Sari-Sarraf, H., & Goddard, J. S. (1999). Goddard Vision system for on-loom fabric inspection. *IEEE Transactions Industry Application*. Available: http://www.ieeexplore.ieee.org/stamp/stamp.jsp?arnumber=00806035

Schiffaueroval, A., & Thomson, V. (2006). A review of research on cost of quality models and best practices. *International Journal of Quality & Reliability Management, 23*(4).

Selvaraj, A., Ganesan, L., & Bama, S. (2006). Fault segmentation in fabric images using Gabor wavelet transform. *Machine Vision and Applications, 16*(6), 356–363. doi:10.1007/s00138-005-0007-x

Serdaroglu, Ertuzun, A., & Ercil, A. (2006). Defect Detection in Textile Fabric Images Using Wavelet Transforms and Independent Component Analysis. *Pattern Recognition and Image Analysis, 16*(1), 61–64.

Shu, Y., & Tan, Z. (2004). Fabric defects automatic detection using gabor filters. *Intelligent Control and Automation, WCICA 2004. Fifth World Congress on IEEE, 4*, 3378-3380.

Siew, L. H., Hodgson, R. M., & Wood, E. J. (1988). Texture measures for carpet wear assessment. *IEEE Transactions on Pattern Analysis and Machine Intelligence, 10*(6), 92–105. doi:10.1109/34.3870

Song, K. Y., Petrou, M., & Kittler, J. (1995). Texture crack detection. *Machine Vision and Applications, 8*(1), 63–76. doi:10.1007/BF01213639

Srinivasan, K., Dastoor, P. H., Radhakrishnaiah, P., & Jayaraman, S. (1992). FDAS: A knowledge-based framework for analysis of defects in woven textile structures. *J. Textile Inst., 83*(3), 431–1448.

Stojanovic, R., Mitropulis, P., Koulamas, C., Karayiannis, Y., Koubias, S., & Papadopoulos, G. (2000). An Approach for Automated Defect Detection and Neural Classification of Web Textile Fabric. *Machine Graphics and Vision, 9*(3), 587–607.

Sylla, C. (n.d.). Experimental investigation of human and machine –vision arrangements in inspection tasks. *Control Engineering Practice,* 10(3), 347-361.

Tolba, A. S. (2011). Fast defect detection in homogeneous flat surface products. Expert Systems with Appl. *International Journal (Toronto, Ont.), 38*(10), 12339–12347.

Tsai, D.-M., & Hsieh, C.-Y. (1999). Automated surface inspection for directional textures. *Image and Vision Computing, 18*(1), 49–62. doi:10.1016/S0262-8856(99)00009-8

Zhang, Y., Lu, Z., & Li, J. (2010). Fabric defect classification using radial basis function network. *Pattern Recognition Letters, 31*(13), 2033–2042. doi:10.1016/j.patrec.2010.05.030

Zhen, H., & Parker, J. M. (2005). *Texture Defect Detection Using Support Vector Machines with Adaptive Gabor Wavelet Features, Application of Computer Vision, WACV/MOTIONS '05* (Vol. 1). Seventh IEEE Workshops.

Zhi, Y. X., Pang, G. K. H., & Yung, N. H. C. (2001). Fabric defect detection using adaptive wavelet. *Icassp, Ieee International Conference On Acoustics, Speech And Signal Processing - Proceedings, 6,* 3697-3700.

Chapter 15

A Holistic–Based Multi–Criterion Decision–Making Approach for Solving Engineering Sciences Problem Under Imprecise Environment

Syed Abou Iltaf Hussain
NIT Agartala, India

Sankar Prasad Mondal
Midnapore College (Autonomous), India

Uttam Kumar Mandal
NIT Agartala, India

ABSTRACT

Multi-Criteria Decision Making has evolved as an important tool for taking some of the most important decisions in the today's hi-tech engineering world. But due to some reasons like measurement difficulty, lack of data, faulty instruments, etc., or due to lack of absolute information about the topic, alternatives present and the criteria, decision making becomes very difficult as all parameter for modeling a decision making problem are not precise. In such scenario the importance of one with respect to the others are represented in terms of linguistic factor. Such cases could be tackled by considering the problem in fuzzy environment. In this chapter, the different hybrid fuzzy MCDM techniques are shown along with their application in different engineering problems. One problem is randomly selected and solved using different fuzzy MCDM techniques and compared the result with the existing literature.

DOI: 10.4018/978-1-5225-2857-9.ch015

1. INTRODUCTION

1.1. Fuzzy MCDM

In engineering, MCDM has become one of the major tools of decision making in a scenario where decision makers have to take a decision which is guided by various criteria. Due to different reasons some known and some unknown, modelling by MCDM for decision making problem are not precise. One of the major reasons for this impreciseness is the lack of concrete rule for converting linguistic terms into quantitative values. In such case we can take the help of fuzzy set theory. Hybrid fuzzy-MCDM models are applied in different engineering fields such as reliability engineering, robotics, scheduling, manufacturing, etc. (Kumar and Gag, 2010; KeshavarzGhorabaee et al., 2015a, 2015c; Amiri et al., 2014), machine selection (Kemal Vatansever and YiğitKazançoğlu, 2014), selection of machining tools etc.

1.2. Motivation of the Chapter

Decision making theory is very important for engineering science problem. When some complication comes to some model or problem, then there we have to take multi criteria decision, in other words the problem belongs to MCDM problem. For practical point of view some of the parameter or some conditions may not be precisely known. For that cases, we have to consider impreciseness. Fuzzy set theory is one of the tool to define such impreciseness. Our main aim is to discuss how MCDM problem behave in fuzzy environment, also how can we solve the problem. In engineering sciences, the fuzzy MCDM problem play an important role, how it works.

1.3. Novelties

A lot of works on fuzzy MCDM have been done over the globe by different researchers and scientists. Yet a lot of work still has to be done in this field. In our chapter, we try to find some new links and some new result, comparison of results with different examples is as follows:

1. How fuzzy set theory are considered for measuring the uncertainty.
2. How MCDM problem is different with fuzzy MCDM problem.
3. Comparison between different fuzzy MCDM techniques.
4. Application of fuzzy MCDM techniques in engineering sciences.

1.4. Structure of the Chapter

The organization of the paper is as follows. In the first section, it is an introduction to the chapter followed by motivation which led to the selection of the particular topic and novelties. The second section consists of basic concept of the MCDM and fuzzy set theory and their application in the engineering science problem. The second section also contains different types of environment. Section 3 and section 4 contains different types of fuzzy MCDM models and the models are used for solving a problem respectively which is further compared with the existing literature in section 4. Section 5 is the conclusion part of the chapter.

2. PRELIMINARIES

2.1. Basic Concept of MCDM

Definition 2.1.a: Decision is defined as the final submission or the conclusion reached after consideration.
Definition 2.1.b: In cognitive science, selection of an action or a belief from a set of alternatives is called Decision Making.

Selecting an action from a set of alternatives by considering various criteria effecting the judgement either to the same or different extent is called Multi-Criteria Decision Making. In MCDM, set of alternatives are the available possibilities or the choices from which the best possibility is to be selected by considering different factors influencing the outcome. Ranking of the alternative is done in ascending order starting from the best to the worst alternative. The alternatives are ranked in on the basis of some factors influencing the results. These factors are called Criteria. Criterion is defined as the factors on the basis of which a decision is taken. In MCDM, there is a number of criterion. Each criterion effects the final judgement either to the same or different extent.

2.2. Steps Involved In Decision Making

2.2.1. GOFER Method for Taking Decision

In 1980s psychologist Leon Mann and his colleagues have developed a method named GOFER for decision making. GOFER[1] is an acronym for five decision-making steps.

G – Goal: What is the ultimate objective?
O – Options: Collecting all the options available.
F – Facts: Looking for fact and information.
E – Effect: How the options are effected?
R – Review: Reviewing the different facts related to the options.

2.2.2. DECIDE Method for Taking Decision

Kristina Guo (2008) developed another method of decision making named as DECIDE. DECIDE model of decision making consists of six parts:

D: Defining the problem.
E: Establishing all the criteria or factors on which basis decision is to be made.
C: Collecting different alternatives among which the best alternative is to be selected.
I: Identify the best alternative from the sets of alternative.
D: Developing a plan of action for choosing the best alternative.
E: Evaluation of the result or choosing the best alternative.

In both the models, steps for decision making are the same and both provide the concept of making decision for a MCDM.

2.2.3. Working Principle

All of the MCDM techniques have some common working principles which are as follows:

1. Selection of criteria:
   a. All the criteria must be related to the alternatives.
   b. The criteria must be well-organized with the decision.
   c. The criteria must be of some importance either equally or not.
   d. The criteria must be independent of each other.
2. Selection of Alternatives:
   a. The alternatives selected must be real.
   b. The selected alternatives should be available.
3. Selection of method to provide weightage to the criteria:
   a. Outranking method - The outranking relation is built through a series of pairwise comparisons of the alternatives.
   b. Compensatory method – Method where strengths and abilities are emphasized over the weakness.

2.3. Classification of MCDM

MCDM is a sub-group of Operation Research that only considers multiple criteria in decision making environments. MCDM is broadly classified into two groups:

2.3.1. Multi-Objective Decision Making (MODM)

MODM approach concentrates decision making in continuous decision space for getting the best solution. In a set of given conflicting objectives MODM searches for the best possible solution. Multi-Objective Decision Making problem is used to design the optimal solution through mathematical modelling. Linear Programming Problem is an example of MODM.

2.3.2. Multi-Attribute Decision Making (MADM)

MADM approach concentrates decision making in discrete decision space for getting the best solution. According to Zimmermann, 1987 MADM problem can be associated with a problem of choice or ranking of the existing alternatives. Some of the MADM techniques are Analytical Hierarchy Process (AHP), Analytical Network Process (ANP), PROMETHEE, ELECTRE, VIKOR, COPRAS etc. The MADM methods usually considers the fact that all the criteria and the weights are expressed in crisp values for appropriate rating and ranking of the alternatives without any difficulty.

MCDM methods are also classified on the basis of the method used to give weightage to the criteria. On such basis MCDM is classified as:

2.3.3. Compensatory Method

A compensatory decision making method involves the concept of "trading off" good and bad attributes of an object. For example, a motorcycle may have a high price and low mileage but high acceleration and good looks. Another motorcycle with low price, good mileage but acceleration with similar looks then the second motorcycle is mostly preferred over the first on as the second motorcycle is more economical than the first one.

2.3.4. Outranking Method

The outranking relation is built through a series of pairwise comparisons of the alternatives. At a time two alternatives are considered and both of them are compared with each other. Although pairwise comparison is done in a lot of ways but the concept of concordance-discordance is widely considered. According to the concept of concordance-discordance an alternative α is better than the alternative β when

1. Majority of the attributes support the assertion.
2. Minority or opposition of the other attributes is not too strong.

2.4. Fuzzy Set and Fuzzy Logic

2.4.1. Fuzzy Logic

Fuzzy logic is a form of many-valued logic which is implemented to take care of the situation where decisions have to be taken in a fuzzy environment. Decision making in fuzzy environment is meant a decision made in an environment where the boundaries of the goals and (or) constraints are not sharply defined. In Fuzzy logic, the truth values of variables may be any real number between 0 and 1. Fuzzy logic concept is more an approximate rather than exact. The importance of fuzzy logic derives from the fact that most modes of human reasoning and especially common sense reasoning are approximate in nature. Some of the characteristics of the fuzzy logic are as follows:

1. Fuzzy logic is more an approximate case rather than exact case.
2. In fuzzy logic, everything is a matter of degree.
3. All the types of logic system can be fuzzified.

2.4.2. Fuzzy Sets

Fuzzy set was first introduced in the year 1965 by Lotfi A. Zadeh and Dieter Klaua. Fuzzy set theory is a set with a smooth or not sharply defined boundary. It generalizes the notion of membership from a black and white binary categorization in classical set theory into one that allows partial membership. The notion of membership in fuzzy sets thus become a matter of degree, which is a number between 0 and 1. A membership degree of 0 represents complete false or complete non-membership whereas a membership degree of 1 represents complete true or complete membership. Mathematically, a fuzzy set is characterized by a mapping from universe of discourse into the interval [0,1]. This mapping is the membership function of the set. Usually, the membership or characteristic function is denoted by the letter μ.

2.4.3. Representation of Fuzzy Sets

Fuzzy sets can be represented in two different ways. The first way is by listing membership values of the elements in the set and the second way is by defining the membership function mathematically.

Representing a fuzzy set by listing membership values of the elements in the set is possible only if the set is discrete. In a continuous fuzzy set has infinite number of elements. Generally, a fuzzy set A can be defined through enumeration using the expression

$$A = \frac{\sum_i \left(\mu_A x_i \right)}{x_i}$$

In the expression the summation operator refers to the union operation and the notation $\frac{\mu_A x_i}{x_i}$ refers to a fuzzy set containing exactly one (partial) element x with a membership function μ_A. Those elements x_i, whose membership function degree is equal to zero are not considered.

The second way of representing a fuzzy set is defining the membership function mathematically. In fuzzy sets there are six membership functions:

1. **Triangular Membership Function:** A triangular membership function is defined as follows:

$$Triangle; \left(\mu : a, b, c \right) = \begin{cases} \dfrac{x - a}{b - a}; a \leq x \leq b \\ \qquad 1; x = b \\ \dfrac{c - x}{c - b}; b \leq x \leq c \\ \qquad 0; otherwise \end{cases}$$

where [a, b, c] are parameters.

2. **Trapezoidal Membership Function:** Trapezoidal membership function is defined as:

$$Trapezoidal; \left(\mu : a, b, c, d \right) = \begin{cases} \dfrac{x-a}{b-a}; a \leq x \leq b \\ 1; b \leq x \leq c \\ \dfrac{d-x}{d-c}; c \leq x \leq d \\ 0; otherwise \end{cases}$$

where [a, b, c, d] are parameters.

3. **Gaussian Membership Function**: Gaussian membership function is defined as:

$$Gaussian; \left(\mu : m, \sigma \right) = \exp \left[-\dfrac{\left(x-m \right)^2}{\sigma^2} \right]$$

where m and σ denotes the centre and width of the function respectively.

4. **Bell-shaped Membership Function:** Bell-shaped membership function is defined as:

$$Bell; \left(\mu : a, b, c \right) = \dfrac{1}{1 + \left| \dfrac{x-c}{a} \right|^{2b}}$$

where [a, b, c] are parameters and the parameter b is usually positive.

5. **Sigmoidal Membership Function:** Sigmoidal Membership Function is defined as:

$$Sigma; \left(\mu : a, c \right) = \dfrac{1}{1 + e^{-a \left(x-c \right)}}$$

where [a, c] are parameters.

6. **S Membership Function:** S Membership Function is defined as:

$$S;(\mu:a,b) = \begin{cases} 0; x < a \\ 2.\left(\dfrac{x-a}{b-a}\right)^2; a \leq x \leq \dfrac{a+b}{2} \\ 1-2.\left(\dfrac{x-a}{b-a}\right)^2; \dfrac{a+b}{2} \leq x \leq b \\ 1; x \geq b \end{cases}$$

where [a, b] are parameters. The S membership function curve is a smooth curve. The membership value is 0 for points below a, 1 for points above b and 0.5 for points in between a and b.

2.5. Application of Fuzzy Set Theory in Engineering Sciences Problem

In 1965, Zadeh introduced fuzzy set theory to represent uncertainty in human cognitive process. Later it was applied to solve different problems of the real world in engineering, business, medical, management, finance and many other fields. Over the years fuzzy set theory has been recognized as an important problem modelling and solution technique. A summary of the applications of fuzzy set theory by different researchers are listed.

A lot of literatures are available for application of fuzzy set theory in the engineering science. Some of the works which shows general application of fuzzy set theory were that of Gaines and Kohout (1977), Kandel and Yager (1979), Kandel (1986), and Kaufmann and Gupta (1988). In the year 1983, Zimmerman and Lai and Hwang (1994) reviewed the application of fuzzy set theory in operation research and MCDM. In 1985, Maiers and Sherif reviewed the application of fuzzy set theory in industrial controllers and its application on decision making, economics, engineering and nine other subject areas. Karwowski and Evans (1986) were successful in applying fuzzy set theory in different topics of production engineering and management topics like new product development, facilities design and layout, production scheduling and control, inventory management, quality and cost benefit analysis. According to Karwowski and Evans,the key reason why fuzzy set theory is relevant to production management is because of research imprecision and vagueness, incomplete information and personal bias and subjective opinion.

It is very difficult to review all published works on hybrid fuzzy set theory application in engineering sciences problem. Few works are review as follows:

1   McCahon and Lee (1990), studied the job sequencing problem where job processing times were represented with fuzzy numbers. In the model developed by McCahon and Lee the traditional algorithm was modified to accept triangular and trapezoidal fuzzy processing times. In the model make span and mean flow is used for measuring the performance criteria of the work. In 1992, McCahon and Lee modified the job sequencing heuristic method to accept fuzzy processing time. The job processing times were defined by the triangular fuzzy numbers which were further used in n job and m workstation environment. In the model make span and mean flow is used for measuring the performance criteria of the work. Make span and mean flow time are used to compare alternative sequences and to interpret the impact of the fuzzy processing times on job completion time, flow time and make span.

2. Bhattacharya et al. (1992), developed a fuzzy goal programming model for selecting a single facility location within a given convex region subject by considering three criteria: (i) maximizing the minimum distances required to cover to avail the facility; (ii) minimizing the maximum distances from the facilities to the demand points; and (iii) minimizing the sum of all transportation costs.

3. Chakraborty (1992, 1994), studied the problem of designing single stage. The main aim of the model is to minimize average total inspection subject to a constraint based on the lot tolerance percent defective (LTPD) and the level of consumer's risk. His model developed consists of triangular fuzzy numbers. Dodge-Romig LTPD sampling plans when the lot tolerance percent defective, consumer's risk and incoming quality level are modeled using triangular fuzzy numbers.

4. Gen et al. (1992), developed a fuzzy multiple objective aggregate planning model. The model is used as a fuzzy multiple objective programming model. In the model, objective function coefficients, technological coefficients, and resource right-hand side values are represented by triangular fuzzy numbers. The fuzzy multiple objective aggregate planning models is transformed into crisp model by some kind of transformation procedure. The main aim of the model is to minimize total production costs, inventory costs and changes in the work force level.

5. Ishii et al. (1992), studied the scheduling of jobs under two shop configurations when job due dates are modelled using fuzzy numbers. They developed two models. The aim of the first model is to determine the optimal speed of each machine and an optimal schedule with respect to an objective function consisting of the minimum degree of satisfaction among all jobs and costs of machine speed. The aim of the second model is to develop a schedule that minimizes the maximum job lateness.

6. Ishikawa et al. (1993), proposed the New Fuzzy Delphi Method (NFDM) overcoming the disadvantages in the traditional and fuzzy Delphi methods. The NFDM has the following advantages: (i) fuzziness is inescapably incorporated in the Delphi findings; (ii) the number of rounds in the Delphi is reduced; (iii) the semantic structure of forecast items is refined; and (iv) the individual attributes of the expert are clarified. The NFDM consists of two methodologies: the Min-Max Delphi Method, and the Fuzzy Delphi Method via Fuzzy Integration. The Max-Min Delphi Method involves the opinion of experts on the data, pursues the accuracy of the forecast from the standpoint of an interval representing possibility and impossibility, and identifies the cross point as the most attainable period. The Fuzzy Delphi Method via Fuzzy Integration employs the expertise of each expert as a fuzzy measure and identifies a point estimate as the most attainable period by the fuzzy integration of each membership function.

7. Zhang and Huang (1994), used fuzzy logic to model selecting the process plan problem. The main objectives of the model are imprecise and conflicting. Fuzzy membership functions are used to evaluate the contribution of competing process plans to shop floor performance objectives. The optimal process plan for each part is determined by the solution of a fuzzy integer programming model.

8. Wang and Chen (1995), developed a hybrid fuzzy-heuristic mathematical programming model for the economic design of statistical control charts. To minimize the expected lost cost per hour of operation is the main objective of the model.

9. Shipley et al. (1996), incorporate fuzzy logic and fuzzy probability distributions along with belief functions and extension principles and developed the fuzzy PERT algorithm, called 'Belief in Fuzzy Probabilities of EstimateTime' (BIFPET). BIFPET is used to determine the project critical

path and expected project completion time. In the paper authors used triangular fuzzy numbers are used to define activity durations.

10. Song and Chissom (1993), proposed a fuzzy time series modelling and applied in a dynamic process and on historical data that are fuzzy set linguistic values. Song and Chissom also developed two fuzzy time series modelsout of whichone is time-variant and other is time-invariant. A seven-step procedure is outlined for conducting a forecast using the time-invariant fuzzy time series model. In 1993, Song and Chissom applied a first order, time-invariant time series model based on twenty years of historical data to forecast enrollments of the University of Alabama. The data was fuzzified and the corresponding linguistic values ranged from "not many" to "too many". The seven-step procedure is used for fuzzy data, develop the time series model, and calculate and interpret the output.

2.6. Application of MCDM in Engineering Science Problem

A lot of literatures are available where the researchers have used fuzzy set theory along with the MCDM problems for solving the engineering problems. The earliest application of fuzzy MCDM known was in the year 1970 by Bellman and R. Zadeh (1970) in their research paper "Decision Making in Fuzzy Environment". After the application done by Bellman and Zadeh in 1970, fuzzy MCDM techniques became one of the major tools for decision making in a fuzzy environment. Yager et al (1984) suggested a methodology of converting the linguistic terms or the qualitative into quantitative values. In their research paper the methodology used converted the information obtained from market survey to predict the values of linguistic variables. Cheng and Mon (1994) applied fuzzy Analytical Hierarchy Process (AHP) for weapon selection. Cheng and Chan (1994) applied fuzzy MCDM techniques to the selection of technology transfer strategies in the area of biotechnology management. Yager et al (1994), constructed a model to best aggregate the respondents' answers to the questions on economic conditions as a predictor of their purchasing a house, car etc. As a result of this process the authors have come to the best predictor of the home purchases was consumers who rated three economic conditions as good, while the best predictor of car purchases was consumers who rated only two economic conditions as good. In the field of machine selection, according to Alberti et. al. (2011) one of the most frequent problems faced by different companies is the selection of the appropriate machine tool because improper selection of machine tool may lead to low quality product which further affects the company image and reputation. The speed, cost of production of an item and quality of an item is largely effected by the proper machine tool selection (Arslan et. al. 2004; Ayağ and Özdemir, 2006). For proper selection of machine tools when it is guided by so much of criteria is a MCDM problem. A mostly used MCDM technique in the selection of machine tool is the Analytical Hierarchy Process (AHP). In the year 2004, an integrated AHP/ANP methodology was proposed by Yurdakul for machine selection decision in accordance with product strategies. Fuzzy AHP and cost-benefit ratio analysis was used by Ayağ and Özdemir (2006) for the machine selection problem. Fuzzy AHP method was also used by Çimren et.al. in the year 2007. Duran and Aquila (2008) dveloped a fuzzy AHP approach to computer aided machine selection decisions. In the year 2008, Önüt et al. computed the criteria weights using fuzzy AHP and ranked the alternatives usıng the fuzzy TOPSIS. Gopalkrishnan et al (2004) develop a decision support system for machining centre selection which was further developed by İç and Yurdakul (2009) where they used fuzzy AHP and fuzzy TOPSIS or the purpose. Taha and Rostam (2011) employed fuzzy AHP and Artificial Neural Networks for machine selection decisions for flexible manufacturing cells. Mishra et.al. (2006) applied a new type of fuzzy goal programming model called Quick Converging Simulated Annealing (QCSA) method for machine selection. In 2010, Tuzkaya et al developed a fuzzy PROMETHEE model to evaluate alternatives for material handling equipment. In his model, he weighted the criteria using the fuzzy ANP model. Prego and Rangone (1998) compared linguistic variable concepts based on linguistic models, fuzzy goal theory and pairwise comparison based on fuzzy hierarchical models for advanced manufacturing technologies selection.

Fuzzy based MCDM method is used in a lot of engineering problems. Keramati et al. (2013) evaluated the risk of customer relationship management (CRM) projects by using fuzzy AHP. Yeh et al. (2014) presented a new hybrid multi-criteria decision-making model to determine critical factors in new-product development based on fuzzy DEMATEL and fuzzy AHP. In 2005, Peldschus and Zavadskas proposed a new multi-criteria decision-making method for evaluating and selecting water supply resources which was based on fuzzy sets and matrix games. Wadhwa et al. (2009) proposed a fuzzy set based multi-criteria decision-making model for determining a suitable reverse manufacturing option. The proposed model is also capable of designing effective and efficient flexible return policy with respect to various criteria. Lin et al. (2010) proposed a fuzzy analytic hierarchy process method which can be used as an analytical tool for determining the competitive marketing strategy for a small tourism venture. Liou et al. (2011) developed a new hybrid MCDM model based on the DEMATEL and analytic network process (ANP) methods for selection of an outsourcing provider. In 2011, Nieto-Morote and Ruz-Vila developed a fuzzy AHP method which considers both quantitative as well as qualitative criteria in the decision-making process and applied it in evaluation of cooling, heating, and power production systems. Su (2011) developed a hybrid fuzzy multi-criteria group decision-making (MCGDM) method based on the VlsekriterijumskaOptimizacija I KompromisnoResenje (VIKOR) method and grey relational analysis (GRA). They applied the tool for problems in reverse logistic management Wang et al. (2012) developed a MCGDM method in fuzzy environment to determine the weights when complete information is not available. Kim and Chung (2013) proposed a fuzzy VIKOR approach for computing the vulnerability of the water supply to climate change and variability in South Korea. Tanselİç et al. (2013) developed a decision support system which was named as ROBSEL for two-phase robot selection. For the development of ROBSEL, a set of criteria and the fuzzy AHP were used to obtain the best alternative. In 2013, Roshandel et al. used a hierarchical fuzzy TOPSIS for evaluation of suppliers and selecting the best alternative among the different alternatives in a production industry. Vinodh et al. (2013) developed a fuzzy VIKOR method for evaluation and selection of the best concept in an agile environment. Moghimi and Anvari (2014) developed an integrated fuzzy AHP and fuzzy TOPSIS methods for evaluation of the financial performance of Iranian cement manufacturing companies. Rezaie et al. (2014) proposed a fuzzy VIKOR method to evaluate performance of cement manufacturing companies and thereby compare the result with the result obtained by Moghimi and Anvari. Mehlawat and Gupta (2015) proposed a new fuzzy MCGDM method for determining the critical path in a project network. Sangaiah et al. (2015) developed a fuzzy approach by integrating the Decision-Making Trial and Evaluation Laboratory Model (DEMATEL) and TOPSIS model to evaluate partnership quality and team service climate aspects with respect to the global software development project outcomes.

In the recent a lot of applications of fuzzy MCDM were seen in various fields ranging from engineering to economics, medical science to different mathematical fields. Abdulla and Jamal (2010) conducted an experiment of converting the linguistic judgement of over the health related problematic status of elderly people. Zakaria et al (2012), developed fuzzy programming to investigate the relationship between variables that impacting car sales volume.

In the recent trend, researchers have shifted their interest from interval type-1fuzzy based MCDM to interval type-2 fuzzy sets based MCDM for making decision. Chen and Lee (2010) proposed a new ranking method for interval type-2 fuzzy sets and used it in a new fuzzy MCDM method. Chen et al further developed the in 2012. Celik et al. (2013) developed fuzzy TOPSIS and fuzzy GRA to evaluate and improve customer satisfaction in Istanbul public transportation. They used fuzzy interval type-2 for the purpose. Chen et al. (2013) developed a method for handling multi-criteria decision-making problems in the context of the interval type-2 fuzzy sets which he named as QUALIFLEX (QUALItative FLEX-ible). In 2013, Hu et al. proposed a new ranking method which was based on the possibility degree for interval type-2 fuzzy sets and applied it in multi-criteria decision-making process. In 2014, Abdullah and Najib proposed a fuzzy AHP method and interval type-2 fuzzy sets and evaluated for work safety. Celik et al. (2014) developed a fuzzy MCDM method based on interval type-2 fuzzy sets for identifying and evaluating critical success factors for humanitarian relief logistics management. Kahraman et al., 2014) developed a ranking method and applied it for developing an AHP method with interval type-2 fuzzy sets. In 2014, Keshavarz Ghorabaee et al developed an interval type-2 fuzzy sets based COPRAS (Complex Proportional ASsessment) method to evaluate suppliers in a supply chain. In 2015, Dymova et al. used alpha cuts to extend the interval type-2 fuzzy sets based TOPSIS method for multi-criteria decision-making. Chen (2015) proposed a new likelihood-based outranking comparison approach with interval type-2 fuzzy PROMETHEE method. Keshavarz Ghorabaee (2015) introduced a new interval type-2 fuzzy VIKOR method to evaluate and select industrial robots. In the same year Keshavarz Ghorabaee used his model for project selection. Kiliç and Kaya (2015) proposed a type-2 fuzzy AHP and type-2 fuzzy TOPSIS methods for evaluating investment projects. Wang et al. (2015) introduced a new fuzzy multi-criteria decision-making likelihood-based QUALIFLEX method in context with interval type-2 fuzzy sets.

2..7. Uncertainty in MCDM Problem

Decision making is very important for engineering sciences problem. For modeling a real-world situation, the values or information of various parameters are not precisely known. So, in order to tackle scenario of incomplete information the concept of impreciseness is introduced. Similarly, for multi criteria group decision making problem uncertainty is an important theme. Now the problem is that how can we measure the uncertainty. There exists different concept to define the uncertainties or impreciseness. In this paper, we solve a hybrid MCGDM problem in parametric intuitionistic interval type uncertainty.

Sahoo et al. (2015) consider Reliability optimization with and low level redundancies with interval environment and solved with the help of genetic algorithm. Pal and Mahapatra (2013) represent the interval number in two parametric form and finds its all arithmetic operation. Karmakar and Bhunia (2013) solved uncertain constrained optimization by interval- oriented algorithm. Pal et al. (2013) take a bio economic model associated with pre-predator with interval biological parameter. Bhunia and Samanta (2014) describe a study of interval metric and its application in multi-objective optimization with interval objectives. Karmakar et al. (2008) take interval oriented multi-section techniques for global optimization. Rao and Berke (1997) deduced uncertain parameter by interval number in engineering analysis/design problems. Kulpa et al. (1998) described interval analysis in mechanical engineering. Oppenheimer and Michel (1988, 1988, 1988) proposed a basic interval analysis of linear electrical systems. Kolev (1993) used interval methods for circuit analysis. Shaocheng and Hladik (1994) apply the interval-number in linear programming problem.

3. DIFFERENT FUZZY MCDM TECHNIQUES

In different literature, a lot of fuzzy MCDM techniques have been modelled which are further applied in different engineering problems to solve and validate the results. Some of the different fuzzy MCDM techniques are as follows:

3.1. Fuzzy Analytical Hierarchy Process (FAHP)

FAHP uses the basic concept of AHP. Since traditional AHP does not include vagueness for personal judgments, it has been improved by involving the concept fuzzy logic approach. In FAHP, the pair wise comparisons of both criteria and the alternatives are performed through the linguistic variables, which are represented by triangular numbers (2011). One of the first appliers of FAHP is van Laarhoven and Pedrycz (1983). They defined the triangular membership functions for the pair wise comparisons. Then, Buckley (1985) has contributed to the FAHP by determining the fuzzy priorities of comparison ratios having triangular membership functions. Chang (1996) also developed a new method related with the usage of triangular numbers in pair-wise comparisons. Buckley's method is implemented to determine the relative importance weights for both the criteria and the alternatives. The steps to calculate FAHP are as follows (2013):

Step 1: Decision Maker compares the criteria or alternatives via linguistic terms (presented in Table 1).

Table 1. Linguistic terms and corresponding fuzzy numbers (Assumption)

Satty Scale	Satty Fuzzy Scale	Definition	Triangular Fuzzy Numbers
1	$\tilde{1}$	Equally Important	(1, 1, 1)
3	$\tilde{3}$	Weakly Important	(2, 3, 4)
5	$\tilde{5}$	Fairly Important	(4, 5, 6)
7	$\tilde{7}$	Strongly Important	(6, 7, 8)
9	$\tilde{9}$	Absolutely Important	(9, 9, 9)
2	$\tilde{2}$	The intermittent values between two adjacent scales	(1, 2, 3)
4	$\tilde{4}$		(3, 4, 5)
6	$\tilde{6}$		(5, 6, 7)
8	$\tilde{8}$		(7, 8, 9)

If one criterion is strongly recommended over the other, then the triangular fuzzy numbers (6, 7, 8) is taken. On the contrary the later criterion to the former criterion takes the triangular fuzzy set numbers (1/8, 1/7, 1/6).

The pair wise contribution matrix is shown in Eq.1, where $\widetilde{d}_{ij}^{k}$ indicates the kth decision maker's preference of ith criterion over j^{th} criterion, via fuzzy triangular numbers

$$\widetilde{A}^{k} = \begin{bmatrix} \widetilde{d}^{k}_{11} & \widetilde{d}^{k}_{12} & \widetilde{d}^{k}_{13} & \cdots & \widetilde{d}^{k}_{1n} \\ \widetilde{d}^{k}_{21} & \widetilde{d}^{k}_{22} & \widetilde{d}^{k}_{23} & \cdots & \widetilde{d}^{k}_{2n} \\ \widetilde{d}^{k}_{31} & \widetilde{d}^{k}_{32} & \widetilde{d}^{k}_{33} & \cdots & \widetilde{d}^{k}_{3n} \\ \vdots & \vdots & \vdots & \ddots & \vdots \\ \widetilde{d}^{k}_{m1} & \widetilde{d}^{k}_{m2} & \widetilde{d}^{k}_{m3} & \cdots & \widetilde{d}^{k}_{mn} \end{bmatrix} \tag{1}$$

Step 2: If there is more than one decision maker, preferences of each decision maker $\left(\widetilde{d}^{k}_{ij} \right)$ are averaged and $\widetilde{d}_{ij}$ is calculated:

$$\widetilde{d}_{ij} = \frac{\sum_{k=1}^{K}\left(\widetilde{d}^{k}_{ij} \right)}{K}$$

Step 3: According to averaged preferences, pair wise contribution matrix is updated:

$$\widetilde{A} = \begin{bmatrix} \widetilde{d}_{11} & \widetilde{d}_{12} & \widetilde{d}_{13} & \cdots & \widetilde{d}_{1n} \\ \widetilde{d}_{21} & \widetilde{d}_{22} & \widetilde{d}_{23} & \cdots & \widetilde{d}_{2n} \\ \widetilde{d}_{31} & \widetilde{d}_{32} & \widetilde{d}_{33} & \cdots & \widetilde{d}_{3n} \\ \vdots & \vdots & \vdots & \ddots & \vdots \\ \widetilde{d}_{m1} & \widetilde{d}_{m2} & \widetilde{d}_{m3} & \cdots & \widetilde{d}_{mn} \end{bmatrix}, \left[m = n \right]$$

Step 4: According to Buckley (1985), the geometric mean of fuzzy comparison values of each criterion is calculated. Here $\widetilde{r}_{i}$ still represents triangular values:

$$\widetilde{r}_{i} = \left[\prod_{j=1}^{n}\left(\widetilde{d}_{ij} \right) \right]^{\left(\frac{1}{n} \right)}, \left[i = 1, 2, 3, ..., n \right]$$

Step 5: The fuzzy weights of each criterion can be found by incorporating next 3 sub-steps.

    Step 5a: Find the vector summation of each $\widetilde{r}_{i}$

Step 5b: Find the inverse of summation vector. Replaced the fuzzy triangular number to arrange it in an ascending order.

Step 5c: To find the fuzzy weight of criterion i, $\widetilde{w_i}$ multiply with each $\widetilde{r_i}$ with this reverse vector.

$$\widetilde{w_i} = \widetilde{r_i} \otimes \left(\widetilde{r_i} \oplus \widetilde{r_i} \oplus \widetilde{r_i} \oplus \cdots \oplus \widetilde{r_i} \right)^{(-1)}$$
$$= \left(lw_i, mw_i, uw_i \right)$$

Step 6: Since $\widetilde{w_i}$ are still fuzzy triangular numbers, they need to de-fuzzified by Centre of area

Method:

$$M_i = \frac{lw_i + mw_i + uw_i}{3}$$

Step 7: M_i is a non-fuzzy number which required to be normalized:

$$N_i = \frac{M_i}{\sum_{i=1}^{n} M_i}$$

In this way normalize weights of both criteria and alternatives are found and then by multiplying each alternative weight with related criteria, the scores for each alternative is calculated. The alternative with the highest score is the best alternative amongst the number of alternatives present.

3.2. Fuzzy ELECTRE

The fuzzy ELECTRE method provides the best alternative by quantifying the decision makers' opinion. The ELECTRE method is based upon three concepts namely, the concordance index, the discordance index and the threshold value. The procedure for finding the best alternative through fuzzy ELECTRE ranking model is as follows (2012):

Step 1: Determination of weights by the decision makers.

Considering that the decision group contains 'l' decision makers' criteria and provides each criterion some linguistic term. The linguistic term is then quantified using triangular fuzzy number. Table 2 represents the linguistic term and the corresponding fuzzy numbers (Assumption).

Step 2: Calculation triangular fuzzy number.

Table 2. Represents the linguistic term and the corresponding fuzzy numbers

Linguistic Term	Scale	Triangular Fuzzy Number (Assumed)
Very bad	1	(1, 1, 1)
Bad	2	(1.6, 2.0, 2.4)
Medium bad	3	(2.4, 3.0, 3.6)
Good	5	(4, 5, 6)
Very good	7	(5.6, 7, 8.4)
Extremely good	9	(8.0, 8.5, 9)

Each expert makes an opinion about the alternatives on the basis of the each criterion. After that the linguistic terms are quantified according to the table 2, then each of the criterion are weighted $\widetilde{G}_j = \left(l_j, m_j, u_j \right)$

$$l_j = \left(l_{1j} \times l_{2j} \times l_{3j} \times \cdots \times l_{kj} \right)^{\left(\frac{1}{k} \right)}$$

$$m_j = \left(m_{1j} \times m_{2j} \times m_{3j} \times \cdots \times m_{kj} \right)^{\left(\frac{1}{k} \right)}$$

$$n_j = \left(n_{1j} \times n_{2j} \times n_{3j} \times \cdots \times n_{kj} \right)^{\left(\frac{1}{k} \right)}$$

where j = 1, 2, 3, ... k

Now $\widetilde{w}_j$ is calculated as:

$$\widetilde{w}_j = \frac{\widetilde{G}_j}{\widetilde{G}_r} = \left(\frac{l_j}{\sum\limits_{j=1}^{k} u_j}, \frac{m_j}{\sum\limits_{j=1}^{k} m_j}, \frac{u_j}{\sum\limits_{j=1}^{k} l_j} \right)$$

Aggregate fuzzy index weighted matrix is constructed as follows:

$$\widetilde{W} = \left[\widetilde{w}_1, \widetilde{w}_2, \widetilde{w}_3, \cdots, \widetilde{w}_n \right]$$

Step 3: Calculation of decision matrix:

$$X = \begin{bmatrix} x_{11} & x_{12} & \cdots & x_{1n} \\ x_{21} & x_{22} & \cdots & x_{2n} \\ \vdots & \vdots & \ddots & \vdots \\ x_{m1} & x_{m2} & \cdots & x_{mn} \end{bmatrix}$$

Step 4: Calculation of normalized decision matrix and the weighted normalized decision matrix.

The normalized decision matrix can be calculated as:

$$r_{ij} = \begin{cases} \dfrac{\dfrac{1}{x_{ij}}}{\sqrt{\displaystyle\sum_{i=1}^{m}\left(\dfrac{1}{x_{ij}^{2}}\right)}}, \min imization \\[3em] \dfrac{x_{ij}}{\sqrt{\displaystyle\sum_{i=1}^{m}\left(x_{ij}^{2}\right)}}, \max imization \end{cases}, \left(i = 1,2,3,\cdots,m\right) \& \left(j = 1,2,3,\cdots,n\right)$$

$$r_{ij} = \begin{bmatrix} r_{11} & r_{12} & \cdots & r_{1n} \\ r_{21} & r_{22} & \cdots & r_{2n} \\ \vdots & \vdots & \ddots & \vdots \\ r_{m1} & r_{m2} & \cdots & r_{mn} \end{bmatrix}$$

The weighted normalized decision matrix based on the normalized decision matrix is constructed as follows:

$$\widetilde{V} = \left[\widetilde{v}_{ij}\right]_{(m \times n)}$$

$\widetilde{v}_{ij}$ is the normalized positive fuzzy number where i = 1, 2, 3.... m and j = 1, 2, 3....n

$$\widetilde{v}_{ij} = r_{ij} \times \widetilde{w}_{j}$$

Step 5: Calculation of concordance and discordance indexes.

The concordance and discordance indexes are calculated for different weights of each criterion. The concordance index C_{a_1a2} represents the degree of confidence in pairwise judgements $(A_{a1} \rightarrow A_{a2})$. The formula for finding the concordance index to satisfy the measured problem can be written as:

$$C^1_{a_1a_2} = \sum\nolimits_{j*} w_{j1}, C^2_{a_1a_2} = \sum\nolimits_{j*} w_{j2}, C^3_{a_1a_2} = \sum\nolimits_{j*} w_{j3}$$

where j* is the attribute contained in the concordance set $C(a_1, a_2)$

On the other hand, the preference of the dissatisfaction can be measured by discordance index D(a_1, a_2), which represents the degree of disagreement in $A_{a_1} \rightarrow A_{a_2}$ as follows:

$$D^1_{a_1a_2} = \frac{\sum\limits_{j+} \left| v^1_{a1j+} - v^1_{a2j+} \right|}{\sum\limits_{j} \left| v^1_{a1j} - v^1_{a2j} \right|}$$

$$D^2_{a_1a_2} = \frac{\sum\limits_{j+} \left| v^2_{a1j+} - v^2_{a2j+} \right|}{\sum\limits_{j} \left| v^2_{a1j} - v^2_{a2j} \right|}$$

$$D^3_{a_1a_2} = \frac{\sum\limits_{j+} \left| v^3_{a1j+} - v^3_{a2j+} \right|}{\sum\limits_{j} \left| v^3_{a1j} - v^3_{a2j} \right|}$$

J$^+$ are the attributes contained in the discordance matrix $D(a_1, a_2)$ and v$_{ij}$ is weighted normalized evaluation of the alternative I to the criterion j

Step 6: Calculating the concordance and discordance indexes.

This is the defuzzification step using the formula:

$$C^*_{a_1a_2} = \sqrt[z]{\prod_{z=1}^{z} C^z_{a_1a_2}}$$

$$D^*_{a_1a_2} = \sqrt[z]{\prod_{z=1}^{z} D^z_{a_1a_2}}$$

The dominance of A_{a_1} over the A_{a_2} becomes stronger with a larger final concordance index $C_{a_1a_2}$ and a smaller discordance index $D_{a_1a_2}$

The best alternative is given by:

$$C(a_1,a_2) \geq \overline{C}, \ D(a_1,a_2) \geq \overline{D}$$

$\overline{C}$: The averages of $C_{a_1 a_2}$

$\overline{D}$: The averages of $D_{a_1 a_2}$

3.3. Fuzzy TOPSIS

In order to solve different MCDM problem under uncertain environment Chen (1997) [31] developed the fuzzy TOPSIS method. The decision makers' uses linguistic term which are further converted into weights by fuzzy set theory. $\widetilde{W_r^j}$ is the weight given to the jth criterion, C_j (j = 1, 2, 3, ..., n) by the rth decision maker. Similarly, $\widetilde{x_{ij}^r}$ is the importance of i$_{th}$ alternative, A_i (i = 1, 2 3, ..., m) with respect to the jth criterion. Procedure for calculating the best alternative by fuzzy TOPSIS is as follows (2014):

Step 1: Making a committee of decision makers for identifying the evaluation criteria.
Step 2: Choosing of the appropriate language by the decision makers for providing weights to the criteria.
Step 3: Calculating the average weight of each criterion and ratings of alternatives as given by k decision makers are calculated as follows:

$$\widetilde{w}_j = \frac{1}{k}\left[\widetilde{w}_j^1 + \widetilde{w}_j^2 + \widetilde{w}_j^3 + \cdots + \widetilde{w}_j^k\right]$$

$$\widetilde{x}_{ij} = \frac{1}{k}\left[\widetilde{x}_{ij}^1 + \widetilde{x}_{ij}^2 + \widetilde{x}_{ij}^3 + \cdots + \widetilde{x}_{ij}^k\right]$$

Step 4: Forming of the decision matrix:

$$\widetilde{D} = \begin{array}{c} \\ A_1 \\ A_2 \\ \vdots \\ A_m \end{array} \begin{array}{cccc} C_1 & C_2 & \cdots & C_n \\ \left[\begin{array}{cccc} \widetilde{x}_{11} & \widetilde{x}_{12} & \cdots & \widetilde{x}_{1n} \\ \widetilde{x}_{21} & \widetilde{x}_{22} & \cdots & \widetilde{x}_{2n} \\ \vdots & \vdots & \ddots & \vdots \\ \widetilde{x}_{m1} & \widetilde{x}_{m2} & \cdots & \widetilde{x}_{mn} \end{array}\right] \end{array}$$

$$\widetilde{W} = \left[\widetilde{w}_1, \widetilde{w}_2, \widetilde{w}_3, \cdots, \widetilde{w}_n\right]$$

Step 5: Normalizing of the fuzzy decision matrix by linear scale transformation as follows:

$$\widetilde{R} = \left[\tilde{r}_{ij}\right]_{(m \times n)}$$

$$\tilde{r}_{ij} = \left(\frac{l_{ij}}{u_j^+}, \frac{m_{ij}}{u_j^+}, \frac{u_{ij}}{u_j^+}\right); u_j^+ = \max_i\left(u_{ij}\right)$$

for benefit criteria

$$\tilde{r}_{ij} = \left(\frac{l_{ij}}{l_j^-}, \frac{m_{ij}}{l_j^-}, \frac{u_{ij}}{l_j^-}\right); l_j^- = \max_i\left(l_{ij}\right)$$

for cost criteria

Step 6: Calculation of the weighted normalize matrix.

$$\widetilde{V} = \left[\tilde{v}_{ij}\right]_{(m \times n)}$$

where $\tilde{v}_{ij}$ is given by

$$\tilde{v}_{ij} = r_{ij} \times \tilde{w}_j$$

Step 7: Calculation of Fuzzy Positive Ideal Solution (FPIS, A⁺) and Fuzzy Negative Ideal Solution (FNIS, A⁻) accordingly as:

$$A^+ = \left[\tilde{v}_1^+, \tilde{v}_2^+, \tilde{v}_3^+, \cdots, \tilde{v}_n^+\right]$$

$$A^- = \left[\tilde{v}_1^-, \tilde{v}_2^-, \tilde{v}_3^-, \cdots, \tilde{v}_n^-\right]$$

where

$$\tilde{v}_j^+ = (1,1,1) \,\&\, \tilde{v}_j^- = (0,0,0)$$

Step 8: Calculation of distances d_j^+ and d_j^- of each alternative from the $\widetilde{v}_j^+$ and $\widetilde{v}_j^-$ respectively accordingly as:

$$d_j^+ = \sum_{j=1}^{n} d_v\left(\tilde{v}_{ij}, \tilde{v}_j^+\right)$$

$$d_j^- = \sum_{j=1}^{n} d_v\left(\tilde{v}_{ij}, \tilde{v}_j^-\right)$$

where d_j^{+-} represent distance between two fuzzy numbers according to vertex method.

$$d\left(\tilde{x}, \tilde{z}\right) = \sqrt{\frac{1}{3}\left[\left(l_x - l_z\right)^2 + \left(m_x - m_z\right)^2 + \left(u_x - u_z\right)^2\right]}$$

Step 9: Calculation of closeness co-efficient CC_i

$$CC_i = \frac{d_i^-}{d_i^- + d_i^+}$$

Step 10: Smaller the closeness co-efficient value of the alternatives better the ranking of the alternative.

3.4. Fuzzy MOORA

The procedure for calculation of fuzzy MOORA method is as follows:

Step 1: Decision matrix is formed using triangular fuzzy numbers

$$\widetilde{X} = \begin{array}{c} \\ A_1 \\ A_2 \\ \vdots \\ A_m \end{array} \begin{array}{c} C_1 \quad C_2 \quad \cdots \quad C_n \\ \left[\begin{array}{cccc} \tilde{x}_{11} & \tilde{x}_{12} & \cdots & \tilde{x}_{1n} \\ \tilde{x}_{21} & \tilde{x}_{22} & \cdots & \tilde{x}_{2n} \\ \vdots & \vdots & \ddots & \vdots \\ \tilde{x}_{m1} & \tilde{x}_{m2} & \cdots & \tilde{x}_{mn} \end{array}\right] \end{array}$$

A$_i$: Alternatives
C$_j$: Criteria

Step 2: Normalizing the decision matrix x_{ij}^n

$$x_{l_{ij}}^n = \frac{x_{lij}}{\sqrt{\sum_{i=1}^m \left[\left(x_{l_{ij}}^2 + x_{m_{ij}}^2 + x_{u_{ij}}^2 \right) \right]}}$$

$$x_{m_{ij}}^n = \frac{x_{mij}}{\sqrt{\sum_{i=1}^m \left[\left(x_{l_{ij}}^2 + x_{m_{ij}}^2 + x_{u_{ij}}^2 \right) \right]}}$$

$$x_{u_{ij}}^n = \frac{x_{uij}}{\sqrt{\sum_{i=1}^m \left[\left(x_{l_{ij}}^2 + x_{m_{ij}}^2 + x_{u_{ij}}^2 \right) \right]}}$$

Step 3: Calculation of weighted normalized fuzzy decision matrix

$$V_{ij} = \left(V_{l_{ij}}, V_{m_{ij}}, V_{u_{ij}} \right)$$
$$V_{l_{ij}} = w_j . x_{l_{ij}}^n$$
$$V_{m_{ij}} = w_j . x_{m_{ij}}^n$$
$$V_{u_{ij}} = w_j . x_{u_{ij}}^n$$

where w_j is the weight of the criteria which is calculated in similar way as that in fuzzy AHP.

Step 4: Calculation of normalized performance values:

$$\widetilde{y}_i = \sum_{j=1}^k \widetilde{V}_{ij} - \sum_{j=k+1}^n \widetilde{V}_{ij}$$

where k stands for the benefit criteria and remaining for the cost criteria

Step 5: Converting to non-fuzzy performance values:

$$\widetilde{y}_i = \left(y_{l_i}, y_{m_i}, y_{u_i} \right)$$

Non-fuzzy performance $y_i = \dfrac{\left(y_{u_i} + y_{m_i} + y_{l_i} \right)}{3}$

Step 6: Ranking of the alternatives. The alternative with the largest value of y_i is the best alternative

3.5. Fuzzy COPRAS

In 1994, Zavadskas and Kaklauskas presented the COPRAS (**CO**mplex**Pr**oportional **AS**sessment) method for ranking different alternatives (Zavadskas et al., 1994). A large number of literature is present describing the COPRAS method and its application (Zavadskas et al., 2001; Vilutiene & Zavadskas, 2003; Zavadskas et al., 2004; Kaklauskas et al., 2005; Kaklauskas et al., 2006; Zavadskas et al., 2008b). The COPRAS technique of ranking multiple alternatives in fuzzy environment is called fuzzy COPRAS. Steps to rank alternatives by the fuzzy COPRAS method is as follows:

Step 1: Decision makers determine the ratings of the alternatives with respect to each criterion in term of linguistic variables.

Step 2: Considering the opinion of all the decision makers and integrating it triangular fuzzy weight of each criterion is obtained as:

$$\tilde{w} = \left(w_1, w_2, w_3 \right)$$

where

$$w_1 = \min\left(w_{i1} \right), i = 1, 2, 3 \ldots m$$

$$w_2 = \frac{1}{k}\left(\sum_{i=1}^{m} w_{i2} \right), i = 1, 2, 3 \ldots m$$

$$w_3 = \max\left(w_{i3} \right), i = 1, 2, 3 \ldots m$$

Step 3: Establishing triangular fuzzy decision making matrix $\tilde{D}$

$$\tilde{D} = \left[\tilde{x}_{ij} \right]_{m \times n}$$

where

$$\tilde{x}_{ij} = \left(x_{l_{ij}}, x_{m_{ij}}, x_{u_{ij}} \right)$$

where

$$x_{l_{ij}} = \min\left(x_{l_{ij}}\right); \; i = 1, 2, 3 \ldots m \; \& \; j = 1, 2, 3 \ldots n$$

$$x_{m_{ij}} = \frac{1}{k}\left(\sum_{i=1}^{m} x_{m_{ij}}\right); \; i = 1, 2, 3 \ldots m \; \& \; j = 1, 2, 3 \ldots n$$

$$x_{u_{ij}} = \max\left(x_{u_{ij}}\right); \; i = 1, 2, 3 \ldots m \; \& \; j = 1, 2, 3 \ldots n$$

Step 4: Normalizing the fuzzy decision matrix $\tilde{N} = \left[\tilde{n}_{ij}\right]_{m \times n}$ where $\tilde{n}_{ij}$ is given by:

$$\tilde{n}_{ij} = \left[\frac{x_{l_{ij}}}{x_{u_{ij}}^*}, \frac{x_{m_{ij}}}{x_{u_{ij}}^*}, \frac{x_{u_{ij}}}{x_{u_{ij}}^*}\right], j = 1, 2, 3 \ldots n$$

where

$$x_{u_{ij}}^* = \max\left\{x_{u_{ij}}\right\}, j = 1, 2, 3 \ldots n$$

Step 5: Determination of weighted normalized decision matrix $\tilde{V} = \left[\tilde{v}_{ij}\right]_{m \times n}$. The value of weighted normalized element is calculated as:

$$\tilde{v}_{ij} = \tilde{n}_{ij} \otimes \tilde{w}_i$$

Step 6: Calculation of sum of weighted normalize elements for all the benefit criteria $\tilde{S}^+$ and non-benefit criteria $\tilde{S}^-$.

$$\tilde{S}^+ = \left(\sum_{i=1}^{k} v_{i_1}, \sum_{i=1}^{k} v_{i_2}, \sum_{i=1}^{k} v_{i_3}\right)$$

$$\tilde{S}^- = \left(\sum_{i=k+1}^{m} v_{i_1}, \sum_{i=k+1}^{m} v_{i_2}, \sum_{i=k+1}^{m} v_{i_3}\right)$$

Step 7: Defuzzification of the fuzzy numbers using one of the various defuzzification method like centre of gravity method.

$$Q_i^* = \frac{\int \mu(x) x dx}{\int \mu(x) dx}$$

Step 8: Determining the priority order (Pri):

$$Pr_i = \frac{Q_i}{maxQ_i}$$

Maximum value of Pr_i is given maximum priority and ranked 1, second largest value of Pr_i is given second priority and ranked 2 and so on.

4. NUMERICAL EXAMPLE

Considering an example to show its application with fuzzy MOORA and fuzzy COPRAS, presented in Table 3, Table 4, Table 5, and Table 6. [The data given below is taken from Junior F. R. L., Osiro L. and Carpinetti L. C. R. (2014)]

4.1 Ranking the Alternatives by Fuzzy MOORA Method

Calculation normalized decision matrix presented in Table 7.

Calculation of weighted normalize decision matrix presented in Table 8.

Calculation of normalized performance values:

Criteria C_1, C_3 and C_5 are benefit criteria and criteria C_2 and C_4 are non-benefit criteria (Assumption)

$$\widetilde{y}_1 = (0.12, \ 0.4, \ 0.73), \ \widetilde{y}_2 = (0.22, \ 0.45, \ 0.6), \ \widetilde{y}_3 = (0.35, \ 0.56, \ 0.36)$$

Table 3. Linguistic scale to evaluate the weight of the criteria

Linguistic Term	Triangular Fuzzy Number
Very little important (VL)	(0.0, 0.0, 0.25)
Moderately important (MI)	(0.0, 0.25, 0.50)
Important (I)	(0.25, 0.5, 0.75)
Very important (VI)	(0.50, 0.75, 1.0)
Absolutely important (AI)	(0.75, 1.0, 1.0)

Table 4. Linguistic scale to evaluate the ratings of the alternative supplier

Linguistic Term	Triangular Fuzzy Number
Very low (VL)	(0.0, 0.0, 2.5)
Low (L)	(0.0, 2.5, 5.0)
Good (G)	(2.5, 5.0, 7.5)
High (H)	(5.0, 7.5, 10.0)
Excellent (Ex)	(7.5, 10.0, 10.0)

Table 5. Linguistic ratings of the alternative suppliers by different decision makers

	C_1	C_2	C_3	C_4	C_5
DECISION MAKER 1					
A_1	G	H	G	G	L
A_2	VH	VH	VH	VH	H
A_3	H	H	VH	G	H
A_4	G	H	G	H	H
A_5	G	H	H	G	G
Weights of criteria	VI	AI	VI	I	VI
DECISION MAKER 2					
A_1	G	G	G	H	G
A_2	VH	VH	VH	VH	H
A_3	VH	H	VH	H	VH
A_4	H	VH	H	H	H
A_5	H	H	H	H	H
Weights of criteria	AI	AI	VI	I	I
DECISION MAKER 3					
A_1	H	G	G	G	H
A_2	VH	VH	VH	VH	VH
A_3	VH	H	VH	G	VH
A_4	G	VH	H	H	G
A_5	L	G	G	G	G
Weights of criteria	AI	AI	AI	VI	I

Table 6. Fuzzy number of the aggregated ratings of the alternative suppliers

	C_1	C_2	C_3	C_4	C_5
A_1	(3.33, 5.83, 8.33)	(3.33, 5.83, 8.33)	(2.5, 5, 7.5)	(3.33, 5.83, 8.33)	(2.5, 5, 7.5)
A_2	(7.5, 10, 10)	(7.5, 10, 10)	(7.5, 10, 10)	(7.5, 10, 10)	(6.67, 9.17, 10)
A_3	(6.67, 9.17, 10)	(5, 7.5, 10)	(7.5, 10, 10)	(3.33, 5.83, 8.33)	(6.67, 9.17, 10)
A_4	(3.33, 5.83, 8.33)	(6.67, 9.17, 10)	(4.17, 6.67, 9.17)	(5, 7.5, 10)	(4.17, 6.67, 9.17)
A_5	(2.5, 5, 7.5)	(4.17, 6.67, 9.17)	(4.17, 6.67, 9.17)	(3.33, 5.83, 8.33)	(3.33, 5.83, 8.33)
Weights of criteria	(0.67, 0.92, 1)	(0.75, 1, 1)	(0.67, 0.92, 1)	(0.42, 0.67, 0.92)	(0.33, 0.58, 0.83)

Table 7. Normalized decision matrix

	C_1	C_2	C_3	C_4	C_5
A_1	(0.31, 0.54, 0.79)	(0.31, 0.54, 0.79)	(0.27, 0.53, 0.8)	(0.31, 0.54, 0.79)	(0.27, 0.53, 0.8)
A_2	(0.47, 0.62, 0.62)	(0.47, 0.62, 0.62)	(0.47, 0.62, 0.62)	(0.47, 0.62, 0.62)	(0.44, 0.61, 0.66)
A_3	(0.44, 0.61, 0.66)	(0.37, 0.56, 0.74)	(0.47, 0.62, 0.62)	(0.31, 0.54, 0.79)	(0.44, 0.61, 0.66)
A_4	(0.31, 0.54, 0.79)	(0.44, 0.61, 0.66)	(0.35, 0.55, 0.76)	(0.37, 0.56, 0.74)	(0.35, 0.55, 0.76)
A_5	(0.27, 0.53, 0.8)	(0.35, 0.55, 0.76)	(0.35, 0.55, 0.76)	(0.31, 0.54, 0.79)	(0.31, 0.54, 0.79)

Table 8. Weighted normalize decision matrix

	C_1	C_2	C_3	C_4	C_5
A_1	(0.21, 0.5, 0.79)	(0.23, 0.54, 0.79)	(0.18, 0.49, 0.8)	(0.13, .36, 0.73)	(0.09, 0.31, 0.66)
A_2	(0.31, 0.57, 0.62)	(0.35, 0.62, 0.62)	(0.31, 0.57, 0.62)	(0.20, 0.42, 0.57)	(0.15, 0.35, 0.55)
A_3	(0.3, 0.56, 0.66)	(0.28, 0.56, 0.74)	(0.31, 0.57, 0.62)	(0.13, 0.36, 0.73)	(0.15, 0.35, 0.55)
A_4	(0.21, 0.5, 0.79)	(0.33, 0.61, 0.66)	(0.23, 0.51, 0.76)	(0.16, 0.38, 0.68)	(0.12, 0.32, 0.63)
A_5	(0.18, 0.49, 0.8)	(0.26, 0.55, 0.76)	(0.23, 0.51, 0.76)	(0.13, 0.36, 0.73)	(0.10, 0.31, 0.66)

$$\widetilde{y_4} = (0.07,\ 0.34,\ 0.84),\ \widetilde{y_5} = (0.12,\ 0.4,\ 0.73)$$

Conversion into non-fuzzy values:

$y_1 = 0.4167$, $y_2 = 0.4233$, $y_3 = 0.4233$, $y_4 = 0.4167$, $y_5 = 0.4167$

Ranking of the alternatives presented in Table 9.

Remark: According to the fuzzy MOORA method the second and the third alternatives are the best alternatives and the remaining are rank second. As the MOORA method mostly concentrates on the best and the worst alternative from the given set of alternatives under certain criteria. Hence the second and the third alternatives are the most preferable alternatives and the remaining are the least preferable.

Table 9. Ranking of the alternatives

Alternatives	Performance	Rank
A_1	0.4167	2nd
A_2	0.4233	1st
A_3	0.4233	1st
A_4	0.4167	2nd
A_5	0.4167	2nd

4.2. Solving by Fuzzy COPRAS

Presented in Table 10, Table 11, Table 12, Table 13, Table 14, and Table 15.

Remarks: According to the fuzzy COPRAS method third is best alternative and the second alternative ranks second whereas the fourth alternative is the least preferred from the given set of alternatives (presented in Table 16).

According to the fuzzy MOORA method the second and the third alternatives are the best alternatives which is further supported by the existing literature (2014) where second alternative is the best and the third alternative ranks second. But according to the fuzzy COPRAS method third is best alternative and the second alternative ranks second. Hence from the table number 16 we can conclude that the second and third alternatives are the most preferred from the given set of alternatives.

5. CONCLUSION AND FUTURE RESEARCH SCOPE

Fuzzy concept is a very important tool in decision making when applied to engineering problems. In engineering sometimes taking the correct decision is all what matters. In such a scenario, Multi-Criteria Decision Making is the perfect tool. Although MCDM is perfect but the decision makers always find it difficult while converting the linguistic decision about an alternative with respect to a criterion into quantitative values. In order to overcome such difficulty fuzzy concepts play a very important role. When fuzzy concept is considered along with MCDM techniques, ranking of alternatives which is difficult to quantify is done. In engineering problems, ranking of different alternative where the degree

Table 10. Fuzzy normalized decision matrix

	C_1	C_2	C_3	C_4	C_5
A_1	(0.25, 0.58, 1)	(0.5, 0.5, 0.75)	(0.25, 0.5, 0.75)	(0.25, 0.58, 1)	(0, 0.5, 1)
A_2	(0.75, 1, 1)	(0.75, 1, 1)	(0.75, 1, 1)	(0.75, 1, 1)	(0.5, 0.83, 1)
A_3	(0.5, 0.92, 1)	(0.5, 0.75, 1)	(0.75, 1, 1)	(0.33, 0.58, 0.83)	(0.67, 0.917, 1)
A_4	(0.33, 0.58, 0.83)	(0.67, 0.917, 1)	(0.417, 0.67, 0.92)	(0.5, 0.75, 1)	(0.417, 0.67, 0.92)
A_5	(0.27, 0.54, 0.82)	(0.45, 0.73, 1)	(0.45, 0.73, 1)	(0.36, 0.64, 0.91)	(0.36, 0.64, 0.91)
Weights of criteria	(0.67, 0.92, 1)	(0.75, 1, 1)	(0.67, 0.92, 1)	(0.42, 0.67, 0.92)	(0.33, 0.58, 0.83)

Table 11. Weighted fuzzy normalized decision matrix

	C_1	C_2	C_3	C_4	C_5
A_1	(0.17, 0.53, 1)	(0.38, 0.5, 0.75)	(0.17, 0.46, 0.75)	(0.11, 0.39, 0.92)	(0, 0.29, 0.83)
A_2	(0.5, 0.92, 1)	(0.56, 1, 1)	(0.5, 0.92, 1)	(0.32, 0.67, 0.92)	(0.17, 0.48, 0.83)
A_3	(0.33, 0.85, 1)	(0.38, 0.75, 1)	(0.5, 0.92, 1)	(0.14, 0.39, 0.76)	(0.22, 0.53, 0.83)
A_4	(0.22, 0.53, 0.83)	(0.5, 0.917, 1)	(0.28, 0.62, 0.92)	(0.21, 0.5, 0.92)	(0.14, 0.39, 0.76)
A_5	(0.18, 0.5, 0.82)	(0.34, 0.73, 1)	(0.3, 0.67, 1)	(0.15, 0.43, 0.84)	(0.12, 0.37, 0.76)

Table 12. Calculation of sum of weighted normalized index

	A_1	A_2	A_3	A_4	A_5
$\tilde{S}^+$	(0.34, 1.28, 2.58)	(1.17, 2.32, 2.83)	(1.05, 2.3, 2.83)	(0.64, 1.54, 2.51)	(0.6, 1.54, 2.58)
$\tilde{S}^-$	(0.49, 0.89, 1.67)	(0.88, 1.67,1.92)	(0.52, 1.14, 1.76)	(0.71, 1.417, 1.92)	(0.49, 1.16, 1.84)

Table 13. Calculation of the significance

	A_1	A_2	A_3	A_4	A_5
$\widetilde{Q_j}$	(1.08, 2.97, 4.56)	(1.58, 3.22, 4.55)	(1.75, 3.62, 4.71)	(1.15, 2.6, 4.23)	(1.34, 2.84, 4.38)

Table 14. Defuzzification of the fuzzy significance

	A_1	A_2	A_3	A_4	A_5
Q^*	2.87	3.12	3.36	2.66	2.85

Table 15. Ranking of the alternatives

Alternatives	Performance	Rank
A_1	85.41%	3rd
A_2	92.86%	2nd
A_3	100.00%	1st
A_4	79.16%	5th
A_5	84.82%	4th

Table 16. Comparisons of results

Alternatives	Fuzzy MOORA	Fuzzy COPRAS	Fuzzy TOPSIS
A_1	2nd	3rd	5th
A_2	1st	2nd	1st
A_3	1st	1st	2nd
A_4	2nd	5th	3rd
A_5	2nd	4th	4th

of goodness or meanness is difficult to express when one object is compared with another on the basis of different criteria. For such situation, fuzzy MCDM techniques is used. Fuzzy removes the difficulty from the conversion of linguistic part to quantitative values and MCDM ranks the different alternatives on the basis of the different criteria.

In this chapter, different fuzzy MCDM techniques are studied and it steps for solving problems are laid down. For better understanding of the methods an example is solved by two fuzzy MCDM techniques and the result obtained is compared with the existing result. At first for making the decision matrix three decision makers or experts are chosen. The decision makers are asked for their opinion about the subject matter to which they respond it in linguistic terms. The fuzzy set theory is used for converting the linguistic terms into quantitative values. Defuzzification of the fuzzy numbers is done by using the centre of gravity method.

The alternatives of the example are ranked by MOORA and COPRAS method. The result is then compared to the already established result. By fuzzy MOORA alternatives 2 & 3, by fuzzy COPRAS alternative 3 and by fuzzy TOPSIS alternative 2 is mostly preferred. Hence alternative 2 and 3 are the mostly preferred alternatives. Although fuzzy TOPSIS is an ideal method for solving but it contains a bit more calculations which increases the chances of committing mistakes. On the other hand, fuzzy MOORA contains less mathematical calculations and the result obtained by this method is same as that obtained from the fuzzy TOPSIS method. Fuzzy COPRAS is also a good method but its result does not matches with the result obtained from the fuzzy TOPSIS method.

Lastly, we can say that all of the fuzzy MCDM techniques are good in their own respective ways and help the researchers in ranking the different alternatives and taking decisions in the engineering and sciences application.

REFERENCES

Abdullah, L., & Jamal, J. (2010). Centroid-point of ranking fuzzy numbers and its application to health related quality of life indicators. *International Journal on Computer Science and Engineering*, *2*(08), 2773–2777.

Ayhan, M. B. (2013). Fuzzy AHP Approach for Supplier Selection Problem: A Case Study in a Gearmotor Company. *International Journal of Managing Value and Supply Chains*, *4*(3), 11–23. doi:10.5121/ijmvsc.2013.4302

Bellman, R., & Zadeh, L. A. (1970). Decision-making in a fuzzy environment. *Management Science*, *17B*(4), 141–164. doi:10.1287/mnsc.17.4.B141

Bhattacharya, U., Rao, J. R., & Tiwari, R. N. (1992). Fuzzy multi-criteria facility location problem. *Fuzzy Sets and Systems*, *51*(3), 277–287. doi:10.1016/0165-0114(92)90018-Y

Bhunia, A. K., & Samanta, S. S. (2014). A study of interval metric and its application in multi-objective optimization with interval objectives. *Computers & Industrial Engineering*, *74*, 169–178. doi:10.1016/j.cie.2014.05.014

Buckley, J. J. (1985). Fuzzy hierarchical analysis. *Fuzzy Sets and Systems*, *17*(1), 233–247. doi:10.1016/0165-0114(85)90090-9

Chakraborty, T. K. (1992). A class of single sampling plans based on fuzzy optimization. *Opsearch, 29*(1), 11–20.

Chakraborty, T. K. (1994a). Possibilistic parameter single sampling inspection plans. *Opsearch, 31*(2), 108–126.

Chakraborty, T. K. (1994b). A class of single sampling inspection plans based on possibilistic programming problem. *Fuzzy Sets and Systems, 63*(1), 35–43. doi:10.1016/0165-0114(94)90143-0

Chang, D.-Y. (1996). Applications of the extent analysis method on fuzzy AHP. *European Journal of Operational Research, 95*(3), 649–655. doi:10.1016/0377-2217(95)00300-2

Chang, P. L., & Chen, Y. C. (1994). A fuzzy multi-criteria decision making method for technology transfer strategy selection in biotechnology. *Fuzzy Sets and Systems, 6*(2), 131–139. doi:10.1016/0165-0114(94)90344-1

Chen, C. T. (2000). Extensions of the TOPSIS for group decision-making under fuzzy environment. *Fuzzy Sets and Systems, 114*(1), 1–9. doi:10.1016/S0165-0114(97)00377-1

Cheng, C. H., & Mon, D. L. (1994). Evaluating weapon system by Analytical Hierarchy Process based on fuzzy scales. *Fuzzy Sets and Systems, 63*(1), 1–10. doi:10.1016/0165-0114(94)90140-6

Gen, M., Tsujimura, Y., & Ida, K. (1992). Method for solving multi-bjective aggregate production planning problem with fuzzy parameters. *Computers & Industrial Engineering, 23*(1-4), 117–120. doi:10.1016/0360-8352(92)90077-W

Guo, K. L. (2008, June). DECIDE: A decision-making model for more effective decision making by health care managers. *The Health Care Manager, 27*(2), 118–127. doi:10.1097/01.HCM.0000285046.27290.90 PMID:18475113

Ishii, H., Tada, M., & Masuda, T. (1992). Two scheduling problems with fuzzy due-dates. *Fuzzy Sets and Systems, 6*(3), 339–347. doi:10.1016/0165-0114(92)90372-B

Ishikawa, A., Amagasa, M., Tomizawa, G., Tatsuta, R., & Mieno, H. (1993). The max-min Delphi method and fuzzy Delphi method via fuzzy integration. *Fuzzy Sets and Systems, 55*(3), 241–253. doi:10.1016/0165-0114(93)90251-C

Janis, I. L., Mann, & Leon. (1977). Decision making: A psychological analysis of conflict, choice, and commitment. New York: Free Press.

Junior, F. R. L., Osiro, L., & Carpinetti, L. C. R. (2014). A comparison between Fuzzy AHP and Fuzzy TOPSIS methods to supplier selection. *Applied Soft Computing, 21*, 194–209. doi:10.1016/j.asoc.2014.03.014

Karmakar, S., & Bhunia, A. K. (2013). Uncertain constrained optimization by interval- oriented algorithm. *The Journal of the Operational Research Society*, 1–15.

Karmakar, S., Mahato, S.K., & Bhunia, A.K. (2008). Interval oriented multi-section techniques for global optimization. *Journal of Computational and Applied Mathematics*.

Kilincci, O., & Onal, S. A. (2011). Fuzzy AHP approach for supplier selection in a washingmachine company. *Expert Systems with Applications, 38*(8), 9656–9664. doi:10.1016/j.eswa.2011.01.159

Kolev, L. V. (1993). *Interval Methods for Circuit Analysis*. Singapore: World Scientific. doi:10.1142/2039

Kulpa, K., Pownuk, A., & Skalna, I. (1998). Analysis of linear mechanical structures with uncertainties by means of interval methods. *Comput. Assist. Mech. Eng. Sci., 5*, 443–477.

McCahon, C. S., & Lee, E. S. (1990). Job sequencing with fuzzy processing times. *Computers & Mathematics with Applications (Oxford, England), 19*(7), 31–41. doi:10.1016/0898-1221(90)90191-L

Narayansahoo, L., Bhunia, A. K., & Roy, D. (2014). Reliability optimization with and low level redundancies in interval environment via genetic algorithm. *Int J syst Assur Manag, 5*(4), 513-523.

Oppenheimer, E. P., & Michel, A. N. (1988). Application of interval analysis techniques to linear systems: Part-I—fundamental results. *IEEE Transactions on Circuits and Systems, 35*, 1243–1256. doi:10.1109/31.7599

Oppenheimer, E. P., & Michel, A. N. (1988). Application of interval analysis techniques to linear systems: part-II—the interval matrix exponential function. *IEEE Transactions on Circuits and Systems, 35*(10), 1230–1242. doi:10.1109/31.7598

Oppenheimer, E. P., & Michel, A. N. (1988). Application of interval analysis techniques to linear systems: part-III— interval value problems. *IEEE Transactions on Circuits and Systems, 35*(10), 1243–1256. doi:10.1109/31.7599

Pal, D., & Mahapatra, G. S. (2015). *Parametric functional representation of interval number with arithmetic operations. Int. J. comput. Math.*

Pal, D., Mahapatra, G. S., & Samanta, G. P. (2013). Optimal harvesting of pre-predator system with interval biological parameters: A biological model. *Mathematical Biosciences, 241*(2), 181–187. doi:10.1016/j.mbs.2012.11.007 PMID:23219573

Rajesri, G., Muhammad, I. A., Leksananto, G., & Tota, S. (2015). The Application of a Decision-making Approach based on Fuzzy ANP and TOPSIS for Selecting a Strategic Supplier. *Journal of Engineering Technology Sci., 47*(4), 406-425.

Rao, S. S., & Berke, L. (1997). Analysis of uncertain structural systems using interval analysis. *J. Am. Inst. Aeronaut. Astronaut., 35*(4), 727–735. doi:10.2514/2.164

Rouyendegh, B. D., & Erol, S. (n.d.). Selecting the Best Project Using the Fuzzy ELECTRE Method. *Mathematical Problem in Engineering*, 1-12.

Shaocheng, T. (1994). Interval number and fuzzy number linear programming. *Fuzzy Sets and Systems, 66*(3), 301–306. doi:10.1016/0165-0114(94)90097-3

Shipley, M. F., De Korvin, A., & Omer, K. (1996). A fuzzy logic approach for determining expected values: A project management application. *The Journal of the Operational Research Society, 47*(4), 562–569. doi:10.1057/jors.1996.61

Song, Q., & Chissom, B. S. (1993a). Fuzzy time series and its models. *Fuzzy Sets and Systems*, *54*(3), 269–277. doi:10.1016/0165-0114(93)90372-O

Song, Q., & Chissom, B. S. (1993b). Forecasting enrollments with fuzzy time series - part I. *Fuzzy Sets and Systems*, *54*(1), 1–9. doi:10.1016/0165-0114(93)90355-L

Song, Q., & Chissom, B. S. (1994). Forecasting enrollments with fuzzy time series - part II. *Fuzzy Sets and Systems*, *62*(1), 1–8. doi:10.1016/0165-0114(94)90067-1

Van Laarhoven, P. J. M., & Pedrycz, W. (1983). A fuzzy extension of Saaty"s priority Theory. *Fuzzy Sets and Systems*, *11*(1-3), 199–227. doi:10.1016/S0165-0114(83)80082-7

Wang, R. C., & Chen, C. H. (1995). Economic statistical np-control chart designs based on fuzzy optimization. *International Journal of Quality & Reliability Management*, *12*(1), 82–92. doi:10.1108/02656719510076276

Yager, R. R. (1984). General multiple objective decision-making and linguistically quantified statements. *International Journal of Man-Machine Studies*, *21*(5), 389–400. doi:10.1016/S0020-7373(84)80066-8

Yager, R. R., Goldstein, L. S., & Mendels, E. (1994). FUZMAR: An approach to aggregating market research data based on fuzzy reasoning. *Fuzzy Sets and Systems*, *68*(1), 1–11. doi:10.1016/0165-0114(94)90269-0

Zakaria, L., & Abdulllah, N. (2012). Matrix Driven Multivariate Fuzzy Linear Regression Model in Car Sales. *Journal of Applied Sciences*, *12*(1), 56–63. doi:10.3923/jas.2012.56.63

Zhang, H. C., & Huang, S. H. (1994). A fuzzy approach to process plan selection. *International Journal of Production Research*, *32*(6), 1265–1279. doi:10.1080/00207549408956999

Chapter 16
A Comprehensive Review of Nature–Inspired Algorithms for Feature Selection

Kauser Ahmed P
VIT University, India

Senthil Kumar N
VIT University, India

ABSTRACT

Due to advancement in technology, a huge volume of data is generated. Extracting knowledgeable data from this voluminous information is a difficult task. Therefore, machine learning techniques like classification, clustering, information retrieval, feature selection and data analysis has become core of recent research. These techniques can also be solved using Nature Inspired Algorithms. Nature Inspired Algorithms is inspired by processes, observed from nature. Feature Selection is helpful in finding subset of prominent components to enhance prescient precision and to expel the excess features. This chapter surveys seven nature inspired algorithms, namely Particle Swarm Optimization, Ant Colony Optimization Algorithms, Artificial Bees Colony Algorithms, Firefly Algorithms, Bat Algorithms, Cuckoo Search and Genetic Algorithms and its application in feature selections. The significance of this chapter is to present comprehensive review of nature inspired algorithms to be applied in feature selections.

INTRODUCTION

Bio Inspired Computing

Huge volume of data is generated from variety of sources at a high speed of velocity in day to day life. Extracting knowledgeable data from this voluminous information is a difficult task. Therefore, machine learning techniques like classification, clustering, information retrieval, feature selection and data analysis has become core of recent research. These techniques can also be solved using Nature Inspired Algorithms.

DOI: 10.4018/978-1-5225-2857-9.ch016

Nature Inspired Algorithms is inspired by processes, observed from nature. Nature inspired algorithms will tackle hard real world problems and solve complex optimization problems. Depends on the inspirations, nature inspired algorithms are classified as biology, physics and chemistry based algorithms. Majority of these algorithms are developed based on the characteristics and behavior of biological systems. This fraction of algorithms is called as bio inspired algorithms and the implementation of these algorithms in computing is known as bio inspired computing. Bio inspired computing is a field that learning from nature; the application of methods and systems found in nature to the study and design of engineering systems and modern technology. Bio-inspired computing is gradually gaining prominence since these algorithms are intelligent, can learn and adapt like biological organisms. Bio-inspired algorithms form a majority of all the nature-inspired algorithms. From the set theory point of view, the swarm intelligence based algorithms are a subset of bio-inspired algorithms, while the bio inspired algorithms are a subset of the nature-inspired algorithms.

Among the bio-inspired algorithms, a special class of algorithms has been developed by drawing inspiration from swarm intelligence. Therefore, some of the bio inspired algorithms can be called as swarm-intelligence based algorithms. In fact, algorithms based on swarm intelligence are among the most popular. Good examples of bio inspired computing algorithms are namely (Arpan, 2016), (Cholavendhan, SivaKumar & Karnan 2014), (Binitha & Siva,2012), Particle Swarm Optimization (PSO), Ant Colony Optimization Algorithms (ACO), Artificial Bees Colony Algorithms (ABC), Firefly Algorithms (FA), Bat Algorithms (BA), Cuckoo Search (CS) and Genetic Algorithms (GA).

FEATURE SELECTION

Feature Selection is helpful in finding subset of prominent components to enhance prescient precision and to expel the excess features. Thus, the learning model receives a concise structure without forfeiting the predictive accuracy built by using only the selected prominent features. Feature selection reduces dimensionality of the data by eliminating features which are noisy, redundant, and irrelevant for a classification problem. It is most often a challenge for the researchers due to its computational complexity. The process of eliminating these types of features from a dataset is referred to as feature selection. This helps us to simplify the models, reduce the computation cost of model training, and enhance the generalization abilities of the model and prevention of over-training. Feature selection techniques are broadly classified into three types. They are:

- Filter approach;
- Wrapper approach;
- Embedded approach.

Feature selection algorithms that perform the selection process separately without any learning algorithms involvement are called as a *filter* approach. In this approach, irrelevant features are filtered before using an induction algorithm. This technique can be applied to most real world problems where it is not interrelated with particular induction process. Feature selection algorithms that are bound together with the learning algorithms to select the subset of features are called as *wrapper* approach. In this method, the selection process is based on the estimated accuracy from an induction process. *Embedded* approach is similar to wrapper approach, where the selection process is built into the classifier model. Here, the searching process takes place in the combined space of hypotheses and feature subsets.

Advantages of Feature Selection

1. It reduces feature space dimensionality;
2. It removes redundant/irrelevant/noisy data;
3. The running time complexity of the learning algorithms can be accelerated instantly using the effective data analysis process;
4. Improving data quality;
5. Increasing the resulting model's accuracy;
6. Feature set reduction, to save resources in next data collection round or when utilized; and
7. Performance improvement resulting in predictive accuracy.

The chapter is structured as follows. The chapter starts with a general introduction to nature-inspired computing followed by preliminary ideas and fundamental concepts of bio inspired computing. This will be further followed by relevant concept of feature selection that is used in bio-inspired computing. In succession, various applications of these algorithms in real life situations are presented. Further, few open ended research problems are presented in the context of bio-inspired algorithms that can be solved by using swarm intelligence techniques. Finally, the chapter will be concluded with a conclusion.

Highlights of this chapter include:

- Review of applications of algorithms in bio-inspired computing;
- Brief description of algorithms without mathematical notations;
- Applications of bio inspired computing algorithms;
- Identification of algorithms on which theory development may be explored.

RELATED WORK

Particle Swarm Optimiztion (PSO)

PSO is initialized with a population of random solutions, each potential solution is also assigned a randomized velocity, and the potential solutions, called *particles,* which would flown through the problem space. Each particle keeps track of its coordinates in the problem space which are associated with the best solution(fitness) it has been achieved so far. (The fitness value is also stored.) This value is called *pbest.* Another "best" value that is tracked by the *global* version of the particle swarm optimizer is the overall best value, and its location, obtained so far by any particle in the population. This location is called *gbest.* The particle swarm optimization concept consists of, at each time step, changing the velocity (accelerating) each particle toward its *pbest* and *gbest* locations (global version of PSO). Acceleration is weighted by a random term, with separate random numbers being generated for acceleration toward *pbest* and *gbest* locations.

There is also a *local* version of PSO in which, in addition to pbest, each particle keeps track of the best solution, called/best, attained within a *local* topological neighborhood of particles.

The (original) process for implementing the global version of PSO is as follows:

- Initialize a population (array) of particles with random positions and velocities on *d* dimensions in the problem space;
- For each particle, evaluate the desired optimization fitness function in d variables;
- Compare particle's fitness evaluation with particle's pbest. If current value is better than pbest, then set pbest value equal to the current value, and the pbest location equal to the current location in d-dimensional space;
- Compare fitness evaluation with the population's overall previous best. If current value is better than gbest, then reset gbest to the current particle's array index and value.

Applications of PSO include (Arpan, 2016) Distributed resource management, search, location identification, resource allocation, regulation, chaotic systems, oscillatory systems, global optimization, path optimization, adaptive learning, job scheduling, thresh-holding, network training, minimization, maximization, migration.

Ant Colony Optimization Algorithms (ACO)

Ant colony optimization technique is a probabilistic technique generally used for problems that deal with finding better paths through graphs. In this technique, simulation agents (artificial ants) locate optimal solutions by moving through a parameter space representing all possible solutions. This computing technique is developed based on the behavior of natural ants which lay down pheromones while exploring their environment to resources. In similar to natural ants, the simulated agents record their positions and the quality of their solutions. This helps in later simulation iterations more ants locate better solutions (Dorigo & Thomas, 2004). The basic flow of ant colony optimization (Dorigo & Thomas, 2004) is presented below.

```
Algorithm 1
1.       Represent the solution space by a construction graph.
2.        Set ant colony optimization parameters and initialize pheromone
trails.
3.         Generate simulation agent (ant) solutions from each simulation
agents walk on the construction graph mediated by pheromone trails.
4.        Update pheromone intensities.
5.        Go to step 3, and repeat the process until convergence or termina-
tion conditions are met.
```

Application of ACO Algorithms (Arpan, 2016) and (ChandraMohan & Baskaran, 2012), include Network analysis, travelling salesman problem, scheduling, routing, clustering, data compression, environmental and economic dispatch problems, routing, data reconciliation, parameter estimation, gaming theory, objective tracking, demand forecasting, layout design, continuous optimization, timing optimization, resource consumption optimization.

Artificial Bees Colony Algorithms (ABC)

Artificial bee colony algorithm (ABC) proposed by Karaboga (2008) is a biological-inspired optimization algorithm, which has been shown to be competitive with some conventional biological-Inspired algorithms, such as differential evolution and particle swarm optimization. This algorithm is very simple and flexible, which does not require external parameters like crossover rates, especially suitable for engineering application.

The Artificial Bee Colony (ABC) algorithm uses a colony of artificial bees. The bees are classified into three types: employed bees, onlookers and scouts. Each employed bee is associated with a food source, in other words, the number of the employed bees is equal to the food sources.

Onlooker bees share the information of the food sources found by employed bees to choose better ones and explore around them. If some food sources are not improved for several cycles, the scouts are translated into a few employed bees, which abandon their food sources and search new ones.

By simulating the behaviors of bee swarm, Karaboga proposed Artificial Bee Colony algorithm for numerical function optimization. The nectar amount of a food source corresponds to the quality of the solution, while the locations of employed bees or onlookers represent solutions.

The main steps of the algorithm can be described as follows:

Step 1: Initialize the population of solutions and evaluate them.
Step 2: Produce new solutions for the employed bees, evaluate them and apply the greedy selection process.
Step 3: Calculate the probabilities of the current sources with which they are preferred by the onlookers.
Step 4: Assign onlooker bees to employed bees according to probabilities, produce new solutions and apply the greedy selection process.
Step 5: Stop the exploitation process of the sources abandoned by bees and send the scouts in the search area for discovering new food sources, randomly.
Step 6: Memorize the best food source found so far.
Step 7: If the termination condition is not satisfied, go to step 2, otherwise stop the algorithm.

Applications of ABC algorithms includes (Arpan, 2016) Numerical function optimization, multilevel thresh-holding, network routing, allocation / assignment, test suite optimization, search, bench-marking, probability distribution, feature selection, single and multi-objective optimization, discrete and continuous optimization.

Firefly Algorithms (FA)

The firefly algorithm (FA) was proposed by (Yang, 2008) and uses three main basic rules:

1. A firefly will be attracted by other fireflies regardless their sex;
2. Attractiveness is proportional to their brightness and decreases as the distance among them increases;
3. The landscape of the objective function determines the brightness of a firefly.

Applications of FA includes (Arpan, 2016) (Iztok, Iztok, Xin-She and Janez, 2013), dispatch problems, job scheduling, chaotic problems, structural optimization, continuous optimization, vector quantization, clustering, price forecasting, discrete optimization, load forecasting, network analysis, travelling salesman problem, non-linear optimization, dynamic environment problems.

Bat Algorithms (BA)

The bat algorithm (BA) was first presented by (Yang, 2010). The basic idea behind the BA is that a population of bats (possible solutions) use echolocation to sense distance and fly randomly through a search space updating their positions and velocities. The bats' flight aims at finding food/prey (best solutions). A loudness decay factor acts in a similar role as the cooling schedule in the traditional simulated annealing optimization method, and a pulse increase factor regulates the pulse frequency. As the loudness usually decreases once a bat has found its prey/solution (in order to not to lose the prey), the rate of pulse emission increases in order to raise the attack accuracy.

The BA uses the following main basic rules:

1. All bats use echolocation to sense distance, and they also 'know' the difference between food/prey and background barriers in some magical way;
2. Bats fly randomly with velocity v_i at position x_i with a frequency f_{min}, varying wavelength and loudness A_0 to search for prey. They can automatically adjust the wavelength (or frequency) of their emitted pulses and adjust the rate of pulse emission $r \in [0, 1]$, depending on the proximity of their target;
3. Although the loudness can vary in many ways, we assume that the loudness varies from a large (positive) A_0 to a minimum constant value A_{min}.

Application of BA (Arpan, 2016) includes structural design optimization, multi-objective optimization, numerical optimization problems, network path analysis, multi-constrained operations, adaptive learning problems, environmental/economic dispatch, scheduling, effort estimation, classification, vector matching and association rule mining.

Cuckoo Search Algorithm (CSA)

Cuckoo search algorithm (CSA) (Yang & Deb, 2009) is based on the brood parasitism of some cuckoo species. The algorithm uses the Levy flights rather than simple random walk. It was inspired by cuckoos' breeding behavior of parasitic cuckoo species, and in the meantime combining the Lévy flight behavior discovered in some birds and fruit flies. In addition, this algorithm uses a balanced combination of a local random walk with permutation and the global explorative random walk, controlled by a switching parameter which is related to similarity of the egg/ solution to the existing egg/solution. As a result, more similar eggs will be more likely to be survived and be part of the next generation.

The CSA uses the following main basic rules:

1. Each cuckoo lays one egg at a time and dumps its egg in a randomly chosen nest;
2. The best nests with high-quality eggs will continue to the next generation;
3. The number of available host nests is fixed, and the egg laid by a cuckoo is discovered by the host bird with a probability p_a. In this case, the host bird can either get rid of the egg or simply abandon the nest and build a new nest.

Applications of CSA includes (Arpan, 2016) search problems, multi-objective problems, optimization among designs, gradient based optimization, gradient free optimization, multi-objective scheduling, multi-objective allocation, phase equilibrium problems, reliability optimization, path identification for network analysis, knapsack problems.

Genetic Algorithms (GA)

Genetic Algorithms (GAs) proposed by John Holland in1975 are adaptive heuristic search algorithm based on the evolutionary ideas of natural selection and genetics. As such they represent an intelligent exploitation of a random search used to solve optimization problems. Although randomized, GAs are by no means random, instead they exploit historical information to direct the search into the region of better performance within the search space. Genetic algorithms use the principles of selection and evolution to produce several solutions to a given problem. Genetic algorithm is a kind of method to simulate the natural evolvement process to search the optimal solution, and the algorithm can be evolved by four operations including coding, selecting, crossing and variation.

The general flow of Genetic Algorithm is described as follows:

1. Randomly initialize population (t);
2. Determine fitness of population (t);
3. Repeat:
    a. Select parents from population (t);
    b. Perform crossover on parents creating population (t+1);
    c. Perform mutation of population (t+1);
    d. Determine fitness of population (t+1);
4. Until best individual is good enough.

Applications of Genetic Algorithm includes (Arpan, 2016) search, maximization or minimization, sorting, multi-criteria selection, job allocation, process scheduling, network analysis parallel computation, prioritization, classification, network path routing, layout planning, anomaly detection, signal coordination, sorting, structural systems, state assignment problem, economics and computer-aided design (see Table 1).

Applications of Bio Inspired Algorithms in Feature Selection

In this paper (Hannah, Ahmad & Jothi, 2014), new supervised feature selection methods based on hybridization of Particle Swarm Optimization (PSO), PSO based Relative Reduct(PSO-RR) and PSO based Quick Reduct (PSO-QR) are presented for the diseases diagnosis. The experimental result on several standard medical datasets proves the efficiency of the proposed technique as well as enhancements over the existing feature selection techniques. Hence in this methodology, discretization is applied as the first (preprocessing) step. When all the continuous attributes are discretized, attribute Selection attributes relevant for mining, among all original attributes, are selected. Feature selection, as preprocessing step to machine learning, is effective in reducing dimensionality, removing irrelevant data, increasing learning accuracy and improving result comprehensibility. In the second step, SPSO-QR and SPSO-RR are applied to select relevant features from the data set. Best subset of features selected by Feature selection

Table 1. Applications of bio - inspired computing algorithms in feature selection, clustering and classification

Bio - Inspired Algorithms	Purpose	Techniques
Particle Swarm Optimization	Hybrid feature selection Attribute reduction Classification	PSO and Rough set. Multi-granularity Rough set for attribute reduction through PSO. PSO.
Ant Colony Optimization	Feature selection Clustering Classification	ACO and Rough set. ACO, PSO and K means. FUZZY ACO.
Firefly Algorithms	Feature selection Clustering Classification	FA and Rough Set. FA. FA FUZZY.
Artificial Bees Colony	Feature selection Clustering	ABC. ABC.
Cuckoo Search	Feature selection Clustering	CS and Rough Set. CS
Bat Algorithms	Feature selection	BA and Rough Set.
Genetic Algorithms	Feature Selection	GA

methods improves classification accuracy. Hence the third step applies classification methods to diagnose the diseases and classification accuracy measures are used to evaluate performance of the Feature selection methods. The proposed methods are compared with existing rough set based supervised algorithms and classification accuracy measures are used to evaluate the performance of the proposed approaches. Hence the analysis section clearly proved the effectiveness of hybridized PSO and RST based approaches for diagnosis the disease over the other existing approaches. Feature selection based on rough set and PSO is also discussed by (Xiangyang, Jie, Xiaolong, Weijun & Richard, 2007).

In this paper (Guangyao, Zongmei, Chao, Hongbo, Aboul & Wanqing, 2015), a multi-granularity rough set algorithm for attribute reduction through particle swarm optimization was developed. They evaluated the performance of their approach using the Statlog (Heart) Data Set by the corresponding computational experiments. The empirical results indicate that their approach is effective at identifying multiple factors and can the multiple candidates reducts.

Ant colony optimization (ACO) has been successfully applied to many difficult combinatorial problems like quadratic assignment, traveling salesman, scheduling, etc. It is particularly attractive for feature selection since there is no heuristic information that can guide search to the optimal minimal subset every time. However, ants can discover the best feature combinations as they traverse the graph. In this paper (Yumin, Duoqian & Ruizhi, 2010) they proposed a new rough set approach to feature selection based on ACO, which adopts mutual information based feature significance as heuristic information. A novel feature selection algorithm is also given. Their approach starts from the feature core, which changes the complete graph to a smaller one. To verify the efficiency of algorithm, experiments are carried out on some standard UCI datasets. The results demonstrate that their algorithm can provide efficient solution to find a minimal subset of the features.

This paper aims at investigating, implementing, and analyzing a feature selection method using the Artificial Bee Colony approach to classification of different data sets. Various UCI data sets have been used to demonstrate the effectiveness of the proposed method against other relevant approaches available in the literature.

A novel hybrid supervised feature selection algorithm (Jothi & Hannah, 2016), called TRSFFQR (Tolerance Rough Set Firefly based Quick Reduct), is developed and applied for MRI brain images. The hybrid intelligent system aims to exploit the benefits of the basic models and at the same time, moderate their limitations. Different categories of features are extracted from the segmented MRI images, i.e., shape, intensity and texture based features. The features extracted from brain tumor Images are real values. Hence Tolerance Rough set is applied in this work. In this study, a hybridization of two techniques, Tolerance Rough Set(TRS) and Firefly Algorithm (FA) are used to select the imperative features of brain tumor. Performance of TRSFFQR is compared with Artificial Bee Colony (ABC), Cuckoo Search Algorithm (CSA), Supervised Tolerance Rough Set–PSO based Relative Reduct (STRSPSO-RR) and Supervised Tolerance Rough Set–PSO based Quick Reduct (STRSPSO-QR). The experimental result shows the effectiveness of the proposed technique as well as improvements over the existing supervised feature selection algorithms. Rough set based feature selection using fire fly algorithm is also discussed in (Hema & Monika, 2011).

This paper (Emaryl,Waleed & Aboul, 2014), presents a new feature selection technique based on rough sets and bat algorithm (BA). BA is attractive for feature selection in that bats will discover best feature combinations as they fly within the feature subset space. Compared with GAs, BA does not need complex operators such as crossover and mutation, it requires only primitive and simple mathematical operators, and is computationally inexpensive in terms of both memory and runtime. A fitness function based on rough-sets is designed as a target for the optimization. The used fitness function incorporates both the classification accuracy and number of selected features and hence balances the classification performance and reduction size. This paper makes use of four initialization strategies for starting the optimization and studies its effect on bat performance. The used initialization reflects forward and backward feature selection and combination of both. Experimentation is carried out using UCI data sets which compares the proposed algorithm with a GA-based and PSO approaches for feature reduction based on rough-set algorithms. The results on different data sets show that bat algorithm is efficient for rough set-based feature selection. The used rough-set based fitness function ensures better classification result keeping also minor feature size. Other similar implementations are also discussed in (Ahmed, Aida & Soong, 2013).

In this paper (Mohamed & Aboul, 2016), a modified cuckoo search algorithm with rough sets is presented to deal with high dimensionality data through feature selection. The modified cuckoo search algorithm imitates the obligate brood parasitic behavior of some cuckoo species in combination with the Lévy flight behavior of some birds. The modified cuckoo search uses the rough sets theory to build the fitness function that takes the number of features in reduct set and the classification quality into account. The proposed algorithm is tested and validated benchmark on several benchmark datasets drawn from the UCI repository and using different evaluation criteria as well as a further analysis is carried out by means of the analysis of variance test. In addition, the proposed algorithm is experimentally compared with the existing algorithms on discrete datasets. Finally, two learning algorithms, namely K-nearest neighbors and support vector machines are used to evaluate the performance of the proposed approach. The results show that the proposed algorithm can significantly improve the classification performance.

Genetic algorithm can help banks in credit scoring of customers by selecting appropriate features and building optimum decision trees. The new proposed hybrid classification model (Mohammad & Mahmood, 2013), is established based on a combination of clustering, feature selection, decision trees, and genetic algorithm techniques. They used clustering and feature selection techniques to pre-process the input samples to construct the decision trees in the credit scoring model. The proposed hybrid model choose and combines the best decision trees based on the optimality criteria. It constructs the final decision tree for credit scoring of customers. Using one credit dataset, results confirm that the classification accuracy of the proposed hybrid classification model is more than almost the entire classification models that have been compared in this paper. Furthermore, the number of leaves and the size of the constructed decision tree (i.e. complexity) are less, compared with other decision tree models.

Applications of Bio Inspired Algorithms in Clustering

This paper (Taher & Babek, 2010), presents a new hybrid evolutionary algorithm to solve nonlinear partitional clustering problem. The proposed hybrid evolutionary algorithm is the combination of FAPSO (fuzzy adaptive particle swarm optimization), ACO (ant colony optimization) and k-means algorithms, called FAPSO-ACO–K, which can find better cluster partition. The performance of the proposed algorithm is evaluated through several benchmark data sets. The simulation results show that the performance of the proposed algorithm is better than other algorithms such as PSO, ACO, simulated annealing (SA), combination of PSO and SA (PSO–SA), combination of ACO and SA (ACO–SA), combination of PSO and ACO (PSO–ACO), genetic algorithm (GA), Tabu search (TS), honey bee mating optimization (HBMO) and k-means for partitional clustering problem.

In this work (Karaboga & Celal, 2011), ABC is used for data clustering on benchmark problems and the performance of ABC algorithm is compared with Particle Swarm Optimization (PSO) algorithm and other nine classification techniques from the literature. Thirteen of typical test data sets from the UCI Machine Learning Repository are used to demonstrate the results of the techniques. The simulation results indicate that ABC algorithm can efficiently be used for multivariate data clustering.

This study (Athraa, Yuhanis & Husniza, 2015), explores the adaptation of another swarm algorithm which is the Firefly Algorithm (FA) in text clustering. They presented two variants of FA; Weight- based Firefly Algorithm (WFA) and Weight-based Firefly Algorithm II (WFAII). The difference between the two algorithms is that the WFAII, includes a more restricted condition in determining members of a cluster. The proposed FA methods are later evaluated using the 20Newsgroups dataset. Experimental results on the quality of clustering between the two FA variants are presented and are later compared against the one produced by particle swarm optimization, K-means and the hybrid of FA and -K-means. The obtained results demonstrated that the WFAII outperformed the WFA, PSO, K-means and FA-Kmeans. This result indicates that a better clustering can be obtained once the exploitation of a search solution is improved.

This paper (Carlos, Henry, Richar, Martha, Elizabeth & Enrique, 2014) introduces a new description-centric algorithm for the clustering of web results, called WDC-CSK, which is based on the cuckoo search meta-heuristic algorithm, k-means algorithm, Balanced Bayesian Information Criterion, split and merge methods on clusters, and frequent phrases approach for cluster labeling. The cuckoo search meta-heuristic provides a combined global and local search strategy in the solution space. Split and merge methods replace the original Lévy flights operation and try to improve existing solutions (nests), so they can be considered as local search methods. WDC-CSK includes an abandon operation that provides diversity and prevents the population nests from converging quickly. Balanced Bayesian Information Criterion is used as a fitness function and allows defining the number of clusters automatically. WDC-CSK was tested with four data sets (DMOZ-50, AMBIENT, MORESQUE and ODP-239) over 447 queries. The algorithm was also compared against other established web document clustering algorithms, including Suffix Tree Clustering (STC), Lingo, and Bisecting k-means. The results show a considerable improvement upon the other algorithms as measured by recall, F-measure, fall-out, accuracy and SSLk.

Applications of Bio Inspired Algorithms in Classification

In this paper (Tiago, Arlindo & Ana, 2004), three different Particle Swarm Data Mining Algorithms were implemented and tested against a Genetic Algorithm and a Tree Induction Algorithm (J48). From the obtained results, Particle Swarm Optimisers proved to be a suitable candidate for classification tasks.

The aim of this paper (Mostafa and Mohammad, 2011) is to use an Ant Colony-based classification system to extract a set of fuzzy rules for diagnosis of diabetes disease, named FCS-ANTMINER. The FCS-ANTMINER has new characteristics that make it different from the existing methods that have utilized the Ant Colony Optimization (ACO) for classification tasks. The obtained classification accuracy is 84.24% which reveals that FCS-ANTMINER outperforms several famous and recent methods in classification accuracy for diabetes disease diagnosis.

A Hybrid Fuzzy-Firefly Approach for Rule-Based Classification is discussed by (Baran, Yousefi, Ostadabbas & Nourani, 2014).

APPLICATIONS OF BIO INSPIRED ALGORITHMS FOR HANDLING UNCERTAINTY MODELS IN BIG DATA CLUSTERING FOR FEATURE SELECTION

According to (Shi, Bin, Ting, Quande, Yuhui, & Kaizhu, 2016), the amount of data are growing exponentially, So the traditional computational models are not suitable to process this massive data. To handle these massive data problem, more effective and efficient methods should be developed. Swarm intelligence or Nature inspired algorithms are most suitable to handle the uncertainty in big data. These algorithms are updated based on few iterative processes and the evaluation of solution is also very simple. The big data analytics may be benefited from these algorithms because handling uncertainty in big data through mathematical models is a difficult task.

(Sujata Dash, 2015) focuses on developing hybrid intelligence techniques for feature selection in big data like micro array data and other biological data sets. Experiments are conducted on big datasets related to micro array and the experimental results show that proposed methods are highly effective for feature selection and attribute reduction. It has been proved that swarm intelligence algorithms give significant improvements in big data feature selection.

(Lipo, Yaoli, & Qing, 2016) surveys main beliefs of feature selection and their recent applications in big data bioinformatics. According to them, common feature selections like filter, wrapper, and embedded feature selection are not suitable for big data applications and uncertainty handling. They formulate feature selection as a combinatorial optimization or search problem and categorize feature selection methods into exhaustive search, heuristic search, and hybrid methods.

FUTURE RESEARCH DIRECTIONS

The challenge now is to develop feature selection applications based on bio- inspired computing algorithms. Amalgamation of various technologies has become one of the most promising tasks in bio-inspired computing research. In addition, some authors discussed about the hybridization of rough set and fuzzy set with swarm intelligence. But, rough set has generalized to many extent such as rough fuzzy set, fuzzy rough set, intuitionistic fuzzy rough set, rough set on fuzzy approximation space, rough set on intuitionistic fuzzy approximation space, rough set with formal concept analysis, rough set on two universal sets, multigranular rough set to name a few. From the perspective and features of computational intelligence, swarm intelligence can be hybridized to any of the techniques mentioned above. This has not been discussed by authors. This provides ample scope of research in bio-inspired computing for feature selection.

CONCLUSION

This chapter surveys seven nature inspired algorithms, namely Particle Swarm Optimization (PSO), Ant Colony Optimization Algorithms (ACO), Artificial Bees Colony Algorithms (ABC), Firefly Algorithms (FA), Bat Algorithms (BA), Cuckoo Search (CS) and Genetic Algorithms (GA) and its application in feature selections, clustering and classification. Besides, there are methods which hybridize rough set and fuzzy set with above mentioned optimization techniques to get better results. Rough set theory is an extensive tool that have been applied to discover the data dependencies, feature selection, pattern selection, decision support system and classification of sample data. Most of the current literature on rough set based tools in bio-inspired computing focuses on classification and reduction issues. This chapter discusses various swarm intelligence methods available for bio-inspired computing and its application to feature selection, clustering and classification. From the review, it is evident that the swarm intelligence approach offers a promising way of solving a number of bio-inspired computing problems. It is also observed that swarm intelligence by itself or in combination with other computational intelligence technologies works remarkably well in many optimization problems, feature selection, clustering and classification problems.

REFERENCES

Agarwal, P., & Mehta, S. (2014). Nature-Inspired Algorithms: State-of-Art, Problems and Prospects. *Nature*, *100*(14).

Banati, H., & Bajaj, M. (2011). Fire fly based feature selection approach. *International Journal of Computer Science Issues*, *8*(4), 473–480.

Binitha, S., & Sathya, S. S. (2012). A survey of bio inspired optimization algorithms. *International Journal of Soft Computing and Engineering*, *2*(2), 137–151.

Chen, Y., Miao, D., & Wang, R. (2010). A rough set approach to feature selection based on ant colony optimization. *Pattern Recognition Letters*, *31*(3), 226–233. doi:10.1016/j.patrec.2009.10.013

Cobos, C., Muñoz-Collazos, H., Urbano-Muñoz, R., Mendoza, M., León, E., & Herrera-Viedma, E. (2014). Clustering of web search results based on the cuckoo search algorithm and Balanced Bayesian Information Criterion. *Information Sciences*, *281*, 248–264. doi:10.1016/j.ins.2014.05.047

Dai, G., Wang, Z., Yang, C., Liu, H., Hassanien, A. E., & Yang, W. (2015). A multi-granularity rough set algorithm for attribute reduction through particles particle swarm optimization. *11th IEEE International Computer Engineering Conference (ICENCO)*, 303-307.

Emary, E., Yamany, W., & Hassanien, A. E. (2014). New approach for feature selection based on rough set and bat algorithm. *9th IEEE International Conference on Computer Engineering & Systems (ICCES)*, 346-353. doi:10.1109/ICCES.2014.7030984

Fister, I., Jr., Yang, X. S., Fister, I., Brest, J., & Fister, D. (2013). *A brief review of nature-inspired algorithms for optimization.* arXiv preprint arXiv:1307.4186

Fister, I., Yang, X. S., & Brest, J. (2013). A comprehensive review of firefly algorithms. *Swarm and Evolutionary Computation*, *13*, 34–46. doi:10.1016/j.swevo.2013.06.001

Ganji, M. F., & Abadeh, M. S. (2011). A fuzzy classification system based on Ant Colony Optimization for diabetes disease diagnosis. *Expert Systems with Applications*, *38*(12), 14650–14659. doi:10.1016/j.eswa.2011.05.018

Inbarani, H. H., Azar, A. T., & Jothi, G. (2014). Supervised hybrid feature selection based on PSO and rough sets for medical diagnosis. *Computer Methods and Programs in Biomedicine*, *113*(1), 175–185. doi:10.1016/j.cmpb.2013.10.007 PMID:24210167

Jothi, G. (2016). Hybrid Tolerance Rough Set–Firefly based supervised feature selection for MRI brain tumor image classification. *Applied Soft Computing*, 639–651.

Kar, A. K. (2016). Bio inspired computing–A review of algorithms and scope of applications. *Expert Systems with Applications*, *59*, 20–32. doi:10.1016/j.eswa.2016.04.018

Karaboga, D., & Akay, B. (2009). A comparative study of artificial bee colony algorithm. *Applied Mathematics and Computation*, *214*(1), 108–132. doi:10.1016/j.amc.2009.03.090

Karaboga, D., & Ozturk, C. (2011). A novel clustering approach: Artificial Bee Colony (ABC) algorithm. *Applied Soft Computing*, *11*(1), 652–657. doi:10.1016/j.asoc.2009.12.025

Khanbabaei, M., & Alborzi, M. (2013). The use of genetic algorithm, clustering and feature selection techniques in construction of decision tree models for credit scoring. *International Journal of Managing Information Technology*, *5*(4), 13–32. doi:10.5121/ijmit.2013.5402

Li, Z., Liu, X., Duan, X., & Huang, F. (2010). Comparative research on particle swarm optimization and genetic algorithm. *Computer and Information Science*, *3*(1), 120. doi:10.5539/cis.v3n1p120

Lipo, W., Yaoli, W., & Qing, C. (2016). Feature selection methods for big data bioinformatics: A survey from the search perspective. *Methods (San Diego, Calif.)*, *111*, 21–31. doi:10.1016/j.ymeth.2016.08.014 PMID:27592382

Mohammed, A. J., Yusof, Y., & Husni, H. (2015). Document clustering based on firefly algorithm. *Journal of Computer Science*, *11*(3), 453–465. doi:10.3844/jcssp.2015.453.465

Mohan, B. C., & Baskaran, R. (2012). A survey: Ant Colony Optimization based recent research and implementation on several engineering domain. *Expert Systems with Applications*, *39*(4), 4618–4627. doi:10.1016/j.eswa.2011.09.076

Niknam, T., & Amiri, B. (2010). An efficient hybrid approach based on PSO, ACO and k-means for cluster analysis. *Applied Soft Computing*, *10*(1), 183–197. doi:10.1016/j.asoc.2009.07.001

Parsons, S. (2005). *Ant Colony Optimization by Marco Dorigo and Thomas Stützle*. MIT Press.

Pawlak, Z. (1982). Rough sets. *International Journal of Computer & Information Sciences*, *11*(5), 341–356. doi:10.1007/BF01001956

Pawlak, Z. (1997). Rough set approach to knowledge-based decision support. *European Journal of Operational Research*, *99*(1), 48–57. doi:10.1016/S0377-2217(96)00382-7

Pouyan, M. B., Yousefi, R., Ostadabbas, S., & Nourani, M. (2014, May).A Hybrid Fuzzy-Firefly Approach for Rule-Based Classification.In *FLAIRS Conference*.357 – 362.

Schiezaro, M., & Pedrini, H. (2013). Data feature selection based on Artificial Bee Colony algorithm. *EURASIP Journal on Image and Video Processing*, (1): 1–8.

Selvaraj, C., Siva Kumar, R., & Karnan, M. (2014). A survey on application of bio-inspired algorithms. *International Journal of Computer Science and Information Technologies*, *5*(1), 366–370.

Shi, C., & Bin, L., Ting, Quande, Q., Yuhui, S., & Kaizhu, H. (2016). Survey on data science with population-based algorithms. *Big Data Analytics*, *1*(3), 1–20.

Shi, Y. (2004). Particle swarm optimization. *IEEE Connections*, *2*(1), 8–13.

Sousa, T., Silva, A., & Neves, A. (2004). Particle swarm based data mining algorithms for classification tasks. *Parallel Computing*, *30*(5), 767–783. doi:10.1016/j.parco.2003.12.015

Sujata, D. (2015). Learning Using Hybrid Intelligence Techniques. *Computational Intelligence for Big Data Analysis*, 73-96.

Taha, A. M., Mustapha, A., & Chen, S. D. (2013). Naive bayes-guided bat algorithm for feature selection. *The Scientific World Journal, 2013*, 1-10.

Wang, X., Yang, J., Teng, X., Xia, W., & Jensen, R. (2007). Feature selection based on rough sets and particle swarm optimization. *Pattern Recognition Letters*, *28*(4), 459–471. doi:10.1016/j.patrec.2006.09.003

Zadeh, L. A. (1965). Fuzzy sets. *Information and Control*, *8*(3), 338–353. doi:10.1016/S0019-9958(65)90241-X

KEY TERMS AND DEFINITIONS

Classification: Objects that are indiscernible based on their attribute values are belongs to same class and we call it as classification.

Clustering: Grouping of objects according to some pre-defined criteria based on some algorithm techniques is known as clustering.

Evolutionary Algorithms: Systems made by writing an algorithm that generate a random set of solutions for the given problem which can be optimized by iteration.

Global Optimization: An algorithm that deals with problems in which a best solution can be represented as a point in an n-dimensional space.

Indiscernibility: Objects for which attribute values are exactly same are termed as indiscernible.

Information Systems: A dataset which provides information about objects and its attributes in a given context is called as information system.

Rough Set: A model, proposed by Pawlak to capture imprecision in data through boundary approach.

Swarm Intelligence: The behavioural models of social insects such as ant colonies, honey bees, firefly, and bird flocks are termed as swarm intelligence.

Chapter 17
Nature-Inspired-Algorithms-Based Cellular Location Management:
Scope and Applications

Swati Swayamsiddha
Indian Institute of Technology Kharagpur, India

Chetna Singhal
Indian Institute of Technology Kharagpur, India

Rajarshi Roy
Indian Institute of Technology Kharagpur, India

ABSTRACT

Nature-Inspired algorithms have gained relevance particularly for solving complex optimization problems in engineering domain. An overview of implementation modeling of the established algorithms to newly developed algorithms is outlined. Mobile location management has vital importance in wireless cellular communication and can be viewed as an optimization problem. It has two aspects: location update and paging where the objective is to reduce the overall cost incurred corresponding to these two operations. The potential application of the Nature-Inspired algorithms to mobile location management is studied. Many such algorithms are recently being explored along with incremental modifications to the existing techniques. Finally, analysis and insights highlight the further scopes of the Nature-Inspired algorithms to mobile location management application.

1. MISSION AND CONCERNS

The purpose of this chapter is to introduce the existing as well as recently developed Nature-Inspired algorithms with their implementation details and flowcharts. This chapter also provides a survey analysis of Nature-Inspired algorithms for cost optimization in mobile location management (MLM) problem and

DOI: 10.4018/978-1-5225-2857-9.ch017

their further potential scope of application. The objective of this work is to introduce the importance of these algorithms for solving the real time applications and also provides initial food for thought in terms of the scope of these algorithms in MLM. In recent years, these metaheuristic nature-inspired optimization algorithms have witnessed a lot of attention in this domain except the newly developed ones whose applicability still remains unexplored. The various sections of this chapter are divided as: Introduction and background, problem formulation and modelling mobile location management as optimization problem and MLM schemes. Subsequently nature-inspired algorithms are explored in general context. Then based on the location management applications and scope of the algorithms, we provide insights on the potential applications of recently developed nature-inspired algorithms for future research directions.

2. INTRODUCTION AND BACKGROUND

The nature-inspired algorithms owe their significance due to the ability to adapt to the changing behavior of the objective function and automatic adjustment from exploration to exploitation to find the global optimal solution and at the same time fine-tuning the control parameters to increase the convergence speed and decrease the computational cost. There is extensive use of these algorithms principally due to their simplicity, easy implementation and diverse solutions (Yang 2012b). Recently, the wireless communication technology has undergone tremendous growth and since the numbers of mobile users are rising rapidly, the mobile location management (MLM) has captured the attention of the researchers which is a key issue in mobile computing. The importance of cellular network lies in managing the traffic efficiently and effectively. Since metaheuristic techniques allow for a variety of possibilities for solving a problem, hence it is employed in optimizing location management cost. This cost must be optimized to minimize lag and bloat in the network and increase profit and cellular capacity. This may be done by resorting to nature-inspired algorithms which are usually robust and natural to implement (Alba et al. 2008).

Location Management is the dynamic tracking of current location of mobile users in a cellular network. It also deals with minimizing cost and overhead associated with the process. It broadly consists of two processes: Location update and Paging (Wong and Leung 2009). In some research work, Location update is also referred to as 'Registration' or 'Location Registration', whereas Paging is also referred to as 'Location Lookup' or 'Search'. Location update is performed by the user equipment which informs the network of the user's current location. Paging is performed by the base station which polls a group of cells to determine the precise location of the user so that an incoming call can be diverted to it without much delay. There is utmost need for efficient cellular network design such that the cost and delay involved in location mobility management is optimized. Thus, many schemes have been proposed for solving this issue which is discussed in detail in section 4, the principal ones being location area (LA) scheme and reporting cell planning (RCP) strategy which differ in subtle ways. The LA refers to a cluster of cells in a cellular network and the location update is performed only when the mobile terminal (MT) crosses the boundary of one LA to another and the paging is also limited to that LA where the MT currently resides. LA is a group of cells within which no registration occurs, whereas Reporting Cell is that only within which registration occurs.

Thus, a network with N cells can be divided into several disjoint location areas such that:

$$L.A_i \cap L.A_j = \varphi \forall i, j \in N$$

and

$$\cup_{i=1}^{P} L.A_i = Area(N) \tag{1}$$

where P number of L.A exists or, a network can be divided into Reporting Cells (R.C) and Non Reporting Cells (N.R.C) such that:

$$R.C \cap N.R.C = \varphi$$

and

$$\sum R.C + \sum N.R.C = Area(N) \tag{2}$$

In a similar fashion, Location Update and Handoff are different in the sense that when the Mobile User changes a cell, it is called Handoff. When the user changes Location Area, it is called Location Update. In context of Location Management, another term crops up, called Mobility Management. Mobility Management is a larger concept which may be broadly divided into two categories: Location Management and Handoff Management.

In context of research, three artificial life techniques such as Genetic algorithm, Tabu Search and Ant Colony Algorithm have been used for location management cost optimization (Subrata and Zomaya 2003a). Differential Evolution has been employed (Almeida et al. 2011) for solving the mobile location management problem. The Binary Particle Swarm Optimization for reporting cell planning problem has been proposed and compared with the earlier works (Kim et al. 2012). A hybrid swarm optimization technique is suggested for location area registration based on intelligent foraging of artificial bee colony swarm (Chaurasia and Singh 2015). Similarly various other naturally occurring phenomenons have been taken into account albeit at a gradual pace. The developing stages of Nature-inspired computing techniques are introduced (Kar 2016) from its application perspective to MLM by describing the upgrades of its importance in cellular networks design, and the relationship between mobility management technology and Nature-inspired optimization.

In this work we first discuss in brief the various bio-inspired optimization algorithms in a qualitative point of view. Then we try to review the work done related to bio-inspired algorithms for MLM for helping to carry out future research work in this field.

3. MLM AS OPTIMIZATION PROBLEM

As discussed in (Subrata and Zomaya 2003b, Kim et al. 2012), mobile location management cost broadly consists of registration cost and lookup cost, i.e.:

$$Cost_{total} = \gamma Cost_{registration} + Cost_{lookup} \tag{3}$$

The registration cost is the cost incurred in sending a message from the mobile user to the base station informing it of its current location. Lookup cost is the cost incurred when the base station searches for the mobile user to forward an incoming call. γ is a factor which is multiplied with registration cost as a weight factor as usually the registration cost is much higher than the lookup cost. The registration cost is incurred when the mobile terminal updates its current cellular location whereas the lookup cost is cost incurred by the network while paging and locating the precise position of the mobile terminal in order to route the incoming call to the intended user. If the mobile terminal updates its location every time it enters a new cell, then the registration cost increases and at the same time the paging cost decreases as the network has to do the least to locate the current position of the mobile user. Whereas, if the mobile terminal does not update the location frequently the registration cost comes down but the network has to page cells to a greater extent thereby increasing the lookup cost. So, when the registration cost increases the lookup cost decreases and vice-versa and a trade-off between the two optimizes the total cost incurred due to the location update and paging. Thus, mobile location management can be developed as an optimization problem where the goal is to minimize the total cost incurred due to location update and paging as illustrated in Equation (3).

4. MLM SCHEMES

The coverage of the location management strategies provides an impetus for selection of effective and efficient schemes for location registration and location inquiry so as to ensure minimal communication and processing costs (Mukherjee and De 2016). Figure 1 shows the location management strategies.

Figure 1. Location management strategies

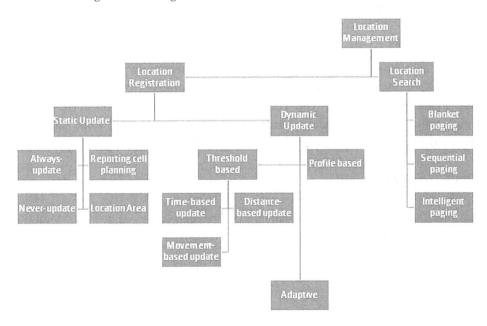

4.1. Location Update

The location registration involves updating of location of the mobile terminal whenever it enters a new cell. It is a costly affair as network spectrum communication channel is used and as well as the signal power is required for information transmission. Location update schemes are categorized into static schemes and dynamic schemes where the static schemes are computationally efficient but cost reduction is lower compared to that of dynamic schemes which are computationally more complex.

4.1.1. Static Schemes

In this scheme the location update takes place in fixed time intervals or upon every cell change. Presently most of the schemes are static in nature.

4.1.1.1. Always-Update vs. Never-Update

In Always-update scheme, the mobile user updates its location whenever it enters a new cell which consumes large resources but the network is able to know the exact position of the mobile terminal to route the incoming call. This scheme is suitable for less mobile and low call arrival systems. The Never-update scheme is logically opposite to the prior one which does not involve location update as a result the paging cost is very high for high call arrival rates. Thus, the Always-update minimizes the location search cost whereas the Never-update scheme minimizes the location registration cost which represents the extremes of location management.

4.1.1.2. Reporting Cell Planning

In this scheme, the mobile device updates its location only when it enters the pre-defined cells called reporting cells. The search operation is carried out for routing a call arrival at the neighborhood of the last updated reporting cell (Subrata and Zomaya 2003a). Thus, the optimal number and position of the reporting cells in this configuration is detrimental to minimize the location update cost and paging cost.

4.1.1.3. Location Areas

The location area scheme involves partitioning of the cellular mobile network into location areas or meta-cells which constitutes a group of cells. The mobile user updates its location only when leaving its current location area (Almeida et al 2011). This reduces the paging cost as the network searches for the mobile terminal only within the particular location area. The disadvantage of this scheme is ping-pong effect. However, this location management strategy is largely been used.

4.1.2. Dynamic Schemes

These are advanced schemes and is modified to best fit the individual users and the conditions. Presently the ongoing research focusses on dynamic schemes.

4.1.2.1. Threshold Based

In threshold based scheme, the location update takes place when a particular parameter exceeds a certain level. The parameters here may be time, movement or distance:

1. **Time-Based Update:** The mobile user updates its location at certain time interval. This requires a simple timer for its implementation but the number of redundant updates has to be minimized by optimizing the timer interval on per-user basis;
2. **Movement-Based Update:** The location update takes place at a certain threshold of boundary crossings of the mobile user. The paging area is restricted around the radius of last updated location;
3. **Distance-Based Update:** Here the mobile user updates its location after travelling a certain radii from its last updated position. This distance threshold is optimized for per-user on basis of call arrival and mobility rate.

4.1.2.2. Profile Based

In this scheme the cellular network maintains a per-user profile based on previous movements containing a list of probable cells at which the user can reside. The mobile device updates its location only when entering a cell not contained in the list. This performs better if the predictability is high otherwise the overhead cost outweighs the cost reduction by profile based scheme.

4.1.2.3. Adaptive

In adaptive scheme a number of parameters are taken into consideration while assigning location area for the mobile user. The predictive distance based update scheme and activity based location update scheme are adaptive where the size of location area changes with call arrival rate and mobility rate.

4.2. Paging

The paging operation is performed by the cellular mobile network in order to determine the exact cellular location of the mobile user so that the incoming call can be routed without much delay. The paging cost involved can be minimised if the polling area is reduced which can be effectively achieved by the following paging strategies.

4.2.1. Simultaneous Paging

Also called as blanket paging, where all the cells of the location area where the mobile user is expected are enquired simultaneously to determine the exact cellular position of the user. It involves excessive amount of traffic and is suitable for cellular networks consisting of bigger cells with less population density and low rate of calls.

4.2.2. Sequential Paging

This mechanism involves polling of different segments of a location area called paging area one after another instead of paging the total location area. The order of paging according to decreasing probability of mobile user's residence is an important factor for optimal performance in terms of paging delay.

4.2.3. Intelligent Paging

It involves determining the order of paging by intelligent algorithms according to the probability of user's residence. It involves paging the right location area in the first go with high success rate. However, the computational overhead is high and it's not feasible for large networks.

5. REVIEW OF NATURE-INSPIRED METAHEURISTIC ALGORITHMS

The nature-inspired metaheuristic algorithms are broadly classified into evolutionary algorithms and swarm intelligence algorithms. These algorithms are inspired from the processes of Nature to solve optimization problems. The popular as well as newly developed algorithms are highlighted and discussed briefly as follows.

5.1. Artificial Neural Algorithms (ANN)

It is a class of adaptive learning that is inspired from the human nervous system and human brain. It is adaptive to the changing environment where a number of networks are connected to each other in different layers (Grossberg 1988). The neural network is basically a black box comprising of inputs which are dependent on feedback received and weights which are adjustable parameters. It has an input/output relationship as it learns from the feedback.

5.2. Genetic Algorithm (GA)

Described by (Holland 1975) and developed by Goldberg and De Jong, it is a population based algorithm where the set of chromosomes act as potential solutions to optimization problems. It works on the concept of "Survival of the fittest" criterion of Darwin. Genetic algorithms are basically heuristic search mechanisms applied for solving optimization problems.

Steps of the algorithm:

1. The algorithm begins with initialization of the population (chromosomes). Then the fitness of each chromosome is tested using a specific fitness function and the fittest chromosomes are selected;
2. **Cross Over:** The selected chromosomes undergo crossover and reproduce off springs. Now the population consists of better individuals. Clones of good strings are made and send to the matting pool to produce better strings;
3. **Mutation:** In this step the strings undergo mutation to introduce variation in the population. Here the bits are flipped;
4. **Selection:** The new population replaces the earlier one if it is fitter. At the end a new set of population is obtained.

This iterative process continues till the stopping criterion is met or the maximum generation is reached.

5.3. Differential Evolution (DE)

Described by (Storn and Price 1997), the method of DE is similar to GA with a small change of mutation occurring prior to crossover unlike GA where first cross over is done and then mutation takes place. Mutation here is not dependent on any predefined function. DE optimization algorithm is faster in comparison to GA. The steps involved in DE are initialization, differential mutation, crossover and selection. In the initialization step, a population of random vectors are generated which represents the potential solutions and these are evaluated using the fitness function. The next step involves generation of a mutant vector which is evaluated by adding the weighted difference of two randomly chosen vectors to a third random vector. In the crossover step, there is exchange of parameters between the mutant vector and a pre-determined target vector on the basis of crossover probability. The resultant is called a trial vector which introduces diversity in the population. If the trial vector yields better cost function than the target vector, then it replaces the latter in the next generation which is the selection step. The performance of the algorithm depends on the population size, the parameter selection and dimensionality of the problem.

5.4. Particle Swarm Optimization (PSO)

Proposed by (Kennedy and Eberhart 1995) it is inspired by the behavior of folk of birds searching for their food in multi-dimensional search space. PSO is a population based iterative optimisation technique where the initial particles or solutions which are randomly initialised progresses towards better solution in every iteration. The birds or particles represents the candidate solutions. The population of such particles represents the swarm. The basic principle is to follow the bird nearest to the food source. The solutions in the search space are considered to be birds having their unique fitness value. Each particle is characterized by position vector and velocity vector (Shi and Eberhart 1999). An individual particle's best fitness value so far is called personal best (pbest) and the best fitness value among its neighbors' is termed as global best(gbest) which are evaluated in each iteration. If the current pbest and gbest are better than that of previous iterations then the former values are replaced with the current ones. The movement of the particles is directed by the pbest which represents the best value of each particle achieved so far and gbest which represents the global best solution among all the particles. The fitness value is obtained for every particle along with location and velocity update for every iteration. The optimal solution corresponds to the gbest solution obtained after the final iteration.

5.5. Ant Colony Optimization (ACO)

It was first introduced by (Dorigo and Blum 2005). This algorithm is inspired by the ants and the way they search their food. Ants secrete a chemical called pheromone when they move in search of food (Dorigo, Birattari and Stützle 2006). This chemical serves as a path selector for its peers. More the pheromone in a path has more probability of being chosen by the other ants.

5.6. Artificial Bee Algorithm (ABA)

It was proposed by (Karaboga and Basturk 2007). It is related to the way honey bees look for nectar. Bees are divided into three groups:

- **Employed Bees:** These bees select the food sources;
- **Onlooker Bees:** These bees select the food sources with better fitness value from those selected by the employed bees;
- **Scouts:** These are the third category of bees which perform random search for discovering new sources.

5.7. Bacteria Foraging Optimization (BFO)

It was suggested by (Passino 2002). Foraging is a phenomena of a bacteria colony. The three basic principle mechanisms are:

- **Chemotaxis:** It is the gathering of bacteria in nutrient rich areas;
- **Reproduction:** Only the best bacteria survive and transmit their genetic characteristics;
- **Elimination-Dispersion:** Part of the bacteria population diminishes through dispersion. This way it ensures diversity of their species.

5.8. Leaping Frog Algorithm (LFA)

It is based on the hunting nature of frogs (Snyman 2000). In the initial stage a set of virtual frogs are taken into consideration. Then they are divided into a number of memeplex which is further divided into sub memeplex. Here the worst frog jumps in the same manner as the best frog in that memeplex. If the jump finds better results than the previous, the process is repeated by the frog, else a new frog is randomly created.

5.9. Cuckoo Search (CS)

Introduced in 2009 this algorithm is based on the breeding habit of cuckoos who lay their eggs in the nests of other birds and has lot of potential applications (Yang and Deb 2009). Under this mechanism every egg is treated as a solution and a cuckoo egg as a new solution. Cuckoos stealthily drop their egg into other birds' nest. The discovery of this egg by the host bird has a certain probability. Best nests with better eggs carry over to the future generations.

5.10. Firefly Algorithm (FA)

Yang formulated this algorithm which uses the blinking habit of fireflies based on process of bioluminescence (Yang 2010a). The fireflies glow to either to attract the mating partners, or potential prey or to signal protection from predators. The attraction of the fireflies is proportional to the brightness or intensity of flashing light. The stronger fireflies glow more, resulting in meeting a partner which results in more efficient exploration. Also the light intensity varies inversely with respect to distance and light absorption in air. So, the attractiveness varies accordingly and the less bright firefly moves towards the brighter one. The brightness of the flash light of the fireflies serve as the objective function and according to the formulation of the attractiveness of the fireflies new solutions are evaluated and light intensity is updated till the global best is reached.

5.11. Cat Swarm Optimization (CSO)

It was proposed by (Chu, Tsai and Pan 2006) based on the behaviour of cats. It has two modes:

1. **Seeking Mode:** It replicates the resting mode of the cat where actually it alertly prepares itself for its next movement;
2. **Tracing Mode:** In this mode the cat traces its food during which its velocity and position update takes place.

5.12. Artificial Bat Algorithm (ABA)

It was introduced by (Yang 2010b). It uses the sonic imaging of bats based on echolocation. Frequencies, loudness and pulse emission rates are the parameters that control the generation of new solution close to global optimization. It has the unique feature of balancing the global exploration and local exploitation. The echolocation principle is used by the bat which is the only flying mammal in dark by emitting a sound pulse of certain loudness and hearing the echo of it to detect the nearness of the food or to avoid obstacles. The bats randomly fly with certain velocity at a particular position with fixed frequency and varying loudness to estimate the location of their prey. The bat reaches its food by fine-tuning the frequency and rate of pulse emission and consequently updating its velocity and position (Huang 2016).

5.13. Artificial Immunological Computation (AIC)

AIC uses the action of immune cells in the human body. It is a network of interconnected cells for the recognition of antigens. They established the network by stimulating and suppressing each other (Castro and Timmis, 2002).

5.14. Flower Pollination Algorithm (FPA)

In (Yang, 2012) explained how flowering plants disperse the pollen grains. This algorithm is based on two optimization processes:

1. **Cross Pollination:** It is a global optimization problem with pollen carriers performing random flights. This involves the transfer of the pollens between flowers of different plants using biotic vectors like insects and birds;
2. **Self-Pollination:** It is a local optimization process. It involves transfer of pollens between flowers of same plant using abiotic factors like wind or water.

5.15. Artificial Plant Optimization (APO)

Artificial Plant Optimization (APO) is based on the growing parts that would address the multimodal optimization problems. The branches of the plant provide potential solutions. Here the growing plant corresponds to the search space. The fitness of the branches is calculated and subsequently the photosynthesis mechanisms are used to determine new solutions (Cui and Cai 2013).

Figure 2 summarizes the flow- diagram of some of the lesser known algorithms discussed above and the popular ones can be referred in (Nanda and Panda 2014).

6. APPLICATION OF NATURE-INSPIRED METAHEURISTICS FOR MLM-A SURVEY

The main objective of mobile location management using nature-inspired algorithms is to optimize the total location registration cost and location search cost. Various methods have been used for achieving cost optimization in mobile location management but there is significant scope for application of nature-inspired techniques.

Figure 3 represents the year wise analysis of location management from year 2006 to 2016 based on the IEEE publications. The first peak has been achieved in the year 2007, followed by 2006 and 2008. Lately, there has been a decrease in the amount of work done in this vast area. As this is the era of wireless, there exists a lot of scope for research in this field.

Mobile location management being a vast and very important field of research only 14.88% (Figure 4) of work had been done on its cost optimization. As cost being an important factor a lot of work can be done to optimize it so that the technology is helpful to serve the needs of the population. The mobile location cost comprises of location update cost and paging cost and since both are conflicting objective functions a trade-off between the two gives the optimal solution.

Figure 2. Flowchart representations of some of the nature-inspired algorithms

	Flow steps					
L.F.A:	Begin →	Specify parameters (Population size, memeplexes, evolution steps) →	Initialize Frog population →	Arrange in Descending order →	Divide population into memeplex →	Update worst frog
			↑ Next Gen. ↑			↓ ↓ ↓
			Cl. Op. ←	Selection ←	Fitness ←	Rearrange Memeplex ←
F.A:			← ← Next Gen. ← ←			
	Begin →	Specify Parameters, Iteration (max) →	Arrange by Brightness →	Selection →	Update location of shiniest & dullest firefly →	Cl. Op.
C.S.O:			← ← ← Next Gen. ←		← ←	
	Initialize Cats →	Velocity Update →	Set to tracing mode/ seeking mode →	Fitness →	Selection →	Cl. Op.
A.B.A:			← ← ← Next Gen. ←		← ←	
	Initialize Bat Population & Individual Velocities →	Set constraints, Set Parameters (Pulse Rate, Loudness etc) →	Velocity Update, Location Update →	Fitness →	Selection →	Cl. Op.
F.P.A:			← ← ← Next Gen. ← ← ← ←			
	Initialize pollens →	Identify Best Pollen →	Identify normalized ratio of global and local pollination →	Apply Global Pollination/ Local Pollination →	Fitness →	Selection → Cl. Op.
A.P.O:			← ← ← ← Next Gen. ← ← ← ←			
	Initialize Plant Growth →	Set lower & upper bounds →	Branch Position Update →	Apply Photosynthesis →	Phototropism →	Evaluate Growth Trajectory → Cl. Op.

Figure 3. Year-wise analysis of publications based on mobile location management (2006-16) (IEEE publications)

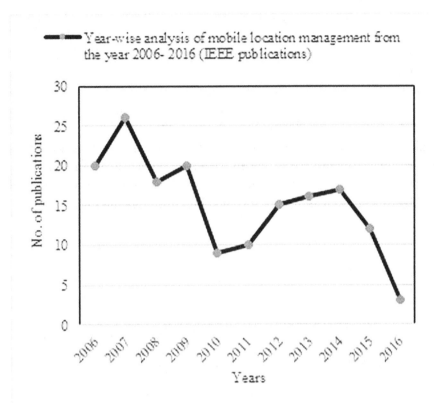

Figure 4. Pie-chart representation of work done in location management for cost optimization (year 2006-2016) based on IEEE publications

2006-2016

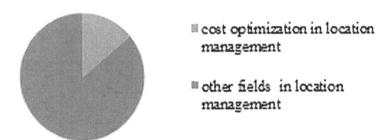

Nature-inspired algorithms, also known as bio-inspired algorithms, are adaptive in nature in comparison to other algorithms. From Figure 5 it can be concluded that approximately 23% of work has been done in location management using nature-inspired algorithms in comparison to the vast field of location management. More is yet to be worked on in this field of location management.

Figure 6 shows the percentage distribution based on publications in IEEE on mobile location management using various nature-inspired algorithms. Some reviews are available on the classic nature-inspired algorithms like Neural Networks, Genetic Algorithm, Ant Colony Optimization, Differential Evolution, Particle Swarm Optimization, Artificial Bee Colony (Taheri & Zomaya, 2007; Subrata & Zomaya 2003a; Subrata & Zomaya 2003b; Almeida et al. 2011; Kim et al. 2012; Chaurasia & Singh 2015, Parija et al. 2017a; Parija et al. 2017b) but no work has been done using the new nature-inspired algorithms. The recently developed algorithms like Bat Algorithm, Cat Swarm Optimization, Bacterial Foraging Optimization, Firefly algorithm, Elephant Herd Algorithm, Flower Pollination Algorithm, Artificial Plant Algorithm as well as the modified and improved versions of the existing algorithms can

Figure 5. Work done in mobile location management using bio inspired algorithms (year 2006-2016) from IEEE publications

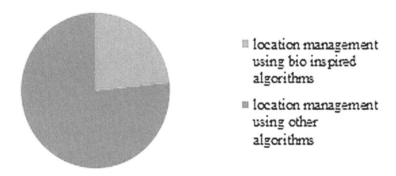

Figure 6. IEEE search results for location management with algorithm names in the title (2006-2016)

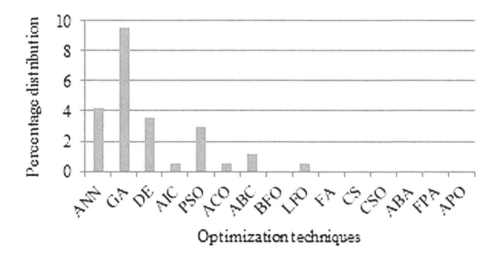

be incorporated for the optimization of cost. These heuristic approaches perform well even for complex cellular network optimization problems. In this wireless era the bandwidth is an important resource and need to be optimized. So, if the number of location updates and paging are reduced for efficient location management the signaling is reduced too which saves the bandwidth requirement. Thus, the location management in cellular networks is an important area of research for tracking the mobile users such that the overhead signaling cost in location registration and location search are optimized. Therefore, this chapter makes a review on the work done and further scope of application to MLM for cost optimization which shows the gaps in current research and gives a new direction to location management problem using nature-inspired techniques.

7. CONCLUSION AND FUTURE DIRECTION

This chapter in general introduces the location management issue in cellular networks and the application of nature-inspired algorithms for optimization of the cost function. The background literature review is provided to give an idea how the nature inspired algorithms are explored for wireless communication problems particularly in the domain of location management. The development of this issue as an optimization problem is discussed in the problem formulation section. The various MLM schemes such static and dynamic schemes are precisely discussed. Then the popular as well as newly proposed nature-inspired algorithms are highlighted and briefly introduced. Then the scope of application of these algorithms to MLM is discussed which provides key areas of research in this direction.

Nature-inspired algorithms look quite promising in terms of the subtle variety that each one offers. This means several algorithms can be potentially combined to a single network to remain entirely flexible at different scenarios. At the same time it can't be emphasized enough how diverse this area is in terms of research yet to be done. With the advent of powerful smartphones, one can only think of the possibilities that portable computing power can bring towards improving the communication capability of cellular networks. Further, it may be pointed out that the advent of solid state storage has drastically reduced the latency, thus the network can potentially transmit at high data rate in bursts, and remain idle the rest of the time. An idling system would consume lower power, which would mean better power efficiency.

The conventional gradient based algorithms which are used for optimization are deterministic, however if there lies a discontinuity in the objective function the derivative-free stochastic methods comes into picture which are heuristic and metaheuristic in nature and gives global optimal solutions. The inspiration from Nature has led to development of several Nature-inspired algorithms which are able to tackle tough, complex and hard optimization problems in different areas of engineering especially in telecommunication domain.

Thus, this chapter gives an overall idea on potential use of Nature-inspired algorithms for mobile location management application which can be used as initial step for exploration of more of such algorithms in this direction. These algorithms are extensively been used for practical applications but the theoretical perspective needs more analysis. More theoretical investigations leading to real-world applications spans the future direction. For further work, hybrid Nature-inspired algorithms can be thought of which takes into account the advantages of different algorithms.

REFERENCES

Alba, E., Garcia-Nieto, J., Taheri, J., & Zomaya, A. Y. (2008). New research in Nature Inspired Algorithms for Mobility Management in GSM Networks. Lecture Notes in Computer Science, 4974, 1-10.

Almeida-Luz, S. M., Vega-Rodríguez, M. A., Gómez-Púlido, J. A., & Sánchez-Pérez, J. M. (2011). Differential Evolution for Solving the Mobile Location Management. *Applied Soft Computing*, *11*(1), 410–427. doi:10.1016/j.asoc.2009.11.031

Chaurasia, S. N., & Singh, A. (2015). A hybrid swarm intelligence approach to the registration area planning problem. *Information Sciences*, *302*, 50–69. doi:10.1016/j.ins.2015.01.012

Chu, S. C., Tsai, P., & Pan, J. S. (2006). Cat swarm optimization. In Q. Yang, & G. Webb (Eds.), Trends in artificial intelligence. Berlin: Springer.

Cui, Z., & Cai, X. (2013). Artificial plant optimization algorithm. Swarm intelligence and bio-inspired computation: Theory and applications, 351–365.

De Castro, L. N., & Timmis, J. (2002). *Artificial immune systems: A new computational intelligence approach*. London: Springer.

Dorigo, M., Birattari, M., & Stützle, T. (2006). Ant colony optimization. *IEEE Computational Intelligence Magazine*, *1*(4), 28–39. doi:10.1109/MCI.2006.329691

Dorigo, M., & Blum, C. (2005). Ant colony optimization theory: A survey. *Theoretical Computer Science*, *344*(2), 243–278. doi:10.1016/j.tcs.2005.05.020

Grossberg, S. (1988). Nonlinear neural networks: Principles, mechanisms, and architectures. *Neural Networks*, *1*(1), 17–61. doi:10.1016/0893-6080(88)90021-4

Holland, J. H. (1975). *Adaptation in natural and artificial systems: An introductory analysis with applications to biology, control, and artificial intelligence*. University of Michigan Press.

Huang, H.-C. (2016). Fusion of Modified Bat Algorithm Soft Computing and Dynamic Model Hard Computing to Online Self-Adaptive Fuzzy Control of Autonomous Mobile Robots. *IEEE Transactions on Industrial Informatics*, *12*(3), 972–979. doi:10.1109/TII.2016.2542206

Kar, A. K. (2016). Bio inspired computing –A review of algorithms and scope of applications. *Expert Systems with Applications*, *59*, 20–32. doi:10.1016/j.eswa.2016.04.018

Karaboga, D., & Basturk, B. (2007). A powerful and efficient algorithm for numerical function optimization: Artificial bee colony (ABC) algorithm. *Journal of Global Optimization*, *39*(3), 459–471. doi:10.1007/s10898-007-9149-x

Kennedy, J., & Eberhart, R. (1995). Particle Swarm Optimization. *Proceedings of IEEE International Conference on Neural Networks, 4*, 1942–1948. doi:10.1109/ICNN.1995.488968

Kim, S. S., Kim, G., Byeon, J. H., & Taheri, J. (2012). Particle Swarm Optimization for Location Mobility Management. *International Journal of Innovative Computing, Information, & Control*, *8*(12), 8387–8398.

Mukherjee, A., & De, D. (2016). Location Management in Mobile Network: A Survey. *Computer Science Review*, *19*, 1–14. doi:10.1016/j.cosrev.2015.12.001

Nanda, S. J., & Panda, G. (2014). A survey on nature inspired metaheuristic algorithms for partitional clustering. *Swarm and Evolutionary Computation, 16,* 1–18. doi:10.1016/j.swevo.2013.11.003

Parija, S. R., Sahu, P. K., & Singh, S. S. (2017). Cost Reduction in Location Management Using Reporting Cell Planning and Particle Swarm Optimization. *Wireless Personal Communication,* 1–21.

Parija, S.R., Singh, S.S., & Swayamsiddha, S. (2017). Particle Swarm Optimization for Cost Reduction in Mobile Location Management Using Reporting Cell Planning Approach. *Recent Developments in Intelligent Nature-Inspired Computing,* 171-189.

Passino, K. M. (2002). Biomimicry of bacterial foraging for distributed optimization and control. *Control Systems, IEEE, 22*(3), 52–67. doi:10.1109/MCS.2002.1004010

Shi, Y., & Eberhart, R. C. (1999). Empirical study of particle swarm optimization. *Proceedings of the 1999 IEEE Congress on Evolutionary Computation,* 1945– 1950. doi:10.1109/CEC.1999.785511

Snyman, J. A. (2000). The LFOPC leap-frog algorithm for constrained optimization. *Computers & Mathematics with Applications (Oxford, England), 40*(8), 1085–1096. doi:10.1016/S0898-1221(00)85018-X

Storn, R., & Price, K. (1997). Differential evolution - a simple and efficient heuristic for global optimization over continuous spaces. *Journal of Global Optimization, 11*(4), 341–359. doi:10.1023/A:1008202821328

Subrata, R., & Zomaya, A. Y. (2003a). A Comparison of Three Artificial Life Techniques for Reporting Cell Planning in Mobile Computing. *IEEE Transactions on Parallel and Distributed Systems, 14*(2), 142–153. doi:10.1109/TPDS.2003.1178878

Subrata, R., & Zomaya, A. Y. (2003b). Evolving Cellular Automata for Location Management in Mobile Computing Networks. *IEEE Transactions on Parallel and Distributed Systems, 14*(1), 13–26. doi:10.1109/TPDS.2003.1167367

Taheri, J., & Zomaya, A. Y. (2007). A Combined Genetic-neural Algorithm for Mobility Management. *Journal of Mathematical Modelling and Algorithms, 6*(3), 481–507. doi:10.1007/s10852-007-9066-5

Wong, V., & Leung, V. (2000). Location management for next generation personal communication networks. *IEEE Network, 14*(5), 18–24. doi:10.1109/65.871336

Yang, X. S. (2010a). Firefly algorithm, stochastic test functions and design optimisation. *International Journal of Bio-inspired Computation, 2*(2), 78–84. doi:10.1504/IJBIC.2010.032124

Yang, X. S. (2010b). A new metaheuristic bat-inspired algorithm. In Nature inspired cooperative strategies for optimization (NICSO 2010). Berlin: Springer.

Yang, X. S. (2012a). Flower pollination algorithm for global optimization. In Unconventional computation and natural computation. Berlin: Springer.

Yang, X. S. (2012b). Nature-Inspired Mateheuristic Algorithms: Success and New Challenges. *J Comput. Eng. Inf. Technol., 1*(1), 1–3. doi:10.4172/2324-9307.1000e101

Yang, X. S., & Deb, S. (2009). Cuckoo search via levy flights. *Proceedings of the world congress on nature & biologically inspired computing,* 210– 214.

KEY TERMS AND DEFINITIONS

Evolutionary Algorithm: Sub-class of Nature-Inspired algorithms based on Darwin's theory of survival of the fittest and natural selection.

Location Update: Performed by mobile station to convey its current up-to-date cellular location.

Mobile Location Management: Tracking the current location of the mobile station in a cellular network.

Nature-Inspired Algorithms: Algorithms mimicking the processes of Nature to solve complex problems.

Optimization: Process of finding the effective solution by minimizing or maximizing the fitness function.

Paging: Performed by the base station by polling a group of cells to determine the precise location of the mobile user.

Swarm Intelligence: Sub-class of Nature-Inspired algorithms based on behavioral models of social creatures such as ant colonies, honey bees, firefly, fish school, bird flocks etc.

Chapter 18
Fuzziness in Ant Colony Optimization and Their Applications

Deepthi P. Hudedagaddi
VIT University, India

B. K. Tripathy
VIT University, India

ABSTRACT

Nature-inspired algorithms are still at a very early stage with a relatively short history, comparing with many traditional, well-established methods. Metaheuristics, in their original definition, are solution methods that orchestrate an interaction between local improvement procedures and higher level strategies to create a process capable of escaping from local optima and performing a robust search of a solution space. One major algorithm is Ant Colony Optimization which has been applied in varied domains to better the performance. Fuzzy Linear Programming models and methods has been one of the most and well-studied topics inside the broad area of Soft Computing. Its applications as well as practical realizations can be found in all the real-world areas. Here we wish to introduce how fuzziness can be included in a nature inspired algorithm like ant colony optimization and thereby enhance its functionality. Several applications of ACO with fuzzy concepts will be introduced in the chapter.

1. INTRODUCTION

Since the fuzzy boom of the 1960s, methodologies based on fuzzy sets (Mousa, 2014) have become a permanent part of all areas of research, development and innovation, and their application has been extended to all areas of our daily life: health, banking, home, and are also the object of study on different educational levels. Similarly, there is no doubt that thanks to the technological potential that we currently have, computers can handle problems of tremendous complexity (both in comprehension and

DOI: 10.4018/978-1-5225-2857-9.ch018

dimension) in a wide variety of new fields. Also since the mid 1970s, GA (or EA from a general point of view) have proved to be extremely valuable for finding good solutions to specific problems in these fields, and thanks to their scientific attractiveness, the diversity of their applications and the considerable efficiency of their solutions in intelligent systems, they have been incorporated into the second level of soft computing components. EA, however, are merely another class of heuristics, or metaheuristics, in the same way as Taboo Search, Simulated Annealing, Hill Climbing, Variable Neighbourhood Search, Estimation Distribution Algorithms (EDA), Scatter Search, GRASP, Reactive Search and very many others are. Generally speaking all these heuristic algorithms (metaheuristics) usually provide solutions which are not ideal, but which largely satisfy the decision-maker or the user. When these act on the basis that satisfaction is better than optimization, they perfectly illustrate Zadeh's famous sentence: "...in contrast to traditional hard computing, soft computing exploits the tolerance for imprecision, uncertainty, and partial truth to achieve tractability, robustness, low solution-cost, and better rapport with reality". Consequently, among the soft computing components, instead of EA (which can represent only one part of the search and optimization methods used), heuristic algorithms and even metaheuristics should be considered. Consequently we could say that the most important second-level Soft Computing components are probabilistic reasoning, fuzzy logic and sets, neural networks and in view of what we have explained, metaheuristics (which would typically encompass EA but would not be confined to these exclusively). As it is patent, all these four main components have common factors as it is Data Mining, essential for learning process, as well as real applications.

2. METAHEURISTICS

The metaheuristics are by far the most popular and define mechanisms for developing an evolution in the search space of the sets of solutions in order to come close to the ideal solution with elements which will survive in successive generations of populations. In the context of soft computing, the hybridizations (Dubois et al, 1990) which take these metaheuristics as a reference are fundamental. A very active area of research is the design of nature-inspired metaheuristics. Many recent metaheuristics, especially evolutionary computation-based algorithms, are inspired by natural systems. Such metaheuristics include Ant colony optimization, particle swarm optimization, cuckoo search, and artificial bee colony to cite a few. Metaheuristics are used for combinatorial optimization in which an optimal solution is sought over a discrete search-space. An example problem is the travelling salesman problem where the search-space of candidate solutions grows faster than exponentially as the size of the problem increases, which makes an exhaustive search for the optimal solution infeasible. Additionally, multidimensional combinatorial problems, including most design problems in engineering (Kirkpatrick, 1983; Holland, 1976; Glover 1977) such as form-finding and behavior-finding, suffer from the curse of dimensionality, which also makes them infeasible for exhaustive search or analytical methods. Popular metaheuristics for combinatorial problems includesimulated annealing by Kirkpatrick et al., genetic algorithms by Holland et al., scatter search (Glover, 1986) and tabu search (Robbins, 1951) by Glover. Literature review on metaheuristic optimization, (Barricelli, 1954) suggested that it was Fred Glover who coined the word metaheuristics (Rastrigin, 1963).

3. ANT COLONY OPTIMIZATION(ACO)

Ant Colony Optimization (ACO) is a recent metaheuristic approach for solving hard combinatorial optimization problems. The inspiring source of ACO is the pheromone trail laying and following behavior of real ants which use pheromones as a communication medium. In analogy to the biological example, ACO is based on the indirect communication of a colony of simple agents, called (artificial) ants, mediated by (artificial) pheromone trails. The pheromone trails in ACO serve as a distributed, numerical information which the ants use to probabilistically construct solutions to the problem being solved and which the ants adapt during the algorithm's execution to reflect their search experience. The first example of such an algorithm is Ant System(AS) which was proposed using as example application, the well-known Traveling Salesman Problem(TSP).

4. FUZZINESS IN ACO

Chandgar et.al developed a novel ant colony optimization algorithm to solve binary knapsack problem. In the developed algorithm for n objects, n candidate groups are created, and each candidate group has exactly m values (for m ants) as 0 or 1. For each candidate value in each group a pheromone is initialized by the value between 0.1 and 0.9, and each ant selects a candidate value from each group. Therefore, the binary solution is generated by each ant by selecting a value from each group. In each generation, pheromone update and evaporation is done. During the execution of algorithm after certain number of generation the best solution is stored as a temporary population. After that, crossover and mutation is performed between the solution generated by ants. We consider profit and weight are fuzzy in nature and taken as trapezoidal fuzzy number. Fuzzy possibility and necessity approaches are used to obtain optimal decision by the proposed ant colony algorithm (Changdar, 2013).

Abd et.al 's approach integrates the merits of both ant colony optimization and steady state genetic algorithm and it has two characteristic features. Firstly, since there is instabilities in the global market and the rapid fluctuations of prices, a fuzzy representation of the economic emission load dispatch (EELD) problem has been defined, where the input data involve many parameters whose possible values may be assigned by the expert. Secondly, by enhancing ant colony optimization through steady state genetic algorithm, a strong robustness and more effectively algorithm was created. Also, stable Pareto set of solutions has been detected, where in a practical sense only Pareto optimal solutions that are stable are of interest since there are always uncertainties associated with efficiency data (Mousa, 2014).

In general, ACO can effectively handle the optimization and clustering problems due to the parallel searching capability. On the other hand, it is well-known to suffer from high computational complexity for a large amount of data. Since each ant (i.e., an image pixel) should estimate the distances and the amount of pheromone on the connected paths, the running cost of ACO can be quite high in the image segmentation. Also, to achieve high-quality segmentation, we need the appropriate number of clusters and their centroids in the clustering algorithm. Commonly, we have assumed or manually determined the relevant number of clusters by investigating the image grayscale histogram. However, the outcomes could not guarantee the optimum. In order to reduce the time complexity of ACO and obtain the more correct number of clusters, we roughly choose the tentative number of clusters based on pixel intensity statistics as the preprocessing step.

In the following section, a couple of applications showing how fuzzy concepts along with ACO are being used is explained.

4.1. Case Study 1: ACO-Based Fuzzy Clustering Algorithm for Noisy Image Segmentation (Yu et al, 2012)

In this paper, a new hybrid clustering algorithm is developed that incorporates ACO-based clustering into PCM, namely ACOPCM which is robust to noise. ACOPCM has three principal advantages:

1. ACOPCM automatically computes the appropriate number of clusters and their centroids by adopting ACO-based clustering without any pre-definition or assumption, which greatly affects the segmentation accuracy, cluster compactness, and coincident clustering problem of PCM;
2. Although existing hybrid swarm-based fuzzy clustering methods could not deal with the coincident clustering problem of PCM, ACOPCM overcomes this problem using pre-classification pixel information derived from ACO-based clustering. The pre-classification pixels are composed of classified and unclassified ants (pixels). The former plays the role as base pixels for preventing coincident clusters, and the latter is classified by PCM;
3. In comparison of ACOPCM with other swarm-based hybrid fuzzy clustering methods, our algorithm is more robust especially to the high level of noise and bias field in image segmentation.

4.2. FCM and PCM Clustering Algorithms

In unsupervised fuzzy clustering, FCM has been a well-known and widely used clustering method, since it was initially proposed by Ruspini and improved by Dune. The algorithm performs clustering by minimizing the objective function JFCM, which as defined in below equation, is the weighted sum of squared errors within each cluster. Let N be the number of pixels, M the cluster number and m the weighted exponent (fuzzifier) that establishes the degree of fuzziness, and then the related optimization problem can be described as follows:

$$\min J_{FCM}(U,C) = \sum_{i=1}^{M} \sum_{j=1}^{N} \mu_{ij}^{m} d_{ij}^{2}$$

$$subject\ to\ 0 \leq \mu_{ij} \leq 1, \sum_{i=1}^{M} \mu_{ij} = 1, \sum_{j=1}^{N} \mu_{ij} > 0 \tag{1}$$

where μ_{ij} is the membership degree of x_j (the intensity of pixel j) to c_i (the intensity of the cluster center i), and $U = [\mu_{ij}]_{MxN}$ is the fuzzy partition matrix, $d_{ij} = \|c_i - x_j\|$ represents the intensity difference between the centroid of cluster i and the pixel j, and $C = \{c_1, c_{2,\ ...}\ c_M\}$ is the set of intensities of cluster centers. The necessary conditions for minimizing J_{FCM} follow the update equations:

$$\mu_{ij} = \left(\sum_{k=1}^{M} \left(\frac{d_{ij}}{d_{kj}} \right)^{2/(m-1)} \right)^{-1}$$

$$\qquad (2)$$

$$c_i = \frac{\sum_{j=1}^{N} \mu_{ij}^{m} \cdot x_j}{\sum_{j=1}^{N} \mu_{ij}^{m}}$$

Note that FCM iteratively optimizes the objective function J_{FCM} by updating μ_{ij} and c_i until $\|U(t+1)-U(t)\| \le \epsilon$ for some small positive number ϵ. Although FCM is a useful method in the image segmentation, membership of each data point does not always reflect well its actual membership to clusters, and may be inaccurate in a noisy environment. To improve this weakness, Krishnapuram and Keller proposed a new clustering algorithm, called possibilistic c-means (PCM). PCM relaxes the column sum constraint in FCM that the memberships of a data point over clusters sum to 1 for giving the low (or even no) membership of noise data, resulting in the related optimization problem described as follows:

$$\min J_{PCM}(U,C) = \sum_{i=1}^{M} \sum_{j=1}^{N} \mu_{ij}^{m} d_{ij}^{2} + \sum_{i=1}^{M} \eta_i \sum_{j=1}^{N} \left(1 - \mu_{ij} \right)^{m}$$

$$subject \ to \ 0 \le \mu_{ij} \le 1, \sum_{j=1}^{N} \mu_{ij} > 0 \qquad (3)$$

In this case, μ_{ij} is defined as:

$$\mu_{ij} = \left(1 + \left(\frac{d_{ij}^{2}}{\eta_i} \right)^{1/(m-1)} \right)^{-1} \qquad (4)$$

where η_i is the scale parameter defined as:

$$\eta_i = K \frac{\sum_{j=1}^{N} \mu_{ij}^{m} \cdot d_{ij}^{2}}{\sum_{j=1}^{N} \mu_{ij}^{m}} \qquad (5)$$

with $K > 0$ and in general $K = 1$.

PCM adopts possibilistic approach in which the membership value of a data represents possibility of a data belonging to a cluster. The possibilistic membership value is often interpreted as the typicality of a data point associated with each cluster rather than its relative memberships to the clusters in FCM. The advantage of PCM over FCM is robustness against outliers. However, by relaxing column sum constraint in FCM, PCM often causes the coincident clustering problem which generates identical clusters. Also, PCM is still fragile to the high level of noise and the initialization of parameters such as inappropriate the number of clusters and their centroids. Figure 1 shows such problems of PCM in brain image segmentation.

Ant colony optimization: Mimicking real ants behavior, ant colony optimization (ACO) algorithm was first proposed by Dorigo et al.. Since then, it has been applied successfully to a wide range of optimization problems such as Traveling Salesman Problem (TSP), Quadratic Assignment Problem (QAP), and Job Shop Scheduling (JSS). Recently, there have been attempts applying ACO to clustering problems. The key strength of ACO is in the direct communication among the individual ants based on pheromone amount and heuristic value, which is calculated by problem-dependent heuristic function that measures the trail quality.

In ACO, the path construction and pheromone update are the main steps. Let path (i, j) denote the path which connects node i to j. Each ant going from node i to j lays pheromone τ_{ij} on path (i, j). In the construction of a path solution, the ant chooses its path based on the following probability:

$$P_{ij} = \frac{\tau_{ij}^{\alpha}(t) \cdot \eta_{ij}^{\beta}(t)}{\Sigma_{s \in S} \tau_{ij}^{\alpha}(t) \cdot \eta_{ij}^{\beta}(t)}, \; j \in S$$

$$\tau_{ij} = \begin{cases} 1 & l_{ij} \leq r \\ 0 & otherwise \end{cases} \tag{6}$$

where $\eta_{ij}(t) = r/l_{ij}$ denotes heuristic information at time t and l_{ij} is the intensity difference between i and j nodes (pixels), and $\tau_{ij}(t)$ denotes the pheromone concentration on path (i, j) at time t. The control parameters α and β explain the relative importance of pheromone versus the heuristic value, r is the

Figure 1. Segmentation problems of PCM: (a) Original simulated brain MR image; (b) Discrete anatomical model (ground truth); (c) Segmentation result with inappropriate cluster centers; (d) Segmentation result with high level of noise (9% Gaussian noise)

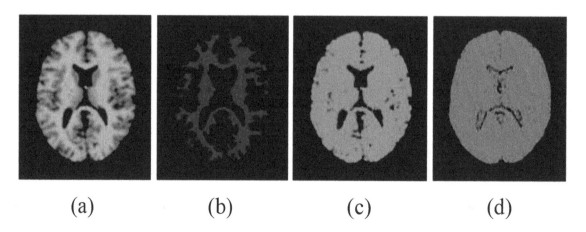

(a)   (b)   (c)   (d)

clustering radius, and $S = \{s \| l_{is} \leq r, s = 1, 2, \ldots, N\}$ is set of feasible nodes. After all ants have finished path construction, the quantity of pheromone is updated according to the following equation:

$$\tau_{ij}(t) = \rho \cdot \tau_{ij}(t) + \sum_{k=1}^{N} \Delta\tau_{ij}^{k} \tag{7}$$

where ρ is the evaporation rate, N is the number of ants, and $\Delta\tau_{ij}^{k}$ is the amount of increased pheromone laid on path (i, j) by the kth ant.

4.3. Adaptive ACO-Based Fuzzy Clustering Algorithm

Initialization of tentative cluster centers. In general, ACO can effectively handle the optimization and clustering problems due to the parallel searching capability. On the other hand, it is well-known to suffer from high computational complexity for a large amount of data. Since each ant (i.e., an image pixel) should estimate the distances and the amount of pheromone on the connected paths, the running cost of ACO can be quite high in the image segmentation. Also, to achieve high-quality segmentation, we need the appropriate number of clusters and their centroids in the clustering algorithm. Commonly, we have assumed or manually determined the relevant number of clusters by investigating the image grayscale histogram. However, the outcomes could not guarantee the optimum. In order to reduce the time complexity of ACO and obtain the more correct number of clusters, we roughly choose the tentative number of clusters based on pixel intensity statistics as the preprocessing step. The procedure of obtaining pixel statistics is described below.

Determine the tentative initial number of clusters and their centroids.

The time complexity of ACO is approximately O(N2), but with the above preprocessing step, obtaining the tentative cluster number M0, the time complexity of ACO is reduced to approximately O(N). The tentative initial cluster centers should be more compact and optimal through the proposed ACOPCM.

The ant colony-possibilistic c-means hybrid algorithm.

PCM has a strong inherent capability for local search, but it is likely to obtain local optima when the inappropriate initial number of the clusters and centroids are used. They substantially affect the overall segmentation accuracy and cluster compactness, and also decide the parameter η_i of PCM which affects the final segmentation result.

In this approach, ACO-based clustering is adopted to provide the appropriate number of clusters and centroids automatically, thereby mitigating the problem of getting trapped in local optima of PCM. Through the ACO-based clustering, the tentative initial cluster centers could be more compact and optimal as in Figure 2.

Even though this algorithm provides the appropriate initialization of parameters, it does not solve the coincident clustering problem of PCM. To overcome the problem, we apply pre-classified ants (pixels) derived from the ACO-based clustering to PCM. The pre-classified ants are composed of the classified and unclassified ants. The classified ants are clustered by the ACO-based clustering utilizing its strong capability to converge to the global optimum. All classified ants with the centroid information belong to each cluster set. The remaining members are defined as unclassified ants. When we carry out PCM, the classifiants are assigned to the image and play a key role as base pixels in preventing the coincident clustering problem, and the unclassified ants will be positioned into any discovered cluster by means of

Figure 2. Illustration of cluster centers

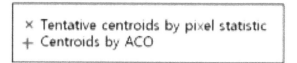

PCM. The classified ants are shown as their centroid value and the unclassified ants are shown as white pixels, as illustrated in Figure 3(c). Figure 3(d) shows the proposed ACOPCM overcomes coincident clustering problem, and stably segments the brain MR image.

4.4. Case Study 2: Fuzzy Based ACO for Optimal Flow Problem[12]

This section presents a new hybrid algorithm for solving optimal power flow under fuzziness. The proposed approach integrates the merits of both ACO and GA and by enhancing ACO through GA, a strong robustness and more effectively algorithm was created. The main steps of the MACO are summarized as follows:

Step 1 - Construct Q Colonies: In a multiobjective optimization problem, multiobjective functions. $F=\{f_1,f_2,...f_Q\}$ need to be optimized simultaneously, there does not necessarily existence a solution that is best with respect to all objectives because of incommensurability and confliction among

Figure 3. Illustration of pre-classified ants: (a) Original simulated MR image; (b) Original simulated MR image with 7% Gaussian noise; (c) Pre-classified ants image derived from ACO; (d) Segmentation result of ACOPCM

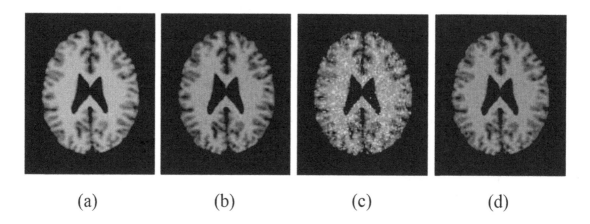

(a)   (b)   (c)   (d)

objectives. For this step, the number of colonies is set to Q with its own pheromone structure, where Q =| F | is the number of objectives to optimize.

Step 2 – Initialization: First, pheromones trails are initialized to a given value where $\tau_0{}^q$(q=1,2,...Q) is the pheromone information in the current iteration and Pareto set are initialized to an empty set.

Step 3 – Evaluation: The MACO parameterized by the number of ant colonies and the number of associated pheromone structures. All the colonies have the same number of ants. Each colony tries to optimize an objective considering the pheromone information associated for each colony, where each colony is determined knowing only the relevant part of a solution. This methodology enforces both colonies to search in different regions of the nondominated front.

Step 4 - Trail Update and Reward Solutions: When updating pheromone trails, one has to decide on which of the constructed solutions laying pheromone. The quantity of pheromone laying on a component represents the past experience of the colony with respect to choosing this component. Then, at each cycle every ant constructs a solution, and pheromone trails are updated. Once all ants have constructed their solutions, pheromone trails are updated first, pheromone trails are reduced by a constant factor to simulate evaporation to prevent premature convergence; then, some pheromone is laid on components of the best solution. Accordingly, pheromone concentration associated with each possible route (variable value) is changed in a way to reinforce good solutions, and the change in pheromone concentration is expressed in equation:

$$\Delta\tau_{ij}^q = \begin{cases} C/f_q, & for\ \text{Min}\ f_q \\ C*f_q, & for\ \text{Max}\ f_q,\ if\ l_{ij}\ is\ chosen\ by\ ant\ K \\ 0, & otherwise \end{cases} \tag{8}$$

A possibility is to reward every nondominated solution of the current cycle as follows:

Figure 4. Ant representation to the associated pheromone with this value. This process continues for each objective. Consequently, path of each ant was consisted of n nodes with a value l_{ij} for each node.

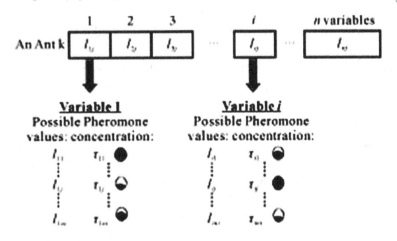

$$\Delta\tau_{ib}^{q}(t) \leftarrow (1-\rho)\tau_{ib}^{q}(t-1) + \Delta\tau_{ib}^{q}$$

$b = 1, 2, ..., B \ \ and \ \ B \subseteq ni$ (9)

Step 5 - Solution Construction: Once the pheromone is updated after an iteration, the next iteration starts by changing the ants' paths (i.e. associated variable values) in a manner that respects pheromone concentration and also some heuristic preference. For each ant and for each dimension construct a new candidate group to replace the old one. As such, an ant will change the value for each variable according to the transition probability. The transition probability is done for each colony.

Step 6 - Nondominated Solutions: The set of nondominated solutions is stored in an archive. During the optimization search, this set, which represents the Pareto front, is updated. At each iteration, the current solutions obtained are compared to those stored in the Pareto archive; the dominated ones are removed and the nondominated ones are added to the set.

Step 7 - Steady State Genetic Algorithm: Steady state genetic algorithm was implemented in such a way that, two offspring are produced in each generation. Parents are selected to produce offspring and then a decision is made as to which individuals in the population to select for deletion to make room for the new offspring. A replacement/deletion strategy defines which member of the population will be replaced by the new offspring. Steady state genetic algorithms overlapping systems, since parents and offspring compete for survival (see Figure 5):

1. **Selections:** Selection determines which individuals of the population will have all or some of their genetic material passed on to the next generation of individuals. The mechanism for selecting the parents is based on a tournament selection. Tournament selection operates by choosing some individuals randomly from a population and selecting the best from this group to survive into the next generation. For example, pairs of parents are randomly chosen from the initial population. Their fitness values are compared and a copy of the better performing individual becomes part of the mating pool. The tournament will be performed repeatedly until the mating pool is filled. That way, the worst performing patent in the population will never be selected for inclusion in the mating pool. Tournaments are held between pairs of individuals are the most common. In this way all parents necessary for a reproduction operator are selected;

2. **Recombination Through Crossover and Mutation:** After selection has been carried out, then the mechanisms of crossover and mutation are applied to produce an offspring, the following subsection outlines these genetic operators:

   a. **Crossover:** Once the parents are created, the crossover step is carried out by replacing the current value with a new one which produced stochastically with a probability proportional to the crossover probability. Suppose the crossover probability set by the system is c;

   b. **Mutation:** Once the, the crossover is performed, the mutation step is carried out by replacing the current value with a new one which produced stochastically with a probability proportional to the mutation probability m;

3. **Replacement/Deletion Strategy:** A widely used combination is to replace the worst individual only if the new individual is better. In the paper, this strategy will be suggested that the individual will be deleted if it was dominated by the new offspring as in Algorithm 1.

Algorithm 1. The strategy of deletion

---

1. INPUT: POP, x

2. if $\exists x' \in POP | x' \succ x$, then

3. $POP' = POP$

4. else if $\exists x' \in POP | x \succ x'$, then

5. $POP' @ POP \cup \{x\} / \{x'\}$

6. end if

7. Output: POP'

Figure 5. The model for steady state for genetic algorithms

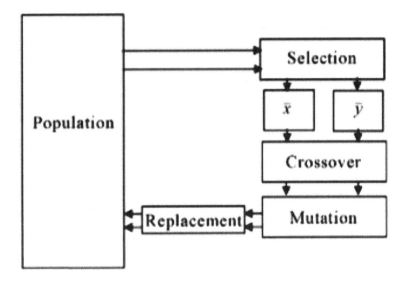

The described methodology has been described for M-objective function, but it is applied to the standard IEEE 30-bus 6-generator test system with two objectives. The single-line diagram of this system is shown in Figure 3 and the detailed data are given in (Kirkpatrick, 1983; Holland, 1975). The values of fuel cost and emission coefficients are given in Table 1. For comparison purposes with the reported results, the system is considered as losses and the security constraint is released.

The techniques used in this study were developed and implemented on 1.7-MHz PC using MATLAB environment. Table 2 lists the parameter setting used in the algorithm for all runs. Naturally, these data (cost and emission) involve many controlled parameters whose possible values are vague and uncertain. Consequently, each numerical value in the domain can be assigned a specific "grade of membership" where 0 represents the smallest possible grade of membership, and 1 is the largest possible grade of membership.

Table 1. Generator cost and emission coefficients

		G1	G2	G3	G4	G5	G6
Cost	a	10	10	20	10	20	10
	b	200	150	180	100	180	150
	c	100	120	40	60	40	100
Emission	α	4.091	2.543	4.258	5.426	4.258	6.131
	β	−5.554	−6.047	−5.094	−3.550	−5.094	−5.555
	γ	6.490	4.638	4.586	3.380	4.586	5.151
	ς	2.0E−4	5.0E−4	1.0E−6	2.0E−3	1.0E−6	1.0E−5
	λ	2.857	3.333	8.000	2.000	8.000	6.667

Table 2. Parameters of the approach

Parameters	
Number of objective function (Q)	2
Number of colonies	2
m	100
ρ	0.5
α	1
β	0
C	100
τ_0	10
p_c	0.85
p_m	0.02

Thus, fuzzy parameters can be represented by its membership grade ranging between 0 and 1.

The fuzzy numbers shown in Figure 4 have been obtained from interviewing DMs or from observing the instabilities in the global market and rate of prices fluctuations. The idea is to transform a problem with these fuzzy parameters to a crisp version.

This membership function can be rewritten as follows:

$$
u\left(a_{ij}\right) = \begin{cases} 1, & a = a_{ij} \\ \dfrac{20a}{a_{ij}} - 19, & 0.95a_{jk} \leq a \leq a_{ij} \\ 21 - \dfrac{20a}{a_{ij}}, & a_{ij} \leq a \leq 1.05a_{ij} \\ 0, & a < 0.95a_{ij} \text{ or } a > 1.05a_{ij} \end{cases}
$$

So, every fuzzy parameter a_{ij} can be represented using the membership function.

5. CONCLUSION

With the advent of several nature inspired metaheuristic algorithms for finding optimized solutions, researchers are now improvising them with the inclusion of several hybrid techniques. Since fuzzy concepts deal with the uncertainty in data, the improvement of fuzzy based algorithms can be made by metaheuristic algorithms. Like finding initial centroids in fuzzy c-means using ant colony optimization, several other applications can be found.

REFERENCES

Barricelli, N.A. (1954). Esempi numerici di processi di evoluzione. *Methodos*, 45–68.

Changdar, C., Mahapatra, G. S., & Pal, R. K. (2013). An Ant colony optimization approach for binary knapsack problem under fuzziness. *Applied Mathematics and Computation*, *223*, 243–253. doi:10.1016/j.amc.2013.07.077

Dubois & Prade. (1990). Rough fuzzy sets and fuzzy rough sets. *International Journal of General System, 17*(2-3), 191-209.

Galal, Mousa, & Al-Matrafi. (2013). Ant Colony Optimization Approach Based Genetic Algorithms for Multiobjective Optimal Power Flow Problem under Fuzziness. *Applied Mathematics, 4*, 595.

Glover, F. (1977). Heuristics for Integer programming Using Surrogate Constraints. *Decision Sciences*, *8*(1), 156–166. doi:10.1111/j.1540-5915.1977.tb01074.x

Glover, F. (1986). Future Paths for Integer Programming and Links to Artificial Intelligence. *Computers & Operations Research*, *13*(5), 533–549. doi:10.1016/0305-0548(86)90048-1

Glover, F. (1986). Future paths for integer programming and links to artificial intelligence. *Computers & Operations Research*, *13*(5), 533–549. doi:10.1016/0305-0548(86)90048-1

Holland, J. H. (1975). *Adaptation in Natural and Artificial Systems*. University of Michigan Press.

Kirkpatrick, S., Gelatt, C.D., Jr., & Vecchi, M.P. (1983). Optimization by Simulated Annealing. *Science, 220*(4598), 671–680. doi:10.1126/science.220.4598.671

Matyas, J. (1965). Random optimization. *Automation and Remote Control, 26*(2), 246–253.

Mousa, A. A. A. (2014). Hybrid ant optimization system for multiobjective economic emission load dispatch problem under fuzziness. *Swarm and Evolutionary Computation, 18*, 11–21. doi:10.1016/j.swevo.2014.06.002

Rastrigin, L. A. (1963). The convergence of the random search method in the extremal control of a many parameter system. *Automation and Remote Control, 24*(10), 1337–1342.

Robbins, H., & Monro, S. (1951). A Stochastic Approximation Method. *Annals of Mathematical Statistics, 22*(3), 400–407. doi:10.1214/aoms/1177729586

Yang, X. S. (2011). Metaheuristic optimization. *Scholarpedia, 6*(8), 11472. doi:10.4249/scholarpedia.11472

Yu, J., Lee, S.-H., & Jeon, M. (2012). An adaptive ACO-based fuzzy clustering algorithm for noisy image segmentation. *International Journal of Innovative Computing, Information, & Control, 8*(6), 3907–3918.

Zadeh, L. A. (1965). Fuzzy sets. *Information and Control, 8*(3), 338–353. doi:10.1016/S0019-9958(65)90241-X

Chapter 19
Application of Natured–Inspired Technique to Odia Handwritten Numeral Recognition

Puspalata Pujari
Guru Ghasidas Vishwavidyalaya, India

Babita Majhi
Guru Ghasidas Vishwavidyalaya, India

ABSTRACT

In this chapter an effort has been made to develop a hybrid system using functional link artificial neural network (FLANN) and differential evolution (DE) for effective recognition of Odia handwritten numerals. The S-transform (ST) is chosen for feature extraction from handwritten numerals and these are further reduced by using principal component analysis (PCA). After reduction of feature the reduced features are applied to FLANN model for recognition of each numeral. Further differential evolution algorithm (DE) is used for the optimization of weights of FLANN classifier. For performance comparison, genetic algorithm (GA) and particle swarm optimization (PSO) based FLANN models (FLANN_GA and FLANN_PSO) are also designed and simulated under similar condition. The efficiency of proposed DE based FLANN (FLANN_DE) method is assessed through simulation with standard dataset consisting of 4000 handwritten Odia numerals. The results of three models are compared and it is observed that the FLANN_DE model provides the best result as compared to other models.

INTRODUCTION

Over the last ten decades optical character recognition (OCR) is the most demanding area which comes under the field of pattern recognition, artificial intelligence and machine vision. There are varieties of applications of handwritten character such as postal pin code verification, passport verification, digital library system, document processing, forgery detection in banks and many more. OCR is the translation of handwritten and printed images of character into editable character. The challenging task lies in the recognition of optically processed characters. In off-line recognition method characters are recognized

DOI: 10.4018/978-1-5225-2857-9.ch019

later, after their creation. But the characters are recognized immediately after their creation in an on-line method. OCR can recognize both printed and handwritten characters, but the efficiency of recognition precisely depends on the constraints associated with the characters. More constrained the character is, greater is the efficiency of the OCR system. It is very difficult to develop OCR system for totally unconstrained handwritten characters. Recognition of handwritten characters and numerals is more complex task than the printed character. Many variations are observed in handwritten character due to the style of writing, added noise, missing part, devices and medias used for image acquisition. These may be due to different size, stroke and slant of the image. Therefore there is a requirement to develop robust system which can recognize effectively any handwritten characters. This chapter develops a recognition model for offline handwritten Odia numerals using FLANN as classifier and a bio-inspired technique such as differential evolution (DE) for the weight optimization of the FLANN model. Preprocessing is the first step of OCR followed by feature extraction and classification. Before developing the recognition model preprocessing and feature extraction tasks are performed. The numeral images are preprocessed first. Then feature based recognition method is applied to measure and extract significant features from the numerals image. Then a hybrid system is developed by using FLANN classifier where the weights of FLANN classifier are optimized with DE algorithm. The features are compared to the prototypes developed in training phase. The description which provides the closest match provides the recognition. For feature extraction the recently developed S-transform (M. Hariharan et.al, 2014) is applied which retains the significant features of the pattern. These features being more in dimensions are then reduced by applying principal component analysis (PCA). For the classification task FLANN model is used, the weights of which are adjusted by minimizing the squared error value using the DE algorithm.

BACKGROUND

A concise study of the chronicle background related to the advancement of OCR is as follows. A hybrid system (S. Rajasekaran, 2003) is the integration of one or more techniques to solve complex problem in efficient way. The objective of hybrid system is to provide a better solution by suitably mixing various techniques so as to overcome the weakness of each technique. In literature several research works have been reported for recognition of characters by using hybrid techniques. A hybrid of GA and Harmony Search algorithm (HS) is suggested in (M.Y.Potrus, 2014) for online Arabic text Recognition. The problem is solved in two phases: text segmentation using dominant point detection, and recognition-based segmentation using GA and HS. The performance of the system is evaluated on 4500 Arabic words and benchmark (ADAB) dataset consisting of 7851 Arabic words with a recognition rate of 93.4% and 94–96% respectively. A feed forward neural network with evolutionary algorithms has been employed by the authors (S.Srivastava et.al, 2011) for recognition of handwritten English alphabet. A new method has been developed in (T. Pourhabibi et.al, 2011) by combining Simulated Annealing (SA) and GA for selection of feature subset using Persian fonts and a good recognition performance is suggested. The convergence rate of Guided Evolutionary Simulated Annealing is found to be better than the GA. A hybrid approach has been proposed in (N. Ozturk et.al, 2004) for feature recognition problem to step down the computational complexity with neural networks (NNs) and GAs to step down the computational complexity. Optimum network architecture has been developed by using GA based input selection approach. In (N.Das et.al, 2012) for recognition of Bangla compound character the authors have developed a multistage recognition system. GA and Support Vector Machine (SVM) are used for the multi stage recognition system. The system has been employed on 8254 numbers of samples of *Bangla* handwritten Compound characters belonging to 171 character classes and an accuracy of 78.93% has been reported. In (R.R. Zheng, 2009) the authors have employed an adaptive genetic algorithm method for segmentation of offline handwritten Chinese characters. The method has been used for accurate segmentation of Chinese numbers, characters, and punctuations. The experiment has been carried on Hirbin Institute of Technology Multiple writer (HIW-MW) database and segmentation rate of 74.55% is reported. A method for feature selection in unsupervised learning is proposed in (L.M. Al-zoubaidy, 2006) where multi objective genetic algorithm has been employed to enhance the recognition speed and efficiency of the system. The proposed strategy has been applied to Arabic handwritten characters recognition. A neural network (NN) approach is proposed in (M.T. Das et.al, 2009) for analysis of signature. In the classification stage the neural network has been trained with PSO algorithm to test unskilled and skilled forgeries. In (X. Pan et.al, 2005) the authors combined two recognition methods based on statistical and structural approach to develop a two stage hybrid recognition system. Then the system has been optimized with GA. The hybrid system is found to be more efficient than the conventional back-propagation based neural network model. A hybrid model has been proposed in (X.X. Niu & C.Y. Suen, 2012) by integrating convolution neural network (CNN) and SVM where the CNN and SVM have been used as feature extractor and classifier respectively. The proposed model has been employed on MNSIT database and achieved 99.81% recognition rate without rejection and 94.40% with 5.60% rejection. In (Z.Man et.al, 2013), for input and output weight optimization of single layer feed forward network (SLFN) an optimal weight learning technique has been developed. The model has been applied on MNIST and United States postal service (USPS) database and a high degree of accuracy has been achieved by the proposed system. In (S.Dehuri, 2012), PSO approach has been used to train FLANN classifier. In (L.Wang et.al, 2015) the authors have proposed a hybrid approach for time series forecasting. They have employed adaptive DE (ADE) based training scheme with back propagation neural network to enhance the forecasting accuracy. A comparative study has been carried out with those obtained from basic ANN and autoregressive integrated moving average (ARIMA) model. A DE algorithm based neural network is proposed to remove stagnation problem in (A.P. Piotrowski, 2014). In (Ritesh Sarkhel et.al, 2016) the authors have presented a multi-objective approach to maximize recognition rate of the system and at the same time to reduce the recognition cost. The system has been applied on compound Bangla characters and numerals with SVM classifier. Good recognition accuracy with minimum recognition cost has been achieved with the proposed system. Prashant M. Kakde and S.M.Gulhane, 2016 have proposed a system for recognition of Devanagari character using PSO and SVM. They have achieved an accuracy of 90% with PSO technique. A novel method has been proposed by Narahari Sastry Panyam, Vijaya Lakshmi T.R, RamaKrishnan Krishnan & Koteswara Rao N.V (2016, December) for recognition of Telugu manuscripts written on palm leafs. Features based on two-dimensional discrete wavelet transform, fast fourier transform, discrete cosine transform along with 3D feature of each pixel proportional to the pressure applied by the writer have been used for feature extraction. A recognition accuracy of 96.4% has been achieved with the proposed model.

The FLANN classifier possesses low computational complexity compared to its MLP counterpart. Most of the recognition task involves highly non-linear data. The FLANN provides the nonlinear solution by way of functionally extending its input vector. As a result the FLANN model finds several applications such as channel equalization (W.D. Weng, 2007), data classification (B. Naik,2015), stock market prediction (C.M. Anish & B. Majhi, 2015), detection of impulsive noise in images (B. Majhi & P.K Sa, 2007), modeling of intelligent pressure sensor (J.C. Patra & A.C. Bos, 2000), noise control (S. K. Behera et.al, 2014), mechanical system design (H. Saruhan, 2014) etc. The FLANN classifier has been applied to many problems related to classification with low computational involvement and providing better solution. Thus in this chapter the FLANN model is chosen for the recognition of handwritten Odia numerals. Feature extraction plays an important role in character recognition. Several authors have employed number of feature extraction techniques to extract important features from the characters and numerals. It is observed from the literature that the S-transform (ST) has been successfully applied to many fields like classification of mental task (M. Hariharan, 2014), ECG signal enhancement (S. Ari, 2013), fringe pattern analysis (M. Ziang, 2012), fault diagnosis of electronic circuits (R. Wang, 2012), denoising of ECG signal (M.K. Das & S. K. Ari, 2013) and time series data mining (H.S. Behera, 2010). Being motivated by these applications, ST has been chosen to extract the features of the handwritten Odia numerals in this chapter. The DE algorithm has been successfully applied for solving many optimization techniques for many applications such as functionally graded beam (C.M.C. Roque & P.A.L.S. Martins, 2015), noisy multiobjective optimization (P. Rakshit & A. Konar, 2015), complementary metal oxide-conductor (CMOS) inverter design (B.P. De et.al, 2015), parametric identification of seismic isolation (G. Quaranta, 2014) etc.

From literature it is noticed that the DE optimization technique has not been applied to earlier Odia numeral recognition. Hence in this chapter this problem is addressed and suitable solution is proposed for recognition of the handwritten Odia numerals. From literature S-transform has been successfully applied to many classification tasks. Hence in this chapter S-transform based feature extraction technique is applied to extract import features from the numerals. As FLANN classifier has low computational complexity, it is used for the classification of numerals. The current study is focused on exploration of possible techniques to develop an OCR system for recognition of Odia numerals.

The chapter is composed of twelve sections. Section II describes the dataset used, preprocessing and feature extraction method for the numeral figures using S-transform. The structure of the FLANN classifier is presented in Section III. Section IV explains the general DE algorithm. The proposed DE based FLANN hybrid recognition model FLANN_DE is discussed in Section V. PSO algorithm and PSO based FLANN model are described in section VI and VII respectively. GA algorithm and GA based FLANN model are described in section VIII and IX respectively. Simulation based experimental study of FLAN_DE model is discussed in section X followed by scope of further research work and conclusion.

DATASET, PREPROCESSING AND FEATURE EXTRACTION

Dataset Used for the Proposed Study

The system is developed and evaluated with standard Odia database for measuring the performance of the system. The database contains 4000 samples of Odia handwritten numerals ranging from (0-9). All samples of the dataset are categorized into ten classes from (0-9). Each numeral (0-9) appears 400 times in the database. For training of the hybrid model 90% of the dataset is used and the remaining 10% for the purpose of testing. Figure 1 shows one sample of Odia handwritten numerals (0-9).

Figure 1. Handwritten Odia numerals from the database

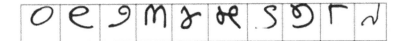

Preprocessing

Pre-processing is the initial step of character recognition system. This step is used to processes the inputs into a suitable form for the next phase. Large number of variations found in handwritten numerals may cause a poor recognition rate. Hence, in this step all type of irregularities present in the numerals are removed. Pre-processing includes the operation like background noise reduction, filtering, original image restoration etc. Normalization is a preprocessing step which is used to remove all types of variation related to non uniform size, slant and rotation during writing like and to obtain standardized data. Normalization includes skew, size, slant and curve smoothing. In this chapter the images are also normalized to a standard pixel size of 64 X 64 to get uniform images of each numeral. Then the gray scale image of the image is generated by using mean filtering method. The gray scale images of one set of numerals are shown in Figure 2.

Feature Extraction Using S-Transform

This step is carried out to extract relevant information from the characters. This step extracts significant features from the input image so that they can be used in the recognition phase with less complexity. The extracted features are represented in the form of a feature vector. The extracted features are further reduced to improve the recognition rate of the system. In this chapter, S-transform (ST) based approach is used for feature extraction. The ST (M. Hariharan et.al, 2014; S. Ari et.al, 2013; M. Jiang et.al, 2012; R.Wang et.al, 2012, M.K. Das 7 S. ari, 2013; H.S. Behera, 2010); H. Pal. Thethi et.al, 2011, G.S. Badrinath & P. Gupta, 2011) is a time-frequency representation which is an improvement over short-time fourier transform (STFT) and the wavelet transform (WT). It combines the features of STFT and WT. In ST a Gaussian window is used to produce progressive resolution. It uniquely combines the time frequency localization capability and local phase information of the signal or image. The performance of ST is found to be better as compared to other time-frequency methods. The ST can be derived from the STFT. By using standard Fourier analysis the spectrum $U(f)$ of a time series $u(t)$ is represented as:

$$U(f) = \int_{-\infty}^{+\infty} u(t)\exp(-i2\pi ft)dt \tag{1}$$

Figure 2. Odia numerals in gray scale image

If $g(t)$ represents the windowed version of $u(t)$, the resultant spectrum is given as:

$$U(f) = \int_{-\infty}^{+\infty} u(t)g(t)\exp(-i2\pi ft)dt \tag{2}$$

Let a normalized Gaussian window is represented as:

$$g(t) = \frac{1}{\sigma\sqrt{2\pi}}\exp\left(-\frac{t^2}{2\sigma^2}\right) \tag{3}$$

If the Gaussian window is a function of window width (or dilation) σ and translation parameter τ the S-transform is defined as:

$$S(\tau, f, \sigma) = \int_{-\infty}^{+\infty} u(t)\frac{1}{\sigma\sqrt{2\pi}}\exp\left(-\frac{(t-\tau)^2}{2\sigma^2}\right)\exp(-i2\pi ft)dt \tag{4}$$

By imposing a constraint which is proportional to the width of the window:

$$\sigma(f) = \left(\frac{1}{|f|}\right)^n \tag{5}$$

Then the ST is given as:

$$S(\tau, f, \sigma) = \int_{-\infty}^{+\infty} u(t)\frac{|f|}{\sqrt{2\pi}}\exp\left(-\frac{(t-\tau)^2 f^2}{2}\right)\exp(-i2\pi ft)dt \tag{6}$$

Feature Reduction Using PCA

By using the ST each numeral image generates 2519 numbers of features which is large in size and hence computational complexity is more while designing a classifier. Therefore, the number of features is further reduced from 2519 numbers to 128 by using the PCA. These features are then fed to the FLANN model for recognition purpose.

FUNCTIONAL LINK ARTIFICIAL NEURAL NETWORK (FLANN) MODEL FOR RECOGNITION

One of the advantages of ANN is to solve highly non-linear problems. The more weights of MLP model need more time to adjust its weight vector. There is a proportional increase in the computational complexity of the neural network with the increase in the number of hidden layers. Hence in this chapter, a FLANN model is chosen for the recognition purpose. FLANN (W.D. Weng, 2007; B. Naik,2015; C.M. Anish & B. Majhi, R. Majhi et.al, 2012; B. Majhi & P.K Sa, 2007; J.C. Patra & A.C. Bos, 2000; S. K. Behera et.al, 2014; H. Saruhan, 2014; S. Rajasekaran & G.A. Vijayalakshmi, 2003) is a higher order neural network without any hidden layer. It generates non-linear decision boundaries for performing complex decision because of nonlinear expansion scheme. In FLANN, the dimension of input vector is increased functionally by expanding the inputs in a nonlinear fashion such as trigonometric, power series, Legendre polynomial or Chebyshev functional expansion (R. Majhi et.al, 2012). It associates less computational load and offers better convergence rate. Figure 3 shows the architecture of FLANN model. The extracted features reduced by using PCA are applied to the FLANN model for generating the enhanced intermediate pattern. In this case the functional expansion block includes original patterns and sin and cosine expansion based terms. The input z_i trigonometrically expanded into five terms is represented as:

$$z_i = [z_i \quad \sin(\pi z_i) \quad \cos(\pi z_i) \quad \sin(3\pi z_i) \quad \cos(3\pi z_i)] \tag{7}$$

where $0 \leq i \leq n$.

Figure 3. An input trigonometric expansion based FLANN adaptive model using DE algorithm

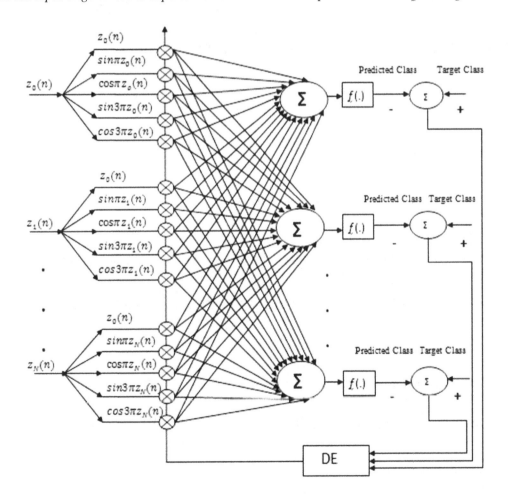

DIFFERENTIAL EVOLUTION (DE)

It is not easy to solve complex problems analytically when the function is not differentiable, not continuous and not linear. The complexity of the system increases with multi-dimension, many local minima and large number constraints in the variables. The bio-inspired technique such as the DE can be chosen (P. Rakshit & A. Konar) as an adaptive scheme over continuous space for global optimization. It does not belong to gradient based algorithm group. For finding best possible solution the bio-inspired techniques use population based method. It uses iterative method to modify each candidate solutions to achieve best possible solution. In the mutation process for each target vector three other vectors are selected randomly. The difference of the two vectors is calculated and the weighted difference is added to the third vector to form a mutant vector. In the crossover operation the trial vector is formed from each pair of target and mutant vector. Basing on the fitness value the better of the target and trial vectors are chosen for the next generation.

Basic Steps of DE Algorithm

Step 1: Select N_p number of individuals $\vec{Y}_{i,gen}$ randomly, where $\vec{Y}_{i,gen}$ is the ith individual of gen^{th} generation.

Step 2: Let $f_i = f(\vec{Y}_{i,gen})$ for $i = 1$ to N_p, represents the fitness value of ith individual solution at gen^{th} generation.

Step 3: While stopping criteria is not reached repeat steps from 4 to 10.

Step 4: Repeat steps from 5 to 10 for $i = 1$ to N_p.

Step 5: Choose three random indices $rand_0, rand_1, rand_2$ between 1 to N_p $\left(i \neq rand_0 \neq rand_1 \neq rand_2\right)$.

Step 6: Compute the mutant vector as:

$$\vec{V}_{i,gen} = \vec{Y}_{rand_0,gen} + F\left(\vec{Y}_{rand_1,gen} - \vec{Y}_{rand_2,gen}\right) \tag{8}$$

where F is a real value within the range $[0.0 \quad 1.0]$.

Step 7: Repeat steps 8 to 9 for $j = 1$ to n.

Step 8: Choose a random number $rand_j$ where $\left(0 \leq rand_j < 1\right)$ and j_{rand} index greater than or equal to 1 and less than n i.e. $(1 \leq r_{rand} < n)$.

Step 9: Compute the trial vector $\vec{U}_{i,gen}$. If $rand_j \leq Cross_r$ or $j = j_{rand}$ then $U_{j,i,gen} = V_{j,i,gen}$ else:

$$U_{j,i,gen} = V_{j,i,gen} \tag{9}$$

where $Cross_r$ is a real valued crossover factor from $0.0 \quad 1.0$.

Step 10: Selection process is carried out as, if $f(\vec{U}_{i,gen}) \leq f_{i,gen}$ then $\vec{Y}_{i,gen+1} = \vec{U}_{i,gen}$ and $f_i = f(\vec{U}_{i,gen})$ else $\vec{Y}_{i,gen+1} = \vec{Y}_{i,gen}$.

The flowchart of DE algorithm is shown in Figure 4.
The generic steps of DE algorithm is as follows:

```
Initialization
Evaluation
While (Not Termination)
{
Mutation
Recombination or crossover
Evaluation
Selection
}
```

Figure 4. Flow chart of differential evolution algorithm

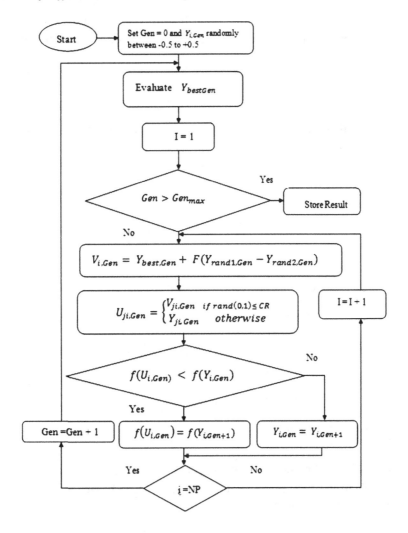

DEVELOPMENT OF FLANN_DE HYBRID MODEL FOR RECOGNITION OF ODIA HANDWRITTEN NUMERALS

There are essentially derivative based or derivative free training schemes for the weight updating of FLANN adaptive model. But most of the derivative based algorithms sometimes provide local minima solution. Further, the convergence characteristics of the derivative based algorithm depends on the weights of the model initially chosen. For these reasons the weights of the FLANN model needs to be updated with bio-inspired based algorithm to improve the learning quality. In this chapter the DE based learning scheme is proposed to overcome the limitation of derivative based learning algorithm. The steps involved in DE based weight optimization of FLANN model during training are:

Step 1: Initialize the target population of size M randomly of which each mth individual represents the coefficients or weights of the FLANN classifier. Each individual of the population consists of N number of weights of the FLANN classifier.

Step 2: Create K numbers of input samples; each contains 128 features extracted from handwritten numerals. Expand each element of feature vector trigonometrically to five non-linear values.

Step 3: Multiply each element of the expanded input feature vector with each element of the member of population and then the partial sums add together to determine the estimated outputs y_i as:

$$y_i = \sum\nolimits_{n=1}^{N} weight_n x_n \tag{10}$$

Step 4: Compare the calculated i^{th} output with the corresponding desired outputs and generate K errors. The ith error is computed as:

$$error_i(k) = d(k) - y_i(k) \tag{11}$$

where $k = 1$ to K.

Step 5: Calculate the fitness value in terms of the mean square error (MSE). Calculate the MSE of nth member using (12) for a set of parameters. Repeat it for M times:

$$MSE(n) = \frac{\sum_{k=1}^{K} error_i^2}{k} \tag{12}$$

Repeat the process for N times:

Step 6: Minimize the MSE using the DE algorithm.
Step 7: Obtain the mutant vector by using (8).
Step 8: Carryout the crossover operation using (9) and obtain trial vectors.
Step 9: Perform the selection of members for the next generation based on minimum MSE criterion. Repeat the total process for a number of generations.

Step 10: Obtain learning characteristics of the classification model by plotting the minimum MSE (MMSE) against the number of generations. When the MMSE has reached the possible minimum value and almost remains constant the training process is stopped. At this stage all the members of the population almost acquire same value which represents the best possible weights of the FLANN model.

BASICS OF PSO ALGORITHM

PSO is an evolution algorithm based on social interaction concept for problem solving. It consists of potential solutions in the form of metaphor of birds in flocks known as particles. First of all each particle of the population is initialized with random position and velocity. The best position attained by an individual particle is known as P_ibest. The best position attained by the total population is known as $Gbest$. The particles are allowed to fly freely across the multidimensional search space. PSO maintains a fixed population size over the search space. The particles updates their own position and velocity basing on their own best experience and the best experience of entire population during flight (R.R. Zheng, 2009 & S. Dehuri et.al, 2012) which guides the particles to move towards the $Gbest$. Finally all particles attain same $Gbest$ value which gives the final solution to a problem. Figure 5 shows the flow chart of PSO model.

Basic Steps of PSO Algorithm

Step 1: Randomly initialize the velocity and position of all particles.
Step 2: Update the velocity of all particles using following equation:

$$vel_i(t+1) = weight * vel_i(t) + coef_1 * rand_1 * (P_ibest(t) - pos_i(t)) \\ + coef_2 * rand_2 * (Gbest(t) - pos_i(t)) \tag{13}$$

where $pos_i(t)$ is the position and $vel_i(t)$ is the velocity of the particle corresponding to t^{th} iteration; p_ibest is the position attained by an individual particle i which is best for the particle so far and $Gbest$ is the position attained by the whole population which is best for the whole population so far; $weight$ is a inertia weight factor which controls the flying dynamics; $coef_i$ and $coef_2$ are acceleration coefficients factors; $rand_1$ and $rand_2$ are two numbers randomly distributed from 0 to 1.

Step 3: Update the position of all particles as given below:

$$pos_i(t+1) = pos_i(t) + vei_i(t+1) \tag{14}$$

Step 4: Update $Pbest$ and $Gbest$ when condition is met using following equation:

$$P_ibest = pos_i \quad if \quad f(pos_i) < f(P_ibest) \tag{15}$$

Figure 5. Flowchart of PSO model

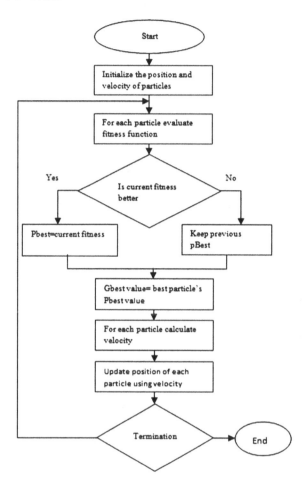

$$Gbest = G_i \quad if \quad f(G_i) < f(G_i best) \tag{16}$$

Step 5: Step 2 to step 4 are repeated until termination criteria is reached. After termination, the GBest gives the best solution.

WEIGHT OPTIMIZATION USING FLANN_PSO MODEL

Steps for weight optimization of PSO_FLANN are as follows:

Step 1: Initialize the positions and velocities of the model corresponding to N particles randomly. Each position vector represents one weight vector of the FLANN architecture.

Step 2: Take k numbers of input samples and functionally expand each input trigonometrically to five numbers of non-linear values using (7). The FLANN model is trained for each particle. Pass the inputs x_n through the input layer of the FLANN and multiply the inputs with the corresponding weights to get the estimated output. Compare the generated outputs of the FLANN model with the target outputs to produce k errors.

Step 3: Calculate the fitness in terms of Mean Square Error (MSE). Using (12) calculate the MSE of nth particle taking same set of parameters and repeat the process M times. This is repeated N times.

Step 4: Use PSO algorithm to minimize the MSE.

Step 5: The velocity and position of each particle is updated using (13) and (14):

$$vel_i(t+1) = weight * vel_i(t) + coef_1 * rand_1 * (P_i best(t) - pos_i(t))$$
$$+ coef_2 * rand_2 * (Gbest(t) - pos_i(t)) \tag{17}$$

$$pos_i(t+1) = pos_i(t) + vei_i(t+1) \tag{18}$$

Step 6: Store the minimum MSE (MMSE) in each iteration. MMSE shows the learning behavior of the model. Repeat the total process for sufficient number of iterations. Stop the optimization process when the required criterion is fulfilled. At this stage the MMSE has reached the pre specified level and all the particles attend almost identical position. This represents the desired optimized weights of the FLANN model.

In this chapter to reach the convergence level the process of generation is repeated for 1000 times. After 1000 number of generations final weights are extracted from the population. The parameters used for FLANN_PSO are population size = 700, weight = 0.5, $coef_1 = 0.7$, $coef_2 = 0.7$.

BASICS OF GENETIC ALGORITHM

Genetic algorithm(GA) is inspired by the principle of "Survival of the fittest" – Darwin's theory about evolution. The fittest individuals dominate over the weaker one competing among individuals for scanty resources. It is an adaptive heuristic search based evolutionary algorithm which mimics the process of nature selection, crossover, mutation and accepting for global optimum solution. The detail steps of GA is given below:

Step 1 - Initialization: Take initial population randomly so as to include all possible range of solutions for the problem. Let N be the randomly created chromosomes in the population taken as initial solution. Choose the probability of crossover P_{cross}, the probability of mutation $P_{mutation}$, size of the chromosome and number of generations.

Step 2: Repeat step 3 through step 7 until required number of generations is met or stopping criteria met.

Step 3 - Fitness Calculation: Evaluate the fitness function $f(chrom)$ by calculating objective function i.e. $f(Chrom_1), f(Chrom_2), ..., f(Chrom_N)$ where $Chrom = Chrom_1, Chrom_2, ..., Chrom_N$ for each chromosome $Chrom$ in the population.

Step 4 - Chromosome Selection: Choose the best-fit chromosomes from the entire population for reproduction.

Step 5 - Crossover: Using crossover probability P_{cross} the chromosomes are selected to produce new offspring.

Step 6 - Mutation: Change the chromosomes at selected alleles with mutation probability $P_{mutation}$ to ensure that the offspring are not exactly same as the parents.

Step 7 - New Population: Replace all worst fit chromosomes with the best fit chromosomes basing on their fitness value. Use the newly generated population for next generation.

Step 8 - Solutions: Return the best solution for the problem. Figure 6 shows the flow chart of GA.

Figure 6. Flow chart of genetic algorithm

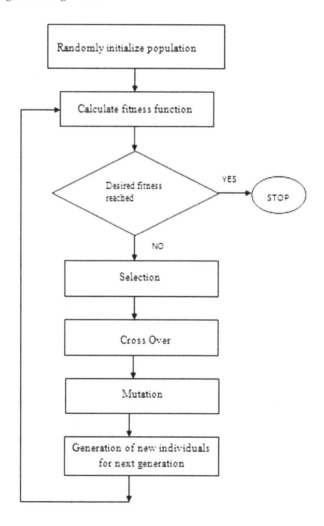

DEVELOPMENT OF FLANN_GA MODEL FOR RECOGNITION OF ODIA HANDWRITTEN NUMERALS

Weight Optimization by FLANN_GA Model

For better discrimination among the classes, real coded genetic algorithm (RCGA) and FLANN classifier are hybridized to obtain suitable weight values for the FLANN classifier. Each input sample containing 128 features extracted from handwritten numerals are expanded trigonometrically to five non linear values where each mth individual of the population represents the coefficients or weights of the FLANN model. Architecture $(75-4-3)(75-4-3)$ of the classifier is 640:10 with 640 X 10 numbers of weights. The gene length is choosen as 5 with 640 X 10 number of gene in each chromosome. Initially a population P_0 is generated with size p. Two algorithms RCGA_FLANN_WT( ) and FITCAL( ) are used for weight optimization and evaluation of fitness function respectively. Using the algorithm RCGA_FLANN_WT () the optimum weights of the FLANN model are obtained. At first the FLANN classifier is trained with all input samples taking each set of weights common to all samples. Errors are generated comparing target and predicted output. The fitness function of each chromosome is calculated using generated error as given in algorithm FITCAL( ). A two point cross over with probability parameter $P_{cross} = 0.8$ is carried out to produce the offspring. Then with probability parameter $P_{mutation} = 0.1$ mutation is carried out. The offspring so formed is combined with parent population and sorted according to the fitness values. From the total population p numbers of chromosomes having minimum fitness values are choosen for the next generation. The process of fitness evaluation, selection, crossover, mutation and generation of new individuals are carried out from generation to generation till all the chromosomes achieve same value. The algorithms for weight optimization and calculation of fitness function are given as follows.

Let $c_1, c_2, ..., c_d, ..., c_l$ represent a chromosome and $c_{rd+1}, c_{rd+2}, ..., c_{(r+1)d}$ represent the rth gene $(r \geq 0)$ in the chromosome. The weight, $weight_r$ is calculated as follows:

$$weight_r = \begin{cases} +\dfrac{c_{rd+2}10^{d-2} + c_{rd+3}10^{d-3} + ... + c_{(r+1)d}}{10^{d-2}}, & if \quad 5 \leq c_{rd+1} \leq 9 \\ -\dfrac{c_{rd+2}10^{d-2} + c_{rd+3}10^{d-3} + ... + c_{(r+1)d}}{10^{d-2}}, & if \quad 0 \leq c_{rd+1} \leq 5 \end{cases} \tag{19}$$

Algorithms for Weight Optimization by RCGA (RCGA_FLANN_WT)

```
{
Set u ← 0 ;
Generate initial population p_u consisting of m number of real coded chromo-
somes C_v^u . Each chromosome represents a weight vector for the FLANN.
While the current population P_u has not converged
{
Obtain the fitness F_v^u value of each chromosome, C_v^u ∈ P_u by using the algorithm
```

```
FITCAL ();
Create the mating pool by replacing the chromosomes with minimum fitness with
the high fitness chromosome;
Use two point crossover mechanisms to reproduce offspring from the parent
chromosomes;
Carry out mutation;
Perform selection for the next generation;
```
$u \leftarrow u + 1;$
```
Make the new population obtained as
```
P_u ;
```
}
Extract weights from
```
P_u to be used finally by FLANN;
```
}
```

Algorithm FITCAL()

Let $Inp_u = (Inp_{1u}, Inp_{2u}, Inp_{3u}, ..., Inp_{lu})$ and $Target_u = (Target_{1u}, Target_{2u}, Target_{3u}, ..., Target_{nu})$ represents the input and output pairs for a $l-n$ FLANN architecture, where *l=640, n=10* and $u = 1, 2, 3, ..., N$.

For each chromosome $C_u, u = 1, 2, ..., p$ of current population P_u with population size p
```
{
Extract weights
```
$weight_u$ from C_u using (19)
```
Train FLANN for
```
N ```
input samples keeping
```
$Weight_u$ as a fixed set of weight
```
For each input instances calculate the error by using the formula
```

$$Error_u = \sum_v \left(Target_{vu} - Out_{vu}\right)^2 \tag{20}$$

```
where
```
$Out_u$ ```
represents the calculated output by FLANN
Find the root mean square error, as
```

$$Error = \sqrt{\frac{\sum_u Error_u}{N}} \tag{21}$$

```
where
```
$u = 1, 2, ..., p$
```
The fitness value
```
F_u ```
of each chromosome is calculated as
```

$$F_u = \frac{1}{Error} \tag{22}$$
```

```
}
Output  F_u  for each  C_u, u = 1, 2, ..., p
}
```

SIMULATION STUDY FOR FLANN_DE MODEL

For the performance evaluation of proposed adaptive nonlinear FLANN_DE model, simulation based experiment is conducted using Matlab software. The handwritten Odia numerals of ISI Kolkata, India dataset comprising of 4000 handwritten numerals belonging to ten target classes (0-9) are used for identification purpose. Each target class contains 400 samples. In the preprocessing stage the scanned image of numerals are normalized to lie within the standard size of 64 X 64 pixels. Then the mean filtering technique is applied to the images for converting them into gray scale images. From each image 2519 numbers of feature vectors are extracted by employing the ST feature extraction technique. Further to lower the computational complexity the features are reduced by using PCA from 2519 to 128 numbers. Each set of reduced feature set belongs to one of ten classes (0-9). The reduced features are applied to FLANN_DE model. The adaptive recognition model is chosen as trigonometric expansion based FLANN and its weights are updated with DE optimization algorithm. Out of the total number of samples 3600 number of samples each with 128 attributes is used for training of the FLANN model and the remaining are used for validation purpose. Each feature is trigonometrically expanded to five terms to make the recognition model nonlinear. The FLANN model employs one sigmoid activation function to add additional nonlinearity to the model. The error term is generated for each input sample by comparing the estimated output with the desired. Using the set of error terms the MSE is computed. In the present simulation study the minimum mean square error is considered as the fitness value which is progressively reduced by varying each weight vector of the population using DE based minimization technique. The parameters of DE used in the simulation study are: The population size is 40, value of F is 0.05, c_r =0.67, number of generations taken is 1000 and number of independent run is 10. The experimental results are also obtained for FLANN_GA and FLANN_PSO models under similar condition for comparison purpose. Figure 7 represents the comparison of convergence characteristics of all three adaptive models. It is observed from the figure that the FLANN_DE model gives minimum MMSE level in comparison to other two models. The confusion matrix obtained during training of FLANN_DE model is given in Table 1 which exhibits the improved recognition accuracy of the model. Comparison of recognition accuracy of the three models during validation is shown in Table 2. The recognition accuracies obtained are 92.5%, 89% and 87.75% for FLANN_DE, FLANN_PSO and FLANN_GA model respectively. From the experiment it is noticed that the proposed FLANN_DE model exhibits well as compared to the other two models for recognition of handwritten Odia numerals.

FEATURE RESEARCH DIRECTIONS

In this chapter, FLANN classifier is used for the recognition of Odia handwritten numerals where the weights of the classifier is optimized with DE approach. Hybrid models can be developed with other evolutionary approaches like Bacterial Foraging algorithm, Cat Swarm algorithm and Ant Colony al-

Figure 7. Comparison of convergence characteristics of three adaptive models during training period

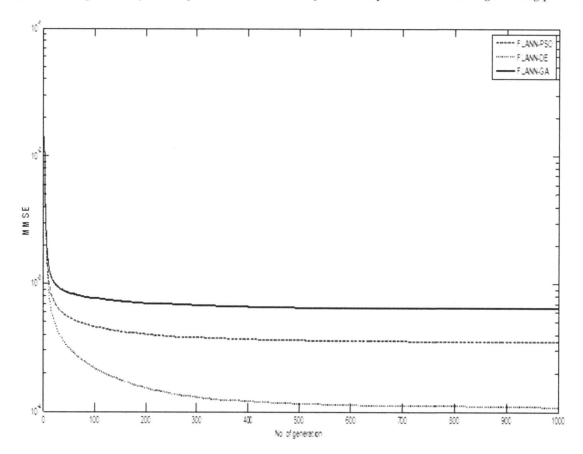

Table 1. Confusion Matrix achieved for all classes by the three adaptive models during training

Class	No of Samples in All Cases	FLANN_DE		FLANN_PSO		FLANN_GA	
		No. of Correct Prediction	Accuracy in %	No. of Correct Prediction	Accuracy in %	No. of Correct Prediction	Accuracy in %
0	360	358	99.44	345	95.83	340	94.44
1	360	356	98.89	347	96.39	347	96.39
2	360	347	96.39	356	98.89	337	93.61
3	360	350	97.22	349	96.94	339	94.17
4	360	354	98.33	348	96.67	345	95.83
5	360	353	98.06	352	97.78	348	96.67
6	360	354	98.33	343	95.28	344	95.56
7	360	358	99.44	350	97.22	346	96.11
8	360	355	98.61	356	98.89	342	95
9	360	348	96.67	325	90.28	323	89.72
		Overall accuracy in % = 98.14		Overall accuracy in % = 96.42		Overall accuracy in % = 94.75	

Table 2. Comparison of recognition accuracy during validation of three adaptive models

Class	No of Samples in All Cases	FLANN_DE		FLANN_PSO		FLANN_GA	
		No. of Correct Prediction	Accuracy in %	No. of Correct Prediction	Accuracy in %	No. of Correct Prediction	Accuracy in %
0	40	40	100	33	82.5	34	85
1	40	35	87.5	40	100	34	85
2	40	37	92.5	35	87.5	40	100
3	40	38	95	40	100	32	80
4	40	36	90	32	80	40	100
5	40	40	100	36	90	32	80
6	40	37	92.5	37	92.5	33	82.5
7	40	34	85	35	87.5	37	92.5
8	40	37	92.5	36	90	34	85
9	40	36	90	32	80	35	87.5
		Overall accuracy in % = 92.5		Overall accuracy in % = 89		Overall accuracy in % = 87.75	

gorithm for optimizing the parameters of the classifiers used for the recognition. This work is limited to FLANN for recognition. Beside FLANN other NNs (Neural networks) can be employed to achieve a higher recognition rate. The system can be extended for recognition of printed Odia characters and on other standard databases. From literature, a number of approaches can be applied on each phase of character recognition to build a more robust recognition system. Ensemble of classifiers can be built where the performances of two or more classifiers can be combined to enhance the performance of the recognition system. After recognition, post-processing operations can be applied to further enhance the recognition rate of the system.

CONCLUSION

This chapter has developed three hybrid soft computing based nonlinear models for improved recognition of handwritten Odia (an old recognized language of India) numerals using a standard database. The accuracy of recognition of these three models has been compared. Comparing the average accuracy obtained from these models the ranking observed is FLANN_DE (92.5%), FLANN_PSO (89%) and FLANN_GA (87.75%). The present work is a first attempt using soft and evolutionary computing based approach for recognition of handwritten Odia numerals using standard database. Further work can be carried out by using different feature extractions and classifiers to improve the classification performance. Similar techniques can be applied for recognition of handwritten Odia characters. Till date no standard database for Odia characters is available for comparing the recognition performance of different methods. This clearly shows that very limited standard ground work has been explored in the field of processing of Odia language particularly in the area of handwritten line and word segmentation, character and numeral recognition.

REFERENCES

Al-zoubaidy, L. M. (2006). Efficient genetics algorithms for Arabic handwritten characters recognition. *Advances in Intelligent and Soft Computing, Springer, 36*, 3–14. doi:10.1007/978-3-540-36266-1_1

Anish, C. M., & Majhi, B. (2015). Hybrid nonlinear adaptive scheme for stock market prediction using feedback FLANN and factor analysis. *Journal of the Korean Statistical Society.*

Ari, S., Das, M. K., & Chacko, A. (2013, July). ECG signal enhancement using S-Transform. *Computers in Biology and Medicine, 43*(6), 649–660. doi:10.1016/j.compbiomed.2013.02.015 PMID:23668340

Badrinath & Gupta. (2011, October). A stockwell transform based palm-print recognition. *Applied Soft Computing, 11*(7), 4267-4281.

Behera, Dash, & Biswal. (2010, June). Power quality time series data mining using S-transform and fuzz expert system. *Applied Soft Computing, 10*(3), 945-955.

Behera, Das, & Subudhi. (2014, October). Functional link artificial neural network applied to active noise control of a mixture of tonal and chaotic noise. *Applied Soft Computing, 23*, 51-60.

Das, M. K., & Ari, S. (2013). Analysis of ECG signal denoising method based on S-transform. *IRBM, Elsevier, 34*(6), 362–370. doi:10.1016/j.irbm.2013.07.012

Das, M. T., & Dulger, L. C. (2009). Signature verification (SV) toolbox. *Application of PSO-NN, Engineering Applications of Artificial Intelligence, Elsevier, 22*(4-5), 688–694. doi:10.1016/j.engappai.2009.02.005

Das, N., Acharya, K., Shankar, R., Basu, S., Kundu, M., & Nasipuri, M. (2012, January). A novel GA-SVM based multistage approach for recognition of handwritten Bangla compound characters. *Proc. of the International Conference on Information Systems, Design and Intelligent Applications, Visakhapatnam,* 1-6. doi:10.1007/978-3-642-27443-5_17

De, Kar, Mandal, & Ghosal. (2015, September). Optimal CMOS inverter design using differential evolution algorithm. *Journal of Electrical Systems and Information Technology, 2*(2), 219-241.

Dehuri, S., Roy, R., Cho, S.-B., & Ghosh, A. (2012, June). An improved swarm optimized functional link artificial neural network (ISO-FLANN) for classification. *Journal of Systems and Software, Elsevier, 85*(6), 1333–1345. doi:10.1016/j.jss.2012.01.025

Hariharan, M., Vijean, V., Sindhu, R., Divakar, P., Saidatul, A., & Yaacob, S. (2014, July). Classification of mental tasks using stockwell transform. *Computer and Electrical Engineering, Elsevier, 40*(5), 1741–1749. doi:10.1016/j.compeleceng.2014.01.010

Jiang, M., Chen, W., Zheng, Z., & Zhong, M. (2012, June). Fringe pattern analysis by S-transform. *Optics Communications, Elsevier, 285*(3), 209–217. doi:10.1016/j.optcom.2011.09.015

Majhi & Sa. (2007, July). FLANN-based adaptive threshold selection for detection of impulsive noise in images. *AEU- International Journal of Electronics and Communications, 61*(7), 478-484.

Majhi, R., Panda, G., & Sahoo, G. (2012, June). Development and performance evaluation of FLANN based model for forecasting of stock markets. *Expert Systems with Applications, Elsevier, 36*(3), 6800–6808. doi:10.1016/j.eswa.2008.08.008

Man, Z., Lee, K., Wang, D., Cao, Z., & Khoo, S. (2013, June). An optimal weight learning machine for handwritten digit image recognition. *Signal Processing, Elsevier, 93*(6), 1624–1638. doi:10.1016/j.sigpro.2012.07.016

Naik, B., Nayak, J., & Behera, H. S. (in press). A global-best harmony search based gradient descent learning FLANN (GbHS-GDL-FLANN) for data classification. *Egyptian Informatics Journal, Elsevier.*

Niu, X.-X., & Suen, C. Y. (2012, April). A novel hybrid CNN-SVM classifier for recognizing handwritten digits. *Pattern Recognition, Elsevier, 45*(4), 1318–1325. doi:10.1016/j.patcog.2011.09.021

Ozturk & Ozturk. (2014, June). Hybrid neural network and genetic algorithm based machining feature recognition. *Journal of Intelligent Manufacturing, 15*(3), 287-298.

Pal Thethi, H., Roy, S. S., Mondal, S., Majhi, B., & Panda, G. (2011, April). Improved Identification Model for Nonlinear Dynamic Systems Using FLANN and Various Types of DE. *Proc. of International Symposium on Devices, MEMS, intelligent Systems, Communications, Sikkim*, 1-6.

Pan, X., Ye, X., & Zhang, S. (2005, December). A hybrid method for robust car plate character recognition. *Engineering Applications of Artificial Intelligence, Elsevier, 18*(8), 963–972. doi:10.1016/j.engappai.2005.03.011

Panyam, Lakshmi, Krishnan, & Rao. (2016, December). Modelling of palm leaf character recognition system using transorm based techniques. *Pattern Recognition Letters, 84*, 29–34. doi:10.1016/j.patrec.2016.07.020

Patra & Bos. (2000, February). Modelling of an intelligent pressure sensor using functional link artificial neural networks. *ISA Transactions, 39*(1), 15-17.

Piotrowski. (2014, August). Differential Evolution algorithms applied to neural network training suffer from stagnation. *Applied Soft Computing, 21*, 382-406.

Potrus, M. Y., Ngah, U. K., & Ahmed, B. S. (2014, December). An evolutionary harmony search algorithm with dominant point detection for recognition-based segmentation of online Arabic text recognition. *Ain Shams Engineering Journal, Elsevier, 5*(4), 1129–1139. doi:10.1016/j.asej.2014.05.003

Pourhabibi, T., Imani, M. B., & Haratizadeh, S. (2011). Feature selection on Persian fonts: A comparative analysis on GAA. *Procedia Computer Science, 3*, 1249–1255. doi:10.1016/j.procs.2010.12.200

Prashant, Kakde, & Gulhane. (2016). A Comparative Analysis of Particle Swarm Optimization and Support Vector Machines for Devnagri Character Recognition: An Android application. *Proceedings of International Conference on Communication, Computing and Virtualization (ICCCV) 2016, 79*, 337-343. doi:10:1016:/j.procs2016.03.044

Quaranta, G., Carlo Marano, G., Greco, R., & Monti, G. (2014, September). Parametric identification of seismic isolators using differential evolution and particle swarm optimization. *Applied Soft Computing, Elsevier, 22*, 458–464. doi:10.1016/j.asoc.2014.04.039

Rajasekaeran, S., & Vijayalakshmi, G. A. (2003). *Neural networks, Fuzzy logic, and Genetics Algorithms Synthesis and Applications*. New Delhi: PHI Publication.

Rakshit, P., & Konar, A. (2015, October). Differential evolution for noisy multiobjective optimization. *Artificial Intelligence, Elsevier, 227*, 165–189. doi:10.1016/j.artint.2015.06.004

Roque, C. M. C., & Martins, P. A. L. S. (2015, December). Differential evolution for optimization of functionally graded beams. *Composite Structures, 133*, 1191–1197. doi:10.1016/j.compstruct.2015.08.041

Sarkhel, R., Das, N., Saha, A. K., & Nasipuri, M. (2016, October). A Multi-Objective Approach Towards Cost Effective Isolated Handwritten Bangla Character and Digit Recognition. *Pattern Recognition, 58*, 172–189. doi:10.1016/j.patcog.2016.04.010

Saruhan. (2014, September). Differential evolution and simulated annealing algorithms for mechanical systems design. *Engineering Science and Technology, 17*(3), 131-136.

Shrivastava, S., & Singh, M. P. (2011, January). Performance evaluation of feed-forward neural network with soft computing techniques for hand written English alphabets. *Applied Soft Computing, Elsevier, 11*(1), 1156–1182. doi:10.1016/j.asoc.2010.02.015

Stockwell, R. G. (2007). A basis of efficient representation of the S-transform. *Digital Signal Processing, 17*(1), 371–393. doi:10.1016/j.dsp.2006.04.006

Wang, L., Zeng, Y., & Chen, T. (2015). Back propagation neural network with adaptive differential evolution algorithm for time series forecasting. Expert Systems With Applications, 42, 855-863.

Wang, R., Zhan, Y., & Zhou, H. (2012, December). Application of S-transform in fault diagnosis of power electronic circuits. *Scientia Iranica, 19*(3), 721–726. doi:10.1016/j.scient.2011.06.013

Weng, W.-D., Yang, C.-S., & Lin, R.-C. (2007, July). A channel equalizer using reduced decision feedback Chebyshev functional link artificial neural networks. *Information Sciences, Elsevier, 177*(13), 2642–2654. doi:10.1016/j.ins.2007.01.006

Zheng, R.-R., Zhao, J.-Y., & Wu, B.-C. (2009). Multi Step Offline Handwritten Chinese Characters Segmentation with GA. Advances in Intelligent and Soft Computing, 62, 1-11.

KEY TERMS AND DEFINITIONS

Differential Evolution (DE): DE is a bio inspired techniques which optimizes a problem by iteratively modifying each candidate solutions.

Functional Link Artificial Neural Network (FLANN): FLANN is a higher order neural network with low computational complexity. It has no hidden layers. The input vector of FLANN is functionally expanded to get non-linear solutions.

OCR: Optical character recognition is the recognition of scanned images of hand written or printed characters.

S-Transform (ST): ST is a time frequency analysis method for the extraction of important features from the characters. It combines the features of short time fourier transform (STFT) and wavelet transform (WT).

Chapter 20
Intelligent Technique to Identify Epilepsy Using Fuzzy Firefly System for Brain Signal Processing

Sasikumar Gurumoorthy
Sree Vidyanikethan Engineering College (Autonomous), India

B. K. Tripathy
VIT University, India

ABSTRACT

In the new direction of understand the signal that is created from the brain organization is one of the main chores in the brain signal processing. Amid all the neurological disorders the human brain epilepsy is measured as one of the extreme prevalent and then programmed artificial intelligence detection technique is an essential due to the crooked and unpredictable nature of happening of epileptic seizures. We proposed an Improved Fuzzy firefly algorithm, which would enhance the classification of the brain signal efficiently with minimum iteration. An important bunching technique created on fuzzy logic is the Fuzzy C means. Together in the feature domain with the spatial domain the features gained after multichannel EEG signals remained combined by means of fuzzy algorithms. And for better precision segmentation process the firefly algorithm is applied to optimize the Fuzzy C-means membership function. This proposed algorithm result compared with other algorithms like fuzzy c means algorithm and PSO algorithm.

INTRODUCTION

Epilepsy captures is considered as the maximum collective neurological disorder that disturbs 1–3% of the world's inhabitants. This one is considered through the amount of two or supplementary meaningless epileptic captures that remain irregular rhythmic exoneration of electrical movement of the brain. This range of brain syndromes sorts from severe, life-threatening and spiking, to ones that are much

DOI: 10.4018/978-1-5225-2857-9.ch020

more beginning. Ahmed Fazle Rabbi and Reza Fazel-Rezai Fuzzy (2012) reported that in epilepsy; the standard pattern of neuronal action becomes uneasy, causing peculiar sensations, feelings and behavior or sometimes seizures, muscle ripples and loss of cognizance. There are many possible causes of epilepsy with several types of seizures. Whatever that interrupts the standard pattern of neuron action (from disease to brain injury to irregular brain enlargement) can tip to captures. Epilepsy might improve since of a difference in brain wiring, an unevenness of nerve signing chemicals named neurotransmitters, alterations in the dynamic structures of brain cells called channels or a combination of these factors and other possible features. Ensuring a particular seizure as the outcome of an extraordinary fever (named febrile seizure) mutual analytic tests for epilepsy are quantity of electrical action in the brain then brain shots such as magnetic resonance imaging (MRI) or computed tomography (CT).

Paroxysmal alteration of single or extra neurological occupations such as motor, behavior and autonomic occupations is definite as a seizure. Epileptic seizures remain episodic, quickly developing fleeting actions, normally enduring for less than a minute. There are numerous studies to understand the machine after epileptic capture and however it is not entirely known yet, a seizure event can be developed as the inflamed link excitation of the neural networks through synchronous release in addition to mutable transmission in the brain. In crucial epilepsy, a specific brain region may candidate for the epilepsy event, but in comprehensive epilepsy the complete brain might remain candidate aimed at seizure events.

The utmost broadly castoff quantity aimed at analysis of neurological syndromes such as epilepsy in medical backgrounds is electroencephalogram (EEG). Enduring intensive care of EEG is one of the best skilled conducts aimed at analysis of epilepsy. This one delivers evidence almost forms of brain electrical movement, category then occurrence of captures and seizure emphasis laterality. In abiding monitoring, ictal EEG footage is typically connected through the medical appearance of removal. Maryann D'Alessandro et al (2014) reported that the one of the greatest defining features in seizure recognition before primary recognition is Maryann D'Alessandro et al (2014) reported that the the assignment of electrodes. Unknown footage location is where the capture attention is placed; the variations in EEG can happen earlier the medical appearances. Sudarshan Nandy et al (2012) reported that if the electrodes are located in remote place after the seizure beginning spot, the medical appearances could transpire earlier any graphic variations in EEG. Professionals observing abiding EEG footages typically look on behalf of initial visually specious variations in EEG to classify ictal arrival. This data benefits doctor or caregiver toward treat patients initial in period with the accessible medicines. But, the graphic review of lasting EEG through clinicians is stimulating for it is achieved over numerous times to weeks due to the indefinite landscape of the period of manifestation of seizures. So, a capture recognition apparatus with great recognition amount and significantly little incorrect recognition amount would be an enormous development in the medical surroundings of epilepsy behavior thus overcoming the time consuming and monotonous nature of the graphic assessment of the huge volume of information to classify seizure.

RELATED WORK

Epilepsy is one of the neurological disorders under extensive research and over the years there has been several methods of seizure detection. One of method was based on detecting strong rhythmic movements of the patient. The drawback in these methods is that, seizures do not always present strong movements. This setback led the detection problem to apply methods based on EEG signal analysis, for example, J.R. Ives & Woods (1974) described detection of large seizures discharges in several EEG channels by amplitude discrimination; T.L. Babb & Crandall (1974) designed an electronic circuit for seizures detection from intracranial electrodes. However, not all seizures present EEG changes. So seizure detection completely dependent only on EEG analysis was not at all reliable and it was mandatory to coalesce it with other efficient methods. For example, P.F. Prior & Maynard (1973) identified on the EEG signal a large increase followed by a clear decrease in the amplitude and at the same time by large electromyogram (EMG) activity; A.M. Murro& Meador (1991) described a method based on spectral parameters and discriminant analysis. From the point of view of pattern recognition, new alternatives for the detection problem have been tackled. Gotman (1982) presented an automatic detection system based on seizure patterns. Unfortunately the setback for this method was the requirement of traditional visual inspection of the patterns by a specialist. Presently, EEG epileptic detectors have evolved including new techniques such as neural networks, non-linear models, independent component analysis (ICA), Bayesian methods, support vector machines and variance-based methods, as described in Guerrero-Mosquera, Trigueros, Franco and Navia-Vazquez (2010). Additional collections of approaches possibly valuable for noticing and examining non-stationary signals are time-frequency distributions (TFDs) Cohen (1995). These methods allow us to visualize the evolution of the frequency behavior during some non-stationary event by mapping a one dimensional (1-D) time signal into a two-dimensional (2-D) function of time and frequency. F Lotte et al (2007) reported that therefore, methods such as peak matching, filter banks, energy estimation, etc from the time-frequency (TF) plane enable to obtain appropriate information.

Feature Extraction

Discovering a set of capacities or a chunk of material with the purpose of illuminating in a healthy-distinct way the data or an event present in a signal is called feature extraction. Saibal k.Pal et al (2012) reported that for detection, a classification or regression task in biomedical signal processing these quantities or structures are the essential origin and remain one of the main phases in the data analysis method.These types establish a new method of uttering the data, and can be binary, definite or constant, and similarly signify qualities or straight capacities of the signal. Maryann D'Alessandro et al (2014) reported that for instance, features might be age, healthiness position of the patient, personal history, electrode location or EEG signal descriptors (voltage, amplitude, frequency, phase etc.).

Other correctly, feature removal accepts we need for N models and D structures, a matrix N×D, where D signifies the quantity of the feature matrix. That funds, at the sample n after the feature matrix, we might gain a unidimensional vector $x = [x_1, x_2, ... x_D]$ named as "pattern vector." Guyon et al. (2006) consists several methods in EEG feature extraction. More explicitly in EEG recognition and classification backdrops, features created on power spectral solidity are presented in Lehmanna et al. (2007); Lyapunov exponents are introduced in Güler & Übeyli (2007); wavelet transform remain defined in Hasan (2008); Lima et al. (2009); Subasi (2007) and Xu et al. (2009); sampling techniques are used in Siuly & Wen (2009) and time frequency analysis are presented on Boashash (2003); Guerrero-Mosquera, Trigueros, Franco & Navia-Vazquez (2010); Tzallas et al. (2009) and Boashash & Mesbah (2001). Other method in feature extraction created in the fractional Fourier transform remains defined in Guerrero-Mosquera, Verleysen and Navia-Vazquez 2010. In this method of feature extraction, the features extracted are directly dependent on the application and also to consider that there are significant possessions of these features to require into account, for example, dimensionality, noise, time information, set size, nonstationarity, and so on Lotte et al. 2007. The frequency domain features, entropy-based features and Time domain were mined from EEG segments. The four structures used in this training were average dominant frequency, amplitude, rhythmicity (coefficient of variation of amplitude) and entropy. These features are recognized to have the most discriminant data for identifying seizure measures. Features extraction methods are expounded briefly in the following sections.

Average Amplitude

For time-based development of limited seizures, average amplitude (AVA) is a decent amount. EEG signals display rhythmic movement with a recurrence frequency among 3 and 30 Hz throughout limited seizures. Consequently, to calculate regular amplitude, EEG divisions were initially high-pass cleaned overhead 3 Hz to eliminate low-frequency sound. Then to identify peaks, a peak recognition algorithm produced on the zero crossings of the initial derived of EEG signals was castoff. Then, by compelling the average of the amplitudes of their half waves the amplitudes of the peaks were calculated. Ahmed Fazle Rabbi and Reza Fazel-Rezai Fuzzy (2012) reported that finally the average amplitude was considered by compelling the average of the amplitudes of the recognized points.

Rhythmicity

Coefficient variation amplitude (CVA) is a degree of rhythmicity or symmetries of ictal activities. Through seizure development, the symmetry of the amplitude of EEG inclines to growth slowly; this escalation is categorized by the CVA. Just in case of partial seizures, the signals display tough rhythmic features that are possible to have symmetry in amplitude. The coefficient variation amplitude (CVA) counts the increased regularity experimental through partial seizures. Ahmed Fazle Rabbi and Reza Fazel-Rezai Fuzzy (2012) reported that the CVA is distinct as the relation of the standard deviation of complete amplitude to the mean complete amplitude as where is the standard deviation and is the mean of apiece EEG segment.

Entropy

Entropy was initially introduced by Shannon in 1948 and is briefly defined as a measure of "irregularity" or "uncertainty". The Shannon entropy () is computed as where are the probabilities of a datum in bin. Pincus and Goldberger introduced approximate entropy (ApEn) are measured additional suitable to calculate the entropy aimed at small and deafening time series data. A squat worth of the entropy designates that the time series is deterministic, while an extraordinary worth designates uncertainty. So, a high importance of entropy designates the anomalies in the EEG information. Parisut jitpakdee and pakinee aimmanee (2014) reported that to calculates ApEn, it is obligatory to regulate a run measurement and an acceptance window to amount the likelihood among runs of shapes. The acceptance window and inserting dimension are the two significant limits in calculation of ApEn. In this training, Sample Entropy (SampEn), which is an irregular of approximate entropy to measure entropy of EEG, was castoff as its robustness over ApEn. Model Entropy is the destructive natural logarithm of an approximation of the restricted probability that segments of length that contest point sensible within a tolerance also contest at the resulting point. Ahmed Fazle Rabbi and Reza Fazel-Rezai Fuzzy (2012) reported that consequently, for investigating dynamics of biomedical signal then additional time series this quantity is a valuable tool.

Domain Frequency

The highest with the maximum spectral control in the power spectrum of a signal is distinct as dominant frequency. This feature is predominantly significant in unique ictal activities after mixed activities by quantizing the frequency signature data mostly found in partial seizures. This is categorized by a high frequency movement at capture onset and a low-frequency action at the end of the captures. In this training, parametric spectrum valuation method, autoregressive-modeling (AR) method was used to assessment the spectral frequency band of the short EEG segments.

The AR model demand was selected rendering to Akaike data criterion. The Burg technique was castoff for calculating the AR coefficients for short EEG segments. Then, the spectral power of an assumed segment is assessed by means of these AR coefficients. For each spectral peak, the spectral frequency band was distinct as the frequencies at increasing and decreasing slopes of the highest with half the amplitude of the greatest.

FUZZY C-MEANS CLUSTERING

Fuzzy c-means (FCM) is a method of clustering which allows a datum to belong to more than one cluster by varying degree of membership described by a fuzzy matrix with n rows and c columns in which n is the number of data and c is the number of clusters.

Runkler and T.A., Katz (2006) reported that the Fuzzy c-means algorithm is popularly used clustering algorithm and introduced by Bezek in 1974, FCM algorithm result totally depend on the initialization of center, the random selection of the center causes the local optima problem. To solve the shortcoming of the FCM algorithm, this proposal integrate the optimization algorithm with FCM.

Consider the set of vectors $X = (x_1, x_2, \ldots x_n)$; where $n \geq 2$, which are to be clustered into c groups. The set of fuzzy partition matrices is denoted as:

$$M_{f_c} = \{W \in R^{cn} \mid W_{ik} \in [0,1], \forall i, k; \sum_{i=1}^{c} W_{ik} = 1, \forall k\} ;$$

$$0 < \sum_{k=1}^{n} W_{ik} < n, \forall i \tag{1}$$

where $1 \leq i \leq c; 1 \leq k \leq n$.

FCM objective function computed by using following equation and Euclidian distance:

$$J_m(W, P) = \sum_{\substack{1 \leq k \leq n \\ 0 \leq i \leq c}} (W_{ik})^m (d_{ik})^2$$

$$(d_{ik}) = \|x_k - p_i\| \tag{2}$$

FIREFLY ALGORITHM

First proposed by Yang (2010), a Firefly Algorithm (FA) is an optimization algorithm, which simulates the flash pattern and features of fireflies. The Firefly Algorithm is a population-based algorithm to discover the global optima of objective functions based on swarm intelligence. Individually firefly is enticed by the brighter luminosity of additional adjacent fireflies. Yang (2007) reported that the attractiveness decreases when far between the couples of fireflies.

Three idealized rules in firefly algorithm distinct by Yang:

1. Entire fireflies are unisex so as to one firefly will be engrossed to other firefly nevertheless of their sex;
2. Attractiveness is proportional to their brightness. Thus, for any two fireflies, the less positive one will change to the brighter one. If there is certainly not brighter one than a specific firefly, it will transfer casually;
3. The brightness of a firefly is from the objective function. For a maximization problem, the brightness can simply be proportional to the value of the objective function.

X-S Yang (2010) made use of firefly algorithm like an optimization algorithm for different purposes. In the design of real-world engineering problems, Azad and Azad and Gandomi showed that firefly algorithm shall be a good remedy for multimodal optimization problems. Banati and Bajaj showed that FA should be a potential future prospective for efficient performance in terms of time and optimality for feature selection when compared with other algorithms. Horng qualified that firefly-based method (firefly-based algorithm) illustrated better high speed and good reconstructed images while compressing the digital images.

Chatterjee & Basu and Mahanti have showed a firefly algorithm for the optimization of antenna design problem and evidenced that firefly algorithm outperforms artificial bee colony algorithm and particle swarm optimization. Yukon Zhang compiled the image registration mechanism by FA., FA provides a solution for job shop scheduling problem that comprises of complex combinatorial optimization which can be further divided into non-deterministic polynomial (NP) hard problem. Olympia Roeva ustilized FA for a model parameter identification of an E-coli fed-batch cultivation process and worked out on parameter optimization.

J. Senthilnath et al. (2011) compared FA with eleven different algorithms and reported that FA is superior to other algorithms based on his wide width evaluation study for clustering. Likewise, FA has been applied to neural networking also. Firefly algorithm has been complemented with other algorithms to have additive effect on efficiency.

The key steps of firefly algorithm are as follows: The first step is to initialize firefly agents in which each firefly is characterized by its light intensity. During the pairwise firefly comparison in each loop, the brighter firefly attracts the firefly with lower light intensity. The attraction depends on the distance between the two fireflies. After attraction, the new firefly is assessed for its light intensity and it is updated. Yang (2007) reported that the best-so-far solution obtained at the end of each pairwise loop is updated iteratively. This pairwise loop comparison process is performed till the termination criterion is verified.

The attractiveness function β calculate from the distance $r(i, j)$ of the firefly is determined by:

$$\beta(r(i,j)) = \beta_0 e^{-\gamma r(i,j)^2} \tag{3}$$

where, β_0 is the attractiveness at r = 0 and γ is the light absorption coefficient at the source. It should be noted that $r(i,j)$ which is the Euclidean distance between any two fireflies at x_i and x_j, where x_i and x_j are the spatial coordinate of the fireflies i and j, respectively.

The movement of a firefly i, which is attracted to another more attractive firefly j, is decided by:

$$\beta\big(r(i,j)\big)x_i = x_i + \beta_0 e^{-\gamma r(i,j)^2}\big(x_i - x_j\big) + \alpha\big(rand(-1/2)\big) \tag{4}$$

α is the randomization parameter, in most of cases α between [0,1], $\beta_0 = 1$ and $\gamma \in [0.01, 100]$. Pseudo code of the firefly algorithm:

objective function $f(x), x = (x_1, \dots x_d)^T$
define the parameters
Generete initial population of fireflies $x_i (i = 1, 2 \dots n)$
```
 Calculate light intensity I_i  at x_i is decided by f(x_i)
Repeat:
For i=1:n all n fireflies
    For j=1:n all n fireflies
        If(I_i > I_j)
          Move firefly I towards j in d-dimension
```
Attractiveness varies with distance r via exp[-³r]
```
          Calculate new solution and update light intensity
If no one of firefly brighter than Ii, Ii move randomly
Rank the fireflies and find current best one
Until: maximum iteration or minimum changes in the member function
```

In various signal processing and pattern recognition applications fuzzy logic has been extensively used. Fuzzy rules can be defined using specialists information for assessment creation which is simpler to contrivance and modular in addition. Growing the amount of procedures one can surge the correctness of the prototypical. With less complex mathematical analysis and modeling, processing speed can also be significantly improved. Moreover fuzzy logic is a useful method for non- linear input-output mapping which is effective in seizure detection or early detection applications. Artificial neural networks and support vector machines are other prominent detection methods which demands training, complex mathematical analysis, and modeling. All these major setbacks can be avoided in fuzzy logic. Therefore, in this study, we practical adaptive form of fuzzy logic structure with a unique method of inclusion data in feature as well as spatial and temporal dominion.

FUZZY FIREFLY ALGORITHM

Fuzzy-based Firefly algorithm (FFA) for data clustering is proposed. Each solution of the cluster is defined fuzzily and then the solution is updated using firefly algorithm the same way it does with non-fuzzy solution. However, minimization of the objective function is calculated in the same way as FCM algorithm. In the proposed method cluster centers are the decision parameters to minimize the membership function. A single firefly represents the cluster centers vectors. Equation 5 represents each firefly:

$$X_i = (p_{i1}, p_{i2}, ..., p_{ij}, ...p_{ic}), 2 \le j \le c \tag{5}$$

where f_{ij} represents the jth center vector. n number of fireflies represents n candidate solutions. This is a minimize problem the intensity of each firefly is equal to the values of the objective function of FCM. FCM will terminate when there is no scope for further improvement in the member function. FFA will terminate when the no changes in the 5 consecutive iterations. Improved FFA method has 50 is the maximum iteration or no changes in current best in 3 consecutive iterations.

Pseudo code of the algorithm:

```
Initialize the population of n fireflies with C random cluster centers of d-
dimensions
Initialize the algorithm parameters
Repeat:
For i=1:n all n fireflies
  For j=1:n all n fireflies
   Calculate light intensity (membership function value) of each firefly
        If(I_i > I_j)
     Move firefly I towards j to update the position of      fireflies
    Rank the fireflies and find current best one
Until: maximum iteration or minimum changes in the member function
```

RESULTS AND DISCUSSION

Our experimental study is to compare the proposed algorithm with other popular optimization algorithms like PSO, FFA, and FCM. The dataset collected from the "ictal" information records from Freiburg project, which must seizures with as a minimum 50 minutes of preictal information then postictal information with not any quantified period. Subsequently, the false recognition rate per hour is slight complex associating to additional approaches in the works but sensible seeing the assessment dataset. The EEG information was acquired using a Neurofile NT digital video EEG system with 128 channels, 256 Hz sampling rate, and a 16 bit analogue-to-digital converter. Notch or band pass filters have not been applied. This algorithm was implemented using MATLAB and all result were tested offline. We utilize MATLAB *fcm* default function with Firefly algorithm. In Figure 1 the results are shown for the seizure is marked in red line.

Figure 1. Seizure is marked by red line. Corresponding changes in features also shown.

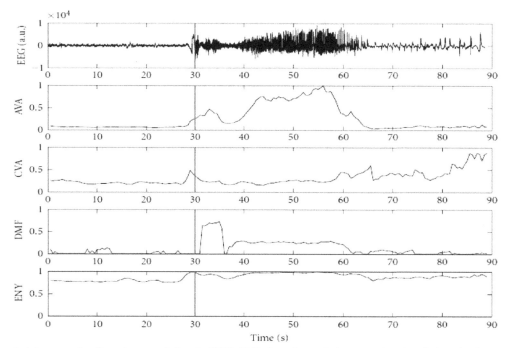

a) Top subplot- a sample of a seizure evolution in iEEG. b) Bottom four subplots- consistent variations in characteristics features- coefficient variation amplitude (CVA), Average amplitude (AVA), entropy (ENY) and dominant frequency (DMF). Seizure beginning is marked by red perpendicular line. Initial electrographic variations are graphic in three of the four structures.

*For a more accurate representation see the electronic version.

For each of the patients in Figure 2, there are datasets called "ictal" and "interictal", the former containing files with epileptic seizures and at least 50 min pre-ictal data.

Consequently, the false discovery rate per hour is slight complex comparing to other approaches in the nonfiction but sensible since the assessment dataset. Till date, numerous algorithms for epilepsy and seizure discovery have been established with different grades of success. Now, we have deliberated momentarily some of these approaches as long as a scope of contrast with our technique. In a current study, Zhang et al. Proposed an automatic patient specific technique for seizure start detection using a novel incremental knowledge system based on nonlinear dimensionality reduction. Feature sets were removed using continuous wavelet transform (CWT). In view of computation time and resources, the optimal of discrete wavelet transform capacity have been improved. Their technique was assessed on iEEG recordings from 21 patients acquired from Freiburg project with period of 193.8 hour then 82 seizures. They must reported average sensitivity of 98.8% through 0.25/h interesting false positive rate and average median recognition delay of 10.8 sec. Aarabi et al. presented a fuzzy rule-based system for epileptic seizure recognition which yielded sensitivity of 98.7% and false detection rate of 0.27/h with detection delay of 11 sec. In this paper, dissimilar thresholds were used for dissimilar patients and a postprocessor was utilized to decrease the false exposures in two steps. First short length detections (less than 5 sec) and artifacts were rejected. Secondly, two successive recognitions were unified given

Figure 2. Seizure development outline in iEEG gained from patient, Seizure start and balance periods are noticeable by red vertical lines, individually. Acronyms-CH$_1$EPT: Epileptic channel 1, CH$_4$RMT: Remote channel 4.

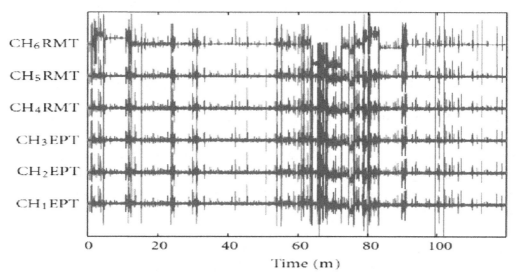

For a more accurate representation see the electronic version.

that they are less than a predefined minimum time interval (set to 30 sec). Chan et al. presented a novel patient-specific algorithm for seizure onset detection and correct onset time determination.

The algorithm abstracts spectral and temporal features in five frequency bands within a sliding window and the feature windows were confidential as encompassing or not containing a seizure onset using support vector machines (SVMs). Support vector machine is a general organization paradigm for epileptic seizure recognition and prediction being used by numerous researchers in this area. Zakian (2011) reported that in order to precisely restrict the seizure onsets in time, the technique creates use of clustering and regression examination. Consequently, their algorithm produced exact discovery in time as stated in five of the six patients, at least 90% of the latencies are less than 3 sec resulting median recognition latency less than 100 msec with standard deviation less than 3 s. However, the technique utilizing user-adjustable parameters allow tuning to achieve high detection sensitivity, low false positive rate, and low recognition latencies. The Standard cross-validation performance measures resulted sensitivities in the range of 80% to 98% and false progressive rates from 0.12 to 2.8/h. Gardner et al. Carlos Guerrero Mosquera et al (2012) reported that offered a detection latency which is negative in time (−7.58 sec) however with a higher false detection rate of 1.56 false detections per hour.

Their scheme was appraised on sample of 29 ictal and 41 interictal epochs and achieved 97.1% sensitivity. Grewal and Gotman proposed an automatic cautionary system with extraordinary sensitivity and low false alarm rates for clinical use. The system essential training and was tested on locally verified dataset yielding 89.4% sensitivity with false detection rate of 0.22 per hour and mean detection latency of 17.1 seconds with user tuning. The presentation of our organization is very much similar to the other approaches. It may not outperform the other approaches in terms of all the performance calculating parameters. However, considering less mathematically complex design and lesser number of tuning parameters we have achieved similar results to other methods and in some cases improved Performance in terms of one or two performance calculating parameters.

Sensitivity

Sensitivity is significant quantity for event based system performance assessment. It measures the capability of a system to identify seizure suitably. It is the amount of true positive rate and different as the ratio of the amount of properly noticed seizure to the total amount of seizures:

$$Sensitivity = (TP/ (TP+FN)) \ 100 \qquad (6)$$

True Positive (TP): The system detects the actual seizures.
False Negative (FN): The System misses the actual seizures.

When compare to the other algorithm Improved version of FFA detect the seizure with minimum iterations. Our method achieved average sensitivity of 96.8% with 0.23/h false detection rates. The average detection latency achieved was 13.5 seconds (see Table 1). Firefly algorithm minimizes the detection latency of the classification process.

Motivation and Advantage of Using Fuzzy Logic

The motivation after our fuzzy rule-based method is that fuzzy logic uses an ample simpler rule-based scheme using natural language. Clinical neurologists mostly look at dissimilar features of capture onset designs as well as dissimilar channels to recognize a seizure properly. This is however multifaceted to model mathematically and implement in computer programs. Fuzzy logic on the other hand provides a simpler design of approximate reasoning which can mimic human reasoning efficiently. We have developed our method in such way to mimic the experts perceptive in detecting seizure onset patterns. Also, the system delivers a possibility of dropping the detection latency by including more sensitive features. Fuzzy logic has been widely used in many signal processing and pattern recognition applications. Fuzzy rules can be defined using experts' data for decision making which are simpler to implement and linked as well. Increasing the number of rules one can growth the accuracy of the model. Processing rapidity can also be better-quality significantly with less multifaceted mathematical examination and modelling. Additionally, fuzzy logic is a useful technique for nonlinear input-output mapping which is operative in seizure discovery or early detection applications. Additional general approaches such as artificial neural networks and support vector machines require exercise, complex mathematical investigation, and modelling.

In this training, we developed adaptive form of fuzzy logic scheme with an original method of merging data in feature as well as three-dimensional and temporal domain. An evaluation of performance of

Table 1. Shows the comparison sensitivity and detection latency for various algorithms

Algorithm	Sensitivity	Average Detection Latency (s)	FDR /h
FCM	94.5	29	0.35
Fuzzy+ PSO	91.3	35	0.32
FFA	94.7	28	0.28
Improved FFA	96.8	13.5	0.23

Table 2. Presentation of adaptive fuzzy system above single technique with conventional hard threshold and non-adaptive fuzzy scheme

Process	SEN(%)	FDR/h
Feature1 - Hard threshold	96.25	1.93
Feature 2 -Hard threshold	93.75	3.62
Feature 3 - Hard threshold	98.75	1.16
Feature 4 - Hard threshold	84.17	1.98
Non-adaptive fuzzy system	91.49	0.35
Adaptive-fuzzy system	95.80	0.26

adaptive fuzzy logic system is exposed over conventional hard threshold based methods and nonadaptive fuzzy system in Table 2. Nonadaptive fuzzy system is where the membership functions were produced in a heuristic way. Adaptive fuzzy system obviously outperforms other approaches by representative improved performance in terms of better sensitivity and significantly reduces false positive amounts.

SUMMARY

After extensive research, we present a strong technique of classifying seizure using fuzzy firefly algorithm classification. Firefly algorithm helps the fuzzy system to obtain the better classification in minimum iteration. This proposed algorithm converge the result faster than the other algorithm with minimum iterations. Considering the challenge and important development in the capacity of seizure recognition, we primarily absorbed in designing effective seizure recognition classification with low complexity. In future our work will compare with other various classification algorithm like SVM and optimization algorithm like Genetic algorithm.

REFERENCES

D'Alessandro, Esteller, Vachtsevanos, Hinson, Echauz, & Litt. (2003). Epileptic Seizure Prediction Using Hybrid Feature Selection over Multiple Intracranial EEG Electrode Contacts: A Report of Four Patients. Academic Press.

EEG Database: Seizure Prediction Project Freilburg. (n.d.). Retrieved from http://epilepsy.uni-freiburg.de/freiburg-seizure-prediction-project/eeg-database

Guerrero Mosquera. (2012). *Armando Malanda Trigueros*. Angel Navia Vazquez EEG Signal Processing for Epilepsy.

Jitpakdee & Aimmanee. (2014). *Image Cluster using fuzzy based firefly algorithm*. Academic Press.

Lotte, Congedo, Lécuyer, Lamarche, & Arnaldi. (2007). A review of classification algorithm for EEG-based brain-computer interfaces. Academic Press.

Nandy, S., Sarkar, P. P., & Das, A. (2012). Analysis of a Nature Inspired Firefly-Algorithm Based Back Propagation Neural Network Training. Academic Press.

Rabbi & Fazel-Rezai. (2012). Fuzzy Logic System for seizure onset detection in intracranial EEG. Academic Press.

Runkler & Katz. (2006). Fuzzy clustering by Particle Swarm Optimization. *Proceedings of 2006 IEEE international Conference on Fuzzy Systems*, 601-608.

Saibal, Pal, Rai, & Singh. (2012). Comparative Study of Firefly Algorithm and Particle Swarm Optimization for Noisy Non Linear Optimization Problems. Academic Press.

Senthilnath, J., Omkar, S. N., & Mani, V. (2011). Clustering using Firefly algorithm: Performance Study. Academic Press.

Yang, X. (2010). Stochastic Test Functions and Design Optimization. *International Journal of Bio-inspired Computation*, 2, 78–84. doi:10.1504/IJBIC.2010.032124

Yang, X. S. (2007). *Nature-inspired metaheuristic Algorithm*. Luniver Press.

Zakian, H. A. (2011). Fuzzy C-means and Fuzzy swarm clustering Problem expert System with Application. Academic Press.

Chapter 21
Analysis and Implementation of Artificial Bee Colony Optimization in Constrained Optimization Problems

Soumya Sahoo
C. V. Raman College of Engineering, India

Sushruta Mishra
C. V. Raman College of Engineering, India

Brojo Kishore Kishore Mishra
C. V. Raman College of Engineering, India

Monalisa Mishra
C. V. Raman College of Engineering, India

ABSTRACT

The growing complexity of real-world problems has motivated computer scientists to search for efficient problem-solving methods. Evolutionary computation and swarm intelligence meta-heuristics are outstanding examples that nature has been an unending source of inspiration. The behaviour of bees, bacteria, glow-worms, fireflies, slime moulds, cockroaches, mosquitoes and other organisms have inspired swarm intelligence researchers to devise new optimisation algorithms. Swarm Intelligence appears in biological swarms of certain insect species. It gives rise to complex and often intelligent behavior through complex interaction of thousands of autonomous swarm members. In this chapter, the ABC algorithm has been extended for solving constrained optimization problems and applied to a set of constrained problems.

DOI: 10.4018/978-1-5225-2857-9.ch021

1. INTRODUCTION

The computer revolution has changed the human societies. Some problems are there which cannot be tackled through traditional hardware and software. So, new computing techniques are needed. Swarm intelligence is an important concept in artificial intelligence and computer science with emergent properties (Blum, 2008). A swarm is a large number of homogenous, simple agents interacting locally among themselves, and their environment, with no central control to allow a global interesting behavior to emerge. Swarm-based algorithms have recently emerged as a family of nature-inspired, population-based algorithms that are capable of producing low cost, fast, and robust solutions to several complex problems. Swarm Intelligence can therefore be defined as a relatively new branch of Artificial Intelligence that is used to model the collective behavior of social swarms in nature, such as ant colonies, honey bees, and bird flocks. Although these agents (insects or swarm individuals) are relatively unsophisticated with limited capabilities on their own, they are interacting together with certain behavioral patterns to cooperatively achieve tasks necessary for their survival. The social interactions among swarm individuals can be either direct or indirect. Examples of direct interaction are through visual or audio contact, such as the waggle dance of honey bees. Indirect interaction occurs when one individual changes the environment and the other individuals respond to the new environment, such as the pheromone trails of ants that they deposit on their way to search for food sources. In 1989, the expression "Swarm Intelligence" was first introduced by G. Beni and J. Wang in the global optimization framework as a set of algorithms for controlling robotic swarm. Swarm intelligence is used in various fields like robotics for controlling robots, automobiles for designing unmanned cars, in NASA for planet or satellite mapping, in medical fraternity for locating and killing tumors or blockages, in genetics, in data mining etc. Various principles of swarm intelligence are:

1. **Proximity Principle:** The basic units of a swarm should be capable of simple computation related to its surrounding environment. Here computation is regarded as a direct behavioral response to environmental variance, such as those triggered by interactions among agents;
2. **Quality Principle:** Apart from basic computation ability, a swarm should be able to response to quality factors, such as food and safety;
3. **Principle of Diverse Response:** Resources should not be concentrated in narrow region. The distribution should be designed so that each agent will be maximally protected facing environmental fluctuations;
4. **Principle of Stability and Adaptability:** Swarms are expected to adapt environmental fluctuations without rapidly changing modes since mode changing costs energy.

Nature is inspiring researchers to develop models for solving their problems. Optimization is an instance field in which these models are frequently developed and applied. Optimization is the science of allocating scarce resources to the best possible effect. The nature-inspired algorithms (Das, 2009) are motivated by a variety of biological and natural processes. Evolutionary computation, neural networks, ant colony optimization, particle swarm optimization, artificial immune systems, and bacteria foraging algorithm are among the algorithms and concepts that were motivated by nature. Swarm behavior is one of the main features of different colonies of social insects (bees, wasps, ants, termites). This type of behavior is principally characterized by autonomy, distributed functioning, and self-organizing. The researchers have been studying the behavior of social insects in an attempt to utilize the swarm intelligence concept and build up various artificial systems. Artificial Bee Colony (ABC) algorithm, proposed by Dervis Karaboga in 2005 is motivated by the intelligent behavior of honey bees (Karaboga, 2005). ABC as an optimization tool provides a population-based search procedure in which individuals called foods positions are modified by the artificial bees with time and the bee's aim is to discover the places of food sources with high nectar amount and finally the one with the highest nectar. The minimal model of swarm-intelligent forage selection in a honey bee colony, that ABC algorithm adopts, consists of three kinds of bees: employed bees, onlooker bees, and scout bees. Half of the colony comprises of employed bees and the other half includes the onlooker bees. Employed bees are responsible from exploiting the nectar sources explored before and giving information to the other waiting bees (onlooker bees) in the hive about the quality of the food source site which they are exploiting. Onlooker bees wait in the hive and decide a food source to exploit depending on the information shared by the employed bees. Communication among bees related to the quality of food sources takes place in the dancing area and the dance is called as the Waggle dance. Scouts randomly search the environment in order to find a new food source depending on an internal motivation or possible external clues or randomly.

1.1. The Advantages and the Disadvantages of the Artificial Bee Colony Optimization Technique (Karaboga et al, nd)

Advantages:
- Simplicity, Flexibility and Robustness;
- Ability to explore local solutions;
- Ease of implementation;
- Ability to handle the objective cost;
- Population of solutions;
- High flexibility, which allows adjustments;
- Broad applicability, even in complex functions;

Disadvantages:
- Lack of use of secondary information;
- Requires new fitness tests on the new algorithm parameters;
- Possibility of losing relevant information;
- High number of objective function evaluations;
- Slow down when used in sequential processing;
- The populations of solutions increases the computational cost.

1.2. This Artificial Bee Colony Algorithm is Applicable to Various Areas (Fahad, 2012)

- Benchmarking optimization;
- Bioinformatics applications;
- Scheduling applications;
- Clustering and Mining applications;
- Image processing applications;
- Economic dispatch problems;
- Engineering designs and applications.

2. BACKGROUND

Swarm intelligence is focused on insect behavior in order to develop some meta-heuristics which can mimic insect's problem solution abilities. Interaction between insects contributes to the collective intelligence of the social insect colonies. These communication systems between insects have been adapted to scientific problems for optimization. One of the examples of such interactive behavior is the waggle dance of bees during the food procuring. By performing this dance, successful foragers share the information about the direction and distance to patches of flower and the amount of nectar within this flower with their hive mates. So this is a successful mechanism which foragers can recruit other bees in their colony to productive locations to collect various resources. Bee colony can quickly and precisely adjust its searching pattern in time and space according to changing nectar sources. The information exchange among individual insects is the most important part of the collective knowledge. Communication among bees about the quality of food sources is being achieved in the dancing area by performing waggle dance. Tereshko developed a model (Tereshko, 2000) of foraging behavior of a honeybee colony based on reaction–diffusion equations. This model that leads to the emergence of collective intelligence of honeybee swarms consists of three essential components: food sources, employed foragers, and unemployed foragers, and defines two leading modes of the honeybee colony behavior: recruitment to a food source and abandonment of a source. After finding the food source, the bee utilizes its own capability to memorize the location and then immediately starts exploiting it. Hence, the bee will become an employed forager. The foraging bee takes a load of nectar from the source and returns to the hive, unloading the nectar to a food store. After unloading the food, the bee has the following options:

- It might become an uncommitted follower after abandoning the food source (UF);
- It might dance and then recruit nest mates before returning to the same food source (EF1);
- It might continue to forage at the food source without recruiting bees (EF2).

Yonezawa and Kikuchi (1996) examine the foraging behavior of honey bees and construct an algorithm to indicate the importance of group intelligence principals. The algorithm (Yonezawa et al, 1996) is simulated with one and three foraging bees and the computational simulation results showed that three foraging bees are faster than the system with one foraging bee at decision making process. They also indicate that the honey bees have an adaptive foraging behavior at complex environment. Seeley and Buhrman (1999) investigated the nest site selection behavior of honey bee colonies. The nest site selection process starts with several hundred scout bees that search for potential nest sites. The scouts then return to the cluster, report their findings by means of waggle dances, and decide the new nest site (Seeley et al, 1999). The type of waggle dance depends on the quality of the site being advertised. The bee colony considers a dozen or more alternative nest sites, evaluates each alternative nest site with respect to at least six distinct attributes with different weightings e.g. cavity volume, entrance height, entrance area, entrance direction etc. Consequently, the bee colony uses this strategy by distributing among many bees both the task of evaluating the alternative sites and the task of identifying the best of these sites. Schmickl et al. (2005) evaluate the robustness of bees' foraging behavior by using a multi-agent simulation platform (Schmickl et al, 2005). They investigate how the time-pattern of environmental fluctuations affects the foraging strategy and the efficiency of the foraging. They conclude that the collective foraging strategy of a honeybee colony is robust and adaptive, and that its emergent features allow the colony to find optimal solutions. Sato and Hagiwara (1997) proposed an improved genetic algorithm

(Sato et al, 1997) based on foraging behavior of honey bees. In a honey bee colony, each bee looks for the feed individually. When a bee finds feed, then it notifies the information to the other many bees by dance and they engage in a job to carry the feed. When they finish the work, each bee tries to find new one individually again. Similarly in the proposed algorithm, named Bee System, global search is done first, and some chromosomes with pretty high fitness (superior chromosomes) are obtained using the simple genetic algorithm. Second, many chromosomes obtain the information of superior chromosomes by the concentrated crossover and they search intensively around there using multiple populations. In the conventional crossover each pair is made randomly, while in the concentrated crossover all of the chromosomes make pair with superior chromosome. Lastly, pseudo-simplex method is contributed to enhance the local search ability of the Bee System. If the solution found by one cycle is not satisfactory, the global search is repeated. As it is known genetic algorithms have good global search ability, however they lack the local search ability. On the other hand with Bee System probability of falling into a local optimum is low because of the combination of local and global search since the aim of the algorithm is to improve the local search ability of genetic algorithm without degrading the global search ability. In the experimental studies Bee System is compared with the conventional genetic algorithm and it is found that Bee System shows better performance than the conventional genetic algorithm especially for highly complex multivariate functions. Karaboga (2005) analyzes the foraging behavior of honey bee swarm and proposes a new algorithm (Karaboga, 2005) simulating this behavior for solving multi-dimensional and multi-modal optimization problems, called Artificial Bee Colony (ABC). The main parts of the entire process include:

Pseudo Code 1 - ABC Algorithm:
- Send the employed bees onto the food sources and determine their nectar amounts;
- Calculate the probability value of the sources with which they are preferred by the onlooker bees;
- Stop the exploitation process of the sources abandoned by the bees;
- Send the scouts into the search area for discovering new food sources, randomly;
- Memorize the best food source found so far.

2.1. ABC Algorithm

The Artificial Bee Colony (ABC), introduced in Karaboga in the year 2005, is a simple population-based optimization algorithm, where a solution population is updated in each iteration. It has been applied in many practical optimization problems Akay, 2013, Draa and Bouaziz, 2014.ABC is a swarm intelligence which is inspired by the behavior of honey bees. Since the development of ABC, it has been applied to solve different kinds of problems. Artificial bee colony (ABC) algorithm is a recently proposed optimization technique which simulates the intelligent foraging behavior of honey bees. A set of honey bees is called swarm which can successfully accomplish tasks through social cooperation. In the ABC algorithm, there are three types of bees: employed bees, onlooker bees, and scout bees. The employed bees search food around the food source in their memory; meanwhile they share the information of these food sources to the onlooker bees. The onlooker bees tend to select good food sources from those found by the employed bees. The food source that has higher quality (fitness) will have a large chance to be selected by the onlooker bees than the one of lower quality. The scout bees are translated from a few employed bees, which abandon their food sources and search new ones.The ABC algorithm simulates the foraging behaviour of the bee swarm, such that each food source represents a possible solution for the optimization problem, and the quality of the source indicates the fitness of the associated solution.It is assumed that there is only one artificial employed bee for each food source. In other words, the number of employed bees in the colony is equal to the number of food sources around the hive. Employed bees go to their food source and come back to hive and dance on this area. The employed bee whose food source has been abandoned becomes a scout and starts to search for finding a new food source. Onlookers watch the dances of employed bees and choose food sources depending on dances.

2.2. The Foraging Process Involves Three Groups of Bees

1. **Employed Bees:** They are responsible for collecting food from food sources, and carrying information about them;
2. **Onlookers:** They search for food sources to exploit according to the information received from the employed bees;
3. **Scouts:** They search randomly, the environment surrounding the hive, for new food sources.

The ABC algorithm converges toward the optimal or near-optimal solution through the operation of the three groups of bees. The overall algorithm is as follows:

- Initial food sources are produced for all employed bees;
- REPEAT;
- Each employed bee goes to a food source in her memory and determines a neighbour source, then evaluates its nectar amount and dances in the hive;
- Each onlooker watches the dance of employed bees and chooses one of their sources depending on the dances, and then goes to that source. After choosing a neighbour around that, she evaluates its nectar amount;
- Abandoned food sources are determined and are replaced with the new food sources discovered by scouts;
- The best food source found so far is registered;
- UNTIL (requirements are met).

The main steps of the algorithm are explained below.

2.2.1. Initialization

Generate randomly the initial solution population of size NS, where each solution X_i has a dimension of D i.e. $X_i = (x_{i,1}, x_{i,2}, …, x_{i,D})$ and i = 1,2, .., NS. All Solutions are bounded between X_{min} and X_{max}, where $X_{min} = (x_{min,1}, x_{min,2}, …, x_{min,D})$ and $X_{max} = (x_{max,1}, x_{max,2}, …, x_{max,D})$. Solution $x_{i,j}$ is generated using the following equation:

$$x_{i,j} = x_{min,j} + rand(0,1) - x_{max,j} - x_{min,j}$$

where j = 1, 2, .., D, and rand(0,1) is a random number between zero and one. After generating all NS solutions, their fitness values are calculated.

2.2.2. Employed Bees Phase

Each employed bee updates its position (solution) (Karaboga et al, 2009) to produce a new one. The old solution is updated according to the following expression: $y_{i,j} = x_{i,j} + \varphi_{i,j} \cdot (x_{i,j} - x_{k,j})$, where j {1, 2, …, D} and k {1, 2, …, NS} are randomly selected indexes, under the condition that the value of k must be different than that of i. The value i,j is a random number between −1 and 1, i.e. i,j [−1,1], and it controls the production of new solutions in the neighbourhood of $x_{i,j}$. Then, the fitness value is calculated for the new solution and is compared with that of the old one. If the new solution has a higher fitness value, then it replaces the old one.

2.2.3. Onlookers Phase

Each bee, in this phase, selects a food source to update using the same expression as in (2). The selection is based on a probability that depends on the fitness value associated to the food source.

2.2.4. Scouts Phase

Scouts phase: The ABC algorithm assigns to each food source a value, referred to as "trials", which is initially set to zero. It represents the number of times that the update, of that source, fails to produce a better one. If a new source replaces an old one, its trials value will be reinitialized. The food source will be abandoned, if its trials exceed a predetermined value, called "limit". Then, its assigned employed bee becomes a scout bee and starts to search randomly for a new source using the formula in (1).

2.2.5. Termination

The ABC algorithm repeats steps 2, 3, and 4 until the number of iterations reaches a predefined value, referred to as MCN (Maximum Cycle Number), or a stopping criterion is met. In ABC, a population based algorithm, the position of a food source represents a possible solution to the optimization problem and the nectar amount of a food source corresponds to the quality (fitness) of the associated solution. The number of the employed bees is equal to the number of solutions in the population. At the first step, a randomly distributed initial population (food source positions) is generated. After initialization, the population is subjected to repeat the cycles of the search processes of the employed, onlooker, and scout bees, respectively. An employed bee produces a modification on the source position in her memory and discovers a new food source position. Provided that the nectar amount of the new one is higher than that of the previous source, the bee memorizes the new source position and forgets the old one. Otherwise she keeps the position of the one in her memory. After all employed bees complete the search process, they share the position information of the sources with the onlookers on the dance area. Each onlooker evaluates the nectar information taken from all employed bees and then chooses a food source depending on the nectar amounts of sources. As in the case of the employed bee, she produces a modification

Figure 1. Behaviour of honey bee foraging for nectar

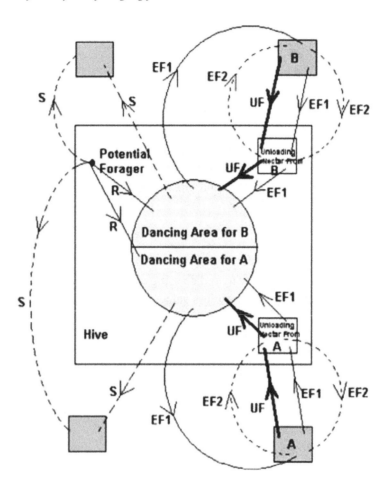

on the source position in her memory and checks its nectar amount. Providing that its nectar is higher than that of the previous one, the bee memorizes the new position and forgets the old one. The sources abandoned are determined and new sources are randomly produced to be replaced with the abandoned ones by artificial scouts. (Karaboga et al, n.d.; Tereshko, 2000).

The exchange of information among bees is the most important occurrence in the formation of collective knowledge. While examining the entire hive it is possible to distinguish some parts that commonly exist in all hives. The most important part of the hive with respect to exchanging information is the dancing area. Communication among bees related to the quality of food sources occurs in the dancing area. The related dance is called waggle dance. (Price et al, 2005; Bonabeau et al, 1999) Since information about all the current rich sources is available to an onlooker on the dance floor, probably she could watch numerous dances and chooses to employ herself at the most profitable source. There is a greater probability of onlookers choosing more profitable sources since more information is circulating about the more profitable sources. Employed foragers share their information with a probability which is proportional to the profitability of the food source, and the sharing of this information through waggle dancing is longer in duration. Hence, the recruitment is proportional to profitability of a food source.

In order to better understand the basic behaviour characteristics of foragers, let us examine Figure 1. Assume that there are two discovered food sources: A and B. At the very beginning, a potential forager will start as unemployed forager. That forager bee will have no knowledge about the food sources around the nest. There are two possible options for such a bee. It can be a scout and starts searching around the nest spontaneously for food due to some internal motivation or possible external clue (S on Figure 1). It can be a recruit after watching the waggle dances and starts searching for a food source.

After finding the food source, the bee utilizes its own capability to memorize the location and then immediately starts exploiting it. Hence, the bee will become an employed forager. The foraging bee takes a load of nectar from the source and returns to the hive, unloading the nectar to a food store. (De Castro et al, 1999; Kennedy et al, 1995) After unloading the food, the bee has the following options:

1. It might become an uncommitted follower after abandoning the food source (UF);
2. It might dance and then recruit nest mates before returning to the same food source (EF1);
3. It might continue to forage at the food source without recruiting bees (EF2).

It is important to note that not all bees start foraging simultaneously. The experiments confirmed that new bees begin foraging at a rate proportional to the difference between the eventual total number of bees and the number of bees presently foraging.

An artificial onlooker bee chooses a food source depending on the probability value associated with that food source is calculated by the following expression:

$$P_i = \sum FIT_i \left/ \left(\sum_{n=1}^{SN} FIT_n \right) \right.$$

where FIT_i is the fitness value of the solution i which is proportional to the nectar amount of the food source in the position i and SN is the number of food sources which is equal to the number of employed bees or onlooker bee. (Karaboga et al, 2009).

3. FITNESS FUNCTION

The proposed fitness function, illustrated in Figure 1, ranks the solutions according to their impact on the defined optimization problem. This is performed through two main processes. The first process is the allocation procedure, applied to each solution individually. In this step, solutions are divided into two groups, where each group is responsible for a different objective (one is for quality and the other is for robustness). In the second step, all the allocated solutions are recombined and ranked in one population (Aseem et al, 2016; Draa et al, 2014). This is explained in more detail in Figure 2.

The proposed solution allocation is illustrated in Figure 2. A solution is allocated to one of two groups according to its achieved quality and the predetermined quality threshold that reflects the distortion limit. For a given solution [k p], the achieved quality Q is evaluated. If the achieved quality is less than the quality threshold Qth, the corresponding solution is assigned to a group, referred to as "Quality group". Otherwise, the robustness objective Rt is evaluated, and the solution is assigned to another group, referred to as "Robustness group".

Figure 2. Demonstration of fitness function

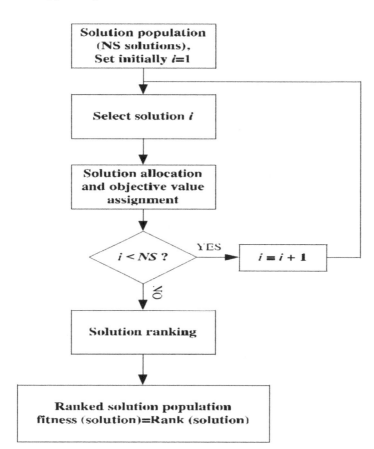

The robustness R_t is calculated as follows:

$$R_t = \sum_{i=1}^{N_a} R_i \tag{1}$$

where R_i is the robustness measured against the ith attack, and Na is the total number of attacks.

In the Quality group, the solution's objective value is its achieved quality Q. Note that, the solutions of this population do not satisfy the quality condition. Therefore, the optimization process will focus on finding solutions with higher quality regard-less of their achieved robustness, until the quality satisfies the de-fined constraint. On the other hand, a solution in the Robustness group is assigned an objective value equal to its achieved robustness Rt. This is because the achieved quality constraint is satisfied. Thus, the robustness is the main objective in this group. Hence, each group is now considered a solution population for a single-objective optimization problem. That is, the multi-objective problem is converted into two single-objective optimization problems.

The proposed allocation is applied to each solution until they are all distributed between the Quality and the Robustness groups. After that, the two groups are recombined in order to complete the optimization process, since the optimization process operates only over one solution population per iteration, and a fitness value must be assigned to each solution. In the following steps, the proposed recombining and ranking process is described:

Step 1: Sort the solutions of the Robustness and the Quality groups according to their assigned objective values, such that:

Sorted Robust population = $[kp_1, kp_2, kp_{Nr}]_R$

Sorted Qualityt population = $[kp_1, kp_2, kp_{Nq}]_Q$

where [.]R and [.]Q are the set of solutions allocated to the Ro-bustness and the Quality groups, respectively. Moreover, Nr and Nq are the total number of solutions in the Robustness and the Quality groups, respectively. The solutions, of each group, are sorted in descending order with respect to their objective values, such that:

Objective $([k\ p]1)R >$ Objective $([k\ p]2)R > \ldots >$ Objective $([kp]Nr)R$ and

Objective $([k\ p]1)Q >$ Objective $([k\ p]2)Q > \ldots >$ Objective $([kp]Nq)Q$ (2)

where Objective $([k\ p]i)R$ and Objective $([k\ p]i)Q$ are the robust-ness objective and the quality objective of the ith solution in the Robustness and Quality group, respectively.

Step 2: Combine the two sorted groups to form one ranked population such that the ranks of its solutions represent their fitness values. The recombined population is ranked such that, the rank of a solution $[k\ p]i$ is higher than that of solution $[k\ p]j$ if one of the following cases is satisfied:

Case 1: $[k\ p]i[.]R$, and $[k\ p]j[.]Q$

In this case, solution $[k\ p]\ i$ satisfies the quality condition, while solution $[k\ p]\ j$ does not. Hence, solution $[k\ p]\ i$ is better than solution$[k\ p]\ j$ in terms of the defined optimization objective, and hence it has a higher rank:

Case 2: Objective $([k\ p]i)R >$ Objective $([k\ p]j)R$

In this case, both solutions belong to the Robustness group. Hence, the solution with the larger robustness is assigned a higher rank:

Case 3: Objective $([k\ p]i)Q >$ Objective $([k\ p]j)Q$

In this case, both solutions are in the Quality group. Therefore, they do not satisfy the quality condition. However, solution $[k\ p]i$ has a higher rank because it achieved higher quality. Thus, solution $[k\ p]\ i$ is selected.

3.1. Comparison of ABC With GA and DE and PSO

While Genetic Algorithm and Differential Evolution employ crossover operators to produce new or candidate solutions from the present ones, ABC algorithm does not. ABC algorithm produces the candidate solution from its parent by a simple operation based on taking the difference of randomly determined parts of the parent and a randomly chosen solution from the population. This process increases the convergence speed of search into a local minimum. In GA, DE and PSO the best solution found so far is always kept in the population and it can be used for producing new solutions in the case of DE and GA, new velocities in the case of Particle Swarm Optimization. However, in ABC, the best solution discovered so far is not always held in the population since it might be replaced with a randomly produced solution by a scout. Therefore, it might not contribute to the production of trial solutions. Both DE and ABC employ a greedy selection process between the candidate and the parent solutions. In ABC, on ''employed bees'' stage atrial solution is produced for each solution in the population as in the case of DE without depending on the quality of solutions. On ''onlooker bees'' stage, the solutions with the higher fitness value are used more often than those with less fitness values to produce trial solutions. It means that the promising regions of the search space are searched in shorter time and in detail. This selection process is similar to the natural selection or to the seeded selection employed in GA. In GA or DE, mutation process creates a modification on a randomly selected part of a solution to provide required diversity in the population. In ABC, there are two types of mechanisms to control the diversity in the population: (a) As in DE or GA, a randomly chosen part of a parent is modified with a magnitude determined randomly to obtain a trail solution. This modification is relatively small and useful for local search and fine tuning. (b) Rather than changing a part of a solution, a whole solution in the population is removed and then a new one produced randomly is inserted into the population by a scout. This mechanism provides the ABC algorithm a global search ability and prevents the search from premature convergence problem. This feature weakens the dependency of the algorithms performance on the population size, too. Hence, there is a good balance between the local search process carried out by artificial onlooker and employed bees and the global search process managed by artificial scouts. Therefore, the ABC algorithm produces better results on multimodal and multivariable problems than other algorithms considered in this paper. Apart from the maximum evaluation number and population size, a standard GA has three more control parameters (crossover rate, mutation rate, generation gap), a standard DE has at least two control parameters (crossover rate, scaling factor) and a basic PSO has three control parameters (cognitive and social factors, inertia weight). Also, limit values for the velocities tmax have a significant effect on the performance of PSO. The ABC algorithm has only one control parameter(limit) apart from Colony Size and Maximum Cycle Number. In the present work, we described an expression for determining the value of ''limit'' depending on population (colony size) and dimension of problem. Therefore, now ABC has only two common control parameters: maximum cycle number(MCN) and colony size(SN). Consequently, ABC is as simple and flexible as DE and PSO; and also employs less control parameters.ES employ recombination and mutation operators to produce offsprings (new individuals) while ABC uses only mutation operator. Although the basic version of ES is as simple as ABC, the improved versions used for comparison in this work are more complex than ABC. Moreover, all of them employ more control parameters than ABC. This work compared the performance of ABC algorithm with those of GA, DE, PSO and ES algorithms on a large set of unconstrained test functions. From the results obtained in this work, it can be concluded that the performance of ABC algorithm is better than or similar to that of these algorithms although it uses less control parameters and it can be efficiently used for solving multimodal and multidimensional optimization problems.

4. USE OF ABC OPTIMIZATION IN CONSTRAINED OPTIMIZATION DOMAIN

Constrained Optimization problems are encountered in numerous applications. Structural optimization, engineering design, VLSI design, economics, allocation and location problems are just a few of the scientific fields in which CO problems are frequently met [20]. The considered problem is reformulated so as to take the form of optimizing two functions, the objective function and the constraint violation function (Hedar et al, nd). General constrained optimization problem is to find x so as to minimize $f(x)$, $x=x1, x2,...,xn \in Rn$.

The objective function f is defined on the search space $S \subseteq Rn$ and the set $F \subseteq S$ defines the feasible region. Usually, the search space S is defined as a n-dimensional rectangle in n (domains of variables defined by their lower and upper bounds):

$l(i) \leq x(i) \leq u(i), 1 \leq i \leq n$

whereas the feasible region $F \subseteq S$ is defined by a set of m additional constraints $(m \geq 0)$:

$g_j(x) \leq 0$, for $j = 1, ..., q$

$h_j(x) = 0$, for $j = q + 1, ...,m$

At any point $x \in F$, the constraints gk that satisfy $gk(x) = 0$ are called the active constraints at x. By extension, equality constraints h_j are also called active at all points of S (Michalewicz, 1995). Different deterministic as well as stochastic algorithms have been developed for tackling constrained optimization problems. Deterministic approaches such as Feasible Direction and Generalized Gradient Descent make strong assumptions on the continuity and differentiability of the objective function [23,24]. Therefore their applicability is limited since these characteristics are rarely met in problems that arise in real life applications. On the other hand, stochastic optimization algorithms such as Genetic Algorithms, Evolution Strategies, Evolutionary Programming and Particle Swarm Optimization (PSO) do not make such assumptions and they have been successfully applied for tackling constrained optimization problems during the past few years (Joines et al, 1994; Hu et al, 2002, Hu et al 2003, Parasopoulos et al 2005, Zavala et al, 2005, Stanarevic et al, 2011) Karaboga has described an Artificial Bee Colony (ABC) algorithm based on the foraging behavior of honey bees for numerical optimization problems Karaboga and Basturk (Blum et al, 2008) have compared the performance of the ABC algorithm with those of other well-known modern heuristic algorithms such as Genetic Algorithm (GA), Differential Evolution (DE), Particle Swarm Optimization (PSO) on unconstrained problems (Basturk et al, 2006). In this work, ABC algorithm is extended for solving constrained optimization (CO) problems. Extension of the algorithm depends on replacing the selection mechanism of the simple ABC algorithm with Deb's (Goldberg et al, 1991) selection mechanism in order to cope with the constraints. The performance of the algorithm has been tested on 13 well-known constrained optimization problems taken from the literature and compared with Particle Swarm Optimization (PSO) and Differential Evolution (DE) (Storn et al, 1997). The Particle Swarm Optimization (PSO) algorithm was introduced by Eberhart and Kennedy in 1995.

4.1. Handling Constrained Optimization Problems Using ABC Algorithm

In order to adapt the ABC algorithm for solving constrained optimization problems, we adopted Deb's constrained handling method (Karaboga et al, n.d.) instead of the selection process (greedy selection) of the ABC algorithm described in the previous section since Deb's method consists of very simple three heuristic rules. Deb's method uses a tournament selection operator, where two solutions are compared at a time, and the following criteria are always enforced: 1) Any feasible solution is preferred to any infeasible solution, 2) Among two feasible solutions, the one having better objective function value is preferred, 3) Among two infeasible solutions, the one having smaller constraint violation is preferred. Because initialization with feasible solutions is very time consuming process and in some cases it is impossible to produce a feasible solution randomly, the ABC algorithm does not consider the initial population to be feasible. Structure of the algorithm already directs the solutions to feasible region in running process due to the Deb's rules employed instead of greedy selection. Scout production process of the algorithm provides a diversity mechanism that allows new and probably infeasible individuals to be in the population. In order to produce a candidate food position from the old one in memory, the adapted ABC algorithm uses the following expression:

$$v_j = x_{ij} + \Phi_{ij} \left(x_{ij} - x_{kj} \right), if \ R_j < MR$$

$$= x_{ij}, otherwise$$

where $k \in \{1, 2,..., SN\}$ is randomly chosen index. Although k is determined randomly, it has to be different from i. R_j is randomly chosen real number in the range [0,1] and $j \in \{1, 2,...,D\}$. MR, modification rate, is a control parameter that controls whether the parameter xij will be modified or not. In the version of the ABC algorithm proposed for constrained optimization problems, artificial scouts are produced at a predetermined period of cycles for discovering new food sources randomly. This period is another control parameter called scout production period (*SPP*) of the algorithm. At each *SPP* cycle, it is controlled, if there is an abandoned food source or not. If there is, a scout production process is carried out.

Deb's method uses a tournament selection operator, where two solutions are compared at a time, and the following criteria are always enforced:

1. Any feasible solution is preferred to any infeasible solution;
2. Among two feasible solutions, the one having better objective function value is preferred;
3. Among two infeasible solutions, the one having smaller constraint violation is preferred.

4.2. Pseudo-Code of the ABC Algorithm Proposed for Solving Constrained Problems

Step 1: Initialize the population of solutions $x_{i,j}$, i= 1. . .SN, j = 1. . .D

Step 2: Evaluate the population

Step 3: cycle=1

Step 4: repeat

Step 5: Produce new solutions $\upsilon_{i,j}$ for the employed bees by using (4) and evaluate them.

Step 6: Apply selection process

Step 7: Calculate the probability values Pi,j for the solutions $x_{i,j}$ by (1)

Step 8: Produce the new solutions $\upsilon i,j$ for the onlookers from the solutions $x_{i,j}$ selected depending on $P_{i,j}$ and evaluate them

Step 9: Apply selection process

Step 10: Determine the abandoned solution for the scout, if exists, and replace it with a new randomly produced solution $x_{i,j}$ by (3)

Step 11: Remember the best solution achieved so far

Step 12: cycle=cycle+1

Step 13: until cycle=MCN

5. EXPERIMENTAL STUDIES AND DISCUSSIONS

In order to evaluate the performance of the ABC algorithm, we used a set of 13 benchmark problems can be found in (Zavala et al, 2005). This set includes various forms of objective function such as linear, nonlinear and quadratic. The performance of the ABC algorithm is compared with that of the differential evolution (DE) and particle swarm optimization (PSO) algorithms. PSO employs Deb's rules for constraint handling. The swarm size is 50 and the generation number is 7000. Hence, PSO performs 350 000 objective function evaluations. Cognitive and social components are both set to 1. Inertia weight is uniform random real number in the range [0.5,1]. All equality constraints are converted into inequality constraints, $|hj| \leq 0.001$ [16]. In DE, F is a real constant which affects the differential variation between two solutions and set to 0.5 in our experiments. Value of crossover rate, which controls the change of the diversity of the population, is chosen to be 0.9 as recommended in [36]. Population size is 40, maximum generation number is 6000 and it uses Deb's rules. In ABC, the value of modification rate (MR) is 0.8, colony size (2 xSN) is 40 and the maximum cycle number (MCN) is 6000. So, the total objective function evaluation number is 240 000 as in DE. The value of limit" is equal to SN x D where D is the dimension of the problem and SPP is also SNxD. Experiments were repeated 30 times each starting from a random population with different seeds.

5.1. Results and Discussion

The results of the experiments for the ABC algorithm are given in Table 1. Comparative results of the best, mean and worst solutions of the investigated algorithms are presented in Table 2, Table 4 and Table 3, respectively.

5.2. Experimental Results

As seen from Table 2, the ABC algorithm has found the global minimum of the seven of thirteen problems (g01, g03, g04, g06, g08, g11, g12) through 240 000 cycles. On five functions (g02, g04, g05, g07,

Table 1. Statistical results obtained by the ABC algorithm for 13 test functions over 30 independent runs using 240,000 objective function evaluations

Optimal	Best	Mean	Worst	Std. Dev.
-15.000	-15.000	-15.000	-15.000	0.000
0.803619	0.803598	0.792412	0.749797	0.012
1.000	1.000	1.000	1.000	0.000
-30665.539	-30665.539	-30665.539	-30665.539	0.000
5126.498	5126.484	5185.714	5438.387	75.358
-6961.814	-6961.814	-6961.814	-6961.814	0.002
24.306	24.306	24.306	24.306	0.186
0.095825	0.095825	0.095825	0.095825	0.000
680.63	680.63	680.63	680.63	0.004
7049.25	7049.25	7049.25	7049.25	133.870
0.75	0.75	0.75	0.75	0.000
1.000	1.000	1.000	1.000	0.000
0.053950	0.760	0.968	1.000	0.055

Table 2. The best solutions obtained by Differential Evolution(DE), Particle Swarm Optimizations(PSO) and ABC(Artificial Bee colony Optimization) algorithms for 13 test functions over 30 independent runs. – Means that no feasible solutions were found. Na = Not Available.

Problem	Optimal	PSO	DE	ABC
g01	-15.000	-15.000	-15.000	-15.000
g02	0.803619	0.669158	0.472	0.803598
g03	1.000	0.993930	1.000	1.000
g04	-30665.539	-30665.539	-30665.539	-30665.539
g05	5126.498	5126.484	5185.714	5438.387
g06	-6961.814	-6961.814	-6961.814	-6961.814
g07	24.306	24.370153	24.306	24.330
g08	0.095825	0.095825	0.095825	0.095825
g09	680.63	680.63	680.63	680.63
g10	7049.25	7049.341	7049.248	7053.904
g11	0.75	0.749	0.752	0.750
g12	1.000	1.000	1.000	1.000
g13	0.053950	0.085655	0.385	0.760

g10), the ABC algorithm produced results quite close to the global optima. On one problem, g13, the ABC algorithm could not find the optima in the specified maximum number of cycles. As seen from Table 2, PSO algorithm is better than ABC on three problems (g09, g10, g13) while the ABC algorithm shows better performance than PSO on four problems (g02, g03, g07, g12).

Table 3. The worst solutions obtained by Differential Evolution(DE), Particle Swarm Optimizations(PSO) and ABC(Artificial Bee colony Optimization) algorithms for 13 test functions over 30 runs. – Means that no feasible solutions were found. Na = Not Available.

Problem	Optimal	PSO	DE	ABC
g01	-15.000	-13.000	-11.828	-15.000
g02	0.803619	0.299426	0.472	0.749797
g03	1.000	0.464	1.000	1.000
g04	-30665.539	-30665.539	-30665.539	-30665.539
g05	5126.498	5249.825	5534.610	5438.387
g06	-6961.814	-6961.814	-6954.434	-6961.805
g07	24.306	56.055	24.330	25.190
g08	0.095825	0.095825	0.095825	0.095825
g09	680.63	680.631	680.631	680.653
g10	7049.25	7894.812	9264.886	7604.132
g11	0.75	0.749	1.0	0.750
g12	1.000	0.994	1.000	1.000
g13	0.053950	1.793361	0.990	1.000

Table 4. The mean solutions results obtained by Differential Evolution(DE), Particle Swarm Optimizations(PSO) and ABC(Artificial Bee colony Optimization) algorithms for 13 test functions over 30 independent runs and total success numbers of algorithms. A result in boldface indicates a better result or that the global optimum (or best known solution) was reached. – Means that no feasible solutions were found.

Problem	Optimal	PSO	DE	ABC
g01	-15.000	-14.710	-14.555	-15.000
g02	0.803619	0.419960	0.665	0.792412
g03	1.000	0.764813	1.000	1.000
g04	-30665.539	-30665.539	-30665.539	-30665.539
g05	5126.498	5135.973	5264.270	5185.714
g06	-6961.814	-6961.814	-	-6961.813
g07	24.306	32.407	24.310	24.473
g08	0.095825	0.095825	0.095825	0.095825
g09	680.63	680.631	680.630	680.640
g10	7049.25	7205.5	7147.334	7224.407
g11	0.75	0.749	0.901	0.750
g12	1.000	0.998875	1.000	1.000
g13	0.053950	0.569358	0.872	0.968

Four functions (g07, g09, g10, g13) as the ABC algorithm is better than DE on three problems (g02, g06, g11) with respect to the best results. From the worst results given in Table 3, PSO is better than ABC on three problems (g05, g06, g09) while ABC outperforms PSO on eight problems (g01, g02, g03, g07, g10, g11, g12, g13). DE show better performance on two problems with respect to the ABC algorithm on three problems (g07, g09, g13) while ABC is better on six problems (g01, g02, g05, g06, g10, g11). Similarly, with respect to the mean solutions in Table 4, PSO shows better performance with respect to the ABC algorithm on five problems (g05, g06, g09, g10, g13) and ABC algorithm is better than PSO on six problems (g01, g02, g03, g07, g11, g12). DE has better performance than ABC on four problems (g07, g09, g10, g13) while ABC is better than DE on five problems (g01, g02, g05, g06, g11). From the mean results presented in Table 4, it can be concluded that the ABC algorithm performs better than DE and PSO.

6. CONCLUSION

A modified version of the ABC algorithm for constrained optimization problems has been introduced and its performance has been compared with that of the state-of-art algorithms. It has been concluded that the ABC algorithm can be efficiently used for solving constrained optimization problems. The performance of the ABC algorithm can be also tested for real engineering problems existing in the literature and compared with that of other algorithms. Also, the effect of constraint handling methods on the performance of the ABC algorithm can be investigated in future works.

REFERENCES

Aseem, M.A., Hassan, I.S., & Amin, M.N. (2016, November). A quality guaranteed robust image watermarking optimization with Artificial Bee Colony. In *Expert Systems with Applications*. Elsevier.

Basturk, B., & Karaboga, D. (2006, May). An Artificial Bee Colony (ABC) Algorithm for Numeric function Optimization. *IEEE Swarm Intelligence Symposium*, Indianapolis, IN.

Blum, C., & Merkle, D. (Eds.). (2008). *Swarm Intelligence – Introduction and Applications, Natural Computing*. Berlin: Springer.

Bonabeau, E., Dorigo, M., & Theraulaz, G. (1999). *Swarm Intelligence: From Natural to Artificial Systems*. Oxford University Press.

Corne, D., Dorigo, M., & Glover, F. (Eds.). (1999). *New Ideas in Optimization*. McGraw-Hill.

Das, S., Panigrahi, B.K., & Pattnaik, S.S. (2009). Nature-Inspired Algorithms for Multi-objective Optimization. In Handbook of Research on Machine Learning Applications and Trends: Algorithms Methods and Techniques (vol. 1, pp. 95-108). Hershey, PA: IGI Global.

De Castro, L.N., & Von Zuben, F.J. (1999). *Artificial immune systems, Part I. Basic theory and applications, Technical Report RtDca 01/99*. Feec/Unicamp, Brazil.

Draa, A., & Bouaziz, A. (2014). An artificial bee colony algorithm for image contrast enhancement. *Swarm and Evolutionary Computation, 16*, 69–84.

Fahad, S., Abu, M., & Ei, H. (2012, March). Overview of Artificial Bee Colony (ABC) algorithm and its applications. *Systems Conference (SysCon), IEEE International.* 10.1109/SysCon.2012.6189539

Floudas, C. A., & Pardalos, P. M. (1987). A collection of test problems for constrained global optimization algorithms. LNCS, 455.

Goldberg, D. E., & Deb, K. (1991). Chapter. In G. J. E. Rawlins (Ed.), A comparison of selection schemes used in genetic algorithms Foundations of Genetic Algorithms (pp. 69–93). Academic Press.

Hedar, A.R., & Fukushima, M. (n.d.). *Derivative-Free Filter Simulated Annealing Method for Constrained Continuous Global Optimization.* Academic Press.

Himmelblau, D. M. (1972). *Applied Nonlinear Programming.* McGrawHill.

Hu, X., Eberhart, R.C., & Shi, Y.H. (2003). Engineering optimization with particle swarm. *IEEE Swarm Intelligence Symposium*, 53-57.

Hu, X., & Eberhart, R. C. (2002). Solving constrained nonlinear optimization problems with particle swarm optimization. *Proceedings of the Sixth World MulticonferenceonSystemics, Cybernetics and Informatics.*

Joines, J. A., & Houck, C. R. (1994). On the use of nonstationary penalty functions to solve nonlinear constrained optimization problems with gas. *Proc. IEEE Int. Conf. Evol. Comp.*, 579-585.

Karaboga, D. (2005). *An Idea Based On Honey Bee Swarm for Numerical Optimization, Technical Report-TR06.* Erciyes University, Engineering Faculty, Computer Engineering Department.

Karaboga, D., & Akay, B. (2009). A comparative study of Artificial Bee Colony algorithm. *Applied Mathematics and Computation, 214*(1), 108–113. doi:10.1016/j.amc.2009.03.090

Karaboga, D., & Akay, B. (n.d.). *Artificial Bee Colony (ABC), Harmony Search and Bees Algorithms on Numerical Optimization.* Academic Press.

Karaboga, D., & Basturk, B. (n.d.). *Artificial Bee Colony (ABC) Optimization Algorithm for Solving Constrained Optimization Problems.* Springer.

Kennedy, J., & Eberhart, R. C. (1995).Particle Swarm Optimization. *1995 IEEE International Conference on Neural Networks*, 4, 1942–1948.

Kennedy, J., & Eberhart, R. C. (1995). Particle swarm optimization. *1995 IEEE International Conference on Neural Networks*, 4, 1942–1948.

Michalewicz, Z., & Schoenauer, M. (1995). Evolutionary Algorithms for Constrained Parameter Optimization Problems. *Evolutionary Computation, 4*(1), 1–32. doi:10.1162/evco.1996.4.1.1

Parsopoulos, K. E., & Vrahatis, M. N. (2002). *Particle Swarm Optimization Method for Constrained Optimization Problems, Intelligent Technologies - Theory and Applications: New Trends in Intelligent Technologies.* IOS Press.

Parsopoulos, K. E., & Vrahatis, M. N. (2005). A Unified Particle Swarm Optimization for solving constrained engineering optimization problems. *Lecture Notes in Computer Science, 3612*, 582–591. doi:10.1007/11539902_71

Price, K., & Storn, R. (2005). *Differential Evolution a Practical Approach to Global Optimization.* Springer Natural Computing Series.

Sato, T. & Hagiwara, M. (1997 ,October). Bee System: Finding Solution by a Concentrated Search. *Proceedings of the 1997 IEEE International Conference on Systems, Man, and Cybernetics*, 3954-3959. doi:10.1109/ICSMC.1997.633289

Schmickl, T., Thenius, R., & Crailsheim. (2005, June). Simulating swarm intelligence in honey bees: foraging in differently fluctuating environments. *Genetic and Evolutionary Computation Conference, GECCO, Proceedings.*

Seeley, T. D., & Buhrman, S. C. (1999). Group decision making in swarms of honeybees. *Behavioral Ecology and Sociobiology, 45*(1), 19–31. doi:10.1007/s002650050536

Stanarevic, N., Tuba, M., & Bacanin, N. (2011). Modified artificial bee colony algorithm for constrained problems optimization. *International Journal of Mathematical Models and Methods in Applied Sciences, 5*(3), 644-651.

Storn, R., & Price, K. (1997). Differential evolution – a simple and efficient heuristic for global optimization over continuous spaces. *Journal of Global Optimization, 11*(4), 341–359. doi:10.1023/A:1008202821328

Tereshko, V. (2000). Reaction–diffusion model of a honeybee colony's foraging behaviour. In M. Schoenauer (Ed.), Lecture Notes in Computer Science: Vol. 1917. *Parallel Problem Solving from Nature VI* (pp. 807–816). Berlin: Springer–Verlag. doi:10.1007/3-540-45356-3_79

Tereshko, V. (2000). Reaction–diffusion model of a honeybee colony's foraging behaviour. In M. Schoenauer (Ed.), Lecture Notes in Computer Science: Vol. 1917. *Parallel Problem Solving from Nature VI* (pp. 807–816). Berlin: Springer–Verlag. doi:10.1007/3-540-45356-3_79

Yonezawa, Y., & Kikuchi, T. (1996). Ecological algorithm for optimal ordering used by collective honey bee behavior. *Proceedings of the 7th International Symposium on Micro Machine and Human Science*, 249–256. doi:10.1109/MHS.1996.563432

Zavala, A. E. M., Aguirre, A. H., & Diharce, E. R. V. (2005). Constrained optimization via particle evolutionary swarm optimization algorithm (PESO). *Proceedings of the conference on Genetic and evolutionary computation (GECCO'05)*, 209–216.

Zavala, A. E. M., Aguirre, A. H., & Diharce, E. R. V. (2005). Constrained optimization via particle evolutionary swarm optimization algorithm (PESO). *Proceedings of the 2005 conference on Genetic and evolutionary computation (GECCO'05)*, 209–216.

Chapter 22
Escalation of Prediction Accuracy With Virtual Data:
A Case Study on Financial Time Series

Sarat Chandra Nayak
Kommuri Pratap Reddy Institute of Technology, India

Bijan Bihari Misra
Silicon Institute of Technology, India

Himansu Sekhar Behera
Veer Surendra Sai University of Technology, India

ABSTRACT

Random fluctuations occur in the trend of financial time series due to many macroeconomic factors. Such fluctuations lead to sudden fall after a constant raise or a sudden rise after a constant fall, which are difficult to predict from previous data points. At the fluctuation point, previous data points that are not too close to the target price adversely influence the prediction trend. Far away points may be ignored and close enough virtual data points are explored and incorporated in order to diminish the adverse prediction trend at fluctuations. From the given data points in the training set, virtual data positions (VDP) can be explored and used to enhance the prediction accuracy. This chapter presents some deterministic and stochastic approaches to explore such VDPs. From the given data points in the training set, VDPs are explored and incorporated to the original financial time series to enhance the prediction accuracy of the model. To train and validate the models, ten real stock indices are used and the models developed with the VDPs yields much better prediction accuracy.

1. INTRODUCTION

Artificial Neural Networks (ANNs) are data driven and requires sufficient number of examples for training. Insufficient number of training examples reduces the generalization and approximation capability of the model which may leads to suboptimal solutions. In many real life situations sufficient amount of training data may not be available or if so, the correlation between the data points may not be strong.

DOI: 10.4018/978-1-5225-2857-9.ch022

Particularly in case of financial time series, random variations occur in the movement of stock market due to several socio-economical factors. Such random fluctuations lead to sudden fall after a steady increase or a sudden rise after a gradual fall, which are difficult to predict from previous data points. At the fluctuation point, previous data points that are not too close adversely influence the prediction trend. Some researchers attempted to enrich the training volume by adopting the deterministic and stochastic schemes for generating artificial training examples. These schemes are developed for training back propagation neural network for approximating ordinary time series. The details of such schemes will be discussed in the first part of the chapter. In the schemes attempted by the previous researches, artificial training examples are generated by manipulating existing training data and these schemes were validated in function approximation, solving toy problems as well as some benchmark functions. In these methods each training example consists of only artificial or natural data points. Since there is the chance of existence of noise in the artificial training examples, the overall performance of the system may hamper. There are some methods generating artificial training samples by local interpolation of consecutive data points. The coexistence of these artificial sample points with the original data may be able to retain the trend or changes a little. These schemes are claimed to be effective for time series analysis and suggested to adopt where computation cost is not concerned due to increase in volume of training samples. However, the stock movements, which can be visualized as financial time series do not behave like ordinary time series. The existing artificial training sample generation schemes which follow local interpolation may not be able to handle the random fluctuations which occur frequently in the stock movement.

The back propagation neural networks lead to poor performance where there is insufficiency of training examples. One way of achieving improved performance is by generating derived training patterns from the original training data and incorporating them to the original training pattern. Some previous attempts (Abu-Mustafa, 1995; An, 1996; Grandvalet et al., 1997) made in order to address this lacking for time series forecasting. They adopted a method of adding artificial training example points to the training set. But this may reduce the performance of forecasting if they have much noise.

Cho et al. (1996) proposed a scheme of generating artificial training examples randomly within a space of original training examples. Their scheme has been validated empirically that the proposed scheme improves the generalization performance of back propagation in nonlinear regression problems. The scheme had some disadvantage in the sense that it is fragile to very few original training examples, since a committee of neural networks trained by very few training examples labels the generated artificial data. The research work conducted by Taeho Jo (2013) proposed three virtual term generation schemes and validated their effect in using the back propagation for the tasks of multivariate time series prediction. The work considered three artificial and one real data set and it is observed that the prediction errors were reduced at least by 30% as the effect of the virtual term generation schemes. As stock market prediction has been an important challenge due to its uncertainty and nonlinear behavior, in order to forecast the future trend accurately, dependability of such models should be improved. However, hardly any literature is found in support of research attempts in the domain of financial forecasting to enhance the performance of neural based models by exploring and incorporating virtual data points. Nayak et al. (2014) explored the scope of improving prediction accuracy in financial time series by incorporating Virtual Data Position (VDP) in the actual datasets. They observed that incorporation of VDPs helps in reducing prediction error to a substantial extent. The same authors applied VDPs with adaptive neuro-fuzzy inference system for the task of forecasting next day's closing prices of some fast growing stock markets and established the usability of VDPs (Nayak et al., 2014).

Stock market has been studied over and over again to extract useful patterns and predict their movements. Stock market prediction has always had a certain appeal for researchers. The objective of stock market forecasting is to achieve better accuracy with minimum input data and least complex model. However it is difficult to capture the nonlinearity with past and current data due to its inherent noisy and non-stationary characteristics. It is assumed that large historical data possesses these characteristics and can be used to map the non-linearity of the model. Though numerous scientific attempts have been made, but no method has been discovered to accurately predict the price movement. There are various approaches in predicting the movement of stock market and a variety of prediction techniques has been used by stock market analysts. When predicting the future prices of the stock market securities, there are two important theories available. The first one is efficient market hypothesis (EMH) and the second one is random walk theory. The efficient market hypothesis (EMH) was initially proposed by Eugene Fama (1965, 1970). The EMH states that no form of information can be used for generating extraordinary profits from the stock market, as stock prices always "fully reflect" all available information. Any new information which arises will be quickly and efficiently absorbed into the price of the stock. The EMH hypothesizes that the future stock price is completely unpredictable given the past trading history of the stock. The random walk hypothesis claims that stock prices do not depend on past stock. With the advent of more powerful computing infrastructure trading companies now build very efficient algorithmic trading systems that can exploit the underlying pricing patterns when a huge amount of data points are made available to them. Clearly with huge data sets available on hand, machine learning techniques can seriously challenge the EMH. However, random walk theory declares that even with such information, future prediction is ineffective. Many early works (Cootner, 1964; Alexander, 1961; Jensen, 1978) support the presentation of random walk model in the financial market.

A number of studies have been made to forecast the stock market behavior by adopting soft and evolutionary computational techniques. These techniques include ANN, fuzzy systems, rough set theory, genetic algorithm etc. Gradient descent based back propagation (BP) learning has been used by many researchers for training neural based forecasting models. However, BP learning is characterized with several disadvantages such as slow convergence, sticking to local minima and premature convergence. Nowadays, increasing number of efforts has been focused on several derivative free optimization techniques such as genetic algorithm, particle swarm optimization, ant colony optimization, artificial bee colony optimization and so on. Combination of these optimization techniques with ANN based models forms hybrid models and they are found to be more efficient in approximating and generalizing financial time series. These techniques have been applied to large number of computationally complex problems including financial forecasting, pattern recognition, control etc. and justified themselves superior to their conventional counterpart with improved solutions. More specifically, Genetic Algorithm (GA) has several advantages over back propagation based learning. GAs are more flexible, do not require a differentiable error function and they are able to find the global minima in multimodal as well as complex search space. GA has been adopted by many researchers for learning neural network based models and giving better performance (Khashei, & Bijari, 2012; Nayak et al., 2012; Nayak et al., 2012; Nayak et al., 2012; Nayak et al., 2014; Nayak et al., 2015a; Nayak et al., 2016; Kuo et al., 2001).

Chemical reaction optimization (CRO) is one of the recently established meta-heuristics proposed by Lam and Li (2012). It is an evolutionary optimization technique inspired by the nature of chemical reaction. In a short period of time, CRO has been applied to solve many problems successfully, outperforming many existing evolutionary algorithms. There are few applications of CRO to multiple-sequence alignment, data mining, classification rule discovery and some benchmark functions and the efficiency has been demonstrated. This optimization method does not need a local search method to refine the search and includes both local and global search capability. Unlike other optimization techniques, CRO does not require many parameters that must be specified at beginning and only defining number of initial reactants is enough for implementation. As the initial reactants are distributed over feasible global search region, optimal solutions can be obtained with little iteration and hence significant reduction in computational time is achieved. The CRO has been successfully used to solve many complex problems in recent years and found to be outperforming many other evolutionary population based algorithms (Alatas, 2011; Alatas, 2012; Nayak et al., 2015b; Nayak et al., 2015; Nayak et al., 2013; Nayak et al., 2016; Oh, & Kim, 2002).

The main contribution of this chapter is the proposed approaches for exploring VDPs. The VDPs are incorporated to the original training sets with the hope of achieving improved prediction performance. In order to compensate the computational cost due to increase in training volume, the model is trained in an adaptive manner. Hence the computation cost reduced in a large extent without degrading the accuracy. Again to search the optimal weight and bias vectors for the neural models considered, CRO, a metaheuristic has been employed. The main reason behind choosing CRO is its fast convergence capability as well as better approximation. Also it requires less number of tunable parameters.

The contribution of this chapter will be:

- An introduction to CRO;
- Introducing the concept of virtual search space exploration;
- Developing VDPs for exploring virtual data;
- Alleviating the lacunas of existing techniques using CRO;
- Improvising the forecast accuracy using VDPs;
- Experimenting on global stock market data.

2. VDP EXPLORATION TECHNIQUES

This section describes about the three deterministic VDP exploration methods such as linear, Lagrange and Taylor interpolation, three stochastic methods based on uniform, normal and triangle distribution method as well as the proposed VDP exploration method predicted by an evolutionary computing technique. Different approaches to explore virtual search space using the original financial time series. The daily closing prices of four stock markets may be represented as financial time series:

$$x(1), x(2), x(3), \cdots, x(n)$$

where, $x(n)$ is the daily closing price of nth financial day. The process of modeling this problem to estimate a future closing value or values based on the analysis of current and past values and can be represented by the following function:

$$x(n+k) = f(x(n-k), \cdots, x(n))$$

Here $x(n+k)$ is the target closing prices for the forecasting model.

Let the search space and the respective targets of the problem is represented as follows:

$$
\begin{array}{ccccc}
x_i(1) & x_i(2) & \cdots & x_i(m) & \vdots & x_i(m+k) \\
x_i(2) & x_i(3) & \cdots & x_i(m+k) & \vdots & x_i(m+k+1) \\
\cdots & \cdots & \cdots & \cdots & \vdots & \cdots \\
x_i(n-k-m) & x_i(n-k-m+1) & \cdots & x_i(n-k) & \vdots & x_i(n)
\end{array}
$$

Here the total number of closing prices in the data set is n, the window size is m, and k represents the prediction step. The window is sliding only one step toward right in the data series. The number of closing prices included within the sliding window is given as the input vector to the forecasting model. With the objective of improving the forecasting accuracy of the model we have introduced VDPs to the original financial time series. The process of estimation of these virtual positions is described in this section. The training examples generated due to sliding the window over the data set are presented below:

$$
\begin{array}{ccccccc}
x_i(1) & x_i(1.5) & x_i(2) & \cdots & x_i(m) & \vdots & x_i(m+k) \\
x_i(2) & x_i(2.5) & x_i(3) & \cdots & x_i(m+1) & \vdots & x_i(m+k+1) \\
\cdots & \cdots & \cdots & \cdots & \cdots & \vdots & \cdots \\
x_i(n-k-m) & x_i(n-k-m+0.5) & x_i(n-k-m+1) & \cdots & x_i(n-k) & \vdots & x_i(n)
\end{array}
$$

Different interpolation methods and the proposed approach adopted to explore the virtual data positions for the original financial time series are discussed by the following subsections. The VDP exploration scheme is broadly divided into two categories in this research work. The first scheme is the deterministic interpolation based approach which includes linear interpolation, Lagrange interpolation and Taylor interpolation method. The second approach is the stochastic method which includes uniform as well as the Gaussian interpolation based VDP exploration.

2.1. Deterministic Interpolation Based VDP Exploration

In the case of deterministic VDP exploration method, the estimated VDPs are computed by a particular equation defined by linear interpolation, 2nd LaGrange interpolation and 1st Taylor series.

2.1.1. Linear Interpolation Method

Linear interpolation is a method of curve fitting using linear polynomials. If the two known points are (x_0, y_0) and (x_1, y_1), then the linear interpolant is the straight line between these two points. For a value x in the interval (x_0, x_1), the value y along the straight line is given by Equation (1):

$$
\frac{y - y_0}{x - x_0} = \frac{y_1 - y_0}{x_1 - x_0}
\tag{1}
$$

Solving this equation for y, gives Equation (2) which is as follows:

$$y = y_0 + (y_1 - y_0) \frac{(x - x_0)}{(x_1 - x_0)} \tag{2}$$

The linear interpolation method can be applied to the financial time series by considering two consecutive terms, $(1, x(i))$ and $(2, x(i+1))$ as input. In order to find out the value of the mid-position $x(i+0.5)$, it's coordinate $(1.5, x(i+0.5))$ may be taken and Equation (2) is applied. The result value is presented as Equation (3):

$$x(i+0.5) = x(i) + \frac{1}{2}(x(i+1) - x(i)) \tag{3}$$

The $x(i+0.5)^{th}$ VDP is explored from two adjacent actual closing prices. After incorporation of the VDP, the financial time series may be represented as follows:

$$x(1), x(1+0.5), x(2), x(2+0.5), \cdots, x(n-0.5), x(n)$$

2.1.2. Second Lagrange Method

The 2nd Lagrange method for exploring the VDPs is discussed here. The general form of Lagrange interpolation can be represented as Equation (4):

$$P(x) = \sum_{k=0}^{n} \prod_{\substack{i=0 \\ i \neq k}} \frac{(x - x_i)}{(x_k - x_i)} y_i \tag{4}$$

This method is based on "Weierstrass Approximation Theorem", where every nonlinear function is approximated with an nth order polynomial. Based on this theorem, the interpolation is defined as the process of defining a polynomial which approximates a nonlinear function. Sample points passing a curve represented by a nonlinear function are given as the input of interpolation. A polynomial generated as the output by interpolation is used for estimating other points of the curve. Lagrange interpolation uses $n+1$ sample points, as input and generates an nth order polynomial. This method can be applied locally for exploration of VDPs in time series by setting $n+1$ sample points, $(0, x(k))$, $(1, x(k+1))$, ..., $(n, x(k+n))$. The Lagrange interpolation used here is restricted to 2nd order only and the output is represented as follows by Equation (5):

$$P(x) = \frac{(x - x_2)(x - x_3)}{(x_1 - x_2)(x_1 - x_3)} y_1 + \frac{(x - x_1)(x - x_3)}{(x_2 - x_1)(x_2 - x_3)} y_2 + \frac{(x - x_1)(x - x_2)}{(x_3 - x_1)(x_3 - x_2)} y_3 \tag{5}$$

In order to build an equation for estimating a mid-term $x(i+0.5)$, two sets of sample points can be defined and Lagrange interpolation can be applied locally on this. The two sets are represented as $\{(0, x(i-1)), (1, x(i)), (2, x(i+1))\}$ and $\{(0, x(i)), (1, x(x+1)), (2, x(i+2))\}$. By applying Equation (5) on the set of first three points, we get an estimator of mid-terms represented by Equation (6):

$$P_1(x) = \frac{(x-1)(x-2)}{2} x(i-1) - x(x-2)x(i) + \frac{x(x-1)}{2} x(i+1)$$

$$\approx P_1(1.5) = \frac{1}{8}(-x(i-1) + 6x(i) + 3x(i+1))$$

(6)

Similarly from the second set of three points, another estimator of mid-terms can be derived, which is represented by Equation (7):

$$P_2(x) = \frac{(x-1)(x-2)}{2} x(i) - x(x-2)x(i+1) + \frac{x(x-1)}{2} x(i+2)$$

$$\approx P_1(0.5) = \frac{1}{8}(3x(i) + 6x(i+1) - x(i+2))$$

(7)

The mid-term $x(i+0.5)$ is estimated by using Equation (6) and Equation (7), represented by Equation (8):

$$\hat{x}(i+0.5) = \frac{1}{2}(P_1(1.5) + P_2(0.5))$$

(8)

For the estimation of two end mid-terms, $x(1.5)$ and $x(n-0.5)$, Equation (7) is not applicable. For estimating $x(1.5)$, only second set of three points, $\{(0, x(i)), (1, x(i+1)), (2, x(i+2))\}$ are used. For estimation of $x(n-0.5)$, only first set of three points have been utilized. These mid-terms are represented by Equation (9) and Equation (10):

$$\hat{x}(1.5) = \frac{1}{8}(3x(1) + 6x(2) - x(3))$$

(9)

$$\hat{x}(n-0.5) = \frac{1}{8}(-x(n-2) + 6x(n-1) + 3x(n))$$

(10)

2.1.3. First Taylor Method

This method is based on Taylor interpolation method. It is the process of approximating a nonlinear function, $f(x)$, as a polynomial in the center of the point, $(x_0, f(x))$. The Taylor interpolation requires

n^{th} order derivation of the function, $f(x)$, in order to define an nth order polynomial. The general form of Taylor interpolation can be represented as in Equation (11):

$$P(x) = \sum_{k=0}^{n} \frac{f^{(k)}(x_0)}{k!}(x - x_0)^k \tag{11}$$

Since real differentiations are not applicable to a trend of a time series, we use equations as suggested by Taeho Jo (2013) for approximating a derivative value of a measure in a particular temporal point. To approximate a derivative value of a function, $f'(x_0)$, we use Equation (12):

$$f'(x_0) \approx \frac{1}{2h}(-f(x_0 - h) + f(x_0 + h)) \tag{12}$$

A derivative value, $X'(i)$ to each measure, $X(i)$ is approximated by replacing the involved components, $h, f(x_0-h)$, and $f(x_0+h)$ by $1, X(i-1)$, and $X(i+1)$, respectively. Equation (13) can be derived as follows:

$$\widehat{X'}(i) = \frac{1}{2}(-X(i-1) + X(i+1)) \tag{13}$$

The 1st order Taylor interpolation considered here is given by Equation (14):

$$P(x) = f(x_0) + (x - x_0)f'(x_0) \tag{14}$$

Substituting $(0, X(i))$ and $X'(i)$ for $(x_0, f(x_0))$ and $f'(x_0)$, respectively, in Equation (14), we get an estimator of a mid-term as represented in Equation (15):

$$P(x) = X(i) + x\widehat{X'}(i) = X(i) + \frac{x}{2}(X(i-1) + X(i+1)) \tag{15}$$

For estimating a mid-term, $X(i+0.5)$, the two points $(0, X(i))$ and $(0, X(i+1))$ are involved as center points. From the first center point, an estimator of the mid-term can be defined as in Equation (16):

$$X(i+0.5) \approx P_1(0.5) = X(i) + 0.5\widehat{X'}(i) = \frac{1}{4}(-X(i-1) + 4X(i) + X(i+1)) \tag{16}$$

From the second center point $(0, X(i+1))$, we define another estimator of the mid-term, $X(i+0.5)$ represented in Equation (17):

$$X(i+0.5) \approx P_2(-0.5) = X(i+1) - 0.5\widehat{X}'(i+2) = \frac{1}{4}(X(i) + 4X(i+1) - X(i+2)) \tag{17}$$

The mid-term except the two end points can be estimated by averaging Equation (16) and Equation (17). The expression is given by Equation (18):

$$\widehat{X}(i+0.5) = \frac{1}{2}(P(0.5) + P(-0.5)) \tag{18}$$

For estimating the mid-term $X(1.5)$, the only point $(0, X(2))$ is allowed as a center point, since $X(1)$ and $X(3)$ are involved in approximating the derivative value, $X'(2)$ using Equation (18). The mid-term is represented by Equation (19):

$$\widehat{X}(1.5) = \frac{1}{4}(X(1) + 4X(2) - X(3)) \tag{19}$$

Similarly, for estimating the last mid-term, $X(n-0.5)$, the only point, $(0, X(n-1))$ is allowed since $X(n-2)$ and $X(n)$ are involved into approximating $X'(n-1)$.

The above discussed deterministic based VDP exploration methods have been adopted in the research work carried out by Nayak et al. (2014) for the financial time series forecasting. The impact of these VDPs on ANN BP model as well as ANNGA model has been carried out and found that the forecasting accuracies of these models improved a lot.

2.2. Stochastic Interpolation Based VDP Exploration

In the case of stochastic interpolation based VDP exploration method, the estimated VDPs are related with random value. Therefore, the estimated VDP value is constant with the original input values in deterministic method, while its estimated value is variable in spite of same input values and unpredictable in stochastic method. The merits of the stochastic method over deterministic methods are simplicity in the computation of estimated values of virtual data positions and potential diversity of its values. The base equation of the stochastic VDP method can be represented by Equation (20):

$$\hat{x}(i+0.5) = \frac{1}{2}(X(i) + X(i+1) + \varepsilon) \tag{20}$$

In the above equation, the random value ε is added to the equation of linear interpolation.

In uniform VDP method, the value of ε is randomized based on the uniform distribution. The range of ε in uniform distribution for $x(i)$ and $x(i+1)$ is given as follows:

$$\left[\frac{1}{2}(x(i) - x(i+1)), \frac{1}{2}(x(i+1) - x(i))\right]$$

In Gaussian VDP method, the value of ε is randomized in the basis of Gaussian or normal distribution and can be calculated by Equation (21):

$$f(x,\mu,\sigma) = \frac{1}{\sigma\sqrt{2\pi}} e^{-\frac{(x-\mu)^2}{2\sigma^2}} \tag{21}$$

The parameter μ mean) is set to 0 and the standard deviation σ is calculated as:

$$\sigma = \left| \frac{1}{2}(x(i+1) - x(i)) \right|$$

3. FINANCIAL TIME SERIES FORECASTING AND SOME STYLIZED FACTS

This section describes the problem of financial time series forecasting and some of its characteristics. The second part of the section describes some of the stylized facts of financial time series data which motivated the authors to pursue research in this domain.

3.1. Financial Time Series Forecasting

Generally, a time series is defined as a sequence of values/data points/events separated/occurred by equal interval of time. A time series can be represented as a set of discrete values $\{x_1, x_2, x_3, \cdots, x_N\}$, where N is the total number of observations. A time series possess both deterministic as well as stochastic components characterized by noise interference. The forecasting process can be mathematically represented as:

$$Y_{t+1} = f(y_t, y_{t-1}, \cdots, y_{t-N})$$

where, y_t is the observation at time t, N is the number of past observations and Y_{t+1} is the value to be forecasted.

However financial time series data is prone to random fluctuations as compared to ordinary time series. It is characterized with high nonlinearity, non-stationary and chaotic in nature. It is often desirable to monitor price behavior frequently and to try to understand the probable development of the prices in the future. Stock market indices are an important financial time series and discussed in the following subsections.

Stock index forecasting also known as financial time series forecasting is the process of making prediction about future performance of a stock market based on existing stock market behavior. Stock market behaves very much like a random walk process and their serial correlation is economically and statistically insignificant. Due to the influence of uncertainties involved in the movement of the market, stock market forecasting is regarded as a challenging and difficult task in financial time-series forecasting.

Predicting stock market price movements is quite difficult due to its nonlinearities, highly volatile nature, discontinuities, movement of other stock markets, political influences and other many macro-economical factors even individual psychology (Wang, 2003; Huang et al., 2008; Liu et al., 2009; Ravichandran et al., 2007). Various economic factors such as oil prices, exchange rates, interest rates, stock price indexes in other countries, domestic/global economic situations, etc. has been employed on the study of stock price prediction and found to be important elements for influencing the market.

3.2. Stylized Facts in Financial Time Series

The observations or empirical findings common across a wide range of instruments, markets, and time periods are called as *stylized facts* and can be obtained by taking a common denominator among the properties observed in studies of different markets and instruments (Cont, 2001). Stylized facts are usually formulated in terms of *qualitative properties* of asset returns and may not be precise enough to distinguish among different parametric models. The intension here is not to go the details of stylized facts, rather to study some of those for the financial time series considered, which motivated the authors of this article to design a sophisticated forecasting model. For more exhaustive study about stylized facts, readers may refer to (Danielsson, 2011;

Sewell, 2011; Taylor, 2007; Franses & Van Dijk, 2000). In this chapter the daily closing prices of ten fast growing stock markets such as BSE, DJIA, NASDAQ, FTSE, TAIEX, S&P 500, ASX, LSE, SSE, and NIKKEI for period of fifteen years (01 Jan. 2000 to 31 Dec. 2014) are used. Figure 1 shows the daily closing indices of the stock market data used.

As can be observed from Figure 1, the financial time series generated from ten different stock markets do not seem to have anything in common. In the other hand returns exhibited more attractive statistical properties.

Table 1 summarizes the descriptive statistics of daily closing prices. Table 2 summarizes the descriptive statistics of daily returns. These statistics are used in discussion of some stylized facts exhibited by the financial time series.

The positive skewness value of the closing price as observed from Table 1 implies that all the data sets except FTSE, TAIEX, and SSE are spread out more toward right. The kurtosis analysis implies that stock price of DJIA, NASDAQ, and S&P 500 are more outlier prone where as all other financial time series are less outlier prone. Also, from the Jarque-Bera test statistics, it can be observed that all the stock price data sets are non-normal distributed.

Similarly Table 2 summarizes the descriptive statistics of daily returns from all data sets. The positive skewness value of the return price implies that all data sets except NASDAQ, TAIEX, S&P 500, SSE, and NIKKEI are spread out more toward right. These positive skewness values suggest investment opportunities in these markets. Figure 2 presents the histogram of daily returns of NASDAQ and BSE for an example. The peaks of the histograms are much higher than the corresponding to the normal distribution and it is slightly skewed to the right in case of BSE and slightly skewed to the left in case of NASDAQ stock data. The kurtosis analysis implies that stock price of all data sets are more outlier prone than the normal distribution. Again from the Jarque-Bera test statistics, it can be observed that all the stock price data sets are non-normal distributed.

Figure 1. Daily observations of closing prices of markets (left) from top to bottom DJIA, BSE, S&P 500, LSE, NIKKEI and (right) from top to bottom NASDAQ, FTSE, TAIEX, ASX, and SSE from January 2000 to December 2014

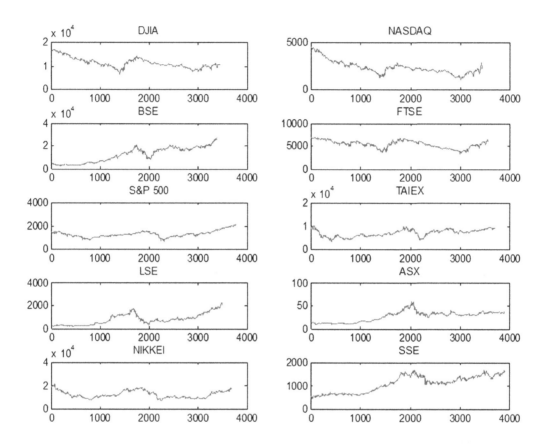

Table 1. Descriptive statistics of closing prices for different stocks

Stock Index	Descriptive Statistics						
	Minimum	Maximum	Mean	Standard Deviation	Skewness	Kurtosis	Jarque-Bera Test Statistics
BSE	792.1800	1.1024e+004	4.6235e+003	2.6947e+003	0.1154	1.7908	236.0430(h=1)
DJIA	6.5471e+003	1.7138e+004	1.1400e+004	2.1801e+003	0.6644	3.0512	253.8134(h=1)
NASDAQ	1.1141e+003	4.5982e+003	2.3858e+003	709.7888	1.0392	4.0027	764.3663(h=1)
FTSE	3287	6.8785e+003	5.4165e+003	836.2381	-0.2837	2.1378	158.4568(h=1)
TAIEX	3.4463e+003	1.0202e+004	6.9835e+003	1.4846e+003	-0.1776	2.0465	159.9786(h=1)
S&P 500	676.5300	2.0906e+003	1.2824e+003	269.6542	0.7109	3.5294	361.8941(h=1)
LSE	186.1040	2255	805.4437	486.4698	0.7035	2.7254	299.6108(h=1)
ASX	9.5989	59.6509	26.9877	11.2061	0.0847	2.3400	75.2181(h=1)
SSE	427.5000	1679	1.0762e+003	350.6077	-0.1679	1.5868	343.2149(h=1)
NIKKEI	7.0550e+003	2.0833e+004	1.2311e+004	3.0587e+003	0.5011	2.1468	266.5799(h=1)

Table 2. Descriptive statistics of daily returns for different stocks

Stock Index	Descriptive Statistics						
	Minimum	Maximum	Mean	Standard deviation	Skewness	Kurtosis	Jarque-Bera Test Statistics
BSE	-14.6179	12.4398	-0.0460	1.5724	0.5305	9.7199	7.2066e+003(h=1)
DJIA	-10.5083	8.2005	-0.0016	1.2983	0.2038	9.8306	7.2907e+003(h=1)
NASDAQ	-13.2546	9.5877	-0.0092	1.5094	-0.0871	9.0069	5.8730e+003(h=1)
FTSE	-9.3842	9.2646	-0.0010	1.1949	0.1516	10.1496	8.3278e+003(h=1)
TAIEX	-9.9360	6.5246	-0.0037	1.4603	-0.2257	5.9269	1.3657e+003(h=1)
S&P 500	-9.4695	10.9572	0.0089	1.2703	-0.1811	11.1322	1.0776e+004(h=1)
LSE	-17.4640	27.7143	0.0593	2.3315	1.0482	22.5719	6.3010e+004(h=1)
ASX	-14.0695	17.7496	0.0293	1.5867	0.3217	14.2521	2.0657e+004(h=1)
SSE	-12.9754	13.4709	0.0304	1.4215	-0.1572	10.0935	8.1989e+003(h=1)
NIKKEI	-12.1110	13.2346	-0.0071	1.5555	-0.3997	9.1350	5.9600e+003(h=1)

Figure 2. Histogram of daily returns of the NASDAQ (left panel) and BSE (right panel) against the theoretical normal distribution

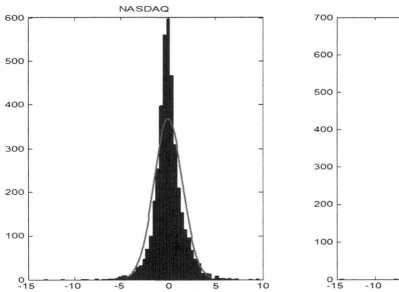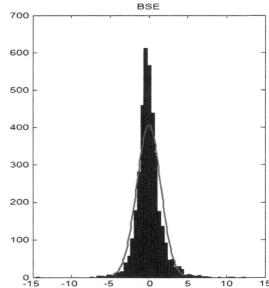

3.2.1. Gain/Loss Asymmetry

This is a stylized fact in financial time series where one observes large draw downs in stock index values but not equally large upward movements. The skewness of a financial time series is a measure of the asymmetry of the distribution of the series. It may be noted that all symmetric distributions including the normal distribution posses skewnees value equal to zero. As observed from the return statistics presented in Table 2, BSE, DJIA, FTSE, LSE, and ASX have positive skewness values which might point to possible investment opportunities in these emerging markets. Positive skewness implies that the right tail of the distribution is fatter than the left tail which indicates that positive returns tend to occur more often than large negative returns. Interested readers may refer to (Cont, 2001).

3.2.2. Fat Tails

The fact that the distribution of stock returns is fat-tailed has important implications in financial time series analysis. Since the probability of observing extreme values is higher for fat-tail distributions compared to normal distributions, it leads to a gross underestimation of risk. A random variable is said to possessing fat tails if it exhibits more extreme outcomes than a normally distributed random variable with the same mean and variance. This indicates that the stock market has more relatively large and small outcomes than one would expect under the normal distribution.

The degree of peakedness of a distribution relative to its tails is measured by its kurtosis value. The normal distribution has kurtosis value 3. Higher kurtosis value (*leptokurtosis*) is a signal of *fat tails*, means that most of the variance is due to infrequent extreme deviations than predicted by the normal distribution. As observed from Table 2, all the stock data sets have excess kurtosis which establishes the fact of *fat tails* and evidence against normality.

The commonly used graphical method for analyzing the tails of a distribution is the quantile-quantile (QQ) plot. Figure 3 presents the QQ plots for NASDAQ, BSE, DJIA, and FTSE for an example. From this it can be observed that returns have fatter tails to fit the normal distribution.

Figure 3. QQ plot of NASDAQ, BSE, DJIA, and FTSE stock data

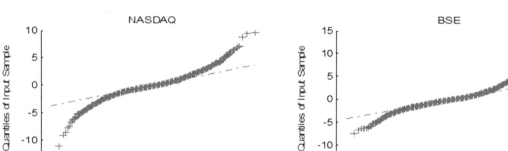

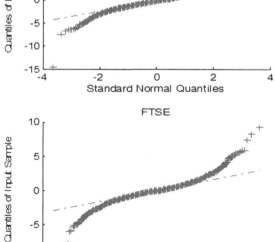

3.2.3. Slow Decay of Autocorrelation in Returns

This fact tells that the autocorrelation function of absolute returns decays slowly as a function of the time lag. It is a well-known fact that price movements in markets do not exhibit any significant linear autocorrelation. The autocorrelation function measures how returns on a given day are correlated with returns on previous days. If such correlations are statistically significant, there is strong evidence for predictability. Figure 4 represents the autocorrelation function for BSE. From Figure 4, it can be clearly seen that the autocorrelation function for BSE rapidly decays to zero after a lag.

3.2.4. Volatility Clustering

This is a well-known stylized fact where different measures of volatility display a positive autocorrelation over several days, which quantifies the fact that high-volatility events tend to cluster in time. This implies that large price variations are more likely to be followed by large price variations; hence returns are not random walk.

Figure 5 shows the autocorrelation function for BSE return series (top), absolute return (middle), and Squared returns (bottom). In the top panel most of the autocorrelations lie within the interval. However in case of absolute return and squared return the autocorrelation function is significant even at long lags which provide the evidence for the predictability.

Figure 4. Autocorrelation plot of BSE returns, along with a 95% confidence interval, for the first 20 lags

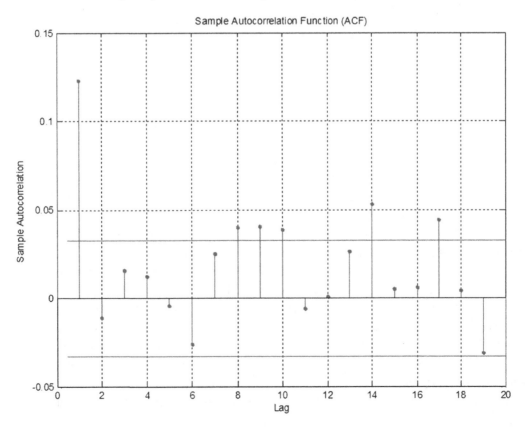

Figure 5. Autocorrelation plots of daily BSE returns (top), absolute returns (middle) and squared returns (bottom) for first 1000 lags

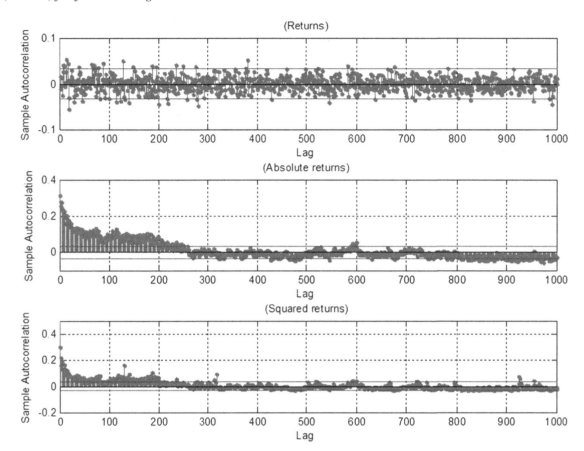

The lag plots of returns of a day r_t against returns of previous day r_{t-1} is another possible way to characterize the stylized fact of volatility/return cluster. Figure 6 presents the lag plots corresponding to returns of DJIA and NASDAQ.

A stylized fact that can be observed from such lag plots is that large returns tend to occur in clusters, i.e., it appears that relatively volatile periods characterized by large returns alternate with more stable periods in which returns remain small.

We studied some stylized facts exhibited by financial time series. We showed that the probability density function of the return series of these stock indices are skewed and fat tailed. The positive skewness shown by BSE, DJIA, FTSE, LSE, and ASX return series implying possible investment opportunities in these markets. For all markets, fat tails existed with kurtosis far in excess of the corresponding to the normal distribution. The linear autocorrelations are insignificant after a few lags and nonlinear autocorrelations prevailed, which was evidence for the existence of volatility clusters.

These preliminary analyses of the stylized facts in financial time series motivated the authors of this article to develop a sophisticated and more accurate model for forecasting stock market behavior. In the first phase a hybrid model has been designed to forecast the next day's closing price. Secondly, the article proposes a novel method to explore virtual data positions estimated by an evolutionary based neural network model.

Figure 6. Lag plots of the returns on the DJIA (left) and NASDAQ (right), on day t, against the return on day t-1

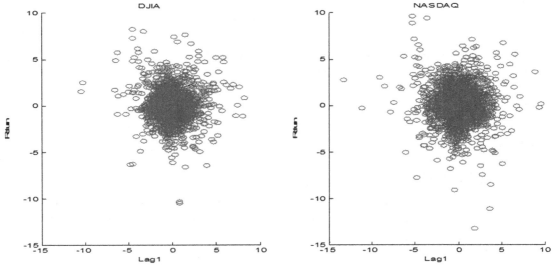

4. CHEMICAL REACTION OPTIMIZATION

This optimization method does not need a local search method to refine the search and includes both local and global search capability. Unlike other optimization techniques, CRO does not require many parameters that must be specified at beginning and only defining number of initial reactants is enough for implementation. As the initial reactants are distributed over feasible global search region, optimal solutions can be obtained with few iterations and hence significant reduction in computational time. The concept loosely couples mathematical optimization techniques with properties of chemical reactions. A chemical reaction is a natural process of transforming the unstable chemical substances (reactants/ molecules) to the stable ones. A chemical reaction starts with some unstable molecules with excessive energy. The molecules interact with each other through a sequence of elementary reactions producing some intermediate chemical products. At the end, they are converted to those with minimum energy to support their existence. The energy associated with a molecule is called as enthalpy (which can be considered as fitness function in case of minimization problem) and/or entropy (which can be considered as fitness function in case of maximization problem). During a chemical reaction this energy changes with the change in intra-molecular structure of a reactant and becomes stable at one point. Most of the reactions can occur in both forward and backward direction, i.e. reversible reaction. These reactions may be monomolecular or bimolecular depending on the number of reactants taking part in the reaction. This property is embedded in CRO to solve optimization problems. CRO algorithm begins with set of initial reactants in a solution. Then reactants are consumed and produced via chemical reactions. Algorithm is terminated when the termination criterion is met similar to the state when no more reactions can take place (the solution becomes inert solution).

Chemical reactions are usually characterized by a chemical change. One or more products having properties different from reactants are produced. *N* different types of molecules or chemical reactants may take part in one or more of *M* types of chemical reactions. Many reactions are reversible. The observable properties and concentrations of all participants become constant when a chemical system reaches a state of equilibrium, i.e. rate of forward reaction = rate of backward reaction. In that state the solution becomes inert. Chemical reactions can be classified into the following categories:

- **Synthesis Reactions:** A synthesis reaction is when two or more reactants combine to produce a single product. In generic terms, synthesis reactions look like the following:

$$2H_2 + O_2 \rightarrow 2H_2O$$

$$6CO_2 + 6H_2O \rightarrow C_6H_{12}O_6 + 6O_2$$

- **Decomposition Reactions:** When a single compound breaks down into two or more elements or compounds on application of some energy source such as heat, light, or electricity, the reaction is termed as decomposition reaction. In general decomposition reaction look like the following:

$$2H_2O \rightarrow 2H_2 + O_2$$

$$2KClO_3 \rightarrow 2KCl + 3O_2$$

- **Single Displacement Reactions:** In this reaction, one element trades places with another element in a compound. In general, single displacement reaction look like the following:

$$Cl + 2KBr \rightarrow 2KCl + Br_2$$

- **Double Displacement Reactions:** This is when the anions and cations of two different molecules switch places, forming two entirely different compounds. In generic terms, double replacement reactions look like the following:

$$NaCO_3 + BaCl_2 \rightarrow NaCl + BaCO_3$$

- **Combustion Reactions:** A combustion reaction is when oxygen combines a substance and releases energy in the form of heat and light:

$$CH_4 + O_2 \rightarrow CO_2 + H_2O$$

- **Redox Reactions:** Redox reactions are the transfer of electrons from one reactant to another. The chemical which gains electrons is reduced and is called an oxidizing agent. The chemical which loses electrons is oxidized and is called the reducing agent:

$$Fe + Cu^{+2} \rightarrow Fe^{+2} + Cu$$

- **Reversible Reactions:** In reversible reactions, products of certain reactions can be converted back to the reactants. Thus, in reversible reactions the products can react with one another under suitable conditions to give back the reactants. In other words, in reversible reactions the reaction takes place in both the forward and backward directions:

$$CaCO_3 \leftrightarrow CaO + CO_2$$

CRO Algorithm begins with set of initial reactants in a solution. Then reactants are consumed and produced via chemical reactions. Algorithm is terminated when the termination criterion is met similar to the state when no more reactions can take place (inert solution). According to the algorithm concept, the major steps of CRO are listed as follows:

Algorithm 1. Major steps of CRO

```
Step 1: Problem and algorithm parameter initialization.
Step 2: Setting the initial reactants and evaluation.
Step 3: Applying chemical reactions.
Step 4: Reactants update.
Step 5: Termination criterion check.
```

The CRO algorithm is discussed by Algorithm 2. The reactants are updated according to enthalpy value associated with them (fitness value).

Algorithm 2. Chemical reaction optimization

```
Set IterationNum = 0
/*Initialize Reactants of size ReacNum randomly from a uniform distribution*/
Create molecules M_i of size ReacNum by uniform population.
for  i = 1 to ReacNum do
Calculate the enthalpy e (M_i)
end for
While (termination criterion not met) do
for I = 1 to ReacNum do
/*Apply all reactions over the reactants of M_i */
Get rand_1 randomly in interval [0,1]
if rand_1 ≤ 0.5 then
Get rand_2 randomly in interval [0, 1]
if rand_2 ≤ 0.5 then
Decomposition (M_i)
else
Redox1 (M_i)
end if
else
Select another molecule M_j (M_i ≠ M_j)
                           Get rand_3 randomly in interval [0, 1]
if 0 ≤ rand_3 ≤ 0.33 then
```

```
Synthesis (M_i, M_j)
else if 0.33 ≤ rand_3 ≤ 0.66 then
Displacement (M_i, M_j)
else
Redox_2 (M_i, M_j)
end if
end if
Apply Reversible Reaction for increased enthalpy to update reactants
end for
IterationNum=IterationNum+1
end while
```

Employ the reactant with best enthalpy as the optimal weight & biases set for the FLN model.

5. MODEL DEVELOPMENT

Two neural network models based on BP and CRO training are presented in this section. The ANN model trained with back propagation technique is termed here as ANNBP and the ANN model trained with CRO termed as ANNCRO. The details of the design and development of these models are discussed below.

5.1. Back Propagation Based ANN Forecasting Model: ANNBP

An ANN is a simplified mathematical and computational model inspired by the structural/ functional aspects of biological neural network. The application of ANNs to financial forecasting problems has become very popular due to their power and potential in modeling nonlinear systems. ANN has a number of data processing elements called neurons or nodes. The neurons in the input layer receive the input vector and transmit the values subsequently to the next layer across connections. This process is continued until the output layer is reached. Figure 7 presents the ANNBP based forecasting model. A three-layer feed forward ANN, shown in Figure 7, has an input layer, an output layer and a hidden middle layer. The solution to the input problem is emanating from the output nodes, when the interconnection weights are modified, the ANN output changes. The back propagation rule propagates the errors through the network and allows adaptation of the hidden neurons. The error correction learning in this case is a supervised learning, i.e. the desired response for the system must be presented at the output neuron.

This model consists of a single output unit to estimate the closing prices. The neurons in the input layer use a linear transfer function, the neurons in the hidden layer and output layer use sigmoid function presented in Equation (22):

$$y_{out} = \frac{1}{1 + e^{-\lambda y_{in}}} \tag{22}$$

where y_{out} is the output of the neuron, λ is the sigmoidal gain and y_{in} is the input to the neuron. The learning rate η influences the rate of convergence. Too large value of η oscillates the search path while

Figure 7. ANNBP based forecasting model

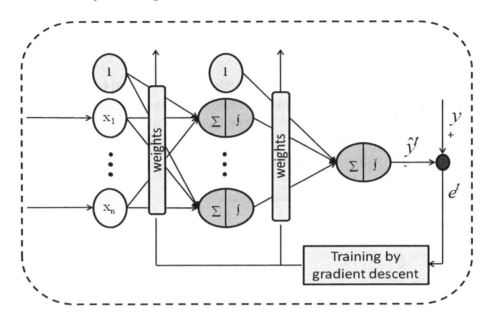

for value of η is too small, the descent will progress in small steps significantly and increases the time to converge. In order to smooth out the descent path by preventing extreme changes in the gradients due to local anomalies a momentum term α has been added to the gradient expression. Let there be *m* neurons in the hidden layer. Since there are *n* input values in an input vector, the number of neurons in the input layer is equal to *n*. The first layer corresponds to the problem input variables with one node for each input variable. The second layer is useful in capturing non-linear relationships among variables. At each neuron *j* in the hidden layer, the weighted output *z* is calculated using Equation 23:

$$z_j = f\left(B_j + \sum_{i=1}^{n} V_{ij} * X_i \right) \tag{23}$$

where X_i is the ith input vector, V_{ij} is the synaptic weight value between i^{th} input neuron and j^{th} hidden neuron and B_j is the bias value and f is sigmoidal activation function. The output y at the single output neuron is calculated using Equation 24:

$$y = f\left(B_0 + \sum_{j=1}^{m} W_j * z_j \right) \tag{24}$$

where, W_j is the synaptic weight from j^{th} hidden neuron to output neuron, z_j is the output of the jth hidden neuron, and B_0 is the output bias. This output y is compared to the desired output and the error is calculated by using Equation 25:

$$e_i = |t_i - y_i| \tag{25}$$

where e_i is the error signal, t_i is the target signal for i^{th} training pattern and y_i is the estimated output for i^{th} pattern.

This error is propagated back to train the ANN model. The weight and other parameter values are adjusted by the gradient descent rule for minimal error signal generation. Because of the gradient descent neural network learning, they are characterized with problems like slow convergence, getting trapped to local minima. Therefore possibilities are there, that it may affect the prediction capabilities of the model. The back propagation algorithm is presented below.

Algorithm 3. Gradient descent based back propagation algorithm

```
Set learning rate, momentum coefficient
Initialize the weight and biases
Repeat
        For each input-output pattern pair
                Present input pattern to input units.
                Compute functional signals for hidden units.
                Compute functional signal for output units.
                Present the target responses to output units.
                Compute error signals.
                Find momentum term using momentum coefficient
                Update all weights and bias values using learning rate, momen-
tum term.
        End for
Until stopping criteria satisfied or maximum epochs reached.
```

5.2. CRO Based ANN Forecasting Model: ANNCRO

Figure 8 presents the architecture of the ANNGA model. This model employ the ANN network presented at Figure 7 with a single hidden layer.

BP learning based on gradient descent suffers from slow convergence, getting trapped to local minima, etc. But CRO performs search over the whole solution space, finds the optimal solution relatively easily. Further CRO does not require continuous differentiable objective functions like gradient descent technique. The reactant includes the weight set between the input-hidden layers, weight set between hidden-output layers, the bias values. Then the search for optimal set of weights can be done by applying CRO. The fitness is obtained from the absolute difference between the target y and the estimated output $\hat{y}$. The less the error value of a reactant, CRO considers it better fit. Figure 9 shows the reactant representation for CRO.

Figure 8. ANNCRO based forecasting model

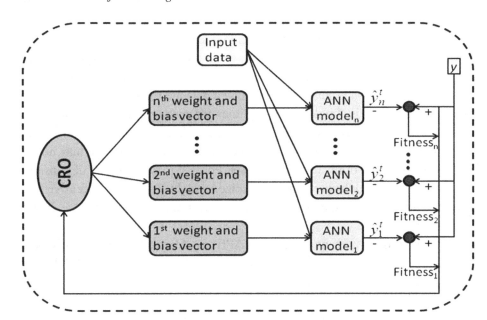

Figure 9. Reactant representations for CRO

Weight Values for							Bias Values for			
links between Input and Hidden layer				links between Hidden and Output layer			Hidden layer			Output layer
V_{11}	V_{12}	...	V_{nm}	W_1	W_2	...	W_m	B_1	... B_m	B_0

Binary encoding scheme has been used for this experimental work. The weight values between input and hidden layer neuron are represented as V_{11} to V_{nm}. Weight values between hidden and output layer are represented by W_1 to W_m. The bias values to the hidden and output layer are represented by B_1 to B_m and B_0 respectively.

6. EXPERIMENTAL RESULTS AND ANALYSIS

In this chapter the daily closing prices of ten fast growing stock markets such as BSE, DJIA, NASDAQ, FTSE, TAIEX, S&P 500, ASX, LSE, SSE, and NIKKEI for period of fifteen years (01 Jan. 2000 to 31 Dec. 2014) are used. The impact of VDP on prediction of the trend of time series data is evaluated using ten real life stock market data mentioned above. After obtaining the results with the original data, the VDPs are explored, incorporated, and tested. As discussed to test the performance, two neural forecasting techniques such as ANNBP and ANNGA are used.

Before conducting the experiments, the datasets are normalized and the normalized data is used for prediction. After prediction, the estimated values are denormalization and compared with the original value for validation. After experimentation with the original data, the VDPs are explored before normalization, incorporated and normalized, and then the data is taken for experimentation.

As discussed, for all the experiments sliding window technique is adopted and also the length of bed is kept fixed for all the experiments. As a result, when the VDPs are incorporated, the data points relatively at a greater distance are dropped and the bed used to forecast the target is constituted of few actual data points and few virtual points. The normalized data are then used to form a training bed for the network model. The model is simulated for 10 times for each training set and the average error is considered for comparative analysis of results. Since each time the sliding window moves one step ahead, only one new closing price data has been included into the training set. So there may not be significant change in nonlinearity behavior of the training data set. For that reason, instead of considering another random weight set, we have used the previously optimized weight set for the successive training. In this way, after the first training set, the number of iteration has been fixed to a small value, hence significant reduction in training time.

In this study, mean absolute percentage error (MAPE) as at Equation (26) is considered as the performance metric. Objective of each model is to reduce the MAPE and the model yields lowest MAPE is treated as a better model:

$$MAPE = \frac{1}{N} \sum_{i=1}^{N} \frac{\left| x_i - \hat{x}_i \right|}{x_i} *100\% \tag{26}$$

where x_i is the actual closing prices, $\hat{x}_i$ is the estimated price and N is the total training patterns.

6.1. Impact of VDP on BP Learning

To test the impact of incorporation of VDPs on financial time series data, it is first tested on the ANN with BP learning. As discussed, three different approaches such as linear interpolation, Lagrange and Taylor method are used for exploration of VDP and after incorporation separate data sets are formed for each exploration technique. Each data set is simulated 10 times and the average results obtained for the three different approaches of exploration are presented in Table 3.

It is observed that after incorporation of VDPs the prediction accuracy improves for all the exploration techniques. Also, it can found that the linear interpolation method obtains lowest MAPE values maximum times (i.e. 4 times). The Lagrange, Uniform, and Gaussian method generated minimal MAPE values twice each.

6.2. Impact of VDP on CRO Learning

Similarly possibility of performance improvement with CRO learning is also explored before and after incorporation of VDPs for different exploration techniques. The result obtained is presented in Table 4.

From the MAPE values presented in Table 4 it can be observed that the prediction accuracies of both ANNBP as well as ANNCRO improves a lot when VDPs are adopted. Here, the Linear, Uniform, and Gaussian method generated lowest error signals twice each. However, the Lagrange interpolation method generated lowest error signals four times. The Taylor interpolation method generated lowest MAPE once.

Table 3. Comparison of MAPE obtained from BP learning for different datasets

Data Set	Without VDPs	VDP Exploration By				
		Deterministic			Stochastic	
		Linear Interpolation	Lagrange	Taylor	Uniform	Gaussian
BSE	1.2420	**0.9128**	1.0026	1.0207	0.9628	0.9822
DJIA	2.0071	**1.0229**	1.1175	1.0715	1.0355	1.0763
NASDAQ	1.8241	1.5533	**1.0241**	1.2055	1.2068	1.0377
FTSE 100	1.2632	**0.8401**	0.9833	0.8532	1.0072	0.9833
S&P 500	1.0762	1.0027	**0.6653**	0.8273	1.0054	1.0146
SSE	2.0073	1.4955	1.7821	1.3062	1.4087	**1.2466**
TAIEX	2.1734	1.4138	1.3762	1.2157	**1.1307**	1.3231
AUX	1.0872	**0.8859**	0.9738	0.9946	0.9729	1.0050
LSE	0.8644	0.4972	0.5723	0.4966	0.5719	**0.4788**
NIKKEI	1.0267	0.9267	0.8999	0.9479	**0.8306**	0.9947

Table 4. Comparison of MAPE obtained from CRO learning for different datasets

Data Set	Without VDPs	VDP Exploration By				
		Deterministic			Stochastic	
		Linear Interpolation	Lagrange	Taylor	Uniform	Gaussian
BSE	0.0963	**0.0473**	0.0552	0.0857	0.0823	0.0805
DJIA	0.7053	0.0860	0.0546	0.6235	**0.0536**	0.5547
NASDAQ	0.0097	0.0092	**0.0050**	0.0095	0.0095	0.0067
FTSE 100	0.2592	0.2381	**0.2295**	0.2375	0.2512	**0.2295**
S&P 500	0.3334	**0.2042**	0.2763	0.3150	0.3188	0.2146
SSE	0.1070	0.0761	0.1027	0.0548	**0.0545**	0.0566
TAIEX	0.4211	0.3888	**0.3671**	0.3785	0.3792	0.3891
AUX	0.5527	0.5309	**0.5500**	0.5337	0.5399	0.5521
LSE	0.8936	0.7728	0.7702	**0.7328**	0.7699	0.7758
NIKKEI	0.6438	0.5855	0.5879	0.6024	0.5933	**0.5825**

7. CONCLUSION

This chapter presents the scope of improving prediction accuracy in financial time series by incorporating VDPs in the actual datasets. At the point of fluctuation, close enough data positions better help in prediction, compared with that of the data points placed relatively away from the point of prediction. As more close enough points are often not recorded, virtual data positions are explored. Different exploration techniques to find the VDPs and the use of such virtual data positions enhance the prediction accuracy to a certain extent. Different existing deterministic and stochastic exploration techniques are used for exploration of VDPs. For the above ten datasets such as BSE, DJIA, NASDAQ, FTSE, TAIEX, S&P 500,

ASX, LSE, SSE, and NIKKEI, the virtual positions are explored by different techniques, incorporated to the training set separately for each data and for each exploration technique.

Findings from this work can be summarized as follows:

1. Incorporation of VDPs shows improvement in prediction accuracy in case of all the databases;
2. The CRO based forecasting models show better forecasting accuracy than back propagation based model irrespective of incorporation of VDPs;
3. None of the VDP exploration methods adversely affect the prediction accuracy, however performance of linear interpolation can be considered superior followed by Lagrange method.

This work may be extended by exploring VDPs with other statistical methods. Other ANNs and metaheuristic can be adopted. Also VDPs can be explored by evolutionary techniques. Applying the concept of VDPs to other areas of forecasting may be considered as further research direction.

REFERENCES

Abu-Mustafa, Y. S. (1995). Financial application of learning from hints. *Advances in Neural Information Processing Systems, 7*, 411–418.

Alatas, B. (2011). ACROA: Artificial Chemical Reaction Optimization Algorithm for global optimization. *Expert Systems with Applications, 38*(10), 13170–13180. doi:10.1016/j.eswa.2011.04.126

Alatas, B. (2012). A novel chemistry based metaheuristic optimization method for mining of classification rules. *Expert Systems with Applications, 39*(12), 11080–11088. doi:10.1016/j.eswa.2012.03.066

Alexander, S. S. (1961, May). Price Movements in Speculative Markets: Trends or Random Walks. *Industrial Management Review*, 7-26.

An, G. (1996). The effect of adding noise during back propagation training on generalization performance. *Neural Computation, 7*(3), 643–674. doi:10.1162/neco.1996.8.3.643

Cho, S., Jang, M., & Chang, S. (1996). Virtual sample generation using a population of neural networks. *Neural Processing Letters, 5*, 83–89.

Cont, R. (2001). Empirical properties of asset returns: Stylized facts and statistical issues. *Quantitative Finance, 1*(2), 223–236. doi:10.1080/713665670

Cootner, P. H. (1964). *The Random Character of Stock Market Prices*. MIT Press.

Danielsson, J. (2011). *Financial Risk Forecasting*. Wiley.

Fama, E. F. (1965). The Behaviour of Stock Market Prices. *The Journal of Business, 38*(1), 34–105. doi:10.1086/294743

Fama, E. F. (1970). Efficient capital markets: A review of theory and empirical work. *The Journal of Finance, 25*(2), 383–417. doi:10.2307/2325486

Franses, P., & van Dijk, D. (2000). *Non-linear time series models in empirical finance*. Cambridge University Press. doi:10.1017/CBO9780511754067

Grandvalet, Y., Canu, S., & Boucheron, S. (1997). Noise injection: Theoretical prospects. *Neural Computation*, *9*(5), 1093–1108. doi:10.1162/neco.1997.9.5.1093

Huang, C.-J., Yang, D.-X., & Chuang, Y.-T. (2008). Application of wrapper approach and composite classifier to the stock trend prediction. *Expert Systems with Applications*, *34*(4), 2870–2878. doi:10.1016/j.eswa.2007.05.035

Jensen, M. C. (1978). Some Anomalous Evidence Regarding Market Efficiency. *Journal of Financial Economics*, *6*(2-3), 95–102. doi:10.1016/0304-405X(78)90025-9

Khashei, M., & Bijari, M. (2012). A new class of hybrid models for time series forecasting. *Expert Systems with Applications*, *39*(4), 4344–4357. doi:10.1016/j.eswa.2011.09.157

Kuo, R. J., Chen, C. H., & Hwang, Y. C. (2001). An intelligent stock trading decision support system through integration of genetic algorithm based fuzzy neural network and artificial neural network. *Fuzzy Sets and Systems*, *118*(1), 21–24. doi:10.1016/S0165-0114(98)00399-6

Lam, A. Y. S. & Li, V. O. K.(2010). Chemical-reaction-inspired metaheuristic for optimization. *IEEE Transactions on Evolutionary Computation, 14*(3), 381-399.

Lam, A. Y. S., & Li, V. O. K. (2012). Chemical Reaction Optimization: A tutorial. *Memtic Computing*, *4*(1), 3–17. doi:10.1007/s12293-012-0075-1

Liu, H-C., Lee, Y.-H., & Lee, M.-C. (2009). Forecasting china stock markets volatility via GARCH models under skewed-GED distribution. *Journal Money Investment Banking*, 5–14.

Nayak, J., Naik, B., & Behera, H. S. (2015). *A novel Chemical Reaction Optimization based Higher order Neural Network (CRO-HONN) for nonlinear classification*. Ain Shams Engineering Journal; doi:10.1016/j.asej.2014.12.013

Nayak, S. C., Misra, B. B., & Behera, H. S. (2012, February). Index prediction with neuro- genetic hybrid network: A comparative analysis of performance. *2012 International Conference on Computing, Communication and Applications*, 1-6. doi:10.1109/ICCCA.2012.6179215

Nayak, S. C., Misra, B. B., & Behera, H. S. (2012, October). Evaluation of normalization methods on neuro-genetic models for stock index forecasting. In *Information and Communication Technologies (WICT), 2012 World Congress on* (pp. 602-607). IEEE. doi:10.1109/WICT.2012.6409147

Nayak, S. C., Misra, B. B., & Behera, H. S. (2012). Stock index prediction with neuro-genetic hybrid techniques. *Int. J. Comput. Sci. Inform*, *2*, 27–34.

Nayak, S. C., Misra, B. B., & Behera, H. S. (2013, September). Hybridzing chemical reaction optimization and artificial neural network for stock future index forecasting. In *Emerging Trends and Applications in Computer Science (ICETACS), 2013 1st International Conference on* (pp. 130-134). IEEE. doi:10.1109/ICETACS.2013.6691409

Nayak, S. C., Misra, B. B., & Behera, H. S. (2014). Exploration and Incorporation of Virtual Data Position for Efficient Forecasting of Financial Time Series. *Int. Journal of Industrial and Systems Engineering*.

Nayak, S. C., Misra, B. B., & Behera, H. S. (2014). Impact of data normalization on stock index forecasting. *Int. J. Comput. Inf. Syst. Ind. Manage. Appl, 6*, 257–269.

Nayak, S. C., Misra, B. B., & Behera, H. S. (2015). Comparison of Performance of Different Functions in Functional Link Artificial Neural Network: A Case Study on Stock Index Forecasting. In Computational Intelligence in Data Mining (vol. 1, pp. 479-487). Springer India. doi:10.1007/978-81-322-2205-7_45

Nayak, S. C., Misra, B. B., & Behera, H. S. (2015). *Artificial chemical reaction optimization of neural networks for efficient prediction of stock market indices*. Ain Shams Engineering Journal.

Nayak, S. C., Misra, B. B., & Behera, H. S. (2016). Efficient forecasting of financial time-series data with virtual adaptive neuro-fuzzy inference system. *International Journal of Business Forecasting and Marketing Intelligence, 2*(4), 379–402. doi:10.1504/IJBFMI.2016.080132

Nayak, S. C., Misra, B. B., & Behera, H. S. (2016). An Adaptive Second Order Neural Network with Genetic-Algorithm-based Training (ASONN-GA) to Forecast the Closing Prices of the Stock Market. *International Journal of Applied Metaheuristic Computing, 7*(2), 39–57. doi:10.4018/IJAMC.2016040103

Nayak, S. C., Misra, B. B., & Behera, H. S. (2016). Improving Performance of Higher Order Neural Network using Artificial Chemical Reaction Optimization: A Case Study on Stock Market Forecasting. *Applied Artificial Higher Order Neural Networks for Control and Recognition*, 253.

Oh, K. J., & Kim, K. J. (2002). Analyzing stock market tick data using piecewise non linear model. *Expert Systems with Applications, 22*(3), 249–255. doi:10.1016/S0957-4174(01)00058-6

Ravichandran, K. S., Thirunavukarasu, P., Nallaswamy, R. R., & Babu, R. (2007). Estimation on return on investment in share market through ANN. *Journal of Theoretical and Applied Information Technology, 3*, 44–54.

Sewell, M. (2011). *Characterization of Financial Time Series*. UCL Department of Computer Science, Research Note.

Taeho, J. (2013). VTG schemes for using back propagation for multivariate time series prediction. *Applied Soft Computing, 13*(5), 2692–2702. doi:10.1016/j.asoc.2012.11.018

Taylor, S. (2007). *Asset Price Dynamics, Volatility, and Prediction*. Princeton University Press.

Wang, Y. (2003). Mining stock prices using fuzzy rough set system. *Expert Systems with Applications, 24*(1), 13–23. doi:10.1016/S0957-4174(02)00079-9

KEY TERMS AND DEFINITIONS

ANN: Artificial Neural Network.
BP: Back Propagation.
BSE: Bombay Stock Exchange.

VDP: Virtual Data Position.

EMH: Efficient Market Hypothesis.

GA: Genetic Algorithm.

GD: Gradient Descent.

CRO: Chemical Reaction Optimization.

MAPE: Mean Absolute Percentage Error.

Chapter 23
Determination of Spatial Variability of Rock Depth of Chennai

Pijush Samui
National Institute of Technology Patna, India

Viswanathan R.
Galgotias University, India

Jagan J.
VIT University, India

Pradeep U. Kurup
University of Massachusetts – Lowell, USA

ABSTRACT

This study adopts four modeling techniques Ordinary Kriging(OK), Generalized Regression Neural Network (GRNN), Genetic Programming(GP) and Minimax Probability Machine Regression(MPMR) for prediction of rock depth(d) at Chennai(India). Latitude (L_x) and Longitude(L_y) have been used as inputs of the models. A semivariogram has been constructed for developing the OK model. The developed GP gives equation for prediction of d at any point in Chennai. A comparison of four modeling techniques has been carried out. The performance of MPMR is slightly better than the other models. The developed models give the spatial variability of rock depth at Chennai.

INTRODUCTION

Rock depth (d) is an important parameter for any civil engineering project. The determination of rock depth has direct influence in the construction and mining works. Hence, the prediction of d is an important task in civil engineering. There are various direct methods for the determination of rock depth, which is not economical. The rock depth has the direct influence on segregating the seismic site. The classifications on seismic sites are utilized for estimation of response spectral ordinates at the surface of the soil

DOI: 10.4018/978-1-5225-2857-9.ch023

(Anabazhagan et al., 2013). Magnetic and resistivity geophysical methods were used to investigate the location and depth of mineral rock, which is also the most expensive methods. This article uses Ordinary Kriging (OK), Generalized Regression Neural Network (GRNN), Genetic Programming (GP) and Minimax Probability Machine Regression (MPMR) for prediction of d at any point in Chennai (India). The latitude and longitude of Chennai are 13.08°N and 90.27°E respectively. The database contains information about Latitude (L_x), Longitude(L_y) and d at 67 different points of Chennai. A comparative study has been carried out between the developed OK, GRNN, GP and MPMR models.

BACKGROUND

Researchers used various random field method for prediction purpose (Yaglom, 1962; Lumb, 1975; Alonso & Krizek, 1975; Vanmarcke, 1977; Tang, 1979; Wu &Wong, 1981; Tabb & Yong, 1981; Asaoka & Grivas, 1982; VanMarcke, 1998; Baecher, 1984; Baker, 1984; Kulatilake & Miller, 1987; Kulatilake, 1989; Fenton, 1998; Phoon & Kulhawy, 1999; Fenton, 1999; Uzielli et al., 2005). In random field method, the science of prediction in the presence of correlation between samples is not at all well developed. Statistical parameters contain uncertainty in random field method. In order to fill the holes of some uncertainty and also to reduce the cost, various intelligent techniques were evolved and utilized according to the requirements.

OK is an interpolation technique (Matheron, 1963; Isaaks & Srivastava, 1989; Davis, 2002). It uses semivariogram for prediction. This technique paved its efficiency in making the super-resolution of an image. Zhang and Wu (2015) had proposed this approach to yield adaptive weight and edge preservation. Dai et al., (2014) has applied OK for the spatial prediction of soil organic matter content in the Tibetan Plateau. There are lots of applications of OK in the literatures (Eldeiry & Garcia, 2012; Clough & Green, 2013; Emadi & Baghernejad, 2014). GRNN is proposed by Specht (1991). It approximates any arbitrary function between the input and output variables. The landslide is one of the major disasters with the worse effects in soil displacement. Jiang & Jiejie (2016) has successfully utilized the GRNN for the prediction of displacement of landslides by incorporating the K-fold cross validation. In the stream of materials engineering, the microstructural studies has great issues. Ozturk & Turan (2012) has adopted GRNN for forecasting the effects of microstructural phases of cement mortaer when it was added with the admixtures. Gaurav & Hasmat (2016) predicted the velocity of wind for the Western region of India by the utilization of GRNN. Many other applications of GRNN are available in the literatures (Kaveh et al., 2012; Singh & Murthy, 2013; Ding et al., 2014). GP is developed based on the concept of genetic algorithm. In order to forecast the flyrock distance, GP was effectively utilized and the effective equations were produced (Roohollah, et al., 2016). Also, GP was employed to predict the stability number of armor blocks due to the rubble-mound breakwaters. The efficiency of this model has outperformed the Van der Meer's stability equations (Mehmet et al., 2016). Researchers use GP for solving many problems (Huang et al., 2012; Danandeh et al., 2013; Zahiri & Azamathulla, 2014). MPMR is developed based on Minimax Probability Machine Classification (Lanckriet et al., 2002). MPMR was resulted as the effective model for forcasting the wireless network traffic in a specific network (Kong et al, 2009). It has been successfully applied to model different problems (Yu et al., 2012; Zhou et al., 2013; Yang & Ju, 2014). These intelligence techniques have successfully employed in various complex problems.

DETAILS OF OK

OK is used to determine d at unknown points based on the available dataset. Semivariogram analysis is the first step for developing OK (Webster, et al., 2001). The value of semivariogram is determined by using the following equation:

$$\gamma(h)\frac{1}{2m(h)}\sum_{i=1}^{m(h)}\left[d\left(x_i\right)-d\left(x_i+h\right)\right]^2 \tag{1}$$

where m(h) is the number of pairs of observations separated by h, $d(x_i)$ is the sample value of the variable d at location xi, and $d(x_i+h)$ is the sample value of the variable d at location x_i+h. OK uses the following equation for determination d. OK uses the following equation for determination d:

$$\hat{d}\left(x_0\right)=\sum_{i=1}^{n}w_i d\left(x_i\right) \tag{2}$$

where w_i is weight. The sum of weights should be equal to one for ensuring unbiased estimation.

In order to construct the OK, the dataset has been cleaved into two as:

- **Training Dataset:** This is adopted to develop the OK. This article uses 47 out of 67 dataset as training;
- **Testing Dataset:** This is employed to verify the developed OK. This article uses the remaining 20 dataset as testing.

The segregation of the dataset was user specific as there are no availability thumb rules. Sitharam et al (2008) had utilized 90% of the available data for the training dataset and the remaining for the testing dataset.

DETAILS OF GRNN

GRNN is developed based on kernel regression. There are four layers in GRNN. It uses the following equation for determination of output (Kurt et al., 1989):

$$\hat{y}_i = \frac{\displaystyle\sum_{i=1}^{n}y_i \exp\left(-D\left(x,x_i\right)\right)}{\displaystyle\sum_{i=1}^{n}\exp\left(-D\left(x,x_i\right)\right)} \tag{3}$$

where n is number of training dataset, xi is input and y_i is corresponding output of x_i. The expression of $D(x,x_i)$ is given below:

$$D(x, x_i) = \sum_{j=1}^{m} \left(\frac{x_j - x_{ij}}{\alpha} \right)^2 \qquad (4)$$

where m is the number of element of an input vector, α is the spread parameter, x_j and x_{ij} are j^{th} element of x and x_i, respectively.

The performance of GRNN model depends on the proper choice of α values. For developing the GRNN, the dataset has been divided into the following two groups:

- **Training Dataset:** This is adopted to develop the GRNN. This article uses 47 out of 67 dataset as training;
- **Testing Dataset:** This is employed to verify the developed GRNN. This article uses the remaining 20 dataset as testing.

The dataset is scaled between 0 and 1. The program of GRNN has been constructed by using MATLAB.

DETAILS OF GP

GP is developed based on the principle of the principle of 'survival of the fittest'. In 1st step, a random population of equation is created. The fitness of each function is computed in 2nd step. 'Parents' are selected in 3rd step. In 4th step, 'offspring's are created from 'parent' through the process of reproduction, mutation and crossover. The best equation after all these process is the solution of the problem. More details about GP is given by Koza (1992).

GP uses the same training dataset, testing dataset, and normalization technique as used by the GRNN model. MATLAB has been adopted to construct the GP model.

DETAILS OF MPMR

MPMR is developed by constructing a dichotomy classifier (Strohmann & Grudic, 2002). It adopts the following relation between input(x) and output(y):

$$y = \sum_{i=1}^{N} \beta_i K(x_i, x) + b \qquad (5)$$

where N is the number of dataset, $K(x_i, x)$ is kernel function, β_i and b are outputs of the MPMR algorithm. MPMR separates the training dataset into the following two classes. MPMR separates the training dataset into the following two classes:

$$u_i = \left(y_i + \varepsilon, x_{i1}, x_{i2}, ..., x_{in} \right) \qquad (6)$$

$$v_i = \left(y_i + \varepsilon, x_{i1}, x_{i2}, ..., x_{in} \right) \tag{7}$$

The classification boundary between u_i and v_i is the regression surface. MPMR adopts the same training dataset, testing dataset and normalization as used by the GP and GRNN models. This article adopts radial basis function as kernel function for developing the MPMR model. The program of MPMR has been constructed by using MATLAB.

RESULTS AND DISCUSSION

The three parameters latitude, longitude and the depth(d) were utilized. In this, the parameter d has much impact than the other parameters. For developing OK, semivariogram is constructed. Gaussian semivariogram is used in this analysis. A gaussian model has been fitted with parameters: 0.95 for range, 0.34 for sill and 0 for nugget. Figure 1 depicts the semivariogram.

The developed gaussian semivariogram has been used to predict d at different points of Chennai. Figure 2 depicts spatial variability of d at Chennai.

A cross validation of the developed OK model has been carried out in this study. The detailed description of the cross-validation methodology is given by Kitanidis (1991). According to the cross validation, the values of Q1 and Q2 are close to 0 and 1 respectively. The procedures for determination of Q1 and Q2 are given by Kitanidis (1991). The developed OK gives Q1=0.01 and Q2=0.974. So, the cross validation indicates the developed OK predicts d reasonable well.

For developing GRNN, the design value of α has been determined by trial and error approach. The future Figure 3 shows the effect of α on Root Mean Square Error (RMSE).

It is observed from Figure 3 that the developed GRNN achieves minimum RMSE at α= 0.71. So, the value of optimum α is 0.71. The value of d has been predicted by using the design value of α for

Figure 1. Semivariogram for developing the OK

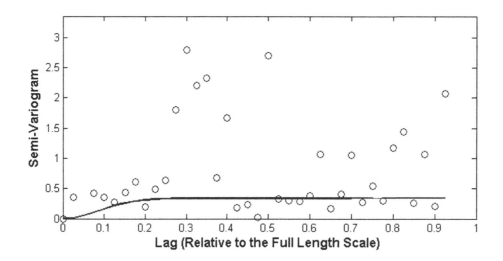

Figure 2. Spatial variability of d using OK

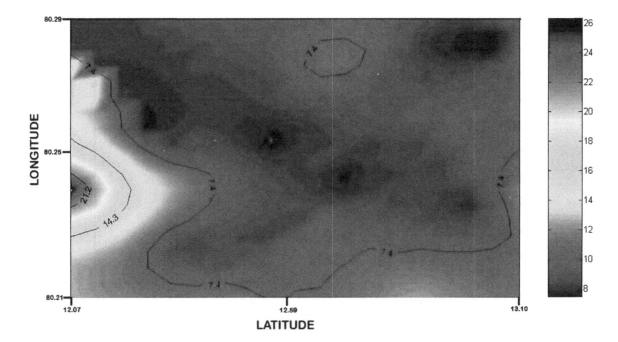

*For a more accurate representation see the electronic version

Figure 3. Effect of α on RMSE for the GRNN

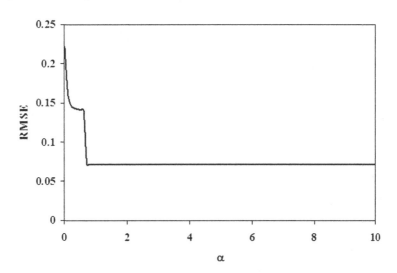

training and testing datasets. Figure 4 illustrates the performance of training and testing datasets of the GRNN model.

The performance of GRNN has been assessed in terms of Coefficient of Correlation (R) value. If the value of R is close to one, then the developed model is good (Samui et al., 2011, Viswanathan & Samui, 2016). As clear from Figure 4 that the value of R is not close to one for the developed GRNN. Therefore, the performance of GRNN is not encouraging.

Figure 4. Performance of the GRNN

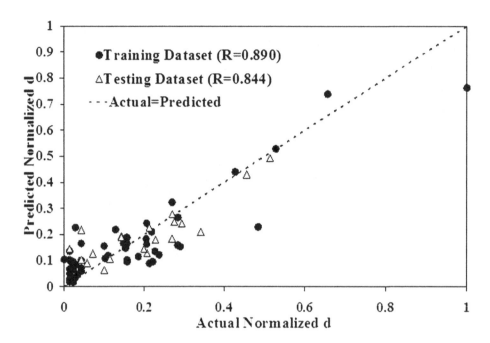

For developing GP, Table 1 shows the different parameters.
The developed GP gives the following equation for prediction of d:

$$d = 0.075\sin\left(\exp\left(L_y + 7.44\right)\right) - 0.103\sin\left(\exp\left(L_x + 2.48\right)\right) + 116.5\cos\left(\left(L_x - L_y\right)\right)$$
$$-6832\cos\left(L_x\left(L_x - L_y\right)\right) - 6831L_x^2 + 6831\cos\left(L_x - L_y\right)\left(L_x\right)^2 + 6716$$

(8)

The above equation has been adopted to determine the performance of GP. Figure 5 shows the performance of GP.

It is observed form the Figure 5 that the value of R is close to one for training as well as testing dataset. Hence, the developed GP proves his ability for prediction of d. Figure 6 shows the spatial variability of d by using the developed GP.

Table 1. Details of the GP

Parameter	Number
Population	700
Generation	100
Mutation Frequency	60
Crossover Frequency	40

Figure 5. Performance of the GP

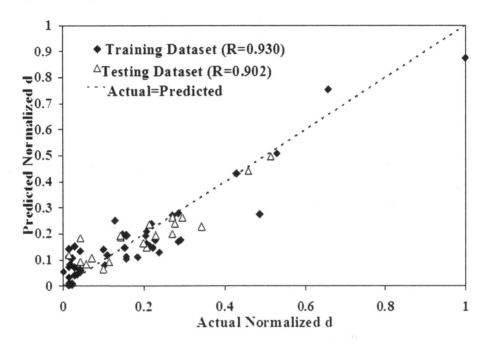

Figure 6. Spatial variability of d by using the GP

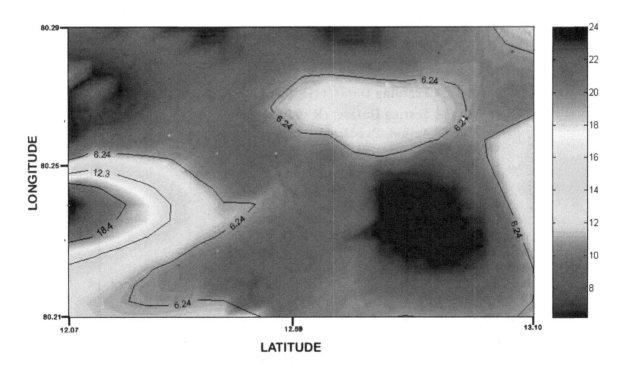

*For a more accurate representation see the electronic version

The performance of MPMR depends on the proper choice of values of ε and width (σ) of radial basis function. The design values of ε and σ have been determined by trial and error approach. Different combinations of ε and σ have been tried to get best performance. The design values of ε and σ are 0.005 and 0.8 respectively. The performance of MPMR has been depicted in Figure 7.

It is clear from Figure 7 that the value of R is close to one for training as well as testing datasets. Therefore, the developed MPMR predicts d reasonable well. A map of spatial variability (see Figure 8) of d has been produced by using the developed MPMR.

A comparative study has been carried out between the developed OK, GRNN, GP and MPMR models. There points have been chosen in Chennai. Table 2 shows the comparison of the above mentioned models.

The performance of OK is not good. The developed GP and MPMR give reasonable performance. The performance of MPMR is slightly better than the GP. The developed GP can take any type of function for developing the final model. So, GP is more flexible than the other models. OK uses statistical parameters of the dataset for prediction. However, MPMR, GP and GRNN do not use any statistical parameter for developing the model.

FUTURE RESEARCH DIRECTIONS

The differences in the dataset ranges tend to the inappropriate outputs. This inadequacy can be resolved by the researchers in the future. Various datasets can be gathered and various technical models can be adopted for predicting the depth of rock at various locations, specifically in the developing areas. It is

Figure 7. Performance of the MPMR

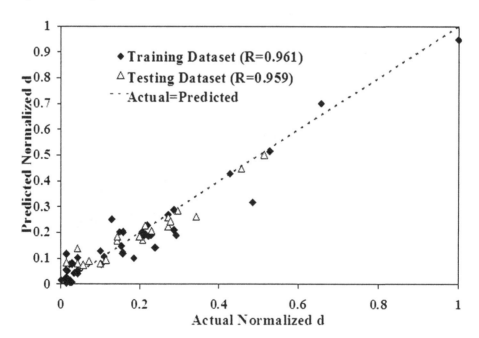

Figure 8. Spatial variability of d by using the MPMR

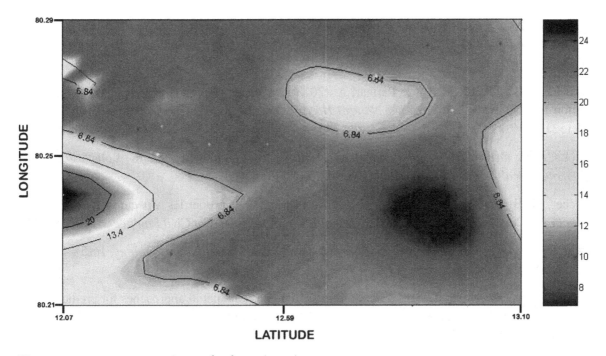

For a more accurate representation see the electronic version

Table 2. Comparison between the developed OK, GRNN, GP and MPMR models

L_x (Degree)	L_y (Degree)	Actual d(m)	Predicted d(m) by OK	Predicted d(m) by GRNN	Predicted d(m) by GP	Predicted d(m) by MPMR
13.0044	80.2625	5.2	7	6.34	4.65	4.90
12.9844	80.2439	12	9.35	13.68	12.85	11.80
13.0231	80.2583	9.5	7.78	11.07	10.24	9.78

also suggested for the scientists and researchers to adopt various techniques like Kalman Filter, Ant Colony Optimization techniques, Fruit fly Optimization algorithm, Adaptive Neuro Fuzzy Inference System, etc for determining at the various crucial and sensitive locations.

CONCLUSION

This article has presented four techniques (Ordinary Kriging, Genetic Programming, Minimax Probability Machine Regression and Generalized Regression Neural Network) for prediction of rock depth (d) at any point in Chennai. The developed models give the spatial variability of rock depth of Chennai. The developed GP gives the equation for prediction of rock depth at Chennai. The comparison between the different methods shows that the developed MPMR gives best performance. The results can provide valuable reference for detecting spatial variability of rock depth in Chennai.

REFERENCES

Alonso, E. E., & Krizek, R. J. (1975). Stochastic formulations of soil properties. *Proceeding of the Second International Conference on Applications of Statistics and Probability in Soil and Structural Engineering,* 15-18.

Anbazhagan, P., Sheikh, M. N., & Parihar, A. (2013). Influence of rock depth on seismic site classification for shallow bedrock regions. *Natural Hazards Review, 14*(2), 108–121. doi:10.1061/(ASCE)NH.1527-6996.0000088

Asaoka, A., & Grivas, D. A. (1982). Spatial variability of the undrained strength of clays. *Journal of the Geotechnical Engineering Division, 108,* 743–745.

Baecher, G. B. (1984). On estimating auto–covariance of soil properties. *Specialty Conference on Probabilistic Mechanics and Structural Reliability, American Society of Civil Engineers, 110,* 214–218.

Baker, R. (1984). Modeling soil variability as a random field. *Mathematical Geology, 16*(5), 435–448. doi:10.1007/BF01886325

Clough, B. J., & Green, E. J. (2013). Comparing spatial and non-spatial approaches for predicting forest soil organic carbon at unsampled locations. *Mathematical and Computational Forestry and Natural Resource Sciences, 5,* 115–125.

Dai, F., Zhou, Q., Lv, Q., Wang, X., & Liu, Q. (2014). Spatial prediction of soil organic matter content integrating artificial neural network and ordinary kriging in Tibetan Plateau. *Ecological Indicators, 45,* 184–194. doi:10.1016/j.ecolind.2014.04.003

Danandeh Mehr, A., Kahya, E., & Olyaie, E. (2013). Stream flow prediction using linear genetic programming in comparison with a neuro-wavelet technique. *Journal of Hydrology (Amsterdam), 505,* 240–249. doi:10.1016/j.jhydrol.2013.10.003

Davis, J. C. (2002). *Statistics and Data Analysis in Geology.* New York: Wiley.

Ding, G., Hu, X., Qiu, W., & Tian, M. (2014). Application of GRNN based on correlation analysis to the real estate valuation. *Journal of Geomatics, 39,* 27–30.

Eldeiry, A. A., & Garcia, L. A. (2012). Evaluating the performance of ordinary kriging in mapping soil salinity. *Journal of Irrigation and Drainage Engineering, 138*(12), 1046–1059. doi:10.1061/(ASCE)IR.1943-4774.0000517

Emadi, M., & Baghernejad, M. (2014). Comparison of spatial interpolation techniques for mapping soil pH and salinity in agricultural coastal areas, northern Iran. *Archives of Agronomy and Soil Science, 60*(9), 1315–1327. doi:10.1080/03650340.2014.880837

Fenton, G. A. (1998). *Random field characterization NGES data.* Paper presented at the Workshop on Probabilistic Site Characterization at NGES, Seattle, WA.

Fenton, G. A. (1999). Random field modeling of CPT data. *Journal of Geotechnical and Geoenvironmental Engineering, 125*(6), 486–498. doi:10.1061/(ASCE)1090-0241(1999)125:6(486)

Gaurav, K., & Hasmat, M. (2016). Generalized Regression Neural Network Based Wind Speed Prediction Model for Western Region of India. *Procedia Computer Science, 93*, 26–32. doi:10.1016/j.procs.2016.07.177

Huang, C. J., Chen, P. W., & Pan, W. T. (2012). Using multi-stage data mining technique to build forecast model for Taiwan stocks. *Neural Computing & Applications, 21*(8), 2057–2063. doi:10.1007/s00521-011-0628-0

Isaaks, E. J., & Srivastava, R. M. (1989). *An introduction to Applied Geostatistics*. New York: Oxford University Press.

Jiang, P., & Jiejie, C. (2016). Displacement prediction of landslide based on generalized regression neural networks with K-fold cross-validation. *Neurocomputing, 198*, 40–47. doi:10.1016/j.neucom.2015.08.118

Kaveh, A., Fahimi-Farzam, M., & Kalateh Ahani, M. (2012). Time-history analysis based optimal design of space trusses: The CMA evolution strategy approach using GRNN and WA. *Structural Engineering & Mechanics, 44*(3), 379–403. doi:10.12989/sem.2012.44.3.379

Kitanidis, P. K. (1991). Orthonormal residuals in geostatistics: Model criticism and parameter estimation. *Mathematical Geology, 23*(5), 741–758. doi:10.1007/BF02082534

Kong, Y., Xing-wei, L., & Zhang, Z. (2009). Minimax probability machine regression for wireless traffic short term forecasting. *Proceedings – 2009 1st UK-India International Workshop on Cognitive Wireless Systems, UKIWCWS*, 1–5. doi:10.1109/UKIWCWS.2009.5749407

Koza, J. R. (1992). *Genetic programming: On the programming of computers by means of natural selection*. MIT Press.

Kulatilake, P. H. S. W. (1989). Probabilistic Potentiometric surface mapping. *Journal of the Geotechnical Engineering Division, 115*(11), 1569–1587. doi:10.1061/(ASCE)0733-9410(1989)115:11(1569)

Kulatilake, P. H. S. W., & Miller, K. M. (1987). A scheme for estimating the spatial variation of soil properties in three dimensions. *Proceedings of the Fifth International Conference on Application of Statistics and Probabilities in Soil and Structural Engineering*, 669–677.

Kurt, H., Maxwell, S., & Halbert, W. (1989). Multilayer feed forward networks are universal approximators. *Neural Networks, 2*(5), 359–366. doi:10.1016/0893-6080(89)90020-8

Lanckriet, G. R. G., Ghaoui, L. E., Bhattacharyya, C., & Jordan, M. I. (2002). A Robust minimax approach to classification. *Journal of Machine Learning Research, 3*, 555–582.

Lumb, P. (1975). Spatial variability of soil properties. *Proceedings Second International Conference on Application of Statistics and Probability in Soil and Structural Engineering*, 397–421.

Matheron, G. (1963). Principles of geostatistics. *Economic Geology and the Bulletin of the Society of Economic Geologists, 58*(8), 1246–1266. doi:10.2113/gsecongeo.58.8.1246

Mehmet, L. K., Balas, C. E., & Dilek, I. K. (2016). Stability assessment of rubble-mound breakwaters using genetic programming. *Ocean Engineering, 111*, 8–12. doi:10.1016/j.oceaneng.2015.10.058

Ozturk, U. A., & Turan, M. E. (2012). Prediction of effects of microstructural phases using generalized regression neural network. *Construction & Building Materials*, *29*, 279–283. doi:10.1016/j.conbuildmat.2011.10.015

Phoon, K. K., & Kulhawy, F. H. (1999). Characterization of geotechnical variability. *Canadian Geotechnical Journal*, *36*(4), 612–624. doi:10.1139/t99-038

Pijush, S., Sarat, D., & Dookie, K. (2011). Uplift capacity of suction caisson in clay using multivariate adaptive regression spline. *Ocean Engineering*, *38*(17–18), 2123–2127.

Roohollah, S. F., Danial, J. A., Masoud, M., & Edy, T. M. (2016). Genetic Programming and gene expression programming for flyrock assessment due to mine blasting. *International Journal of Rock Mechanics and Mining Sciences*, *88*, 254–264. doi:10.1016/j.ijrmms.2016.07.028

Singh, S., & Murthy, T. V. R. (2013). Neural network-based sensor fault accommodation in flight control system. *Journal of Intelligent Systems*, *22*(3), 317–333. doi:10.1515/jisys-2013-0032

Sitharam, T. G., Pijush, S., & Anbazhagan, P. (2008). Spatial variability of rock depth in Bangalore using geostatistical, neural network and support vector machine models. *Geotechnical and Geological Engineering*, *26*(5), 503–517. doi:10.1007/s10706-008-9185-4

Specht, D. F. (1991). A general regression neural network. *IEEE Transactions on Neural Networks*, *2*(6), 568–576. doi:10.1109/72.97934 PMID:18282872

Strohmann, T. R., & Grudic, G. R. (2002). A Formulation for minimax probability machine regression. In Advances in Neural Information Processing Systems (NIPS) 14. Cambridge, MA: MIT Press.

Tabba, M. M., & Yong, R. N. (1981). Mapping and predicting soil properties: Theory. *Journal of the Engineering Mechanics Division*, *107*, 773–793.

Tang, A. M. (1979). Probabilistic evaluation of penetration resistance. *Journal of the Geotechnical Engineering Division*, *105*, 117–191.

Uzielli, M., Vannucchi, G., & Phonn, K. K. (2005). Random field characterisation of stress normalised cone penetration testing parameters. *Geotechnique*, *55*(1), 3–20. doi:10.1680/geot.2005.55.1.3

VanMarcke, E. (1998). *Random Fields: Analysis and Synthesis*. Princeton, NJ: MIT Press.

Vanmarcke, E. H. (1977). Probabilistic modeling of soil profiles. *Journal of the Geotechnical Engineering Division*, *102*, 1247–1265.

Viswanathan, R., & Pijush, S. (2016). Determination of rock depth using artificial intelligence techniques. *Geoscience Frontiers*, *7*(1), 61–66. doi:10.1016/j.gsf.2015.04.002

Wabster, R., & Oliver, M. A. (2001). *Geostatistics for Environmental Scientists*. New York: John Wiley and Sons.

Wu, T. H., & Wong, K. (1981). Probabilistic soil exploration: A case history. *Journal of the Geotechnical Engineering Division*, *107*, 1693–1711.

Yaglom, A. M. (1962). Theory of stationary random functions. Englewood Cliffs, NJ: Prentice-Hall.

Yang, L., & Ju, R. (2014). A DC programming approach for feature selection in the Minimax Probability Machine. *International Journal of Computational Intelligence Systems*, *7*(1), 12–24. doi:10.1080/187 56891.2013.864471

Yu, M., Naqvi, S. M., Rhuma, A., & Chambers, J. (2012). One class boundary method classifiers for application in a video-based fall detection system. *IET Computer Vision*, *6*(2), 90–100. doi:10.1049/ iet-cvi.2011.0046

Zahiri, A., & Azamathulla, H. M. (2014). Comparison between linear genetic programming and M5 tree models to predict flow discharge in compound channels. *Neural Computing & Applications*, *24*(2), 413–420. doi:10.1007/s00521-012-1247-0

Zhang, Q., & Wu, J. (2015). Image super-resolution using windowed ordinary kriging interpolation. *Optics Communications*, *336*, 140–145. doi:10.1016/j.optcom.2014.09.060

Zhou, Z., Wang, Z., & Sun, X. (2013). Face recognition based on optimal kernel minimax probability machine. *Journal of Theoretical and Applied Information Technology*, *48*, 1645–1651.

ADDITIONAL READING

Akbar Asadi, T., Farzin Zokaee, A., Karimi, M., & Okhovat, A. (2015). A novel approach for estimation of solvent activity in polymer solutions using genetic programming. *Calphad*, *51*, 35–41. doi:10.1016/j. calphad.2015.07.005

Alexandre Salles da, C., Luidi, S., & Abilio, L. (2015). Optimality cuts and a branch-and-cut algorithm for the *K*-rooted mini-max spanning forest problem. *European Journal of Operational Research*, *16*(2), 16392–16399.

Ali, M., Petra, S., Fong May Chui, T., & Vladan, B. (2015). Development of a modular streamflow model to quantify runoff contributions from different land uses in tropical urban environments using Genetic Programming. *Journal of Hydrology (Amsterdam)*, *525*, 711–723. doi:10.1016/j.jhydrol.2015.04.032

Ali, N., Pathmanathan, R., & Jay, G. S. (2015). Modelling of upheaval buckling of offshore pipeline buried in clay soil using genetic programming. *Engineering Structures*, *101*(15), 306–317.

Amir, H. G., & David, A. R. (2015). Assessment of artificial neural network and genetic programming as predictive tools. *Advances in Engineering Software*, *88*, 63–72. doi:10.1016/j.advengsoft.2015.05.007

Amir Hossein, Z., & Hossein, B. (2015). Application of artificial neural network and genetic programming models for estimating the longitudinal velocity field in open channel junctions. *Flow Measurement and Instrumentation*, *41*, 81–89. doi:10.1016/j.flowmeasinst.2014.10.011

Ardakani, M., Ahmed, S., Ghazal, S., Gerard, E., Moises, G., & Antonio, E. (2016). Imputation of Missing Data with Ordinary Kriging for Enhancing Fault Detection and Diagnosis. *Computer Aided Chemical Engineering*, *38*, 1377–1382. doi:10.1016/B978-0-444-63428-3.50234-4

Carmona, C. J., Ruiz-Rodado, V., Del Jesus, M. J., Weber, A., Grootveld, M., González, P., & Elizondo, D. (2015). A fuzzy genetic programming-based algorithm for subgroup discovery and the application to one problem of pathogenesis of acute sore throat conditions in humans. *Information Sciences*, *20*, 180–197. doi:10.1016/j.ins.2014.11.030

Castro, A., Pérez, J. L., Rabuñal, J. R., & Iglesias, R. (2015). Genetic programming and floating boom performance. *Ocean Engineering*, *104*, 310–318. doi:10.1016/j.oceaneng.2015.05.023

Cheng-Shin, J., Shih-Kai, C., & Ya-Ting, C. (2016). Spatial estimation of the thickness of low permeability topsoil materials by using a combined ordinary-indicator kriging approach with multiple thresholds. *Engineering Geology*, *207*, 56–65. doi:10.1016/j.enggeo.2016.04.008

Chih-Ming, H., Fu-Sheng, C., & Chiung-Hsing, C. (2014). Optimal control for variable-speed wind generation systems using General Regression Neural Network. *International Journal of Electrical Power & Energy Systems*, *60*, 14–23. doi:10.1016/j.ijepes.2014.02.015

Daya Shankar, P., Indranil, P., Saptarshi, D., James, J. L., & Witold, K. (2015). Multi-gene genetic programming based predictive models for municipal solid waste gasification in a fluidized bed gasifier. *Bioresource Technology*, *179*, 524–533. doi:10.1016/j.biortech.2014.12.048 PMID:25576988

Dilek İmren, K., & Mehmet Levent, K. (2015). A genetic programming-based QSPR model for predicting solubility parameters of polymers. *Chemometrics and Intelligent Laboratory Systems*, *144*, 122–127. doi:10.1016/j.chemolab.2015.04.005

Emamgolizadeh, S., Bateni, S. M., Shahsavani, D., Ashrafi, T., & Ghorbani, H. (2015). Estimation of soil cation exchange capacity using Genetic Expression Programming (GEP) and Multivariate Adaptive Regression Splines (MARS). *Journal of Hydrology (Amsterdam)*, *3*, 1590–1600. doi:10.1016/j.jhydrol.2015.08.025

Frits Byron, S., Selen, C., Cem, S., Hariprasad, J. S., Gene, E. K., & Haijing, G. (2016). Estimation of percentiles using the Kriging method for uncertainty propagation. *Computers & Chemical Engineering*, *93*(4), 143–159.

Garg, A., & Siu Lee Lam, J. (2015). Improving environmental sustainability by formulation of generalized power consumption models using an ensemble based multi-gene genetic programming approach. *Journal of Cleaner Production*, *1*, 246–263. doi:10.1016/j.jclepro.2015.04.068

Gaurav, K., & Hasmat, M. (2016). Generalized Regression Neural Network Based Wind Speed Prediction Model for Western Region of India. *Procedia Computer Science*, *93*, 26–32. doi:10.1016/j.procs.2016.07.177

Hadi, S., & Sirous, S. (2015). Adiabatic reactor network synthesis using coupled genetic algorithm with quasi linear programming method. *Chemical Engineering Science*, *137*(1), 601–612.

Haydar, D., & Yasemin, K. A. (2015). New horizontal global solar radiation estimation models for Turkey based on robust coplot supported genetic programming technique. *Energy Conversion and Management*, *106*, 1013–1023. doi:10.1016/j.enconman.2015.10.038

Hon-lun, Y., Hongqin, F., & Yat-hung, C. (2014). Predicting the maintenance cost of construction equipment: Comparison between general regression neural network and Box–Jenkins time series models. *Automation in Construction, 38*, 30–38. doi:10.1016/j.autcon.2013.10.024

Hugo Jair, E., Mauricio, A. G. L., Morales-Reyes, A., Mario, G., Montes-y-Gómez, M., Eduardo, F. M., & Martínez Carranza, J. (2015). Term-weighting learning via genetic programming for text classification. *Knowledge-Based Systems, 83*, 176–189. doi:10.1016/j.knosys.2015.03.025

Jinna, L., Hongping, H., & Yanping, B. (2015). Generalized radial basis function neural network based on an improved dynamic particle swarm optimization and Ada Boost algorithm. *Neurocomputing, 152*, 305–315. doi:10.1016/j.neucom.2014.10.065

Kattan, A., Fatima, S., & Arif, M. (2015, April). learning framework based on genetic programming. *Information Sciences, 301*, 99–123. doi:10.1016/j.ins.2014.12.054

Kuo, R. J., Lee, Y. H., Ferani, E. Z., & Tien, F. C. (2015). Solving bi-level linear programming problem through hybrid of immune genetic algorithm and particle swarm optimization algorithm. *Applied Mathematics and Computation, 1*, 1013–1026. doi:10.1016/j.amc.2015.06.025

Lorena Silva, B., & Henri, P. (2015). Using genetic programming and simulation to learn how to dynamically adapt the number of cards in reactive pull systems. *Expert Systems with Applications, 42*(6), 3129–3141. doi:10.1016/j.eswa.2014.11.052

Mauro, C., Leonardo, T., Leonardo, V., & Popovič, A. (2015). Prediction of energy performance of residential buildings: A genetic programming approach. *Energy and Building, 102*, 67–74. doi:10.1016/j.enbuild.2015.05.013

Mauro, C., Roberto, H., & Leonardo, V. (2015). A geometric semantic genetic programming system for the electoral redistricting problem. *Neurocomputing, 154*, 200–207. doi:10.1016/j.neucom.2014.12.003

Nouredine, D., Jalal, F., Foudel, B., Kamel, B., El-adj, S., & Mohammed, F. (2014). Seismic noise filtering based on Generalized Regression Neural Networks. *Computers & Geosciences, 69*, 1–9. doi:10.1016/j.cageo.2014.04.007

Otis, S., & Lauren, B. (2015). Genetic programming and frequent itemset mining to identify feature selection patterns of iEEG and fMRI epilepsy data. *Engineering Applications of Artificial Intelligence, 39*, 198–214. doi:10.1016/j.engappai.2014.12.008 PMID:25580059

Ping, J., & Jiejie, C. (2016). Displacement prediction of landslide based on generalized regression neural networks with K-fold cross-validation. *Neurocomputing, 198*, 40–47. doi:10.1016/j.neucom.2015.08.118

Purva, G., Sanket, B., Renu, V., Amruta, T., & Sanjeev, S. T. (2015). Genetic programming based quantitative structure–retention relationships for the prediction of Kovats retention indices. *Journal of Chromatography. A, 13*, 98–109. PMID:26460075

Qianying, Z., & Jitao, W. (2015). Image super-resolution using windowed ordinary Kriging interpolation. *Optics Communications, 336*, 140–145. doi:10.1016/j.optcom.2014.09.060

Reisi-Nafchi, M., & Ghasem, M. (2015). A hybrid genetic and linear programming algorithm for two-agent order acceptance and scheduling problem. *Applied Soft Computing*, *33*, 37–47. doi:10.1016/j.asoc.2015.04.027

Saeid, R. D. (2015). Prediction of blast-induced ground vibrations via genetic programming. *International Journal of Mining Science and Technology*, *25*(6), 1011–1015. doi:10.1016/j.ijmst.2015.09.020

Somayeh, M., Akbar, E., & Hossein Fazel Zarandi, M. (2015). MGP-INTACTSKY: Multitree Genetic Programming-based learning of INTerpretable and ACcurate TSK sYstems for dynamic portfolio trading. *Applied Soft Computing*, *34*, 449–462. doi:10.1016/j.asoc.2015.05.021

Viktor, M., Robert, H., & Hafiz, H. (2015). Return predictability and the wisdom of crowds: Genetic Programming trading algorithms, the Marginal Trader Hypothesis and the Hayek Hypothesis. *Journal of International Financial Markets, Institutions and Money*, *37*, 85–98. doi:10.1016/j.intfin.2015.02.009

Wanli, X., Rui, G., Eva, P., & Sean, G. (2015). Participation-based student final performance prediction model through interpretable Genetic Programming: Integrating learning analytics, educational data mining and theory. *Computers in Human Behavior*, *47*, 168–181. doi:10.1016/j.chb.2014.09.034

Xiaojun, W., Mingshuang, Y., Zhizhong, M., & Ping, Y. (2014). Tree-Structure Ensemble General Regression Neural Networks applied to predict the molten steel temperature in Ladle Furnace. *Advanced Engineering Informatics*, *30*(3), 368–375.

Xuyuan, L., Aaron, C. Z., & Holger, R. M. (2014). Selection of smoothing parameter estimators for general regression neural networks – Applications to hydrological and water resources modelling. *Environmental Modelling & Software*, *59*, 162–186. doi:10.1016/j.envsoft.2014.05.010

Zhuo, D., & Xiaoting, Z. (2015). Design of close-loop supply chain network under uncertainty using hybrid genetic algorithm: A fuzzy and chance-constrained programming model. *Computers & Industrial Engineering*, *88*, 444–457. doi:10.1016/j.cie.2015.08.004

KEY TERMS AND DEFINITIONS

Generalized Regression Neural Network: Generalized Regression Neural Network (GRNN) falls under probabilistic neural network category, which is utilized for function approximation.

Genetic Programming: Genetic Programming (GP) is a technique whereby computer programs are encoded as a set of genes that are then modified (evolved) using an evolutionary algorithm.

Minimax Probability Machine Regression: Minimax Probability Machine Regression (MPMR) is defined as the process of maximizing the minimum probability of regression model for all possible distribution with known mean and covariance matrix.

Ordinary Kriging: Ordinary Kriging is the type of kriging method in which the weights of the values sum to unity. It uses an average of a subset of neighboring points to produce a particular interpolation point.

Prediction: Prediction is defined as the action of forecasting something.

Rock Depth: Rock Depth is defined as the distance from top of the surface to the bottom of the rock.

Spatial Variability: Spatial variability occurs when a quantity that is measured at different spatial locations exhibits values that differ across the locations. Spatial variability can be assessed using spatial descriptive statistics such as the range.

Compilation of References

Aarts, E. H. L., Korst, J. H. M., & van Laarhoven, P. J. M. (1997). Simulated annealing. In E. H. L. Aarts & J. K. Lenstra (Eds.), *Local Search in Combinatorial Optimization* (pp. 91–120). Chichester, UK: Wiley-Interscience.

Aarts, E., Korst, J., & Michiels, W. (2014). Simulated annealing. In E. K. Burke & G. Kendall (Eds.), *Search methodologies: Introductory tutorials in optimization and decision support techniques* (2nd ed.). Boston, MA: Springer US; doi:10.1007/978-1-4614-6940-7_10

Abboud, N., Sakawa, M., & Inuiguchi, M. (1998). School scheduling using threshold accepting. *Cybernetics and Systems*, *29*(6), 593–611. doi:10.1080/019697298125533

Abdullah, L., & Jamal, J. (2010). Centroid-point of ranking fuzzy numbers and its application to health related quality of life indicators. *International Journal on Computer Science and Engineering*, *2*(08), 2773–2777.

Abernathy, W. J., & Corcoran, J. E. (1983). Relearning from the old masters: Lessons of the American system of manufacturing. *Journal of Operation Management*, 155-167.

Abu-Mustafa, Y. S. (1995). Financial application of learning from hints. *Advances in Neural Information Processing Systems*, *7*, 411–418.

Acosta, F. M. A. (1995). Radial Basis Functions and Related Models: An Overview. *Signal Processing*, *45*(1), 37–58. doi:10.1016/0165-1684(95)00041-B

Agarwal, P., & Mehta, S. (2014). Nature-Inspired Algorithms: State-of-Art, Problems and Prospects. *Nature*, *100*(14).

Ahmad, A., & Dey, L. (2005). A feature selection technique for classificatory analysis. *Pattern Recognition Letters*, *26*(1), 43–56. doi:10.1016/j.patrec.2004.08.015

Ahuja, R. K., Orlin, J. B., & Tiwari, A. (2000). A greedy genetic algorithm for the quadratic assignment problem. *Computers & Operations Research*, *27*(10), 917–934. doi:10.1016/S0305-0548(99)00067-2

Akadi, A. E., Amine, A., Ouardighi, A. E., & Aboutajdine, D. (2009). Feature selection for Genomic data bycombining filter and wrapper approaches. *INFOCMP Journal of Computer Science, 8*(4), 28-36.

Aladag, C. H. (2011). A new architecture selection method based on tabu search for artificial neural networks. *Expert Systems with Applications*, *38*(4), 3287–3293. doi:10.1016/j.eswa.2010.08.114

Al-Askary, O. (2006). *Coding and iterative decoding of concatenated multi-level codes for the Rayleigh fading channel* (PhD thesis). KTH Information and Communication Technology, Stockholm, Sweden.

Alatas, B. (2011). ACROA: Artificial Chemical Reaction Optimization Algorithm for global optimization. *Expert Systems with Applications*, *38*(10), 13170–13180. doi:10.1016/j.eswa.2011.04.126

Alatas, B. (2012). A novel chemistry based metaheuristic optimization method for mining of classification rules. *Expert Systems with Applications, 39*(12), 11080–11088. doi:10.1016/j.eswa.2012.03.066

Alba, E., Garcia-Nieto, J., Taheri, J., & Zomaya, A. Y. (2008). New research in Nature Inspired Algorithms for Mobility Management in GSM Networks. Lecture Notes in Computer Science, 4974, 1-10.

Albeahdili, H. M., Han, T., & Islam, N. E. (2015). Hybrid Algorithm for the Optimization of Training Convolutional Neural Network. *International Journal of Advanced Computer Science & Applications, 1*(6), 79–85.

Alexander, S. S. (1961, May). Price Movements in Speculative Markets: Trends or Random Walks. *Industrial Management Review*, 7-26.

Alexandridis, A. (2013). RBF network training using a non symmetric partition of the input space and particle swarm optimization. *IEEE Transactions on Neural Networks and Learning Systems, 24*(2), 219–230. doi:10.1109/TNNLS.2012.2227794 PMID:24808277

Alizadeh, A. A., Eisen, M. B., Davis, R. E., Ma, C., Lossos, I. S., Rosenwald, A., & Staudt, L. M. et al. (2000). Distinct types of diffuse large B-cell lymphoma identified by gene expression profiling. *Nature, 403*(6769), 503–511. doi:10.1038/35000501 PMID:10676951

Alizamir, S., Rebennack, S., & Pardalos, P. M. (2008). Improving the Neighborhood Selection Strategy in Simulated Annealing using the Optimal Stopping Problem. In C. M. Tan (Ed.), Simulated Annealing (pp. 363–382). Rijeka, Croatia: InTech. doi:10.5772/5571

Allahyari, S., Salari, M., & Vigo, D. (2015). A hybrid metaheuristic algorithm for the multi-depot covering tour vehicle routing problem. *European Journal of Operational Research, 242*(3), 756–768. doi:10.1016/j.ejor.2014.10.048

Almeida-Luz, S. M., Vega-Rodríguez, M. A., Gómez-Púlido, J. A., & Sánchez-Pérez, J. M. (2011). Differential Evolution for Solving the Mobile Location Management. *Applied Soft Computing, 11*(1), 410–427. doi:10.1016/j.asoc.2009.11.031

Alonso, E. E., & Krizek, R. J. (1975). Stochastic formulations of soil properties. *Proceeding of the Second International Conference on Applications of Statistics and Probability in Soil and Structural Engineering*, 15-18.

Alrefaei, M. H., & Diabat, A. H. (2009). A simulated annealing technique for multi-objective simulation optimization. *Applied Mathematics and Computation, 215*(8), 3029–3035. doi:10.1016/j.amc.2009.09.051

Althöfer, I., & Koschnick, K. (1991). On the convergence of Threshold Accepting. *Applied Mathematics & Optimization, 24*(1), 183–195. doi:10.1007/BF01447741

Al-zoubaidy, L. M. (2006). Efficient genetics algorithms for Arabic handwritten characters recognition. *Advances in Intelligent and Soft Computing, Springer, 36*, 3–14. doi:10.1007/978-3-540-36266-1_1

Anbazhagan, P., Sheikh, M. N., & Parihar, A. (2013). Influence of rock depth on seismic site classification for shallow bedrock regions. *Natural Hazards Review, 14*(2), 108–121. doi:10.1061/(ASCE)NH.1527-6996.0000088

An, G. (1996). The effect of adding noise during back propagation training on generalization performance. *Neural Computation, 7*(3), 643–674. doi:10.1162/neco.1996.8.3.643

Anish, C. M., & Majhi, B. (2015). Hybrid nonlinear adaptive scheme for stock market prediction using feedback FLANN and factor analysis. *Journal of the Korean Statistical Society*.

Anish, C. M., & Majhi, B. (2015a). Multiobjective optimization based adaptive models with fuzzy decision making for stock market forecasting. *Neurocomputing, 167*, 502–511. doi:10.1016/j.neucom.2015.04.044

Anish, C. M., & Majhi, B. (2015b). An ensemble model for net asset value prediction. *Proceeding of IEEE International Conference on Power, Communication and information technology (PCITC)*, 392-396. doi:10.1109/PCITC.2015.7438197

Anish, C. M., & Majhi, B. (2016).Prediction of mutual fund net asset value using low complexity feedback neural network. *Proceeding of IEEE International Conference on Current Trends in advanced Computing (ICCTAC)*, 1-5. doi:10.1109/ICCTAC.2016.7567345

Aote, S. S., Raghuwanshi, M. M., & Malik, L. (2013). A brief review on particle swarm optimization: Limitations & future directions. *International Journal on Computer Science and Engineering*, *14*(1), 196–200.

Araújo, R. A. (2010). Swarm-based translation-invariant morphological prediction method for financial time series forecasting. *Information Science*, *180*, 4784–4805. doi:10.1016/j.ins.2010.08.037

Arbnor, I., & Bjerke, B. (2008). *Methodology for creating business knowledge*. Sage Publications Ltd.

Areibi, S., & Yang, Z. (2004). Effective Memetic Algorithms for VLSI Design Automation = Genetic Algorithms + Local Search + Multi- Level Clustering. *Evolutionary Computation*, *12*(3), 327–353. doi:10.1162/1063656041774947 PMID:15355604

Ari, S., Das, M. K., & Chacko, A. (2013, July). ECG signal enhancement using S-Transform. *Computers in Biology and Medicine*, *43*(6), 649–660. doi:10.1016/j.compbiomed.2013.02.015 PMID:23668340

Armony, M., Klincewicz, J. G., Luss, H., & Rosenwein, M. B. (2000). Design of stacked self-healing rings using a genetic algorithm. *Journal of Heuristics*, *6*(1), 85–105. doi:10.1023/A:1009665726946

Aruna, S., Nandakishore, & Rajagopalan, L. V. S. P. (2012). A Hybrid Feature Selection Method based on IGSBFS and Naïve Bayes for the Diagnosis of Erythemato - Squamous Diseases. *International Journal of Computer Applications, 41*(7).

Asaoka, A., & Grivas, D. A. (1982). Spatial variability of the undrained strength of clays. *Journal of the Geotechnical Engineering Division*, *108*, 743–745.

Aseem, M.A., Hassan, I.S., & Amin, M.N. (2016, November). A quality guaranteed robust image watermarking optimization with Artificial Bee Colony. In *Expert Systems with Applications*. Elsevier.

Atsalakis, G. S., & Valavanis, K. P. (2009a). Surveying stock market forecasting techniques – Part II: Soft computing methods. *Expert Systems with Applications*, *36*(3), 5932–5941. doi:10.1016/j.eswa.2008.07.006

Atsalakis, G. S., & Valavanis, K. P. (2009b). Forecasting stock market short term trends using a neuro-fuzzy based methodology. *Expert Systems with Applications*, *36*(7), 10696–10707. doi:10.1016/j.eswa.2009.02.043

Atta-ur-Rahman, & Qureshi, I.M. (2013). Optimum Resource Allocation in OFDM Systems using FRBS and Particle Swarm Optimization. Nature and Biologically Inspired Computing (NaBIC'13), 174-180.

Atta-ur-Rahman, Qureshi, I.M., Malik, A.N., & Naseem, M.T. (2014). A Real Time Adaptive Resource Allocation Scheme for OFDM Systems using GRBF-Neural Networks and Fuzzy Rule Base System. *International Arab Journal of Information Technology, 11*(6), 593-601. http://ccis2k.org/iajit/PDF/vol.11,no.6/6305.pdf

Atta-ur-Rahman, Qureshi, I.M., Muzaffar, M.Z., & Naseem, M.T. (2012). A Fuzzy Rule Base Aided Rate Enhancement Scheme for OFDM Systems. *IEEE Conference on Emerging Technologies (ICET'12), 151-156.

Atta-ur-Rahman, Qureshi, I.M., Muzaffar, M.Z., & Naseem, M.T. (2012). Adaptive Resource Allocation for OFDM Systems using Fuzzy Rule Base System Water-filling Principle and Product Codes. *12th International Conference on Intelligent Systems Design and Applications (ISDA'12)*, 811-816.

Atta-ur-Rahman, Qureshi, I.M., Muzaffar, M.Z., & Naseem, M.T. (2012). FRBS based Rate Enhancement Scheme for OFDM Systems using Product Codes. *IEEE 15th International Multi-topic Conference (INMIC'12)*, 339-344.

Atta-ur-Rahman, Qureshi, I.M., Naseem, M.T., & Muzaffar, M.Z. (2012). A GA-FRBS based Rate Enhancement Scheme for OFDM based Hyperlans. *10th IEEE International Conference on Frontiers of Information Technology (FIT'12)*, 153-158.

Atta-ur-Rahman, Qureshi, I.M., Naseem, M.T., & Muzaffar, M.Z. (2013). An Intelligent Link Adaptation Scheme for OFDM based Hyperlans. *5th International Conference of SoftComputing for Pattern Recognition (SoCPaR'13)*, 361-366.

Atta-ur-Rahman, Qureshi, I.M., Salam, M.H., & Muzaffar, M. Z. (2013). Adaptive Communication using Soft-computing Techniques. *5th International Conference of Soft-Computing for Pattern Recognition (SoCPaR'13)*, 19-24.

Atta-ur-Rahman, Qureshi, I.M., Salam, M.H., & Naseem, M.T. (2013). Efficient Link Adaptation in OFDM Systems using a Hybrid Intelligent Technique. *13th International Conference on Hybrid Intelligent Systems (HIS'13)*, 12-17.

Atta-ur-Rahman. (2011, December). Adaptive Coding and Modulation for OFDM Systems using Product Codes and Fuzzy Rule Base System. *International Journal of Computers and Applications*, *35*(4), 41–48.

Atta-ur-Rahman. (2012). A Fuzzy Rule Base Assisted Adaptive Coding and Modulation Scheme for OFDM Systems. *J. Basic Appl. Sci. Res.*, *2*(5), 4843–4853.

Atta-ur-Rahman. (2012). Adaptive Resource Allocation in OFDM Systems using GA and Fuzzy Rule Base System. *World Applied Sciences Journal*, *18*(6), 836–844. doi:10.5829/idosi.wasj.2012.18.06.906

Atta-ur-Rahman. (2013). Comparison of Coding Schemes over FRBS aided AOFDM Systems. *Journal of Networking and Innovative Computing*, *1*, 183–193.

Atta-ur-Rahman. (2014). Dynamic Resource allocation for OFDM Systems using Differential Evolution and Fuzzy Rule Base System. *Journal of Intelligent & Fuzzy Systems*, *26*(4), 2035–2046.

Atta-ur-Rahman. (2016). QoS and Rate Enhancement in DVB-S2 using Fuzzy Rule Base System. *Journal of Intelligent & Fuzzy Systems*, *30*(1), 801–810.

Atta-ur-Rahman. (2017). Applications of Softcomputing in Adaptive Communication. *International Journal Control Theory and Applications*, *10*(18), 81–93.

Ayhan, M. B. (2013). Fuzzy AHP Approach for Supplier Selection Problem: A Case Study in a Gearmotor Company. *International Journal of Managing Value and Supply Chains*, *4*(3), 11–23. doi:10.5121/ijmvsc.2013.4302

Babu, G. S., & Suresh, S. (2013). Sequential projection-based meta cognitive learning in a radial basis function network for classification problems. *IEEE Transactions on Neural Networks*, *24*(2), 194–206. doi:10.1109/TNNLS.2012.2226748 PMID:24808275

Badrinath & Gupta. (2011, October). A stockwell transform based palm-print recognition. *Applied Soft Computing*, *11*(7), 4267-4281.

Baecher, G. B. (1984). On estimating auto–covariance of soil properties. *Specialty Conference on Probabilistic Mechanics and Structural Reliability, American Society of Civil Engineers, 110*, 214–218.

Bai, Q. (2010). Analysis of particle swarm optimization algorithm. *Computer and Information Science, 3*(1), 180.

Baker, R. (1984). Modeling soil variability as a random field. *Mathematical Geology*, *16*(5), 435–448. doi:10.1007/BF01886325

Baldi, P., & Hatfield, G. W. (2002). *DNA Microarrays and Gene Expression.* Cambridge Univ. Press.

Banati, H., & Bajaj, M. (2011). Fire fly based feature selection approach. *International Journal of Computer Science Issues*, *8*(4), 473–480.

Banks, A., Vincent, J., & Anyakoha, C. (2008). A review of particle swarm optimization. Part II: Hybridisation, combinatorial, multicriteria and constrained optimization, and indicative applications. *Natural Computing*, *7*(1), 109–124. doi:10.1007/s11047-007-9050-z

Barbalho, H., Rosseti, I., Martins, S. L., & Plastino, A. (2013). A hybrid data mining GRASP with path-relinking. *Computers & Operations Research*, *40*(12), 3159–3173. doi:10.1016/j.cor.2012.02.022

Barricelli, N.A. (1954). Esempi numerici di processi di evoluzione. *Methodos*, 45–68.

Basheer, I. A., & Hajmeer, M. (2000). Artificial neural networks: Fundamentals, computing, design, and application. *Journal of Microbiological Methods*, *43*(1), 3–31. doi:10.1016/S0167-7012(00)00201-3 PMID:11084225

Basturk, B., & Karaboga, D. (2006, May). An Artificial Bee Colony (ABC) Algorithm for Numeric function Optimization. *IEEE Swarm Intelligence Symposium*, Indianapolis, IN.

Baykasoglu, A., Yunusoglu, M. G., & Özsoydan, F. B. (2015). A GRASP based solution approach to solve cardinality constrained portfolio optimization problems. *Computers & Industrial Engineering*, *90*, 339–351. doi:10.1016/j.cie.2015.10.009

Behera, Das, & Subudhi. (2014, October). Functional link artificial neural network applied to active noise control of a mixture of tonal and chaotic noise. *Applied Soft Computing, 23*, 51-60.

Behera, Dash, & Biswal. (2010, June). Power quality time series data mining using S-transform and fuzz expert system. *Applied Soft Computing, 10*(3), 945-955.

Bellman, R., & Zadeh, L. A. (1970). Decision-making in a fuzzy environment. *Management Science*, *17B*(4), 141–164. doi:10.1287/mnsc.17.4.B141

Bender, A. D., Pyle III, E. B., Westlake, W. J., & Douglas, B. (1976). Simulation of R&D investment strategies. *OMEGA, International Journal of Management Science*, 67-77.

Bhattacharjee, A., Richards, W. G., Staunton, J., Li, C., Monti, S., Vasa, P., & Meyerson, M. et al. (2001). Classification of human lung carcinomas by mRNA expression profiling reveals distinct adenocarcinomasubclasses, PNAS. *The National Academy of Sciences, USA*, *98*(24), 13790–13795. doi:10.1073/pnas.191502998 PMID:11707567

Bhattacharya, U., Rao, J. R., & Tiwari, R. N. (1992). Fuzzy multi-criteria facility location problem. *Fuzzy Sets and Systems*, *51*(3), 277–287. doi:10.1016/0165-0114(92)90018-Y

Bhunia, A. K., & Samanta, S. S. (2014). A study of interval metric and its application in multi-objective optimization with interval objectives. *Computers & Industrial Engineering*, *74*, 169–178. doi:10.1016/j.cie.2014.05.014

Bilyk, A., Mönch, L., & Almeder, C. (2014). Scheduling jobs with ready times and precedence constraints on parallel batch machines using metaheuristics. *Computers & Industrial Engineering*, *78*, 175–185. doi:10.1016/j.cie.2014.10.008

Binitha, S., & Sathya, S. S. (2012). A survey of bio inspired optimization algorithms. *International Journal of Soft Computing and Engineering*, *2*(2), 137–151.

Bishop, C. M. (1995). *Neural Networks for Pattern Recognition*. Clarendon Press.

Bishop, J. M. (1989). Stochastic Searching Networks. *Proceedings of the 1st IEE International Conference on Artificial Neural Networks*, 329–331.

Blum, C., & Merkle, D. (Eds.). (2008). *Swarm Intelligence – Introduction and Applications, Natural Computing*. Berlin: Springer.

Blum, Ch., & Roli, A. (2003). Metaheuristics in combinatorial optimization: Overview and conceptual comparison. *ACM Computing Surveys*, *35*(3), 268–308. doi:10.1145/937503.937505

Bockelmann, C., W¨ubben, D., & Kammeyer, K. D. (2009). Rate Enhancement of BICM-OFDM with Adaptive Coded Modulation via a Bisection approach. *IEEE 10th Workshop on Signal Processing Advances in Wireless Communications, SPAWC '09*, 658-662.

Bodnarova, A., Bennamoun, M., & Latham, S. (2002). Optimal gabor filters for textile flaw detection. *Pattern Recognition*, *35*(12), 2973–2991. doi:10.1016/S0031-3203(02)00017-1

Bonabeau, E., Dorigo, M., & Theraulaz, G. (1999). *Swarm Intelligence: From Natural to Artificial Systems*. Oxford University Press.

Booz, E. G., Hamilton, C. L., & Allen, J. L. (1968). *Management of new products*. Chicago: Booz, Allen & Hamilton.

Bors, A. G. (2001). Introduction of the Radial Basis Function Networks. *Online Symposium for Electronics Engineers*, *1*(1), 1-7.

Bors, A. G., & Pitas, I. (1996). Median Radial Basis Functions Neural Network. *IEEE Transactions on Neural Networks*, *7*(6), 1351–1364. doi:10.1109/72.548164 PMID:18263530

Bors, A. G., & Pitas, I. (1999). Object Classification in 3-D images using Alpha-trimmed Mean Radial Basis Function Network. *IEEE Transactions on Image Processing*, *8*(12), 1744–1756. doi:10.1109/83.806620 PMID:18267451

Bourgron, L. (2007). Staffing approach and condition for collective learning in project teams: The case of new product development projects. *International Journal of Project Management*, *25*(4), 413–422. doi:10.1016/j.ijproman.2007.01.014

Bresina, J. L. (1996). Heuristic-biased stochastic sampling. AAAI-96, 271-278.

Brito, J., Martínez, F., Moreno, J., & Verdegay, J. (2015). An aco hybrid metaheuristic for closeopen vehicle routing problems with time windows and fuzzy constraints. *Applied Soft Computing*, *32*, 154–163. doi:10.1016/j.asoc.2015.03.026

Broomhead, & Lowe, D. D. (1998). Multivariable functional interpolation and adaptive networks. *Complex System, 2*, 321-355.

Broomhead, D. S., & Lowe, D. (1988). Multi-variable Functional Interpolation and Adaptive Networks. *Complex Systems*, *2*, 321–355.

Brzakovic, D., & Vujovic, N. (1996). Desiging defect classification systems: A case study. *Pattern Recognition*, *29*(8), 1401–1419. doi:10.1016/0031-3203(95)00166-2

Buckley, J. J. (1985). Fuzzy hierarchical analysis. *Fuzzy Sets and Systems*, *17*(1), 233–247. doi:10.1016/0165-0114(85)90090-9

Bu, H., Wang, J., & Huang, X. (2009). Fabric defect detection based on multiple fractal features and support vector data description. *Engineering Applications of Artificial Intelligence*, *22*(2), 224–235. doi:10.1016/j.engappai.2008.05.006

Buhmann, M. D., & Ron, A. (1994). Radial Basis Functions: Lp-Approximation Orders with Scattered Centers in Wavelets, Images, and Surface Fitting. A. K. Peters.

Buhmann, M. D. (1990). Multivariate Cardinal Interpolation with Radial Basis functions. *Constructive Approximation*, *6*(3), 225–255. doi:10.1007/BF01890410

Buhmann, M. D. (1993a). On Quasi-Interpolation with Radial Basis Functions. *Journal of Approximation Theory, 72*(1), 103–130. doi:10.1006/jath.1993.1009

Buhmann, M. D. (1993b). New Developments in the Theory of Radial Basis Function Interpolation. In K. Jette & F. Utreras (Eds.), *Multivariate Approximation: From CAGD to Wavelets* (pp. 35–75). Singapore: World Scientific Publishing. doi:10.1142/9789814503754_0003

Buhmann, M. D. (1995). Pre-Wavelet on Scattered Knots and from Radial Function Spaces: A Review. In R. R. Martin (Eds.), *6th IMA Conference on the Mathematics of Surfaces*. Clarendon Press.

Buhmann, M. D. (1998). Radial Functions on Compact Support. *Proceedings of the Edinburgh Mathematical Society, 41*(1), 33–46. doi:10.1017/S0013091500019416

Buhmann, M. D. (2000). Radial Basis Functions. *Acta Numerica, Cambridge University Press, 9*(0), 1–38. doi:10.1017/S0962492900000015

Buhmann, M. D. (2003). *Radial Basis Functions: Theory and Implementations.12*. Cambridge University Press. doi:10.1017/CBO9780511543241

Buhmann, M. D., & Chui, C. K. (1993). A Note on the Local Stability of Translates of Radial Basis Functions. *Journal of Approximation Theory, 74*(1), 36–40. doi:10.1006/jath.1993.1051

Buhmann, M. D., & Mehaute, A. L. (1995). Knot Removal with Radial Basis Function Interpolation. *Comptes Rendus de l'Académie des Sciences. Série 1, Mathématique, 320*, 501–506.

Burke, E. K., & Bykov, Y. (2016). An Adaptive Flex-Deluge Approach to University Exam Timetabling. *INFORMS Journal on Computing, 28*(4), 781–794. doi:10.1287/ijoc.2015.0680

Cai, X., Zhang, N., Venayagamoorthy, G. K., & Wunsch, D. C. II. (2007). Time series prediction with recurrent neural networks trained by a hybrid PSO–EA algorithm. *Neurocomputing, 70*(13), 2342–2353. doi:10.1016/j.neucom.2005.12.138

Callan, R. (1998). *The Essence of Neural Networks*. Prentice Hall PTR Upper Saddle River.

Campbell, J.G., Hashim, A. A., & Murtagh, F.D. (1997). *Flaw Detection in Woven Textiles using Space-dependent Fourier Transform*. University of Ulster, Faculty of Informatics, Magee College, 8, Preprint INFM-97-004.

Cauvery, N. K. (2011). Timetable scheduling using graph coloring. International Journal of P2P Network Trends and Technology, 1(2), 57-62.

Censor, Y. (1977). Pareto optimality in multiobjective problems. *Applied Mathematics & Optimization, 4*(1), 41–59. doi:10.1007/BF01442131

Chai, W., & Qiao, J. (2014). Passive robust fault detection using RBF neural modeling based on set membership identification. *Engineering Applications of Artificial Intelligence, 28*, 1–12. doi:10.1016/j.engappai.2013.10.005

Chakraborty, T. K. (1992). A class of single sampling plans based on fuzzy optimization. *Opsearch, 29*(1), 11–20.

Chakraborty, T. K. (1994a). Possibilistic parameter single sampling inspection plans. *Opsearch, 31*(2), 108–126.

Chakraborty, T. K. (1994b). A class of single sampling inspection plans based on possibilistic programming problem. *Fuzzy Sets and Systems, 63*(1), 35–43. doi:10.1016/0165-0114(94)90143-0

Chakrapani, G., & Lokeswara Reddy, V. (2014). Optimized Videotapr Steganography Using Genetic Algorithm (GA). *IJCS, 15*, 1–6.

Chang, D.-Y. (1996). Applications of the extent analysis method on fuzzy AHP. *European Journal of Operational Research*, *95*(3), 649–655. doi:10.1016/0377-2217(95)00300-2

Changdar, C., Mahapatra, G. S., & Pal, R. K. (2013). An Ant colony optimization approach for binary knapsack problem under fuzziness. *Applied Mathematics and Computation*, *223*, 243–253. doi:10.1016/j.amc.2013.07.077

Chang, P. L., & Chen, K. L. (2004). The influence of input factors on new leading product development projects in Taiwan. *International Journal of Project Management*, *22*(5), 415–423. doi:10.1016/j.ijproman.2003.11.002

Chang, P. L., & Chen, Y. C. (1994). A fuzzy multi-criteria decision making method for technology transfer strategy selection in biotechnology. *Fuzzy Sets and Systems*, *6*(2), 131–139. doi:10.1016/0165-0114(94)90344-1

Chang, Y. W. (2013). New parameter-free simplified swarm optimization for artificial neural network training and its application in the prediction of time series. *IEEE Transaction on Neural Networks Learning System*, *24*(4), 661–665. doi:10.1109/TNNLS.2012.2232678 PMID:24808385

Chassaing, M., Fontanel, J., Lacomme, P., Ren, L., Tchernev, N., & Villechenon, P. (2014). A GRASP - ELS approach for the job-shop with a web service paradigm packaging. *Expert Systems with Applications*, *41*(2), 544–562. doi:10.1016/j.eswa.2013.07.080

Chauhan, N. (2010). *Software Testing: Principles and Practices*. Oxford University Press.

Chaurasia, S. N., & Singh, A. (2015). A hybrid swarm intelligence approach to the registration area planning problem. *Information Sciences*, *302*, 50–69. doi:10.1016/j.ins.2015.01.012

Chen, C. W. K., & Yun, D. Y. Y. (1998). Unifying graph-matching problem with a practical solution. *Proceedings of International Conference on Systems, Signals, Control, Computers*.

Chen, T., Hong, Z., Deng, F., Yang, X., Wei, J. & Cui, M. (2015). A novel selective ensemble classificationof microarray data based on teaching-learning-based optimization. *International Journal of Multimedia and Ubiquitous Engineering*, *10*(6), 203-218.

Chen, C. T. (2000). Extensions of the TOPSIS for group decision-making under fuzzy environment. *Fuzzy Sets and Systems*, *114*(1), 1–9. doi:10.1016/S0165-0114(97)00377-1

Cheng, C. H., & Mon, D. L. (1994). Evaluating weapon system by Analytical Hierarchy Process based on fuzzy scales. *Fuzzy Sets and Systems*, *63*(1), 1–10. doi:10.1016/0165-0114(94)90140-6

Chen, L. F., Su, C.-T., Chen, K.-H., & Wang, P.-C. (2011). Particle swarm optimization for feature selection with application in obstructive sleep apnea diagnosis. *Neural Computing & Applications*, *21*(8), 2087–2096. doi:10.1007/s00521-011-0632-4

Chen, S., Gibson, G. J., Cowan, C. F. N., & Grant, P. M. (1991). Reconstruction of Binary Signals using an Adaptive Radial-Basis-Function Equalizer. *EURASIP Signal Processing*, *22*(1), 77–93. doi:10.1016/0165-1684(91)90030-M

Chen, S., Hong, X., Luk, B. L., & Harris, C. J. (2009). Construction of Tunable Radial Basis Function Networks Using Orthogonal Forward Selection. *IEEE Transactions on Systems, Man, and Cybernetics. Part B, Cybernetics*, *39*(2), 457–466. doi:10.1109/TSMCB.2008.2006688 PMID:19095548

Chen, S., McLaughlin, S., & Mulgrew, B. (1994). Complex-valued Radial Basis Function Network, Part I: Network Architecture and Learning Algorithms. *Signal Processing*, *35*(1), 19–31. doi:10.1016/0165-1684(94)90187-2

Chen, S., Wang, X. X., Hong, X., & Harris, C. J. (2006). Kernel Classifier Construction Using Orthogonal Forward Selection And Boosting With Fisher Ratio Class Separability Measure. *IEEE Transactions on Neural Networks*, *17*(6), 1652–1656. doi:10.1109/TNN.2006.881487 PMID:17131680

Chen, T., & Chen, H. (1995). Approximation Capability to Functions of Several Variables, Nonlinear Functional and Operators by Radial Basis Function Neural Networks. *IEEE Transactions on Neural Networks*, *6*(4), 904–910. doi:10.1109/72.392252 PMID:18263378

Chen, Y., Miao, D., & Wang, R. (2010). A rough set approach to feature selection based on ant colony optimization. *Pattern Recognition Letters*, *31*(3), 226–233. doi:10.1016/j.patrec.2009.10.013

Chen, Y., Yang, B., Meng, Q., Zhao, Y., & Abraham, A. (2011). Time-series forecasting using a system of ordinary differential equations. *Information Science*, *181*(1), 106–114. doi:10.1016/j.ins.2010.09.006

Cherrie, J. B., Beatson, R. K., & Newsam, G. N. (2002). Fast Evaluation of Radial Basis Functions: Methods for Generalized Multi-quadrics in Rn. *SIAM Journal on Scientific Computing*, *23*(5), 1549–1571. doi:10.1137/S1064827500367609

Chiang, W. C., & Urban, T. L. (1996). A Neural Network Approach to Mutual Fund Net Asset Value Forecasting. OMEGA. *International Journal of Management Sciences*, *24*(2), 205–215.

Cho, S., Jang, M., & Chang, S. (1996). Virtual sample generation using a population of neural networks. *Neural Processing Letters*, *5*, 83–89.

Chowdhury, H. A. R., Farhat, T., & Khan, H. A. (2013). Memetic Algorithm to solve Graph Coloring Problem. *International Journal of Computer Theory and Engineering*, *5*(6).

Chow, P. S., Cioffi, J. M., & Bingham, J. A. C. (1995). A practical discrete multi-tone transceiver loading algorithm for data transmission over spectrally shaped channels. *IEEE Transactions on Communications*, *48*, 772–775.

Chu, S. C., Tsai, P. W., & Pan, J. S. (2006, August). Cat swarm optimization. In *Pacific Rim International Conference on Artificial Intelligence* (pp. 854-858). Springer Berlin Heidelberg.

Chu, S. C., Tsai, P., & Pan, J. S. (2006). Cat swarm optimization. In Q. Yang, & G. Webb (Eds.), Trends in artificial intelligence. Berlin: Springer.

Clough, B. J., & Green, E. J. (2013). Comparing spatial and non-spatial approaches for predicting forest soil organic carbon at unsampled locations. *Mathematical and Computational Forestry and Natural Resource Sciences*, *5*, 115–125.

Cobos, C., Muñoz-Collazos, H., Urbano-Muñoz, R., Mendoza, M., León, E., & Herrera-Viedma, E. (2014). Clustering of web search results based on the cuckoo search algorithm and Balanced Bayesian Information Criterion. *Information Sciences*, *281*, 248–264. doi:10.1016/j.ins.2014.05.047

Coelho, R. T., Silva, L. R., Braghini, A. Jr., & Bezerra, A. A. (2004). Some effects of cutting edge preparation and geometric modifications when turning Inconel 718 (TM) at high cutting speeds. *Journal of Materials Processing Technology*, *148*(1), 147–153. doi:10.1016/j.jmatprotec.2004.02.001

Coelho, V., Grasas, A., Ramalhinho, H., Coelho, I., Souza, M., & Cruz, R. (2016a). An ils-based algorithm to solve a large-scale real heterogeneous eet fVRPg with multi-trips and docking constraints. *European Journal of Operational Research*, *250*(2), 367–376. doi:10.1016/j.ejor.2015.09.047

Coello, C. C. (2006). Evolutionary multi-objective optimization: A historical view of the field. *IEEE Computational Intelligence Magazine*, *1*(1), 28–36. doi:10.1109/MCI.2006.1597059

Cohen, F. S., Fan, Z., & Attali, S. (1991). Automated inspection of textile fabric using textural models. *IEEE Transactions on Pattern Analysis and Machine Intelligence*, *13*(8), 803–808. doi:10.1109/34.85670

Çolak, O. (2012). Investigation on Machining Performance of Inconel 718 under High Pressure Cooling Conditions. *Journal of Mechanical Engineering*, *5811*(11), 683–690. doi:10.5545/sv-jme.2012.730

Colmenar, J. M., Greistorfer, P., Martí, R., & Duarte, A. (2016). Advanced greedy randomized adaptive search procedure for the obnoxious p-median problem. *European Journal of Operational Research*, *252*(2), 432–442. doi:10.1016/j.ejor.2016.01.047

Conci, A., & Proenca, C. B. (1998). A fractal image analysis system for fabric inspection based on a box-counting method. *Computer Networks and ISDN Systems*, *30*(20-21), 1887–1895. doi:10.1016/S0169-7552(98)00211-6

Consoli, S., & Pérez, J. A. M. (2015). Variable neighbour-hood search for the k-labelled spanning forest problem. *Electronic Notes in Discrete Mathematics*, *47*, 29–36. doi:10.1016/j.endm.2014.11.005

Cont, R. (2001). Empirical properties of asset returns: Stylized facts and statistical issues. *Quantitative Finance*, *1*(2), 223–236. doi:10.1080/713665670

Cootner, P. H. (1964). *The Random Character of Stock Market Prices*. MIT Press.

Cordone, R., & Lulli, G. (2013). A GRASP metaheuristic for microarray data analysis. *Computers & Operations Research*, *40*(12), 3108–3120. doi:10.1016/j.cor.2012.10.008

Corne, D., Dorigo, M., & Glover, F. (Eds.). (1999). *New Ideas in Optimization*. McGraw-Hill.

Costes, J., Guillet, Y., Poulachon, G., & Dessoly, M. (2007). Tool-life and wear mechanisms of CBN tools in machining of Inconel 718. *International Journal of Machine Tools & Manufacture*, *47*(7–8), 1081–1087. doi:10.1016/j.ijmachtools.2006.09.031

Creutz, M. (1983). Microcanonical Monte Carlo simulation. *Physical Review Letters*, *50*(19), 1411–1414. doi:10.1103/PhysRevLett.50.1411 PMID:10047098

Cui, Z., & Cai, X. (2013). Artificial plant optimization algorithm. Swarm intelligence and bio-inspired computation: Theory and applications, 351–365.

Cutello, V., Nicosia, G., & Pavone, M. (2003). A hybrid immune algorithm with information gain for the graph coloring problem. *Proceedings of GECCO 2003*, 171-182.

Cybenko, G. (1989). Approximation by superpositions of a sigmoidal function. *Mathematics of Control, Signals, and Systems*, *2*(4), 303–314. doi:10.1007/BF02551274

Cyzlwik, A. (1996). Adaptive OFDM for wideband radio channels. *Global Telecommunications Conference*, 1, 713-718.

Czyżak, P., & Jaszkiewicz, A. (1998). Pareto simulated annealing - a metaheuristic technique for multiple objective combinatorial optimization. *Journal of Multi-Criteria Decision Analysis*, *7*(1), 34–47. doi:10.1002/(SICI)1099-1360(199801)7:1<34::AID-MCDA161>3.0.CO;2-6

D'Alessandro, Esteller, Vachtsevanos, Hinson, Echauz, & Litt. (2003). Epileptic Seizure Prediction Using Hybrid Feature Selection over Multiple Intracranial EEG Electrode Contacts: A Report of Four Patients. Academic Press.

Dai, F., Zhou, Q., Lv, Q., Wang, X., & Liu, Q. (2014). Spatial prediction of soil organic matter content integrating artificial neural network and ordinary kriging in Tibetan Plateau. *Ecological Indicators*, *45*, 184–194. doi:10.1016/j.ecolind.2014.04.003

Dai, G., Wang, Z., Yang, C., Liu, H., Hassanien, A. E., & Yang, W. (2015). A multi-granularity rough set algorithm for attribute reduction through particles particle swarm optimization. *11th IEEE International Computer Engineering Conference (ICENCO)*, 303-307.

Danandeh Mehr, A., Kahya, E., & Olyaie, E. (2013). Stream flow prediction using linear genetic programming in comparison with a neuro-wavelet technique. *Journal of Hydrology (Amsterdam)*, *505*, 240–249. doi:10.1016/j.jhydrol.2013.10.003

Danielsson, J. (2011). *Financial Risk Forecasting*. Wiley.

Das, S., Panigrahi, B.K., & Pattnaik, S.S. (2009). Nature-Inspired Algorithms for Multi-objective Optimization. In Handbook of Research on Machine Learning Applications and Trends: Algorithms Methods and Techniques (vol. 1, pp. 95-108). Hershey, PA: IGI Global.

Dasgupta, K., Mondal, J. K., & Dutta, P. (2013). *Optimized Video Steganography using Genetic Algorithm (GA)*. Paper presented in International Conference on Computational Intelligence: Modeling, Techniques and Applications (CIMTA) 2013, Department of Computer Science & Engineering, University of Kalyani, West Bengal, India.

Dash, S., & Patra, B. N. (2012). Rough Set Aided Gene Selection for Cancer Classification. *Proceedings of 7th International Conference on Computing and Convergence Technology (ICCCT)*, 290-294.

Dash, S., & Patra, B. N. (2016). Genetic diagnosis of cancer by evolutionary fuzzy-based neural network ensemble. *International Journal of Knowledge Discovery in Bioinformatics, 6*(1).

Dash, C. S. K., Dash, A. P., Dehuri, S., Cho, S. B., & Wang, G. N. (2013). DE+ RBFNs Based Classification: A Special Attention to Removal of Inconsistency and Irrelevant Features. *Engineering Applications of Artificial Intelligence*, *26*(10), 2315–2326. doi:10.1016/j.engappai.2013.08.006

Dash, S. (2015). *A Rule Induction Model Empowered by Fuzzy-Rough Particle Swarm Optimization Algorithm for Classification of Microarray Dataset, Computational Intelligence in Data Mining* (Vol. 3). SIST. doi:10.1007/978-81-322-2202-6_26

Dash, S. (2016). *Hybrid Ensemble Learning Methods for Classification of Microarray Data. In Handbook of research on Computational Intelligence Applications in Bioinformatics* (pp. 17–36). Hershey, PA: IGI Global. doi:10.4018/978-1-5225-0427-6

Dash, S., & Behera, R. (2016). Sampling based Hybrid Algorithms for Imbalanced Data Classification. *International Journal of Hybrid-Intelligent-Systems*, *13*(2), 77–86. doi:10.3233/HIS-160226

Dash, S., & Patra, B. N. (2013). Redundant Gene Selection based on Genetic and Quick-Reduct Algorithms. *International Journal on Data Mining and Intelligent Information Technology Application*, *3*(2), 1–9.

Dash, S., & Patra, B. N. (2016). *Knowledge Discovery using Machine Learning Algorithms*. Lambert Academic Publishing.

Dash, S., Patra, B. N., & Tripathy, B. K. (2012). A Hybrid Data Mining Technique for Improving the Classification Accuracy ofMicroarray Data Set. I.J. *Information Engineering and Electronic Business*, *4*(2), 43–50. doi:10.5815/ijieeb.2012.02.07

Das, K. K., & Satapathy, J. K. (2011). Legendre neural network for non-linear active noise cancellation with non-linear secondary path. *International Conference on Multimedia, Signal Processing and Communication Technologies*, 40–43.

Das, M. K., & Ari, S. (2013). Analysis of ECG signal denoising method based on S-transform. *IRBM, Elsevier*, *34*(6), 362–370. doi:10.1016/j.irbm.2013.07.012

Das, M. T., & Dulger, L. C. (2009). Signature verification (SV) toolbox. *Application of PSO-NN, Engineering Applications of Artificial Intelligence, Elsevier, 22*(4-5), 688–694. doi:10.1016/j.engappai.2009.02.005

Das, N., Acharya, K., Shankar, R., Basu, S., Kundu, M., & Nasipuri, M. (2012, January). A novel GA-SVM based multistage approach for recognition of handwritten Bangla compound characters. *Proc. of the International Conference on Information Systems, Design and Intelligent Applications, Visakhapatnam*, 1-6. doi:10.1007/978-3-642-27443-5_17

Das, S., & Suganthan, P. N. (2011). Differential Evolution: A Survey of the State-of- the- Art. *IEEE Transactions on Evolutionary Computation, 15*(1), 4–31. doi:10.1109/TEVC.2010.2059031

Davis, J. C. (2002). *Statistics and Data Analysis in Geology*. New York: Wiley.

de Armas, J., Lalla-Ruiz, E., Expósito-Izquierdo, C., Landa-Silva, D., & Melián-Batista, B. (2015). A hybrid GRASP-VNS for ship routing and scheduling problem with discretized time windows. *Engineering Applications of Artificial Intelligence, 45*, 350–360. doi:10.1016/j.engappai.2015.07.013

de C. M. Nogueira, J. P., Arroyo, J. E. C., Villadiego, H. M. M., & Gonçalves, L. B. (2014, February). Hybrid GRASP Heuristics to Solve an Unrelated Parallel Machine Scheduling Problem with Earliness and Tardiness Penalties. *Electronic Notes in Theoretical Computer Science, 302*, 53–72. doi:10.1016/j.entcs.2014.01.020

De Castro, L.N., & Von Zuben, F.J. (1999). *Artificial immune systems, Part I. Basic theory and applications, Technical Report RtDca 01/99*. Feec/Unicamp, Brazil.

De Castro, L. N., & Timmis, J. (2002). *Artificial immune systems: A new computational intelligence approach*. London: Springer.

De Natale, F. G. B. (1986). Article. *International Journal of Pattern Recognition and Artificial Intelligence, 10*(8).

De Oliveira, B. M., & Labiche, Y. (2015). *Search-Based Software Engineering: 7th International Symposium*. Springer.

De, Kar, Mandal, & Ghosal. (2015, September). Optimal CMOS inverter design using differential evolution algorithm. *Journal of Electrical Systems and Information Technology, 2*(2), 219-241.

Deb, K. (2001). *Multi-objective optimization using evolutionary algorithms* (Vol. 16). John Wiley & Sons.

Deb, K., Pratap, A., Agarwal, S., & Meyarivan, T. (2002). A Fast and Elitist Multiobjective Genetic Algorithm. *IEEE Transaction Evolutionary Computation, 6*(2), 182–197. doi:10.1109/4235.996017

Dehuri, S., Roy, R., Cho, S. B., & Ghosh, A. (2012). An improved swarm optimized functional link artificial neural network (ISO-FLANN) for classification. *Journal of Systems and Software, 85*(6), 1333–1345. doi:10.1016/j.jss.2012.01.025

Deng, J., Sundararajan, N., & Saratchandran, P. (2000). Complex-valued minimal resource allocation network for nonlinear signal processing. *International Journal of Neural Science, 10*(02), 95–106. doi:10.1142/S0129065700000090

Desell, T., Clachar, S., Higgins, J., & Wild, B. (2015, April). Evolving Deep Recurrent Neural Networks Using Ant Colony Optimization. In *European Conference on Evolutionary Computation in Combinatorial Optimization* (pp. 86-98). Springer International Publishing. doi:10.1007/978-3-319-16468-7_8

Díez-Pastor, J. F., García-Osorio, C., & Rodríguez, J. J. (2014). Tree ensemble construction using a GRASP-based heuristic and annealed randomness. *Information Fusion, 20*, 189–202. doi:10.1016/j.inffus.2014.01.009

Ding, C., & Peng, H. (2005). Minimum redundancy feature selection from microarray gene expression data. *Journal of Bioinformatics and Computational Biology, 3*(2), 185–205. doi:10.1142/S0219720005001004 PMID:15852500

Ding, G., Hu, X., Qiu, W., & Tian, M. (2014). Application of GRNN based on correlation analysis to the real estate valuation. *Journal of Geomatics*, *39*, 27–30.

Dominguez, L. V., & Cirigliano, M. (1997). Chocolates EI Rey: Industrial Modernization and Export Strategy. *Journal of Business Research*, *38*(1), 35–45. doi:10.1016/S0148-2963(96)00116-6

Dorigo, M. (1992). *Optimization, learning and natural algorithms* (Ph. D. Thesis). Politecnico di Milano, Italy.

Dorigo, M. (1992). *Optimization, Learning and Natural Algorithms* (Unpublished doctoral dissertation). Politecnico di Milano, Italy.

Dorigo, M., Birattari, M., & Stützle, T. (2006). Ant colony optimization. *IEEE Computational Intelligence Magazine*, *1*(4), 28–39. doi:10.1109/MCI.2006.329691

Dorigo, M., & Blum, C. (2005). Ant colony optimization theory: A survey. *Theoretical Computer Science*, *344*(2), 243–278. doi:10.1016/j.tcs.2005.05.020

Dorigo, M., Maniezzo, V., & Colorni, A. (1996). Ant system: optimization by a colony of cooperating agents. Systems, Man, and Cybernetics, Part B: Cybernetics. *IEEE Transactions on*, *26*(1), 29–41.

Dowsland, K. A., & Thompson, J. M. (2012). Simulated Annealing. In G. Rozenberg, Th. Bäck, & J. N. Kok (Eds.), *Handbook of Natural Computing* (pp. 1623–1655). Berlin: Springer-Verlag; doi:10.1007/978-3-540-92910-9_49

Draa, A., & Bouaziz, A. (2014). An artificial bee colony algorithm for image contrast enhancement. *Swarm and Evolutionary Computation, 16*, 69–84.

Duarte, A. R., Ribeiro, C. C., Urrutia, S., & Haeusler, E. H. (2006). Referee assignment in sports leagues. In *International Conference on the Practice and Theory of Automated Timetabling* (pp. 158-173). Springer.

Dubois & Prade. (1990). Rough fuzzy sets and fuzzy rough sets. *International Journal of General System, 17*(2-3), 191-209.

Duda, P. O., & Hart, P. E. (1973). *Pattern Classification and Scene Analysis*. New York: Wiley.

Dudzinski, D., Devillez, A., Moufki, A., Larrouquère, D., Zerrouki, V., & Vigneau, J. (2004). A review of developments towards dry and high speed machining of Inconel 718 alloy. *International Journal of Machine Tools & Manufacture*, *44*(4), 439–456. doi:10.1016/S0890-6955(03)00159-7

Dueck, G. (1993). New optimization heuristics, the great deluge and the record to record travel. *Journal of Computational Physics*, *104*(1), 86–92. doi:10.1006/jcph.1993.1010

Dueck, G., & Scheuer, T. (1990). Threshold accepting: A general purpose optimization algorithm appearing superior to simulated annealing. *Journal of Computational Physics*, *90*(1), 161–175. doi:10.1016/0021-9991(90)90201-B

Dutt, D., & Hedge, V. (2015). AAKRITI[ed]: An Image and Data Encryption-Decryption Tool. *International Journal of Computer Science and Information Technology Research, 2*(2), 264-268.

Eberhart, R. C., & Kennedy, J. (1995, October). A new optimizer using particle swarm theory. In *Proceedings of the sixth international symposium on micro machine and human science* (Vol. 1, pp. 39-43). doi:10.1109/MHS.1995.494215

Eberhart, R. C., & Shi, Y. (2001). Particle swarm optimization: Developments, Applications and Resources. *Proceeding of IEEE International Conference on Evolutionary Computation, 1*, 81-86. doi:10.1109/CEC.2001.934374

EEG Database: Seizure Prediction Project Freilburg. (n.d.). Retrieved from http://epilepsy.uni-freiburg.de/freiburg-seizure-prediction-project/eeg-database

Eiben, A. E., & Schippers, C. A. (1998). On evolutionary exploration and exploitation. *Fundamenta Informaticae, 35*(1), 16.

Eiben, A. E., & Schippers, C. A. (1998). On evolutionary exploration and exploitation. *Fundamenta Informaticae, 35*, 1-16.

Eldeiry, A. A., & Garcia, L. A. (2012). Evaluating the performance of ordinary kriging in mapping soil salinity. *Journal of Irrigation and Drainage Engineering, 138*(12), 1046–1059. doi:10.1061/(ASCE)IR.1943-4774.0000517

Electronics Manufacturing Industry Overview. (n.d.). Retrieved June 12, 2016, from http://policy.electronicsb2b.com/industry/electronics-manufacture-industry-overview/

Elghondakly, R., Moussa, S., & Badr, N. (2016, March). A Comprehensive Study for Software Testing and Test Cases Generation Paradigms. *Proceedings of the International Conference on Internet of things and Cloud Computing*, 50. doi:10.1145/2896387.2896435

Elloumi, W., & Alimi, A. M. (2010, May). A more efficient MOPSO for optimization. In *ACS/IEEE International Conference on Computer Systems and Applications-AICCSA 2010* (pp. 1-7). IEEE. doi:10.1109/AICCSA.2010.5587045

Elman, J. L. (1990). Finding structure in time. *Cognitive Science, 14*(2), 179–211. doi:10.1207/s15516709cog1402_1

Emadi, M., & Baghernejad, M. (2014). Comparison of spatial interpolation techniques for mapping soil pH and salinity in agricultural coastal areas, northern Iran. *Archives of Agronomy and Soil Science, 60*(9), 1315–1327. doi:10.1080/03650340.2014.880837

Emary, E., Yamany, W., & Hassanien, A. E. (2014). New approach for feature selection based on rough set and bat algorithm. *9th IEEE International Conference on Computer Engineering & Systems (ICCES)*, 346-353. doi:10.1109/ICCES.2014.7030984

Emery, C. J., Ferenc, S., Mary, P., & Emmanuel, C. (2003). Artificial Neural Network Approach for Predicting Transient Water Levels in Multilayered Groundwater System Under Variable State, Pumping, and Climate Conditions. *Journal of Hydrologic Engineering*, 348–360.

EmreAydemir, M., Gunel, T., & Kumaz, S. (2003). A h'ovcl Approach for Synthetic Aperture Radar Image Processing Based On Genetic Algorithm. *Proceedings of RAST 2003 Conference*.

Escofet, J., Navarro, R., Millan, M. S., & Pladelloreans, J. (1998). Detection of local defects in textiles webs using Gabor filters. *Optical Engineering (Redondo Beach, Calif.), 37*(8), 2297–2307. doi:10.1117/1.601751

EU SME Centre. (2011). *The machinery sector in China*. Retrieved June 12, 2016, from https://www.ccilc.pt: https://www.ccilc.pt/sites/default/files/machinery_sectorreport_v3_en.pdf

Ezugwu, E. O., Fadare, D. A., Bonney, J., Silva, R. B., & Sales, W. F. (2005). Modelling the correlation between cutting and process parameters in high-speed machining of Inconel 718 alloy using an artificial neural network. *International Journal of Machine Tools & Manufacture, 45*(12-13), 1375–1385. doi:10.1016/j.ijmachtools.2005.02.004

Faezah, J., & Sabira, K. (2009). Adaptive Modulation for OFDM Systems. *International Journal of Communication Networks and Information Security, 1*(2), 1–8.

Fahad, S., Abu, M., & Ei, H. (2012, March). Overview of Artificial Bee Colony (ABC) algorithm and its applications. *Systems Conference (SysCon), IEEE International*. 10.1109/SysCon.2012.6189539

Fahlman, S. E. (1988). *Faster-learning variations on back-propagation: An empirical study*. Academic Press.

Fahlman, S. E., & Lebiere, C. (1989). *The cascade-correlation learning architecture*. Academic Press.

Falcao, A., Langlois, T., & Wichert, A. (2006). Flexible Kernels for RBF Networks. *Neurocomputing, 69*(16-18), 2356–2359. doi:10.1016/j.neucom.2006.03.006

Fallahpour, A. R., &Moghassem, A. R. (2013). Yarn Strength Modelling Using Adaptive Neuro-Fuzzy Inference System (ANFIS) and Gene Expression Programming (GEP). *Journal of Engineered Fibers and Fabrics, 8*(4).

Fama, E. F. (1965). The Behaviour of Stock Market Prices. *The Journal of Business, 38*(1), 34–105. doi:10.1086/294743

Fama, E. F. (1970). Efficient capital markets: A review of theory and empirical work. *The Journal of Finance, 25*(2), 383–417. doi:10.2307/2325486

Fausett, L. (1994). *Fundamentals of Neural Networks*. Prentice Hall.

Fei, X., Mahmassani, H. S., & Murray-Tuite, P. (2013). Vehicular network sensor placement optimization under uncertainty. *Transportation Research Part C, Emerging Technologies, 29*, 14–31. doi:10.1016/j.trc.2013.01.004

Fenton, G. A. (1998). *Random field characterization NGES data.* Paper presented at the Workshop on Probabilistic Site Characterization at NGES, Seattle, WA.

Fenton, G. A. (1999). Random field modeling of CPT data. *Journal of Geotechnical and Geoenvironmental Engineering, 125*(6), 486–498. doi:10.1061/(ASCE)1090-0241(1999)125:6(486)

Feo, T. A., & Resende, M. G. (1989). A probabilistic heuristic for a computationally di cult set covering problem. *Operations Research Letters, 8*(2), 67–71. doi:10.1016/0167-6377(89)90002-3

Fernandez-Navarro, F., Hervas-Martinez, C., Cruz-Ramirez, M., Gutierrez, P. A., & Valero, A. (2011). Evolutionary q-Gaussian Radial Basis Function Neural Network to Determine the Microbial Growth/no Growth Interface of Staphylococcus Aureus. *Applied Soft Computing, 11*(3), 3012–3020. doi:10.1016/j.asoc.2010.11.027

Ferreira, C. (2002). Gene Expression Programming: Mathematical Modeling by an Artificial Intelligence. Angra do Heroismo, Portugal

Ferreira, C. (2001). Gene Expression Programming: A New Adaptive Algorithm for Solving Problems. *Complex Systems, 13*(2), 87–129.

Ferreira, C. (2006). *Gene Expression Programming: Mathematical Modeling by an Artificial Intelligence* (2nd ed.). Springer-Verlag.

Ferreira, C. S., Ochi, L. S., Parada, V., & Uchoa, E. (2012). A GRASP-based approach to the generalized minimum spanning tree problem. *Expert Systems with Applications, 39*(3), 3526–3536. doi:10.1016/j.eswa.2011.09.043

Figueiredo, R., & Frota, Y. (2014). The maximum balanced subgraph of a signed graph: Applications and solution approaches. *European Journal of Operational Research, 236*(2), 473–487. doi:10.1016/j.ejor.2013.12.036

Fister, I., Jr., Yang, X. S., Fister, I., Brest, J., & Fister, D. (2013). *A brief review of nature-inspired algorithms for optimization.* arXiv preprint arXiv:1307.4186

Fister, I., Yang, X. S., & Brest, J. (2013). A comprehensive review of firefly algorithms. *Swarm and Evolutionary Computation, 13*, 34–46. doi:10.1016/j.swevo.2013.06.001

Fleurent, C., & Glover, F. (1999). Improved construc-tive multistart strategies for the quadratic assignment problem using adaptive memory. *INFORMS Journal on Computing, 11*(2), 198–204. doi:10.1287/ijoc.11.2.198

Floudas, C. A., & Pardalos, P. M. (1987). A collection of test problems for constrained global optimization algorithms. *LNCS, 455.*

Foroutan, I., & Sklasky, J. (1987). Feature Selection for Automatic Classification of Non-Gaussian Data. *IEEE Transactions on Systems, Man, and Cybernetics, 17*(2), 187–198. doi:10.1109/TSMC.1987.4309029

Francisco, F. N., César, H. M., Roberto, R., & Jose, C. R. (2012). Evolutionary Generalized Radial Basis Function neural networks for improving prediction accuracy in gene classification using feature selection. *Applied Soft Computing, 12*(6), 1787–1800. doi:10.1016/j.asoc.2012.01.008

Frank, A., & Asuncion, A. (2010). UCI Machine Learning Repository. Irvine, CA: University of California, School of Information and Computer Science. Retrieved from http://archive.ics.uci.edu/ml

Franke, C., & Schaback, R. (1998). Convergence Orders of Meshless Collocation Methods using Radial Basis Functions. *Advances in Computational Mathematics, 8*(4), 381–399. doi:10.1023/A:1018916902176

Frankenhoff, W. P., & Granger, C. H. (1971, April). Strategic Management: A new managerial concept for an era of rapid change. *Long Range Planning, 3*(3), 7–12. doi:10.1016/0024-6301(71)90015-X

Frankort, H. T. (2016). When does knowledge acquisition in R&D alliances increase new product development? The moderating roles of technological relatedness and product-market competition. *Research Policy, 45*(1), 291–302. doi:10.1016/j.respol.2015.10.007

Franses, P. H., & Ghijsels, H. (1999). Additive outliers. GARCH and forecasting volatility. *International Journal of Forecasting, 15*(1), 1–9. doi:10.1016/S0169-2070(98)00053-3

Franses, P., & van Dijk, D. (2000). *Non-linear time series models in empirical finance.* Cambridge University Press. doi:10.1017/CBO9780511754067

Frigui, H., & Krishnapuram, R. (1999, May). A Robust Competitive Clustering Algorithm with Applications in Computer Vision. *IEEE Transactions on Pattern Analysis and Machine Intelligence, 21*(5), 450–465. doi:10.1109/34.765656

Fujiwara, Y., Mori, K., Fujii, Y., Sawada, Y., & Okumura, S. (2001). Measurement of surface roughness of coated wood by laser scanning. *Proc. on the 15th Wood Machining Seminar.*

Galal, Mousa, & Al-Matrafi. (2013). Ant Colony Optimization Approach Based Genetic Algorithms for Multiobjective Optimal Power Flow Problem under Fuzziness. *Applied Mathematics, 4*, 595.

Gal, E., Matan, N., Nir, F., & Dale, S. (2002). Data perturbation for escaping local maxima in learning. *Eighteenth National Conference on Artificial Intelligence*, 132-139.

Gamst, A. (1986). Some lower bounds for class of frequency assignment problems. *IEEE Transactions on Vehicular Technology, 35*(1), 8–14. doi:10.1109/T-VT.1986.24063

Ganji, M. F., & Abadeh, M. S. (2011). A fuzzy classification system based on Ant Colony Optimization for diabetes disease diagnosis. *Expert Systems with Applications, 38*(12), 14650–14659. doi:10.1016/j.eswa.2011.05.018

Gaurav, K., & Hasmat, M. (2016). Generalized Regression Neural Network Based Wind Speed Prediction Model for Western Region of India. *Procedia Computer Science, 93*, 26–32. doi:10.1016/j.procs.2016.07.177

Geem, Z. W., Kim, J. K., & Loganathan, G. V. (2001). A new heuristic optimisation: Harmony search. *Simulation, 76*(2), 60–68. doi:10.1177/003754970107600201

Geman, S., & Geman, D. (1984). Stochastic Relaxation, Gibbs Distributions, and the Bayesian Restoration of Images. *IEEE Transactions on Pattern Analysis and Machine Intelligence, 6*(6), 721–741. doi:10.1109/TPAMI.1984.4767596 PMID:22499653

Gen, M., Tsujimura, Y., & Ida, K. (1992). Method for solving multi-bjective aggregate production planning problem with fuzzy parameters. *Computers & Industrial Engineering, 23*(1-4), 117–120. doi:10.1016/0360-8352(92)90077-W

George, N. V., & Panda, G. (2012). A reduced complexity adaptive Legendre neural network for non-linear active noise control. *19th International Conference on Systems, Signals and Image Processing (IWSSIP)*, 560–563.

Ghosh, A., & Dehuri, S. (2004). Evolutionary algorithms for multi-criterion optimization: A survey. *International Journal of Computing & Information Sciences*, *2*(1), 38–57.

Ghosh, A., & Jain, L. C. (Eds.). (2005). *Evolutionary computation in data mining*. Berlin: Springer-Verlag. doi:10.1007/3-540-32358-9

Gilli, M., Këllezi, E., & Hysi, H. (2006). A Data-Driven Optimization Heuristic for Downside Risk Minimization. *Journal of Risk*, *8*(3), 1–18. doi:10.21314/JOR.2006.129

Glick, R. (1982). *R& D effort and US exports and foreign affiliate production of manufactures*. North-Holland Publishing Company.

Glover, F. (1986). Future paths for integer programming and links to artificial intelligence. *Comp. Oper. Res.*, *13*, 533-549.

Glover, F. (1977). Heuristics for Integer programming Using Surrogate Constraints. *Decision Sciences*, *8*(1), 156–166. doi:10.1111/j.1540-5915.1977.tb01074.x

Glover, F. (1986). Future paths for integer programming and links to artificial intelligence. *Computers & Operations Research*, *13*(5), 533–549. doi:10.1016/0305-0548(86)90048-1

Glover, F. (1997). *Tabu Search and Adaptive Memory Programming - Advances*. Applications and Challenges. doi:10.1007/978-1-4615-6089-0_1

Glover, F., & Laguna, M. (1997). *Tabu Search*. Kluwer Academic Publishers. doi:10.1007/978-1-4615-6089-0

Gokul, M., & Umeshbabu, R. (2012). Hybrid Steganography using Visual Cryptography and LSB Encryption Method. *International Journal of Computer Applications*, *59*(14), 5-8.

Goldberg, D. E. (1989). Genetic Algorithms in Search, Optimization, and Machine Learning. Addison-Wesley.

Goldberg, D. E., & Deb, K. (1991). Chapter. In G. J. E. Rawlins (Ed.), A comparison of selection schemes used in genetic algorithms Foundations of Genetic Algorithms (pp. 69–93). Academic Press.

Goldberg, D. E., & Richardson, J. (1987). Genetic Algorithms with Sharing for Multimodal Function Optimization. *Proceedings of Second Int'l Conf. Genetic Algorithms (ICGA '87)*, 41-49.

Goldstein, L., & Waterman, M. (1988). Neighborhood size in the simulated annealing algorithm. *American Journal of Mathematical and Management Sciences*, *8*(3-4), 409–423. doi:10.1080/01966324.1988.10737247

Golub, T. R. (1999). Molecular classification of cancer: Class discovery and class prediction by gene expression monitoring, 1. *Science*, *286*(5439), 531–537. doi:10.1126/science.286.5439.531 PMID:10521349

Gomez, F. J., & Miikkulainen, R. (2003). Active Guidance for a finless rocket using neuroevolution. *Genetic and Evolutionary Computation Conference* (pp. 2084-2095). Chicago, IL: Springer Berlin Heidelberg. doi:10.1007/3-540-45110-2_105

Gooijer, J. G. D., & Hyndman, R. J. (2006). 25 years of time series forecasting. *International Journal of Forecasting*, *22*(3), 443–473. doi:10.1016/j.ijforecast.2006.01.001

Grandvalet, Y., Canu, S., & Boucheron, S. (1997). Noise injection: Theoretical prospects. *Neural Computation*, *9*(5), 1093–1108. doi:10.1162/neco.1997.9.5.1093

Grossberg, S. (1988). Nonlinear neural networks: Principles, mechanisms, and architectures. *Neural Networks*, *1*(1), 17–61. doi:10.1016/0893-6080(88)90021-4

Grupp, H. (1994). *The measurement of technical performance of innovations by technometrics and its impact on established technology indicators*. North-Holland Research Policy.

Guerrero Mosquera. (2012). *Armando Malanda Trigueros*. Angel Navia Vazquez EEG Signal Processing for Epilepsy.

Guo, K. L. (2008, June). DECIDE: A decision-making model for more effective decision making by health care managers. *The Health Care Manager*, 27(2), 118–127. doi:10.1097/01.HCM.0000285046.27290.90 PMID:18475113

Gupta, A. K., & Sapienza, H. J. (1992). Determinants of venture capital firmss preferences regarding diversity and geographic scope of their investments. *Journal of Business Venturing*, 7(5), 347–362. doi:10.1016/0883-9026(92)90012-G

Gupta, J. N., & Sexton, R. S. (1999). Comparing backpropagation with a genetic algorithm for neural network training. *Omega*, 27(6), 679–684. doi:10.1016/S0305-0483(99)00027-4

Guyon, I., Gunn, S., Nikravesh, M., & Zadeh, L. A. (Eds.). (2006). *Feature Extraction: foundations and applications*. Berlin: Springer. doi:10.1007/978-3-540-35488-8

Gwee, B. H., Lim, M. H. & Ho, J. S. (1993). Solving four-colouring map problem using genetic algorithm. *Proceedings of Artificial Neural Networks and Expert Systems*.

Gyorfi, L., Kohler, M., Krzyzak, A., & Walk, H. (2002). *A Distribution Free Theory of Non- Parametric Regression*. Springer Verlag, New York Inc.

Haberman, B. K., & Sheppard, J. W. (2012). Overlapping particle swarms for energy-efficient routing in sensor networks. *Wireless Networks*, 18(4), 351–363. doi:10.1007/s11276-011-0404-1

Hadavandi, E., Shavandi, H., & Ghanbari, A. (2010). Integration of genetic fuzzy systems and artificial neural networks for stock price forecasting. *Knowledge-Based Systems*, 23(8), 800–808. doi:10.1016/j.knosys.2010.05.004

Haddadene, S. R. A., Labadie, N., & Prodhon, C. (2016). A GRASP ILS for the vehicle routing problem with time windows, syn-chronization and precedence constraints. *Expert Systems with Applications*, 66, 274–294. doi:10.1016/j.eswa.2016.09.002

Hagan, M. T., & Menhaj, M. B. (1994). Training feedforward networks with the Marquardt algorithm. *IEEE Transactions on Neural Networks*, 5(6), 989–993. doi:10.1109/72.329697 PMID:18267874

Hagenauer, J., & Hoeher, P. (1989). A Viterbi algorithm with soft-decision outputs and its applications. *Proc. IEEE GLOBECOM*, 11-17. doi:10.1109/GLOCOM.1989.64230

Hajek, B. (1988). Cooling schedules for optimal annealing. *Mathematics of Operations Research*, 13(2), 311–329. doi:10.1287/moor.13.2.311

Hajek, B., & Sasaki, G. (1989). Simulated annealing – to cool or not. *Systems & Control Letters*, 12(5), 443–447. doi:10.1016/0167-6911(89)90081-9

Hale, W. K. (1980). Frequency assignment: Theory and applications. *Proceedings of the IEEE*, 12(12), 1497–1514. doi:10.1109/PROC.1980.11899

Ha, M. H., Bostel, N., Langevin, A., & Rousseau, L.-M. (2014). An exact algorithm and a metaheuristic for the generalized vehicle routing problem with exible eet size. *Computers & Operations Research*, 43, 9–19. doi:10.1016/j.cor.2013.08.017

Hanmandlu, M., Choudhury, D., & Dash, S. (2015). Detection of defects in fabrics using topothesy fractal dimension features. *Signal Image and Video Processing*, 9(7), 1521–1530. doi:10.1007/s11760-013-0604-5

Hanmandlu, M., Choudhury, D., & Dash, S. (2016). Detection of Fabric Defects using Fuzzy Decision Trees. *International Journal of Signal and Imaging Systems Engineering*, 9(3), 184–198. doi:10.1504/IJSISE.2016.076230

Hariharan, M., Vijean, V., Sindhu, R., Divakar, P., Saidatul, A., & Yaacob, S. (2014, July). Classification of mental tasks using stockwell transform. *Computer and Electrical Engineering, Elsevier*, 40(5), 1741–1749. doi:10.1016/j.compeleceng.2014.01.010

Harman, M. (2007). The current state and future of search based software engineering. Future of Software Engineering, 342-357. doi:10.1109/FOSE.2007.29

Harman, M., Mansouri, S. A., & Zhang, Y. (2009). *Search based software engineering: A comprehensive analysis and review of trends techniques and applications*. Department of Computer Science, King's College London, Tech. Rep. TR-09-03.

Harman, M., Jia, Y., & Zhang, Y. (2015). Achievements, open problems and challenges for search based software testing. *Software Testing, Verification and Validation ICST, 8th International Conference*, 1-12.

Harman, M., & Jones, B. F. (2001). Search-based software engineering. *Information and Software Technology*, 43(4314), 833–839. doi:10.1016/S0950-5849(01)00189-6

Harman, M., & Jones, B. F. (2001). The SEMINAL workshop: Reformulating software engineering as a metaheuristic search problem. *Software Engineering Notes*, 26(266), 62–66. doi:10.1145/505532.505548

Harpham, C., Dawson, C. W., & Brown, M. R. (2004). A review of genetic algorithms applied to training radial basis function networks. *Neural Computing & Applications*, 13(3), 193–201. doi:10.1007/s00521-004-0404-5

Hart, J. P., & Shogan, A. W. (1987). Semi-greedy heuristics: An empirical study. *Operations Research Letters*, 6(3), 107–114. doi:10.1016/0167-6377(87)90021-6

Hassanien, A. E., Moftah, H. M., Azar, A. T., & Shoman, M. (2014). MRI breast cancer diagnosis hybrid approach using adaptive ant-based segmentation and multilayer perceptron neural networks classifier. *Applied Soft Computing*, 14, 62–71. doi:10.1016/j.asoc.2013.08.011

Haykin, S. (1994). *Neural Networks: a Comprehensive Foundation*. Upper Saddle River, NJ: Prentice Hall.

Haykin, S. (1999). *Neural Networks: A Comprehensive Foundation* (2nd ed.). Prentice-Hall.

Haykin, S. S. (2001). *Communication Systems*. Wiley Johns and Sons.

Hedar, A.R., & Fukushima, M. (n.d.). *Derivative-Free Filter Simulated Annealing Method for Constrained Continuous Global Optimization*. Academic Press.

Himmelblau, D. M. (1972). *Applied Nonlinear Programming*. McGrawHill.

Hindi, M. M., & Yampolskiy, R. V. (2012). Genetic algorithm applied to the graph coloring problem. *Proceedings of 23rd Midwest Artificial Intelligence and Cognitive Science Conf.*, 61-66.

Hochreiter, S., & Schmidhuber, J. (1997). Long short-term memory. *Neural Computation*, 9(8), 1735–1780. doi:10.1162/neco.1997.9.8.1735 PMID:9377276

Holland, J. (1975). *Adaptation in Natural and Artificial systems*. University of Michigan Press.

Holland, J. H. (1975). *Adaptation in Natural and Artificial Systems*. Ann Arbor, MI: Univ. of Michigan.

Holland, J. H. (1975). *Adaptation in natural and artificial systems: an introductory analysis with applications to biology, control, and artificial intelligence*. University of Michigan Press.

Holland, J. H. (1975). *Adaptation in natural and artificial systems: An introductory analysis with applications to biology, control, and artificial intelligence.* University of Michigan Press.

Höller, H., Melián, B., & Voss, S. (2008). Applying the pilot method to improve VNS and GRASP metaheuristics for the design of SDH/WDM networks. *European Journal of Operational Research, 191*(3), 691–704. doi:10.1016/j.ejor.2006.12.060

Hon, Y. C., & Mao, X. Z. (1999). A Radial Basis Function Method for Solving Options Pricing Model. *Journal of Financial Engineering, 8*, 31–49.

Hon, Y. C., & Schaback, R. (2001). On UnSymmetric Collocation by Radial Basis Functions. *Applied Mathematics and Computation, 119*(2-3), 177–186. doi:10.1016/S0096-3003(99)00255-6

Hon, Y. C., Schaback, R., & Zhou, X. (2003). An Adaptive Greedy Algorithm for Solving Large RBF Collocation Problems. *Numerical Algorithms, 32*(1), 13–25. doi:10.1023/A:1022253303343

Hopfield, J. J. (1982). Neural networks and physical systems with emergent collective computational abilities. *Proceedings of the National Academy of Sciences of the United States of America, 79*(8), 2554–2558. doi:10.1073/pnas.79.8.2554 PMID:6953413

Hornik, K. (1991). Approximation capabilities of multilayer feedforward networks. *Neural Networks, 4*(2), 251–257. doi:10.1016/0893-6080(91)90009-T

Hornik, K., Stinchcombe, M., & White, H. (1989). Multilayer feedforward networks are universal approximators. *Neural Networks, 2*(5), 359–366. doi:10.1016/0893-6080(89)90020-8

Ho, S. C., & Szeto, W. (2016). GRASP with path relinking for the selective pickup and delivery problem. *Expert Systems with Applications, 51*, 14–25. doi:10.1016/j.eswa.2015.12.015

Hu, X., Eberhart, R.C., & Shi, Y.H. (2003). Engineering optimization with particle swarm. *IEEE Swarm Intelligence Symposium*, 53-57.

Huang, F., Zhou, Z., Zhang, H., & Chen, T. (2000). Pose invariant face recognition. *Proceedings of 4th IEEE International Conference. Automatic Face and Gesture Recognition*, 245–250.

Huang, C. J., Chen, P. W., & Pan, W. T. (2012). Using multi-stage data mining technique to build forecast model for Taiwan stocks. *Neural Computing & Applications, 21*(8), 2057–2063. doi:10.1007/s00521-011-0628-0

Huang, C. L., & Tsai, C. Y. (2009). A hybrid SOFM-SVR with a filter-based feature selection for stock market forecasting. *Expert Systems with Applications, 36*(2), 1529–1539. doi:10.1016/j.eswa.2007.11.062

Huang, C.-J., Yang, D.-X., & Chuang, Y.-T. (2008). Application of wrapper approach and composite classifier to the stock trend prediction. *Expert Systems with Applications, 34*(4), 2870–2878. doi:10.1016/j.eswa.2007.05.035

Huang, H.-C. (2016). Fusion of Modified Bat Algorithm Soft Computing and Dynamic Model Hard Computing to Online Self-Adaptive Fuzzy Control of Autonomous Mobile Robots. *IEEE Transactions on Industrial Informatics, 12*(3), 972–979. doi:10.1109/TII.2016.2542206

Huart, J., & Postaire, J. G. (1994). Integration of computer vision onto weavers for quality control in the textile industry. *Proc. SPIE Mach. Vis. Appl. Ind. Insp., 2183*, 155–163. doi:10.1117/12.171205

Hung, C. C., & Chen, I. C. (2001). Article. *Textile Research Journal, 71*(3), 220–224. doi:10.1177/004051750107100306

Hu, X., & Eberhart, R. C. (2002). Solving constrained nonlinear optimization problems with particle swarm optimization. *Proceedings of the Sixth World MulticonferenceonSystemics, Cybernetics and Informatics.*

Hu, Y., Song, Y., Zhao, K., & Xu, B. (2016). Integrated recovery of aircraft and passengers after airline operation disruption based on a GRASP algorithm. *Transportation Research Part E, Logistics and Transportation Review*, *87*, 97–112. doi:10.1016/j.tre.2016.01.002

Ian, P. (n.d.). *Electronics component and Industry forecast for 2016*. Retrieved June 12, 2016, from http://www.radio-electronics.com/articles/distribution-supply/electronics-component-industry-forecast-for-168

Inbarani, H. H., Azar, A. T., & Jothi, G. (2014). Supervised hybrid feature selection based on PSO and rough sets for medical diagnosis. *Computer Methods and Programs in Biomedicine*, *113*(1), 175–185. doi:10.1016/j.cmpb.2013.10.007 PMID:24210167

Ingber, L. (1989). Very fast simulated re-annealing. *Mathematical and Computer Modelling*, *12*(8), 967–973. doi:10.1016/0895-7177(89)90202-1

Isaaks, E. J., & Srivastava, R. M. (1989). *An introduction to Applied Geostatistics*. New York: Oxford University Press.

Ishii, H., Tada, M., & Masuda, T. (1992). Two scheduling problems with fuzzy due-dates. *Fuzzy Sets and Systems*, *6*(3), 339–347. doi:10.1016/0165-0114(92)90372-B

Ishikawa, A., Amagasa, M., Tomizawa, G., Tatsuta, R., & Mieno, H. (1993). The max-min Delphi method and fuzzy Delphi method via fuzzy integration. *Fuzzy Sets and Systems*, *55*(3), 241–253. doi:10.1016/0165-0114(93)90251-C

Jacobson, Sh. H., & Yücesan, E. (2004). Global Optimization Performance Measures for Generalized Hill Climbing Algorithms. *Journal of Global Optimization*, *29*(2), 173–190. doi:10.1023/B:JOGO.0000042111.72036.11

Jain, A. K., & Dubes, R. C. (1988). Algorithms for Clustering Data. Prentice Hall.

Jain, R., & Kumar, N. (2012). Efficient data hiding scheme using lossless data compression and image steganography. *International Journal of Engineering Science and Technology, 4*(8), 3908-3915.

Jain, A. K., & Flynn, P. (1996). *Image Segmentation Using Clustering*. Advances in Image Understanding.

Janis, I. L., Mann, & Leon. (1977). Decision making: A psychological analysis of conflict, choice, and commitment. New York: Free Press.

Jensen, M. C. (1978). Some Anomalous Evidence Regarding Market Efficiency. *Journal of Financial Economics*, *6*(2-3), 95–102. doi:10.1016/0304-405X(78)90025-9

Jia, Z., & Gong, L. (2008, December). Multi-criteria human resource allocation for optimization problems using multi-objective particle swarm optimization algorithm. In *Computer Science and Software Engineering, 2008 International Conference on* (Vol. 1, pp. 1187-1190). IEEE. doi:10.1109/CSSE.2008.1506

Jiang, M., Chen, W., Zheng, Z., & Zhong, M. (2012, June). Fringe pattern analysis by S-transform. *Optics Communications, Elsevier*, *285*(3), 209–217. doi:10.1016/j.optcom.2011.09.015

Jiang, P., Chen, C., & Liu, X. (2016, April). Time series prediction for evolutions of complex systems: A deep learning approach. In *2016 IEEE International Conference on Control and Robotics Engineering (ICCRE)* (pp. 1-6). IEEE. doi:10.1109/ICCRE.2016.7476150

Jiang, P., & Jiejie, C. (2016). Displacement prediction of landslide based on generalized regression neural networks with K-fold cross-validation. *Neurocomputing*, *198*, 40–47. doi:10.1016/j.neucom.2015.08.118

Jianping, D., Sundararajan, N., & Saratchandran, P. (2002). Communication channel equalization using complex-valued minimal radial basis function neural networks. *IEEE Transactions on Neural Networks*, *13*(3), 687–696. doi:10.1109/TNN.2002.1000133 PMID:18244465

Jing, J., Zhang, H., Wang, J., Li, P., & Jia, J. (2013). Fabric defect detection using Gabor filters and defect classification based on LBP and Tamura method. *Journal of the Textile Institute*, *104*(1), 18–27. doi:10.1080/00405000.2012.692940

Jitpakdee & Aimmanee. (2014). *Image Cluster using fuzzy based firefly algorithm*. Academic Press.

Joines, J. A., & Houck, C. R. (1994). On the use of nonstationary penalty functions to solve nonlinear constrained optimization problems with gas. *Proc. IEEE Int. Conf. Evol. Comp.*, 579-585.

Jonathan, G. C., & Fionn, M. (1998). Automatic visual inspection of woven textiles using a two-stage defect detector. *Optical Engineering (Redondo Beach, Calif.)*, *37*(9), 2536–2542. doi:10.1117/1.601692

Jothi, G. (2016). Hybrid Tolerance Rough Set–Firefly based supervised feature selection for MRI brain tumor image classification. *Applied Soft Computing*, 639–651.

Junfeng, Z., & Ping, W. W. (2016). Leveraging internal resources and external business networks for new product success: A dynamic capabilities perspective. *Industrial Marketing Management*.

Junior, F. R. L., Osiro, L., & Carpinetti, L. C. R. (2014). A comparison between Fuzzy AHP and Fuzzy TOPSIS methods to supplier selection. *Applied Soft Computing*, *21*, 194–209. doi:10.1016/j.asoc.2014.03.014

Kalet, I. (1989). The multitone channel. *IEEE Transactions on Communications*, *37*(2), 119–124. doi:10.1109/26.20079

Kar, A. K. (2016). A Bio inspired computing – A review of algorithms and scope of applications. *Expert Systems with Applications*, *59*, 20–32. doi:10.1016/j.eswa.2016.04.018

Karaboga, D. (2005). *An idea based on honey bee swarm for numerical optimization*. Technical report, Technical report-tr06, Erciyes University, Engineering Faculty, Computer Engineering Department.

Karaboga, D., & Akay, B. (n.d.). *Artificial Bee Colony (ABC), Harmony Search and Bees Algorithms on Numerical Optimization*. Academic Press.

Karaboga, D., & Basturk, B. (n.d.). *Artificial Bee Colony (ABC) Optimization Algorithm for Solving Constrained Optimization Problems*. Springer.

Karaboga, D. (2005). *An Idea Based On Honey Bee Swarm for Numerical Optimization, Technical Report-TR06*. Erciyes University, Engineering Faculty, Computer Engineering Department.

Karaboga, D., & Akay, B. (2009). A comparative study of artificial bee colony algorithm. *Applied Mathematics and Computation*, *214*(1), 108–132. doi:10.1016/j.amc.2009.03.090

Karaboga, D., & Basturk, B. (2007). A powerful and efficient algorithm for numerical function optimization: Artificial bee colony (ABC) algorithm. *Journal of Global Optimization*, *39*(3), 459–471. doi:10.1007/s10898-007-9149-x

Karaboga, D., & Ozturk, C. (2011). A novel clustering approach: Artificial Bee Colony (ABC) algorithm. *Applied Soft Computing*, *11*(1), 652–657. doi:10.1016/j.asoc.2009.12.025

Karmakar, S., Mahato, S.K., & Bhunia, A.K. (2008). Interval oriented multi-section techniques for global optimization. *Journal of Computational and Applied Mathematics*.

Karmakar, S., & Bhunia, A. K. (2013). Uncertain constrained optimization by interval- oriented algorithm. *The Journal of the Operational Research Society*, 1–15.

Kaveh, A., Fahimi-Farzam, M., & Kalateh Ahani, M. (2012). Time-history analysis based optimal design of space trusses: The CMA evolution strategy approach using GRNN and WA. *Structural Engineering & Mechanics*, *44*(3), 379–403. doi:10.12989/sem.2012.44.3.379

Kazem, A., Sharifi, E., Hussain, F. K., Saberi, M., & Hussain, O. K. (2013). Support vector regression with chaos-based firefly algorithm for stock market price forecasting. *Applied Soft Computing*, *13*(2), 947–958. doi:10.1016/j.asoc.2012.09.024

Kellerer, H., Pferschy, U., & Pisinger, D. (2004). *Knap-sack problems*. Springer Berlin Heidelberg. doi:10.1007/978-3-540-24777-7

Keller, T., & Hanzo, L. (2000). Adaptive modulation techniques for duplex OFDM transmission. *IEEE Transactions on Vehicular Technology*, *49*(5), 1893–1906. doi:10.1109/25.892592

Kemmoé, S., Lamy, D., & Tchernev, N. (2016). A GRASP embedding a bi-levelels for solving exible job-shop problems. *IFAC-PapersOnLine*, *49*(12), 1749–1754. doi:10.1016/j.ifacol.2016.07.835

Kemmoe-Tchomte, S., & Tchernev, N. (2014). A GRASPxELS for Scheduling of Job-Shop Like Manufacturing Systems and CO2 Emission Reduction. Springer Berlin Heidelberg.

Kennedy, J. (2011). Particle swarm optimization. In Encyclopedia of machine learning (pp. 760-766). Springer US.

Kennedy, J., & Eberhart, R. (1995). Particle swarm optimization. *IEEE Int. Conf Neural Networks - Conf Proc, 4*, 1942–1948. doi:10.1109/ICNN.1995.488968

Kennedy, J., & Eberhart, R. C. (1995). Particle swarm optimization. *1995 IEEE International Conference on Neural Networks*, *4*, 1942–1948.

Kennedy, J., & Eberhart, R. C. (1995).Particle Swarm Optimization. *1995 IEEE International Conference on Neural Networks*, *4*, 1942–1948.

Khamrui, A., & Mandal, J. K. (2013). A Genetic Algorithm based Steganography using Discrete Cosine Transformation (GASDCT). *International Conference on Computational Intelligence: Modeling Techniques and Applications (CIMTA)*. doi:10.1016/j.protcy.2013.12.342

Khanbabaei, M., & Alborzi, M. (2013). The use of genetic algorithm, clustering and feature selection techniques in construction of decision tree models for credit scoring. *International Journal of Managing Information Technology*, *5*(4), 13–32. doi:10.5121/ijmit.2013.5402

Khan, J., Wei, J. S., Ringner, M., Saal, L. H., Ladanyi, M., Westermann, F., & Meltzer, P. S. (2001). Classification and diagnostic of cancers using gene expression profiling and artificial neural networks. *NCBI*, *7*(6), 673–679. PMID:11385503

Khashei, M., & Bijari, M. (2010). An artificial neural network (p, d, q) model for time series forecasting. *Expert Systems with Applications*, *37*(1), 479–489. doi:10.1016/j.eswa.2009.05.044

Khashei, M., & Bijari, M. (2011). A novel hybridization of artificial neural networks and ARIMA models for time series forecasting. *Applied Soft Computing*, *11*(2), 2664–2675. doi:10.1016/j.asoc.2010.10.015

Khashei, M., & Bijari, M. (2012). A new class of hybrid models for time series forecasting. *Expert Systems with Applications*, *39*(4), 4344–4357. doi:10.1016/j.eswa.2011.09.157

Kilincci, O., & Onal, S. A. (2011). Fuzzy AHP approach for supplier selection in a washingmachine company. *Expert Systems with Applications*, *38*(8), 9656–9664. doi:10.1016/j.eswa.2011.01.159

Kim, S. H., & Chun, S. H. (1998). Graded forecasting using an array of bipolar predictions: Application of probabilistic neural networks to a stock market index. *International Journal of Forecasting*, *14*(3), 323–337. doi:10.1016/S0169-2070(98)00003-X

Kim, S. S., Kim, G., Byeon, J. H., & Taheri, J. (2012). Particle Swarm Optimization for Location Mobility Management. *International Journal of Innovative Computing, Information, & Control*, *8*(12), 8387–8398.

Kim, S., Lee, M. H., & Woo, K. B. (1998). Wavelet Analysis to defects detection in weaving processes. *Proc. IEEE Int. Symp. Industrial Electronics*, 3, 1406-1409.

Kirkpatrick, S. (1984). Optimization by simulated annealing – quantitative studies. *Journal of Statistical Physics, 34*(5-6), 975–986. doi:10.1007/BF01009452

Kirkpatrick, S., Gelatt, C. D., & Vecchi, M. P. (1983). Optimization by simulated annealing. *Science, 220*(4598), 671–680. doi:10.1126/science.220.4598.671 PMID:17813860

Kitanidis, P. K. (1991). Orthonormal residuals in geostatistics: Model criticism and parameter estimation. *Mathematical Geology, 23*(5), 741–758. doi:10.1007/BF02082534

Knowles, J. D., & Corne, D. W. (2000). Approximating the nondominated front using the Pareto archived evolution strategy. *Evolutionary Computation, 8*(2), 149–172. doi:10.1162/106365600568167 PMID:10843519

Ko, C. N. (2012). Identification of non-linear systems using radial basis function neural networks with time-varying learning algorithm. *IET Signal Processing, 6*(2), 91–98. doi:10.1049/iet-spr.2011.0025

Kohonen, T. (1990, September). The self-organizing map. *Proceedings of the IEEE, 78*(9), 1464–1480. doi:10.1109/5.58325

Kolev, L. V. (1993). *Interval Methods for Circuit Analysis*. Singapore: World Scientific. doi:10.1142/2039

Kong, Y., Xing-wei, L., & Zhang, Z. (2009). Minimax probability machine regression for wireless traffic short term forecasting. *Proceedings – 2009 1st UK-India International Workshop on Cognitive Wireless Systems, UKIWCWS*, 1–5. doi:10.1109/UKIWCWS.2009.5749407

Koopmans, T., & Beckman, M. (1957). Assignment problems and the location of economic activities. *Econometrica, 25*(1), 53–76. doi:10.2307/1907742

Koza, J. R. (1992). *Genetic programming: On the programming of computers by means of natural selection*. MIT Press.

Kozarzewski, B. (2010). A neural network based time series forecasting system. *3rd International Conference on Human System Interaction*, 59–62. doi:10.1109/HSI.2010.5514591

Krongold, B. S., Ramchandran, K., & Jones, D. L. (2000). Computationally Efficient Optimal Power Allocation Algorithm for Multicarrier Communication Systems. *IEEE Transactions on Communications, 48*(1), 23–27. doi:10.1109/26.818869

Krueger, V., & Sommer, G. (2000), Gabor wavelet network for object representation. *DAGM Symposium*, 13–15.

Kubale, M. (2004). Graph colorings. American Mathematical Society.

Kulatilake, P. H. S. W. (1989). Probabilistic Potentiometric surface mapping. *Journal of the Geotechnical Engineering Division, 115*(11), 1569–1587. doi:10.1061/(ASCE)0733-9410(1989)115:11(1569)

Kulatilake, P. H. S. W., & Miller, K. M. (1987). A scheme for estimating the spatial variation of soil properties in three dimensions. *Proceedings of the Fifth International Conference on Application of Statistics and Probabilities in Soil and Structural Engineering*, 669–677.

Kulpa, K., Pownuk, A., & Skalna, I. (1998). Analysis of linear mechanical structures with uncertainties by means of interval methods. *Comput. Assist. Mech. Eng. Sci., 5*, 443–477.

Kumar, A. (2008). (2008), Computer vision –based fabric defect detection: A syrvetm IEEE. *Transactions on Industrial Electronics, 55*(1), 348–363. doi:10.1109/TIE.1930.896476

Kumar, A., & Pang, G. (2002). Defect detection in textured materials using optimized filters. *IEEE Transactions on Systems, Man, and Cybernetics, 32*(5), 553–570. doi:10.1109/TSMCB.2002.1033176 PMID:18244861

Kumar, A., & Pang, G. K. H. (2002). Defect Detection in Textured Materials Using Gabor Filters. *IEEE Transactions on Industry Applications*, *38*(2), 425–440. doi:10.1109/28.993164

Kumar, P. R., & Ravi, V. (2007). prediction in banks and firms via statistical and intelligent techniques – A review. *European Journal of Operational Research*, *180*(1), 1–28. doi:10.1016/j.ejor.2006.08.043

Kuncheva, L. (2004). *Combining Pattern Classifiers*. John Wiley & Sons. doi:10.1002/0471660264

Kuo, R. J., Chen, C. H., & Hwang, Y. C. (2001). An intelligent stock trading decision support system through integration of genetic algorithm based fuzzy neural network and artificial neural network. *Fuzzy Sets and Systems*, *118*(1), 21–24. doi:10.1016/S0165-0114(98)00399-6

Lacerda, E., Carvalho, A. C., Braga, A. P., & Ludermir, T. B. (2005). Evolutionary radial basis functions for credit assessment. *Applied Intelligence*, *22*(3), 167–181. doi:10.1007/s10791-005-6617-0

Lacomme, P., Moukrim, A., Quilliot, A., & Vinot, M. (2016). The integrated production and transportation scheduling problem based on a GRASPxELS resolution scheme. *IFAC-PapersOnLine*, *49*(12), 1466 - 1471.

Lai, R. K., Fan, C. Y., Huang, W. H., & Chang, P. C. (2009). Evolving and clustering fuzzy decision tree for financial time series data forecasting. *Expert Systems with Applications*, *36*(2), 3761–3773. doi:10.1016/j.eswa.2008.02.025

Lam, A. Y. S. & Li, V. O. K.(2010). Chemical-reaction-inspired metaheuristic for optimization. *IEEE Transactions on Evolutionary Computation*, *14*(3), 381-399.

Lam, A. Y. S., & Li, V. O. K. (2012). Chemical Reaction Optimization: A tutorial. *Memtic Computing*, *4*(1), 3–17. doi:10.1007/s12293-012-0075-1

Lanckriet, G. R. G., Ghaoui, L. E., Bhattacharyya, C., & Jordan, M. I. (2002). A Robust minimax approach to classification. *Journal of Machine Learning Research*, *3*, 555–582.

Laursen, L. N., & Andersen, P. H. (2016). Supplier involvement in NPD: A quasi-experiment at Unilever. *Industrial Marketing Management*, *58*, 162–171. doi:10.1016/j.indmarman.2016.05.023

Lee, C. M., & Ko, C. N. (2009). Time series prediction using RBF neural networks with a non-linear time-varying evolution PSO algorithm. *Neurocomputing*, *73*(1), 449–460. doi:10.1016/j.neucom.2009.07.005

Lee, D. S., Vassiliadis, V. S., & Park, J. M. (2002). List-Based Threshold-Accepting Algorithm for Zero-Wait Scheduling of Multiproduct Batch Plants. *Industrial & Engineering Chemistry*, *41*(25), 6579–6588. doi:10.1021/ie010570n

Lee, D. S., Vassiliadis, V. S., & Park, J. M. (2004). A novel threshold accepting meta-heuristic for the job-shop scheduling problem. *Computers & Operations Research*, *31*(13), 2199–2213. doi:10.1016/S0305-0548(03)00172-2

Lee, H., Hong, S., & Kim, E. (2009). A new genetic feature selection with neural network ensemble. *International Journal of Computer Mathematics*, *86*(7), 1105–1117. doi:10.1080/00207160701724760

Lee, H., Hong, S., & Kim, E. (2009). Neural Network Ensemble with probabilistic fusion and its application to gait recognition. *Neurocomputing*, *72*(7-9), 1557–1564. doi:10.1016/j.neucom.2008.09.009

Leung, F. H., Lam, H. K., Ling, S. H., & Tam, P. K. (2003). Tuning of the structure and parameters of a neural network using an improved genetic algorithm. *IEEE Transactions on Neural Networks*, *14*(1), 79–88. doi:10.1109/TNN.2002.804317 PMID:18237992

Li, H., Zhou, H., & Cai, Q. (2010).An Asset Evalution Method Based on Neural Network. *The 2nd IEEE International Conference on information management and engineering (ICIME)*, 582-585.

Li, Y., Pardalos, P. M., & Resende, M. G. C. (1993). A greedy randomized adaptive search procedure for the quadratic assignment problem. In P. M. Pardalos & H. Wolkowicz (Eds.), *Quadratic Assignment and Related Problems, Proceedings of a DIMACS Workshop* (pp. 237-262). DIMACS/AMS.

Lian, R. J. (2014). Adaptive self-organizing fuzzy sliding-mode radial basis-function neural-network controller for robotic systems. *IEEE Transactions on Industrial Electronics, 61*(3), 1493–1503. doi:10.1109/TIE.2013.2258299

Li, H. Z., Zeng, H., & Chen, X. Q. (2006). An experimental study of tool wear and cutting force variation in the end milling of Inconel 718 with coated carbide inserts. *Journal of Materials Processing Technology, 180*(1-3), 296–304. doi:10.1016/j.jmatprotec.2006.07.009

Li, M., Liu, J., Jiang, Y., & Feng, W. (2012). Complex Chebyshev functional link neural network behavioral model for broadband wireless power amplifiers. *IEEE Transactions on Microwave Theory and Techniques, 60*(6), 1979–1989. doi:10.1109/TMTT.2012.2189239

Lim, A., Zhu, Y., Lou, Q., & Rodrigues, B. (2005). Heuristic methods for graph coloring problems. *Proceedings of Symposium on Applied Computing.*

Lim, E. A., & Zainuddin, Z. (2008). An Improved Fast Training Algorithm for RBF Networks using Symmetry-Based Fuzzy C-Means Clustering. *Matematika, 24*(2), 141–148.

Lin, J., & Zhong, Y. (2015). Multi-agent list-based threshold-accepting algorithm for numerical optimisation. *International Journal of Computing Science and Mathematics, 6*(5), 501–509. doi:10.1504/IJCSM.2015.072970

Lin, Y., Bian, Z., & Liu, X. (2016). Developing a dynamic neighborhood structure for an adaptive hybrid simulated annealing – tabu search algorithm to solve the symmetrical traveling salesman problem. *Applied Soft Computing, 49,* 937–952. doi:10.1016/j.asoc.2016.08.036

Lin, Y.-K. (2014). A data hiding scheme based upon DCT coefficient modification. *Computer Standards & Interfaces, 36*(5), 855–862. doi:10.1016/j.csi.2013.12.013

Li, P., Zhang, H., Jing, J., Li, R., & Zhao, J. (2015). Fabric defect detection based on multi-scale wavelet transform and Gaussian mixture model method. *Journal of the Textile Institute, 106*(6), 587–592. doi:10.1080/00405000.2014.929790

Lipo, W., Yaoli, W., & Qing, C. (2016). Feature selection methods for big data bioinformatics: A survey from the search perspective. *Methods (San Diego, Calif.), 111,* 21–31. doi:10.1016/j.ymeth.2016.08.014 PMID:27592382

Liu, H-C., Lee, Y.-H., & Lee, M.-C. (2009). Forecasting china stock markets volatility via GARCH models under skewed-GED distribution. *Journal Money Investment Banking,* 5–14.

Liu, B., Cui, Q., Jiang, T., & Ma, S. (2004). A combinational feature selection and ensemble neural network method for classification of gene expression data. *BMC Bioinform., 5*(1), 136–147. doi:10.1186/1471-2105-5-136 PMID:15450124

Liu, Y.-H. (2011). Incorporating scatter search and threshold accepting in finding maximum likelihood estimates for the multinomial probit model. *European Journal of Operational Research, 211*(1), 130–138. doi:10.1016/j.ejor.2010.10.038

Li, X. L., Shao, Z. J., & Qian, J. X. (2002). An optimizing method based on autonomous animats: Fish-swarm algorithm. *System Engineering Theory and Practice, 22*(11), 32–38.

Li, Y., & Ryan, W. E. (2007). Mutual Information-Based Adaptive Bit-Loading Algorithms for LDPC-Coded OFDM. *IEEE Transactions on Wireless Communications, 6*(5), 1670–1680. doi:10.1109/TWC.2007.360369

Li, Z., Liu, X., Duan, X., & Huang, F. (2010). Comparative research on particle swarm optimization and genetic algorithm. *Computer and Information Science, 3*(1), 120. doi:10.5539/cis.v3n1p120

Lotte, Congedo, Lécuyer, Lamarche, & Arnaldi. (2007). A review of classification algorithm for EEG-based brain-computer interfaces. Academic Press.

Lu, C. J., & Wu, J. Y. (2011). An efficient CMAC neural network for stock index forecasting. *Expert Systems with Applications*, *38*(12), 15194–15201. doi:10.1016/j.eswa.2011.05.082

Lumb, P. (1975). Spatial variability of soil properties. *Proceedings Second International Conference on Application of Statistics and Probability in Soil and Structural Engineering*, 397–421.

Lundy, M., & Mees, A. (1986). Convergence of an annealing algorithm. *Mathematical Programming*, *34*(1), 111–124. doi:10.1007/BF01582166

Luque-Baena, R. M., Urda, D., Subirats, J. I., Franco, L., & Jerez, J. M. (2014). Application of genetic algorithms and constructive neural networks for the analysis of microarray cancer data. *Theoretical Biology & Medical Modelling*, *11*(Suppl. 1), S7. doi:10.1186/1742-4682-11-S1-S7 PMID:25077572

MacQueen, J. (1967). Some Methods for Classification and Analysis of Multivariate Observations. *Proceedings of Fifth Berkeley Symp. Math. Statistics and Probability*, 281-297.

Madhumita, P. & Partha, S. (2013). Performance Analysis of Test Data Generation for Path Coverage Based Testing Using Three Meta-heuristic Algorithms. *International Journal of Computer Science and Informatics*, (32), 2231–5292.

Madhumita, P., & Durga, P. M. (2014). Generating Test Data for Path Coverage Based Testing Using Genetic Algorithms. *Proceedings of ICICIC Global Conference*.

Majhi & Sa. (2007, July). FLANN-based adaptive threshold selection for detection of impulsive noise in images. *AEU-International Journal of Electronics and Communications, 61*(7), 478-484.

Majhi, R., Panda, G., & Sahoo, G. (2009). Development and performance evaluation of FLANN based model for forecasting of stock markets. *Expert Systems with Applications*, *36*(3), 6800–6808. doi:10.1016/j.eswa.2008.08.008

Maji, P. (2009). f-information measures for efficient selection of discriminative genes from microarray data. *IEEE Transactions on Bio-Medical Engineering*, *56*(4), 1063–1069. doi:10.1109/TBME.2008.2004502 PMID:19272938

Mallick-Goswami, B., & Datta, A. K. (2000). Detecting defects in fabric with laser-based morphological image processing. *Textile Research Journal*, *70*(9), 758–762. doi:10.1177/004051750007000902

Mall, R. (2014). *Fundamentals of software engineering*. PHI Learning Pvt., Ltd.

Mandic, D., & Chambers, J. (2001). *Recurrent Neural Networks for Prediction: Learning Algorithms, Architectures and Stability*. New York: John Wiley & Sons. doi:10.1002/047084535X

Manufacturing & Industrial: Waste Minimization. (n.d.). Retrieved June 12, 2016, from https://www.wm.com/sustainability-services/documents/insights/Waste%20Minimization%20Insight.pdf

Man, Z., Lee, K., Wang, D., Cao, Z., & Khoo, S. (2013, June). An optimal weight learning machine for handwritten digit image recognition. *Signal Processing, Elsevier*, *93*(6), 1624–1638. doi:10.1016/j.sigpro.2012.07.016

Maragathavalli, P. (2011). *Search-based software test data generation using evolutionary computation*. arXiv preprint arXiv:1103.0125

Marini, F. (2009). 3.14 - Neural Networks. *Comprehensive Chemometrics*, 477-505.

Martins de Sá, E., Contreras, I., & Cordeau, J. F. (2015). Exact and heuristic algorithms for the design of hub networks with multiple lines. *European Journal of Operational Research*, *246*(1), 186–198. doi:10.1016/j.ejor.2015.04.017

Martins, S., Resende, M., Ribeiro, C., & Pardalos, P. (2000). A parallel GRASP for the Steiner tree problem in graphs using a hybrid local search strategy. *Journal of Global Optimization, 17*(1), 267–283. doi:10.1023/A:1026546708757

Mateus, G. R., Resende, M. G., & Silva, R. M. (2011). GRASP with path-relinking for the generalized quadratic assignment problem. *Journal of Heuristics, 17*(5), 527–565. doi:10.1007/s10732-010-9144-0

Matheron, G. (1963). Principles of geostatistics. *Economic Geology and the Bulletin of the Society of Economic Geologists, 58*(8), 1246–1266. doi:10.2113/gsecongeo.58.8.1246

Matyas, J. (1965). Random optimization. *Automation and Remote Control, 26*(2), 246–253.

Ma, W., Wang, Y., & Dong, N. (2010). Study on stock price prediction based on BP neural network. *IEEE International conference on Emergency Management and Management Sciences (ICEMMS)*, 57–60.

Mazzola, E., Bruccoleri, M., & Perrone, G. (2015). Supply chain of innovation and new product development. *Journal of Purchasing and Supply Management, 21*(4), 273–284. doi:10.1016/j.pursup.2015.04.006

McCahon, C. S., & Lee, E. S. (1990). Job sequencing with fuzzy processing times. *Computers & Mathematics with Applications (Oxford, England), 19*(7), 31–41. doi:10.1016/0898-1221(90)90191-L

McClelland, D. C. (1973). Testing for competence rather than for" intelligence. *The American Psychologist, 28*(1), 1–14. doi:10.1037/h0034092 PMID:4684069

McCulloch, W. S., & Pitts, W. H. (1943). A Logical Calculus of the Ideas Immanent in Nervous Activity. *The Bulletin of Mathematical Biophysics, 5*(4), 115–133. doi:10.1007/BF02478259

McDougall, P. P. (1989). International versus domestic entrepreneurship: New venture strategic behaviour and industry structure. *Journal of Business Venturing, 4*(6), 387–400. doi:10.1016/0883-9026(89)90009-8

McMinn, P. (2004). Search-based software test data generation: A survey. *Software Testing Verification and Reliability*, (142), 105-156.

McMinn, P., Harman, M., Fraser, G., & Kapfhammer, G. M. (2016, May). Automated search for good coverage criteria: moving from code coverage to fault coverage through search-based software engineering. *Proceedings of the 9th International Workshop on Search-Based Software Testing*, 43-44. doi:10.1145/2897010.2897013

Mehmet, L. K., Balas, C. E., & Dilek, I. K. (2016). Stability assessment of rubble-mound breakwaters using genetic programming. *Ocean Engineering, 111*, 8–12. doi:10.1016/j.oceaneng.2015.10.058

Merz, P., & Freisleben, B. (1998). *Memetic Algorithms and the Fitness Landscape of the Graph Bi-partitioning Problem*. LNCS. doi:10.1007/BFb0056918

Metropolis, N., Rosenbluth, A. W., Rosenbluth, M. N., Teller, A. H., & Teller, E. (1953). Equation of State Calculations by Fast Computing Machines. *The Journal of Chemical Physics, 21*(6), 1087–1092. doi:10.1063/1.1699114

Michalewicz, Z., & Schoenauer, M. (1995). Evolutionary Algorithms for Constrained Parameter Optimization Problems. *Evolutionary Computation, 4*(1), 1–32. doi:10.1162/evco.1996.4.1.1

Michiels, W., Aarts, E., & Korst, J. (2007). *Theoretical aspects of local search*. Springer Science & Business Media.

Mili, F., & Hamdi, M. (2012). A hybrid evolutionary functional link artificial neural network for data mining and classification. *International Journal of Advanced Computer Science and Applications, 3*(8), 89–95. doi:10.14569/IJACSA.2012.030815

Mishra, A., & Johri, P. (2015). A Review on Video Steganography using GA. *International Journal of Innovative & Advancement in Computer Science, 4*(SI), 120-124.

Mishra, S. K., Panda, G., & Meher, S. (2009). Chebyshev functional link artificial neural networks for denoising of image corrupted by salt and pepper noise. *International Journal of Recent Trends in Enginering, 1*(1), 413–417.

Mladenovic, N., & Hansen, P. (1997). Variable neighborhood search. *Computers & Operations Research, 24*(11), 1097–1100. doi:10.1016/S0305-0548(97)00031-2

Mohamad, M. S. (2009). Particle swarm optimization for gene selection in classifying cancer classes. *Proceedings of the 14th International Symposium on Artificial Life and Robotics*, 762–765. doi:10.1007/s10015-009-0712-z

Mohammed, A. J., Yusof, Y., & Husni, H. (2015). Document clustering based on firefly algorithm. *Journal of Computer Science, 11*(3), 453–465. doi:10.3844/jcssp.2015.453.465

Mohan, B. C., & Baskaran, R. (2012). A survey: Ant Colony Optimization based recent research and implementation on several engineering domain. *Expert Systems with Applications, 39*(4), 4618–4627. doi:10.1016/j.eswa.2011.09.076

Mohanty, H., Mohanty, J. R., & Balakrishnan, A. (2016). *Trends in Software Testing.* Springer.

Molodtsov, D. (1999). Soft set theory - First results. *Computers & Mathematics with Applications (Oxford, England), 37*(4-5), 19–31. doi:10.1016/S0898-1221(99)00056-5

Moscato, P., & Fontanari, J. F. (1990). Stochastic versus deterministic update in simulated annealing. *Physics Letters. [Part A], 146*(4), 204–208. doi:10.1016/0375-9601(90)90166-L

Mostafa, M. M. (2010). Forecasting stock exchange movements using neural networks: Empirical evidence from Kuwait. *Expert Systems with Applications, 37*(9), 6302–6309. doi:10.1016/j.eswa.2010.02.091

Mousa, A. A. A. (2014). Hybrid ant optimization system for multiobjective economic emission load dispatch problem under fuzziness. *Swarm and Evolutionary Computation, 18*, 11–21. doi:10.1016/j.swevo.2014.06.002

Muammer, N., Abdullah, A., & Hasan, G. (2007). The effect of cutting speed and cutting tool geometry on machinability properties of nickel-base Inconel 718 super alloys. *Materials & Design, 28*(4), 1334–1338. doi:10.1016/j.matdes.2005.12.008

Mukherjee, A., & De, D. (2016). Location Management in Mobile Network: A Survey. *Computer Science Review, 19*, 1–14. doi:10.1016/j.cosrev.2015.12.001

Musmanno, L. M., & Ribeiro, C. C. (2016). Heuristics for the generalized median graph problem. *European Journal of Operational Research, 254*(2), 371–384. doi:10.1016/j.ejor.2016.03.048

Naik, B., Nayak, J., & Behera, H. S. (in press). A global-best harmony search based gradient descent learning FLANN (GbHS-GDL-FLANN) for data classification. *Egyptian Informatics Journal, Elsevier*.

Naldi, L., & Davidsson, P. (2013). Entrepreneurial growth: The role of international knowledge acquisition as moderated by firm age. *Journal of Business Venturing*, 687–703.

Nanda, S. J., & Panda, G. (2014). A survey on nature inspired metaheuristic algorithms for partitional clustering. *Swarm and Evolutionary Computation, 16*, 1–18. doi:10.1016/j.swevo.2013.11.003

Nandy, S., Sarkar, P. P., & Das, A. (2012). Analysis of a Nature Inspired Firefly-Algorithm Based Back Propagation Neural Network Training. Academic Press.

Narayansahoo, L., Bhunia, A. K., & Roy, D. (2014). Reliability optimization with and low level redundancies in interval environment via genetic algorithm. *Int J syst Assur Manag, 5*(4), 513-523.

Narendra, K. S., & Parthasarathy, K. (1990). Identification and control of dynamic systems using neural networks. *IEEE Transactions on Neural Networks*, *1*(1), 4–27. doi:10.1109/72.80202 PMID:18282820

Narutaki, N., Yamane, Y., Hayashi, K., Kitagawa, T., & Uehara, K. (1993). High speed machining of Inconel 718 with ceramic tools. *Annals of CIRP*, *42*(1), 103–106. doi:10.1016/S0007-8506(07)62402-0

Nascimento, M. C., Resende, M. G., & Toledo, F. M. (2010). Grasp heuristic with path-relinking for the multi-plant capacitated lot sizing problem. *European Journal of Operational Research*, *200*(3), 747–754. doi:10.1016/j.ejor.2009.01.047

Nayak, B. (n.d.). *Lean Manufacturing and Value Management Convergence of Divergent Tools*. Retrieved June 12, 2016, from http://www.value-eng.org/knowledge_bank/attachments/200629.pdf

Nayak, S. C., Misra, B. B., & Behera, H. S. (2012, October). Evaluation of normalization methods on neuro-genetic models for stock index forecasting. In *Information and Communication Technologies (WICT), 2012 World Congress on* (pp. 602-607). IEEE. doi:10.1109/WICT.2012.6409147

Nayak, S. C., Misra, B. B., & Behera, H. S. (2013, September). Hybridzing chemical reaction optimization and artificial neural network for stock future index forecasting. In *Emerging Trends and Applications in Computer Science (ICETACS), 2013 1st International Conference on* (pp. 130-134). IEEE. doi:10.1109/ICETACS.2013.6691409

Nayak, S. C., Misra, B. B., & Behera, H. S. (2014). Exploration and Incorporation of Virtual Data Position for Efficient Forecasting of Financial Time Series. *Int. Journal of Industrial and Systems Engineering*.

Nayak, S. C., Misra, B. B., & Behera, H. S. (2015). Comparison of Performance of Different Functions in Functional Link Artificial Neural Network: A Case Study on Stock Index Forecasting. In Computational Intelligence in Data Mining (vol. 1, pp. 479-487). Springer India. doi:10.1007/978-81-322-2205-7_45

Nayak, S. C., Misra, B. B., & Behera, H. S. (2016). Improving Performance of Higher Order Neural Network using Artificial Chemical Reaction Optimization: A Case Study on Stock Market Forecasting. *Applied Artificial Higher Order Neural Networks for Control and Recognition*, 253.

Nayak, J., Naik, B., & Behera, H. S. (2015). *A novel Chemical Reaction Optimization based Higher order Neural Network (CRO-HONN) for nonlinear classification*. Ain Shams Engineering Journal; doi:10.1016/j.asej.2014.12.013

Nayak, S. C., Misra, B. B., & Behera, H. S. (2012). Stock index prediction with neuro-genetic hybrid techniques. *Int. J. Comput. Sci. Inform*, *2*, 27–34.

Nayak, S. C., Misra, B. B., & Behera, H. S. (2012, February). Index prediction with neuro- genetic hybrid network: A comparative analysis of performance. *2012 International Conference on Computing, Communication and Applications*, 1-6. doi:10.1109/ICCCA.2012.6179215

Nayak, S. C., Misra, B. B., & Behera, H. S. (2014). Impact of data normalization on stock index forecasting. *Int. J. Comput. Inf. Syst. Ind. Manage. Appl*, *6*, 257–269.

Nayak, S. C., Misra, B. B., & Behera, H. S. (2015). *Artificial chemical reaction optimization of neural networks for efficient prediction of stock market indices*. Ain Shams Engineering Journal.

Nayak, S. C., Misra, B. B., & Behera, H. S. (2016). An Adaptive Second Order Neural Network with Genetic-Algorithm-based Training (ASONN-GA) to Forecast the Closing Prices of the Stock Market. *International Journal of Applied Metaheuristic Computing*, *7*(2), 39–57. doi:10.4018/IJAMC.2016040103

Nayak, S. C., Misra, B. B., & Behera, H. S. (2016). Efficient forecasting of financial time-series data with virtual adaptive neuro-fuzzy inference system. *International Journal of Business Forecasting and Marketing Intelligence*, *2*(4), 379–402. doi:10.1504/IJBFMI.2016.080132

Nehru, G., & Dhar, P. (2012). A Detailed look of Audio Steganography Techniques using LSB and Genetic Algorithm Approach. *International Journal of Computer Science Issues, 9*(1), 402-406.

Netjinda, N., Achalakul, T., & Sirinaovakul, B. (2015). Particle Swarm Optimization inspired by starling flock behavior. *Applied Soft Computing, 35*, 411–422. doi:10.1016/j.asoc.2015.06.052

Neto, J. X. V., Reynoso-Meza, G., Ruppel, T. H., Mariani, V. C., & dos Santos Coelho, L. (2017). Solving non-smooth economic dispatch by a new combination of continuous GRASP algorithm and diferential evolution. *International Journal of Electrical Power & Energy Systems, 84*, 13–24. doi:10.1016/j.ijepes.2016.04.012

Newsroom, I. H. S. (n.d.). *Rise of the Machines: Industrial Machinery Market Growth to Double in 2014.* Retrieved June 12, 2016, from http://press.ihs.com/press-release/design-supply-chain/rise-machines-industrial-machinery-market-growth-double-2014

Nicos, M., Telemachos, S., Konstantinos, D., Costas, P., & Michael, S. (1998). ECG pattern recognition and classification using nonlinear transformations and neural networks: A review. *International Journal of Medical Informatics*, 191–208. PMID:9848416

Niknam, T., & Amiri, B. (2010). An efficient hybrid approach based on PSO, ACO and k-means for cluster analysis. *Applied Soft Computing, 10*(1), 183–197. doi:10.1016/j.asoc.2009.07.001

Nimpa, J. L., & Lichter, H. (2016). An Overview on Automated Test Data Generation. *Full-Scale Software Engineering/ Current Trends in Release Engineering, 31.*

Niu, X.-X., & Suen, C. Y. (2012, April). A novel hybrid CNN-SVM classifier for recognizing handwritten digits. *Pattern Recognition, Elsevier, 45*(4), 1318–1325. doi:10.1016/j.patcog.2011.09.021

Obikawa, T., Kamata, Y., Asano, Y., Nakayama, K., & Otieno, A. W. (2008). Micro-liter lubrication machining of Inconel 718. *International Journal of Machine Tools & Manufacture, 48*(15), 1605–1612. doi:10.1016/j.ijmachtools.2008.07.011

Oh, K. J., & Kim, K. J. (2002). Analyzing stock market tick data using piecewise non linear model. *Expert Systems with Applications, 22*(3), 249–255. doi:10.1016/S0957-4174(01)00058-6

Oliveira, F. A., Zarate, L. E., & Reis, M. A. (2011). The use of artificial neural networks in the analysis and prediction of stock prices. *IEEE International Conference on Systems, Man and Cybernetics (SMC)*, 2151–2155.

Oppenheimer, E. P., & Michel, A. N. (1988). Application of interval analysis techniques to linear systems: Part-I—fundamental results. *IEEE Transactions on Circuits and Systems, 35*, 1243–1256. doi:10.1109/31.7599

Oppenheimer, E. P., & Michel, A. N. (1988). Application of interval analysis techniques to linear systems: part-II—the interval matrix exponential function. *IEEE Transactions on Circuits and Systems, 35*(10), 1230–1242. doi:10.1109/31.7598

Orso, A., & Rothermel, G. (2014). Software testing: a research travelogue 2000–2014. In *Proceedings of the on Future of Software Engineering* (pp. 117-132). ACM.

Osman, I. H., & Laporte, G. (1996). Metaheuristics: A bibliography. *Annals of Operations Research, 63*, 513-623.

Ou, P., & Wang, H. (2009). Prediction of stock market index movement by ten data 549 mining techniques. *Modern Applied Science, 3*(12), 28. doi:10.5539/mas.v3n12p28

Özdemir, S., & Erçil, A. (1996). Markov random fields and Karhunen-Loève transforms for defect inspection of textile products. *Proceedings of IEEE Emerging Technologies and Factory Automation Conference (EFTA), 2*, 697-703.

Ozturk & Ozturk. (2014, June). Hybrid neural network and genetic algorithm based machining feature recognition. *Journal of Intelligent Manufacturing, 15*(3), 287-298.

Ozturk, U. A., & Turan, M. E. (2012). Prediction of effects of microstructural phases using generalized regression neural network. *Construction & Building Materials*, *29*, 279–283. doi:10.1016/j.conbuildmat.2011.10.015

Page, A. L. (1994). Result from PDMA's best practices study: The best practices of high impact new product programs. *The EEI/PDMA Conference*.

Page, A. L. (1993). Assessing new product development practices and performance: Establishing crucial norms. *Journal of Product Innovation Management*, *10*(4), 273–290. doi:10.1016/0737-6782(93)90071-W

Pal Thethi, H., Roy, S. S., Mondal, S., Majhi, B., & Panda, G. (2011, April). Improved Identification Model for Nonlinear Dynamic Systems Using FLANN and Various Types of DE. *Proc. of International Symposium on Devices, MEMS, intelligent Systems, Communications, Sikkim*, 1-6.

Pal, D., & Mahapatra, G. S. (2015). *Parametric functional representation of interval number with arithmetic operations. Int. J. comput. Math.*

Pal, D., Mahapatra, G. S., & Samanta, G. P. (2013). Optimal harvesting of pre-predator system with interval biological parameters: A biological model. *Mathematical Biosciences*, *241*(2), 181–187. doi:10.1016/j.mbs.2012.11.007 PMID:23219573

Palmieri, F., Fiore, U., Ricciardi, S., & Castiglione, A. (2016). Grasp-based resource re-optimization for e ective big data access in federated clouds. *Future Generation Computer Systems*, *54*, 168–179. doi:10.1016/j.future.2015.01.017

Pandit, B. L., & Siddharthan, N. S. (1998). Technological acquisition and investment: Lessons from recent indian experience. *Journal of Business Venturing*, *13*(1), 43–55. doi:10.1016/S0883-9026(97)00003-7

Pan, X., Ye, X., & Zhang, S. (2005, December). A hybrid method for robust car plate character recognition. *Engineering Applications of Artificial Intelligence, Elsevier*, *18*(8), 963–972. doi:10.1016/j.engappai.2005.03.011

Panyam, Lakshmi, Krishnan, & Rao. (2016, December). Modelling of palm leaf character recognition system using transorm based techniques. *Pattern Recognition Letters*, *84*, 29–34. doi:10.1016/j.patrec.2016.07.020

Pao, Y. H. (1989). *Adaptive Pattern Recognition and Neural Networks*. Reading, MA: Addison-Wesley Publishing Co., Inc.

Parija, S. R., Sahu, P. K., & Singh, S. S. (2017). Cost Reduction in Location Management Using Reporting Cell Planning and Particle Swarm Optimization. *Wireless Personal Communication*, 1–21.

Parija, S.R., Singh, S.S., & Swayamsiddha, S. (2017). Particle Swarm Optimization for Cost Reduction in Mobile Location Management Using Reporting Cell Planning Approach. *Recent Developments in Intelligent Nature-Inspired Computing*, 171-189.

Park, H. S., Chung, Y. D., Oh, S. K., Pedrycz, W., & Kim, H. K. (2011). Design of information granule-oriented RBF neural networks and its application to power supply for high-field magnet. *Engineering Applications of Artificial Intelligence*, *24*(3), 543–554. doi:10.1016/j.engappai.2010.11.001

Park, J., Gunn, F., Lee, Y. H., & Shim, S. (2015). Consumer acceptance of a revolutionary technology-driven product: The role of adoption in the industrial design development. *Journal of Retailing and Consumer Services*, *26*, 115–124. doi:10.1016/j.jretconser.2015.05.003

Parsons, S. (2005). *Ant Colony Optimization by Marco Dorigo and Thomas Stützle*. MIT Press.

Parsopoulos, K. E., & Vrahatis, M. N. (2002). *Particle Swarm Optimization Method for Constrained Optimization Problems, Intelligent Technologies - Theory and Applications: New Trends in Intelligent Technologies*. IOS Press.

Parsopoulos, K. E., & Vrahatis, M. N. (2005). A Unified Particle Swarm Optimization for solving constrained engineering optimization problems. *Lecture Notes in Computer Science*, *3612*, 582–591. doi:10.1007/11539902_71

Passino, K. M. (2002). Biomimicry of bacterial foraging for distributed optimization and control. *IEEE Control Systems, 22*(3), 52-67.

Passino, K. M. (2002). Biomimicry of bacterial foraging for distributed optimization and control. *Control Systems, IEEE, 22*(3), 52–67. doi:10.1109/MCS.2002.1004010

Patra & Bos. (2000, February). Modelling of an intelligent pressure sensor using functional link artificial neural networks. *ISA Transactions, 39*(1), 15-17.

Patra, J. C., & Bornand, C. (2010). Non-linear dynamic system identification using Legendre neural network. *International Joint Conference on Neural Networks (IJCNN)*, 1–7.

Patra, J. C., Bornand, C., & Meher, P. K. (2009). Laguerre neural network based smart sensors for wireless sensor networks. *IEEE Conference on Instrumentation and Measurement Technology*, 832–837. doi:10.1109/IMTC.2009.5168565

Patrikar, A. M. (2013). Approximating Gaussian Mixture Model on Radial Basis Function Networks with Multilayer Perceptron. *IEEE Transactions on Neural Networks, 24*(7), 1161–1166. doi:10.1109/TNNLS.2013.2249086 PMID:24808530

Pawlak, Z. (1982). Rough sets. *Int. J. Inform. Comput. Sci., 11*(5), 341–356. doi:10.1007/BF01001956

Pawlak, Z. (1997). Rough set approach to knowledge-based decision support. *European Journal of Operational Research, 99*(1), 48–57. doi:10.1016/S0377-2217(96)00382-7

Peiró, J., Corberán, Á., & Martí, R. (2014). Grasp for the uncapacitated r-allocation p-hub median problem. *Computers & Operations Research, 43*, 50–60. doi:10.1016/j.cor.2013.08.026

Peng, F., Zhang, J., & Ryan, W. E. (2007). Adaptive Modulation and Coding for IEEE 802.11n. *IEEE Wireless Communications and Networking Conference*, 656-661. doi:10.1109/WCNC.2007.126

Pen, J. X., Li, K., & Huang, D. S. (2006). A hybrid forward algorithm for RBF neural network construction. *IEEE Transactions on Neural Networks, 17*(6), 1439–1451. doi:10.1109/TNN.2006.880860 PMID:17131659

Pessoa, L. S., Resende, M. G., & Ribeiro, C. C. (2013). A hybrid Lagrangean heuristic with GRASP and path-relinking for set k-covering. *Computers & Operations Research, 40*(12), 3132–3146. doi:10.1016/j.cor.2011.11.018

Phoon, K. K., & Kulhawy, F. H. (1999). Characterization of geotechnical variability. *Canadian Geotechnical Journal, 36*(4), 612–624. doi:10.1139/t99-038

Pijush, S., Sarat, D., & Dookie, K. (2011). Uplift capacity of suction caisson in clay using multivariate adaptive regression spline. *Ocean Engineering, 38*(17–18), 2123–2127.

Piotrowski. (2014, August). Differential Evolution algorithms applied to neural network training suffer from stagnation. *Applied Soft Computing, 21*, 382-406.

Pomeroy, S. L., Tamayo, P., Gaasenbeek, M., Sturla, L. M., Angelo, M., McLaughlin, M. E., & Golub, T. R. et al. (2002). Prediction of central nervous system embryonal tumour outcome based on gene expression. *Nature, 415*(6870), 436–442. doi:10.1038/415436a PMID:11807556

Ponsich, A., Jaimes, A. L., & Coello, C. A. C. (2013). A survey on multiobjective evolutionary algorithms for the solution of the portfolio optimization problem and other finance and economics applications. *IEEE Transactions on Evolutionary Computation, 17*(3), 321–344. doi:10.1109/TEVC.2012.2196800

Potrus, M. Y., Ngah, U. K., & Ahmed, B. S. (2014, December). An evolutionary harmony search algorithm with dominant point detection for recognition-based segmentation of online Arabic text recognition. *Ain Shams Engineering Journal, Elsevier, 5*(4), 1129–1139. doi:10.1016/j.asej.2014.05.003

Pourhabibi, T., Imani, M. B., & Haratizadeh, S. (2011). Feature selection on Persian fonts: A comparative analysis on GAA. *Procedia Computer Science*, *3*, 1249–1255. doi:10.1016/j.procs.2010.12.200

Pouyan, M. B., Yousefi, R., Ostadabbas, S., & Nourani, M. (2014, May). A Hybrid Fuzzy-Firefly Approach for Rule-Based Classification. In *FLAIRS Conference*. 357 – 362.

Powell, M. J. D. (1987a). Radial Basis Functions for Multivariable Interpolation: A Review. In J. C. Mason & M. G. Cox (Eds.), *Algorithms for the Approximation* (pp. 143–167). Clarendon Press.

Powell, M. J. D. (1987b). Radial Basis Function Approximations to Polynomials. In D. F. Griths & G. A. Watson (Eds.), *Numerical Analysis 87* (pp. 223–241). Longman Publishing Group.

Powell, M. J. D. (1992). The Theory of Radial Basis Function Approximation in 1990. *Advances in Numerical Analysis*, *2*, 105–210.

Powell, M. J. D. (1999). *Recent Research at Cambridge on Radial Basis Functions*. New Developments in Approximation Theory, International Series of Numerical Mathematics. doi:10.1007/978-3-0348-8696-3_14

Prais, M., & Ribeiro, C. C. (2000). Reactive GRASP: An application to a matrix decomposition problem in TDMA traffic assignment. *INFORMS Journal on Computing*, *12*(3), 164–176. doi:10.1287/ijoc.12.3.164.12639

Prashant, Kakde, & Gulhane. (2016). A Comparative Analysis of Particle Swarm Optimization and Support Vector Machines for Devnagri Character Recognition: An Android application. *Proceedings of International Conference on Communication, Computing and Virtualization (ICCCV) 2016*, *79*, 337-343. doi:10:1016:/j.procs2016.03.044

Price, K., & Storn, R. (2005). *Differential Evolution a Practical Approach to Global Optimization*. Springer Natural Computing Series.

Price, K., Storn, R., & Lampinen, J. (2005). *Differential Evolution: A Practical Approach to Global Optimization*. Springer.

Primo, M. A., & Amundson, S. D. (2002). An exploratory study of the effects of supplier relationships on new product development outcomes. *Journal of Operation Management*, 33-52.

Quaranta, G., Carlo Marano, G., Greco, R., & Monti, G. (2014, September). Parametric identification of seismic isolators using differential evolution and particle swarm optimization. *Applied Soft Computing, Elsevier*, *22*, 458–464. doi:10.1016/j.asoc.2014.04.039

Qu, Y., & Bard, J. F. (2012). A GRASP with adaptive large neighborhood search for pickup and delivery problems with transshipment. *Computers & Operations Research*, *39*(10), 2439–2456. doi:10.1016/j.cor.2011.11.016

Rabbi & Fazel-Rezai. (2012). Fuzzy Logic System for seizure onset detection in intracranial EEG. Academic Press.

Rajasekaeran, S., & Vijayalakshmi, G. A. (2003). *Neural networks, Fuzzy logic, and Genetics Algorithms Synthesis and Applications*. New Delhi: PHI Publication.

Rajesri, G., Muhammad, I. A., Leksananto, G., & Tota, S. (2015). The Application of a Decision-making Approach based on Fuzzy ANP and TOPSIS for Selecting a Strategic Supplier. *Journal of Engineering Technology Sci.*, *47*(4), 406-425.

Rakshit, P., & Konar, A. (2015, October). Differential evolution for noisy multiobjective optimization. *Artificial Intelligence, Elsevier*, *227*, 165–189. doi:10.1016/j.artint.2015.06.004

Rao, S. S., & Berke, L. (1997). Analysis of uncertain structural systems using interval analysis. *J. Am. Inst. Aeronaut. Astronaut.*, *35*(4), 727–735. doi:10.2514/2.164

Rastrigin, L. A. (1963). The convergence of the random search method in the extremal control of a many parameter system. *Automation and Remote Control, 24*(10), 1337–1342.

Ravichandran, K. S., Thirunavukarasu, P., Nallaswamy, R. R., & Babu, R. (2007). Estimation on return on investment in share market through ANN. *Journal of Theoretical and Applied Information Technology, 3*, 44–54.

Ray, B., Pal, A. J., Bhattacharyya, D., & Kim, T. (2010). An efficient GA with multipoint guided mutation for graph coloring problems. *International Journal of Signal Processing, Image Processing and Pattern Recognition, 3*(2), 51–58.

Reeves, C. R. (Ed.). (1993). Modern Heuristic Techniques for Combinatorial Problems. Blackwell Scientific Publishing.

Reeves, C. R. (Ed.). (1993). *Modern Heuristic Techniques for Combinatorial Problems*. Oxford, UK: Blackwell Scientific Publishing.

Resende, M. G., & Ribeiro, C. C. (2014). GRASP: Greedy randomized adaptive search procedures. In Search methodologies (pp. 287-312). Springer US. ISO 690.

Resende, M. G., & Ribeiro, C. C. (2014). GRASP: Greedy randomized adaptive search procedures. In Search methodologies (pp. 287-312). Springer.

Resende, M. G., Mateus, G. R., & Silva, R. (2012). *Manual da computacao evolutiva e metaheuristica, chapter GRASP: Busca gulosa, aleatorizada e adaptativa*. Coimbra: Coimbra University Press.

Resende, M. G., & Ribeiro, C. C. (2013). *Metaheuristicas em pesquisa operacional, chapter GRASP: Procedimentos de busca gulosos, aleatorios e adaptativos*. Curitiba: Omnipax Editora. doi:10.7436/2013.mhpo.01

Ribas, I., & Companys, R. (2015). Efficient heuristic algorithms for the blocking flow shop scheduling problem with total flow time minimization. *Computers & Industrial Engineering, 87*, 30–39. doi:10.1016/j.cie.2015.04.013

Riedmiller, M., & Braun, H. (1993). A direct adaptive method for faster backpropagation learning: The RPROP algorithm. In *Neural Networks, 1993., IEEE International Conference on* (pp. 586-591). IEEE.

Robbins, A., & Garcia, J. P. (n.d.). *Consumer Willingness to Pay for Renewable Bilding Materials: An Experimental Choice Analysis and Survey*. Retrieved June 12, 2016, from https://digital.lib.washington.edu/researchworks/bitstream/handle/1773/35443/WP96WillingnessToPayRenewableBuildingMatrls.pdf?sequence=1

Robbins, H., & Monro, S. (1951). A Stochastic Approximation Method. *Annals of Mathematical Statistics, 22*(3), 400–407. doi:10.1214/aoms/1177729586

Rodriguez-Cristerna, A., & Torres-Jimenez, J. (2012). A Simulated Annealing with Variable Neighborhood Search Approach to Construct Mixed Covering Arrays. *Electronic Notes in Discrete Mathematics, 39*, 249–256. doi:10.1016/j.endm.2012.10.033

Rodriguez, N. (2009). Multiscale Legendre neural network for monthly anchovy catches forecasting. *Third International Symposium on Intelligent Information Technology Application*, 598–601. doi:10.1109/IITA.2009.466

Roessner, D., Bond, J., Okubo, S., & Planting, M. (2013). The economic impact of licensed commercialized inventions originating in university research. *Research Policy, 42*(1), 23–34. doi:10.1016/j.respol.2012.04.015

Rogen Jang, J. S., & Sun, C. T. (1995). Nuero fuzzy modeling control. *Proc IEEE, 83*, 378-404.

Ron, A. (1992). The L2-approximation Orders of Principal Shift-Invariant Spaces Generated by a Radial Basis function. In D. Braess & L. L. Schumaker (Eds.), *Numerical Methods in Approximation Theory* (pp. 245–268). doi:10.1007/978-3-0348-8619-2_14

Roohollah, S. F., Danial, J. A., Masoud, M., & Edy, T. M. (2016). Genetic Programming and gene expression programming for flyrock assessment due to mine blasting. *International Journal of Rock Mechanics and Mining Sciences*, *88*, 254–264. doi:10.1016/j.ijrmms.2016.07.028

Roque, C. M. C., & Martins, P. A. L. S. (2015, December). Differential evolution for optimization of functionally graded beams. *Composite Structures*, *133*, 1191–1197. doi:10.1016/j.compstruct.2015.08.041

Rosenwald, A., Wright, G., Chan, W. C., Connors, J. M., Campo, E., Fisher, R. I., & Staudt, L. M. et al. (2002). The use of molecular profiling to predict survival after chemotherapy for diffuse large-B-cell lymphoma. *The New England Journal of Medicine*, *346*(25), 1937–1947. doi:10.1056/NEJMoa012914 PMID:12075054

Rosler, R. N. U. (1992). Defect detection in fabrics by image processing. *Melliand Texilber.*, *73*, 635–636.

Roure, J. B., & Keeley, R. H. (1990). Predictors of success in new technology based ventures. *Journal of Business Venturing*, *5*(4), 201–220. doi:10.1016/0883-9026(90)90017-N

Rout, M., Majhi, B., Majhi, R., & Panda, G. (2014). Forecasting of currency exchange rates using an adaptive ARMA model with differential evolution based training. *Journal of King Saud University-Computer and Information Sciences*, *26*(1), 7–18. doi:10.1016/j.jksuci.2013.01.002

Rout, S. S., Misra, B. B., & Samanta, S. (2014). Load Allocation in Academic Environment: A Multi Objective PSO Approach. *GSTF Journal on Computing*, *3*(4), 9. doi:10.7603/s40601-013-0036-7

Rouyendegh, B. D., & Erol, S. (n.d.). Selecting the Best Project Using the Fuzzy ELECTRE Method. *Mathematical Problem in Engineering*, 1-12.

Roy, S., & Venkateswaran, P. (2014). Online Payment System using Steganography and Visual Cryptography. *IEEE Students' Conference on Electrical, Electronics and Computer Science*.

Rubio-Sánchez, M., Gallego, M., Gortázar, F., & Duarte, A. (2016). GRASP with path relinking for the single row facility layout problem. *Knowledge-Based Systems*, *106*, 1–13. doi:10.1016/j.knosys.2016.05.030

Rubio-Solis, A., & Panoutsos, G. (2015). Interval type-2 radial basis function neural network: A modeling framework. *IEEE Transactions on Fuzzy Systems*, *23*(2), 457–473. doi:10.1109/TFUZZ.2014.2315656

Rumelhart, D. E., Hinton, G. E., & Williams, R. J. (1988). Learning representations by back-propagating errors. *Cognitive Modeling, 5*(3), 1.

Rumelhart, D. E., Hinton, G. E., & Williams, R. J. (1985). *Learning internal representations by error propagation (No. ICS-8506)*. California Univ San Diego La Jolla Inst for Cognitive Science.

Runkler & Katz. (2006). Fuzzy clustering by Particle Swarm Optimization. *Proceedings of 2006 IEEE international Conference on Fuzzy Systems*, 601-608.

Sadiq, M., & Sultana, S. (2015). A Method for the Selection of Software Testing Techniques Using Analytic Hierarchy Process. Computational Intelligence in Data Mining, (1), 213-220.

Saeys, Y., Inza, I., & Larranaga, P. (2007). A review of feature selection techniques in Bioinformatics. *Bioinformatics (Oxford, England)*, *23*(19), 2507–2517. doi:10.1093/bioinformatics/btm344 PMID:17720704

Saibal, Pal, Rai, & Singh. (2012). Comparative Study of Firefly Algorithm and Particle Swarm Optimization for Noisy Non Linear Optimization Problems. Academic Press.

Sait, S. M., & Youssef, H. (1999). *Iterative Computer Algorithms with Applications in Engineering: Solving Combinatorial Optimization Problems*. Los Alamitos, CA: IEEE Computer Society Press.

San, P. P., Ling, S. H., & Nguyen, H. (2014). Evolvable rough-block-based neural network and its biomedical application to hypoglycemia detection system. *IEEE Transactions on Cybernetics, 44*(8), 1338-1349.

San, P. P., Ling, S. H., & Nguyen, H. T. (2013). Industrial application of evolvable block-based neural network to hypoglycemia monitoring system. *IEEE Transactions on Industrial Electronics, 60*(12), 5892–5901. doi:10.1109/TIE.2012.2228143

Sareni, B., & Krahenbuhl, L. (1998). Fitness Sharing and Niching Methods Revisited. *IEEE Transactions on Evolutionary Computation, 2*(3), 97–106. doi:10.1109/4235.735432

Sari-Sarraf, H., & Goddard, J. S. (1999). Goddard Vision system for on-loom fabric inspection. *IEEE Transactions Industry Application.* Available: http://www.ieeexplore.ieee.org/stamp/stamp.jsp?arnumber=00806035

Sarkhel, R., Das, N., Saha, A. K., & Nasipuri, M. (2016, October). A Multi-Objective Approach Towards Cost Effective Isolated Handwritten Bangla Character and Digit Recognition. *Pattern Recognition, 58*, 172–189. doi:10.1016/j.patcog.2016.04.010

Saruhan. (2014, September). Differential evolution and simulated annealing algorithms for mechanical systems design. *Engineering Science and Technology, 17*(3), 131-136.

Sastry, K.S., & Babu, M.S.P. (2010). Fuzzy Logic based Adaptive Modulation using Non Data Aided SNR Estimation for OFDM Systems. *International Journal of Engineering Science and Technology, 2*(6), 2384-2392.

Sato, T. & Hagiwara, M. (1997 ,October). Bee System: Finding Solution by a Concentrated Search. *Proceedings of the 1997 IEEE International Conference on Systems, Man, and Cybernetics*, 3954-3959. doi:10.1109/ICSMC.1997.633289

Sawaragi, Y., Nakayama, H., & Tanino, T. (Eds.). (1985). Theory of multiobjective optimization (Vol. 176). Elsevier.

Schiezaro, M., & Pedrini, H. (2013). Data feature selection based on Artificial Bee Colony algorithm. *EURASIP Journal on Image and Video Processing*, (1): 1–8.

Schiffaueroval, A., & Thomson, V. (2006). A review of research on cost of quality models and best practices. *International Journal of Quality & Reliability Management, 23*(4).

Schmickl, T., Thenius, R., & Crailsheim. (2005, June). Simulating swarm intelligence in honey bees: foraging in differently fluctuating environments. *Genetic and Evolutionary Computation Conference, GECCO, Proceedings.*

Schuster, M., & Paliwal, K. K. (1997). Bidirectional recurrent neural networks. *IEEE Transactions on Signal Processing, 45*(11), 2673–2681. doi:10.1109/78.650093

Schwenker, F., & Dietrich, C. (2000). Initialization of Radial Basis Function networks by Means of Classification Trees. *Neural Network World, 10*, 473–482.

Schwenker, F., Kestler, H. A., Palm, G., & Höher, M. (1994). Similarities of LVQ and RBF Learning - A Survey of Learning Rules and the Application to the Classification of Signals from High-Resolution Electrocardiography. *Proceedings IEEE SMC*, 646-651. doi:10.1109/ICSMC.1994.399913

Seeley, T. D., & Buhrman, S. C. (1999). Group decision making in swarms of honeybees. *Behavioral Ecology and Sociobiology, 45*(1), 19–31. doi:10.1007/s002650050536

Selvaraj, A., Ganesan, L., & Bama, S. (2006). Fault segmentation in fabric images using Gabor wavelet transform. *Machine Vision and Applications, 16*(6), 356–363. doi:10.1007/s00138-005-0007-x

Selvaraj, C., Siva Kumar, R., & Karnan, M. (2014). A survey on application of bio-inspired algorithms. *International Journal of Computer Science and Information Technologies, 5*(1), 366–370.

Senthilnath, J., Omkar, S. N., & Mani, V. (2011). Clustering using Firefly algorithm: Performance Study. Academic Press.

Serafini, P. (1994). Simulated annealing for multiple objective optimization problems. In G. H. Tzeng, H. F. Wang, U. P. Wen, & P. L. Yu (Eds.), *Multiple Criteria Decision Making: Proceedings of the Tenth International Conference: Expand and Enrich the Domains of Thinking and Application* (pp. 283–292). New York, NY: Springer-Verlag. doi:10.1007/978-1-4612-2666-6_29

Serdaroglu, Ertuzun, A., & Ercil, A. (2006). Defect Detection in Textile Fabric Images Using Wavelet Transforms and Independent Component Analysis. *Pattern Recognition and Image Analysis, 16*(1), 61–64.

Sewell, M. (2011). *Characterization of Financial Time Series*. UCL Department of Computer Science, Research Note.

Shahhosseini, V., & Sebt, M. H. (2011). Competency-based selection and assignment of human resources to construction projects. *Scientia Iranica, 18*(2), 163–180. doi:10.1016/j.scient.2011.03.026

Shaocheng, T. (1994). Interval number and fuzzy number linear programming. *Fuzzy Sets and Systems, 66*(3), 301–306. doi:10.1016/0165-0114(94)90097-3

Sharif, M. T., & Salari, M. (2015). A GRASP algorithm for a humanitarian relief transportation problem. *Engineering Applications of Artificial Intelligence, 41*, 259–269. doi:10.1016/j.engappai.2015.02.013

Sheng, W., Tucker, A., & Liu, X. (2004). Clustering with Niching Genetic K-Means Algorithm. *Proceedings of Genetic and Evolutionary Computation Conf. (GECCO '04)*, 162-173. doi:10.1007/978-3-540-24855-2_15

Shermon, G. (2004). *Competency based HRM*. McGraw-Hill.

Sheta, A. F., & Jong, K. (2001). Time-series forecasting using GA-tuned radial basis functions. *Information Sciences, 133*(3), 221–228. doi:10.1016/S0020-0255(01)00086-X

Shi, Y. (2001). Particle swarm optimization: developments, applications and resources. *Proceedings of the 2001 Congress on Evolutionary Computatio.*

Shi, C., & Bin, L., Ting, Quande, Q., Yuhui, S., & Kaizhu, H. (2016). Survey on data science with population-based algorithms. *Big Data Analytics, 1*(3), 1–20.

Shi, J., & Malik, J. (2000). Normalized Cuts and Image Segmentation. *IEEE Transactions on Pattern Analysis and Machine Intelligence, 22*(8), 888–905. doi:10.1109/34.868688

Shipley, M. F., De Korvin, A., & Omer, K. (1996). A fuzzy logic approach for determining expected values: A project management application. *The Journal of the Operational Research Society, 47*(4), 562–569. doi:10.1057/jors.1996.61

Shipp, M. A. et al.. (2002). The AP1-dependent secretion of gelectin-1 by Reed-Sternberg cells fosters immune privilege in classical Hodgkin lymphoma, PNAS. *The National Academy of Sciences, USA, 104*(32), 13134–13139.

Shi, Y. (2004). Particle swarm optimization. *IEEE Connections, 2*(1), 8–13.

Shi, Y., & Eberhart, R. C. (1999). Empirical study of particle swarm optimization. *Proceedings of the 1999 IEEE Congress on Evolutionary Computation*, 1945– 1950. doi:10.1109/CEC.1999.785511

Shrivastava, S., & Singh, M. P. (2011, January). Performance evaluation of feed-forward neural network with soft computing techniques for hand written English alphabets. *Applied Soft Computing, Elsevier, 11*(1), 1156–1182. doi:10.1016/j.asoc.2010.02.015

Shu, Y., & Tan, Z. (2004). Fabric defects automatic detection using gabor filters. *Intelligent Control and Automation, WCICA 2004. Fifth World Congress on IEEE, 4*, 3378-3380.

Siew, L. H., Hodgson, R. M., & Wood, E. J. (1988). Texture measures for carpet wear assessment. *IEEE Transactions on Pattern Analysis and Machine Intelligence, 10*(6), 92–105. doi:10.1109/34.3870

Silva, F., & Gao, L. (2013). A joint replenishment inventory-location model. *Networks and Spatial Economics, 13*(1), 107–122. doi:10.1007/s11067-012-9174-2

Singh, S., & Murthy, T. V. R. (2013). Neural network-based sensor fault accommodation in flight control system. *Journal of Intelligent Systems, 22*(3), 317–333. doi:10.1515/jisys-2013-0032

Singla, D., & Syal, R. (2012). Data Security Using LSB & DCT Steganography In Images. *International Journal of Computational Engineering Research, 2*(2), 359-364.

Sitharam, T. G., Pijush, S., & Anbazhagan, P. (2008). Spatial variability of rock depth in Bangalore using geostatistical, neural network and support vector machine models. *Geotechnical and Geological Engineering, 26*(5), 503–517. doi:10.1007/s10706-008-9185-4

Smith, N. C., Read, D., & Rodriguez, S. L. (n.d.). *Consumer Perceptions of Corporate Social Responsibility: The CSR Halo Effect.* Retrieved June 12, 2016, from https://flora.insead.edu/fichiersti_wp/inseadwp2010/2010-16.pdf

Snyman, J. A. (2000). The LFOPC leap-frog algorithm for constrained optimization. *Computers & Mathematics with Applications (Oxford, England), 40*(8), 1085–1096. doi:10.1016/S0898-1221(00)85018-X

Soete, L. (1987). *The impact of technological innovation on international trade patterns: The evidence reconsidered.* North Holland Research Policy.

Soleimanpour, M., Tabeli, S., & Azadi-Motlag, H. (2013). A Novel Technique for Steganography Method Based on Improved Genetic Algorithm Optimization in Spatial Domain. *Iranian Journal of Electrical & Electronics Engineering, 9*(2), 67–74.

Soll, M. (2015). *Fooling deep neural networks using Cuckoo Search.* Academic Press.

Song, M. P., & Gu, G. C. (2004, August). Research on particle swarm optimization: a review. In *Machine Learning and Cybernetics, 2004. Proceedings of 2004 International Conference on* (Vol. 4, pp. 2236-2241). IEEE.

Song, K. Y., Petrou, M., & Kittler, J. (1995). Texture crack detection. *Machine Vision and Applications, 8*(1), 63–76. doi:10.1007/BF01213639

Song, Q., & Chissom, B. S. (1993a). Fuzzy time series and its models. *Fuzzy Sets and Systems, 54*(3), 269–277. doi:10.1016/0165-0114(93)90372-O

Song, Q., & Chissom, B. S. (1993b). Forecasting enrollments with fuzzy time series - part I. *Fuzzy Sets and Systems, 54*(1), 1–9. doi:10.1016/0165-0114(93)90355-L

Song, Q., & Chissom, B. S. (1994). Forecasting enrollments with fuzzy time series - part II. *Fuzzy Sets and Systems, 62*(1), 1–8. doi:10.1016/0165-0114(94)90067-1

Song, Y., Chen, Z., & Yuan, Z. (2007). New chaotic PSO based neural network predictive control for non-linear process. *IEEE Transactions on Neural Networks, 18*(2), 595–600. doi:10.1109/TNN.2006.890809 PMID:17385644

Sooraj, T. R., Mohanty, R. K., & Tripathy, B. K. (2016). Fuzzy soft set theory and its application in group decision making. *Advances in Intelligent Systems and Computing, 452*, 171–178. doi:10.1007/978-981-10-1023-1_17

Sörensen, K., & Vanovermeire, C. (2013). Bi-objective optimization of the intermodal terminal location problem as a policy-support tool. *Computers in Industry, 64*(2), 128–135. doi:10.1016/j.compind.2012.10.012

Soteris, A. K. (2001). Artificial neural networks in renewable energy systems applications: A review. *Renewable & Sustainable Energy Reviews*, 373–401.

Sousa, T., Silva, A., & Neves, A. (2004). Particle swarm based data mining algorithms for classification tasks. *Parallel Computing*, *30*(5), 767–783. doi:10.1016/j.parco.2003.12.015

Specht, D. F. (1991). A general regression neural network. *IEEE Transactions on Neural Networks*, *2*(6), 568–576. doi:10.1109/72.97934 PMID:18282872

Srinivasan, K., Dastoor, P. H., Radhakrishnaiah, P., & Jayaraman, S. (1992). FDAS: A knowledge-based framework for analysis of defects in woven textile structures. *J. Textile Inst.*, *83*(3), 431–1448.

Srivastava, P. R., Ramachandran, V., Kumar, M., Talukder, G., Tiwari, V., & Sharma, P. (2008). Generation of test data using meta heuristic approach. In *TENCON IEEE Region 10 Conference* (pp. 1–6). IEEE. doi:10.1109/TENCON.2008.4766707

Srivastava, P. R., Sravya, C., Ashima, N. A., Kamisetti, S., & Lakshmi, M. (2012). Test sequence optimisation: An intelligent approach via cuckoo search. *International Journal of Bio-inspired Computation*, *4*(43), 139–148. doi:10.1504/IJBIC.2012.047237

Stanarevic, N., Tuba, M., & Bacanin, N. (2011). Modified artificial bee colony algorithm for constrained problems optimization. *International Journal of Mathematical Models and Methods in Applied Sciences*, *5*(3), 644-651.

Stefanowski. (2003). *Changing representation of learning examples while inducing classifiers based on decision rules, Artificial Intelligence Methods*. Bioinformatics Laboratory, University of Ljubljana. Retrieved from http://www.biolab.si/supp/bi-ancer/projections/info/lungGSE1987.htm

Steuer, R. E. (1986). *Multiple criteria optimization: theory, computation, and applications*. Wiley.

Sthamer, H., Wegener, J., & Baresel, A. (2002).Using evolutionary testing to improve efficiency and quality in software testing. *Proceedings of the 2nd Asia-Pacific Conference on Software Testing Analysis& Review*.

Stierstorfer, C., & Fischer, R. F. H. (2007). Gray Mapping for Bit-Interleaved Coded Modulation. *IEEE Vehicular Technology Conference*, 1703-1707. doi:10.1109/VETECS.2007.354

Stockwell, R. G. (2007). A basis of efficient representation of the S-transform. *Digital Signal Processing*, *17*(1), 371–393. doi:10.1016/j.dsp.2006.04.006

Stojanovic, R., Mitropulis, P., Koulamas, C., Karayiannis, Y., Koubias, S., & Papadopoulos, G. (2000). An Approach for Automated Defect Detection and Neural Classification of Web Textile Fabric. *Machine Graphics and Vision*, *9*(3), 587–607.

Storn, R., & Price, K. (1997). Differential Evolution - A Simple and Efficient Heuristic for Global Optimization over Continuous Spaces. *Journal of Global Optimization*, *11*(4), 341–359. doi:10.1023/A:1008202821328

Strohmann, T. R., & Grudic, G. R. (2002). A Formulation for minimax probability machine regression. In Advances in Neural Information Processing Systems (NIPS) 14. Cambridge, MA: MIT Press.

Stron, R., & Price, K. (1995). *Differential Evolution-A Simple and Efficient Adaptive Scheme for Global Optimization over Continuous Spaces*. Technical Report TR-05-012: International Computer Science Institute, Berkeley.

Subrata, R., & Zomaya, A. Y. (2003a). A Comparison of Three Artificial Life Techniques for Reporting Cell Planning in Mobile Computing. *IEEE Transactions on Parallel and Distributed Systems*, *14*(2), 142–153. doi:10.1109/TPDS.2003.1178878

Subrata, R., & Zomaya, A. Y. (2003b). Evolving Cellular Automata for Location Management in Mobile Computing Networks. *IEEE Transactions on Parallel and Distributed Systems*, *14*(1), 13–26. doi:10.1109/TPDS.2003.1167367

Sudkamp, T. A., & Cotterman, A. (1988). *Languages and machines: an introduction to the theory of computer science* (Vol. 2). Addison-Wesley.

Sugeno, M., & Kang, G. T. (1988). Structure identification of fuzzy model. *Fuzzy Sets Syst, 28*, 15-33.

Sujata, D. (2015). Learning Using Hybrid Intelligence Techniques. *Computational Intelligence for Big Data Analysis*, 73-96.

Suman, B. (2003). Simulated annealing based multiobjective algorithm and their application for system reliability. *Engineering Optimization, 35*(4), 391–416. doi:10.1080/03052150310001597765

Suman, B., & Kumar, P. (2006). A survey of simulated annealing as a tool for single and multiobjective optimization. *The Journal of the Operational Research Society, 57*(10), 1143–1160. doi:10.1057/palgrave.jors.2602068

Suppapitnarm, A., Seffen, K. A., Parks, G. T., & Clarkson, P. J. (2000). A simulated annealing algorithm for multiobjective optimization. *Engineering Optimization, 33*(1), 59–85. doi:10.1080/03052150008940911

Suresh, S., Sundararajan, N., & Savitha, R., (2013). A fully complex-valued radial basis function network and its learning algorithm. *Studies in Computational Intelligence, 421*, 49-71.

Swathi, J. N., & Jayant, G. R. (2016). A Review On Metaheuristic Techniques To Train Feedforward Neural Networks And Its Application To Predict Patient Medical Behaviour. *Int J Pharm Bio Sci*, 300-309.

Sylla, C. (n.d.). Experimental investigation of human and machine –vision arrangements in inspection tasks. *Control Engineering Practice, 10*(3), 347-361.

Syulistyo, A. R., Purnomo, D. M. J., Rachmadi, M. F., & Wibowo, A. (2016). Particle swarm optimization (PSO) for training optimization on convolutional neural network (CNN). *Jurnal Ilmu Komputer dan Informasi, 9*(1), 52-58.

Tabba, M. M., & Yong, R. N. (1981). Mapping and predicting soil properties: Theory. *Journal of the Engineering Mechanics Division, 107*, 773–793.

Taeho, J. (2013). VTG schemes for using back propagation for multivariate time series prediction. *Applied Soft Computing, 13*(5), 2692–2702. doi:10.1016/j.asoc.2012.11.018

Taha, A. M., Mustapha, A., & Chen, S. D. (2013). Naive bayes-guided bat algorithm for feature selection. *The Scientific World Journal, 2013*, 1-10.

Taheri, J., & Zomaya, A. Y. (2007). A Combined Genetic-neural Algorithm for Mobility Management. *Journal of Mathematical Modelling and Algorithms, 6*(3), 481–507. doi:10.1007/s10852-007-9066-5

Takagi, T., & Sugeno, M. (1985). Fuzzy identification of systems and its applications to modeling and control. *IEEE Trans Syst Man Cybernet, 15*(1), 116-132.

Talbi, E.-Gh. (2009). *Metaheuristics: From design to implementation.* Hoboken, NJ: John Wiley & Sons. doi:10.1002/9780470496916

Tan, A. C., & Gilbert, D. (2003). Ensemble machine learning on gene expression data for cancer classification. *Applied Bioinformatics, 2*, S75–S83. PMID:15130820

Tang, A. M. (1979). Probabilistic evaluation of penetration resistance. *Journal of the Geotechnical Engineering Division, 105*, 117–191.

Tang, L., Cao, H., Zheng, L., & Huang, N. (2015). RFID network planning for wireless manufacturing considering the detection uncertainty. *IFAC-PapersOnLine, 48*(3), 406–411. doi:10.1016/j.ifacol.2015.06.115

Tarantilis, C. D., & Kiranoudis, C. T. (2002). A list-based threshold accepting method for job shop scheduling problems. *International Journal of Production Economics*, 77(2), 159–171. doi:10.1016/S0925-5273(01)00231-6

Tarantilis, C. D., Kiranoudis, C. T., & Vassiliadis, V. S. (2002). A list based threshold accepting algorithm for the capacitated vehicle routing problem. *International Journal of Computer Mathematics*, 79(5), 537–553. doi:10.1080/00207160210948

Tarantilis, C. D., Kiranoudis, C. T., & Vassiliadis, V. S. (2003). A list based threshold accepting metaheuristic for the heterogeneous fixed fleet vehicle routing problem. *The Journal of the Operational Research Society*, 54(1), 65–71. doi:10.1057/palgrave.jors.2601443

Tavazoie, S., Hughes, D., Campbell, M. J., Cho, R. J., & Church, G. M. (1999). Systematic Determination of Genetic Network Architecture. *Nature Genetics*, 22(3), 281–285. doi:10.1038/10343 PMID:10391217

Taylor, S. (2007). *Asset Price Dynamics, Volatility, and Prediction*. Princeton University Press.

Teghem, J., Tuyttens, D., & Ulungu, E. L. (2000). An intractive heuristic method for multiobjective combinatorial optimization. *Computers & Operations Research*, 27(7-8), 621–634. doi:10.1016/S0305-0548(99)00109-4

Tekinalp, O., & Karsli, G. (2007). A new multiobjective simulated annealing algorithm. *Journal of Global Optimization*, 39(1), 49–77. doi:10.1007/s10898-006-9120-2

Tereshko, V. (2000). Reaction–diffusion model of a honeybee colony's foraging behaviour. In M. Schoenauer (Ed.), Lecture Notes in Computer Science: Vol. 1917. *Parallel Problem Solving from Nature VI* (pp. 807–816). Berlin: Springer–Verlag. doi:10.1007/3-540-45356-3_79

Tolba, A. S. (2011). Fast defect detection in homogeneous flat surface products. Expert Systems with Appl. *International Journal (Toronto, Ont.)*, 38(10), 12339–12347.

Tomkovick, C., & Miller, C. (2000). Perspective-Riding the wind: Managing new products development in an age of change. *Journal of Product Innovation Management*, 17(6), 413–423. doi:10.1016/S0737-6782(00)00056-4

Triki, E., Collette, Y., & Siarry, P. (2005). A theoretical study on the behavior of simulated annealing leading to a new cooling schedule. *European Journal of Operational Research*, 166(1), 77–92. doi:10.1016/j.ejor.2004.03.035

Tripathy, B. K., & Arun, K. R. (2015). A new approach to soft sets, soft multisets and their properties. *International Journal of Reasoning-based Intelligent Systems*, 7(3-4), 244–253. doi:10.1504/IJRIS.2015.072951

Tripathy, B. K., & Ghosh, A. (2011). SDR: An algorithm for clustering categorical data using rough set theory. *IEEE Recent Advances in Intelligent Computational Systems, RAICS 2011*, 867-872.

Tripathy, B. K., Sooraj, T. R., & Mohanty, R. K. (2016). A new approach to fuzzy soft set theory and its application in decision making. *Advances in Intelligent Systems and Computing*, 411, 305–313. doi:10.1007/978-81-322-2731-1_28

Tsai, D.-M., & Hsieh, C.-Y. (1999). Automated surface inspection for directional textures. *Image and Vision Computing*, 18(1), 49–62. doi:10.1016/S0262-8856(99)00009-8

Tsai, K. H., Hsieh, M. H., & Hultink, E. J. (2011). External technology acquistion and product innovativeness: The moderating roles of R&D investment and configurational context. *Journal of Engineering and Technology Management*, 28(3), 184–200. doi:10.1016/j.jengtecman.2011.03.005

Tsai, T. J., Yang, C. B., & Peng, Y. H. (2011). Genetic algorithms for the investment of the mutual fund with global trend indicator. *Expert Systems with Applications*, 38(3), 1697–1701. doi:10.1016/j.eswa.2010.07.094

Uddin, M. I., Tanchi, K. R., & Alam, M. N. (2012). Competency mapping: A tool for hr excellence. *European Journal of Business and Management*, 4(5).

Ulungu, E. L., Teghem, J., Fortemps, P., & Tuyttens, D. (1999). MOSA method: A tool for solving multiobjective combinatorial optimization problems. *Journal of Multi-Criteria Decision Analysis, 8*(4), 221–236. doi:10.1002/(SICI)1099-1360(199907)8:4<221::AID-MCDA247>3.0.CO;2-O

University of Wisconsin-Madison. (n.d.). *A Basic Introduction To Neural Networks*. Retrieved August 22, 2016, from University of Wisconsin-Madison: http://pages.cs.wisc.edu/~bolo/shipyard/neural/local.html

Urade, H. S., & Patel, R. (2012). *Performance Evaluation of Dynamic Particle Swarm Optimization*. IJCSN.

Uzielli, M., Vannucchi, G., & Phonn, K. K. (2005). Random field characterisation of stress normalised cone penetration testing parameters. *Geotechnique, 55*(1), 3–20. doi:10.1680/geot.2005.55.1.3

V., V., R., V., & Y., Y. (1990). Process fault detection and diagnosis using neural networks-I. steady-state processes. *Computers & Chemical Engineering*, 699-712.

van Laarhoven, P. J. M. (1988). *Theoretical and computational aspects of simulated annealing* (Unpublished PhD dissertation). Erasmus University, Rotterdam, The Netherlands.

Van Laarhoven, P. J. M., & Pedrycz, W. (1983). A fuzzy extension of Saaty''s priority Theory. *Fuzzy Sets and Systems, 11*(1-3), 199–227. doi:10.1016/S0165-0114(83)80082-7

VanMarcke, E. (1998). *Random Fields: Analysis and Synthesis*. Princeton, NJ: MIT Press.

Vanmarcke, E. H. (1977). Probabilistic modeling of soil profiles. *Journal of the Geotechnical Engineering Division, 102*, 1247–1265.

Vardhini, K. K., & Sitamahalakshmi, T. (2016). A Review on Nature-based Swarm Intelligence Optimization Techniques and its Current Research Directions. *Indian Journal of Science and Technology, 9*(10).

Villalobos-Arias, M., Coello, C. A. C., & Hernández-Lerma, O. (2006). Asymptotic convergence of a simulated annealing algorithm for multiobjective optimization problems. *Mathematical Methods of Operations Research, 64*(2), 353–362. doi:10.1007/s00186-006-0082-4

Viswanathan, R., & Pijush, S. (2016). Determination of rock depth using artificial intelligence techniques. *Geoscience Frontiers, 7*(1), 61–66. doi:10.1016/j.gsf.2015.04.002

Voß, S., Martello, S., Osman, I. H., & Roucairol, C. (Eds.). (1999). *Meta-Heuristics - Advances and Trends in Local Search Paradigms for Optimization*. Dordrecht, The Netherlands: Kluwer Academic Publishers.

Wabster, R., & Oliver, M. A. (2001). *Geostatistics for Environmental Scientists*. New York: John Wiley and Sons.

Walton, S., Hassan, O., Morgan, K., & Brown, M. R. (2011). Modified cuckoo search: A new gradient free optimisation algorithm. *Chaos, Solitons, and Fractals, 44*(449), 710–718. doi:10.1016/j.chaos.2011.06.004

Wang, L., Zeng, Y., & Chen, T. (2015). Back propagation neural network with adaptive differential evolution algorithm for time series forecasting. Expert Systems With Applications, 42, 855-863.

Wang, Q., & Zheng, H. C. (2011, April). Optimization of task allocation and knowledge workers scheduling based-on particle swarm optimization. In *Electric Information and Control Engineering (ICEICE), 2011 International Conference on* (pp. 574-578). IEEE. doi:10.1109/ICEICE.2011.5778029

Wang, S. Q., Gong, L. H., & Yan, S. L. (2009, July). The allocation optimization of project human resource based on particle swarm optimization algorithm. In *Services Science, Management and Engineering, 2009. SSME'09. IITA International Conference on* (pp. 169-172). IEEE. doi:10.1109/SSME.2009.113

Wang, L. X. (1997). *A Course in Fuzzy Systems and Controls*. Prentice Hall Publications.

Wang, R. C., & Chen, C. H. (1995). Economic statistical np-control chart designs based on fuzzy optimization. *International Journal of Quality & Reliability Management*, *12*(1), 82–92. doi:10.1108/02656719510076276

Wang, R., Zhan, Y., & Zhou, H. (2012, December). Application of S-transform in fault diagnosis of power electronic circuits. *Scientia Iranica*, *19*(3), 721–726. doi:10.1016/j.scient.2011.06.013

Wang, X., Yang, J., Teng, X., Xia, W., & Jensen, R. (2007). Feature selection based on rough sets and particle swarm optimization. *Pattern Recognition Letters*, *28*(4), 459–471. doi:10.1016/j.patrec.2006.09.003

Wang, Y. (2003). Mining stock prices using fuzzy rough set system. *Expert Systems with Applications*, *24*(1), 13–23. doi:10.1016/S0957-4174(02)00079-9

Wang, Y. L. Z., Glover, F., & Hao, J. K. (2013). Probabilistic GRASP-tabu search algorithms for the UBQP problem. *Computers & Operations Research*, *40*(12), 3100–3107. doi:10.1016/j.cor.2011.12.006

Wei, L. Y. (2016). A hybrid ANFIS model based on empirical mode decomposition for stock time series forecasting. *Applied Soft Computing*, *42*, 368–376. doi:10.1016/j.asoc.2016.01.027

Weng, W.-D., Yang, C.-S., & Lin, R.-C. (2007, July). A channel equalizer using reduced decision feedback Chebyshev functional link artificial neural networks. *Information Sciences, Elsevier*, *177*(13), 2642–2654. doi:10.1016/j.ins.2007.01.006

Werbos, P. J. (1990). Backpropagation through time: What it does and how to do it. *Proceedings of the IEEE*, *78*(10), 1550–1560. doi:10.1109/5.58337

Werbos, P. J. (1994). *The roots of backpropagation*. John Wiley & Sons.

Whitley, D. (1995). Modeling Hybrid Genetic Algorithms. In G. Winter, J. Periaux, M. Galan, & P. Cuesta (Eds.), *Genetic Algorithms in Eng. and Computer Science* (pp. 191–201). John Wiley.

Wichmann, M. G. & Spengler, T. S. (2015). Slab scheduling at parallel continuous casters. International Journal of Production Economics. *Current Research Issues in Production Economics*.

Wilamowski, B. M., Cotton, N., Hewlett, J., & Kaynak, O. (2007, June). Neural network trainer with second order learning algorithms. In *2007 11th International Conference on Intelligent Engineering Systems* (pp. 127-132). IEEE. doi:10.1109/INES.2007.4283685

Wilamowski, B. (2002). *Neural networks and fuzzy systems*. The Microelectronic Handbook.

Williams, D. R. G. H. R., & Hinton, G. E. (1986). Learning representations by back-propagating errors. *Nature*, *323*(6088), 533–536. doi:10.1038/323533a0

Winker, P., & Fang, K. (1997). Application of threshold-accepting to the evaluation of the discrepancy of a set of points. *SIAM Journal on Numerical Analysis*, *34*(5), 2028–2042. doi:10.1137/S0036142995286076

Witten, I. H., Frank, E., & Hall, M. A. (2011). Data mining: practical machine learning tools and techniques (3rd ed.). Morgan Kaufmann.

Wong, V., & Leung, V. (2000). Location management for next generation personal communication networks. *IEEE Network*, *14*(5), 18–24. doi:10.1109/65.871336

Wood, R., & Pitt-Payne, T. (1998). *Competency-based recruitment and selection*. John Wiley & Sons.

Wren, B. M., Souder, W. E., & Berkowitz, D. (2000). Market orientation and new product development in global industrial firms. *Industrial Marketing Management*, *29*(6), 601–611. doi:10.1016/S0019-8501(00)00120-6

Wu, J., & Liu, J. C. (2012). A forecasting system for car fuel consumption using a radial basis function neural network. *Expert Systems with Applications*, *39*(2), 1883–1888. doi:10.1016/j.eswa.2011.07.139

Wu, Q., Law, R., Wu, E., & Lin, J. (2013). A hybrid-forecasting model reducing Gaussian noise based on the Gaussian support vector regression machine and chaotic particle swarm optimization. *Information Science*, *238*, 96–110. doi:10.1016/j.ins.2013.02.017

Wu, R. T. (2004). *The Impact of Globalization on Career and Technical Education in Taiwan, Republic of China*. Online Submission.

Wu, S., Liew, A. W. C., Yan, H., & Yang, M. (2004). Cluster Analysis of Gene Expression Database on Self-Splitting and Merging Competitive Learning. *IEEE Transactions on Information Technology in Biomedicine*, *8*(1).

Wu, T. H., & Wong, K. (1981). Probabilistic soil exploration: A case history. *Journal of the Geotechnical Engineering Division*, *107*, 1693–1711.

Wu, X. L. (2007). Consistent Feature Selection Reduction About Classification Dataset. *Computer Engineering and Applications*, *42*(18), 174–176.

Xiaohua, W., Phua, P. K., & Weidong, L. (2003). Stock market prediction using neural networks: Does trading volume help in short-term prediction? *Proceedings of the International Joint Conference on Neural Networks*, 2438-2442. doi:10.1109/IJCNN.2003.1223946

Xue, Q., Yun, F., Zheng, C., Liu, Y., Wei, Y., Yao, Y., & Zhou, S. (2010, October). Improved LMBP algorithm in the analysis and application of simulation data. In *2010 International Conference on Computer Application and System Modeling (ICCASM 2010)* (Vol. 6, pp. V6-545). IEEE.

Xu, H. H., & Wang, Y. H. (2009). Training system design for middle-level manager in coal enterprises based on post competency model. *Procedia Earth and Planetary Science*, *1*(1), 1764–1771. doi:10.1016/j.proeps.2009.09.270

Xu, K., Huang, K. F., & Gao, S. (2012). Technology sourcing, appropriability regimes, and new product development. *Journal of Engineering and Technology Management*, *29*(2), 265–280. doi:10.1016/j.jengtecman.2012.03.003

Yager, R. R. (1984). General multiple objective decision-making and linguistically quantified statements. *International Journal of Man-Machine Studies*, *21*(5), 389–400. doi:10.1016/S0020-7373(84)80066-8

Yager, R. R., Goldstein, L. S., & Mendels, E. (1994). FUZMAR: An approach to aggregating market research data based on fuzzy reasoning. *Fuzzy Sets and Systems*, *68*(1), 1–11. doi:10.1016/0165-0114(94)90269-0

Yaglom, A. M. (1962). Theory of stationary random functions. Englewood Cliffs, NJ: Prentice-Hall.

Yamada, T., & Wrobel, L. C. (1993). Properties of Gaussian Radial Basis Functions in the Dual Reciprocity Boundary Element Method. *Zeitschrift für Angewandte Mathematik und Physik*, *44*(6), 1054–1067. doi:10.1007/BF00942764

Yan, H., Liu, W., Xiuying, Kong, H., & Lv, C. (2010). Predicting Net Asset Value of Investment Fund Based On BP Neural Network. *IEEE International Conference on Computer Application and system modeling (ICCASM)*, *10*, 635-637.

Yang, X. S. (2009). Firefly algorithms for multimodal optimization. In *International symposium on stochastic algorithms* (pp. 169-178). Springer.

Yang, X. S. (2010). A new metaheuristic bat-inspired algorithm. In Nature inspired cooperative strategies for optimization (NICSO 2010) (pp. 65-74). Springer Berlin Heidelberg. doi:10.1007/978-3-642-12538-6_6

Yang, X. S. (2010). A new metaheuristic bat-inspired algorithm. *Nature Inspired Cooperative Strategies for Optimization*, 65-74.

Yang, X. S. (2010b). A new metaheuristic bat-inspired algorithm. In Nature inspired cooperative strategies for optimization (NICSO 2010). Berlin: Springer.

Yang, X. S. (2012a). Flower pollination algorithm for global optimization. In Unconventional computation and natural computation. Berlin: Springer.

Yang, X. S., & Deb, S. (2009). Cuckoo search via levy flights. *Proceedings of the world congress on nature & biologically inspired computing,* 210– 214.

Yang, X. S., & Deb, S. (2009, December). Cuckoo search via Lévy flights. In *Nature & Biologically Inspired Computing, 2009. NaBIC 2009. World Congress on* (pp. 210-214). IEEE.

Yang, X. S., & Deb, S. (2010). Engineering optimisation by cuckoo search. *International Journal of Mathematical Modelling and Numerical Optimisation*, (14), 330-343.

Yang, I. T., & Chou, J. S. (2011). Multiobjective optimization for manpower assignment in consulting engineering firms. *Applied Soft Computing*, *11*(1), 1183–1190. doi:10.1016/j.asoc.2010.02.016

Yang, L., & Ju, R. (2014). A DC programming approach for feature selection in the Minimax Probability Machine. *International Journal of Computational Intelligence Systems*, *7*(1), 12–24. doi:10.1080/18756891.2013.864471

Yang, P., Yang, Y. H., Zhou, B. B., & Zomaya, A. Y. (2010). A review of ensemble methods in bioinformatics. *Bioinformatics (Oxford, England)*, *5*(4), 296–308.

Yang, X. S. (2007). *Nature-inspired metaheuristic Algorithm*. Luniver Press.

Yang, X. S. (2010). Firefly algorithm, stochastic test functions and design optimisation. *International Journal of Bioinspired Computation*, *2*(2), 78–84. doi:10.1504/IJBIC.2010.032124

Yang, X. S. (2011). Metaheuristic optimization. *Scholarpedia*, *6*(8), 11472. doi:10.4249/scholarpedia.11472

Yang, X. S. (2012b). Nature-Inspired Mateheuristic Algorithms: Success and New Challenges. *J Comput. Eng. Inf. Technol.*, *1*(1), 1–3. doi:10.4172/2324-9307.1000e101

Yang, X. S., & Deb, S. (2009). Cuckoo search via L'evy flights. *Proc. of World Congress on Nature & Biologically Inspired Computing*, 210-214. doi:10.1109/NABIC.2009.5393690

Yang, Z., Wang, G., & Chu, F. (2013). An effective GRASP and tabu search for the 0–1 quadratic knapsack problem. *Computers & Operations Research*, *40*(5), 1176–1185. doi:10.1016/j.cor.2012.11.023

Yao, X., Wang, Y., Zhang, X., Zhang, R., Liu, M., Hu, Z., & Fan, B. (2002). Radial basis function neural network-based QSPR for the prediction of critical temperature. *Chemometrics and Intelligent Laboratory Systems*, *62*(2), 217–225. doi:10.1016/S0169-7439(02)00017-5

Yasdi, R. (2000). A Literature Survey on Applications of Neural Networks for Human-Computer Interaction. *Neural Computing & Applications*, *9*(4), 245–258. doi:10.1007/s005210070002

Yenigun, H., Yilmaz, C., & Andreas, U. (2016). Advances in test generation for testing software and systems. *International Journal of Software Tools and Technology Transfer*, *18*(3), 1–5. doi:10.1007/s10009-015-0404-z

Yin, P. Y., & Wang, T. Y. (2012). A GRASP-VNS algorithm for optimal wind turbine placement in wind farms. *Renewable Energy*, *48*, 489–498. doi:10.1016/j.renene.2012.05.020

Yogi, S., Subhashini, K. R., & Satapathy, J. K. (2010). A PSO based functional link artificial neural network training algorithm for equalization of digital communication channels. *5th International Conference on Industrial and Information Systems, ICIIS*, 107–112. doi:10.1109/ICIINFS.2010.5578726

Yonezawa, Y., & Kikuchi, T. (1996). Ecological algorithm for optimal ordering used by collective honey bee behavior. *Proceedings of the 7th International Symposium on Micro Machine and Human Science*, 249–256. doi:10.1109/MHS.1996.563432

Yu, H., Xie, T., Paszczyñski, S., & Wilamowski, B. M. (2011). Advantages of radial basis function networks for dynamic system design. *IEEE Transactions on Industrial Electronics*, 58(12), 5438–5450. doi:10.1109/TIE.2011.2164773

Yu, J., Lee, S.-H., & Jeon, M. (2012). An adaptive ACO-based fuzzy clustering algorithm for noisy image segmentation. *International Journal of Innovative Computing, Information, & Control*, 8(6), 3907–3918.

Yu, L. (2012). An evolutionary programming based asymmetric weighted least squares support vector machine ensemble learning methodology for software repository mining. *Information Science*, 191, 31–46. doi:10.1016/j.ins.2011.09.034

Yu, L. Q., & Rong, F. S. (2010). Stock market forecasting research based on neural network and pattern matching. *International Conference on E-Business and E-Government*, 1940–1943. doi:10.1109/ICEE.2010.490

Yu, L., Lai, K. K., & Wang, S. (2008). Multistage RBF neural network ensemble learning for exchange rates forecasting. *Neurocomputing*, 71(16), 3295–3302. doi:10.1016/j.neucom.2008.04.029

Yu, M., Naqvi, S. M., Rhuma, A., & Chambers, J. (2012). One class boundary method classifiers for application in a video-based fall detection system. *IET Computer Vision*, 6(2), 90–100. doi:10.1049/iet-cvi.2011.0046

Yuvaraj, R. (2011). Competency Mapping. *International Journal of Scientific & Engineering Research*, 2(8).

Zadeh, L. A. (1965). Fuzzy sets. *Information and Control*, 8(3), 338–353. doi:10.1016/S0019-9958(65)90241-X

Zahiri, A., & Azamathulla, H. M. (2014). Comparison between linear genetic programming and M5 tree models to predict flow discharge in compound channels. *Neural Computing & Applications*, 24(2), 413–420. doi:10.1007/s00521-012-1247-0

Zakaria, L., & Abdulllah, N. (2012). Matrix Driven Multivariate Fuzzy Linear Regression Model in Car Sales. *Journal of Applied Sciences*, 12(1), 56–63. doi:10.3923/jas.2012.56.63

Zakian, H. A. (2011). Fuzzy C-means and Fuzzy swarm clustering Problem expert System with Application. Academic Press.

Zamani, M., Manaf, A. A., Ahmed, R. B., Zeki, A. M., & Abdullah, S. (2009). A Genetic Algorithm Based Approach for Audio Steganography, International Journal of Computer, Electrical, Automation. *Control and Information Engineering*, 3(6), 1562–1565.

Zavala, A. E. M., Aguirre, A. H., & Diharce, E. R. V. (2005). Constrained optimization via particle evolutionary swarm optimization algorithm (PESO). *Proceedings of the 2005 conference on Genetic and evolutionary computation (GECCO'05)*, 209–216.

Zavala, A. E. M., Aguirre, A. H., & Diharce, E. R. V. (2005). Constrained optimization via particle evolutionary swarm optimization algorithm (PESO). *Proceedings of the conference on Genetic and evolutionary computation (GECCO'05)*, 209–216.

Zbigniew, M. (1994). GAs: What are they? Genetic Algorithm+ Data Structures = Evolution Programs. *Genetic and Evolutionary Computation Conference* (pp. 13-30). Chicago: Springer Berlin Heidelberg.

Zell, A. (2002). *SNNS Stuttgart Neural Network Simulator*. Retrieved from http://www-ra. informatik. uni-tuebingen. de

Zeng, Z. Y., Xu, W. S., Xu, Z. Y., & Shao, W. H. (2014). A hybrid GRASP+vnd heuristic for the two-echelon vehicle routing problem arising in city logistics. *Mathematical Problems in Engineering*, (1): 1–11.

Zhang, H. C., & Huang, S. H. (1994). A fuzzy approach to process plan selection. *International Journal of Production Research*, *32*(6), 1265–1279. doi:10.1080/00207549408956999

Zhang, Q., & Wu, J. (2015). Image super-resolution using windowed ordinary kriging interpolation. *Optics Communications*, *336*, 140–145. doi:10.1016/j.optcom.2014.09.060

Zhang, S., Lee, C. K., Chan, H. K., Choy, K. L., & Wu, Z. (2015). Swarm intelligence applied in green logistics: A literature review. *Engineering Applications of Artificial Intelligence*, *37*, 154–169. doi:10.1016/j.engappai.2014.09.007

Zhang, Y., Lu, Z., & Li, J. (2010). Fabric defect classification using radial basis function network. *Pattern Recognition Letters*, *31*(13), 2033–2042. doi:10.1016/j.patrec.2010.05.030

Zhan, Sh., Lin, J., Zhang, Z., & Zhong, Y. (2016). List-Based Simulated Annealing Algorithm for Traveling Salesman Problem. *Computational Intelligence and Neuroscience*, *2016*, 1–12. doi:10.1155/2016/1712630 PMID:27034650

Zhan, Z. H., Zhang, J., Li, Y., & Chung, H. S. H. (2009). Adaptive particle swarm optimization. *IEEE Transactions on Systems, Man, and Cybernetics*, *39*(6), 1362–1381. doi:10.1109/TSMCB.2009.2015956 PMID:19362911

Zheng, R.-R., Zhao, J.-Y., & Wu, B.-C. (2009). Multi Step Offline Handwritten Chinese Characters Segmentation with GA. Advances in Intelligent and Soft Computing, 62, 1-11.

Zhen, H., & Parker, J. M. (2005). *Texture Defect Detection Using Support Vector Machines with Adaptive Gabor Wavelet Features, Application of Computer Vision, WACV/MOTIONS '05* (Vol. 1). Seventh IEEE Workshops.

Zhi, Y. X., Pang, G. K. H., & Yung, N. H. C. (2001). Fabric defect detection using adaptive wavelet. *Icassp, Ieee International Conference On Acoustics, Speech And Signal Processing - Proceedings, 6*, 3697-3700.

Zhou, Z.-H., Jiang, Y., Yang, Y.-B., & Chen, S.-F. (2002). Lung cancer cell identification based on artificial neural network ensembles. *Artificial Intelligence in Medicine*, *24*(1), 25–36. doi:10.1016/S0933-3657(01)00094-X PMID:11779683

Zhou, Z., Wang, Z., & Sun, X. (2013). Face recognition based on optimal kernel minimax probability machine. *Journal of Theoretical and Applied Information Technology*, *48*, 1645–1651.

Zhu, X., Li, X., & Wang, Q. (2013). An adaptive intelligent method for manufacturing process optimization in steelworks. In *Computer Supported Cooperative Work in Design (CSCWD), 2013 IEEE 17th International Conference on* (pp. 363-368). doi:10.1109/CSCWD.2013.6580989

Zitzler, E. (1999). *Evolutionary algorithms for multiobjective optimization: Methods and applications*. Academic Press.

Zouadi, T., Yalaoui, A., Reghioui, M., & El Kadiri, K. E. (2015). Lot-sizing for production planning in a recovery system with returns. *RAIRO-Operations Research*, *49*(1), 123–142. doi:10.1051/ro/2014044

About the Contributors

Sujata Dash is currently working as an Associate Professor of Computer Science, Department of North Orissa University, Baripada, Odisha, India. She has 26 years of teaching and 17 years of research experience. She is recipient of Titular Fellowship from Association of Commonwealth Universities, UK. She has published more than 85 technical papers in international journals/ proceedings of international conferences/ edited book chapters of reputed publishers like Springer, Elsevier, IGI Global USA, text books and guiding students for PhD, M.Phil and M.Tech. She is a member of international professional associations like ACM, IRSS, CSI, IMS, OITS, OMS, IACSIT, IST and is a reviewer of around 10 international journals which include World Scientific, Bioinformatics, Springer, Elsevier, Inderscience and Science Direct publications. Also, she is a member of the editorial board of 8 international journals. She has presented and chaired many special sessions in International conferences abroad. Her current research interest includes Machine Learning, Data Mining, Big Data Analytics, Bioinformatics, Fuzzy sets and systems, Rough sets, Soft Computing and Intelligent Agents.

B. K. Tripathy is now working as a Senior Professor in SCOPE, VIT University, Vellore, India. He has received research/academic fellowships from UGC, DST, SERC and DOE of Govt. of India. Dr. Tripathy has published more than 430 technical papers in international journals, proceedings of international conferences and edited research volumes. He has produced 26 PhDs, 13 MPhils and 4 M.S (By research) under his supervision. Dr. Tripathy has published two text books on Soft Computing and Computer Graphics. Dr. Tripathy has served as the member of Advisory board or Technical Programme Committee member of several International conferences inside India and abroad. Also, he has edited two research volumes for IGI publications. He is a life/senior member of IEEE, ACM, IRSS, CSI, ACEEE, OMS and IMS. Dr.Tripathy is an editorial board member/reviewer of more than 60 journals. His research interest includes Fuzzy Sets and Systems, Rough Sets and Knowledge Engineering, Data Clustering, Social Network Analysis, Soft Computing, Granular Computing, Content Based Learning, Neighbourhood Systems, Soft Set Theory, Social Internet of Things, Big Data Analytics, Theory of Multisets and List theory.

Atta ur Rahman is currently working with University of Dammam, Dammam, Saudi Arabia as Assistant Professor. Before that he was with Barani Institute of Information Technology (BIIT), Rawalpindi, Pakistan, as Associate Professor & Deputy Director (R&D). Dr. Atta has completed his BS degree in Computer Science from University of The Punjab, Lahore, Pakistan; MS degree in Electronic Engineering from International Islamic University, Islamabad, Pakistan and PhD degree in Electronic Engineering from ISRA University, Islamabad Campus, Pakistan in years 2004, 2008 and 2012, respectively. He has been actively involved in research and development during last decade or so. His research interests include AI, Hybrid intelligent systems, evolutionary/soft computing, DSP, wireless communication and adaptive resource allocation.

* * *

Khalil Amine received the Licence degree in Applied Mathematics in 2006 and the Master's degree in Operations Research and Computer Science in 2008; both from Faculty of Sciences, University of Moulay Ismaïl, Meknès, Morocco. He was a researcher at Modelling and Scientific Computing Laboratory, Department of Mathematics, Faculty of Sciences and Techniques, University of Sidi Mohamed Ben Abdallah, Fès, Morocco From 2009 to 2011. He is working forward the PhD degree from Mohammadia School of Engineering, Mohammed V University of Rabat, Morocco. His research interests include ad hoc networking, telecommunications, multicriteria optimization, algorithms, graph theory, and transportation. Furthermore, he is a reviewer of the American Journal of Systems Science and the Applied Mathematics and served as a Technical Program Committee member for few international conferences. Mr. Amine has many experiences in teaching Mathematics and Computer Science since 2008. He served as a lecturer in applied mathematics and computer science since October 2009 respectively at University of Moulay Ismaïl, Meknès and University of Hassan II, Casablanca.

C. M. Anish is currently pursuing his Ph.D in the department of Computer Science and Information Technology, Guru Ghasidas Vishwavidyalay, Central University, Bilaspur, India. He did MCA degree from Chattisgarh Swami Vivekananda Technical University, Bhilai in 2009. His research interests are computational finance and Soft computing.

Nikhilesh Barik is an information security specialist in the field of Computer Sc. He is presently working as Deputy Controller of Examinations at Kazi Nazrul University, Asansol, India. He has awarded Ph.D Degree By Burdwan University, India. He holds a Master's degree in Computer Application from North Bengal University, India and Mathematics from Kalyani University and M Phil (Computer Science) from Madurai Kamaraj University . Before that, he did B.Sc (Hons.) degree in Mathematics from University of Calcutta, India. Dr. Barik started his professional career as Assistant Professor in since September, 2000. In his academic career, he published many research papers with good impact factors. His PhD thesis is on STUDIES ON SECURITY ISSUES IN E-LEARNING under supervision of Dr. Sunil Karforma, University of Burdwan, India. His areas of interests are Network Security, E-Learning and Digital Authentication.

Himanshu S. Behera has completed his M. E (Computer Science & Engineering) from National Institute of Technology, Rourkela, India, and Ph.D. (Engineering) from Biju Pattanaik University of Technology. His area of interest includes data mining and soft- computing, software engineering, distributed system. Dr. Behera has more than 100 research publications in National and International journals and conferences. Currently he is working as Associate Professor, department of computer science engineering & information technology, Veer Surendra Sai University of Technology, Burla, India. He has more than 20 years of experiences in teaching as well as research.

Vikas Bhatnagar is currently pursuing his Ph.D. in the Department of School of Management, National Institute of Technology Warangal, India. He did post graduation in Business Administration from the Central University of Himachal Pradesh, India, and graduation in Electronics and Communication Engineering from Kurukshetra University, India. His research interests are Marketing Management and Soft Computing.

Ayan Chatterjee, MCA, is an assistant professor of D.EL.ED section at Sarboday Public Academy, Purba Medinipur, India. He holds a Master's degree in Computer Application from Vidyasagar University, India. Before that, he did B.Sc (Hons.) degree in Mathematics from University of Calcutta, India. Mr. Chatterjee started his professional career since January, 2016. In his academic career, he published some research papers with good impact factors. His Master's thesis is on optimization technique of Travelling Salesman Problem (TSP) using Artificial Neural Network under supervision of Dr. Asit Kumar Das, IIEST, India. His areas of interests are Software Engineering, Computational Methodology, Soft Computing, Steganography and Cryptography.

S.L. Tulasi Devi is associated with School of Management, National Institute of Technology Warangal, India as Assistant Professor from July 2008 onwards. She has 25 years of teaching experience.

Christopher Expósito Izquierdo is an Engineering in computer sciences from the University of La Laguna, Spain, and with research experience in the field of optimization applied to logistics and transportation, especially in the design, implementation, and validation of meta-heuristic algorithms

Airam Expósito Márquez is a Computer Scientist specializing in artificial intelligence and optimization problems.

Sasikumar Gurumoorthy (born on 10th September 1981) is an Indian academician who is serving as a Professor in the Department of Computer Science and Systems Engineering, at Sree Vidhyanikethan Engineering College in Tirupati, Andhra Pradesh. Sasikumar Gurumoorthy is an alumnus of VIT University (VIT), Vellore, Tamil Nadu, India where he completed his Doctoral - Ph.D. (2016) in computer science and engineering. His advisor was Professor Dr. B.K. Tripathy, a famous Indian-born internationally renowned Senior Professor and former Dean from VIT University, Vellore, Tamil Nadu, India. The title of thesis is "Study of Human Brain Signals for Finding Diseases using Soft Computing Techniques". Earlier, he obtained his Post Graduation M.E., degree in Computer Science and Engineering from the Anna University, Chennai, India in 2005. His Under Graduation B.E., degree in Computer science and Engineering from the Madurai Kamaraj University, Madurai, Tamil Nadu in 2003. He has held various senior positions such as Head of the Department, Chief Superintend and Assistant CS of University Exams. He also serves on the Board of examiners and Board of Studies in Indian Universities. He has published over 75 Research papers in different International Journals and Conferences, more in the area of Intelligent System and Interactive Computing. He authored two reference text books, on "Programming in C and Introduction to Data Structures" in the area of UNIX and Windows operating system. He has started guiding many research scholars across the world. He has visited London (U.K). His team of researchers is from Finland, USA, UK, Australia, Malaysia, Singapore and Canada. The team is working on several projects utilizing grants from several organizations across the world. He will be roaming around the world as a resource person or speaker for Conferences and Workshops. He would like to contribute as Invited Speaker, keynote speaker, session chair or for special sessions in conferences and workshops. Also, He would like to be an active member in workshops chairs, program committee board or in reviewing panel of research paper for Conference and Journal. He is a Life Member of CSI-Computer Society of India, IAENG International Association of Engineers, ISTE-Life Member Indian Society for Technical Education, AIRCC- Academy & Industry Research Collaboration Center, IACSIT-International Association of Computer Science and Information Technology, IDES-Life Member, The Institute for Doctors Engineers and Scientists, IFERP-Institute for Engineering Research and Publication, WASET-World Academy of Science Engineering and Technology, INEER-International Network for Engineering Education and Research. He is involved in organizing a number of Research Projects Proposals and workshops, Conferences, Faculty Development Program on topics covering Computer science and research activities. He has lectured extensively in these areas both in India and abroad. He has been a member of editor Board of several Journals in the areas of Computer Science. He organized a number of conferences, workshops in Computer science in J.J. College of Engineering and Technology, Kurinji college of Engineering and Technology, VIT University, Dayananda Sagar College of Engineering and Sree Vidyanikethan Engineering College; in the past eleven years, he conducted similar courses in CCNA, FOSS, Computer Hardware, and SAP in around Tamilnadu. He is serving as a mentor for the Institute for Research and Development India-IRD and IFERP. For his outstanding contributions in the Wipro-Misson10X has been awarded In Pursuit of Excellence in Engineering Education through Innovation (in 2009) and in the WCE 2010 Best Research Paper award (in 2010, London, UK) by the International Association of Engineers.

Deepthi P. Hudedagaddi is pursuing her Masters at Vellore Institute of Technology. She is working on fuzzy clustering techniques on spatial data.

Jagan Jayabalan is currently working as the Assistant Professor in School of Civil Engineering at Galgotias University, UttarPradesh. He pursued the M.S.(ByResearch) at VIT University, Vellore and received B.E. Civil Engineering at Adhiyamaan College of Engineering, Hosur. He also worked as the Junior Research Fellow (JRF) under the sponsored research project by BRNS in Centre for Disaster Mitigation and Management at VIT University, Vellore. His research interests includes the application of artificial intelligence techniques in various fields of Civil Engineering.

Pradeep Kurup is Professor and Chair of the department of Civil and Environmental Engineering, at the University of Massachusetts Lowell. He is a Distinguished University Professor - recognized for his exemplary teaching, for nationally and internationally acclaimed research and for outstanding service to the university community and his profession. His scholarly work has covered a range of areas including, minimally invasive determination of engineering soil properties, evaluation of earthquake liquefaction potential, in-situ interpretation of contaminated sediments, and development of novel sensing systems for direct push technologies. He has developed novel testing devices, equipment, and interpretation methods that provide real-world solutions to industry and various agencies in the United States, including the National Science Foundation, Federal Highway Administration, Department of Defense, and the Environmental Protection Agency.

Babita Majhi is presently working as an Assistant Professor in the department of Computer Science and Information Technology, Guru Ghasidas Vishwavidyalay, Central University, Bilaspur, India. She did her Ph.D. in 2009 from National Institute of Technology Rourkela and Post Doctoral research work at University of Sheffield, UK (Dec.2011-Dec. 2012) under Boyscast Fellowship of DST, Govt. of India. She has guided 02 Ph.D. and 08 M.Tech. theses in the field of adaptive signal processing, computational finance and Soft-computing and has published 100 research papers in various referred International journals and conferences. Her research interests are Adaptive Signal Processing, Soft Computing, Evolutionary Computing, Computational Finance, Distributed Signal Processing and Data Mining.

Ritanjali Majhi is presently working as a Assistant Professor in the department of school of Management at National Institute of Technology Warangal. She has received best PhD thesis award from Pentagram research center in the year 2010. She has published 88 research papers in various national and international journals and conferences. Her total numbers of citations are 558 with h-index: 11 and i10index: 13.She has guided 01 PhD and 40 Master theses. Her area of specialization is marketing intelligence, Application of Soft and Evolutionary Computing to Management and Computational Finance.

Uttam Kumar Mandal is an Assistant Professor in the Department of production engineering of National Institute of Technology, Agartala, Tripura, India. He received his M.TECH in production engineering from the Jadavpur University West Bengal, India and PhD from the Jadavpur University West Bengal, India

Bijan B. Misra is currently working as Dean Research at Silicon Institute of Technology, Bhubaneswar, India. He received Bachelor degree in Textiles from Kanpur University, India in 1984, Master of Technology in Computer Science from Utkal University, Bhubaneswar, India in 2002 and Ph.D. in Engineering from Biju Pattanaik University of Technology, Rourkela, India, in 2011. He has done his Post Doctoral Research during 2013-14, at AJOU University, South Korea under the Technology Research Program for Brain Science of Yonsei University. His areas of interests include Data Mining, Sensor Network, Bioinformatics, Evolutionary Computation, Bio-inspired Computation and Computational Intelligence. He has published one book, three book chapters and more than 80 papers in different journals and conferences of National and International repute. He has been a key note speaker and session chair of different national and international conferences. Dr. Misra has more than 30 years of industrial as well as academics experiences.

Brojo Kishore Mishra is an Associate Professor in the Department of IT and Coordinator IQAC, C. V. Raman College of Engineering, Bhubaneswar, Odisha, India. He is the Regional Student Coordinator (2016-17), CSI Region – IV, India. Also he is the IEEE Day 2016 Ambassador for IEEE Kolkata Section. He has received his Ph. D. (Computer Science) from Berhampur University in 2012 and has supervised more than 08 M. Tech. thesis and currently guiding 04 Ph.D research scholars in the area of Data Mining, Opinion Mining, Soft Computing and Security. Dr. Mishra has published more than 25 research papers in international journals and conference proceedings and 3 invited book chapters. He serves as Guest Editor in IJKDB, IJSE, IJACR and IJRSDA special issue journals and an editorial board member of many international journals. He is associated with a CSI funded research project as a Principal Investigator. He was the Regional Convener of CSI YITP 2015-16, CSI State Student Coordinator (2015-16), Jury Coordination Committee Member of All IEEE Young Engineers' Humanitarian Challenge (AIYEHUM 2015) project competition, organized by IEEE Region 10 (Asia pacific) and IEEE Day 2015 Ambassador for IEEE Kolkata section.

Sankar Prasad Mondal is an Assistant Professor in the Department of Mathematics of Midnapore College (Autonomous), Midnapore, India. He received his MSc in Applied Mathematics from the Indian Institute of Engineering Science and Technology (formerly Bengal Engineering and Science University), Shibpur, West Bengal, India and PhD from the Indian Institute of Engineering Science and Technology, Shibpur, West Bengal, India. His current research interests are in fuzzy differential equation and its applications, Decision making problem, Application of fuzzy sets theory in Engineering.

Swathi J. N. is currently working as Associate Professor in School of Computer Science and Engineering, VIT University, Vellore, India. She is having 10 years of teaching experience. Her research interest includes Soft Computing, Pattern Recognition and Data Mining.

Sarat C. Nayak has received a M. Tech (Computer Science) degree from Utkal University, Bhubaneswar, India, and Ph.D. (Engineering) from Veer Surendra Sai University of Technology, Burla, India. His area of research interest includes data mining, soft computing, evolutionary computation, financial time series forecasting. He has published 25 research articles in various journals, conferences, and books of National and International repute. Dr. Nayak currently associated with computer science & engineering department at Kommuri Pratap Reddy Institute of Technology, Hyderabad, India.

Boominathan P is currently working as Assistant Professor(SG) at School of Computer Science and Engineering, VIT University, Vellore, India. He is having 11 years of teaching experience. His research interest includes optimization, cloud computing, network security.

Kauser Ahmed P received his M.Tech degree in information technology with specialization in networking from VIT University, Vellore, India; M. Sc. Degree in computer science from VIT University, Vellore, India and right now pursuing his PhD in computer science and engineering from VIT University, Vellore, India. Presently he is an Assistant Professor in School of Computer Science and Engineering, VIT University, Vellore, India. He has several peer-reviewed national and international conferences and journals publications. He is associated with many professional bodies like CSI, ISTE, IACSIT, CSTA, IEEE, IRSS and IAENG. He is a reviewer of many international conferences sponsored by IEEE, SPRINGER, IACSIT and IAENG. His current research interests include soft computing, big data analytics, bio-inspired computing and bio informatics.

Puspalata Pujari is an assistant professor in CSIT department, GGV, Central University, Bilaspur, and Chhattisgarh, India. She received her M.C.A Degree from Berhampur University, Berhampur, Odisha, India in 1998. She is currently pursuing her Ph.D in the department of Computer Science and Information Technology, Guru Ghasidas Vishwavidyalaya, Central University, Bilaspur, Chhattisgarh, India. Her areas of interest include Character Recognition, Soft Computing and Data Mining.

Viswanathan R is currently working as the Assistant Professor in Galgotias University, Greater Noida, Uttar Pradesh. He pursued his PhD in VIT University (2015), MBA in International Business Management from Annamalai University (2008), M.Sc in Computer Science (2005) and B.Sc in Computer

Science (2002) from Bharathidasan University, Trichy, India. He also employed in VIT University as the Assistant Professor in School of Information Technology and Engineering (SITE) during the period of 2012-2015. He also worked as a Business Development Manager with MRS Bean House of Desserts (p) Ltd in Singapore from 2009 –2012. Also he worked as a SAP Consultant, with Sundaram-Clayton Limited Chennai 2006 – 2009. His research studies include the implementation of intelligent techniques in disaster oriented problems. His research interest includes data mining techniques, soft computing, cloud computing, artificial intelligence, etc. He has several publications in peer reviewed journals.

Jayant G, Rohra is final Year B.tech student in School of Computer Science and engineering, VIT University, Vellore. His research interest includes machine learning and optimization.

Sushri Samita Rout has completed her BE in Electronics and Instrumentation from Berhampur University in 2001, PGDM in Systems from KIIT University in 2004 and PhD from KIIT University in 2015. Her areas of interest include Computational Intelligence, Application of Computational intelligence in Management. Presently she is continuing as a Associate Professor at Silicon Institute of Technology, Bhubaneswar.

Soumya Sahoo has completed her M.Tech (CSE) under BPUT in the year 2009. Currently she is working as an Asst. Professor (CSE) at C. V. raman College of Engineering, Bhubaneswar.

Pijush Samui is working as the Associate Professor in Department of Civil engineering at NIT Patna, India. He graduated in 2000, with a B.Tech. in Civil Engineering from Indian Institute of Engineering Science and Technology, Shibpur, India. He received his M.Sc. in Geotechnical Earthquake Engineering from Indian Institute of Science, Bangalore, India (2004). He holds a Ph.D. in Geotechnical Earthquake Engineering (2008) from Indian Institute of Science, Bangalore, India. He was a postdoctoral fellow at University of Pittsburgh (USA) (2008-2009) and Tampere University of Technology (Finland) (2009-2010). At University of Pittsburgh, he worked on design of efficient tool for rock cutting and application of Support Vector Machine (SVM) in designing of geostructure. At Tampere University of Technology, he worked on design of railway embankment, slope reliability and site characterization. In 2010, Dr. Pijush joined in the Center for Disaster Mitigation and Management at VIT University as the Associate Professor. He was promoted to a Professor in 2012. Dr. Pijush's research focuses on the application of Artificial Intelligence for designing civil engineering structure, design of foundation, stability of railway embankment, reliability analysis, site characterization, and earthquake engineering. Dr. Pijush is the recipient of the prestigious CIMO fellowship (2009) from Finland, for his integrated research on the design of railway embankment. He was awarded Shamsher Prakash Research Award (2011) by IIT Roorkee for his innovative research on the application of Artificial Intelligence in designing civil engineering structure. He was selected as the recipient of IGS Sardar Resham Singh Memorial. Dr. Pijush is active in a variety of professional organizations including the Indian Geotechnical Society, Indian Science Congress, Institution of Engineers, World federation of Soft Computing, and Geotechnical Engineering for Disaster Mitigation and Rehabilitation. He has organized numerous workshops and conferences on the applications of artificial intelligence in Civil Engineering.

Binayak Sen was born in Agartala, India on 15 June 1991, son of Late. Bikram Sen and Mrs. Dipti Chakraborty (Sen). He has completed his Bachelor of Engineering in Mechanical Engineering from Tripura Institute of Technology, Agartala, Tripura in the year 2014. He entered into the Master Programme of Computer Integrated Manufacturing at National Institute of Technology, Agartala, India in August, 2014 and completed it in May 2016. His master research focuses on the "Development and validation of GEP model to predict the machining parameters of Inconel X-750 super alloy in a CNC assisted 3-axis milling machine under dry machining condition".

Swati Swayamsiddha received the B.Tech degree in Electronics and Telecommunications in 2009 and M.Tech degree in Communications System Engineering in 2011 from KIIT University, Bhubaneswar. She is working as Assistant Professor in School of Electronics Engineering, KIIT University, Bhubaneswar since 2009. She is currently pursuing the Ph.D degree from Department of Electronics & Electrical Communication Engineering, IIT Kharagpur. Her research interests spans the area of mobile communications, adaptive signal processing, cognitive radio networks, nonlinear optimization, soft and evolutionary computing. She is a member of ISC and IET.

Index

Stay Current on the Latest Emerging Research Developments

Become an IGI Global Reviewer for Authored Book Projects

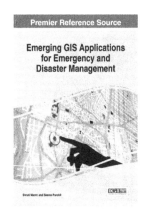

Premier Reference Source

Emerging GIS Applications for Emergency and Disaster Management

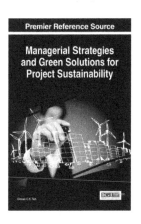

Premier Reference Source

Managerial Strategies and Green Solutions for Project Sustainability

Premier Reference Source

Comparative Approaches to Using R and Python for Statistical Data Analysis

Premier Reference Source

Solutions for High-Touch Communications in a High-Tech World

The overall success of an authored book project is dependent on quality and timely reviews.

In this competitive age of scholarly publishing, constructive and timely feedback significantly decreases the turnaround time of manuscripts from submission to acceptance, allowing the publication and discovery of progressive research at a much more expeditious rate. Several IGI Global authored book projects are currently seeking highly qualified experts in the field to fill vacancies on their respective editorial review boards:

Applications may be sent to:
development@igi-global.com

Applicants must have a doctorate (or an equivalent degree) as well as publishing and reviewing experience. Reviewers are asked to write reviews in a timely, collegial, and constructive manner. All reviewers will begin their role on an ad-hoc basis for a period of one year, and upon successful completion of this term can be considered for full editorial review board status, with the potential for a subsequent promotion to Associate Editor.

If you have a colleague that may be interested in this opportunity, we encourage you to share this information with them.

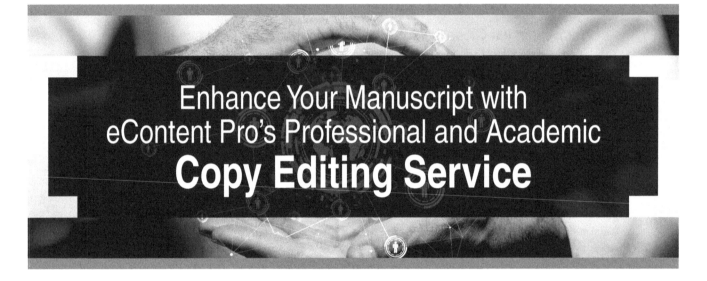

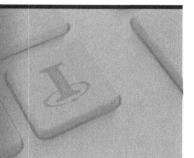

Printed in the United States
By Bookmasters